VICE PRESIDENTS

A BIOGRAPHICAL DICTIONARY

Edited by

L. Edward Purcell

Checkmark Books®

An imprint of Facts On File, Inc.

Vice Presidents: A Biographical Dictionary, Updated Edition

Checkmark Books
An imprint of Facts On File, Inc.
132 West 31st Street
New York, NY 10001

Library of Congress Cataloging-in-Publication Data

Vice presidents: a biographical dictionary / edited by L. Edward Purcell
    p. cm.
Includes bibliographical references (p.) and index.
ISBN 0-8160-4645-X (hardcover: alk. paper)—
ISBN 0-8160-4615-8 (pbk.: alk. paper)
    1. Vice Presidents—United States—Biography—Dictionaries. I. Purcell, L. Edward

E176.49.V52 2001
973'.09'9—dc21
[B]   2001023042

Text design and layout by Grace M. Ferrara
Cover design (hc) by Cathy Rincon
Cover design (pbk) by Max Media

Printed in the United States of America

    MP FOF 10 9 8 7 6 5 4 3 2 1
      (pbk) 10 9 8 7 6 5 4 3 2 1

This book is printed on acid-free paper.

CONTENTS

ACKNOWLEDGMENTS

*M*any people and institutions helped accomplish the tasks of putting this volume together, and especially important were those who suggested authors. In alphabetical order, the following are very gratefully acknowledged: Irving H. Bartlett, Marvin Bergman, Roger Bridges, the George Bush Presidential Materials Project, John Catanzaritti, the Cowles Library at Drake University, Todd Culbertson, Ken Davidson, William C. Davis, Virgil Dean, the Des Moines Public Library, the Grace Doherty Library at Centre College, John Dumville, George C. Edwards, H. Roger Grant, John Robert Greene, Peter Harstad, Mary Holt, Loren N. Horton, Ludwell Johnson III, the M.I. King Library at the University of Kentucky, Richard Kirkendall, James Klotter, John Kolp, the Lexington Public Library, the Library of Congress, Frank Mackaman, Madison House Publishers, Robert McCown, Martin Medhurst, Susan Naulty, the Richard Nixon Library and Birthplace, Nick Noyes, Nancy Osborne, Mark Palmer, Bradley Patterson, Jr., Frances Pollard, the Dan Quayle Center and Museum, Janet Rassweiler, the Regents Press of Kansas, Donald Ritchie, George Robinson, Richard Ryerson, Elizabeth Safly, Edward L. Schapsmeier, Leonard Schlup, Ann Shaller, Robert M. Sutton, Brent Tarter, Tim Walch, Robert Waller, Shirley Anne Warshaw, Clyde Wilson, and Dan Wilson.

This is a book of reference, and it is not intended, nor is it likely, that the biographies of all forty-six American vice presidents will be read through from start to finish, from John Adams to Richard Cheney. Should readers choose to do so, however, they will discover much about the political history of our nation and the role played by the vice presidents. They will also, of course, discover a wealth of interesting facts about these men, from the titillating public innuendo about William Rufus King's sex life to the otherworldly dreams of Henry Wallace.

One of the most striking conclusions to be drawn from considering the lives of the vice presidents is the extremely high quality of the men who have borne that title.

When they devised the Constitution of the United States after the American Revolution, the Founding Fathers intended that the vice presidency go to whomever the electoral voters thought was presumed to be the second-best man in the nation and deserving of a high and mighty office. The writers of the Constitution gave the vice president only the specific task of presiding over the Senate, thus conceiving of the vice presidency as primarily a working legislative office with the major proviso that the vice president would take over the presidency if the chief should die or become incapacitated, what author Richard Zuczek calls the vice president's "ultimate function."

In the more than 200 years since John Adams was sworn in, we have come to view the vice presidency somewhat differently. In fact, in the popular mind, the vice president is often a figure of fun, someone who has no meaningful role in life other than to check on the president's health each morning.

The very idea of the vice presidency calls forth a flow of derision—just look at the titles of the most popular books about the vice presidents. Worse yet, the incumbents themselves have done much to demean the office in what must be an unparalleled tradition of public self-loathing. Virtually all the vice presidents, beginning with Adams, have sooner or later said or written something in public that indicated their viciously low self-opinion: John Nance Garner's pithy comparative reference to a warm bodily fluid was unusual only in its stark directness.

The "second man" has been the butt of jokes for so long that the image of the worthless, bumbling vice president is firmly fixed in the collective understanding of the nation. It is not too difficult to comprehend where this negative view comes from. The actual duties of the office of vice president, unless the incumbent is taken into the confidence of the president and given real work to do (as was frequently the case in the twentieth century), are slight and boring. Active politicians who find themselves thus sidelined, often at the height of their powers, have not taken kindly to the situation.

Yet it seems very clear with only a little serious examination that it is the *office* of the vice president that should be the butt of jokes and not the people elected to it.

There is little profit in protesting the opinion that vice presidents are historical ciphers, but it is quite contrary to historical fact. If the list of vice presidents were presented in some neutral context, without the fatal "vice presidents" label, it would be mistaken for an honor roll of significant American political leaders.

It will probably come as a shock and surprise to most American general readers and even many political scientists and historians who consult the biographies in this volume to learn that the great majority of U.S. vice presidents have been men of extraordinarily high ability and achievement. Even individual authors, all of whom are experts, of the biographies in this volume frequently hint that only *their* subjects were accomplished leaders and therefore must be aberrations.

Nothing could be further from the truth. Only a handful of the forty-six vice presidents have been nonentities, mostly those serving during the so-called Gilded Age, when American politics in general may have hit a historic low. During most of our national history, however, it would have been impossible for politically unimportant men to come to the vice-presidential nomination and election. For example, the list of vice presidents is filled with men who were Speakers of the House of Representatives, distinguished and powerful senators, governors of the most important states, powerful mayors, and military heroes. Even many of the less distinguished came to the office with impressive credentials: Charles Dawes, who performed poorly as vice president, was an international expert on finance and had a Nobel Peace Prize in his portfolio when nominated.

Anyone who doubts the quality of the vice presidents should pause to consider John Adams, Thomas Jefferson, John C. Calhoun, Theodore Roosevelt, Harry Truman, and Lyndon Johnson. Slipping down a notch still produces a list with names such as George Clinton, John Nance Garner, Henry Wallace, Hubert Humphrey, and Nelson Rockefeller. No matter what their overall job rating, Martin Van Buren, John Tyler, Millard Fillmore, Andrew Johnson, Chester Arthur, Calvin Coolidge, Gerald Ford, and George Bush all were presidents of the United States. Even the most notorious of vice presidents, Aaron Burr and Richard Nixon, had immense impact on the nation.

Overall, the following forty-six biographical essays demonstrate the vigor of the office of vice president and of American political life since the founding of the republic, and they will, one hopes, provide ample information and interpretation about the individuals who have served.

JOHN ADAMS (1735–1826)

Vice President, 1789–1797

(President George Washington)

JOHN ADAMS
(Library of Congress)

By Jack D. Warren

A major figure in the patriot cause in Massachusetts before the American Revolution, a leader in the Continental Congress during the Revolutionary War, and one of the United States's first diplomats in Europe, John Adams served for eight years as the first vice president of the United States before succeeding George Washington to become the second president of the United States. Although his career as vice president was overshadowed by his accomplishments as congressman, diplomat, and president, John Adams was among the most important vice presidents in American history. The precedents established during his eight years in office continue to shape the vice presidency more than 200 years later, and his tie-breaking votes in the Senate were decisively important to the establishment of a strong national government during the Washington administration.

John Adams was a man of brilliant intellect, enormous personal integrity, and high principles. He was also ceaselessly ambitious—for professional and political advancement, wealth, and mostly for lasting fame. From the outbreak of the Revolution, he devoted himself to the patriot cause with an industry matched by few of his contemporaries. Although Adams spent most of his adult life in politics, he was temperamentally ill suited to the accommodations and compromises required by political life. Always fiercely independent, he could be stubborn and self-righteous and was often blunt, undiplomatic, impatient, and demanding. He was apparently awkward in social situations and possessed an unfortunate talent for alienating people. Unsparingly critical of himself, he was equally quick to point out shortcomings in those around him. Adams's political principles and his passion for fame and advancement often dictated contradictory actions, and it is a credit to him that at decisive points in his career he consistently sacrificed his ambitions to his principles. He refused to compromise his convictions for popularity or political office, a characteristic that ultimately cost him reelection to the presidency.

John Adams was born on October 19, 1735, in Braintree (later renamed Quincy), Massachusetts, the eldest son of John Adams, a yeoman farmer, and his wife, Susanna Boylston Adams. Educated at Harvard College, from which he graduated in 1755, he then took up the study of law and was admitted to the bar in Boston in November 1758. On October 25, 1764, he married Abigail Smith, the daughter of a Weymouth, Massachusetts, minister. Although she lacked formal education, she was vivacious and possessed a sparkling intellect that made her an ideal partner for Adams through his long and varied public career. During the next ten years the couple had four children: John Quincy, Thomas, Charles, and Abigail II.

John Adams became a major public figure in Massachusetts during the decade-long controversy between Britain and its American colonies that preceded the outbreak of the American Revolution. During the Stamp Act controversy, Adams drafted resolutions of protest for Braintree that were imitated all over Massachusetts. As a lawyer, he was involved in a number of legal cases arising out of the pre-Revolutionary crisis: He defended John Hancock against smuggling charges but also defended the British soldiers involved in the Boston Massacre against charges of murder, an action that marked him as a man of personal integrity, devoted to his principles regardless of personal cost.

In June 1774, Adams was chosen to be one of the three delegates from Massachusetts to the Continental Congress, meeting in Philadelphia. In the First Continental Congress, he counseled moderation and publicly supported reconciliation with Britain, but privately he was becoming impatient with British intransigence; in the Second Continental Congress, he emerged as a most outspoken and determined advocate of independence. Congress adopted a resolution in May 1776, with a preamble written by Adams, that called on the states where no adequate colonial government remained to adopt constitutions independent of British authority. This virtual declaration of independence was followed immediately by a resolution calling for independence, foreign alliances, and a confederation of the states. Adams was appointed to committees to prepare a declaration of independence and to prepare a plan for treaties with foreign powers.

Although Thomas Jefferson wrote the Declaration of Independence, Adams accepted the difficult task of securing its adoption on the floor of Congress, where, according to Jefferson, he "supported the Declaration with zeal and ability, fighting fearlessly for every word of it."

On November 28, 1777, Congress appointed Adams to join Benjamin Franklin as an American commissioner to France, launching Adams on a diplomatic career that would last more than ten years. Adams's first mission to Europe was a frustrating and largely unproductive experience. By the time he reached Paris in April 1778, France had already recognized the United States, and war between France and Britain was imminent, leaving Adams with little to do. He spent most of this first trip abroad reorganizing the U.S. mission, establishing an orderly system of correspondence, and recommending changes in the conduct of American diplomacy to Congress.

Adams returned to the United States in the summer of 1779 and was immediately elected to represent Braintree at the Massachusetts state constitutional convention. The constitution adopted by that convention in 1780 was largely his work, and its principal features—a bicameral legislature, single executive, and an independent judiciary—served as a model for the framers of the federal constitution in 1787.

But Adams was called away from the convention before its work was complete, having been chosen by Congress as a commissioner to negotiate a peace treaty with Great Britain. After this, he was to serve as American minister to Great Britain and to conclude a commercial treaty with the British. Arriving in Paris in February 1780, Adams soon found himself caught up in intrigues with the French ministry and Franklin and then functioned as sole American minister to France. At French Minister Vergennes's urging, he kept his peace mission secret but soon regretted the decision, concluding that the French wished to prolong the war for their own advantage. Adams found himself in the delicate position of intruding on Franklin's prerogatives and soon alienated himself from Vergennes.

In July 1780, Adams went to Holland to seek a loan for the United States. Although this effort met with no immediate success, he was appointed minister to the Dutch republic by Congress in December 1780. Two years later, Adams concluded a treaty with the Dutch republic and made proposals that resulted in the first Dutch loan to the United States. At the same time, Franklin and John Jay were concluding preliminary articles for a peace treaty with Great Britain. Hastening to Paris, Adams made important contributions toward concluding the final peace treaty, signed September 3, 1783.

The British court received Adams as minister from the United States in May 1785. He spent more than two years in fruitless efforts to resolve matters arising out of the peace treaty, but the British, lacking faith in the United States government under the weak Articles of Confederation, paid little attention to these matters or to Adams. Unable to accomplish his primary mission, Adams spent much of his time in London studying the principles of government, publishing the results in a massive, three-volume work entitled *A Defense of the Constitutions of Government of the United States* (1787–88) that was praised by contemporaries as the most thorough disquisition on the principles of American constitutionalism yet published. The work was also criticized by many in the United States as too favorable to monarchical forms in government. Having been frustrated in his tenure as U.S. minister to Britain, Adams was recalled at his own request in February 1788.

Adams returned home to find that he had been chosen as a delegate to the Confederation Congress, but he never took his seat in that expiring body. His future seemed clouded: In his absence, eleven of the original states had ratified the new federal Constitution, drafted by a convention in the summer of 1787. Despite being one of the nation's most important political thinkers, Adams had not been able to participate in this convention. His distinguished record as a lawyer, legislator, and diplomat marked him as a suitable candidate for a position in the new federal government—as vice president, senator, Supreme Court justice, or secretary of state—but his long absence from the domestic political scene made his advancement to any of these posts uncertain.

In the first election under the federal Constitution, George Washington was the universal choice for president, but Adams was just one of several prospective candidates for the vice presidency. In the absence of political parties and a formal nominating method, the process of selecting and advancing candidates for vice president was conducted in private correspondence and behind-the-scenes maneuvering by established political leaders. Eighteenth-century political principle, which held that public servants should be above self-interested motivations, precluded candidates from actively seeking office. At the end of the eighteenth century, candidates for office were typically brought forward by their political allies, agreed upon quietly within coalitions of like-minded men, and then publicly advanced in newspapers.

This manner of selecting a candidate for vice president put Adams at a disadvantage. Although he enjoyed widespread respect, his long absence from domestic politics left Adams with few allies to champion his candidacy. In particular, his absence during the crucial deliberations that produced the federal Constitution and the political struggle over its ratification further hampered his prospects; although his support of the federal Constitution was assumed, he was not associated with the triumphant nationalist leadership that had worked through the 1780s to establish the federal government on a strong basis. Other men were better positioned than Adams to be chosen vice president. With some justification, he regarded his prospects for being elected vice president as poor.

Through the summer of 1788, several possible candidates for vice president were discussed in private correspondence and the press. Benjamin Franklin was widely advanced as the most distinguished American after Washington, but even his most ardent supporters recognized that he was too old. Adams, John Jay of New York, John Rutledge of South Carolina, and John Hancock of Massachusetts were the other candidates most frequently mentioned. Hancock's distinguished record in the Revolution, highly visible public role in New England politics, and extraordinary popularity in Massachusetts, of which he was governor, made him the leading contender, as did the widely held principle that the major offices in the new government ought to be distributed geographically to secure attachment to the new government. Rumors circulated, however, that Hancock had refused to accept second place to any man, and his supporters seem to have held out hope that he would be elected president in the event Washington declined the office.

Adams seemed a suitable New England alternative to Hancock, but leading Federalists, including Alexander Hamilton and James Madison, were uncertain where Adams stood on some most-critical political issues. Madison, in particular, was concerned that Adams had "made himself obnoxious to many particularly in the Southern states by the political principles avowed in his book. Others recollecting his cabal during the war against General Washington." The latter was the main concern of Hamilton, who had served as Washington's military secretary during the Revolution and believed that Adams was "unfriendly in his sentiments to General Washington." In Adams's defense, Massachusetts Federalist Theodore Sedgwick assured Hamilton that Adams was "a man of unconquerable intrepidity & of incorruptible integrity" fully deserving the confidence "of those who wish energy in government." Mollified, Hamilton decided to support Adams for vice president, partly, he explained to Madison, to prevent Adams from being "nominated to some important office for which he is less proper" as well as to prevent him from becoming a "malcontent." Hamilton was then careful to orchestrate, through private correspondence with other Federalist leaders, the disposition of votes in the electoral college to ensure that Adams did not receive more votes that Washington.

During the months of political maneuvering leading up to Adams's election, George Washington did not publicly endorse a candidate for the vice presidency, explaining to a friend that "Whosoever shall be found to enjoy the confidence of the States so far as to be elected Vice President, cannot be disagreeable to me," adding that:

Supposing myself to be connected in that office with any gentleman of character, I would most certainly treat him with perfect sincerity and the greatest candor in every respect. I would give him my full confidence & use my utmost endeavours to cooperate with him, in promoting and rendering permanent the national prosperity—this should be my great—my only aim—under the fixed & irrevocable resolution of leaving to other hands the helm of the State, as soon as my services could possibly with propriety be dispensed with.

This statement, combined with Washington's expressed determination to retire from the presidency after a single term, suggested that he would regard the vice president as his natural successor in the presidency. In January 1789, Washington wrote privately that it was clear "that Mr. John Adams would be chosen Vice President. He will doubtless make a very good one: and let whoever may occupy the first seat, I shall be entirely satisfied with that arrangement for filling the second office."

When Congress convened in New York City on April 6, 1789, Washington was found to have received a vote from each of the sixty-nine electors. Adams received the vote of thirty-four electors, including all ten from Massachusetts, all five from New Hampshire, five of seven from Connecticut, one of six from New Jersey, eight of ten from Pennsylvania, five of ten from Virginia. Other second votes were widely scattered. John Jay received nine votes. Robert H. Harrison of Maryland and John Rutledge of South Carolina received six votes each, all from their respective states. The Antifederalist candidate, George Clinton, received only three votes, all from Virginia.

Adams arrived in New York City on April 20, 1789, and took the oath of office the next day. He then presented a brief address, anticipating the difficulties that lay ahead. Adams noted that he was "unaccustomed to refuse any public service, however dangerous to my reputation, or disproportioned to my talents." He added that he was "not wholly without experience in public assemblies," but that "I have been more accustomed to take a share in their debates, than to preside in their deliberations" and asked the forbearance of the members: "If from inexperience, or inadvertency, any thing should ever escape me, inconsistent with propriety, I must entreat you, by imputing it to its true cause, and not to any want of respect, to pardon and excuse it."

Adams's conduct as president of the Senate was governed by rules adopted before he arrived to take his seat. These rules made it clear that the senators expected Adams to conduct himself much like the presidents of the Continental Congress, managing the flow of business and maintaining order but not actively participating in debates. This would prove to be a role for which Adams—a brilliant intellectual, skilled in debate but also opinionated and lacking in tact—was to prove temperamentally ill suited. Yet, unlike some later vice presidents, Adams took his duties as president of the Senate very seriously and was rarely absent from the chair. During his first six months in office, Adams's attention to the business of the Senate was, in his wife's words, "close and unremitting." He privately acknowledged that he was unsuited to his task: "My office," he wrote to his son John Quincy in July 1789, "requires rather severe duty, and it is a kind of duty which, if I do not flatter myself too much, is not quite adapted to my character—I mean it is too inactive and mechanical." Even when he believed he could throw light on a matter under consideration, "it cannot be done." To a friend, Adams wrote dismally that his new office left him without "the smallest degree of power to do any good either in the executive, legislative, [or] judicial departments."

He had become, he complained, a "'head of wood,' a mere mechanical tool to wind up the clock." To the Senate, he made his contempt for his new post abundantly clear: "I am Vice President," he said during one contentious debate, and "in this I am nothing."

Adams's frustration was compounded by his conviction that the union of the states, and indeed even American independence, remained in jeopardy and depended upon the wisdom of precedents established at the outset by the new government. He had returned to the United States in a mood of black pessimism about the future of the new nation. His experience as a member of Congress during the Revolution had convinced Adams that the American people lacked sufficient willingness to sacrifice enough of their selfish, private interests for the good of the whole. From Europe, he had observed the confederation's gradual disintegration from the unwillingness of the states to provide funds for the payment of U.S. financial obligations at home or abroad. He had experienced, at first hand, the wiliness and duplicity of European diplomats, and he doubted that the federal government would be able to protect the new nation from their machinations. He had little faith that the federal Constitution, in the absence of broad-based public willingness to sacrifice for the country's good, could provide the basis for long-term government stability and fully expected the Union to be torn apart by the competing interests of the different states and sections.

His frustrations were also personal. At the outset of his tenure, he found that Congress had not yet voted a salary for the vice president and he was virtually without funds. He considered resigning and wrote home to Abigail not to join him until he received some assurance of a decent salary. When Congress finally voted a salary, it was only half of what was to be paid to the president, despite the fact that the vice president found himself under a public obligation to entertain nearly as many guests as Washington.

Adams's tenure as vice president was shaped both by his personal relationship with Washington and by Washington's conception of the vice presidency. Adams and Washington had first met as delegates to the Continental Congress, before Washington assumed command of the Continental Army. He had supported Washington's appointment to that post; later he had been openly critical of the defensive strategy adopted by Washington and of the congressional policy of vesting the commander in chief with extensive powers, and he was privately critical of Washington's generalship. At least some of these criticisms probably came to Washington's attention, but relations between the two men remained cordial while Adams was serving in Congress. Between the time Adams first departed for Europe and their meeting in New York in 1789, Washington and Adams do not seem to have had any contact. Adams was thus not one of Washington's circle of advisors, a group that included Jay, Hamilton, and Madison. Washington seems to have consulted Adams infrequently during the early months of the administration. The evidence of such consultation may simply not exist; the two men were in regular contact and would have had infrequent need to resort to letters. Yet, the silence of the documentary record suggests that Adams had little influence in executive appointments or policy. Even on foreign affairs, a subject about which Adams possessed considerable expertise, Washington does not often seem to have appealed for his advice.

One matter about which Washington did seek Adams's advice, along with that of Hamilton, Madison, and Jay, involved the adoption of formal procedures regulating access to the president. Shortly after arriving in New York, Washington was deluged with invitations and visitors. It soon became obvious that he would have to institute formal measures regulating his social life or else have all his time consumed in receiving and returning visits and attending public and private functions. These, he feared, would not only prevent him from accomplishing public business, but would also diminish the dignity of the presidential office. Adams shared Washington's belief that the new government's success relied, to a large extent, on the respect its officials could command. In his reply to Washington, Adams wrote that "neither Dignity, nor Authority, can be Supported in human Minds collected into nations or any great numbers without a Splendor and Majisty, in Some degree, proportioned to them."

Adams approved of Washington's proposal to insulate the presidency from the public and supported his proposal to institute regular levees at which to receive visitors. But Adams went even further than Washington in his efforts to elevate the presidency in the public mind, proposing to endow the president and other high federal officials with formal titles reminiscent of the forms and usages of monarchical governments. The president, Adams maintained, should be referred to as His Excellency or by some other appropriate title and that relations between the Senate and the president should be conducted with the same formality that characterized relations between the House of Lords and the British monarch. Adams first made these proposals in the Senate on April 23, 1789, before Washington arrived in New York (the nation's capital at that time), when the Senate was considering arrangements for Washington's inauguration; the issue was referred to a committee and discussed inconclusively on the floor until May 1, when debate began in earnest.

Most of what is known about this debate, as well as others that occurred in the Senate during the First Congress, comes from the private diary of William Maclay, a senator from Pennsylvania. Maclay had supported Adams for vice president, but the debate over titles made him one of Adams's harshest critics. He took the lead in attacking Adams's proposals on the grounds that they were repugnant to the principles of republican government. "We have lately had a hard struggle for our liberty against Kingly Authority," Maclay reminded Adams, and "everything related to that Species of Government is odious to the People." At this, Maclay wrote,

Adams "expressed the greatest Surprize, that any thing should be objected to on account of its being taken from the Practise of that Government under which we had lived so long and so happily formerly, that he was for a dignifyed and respectable Government, and as far as he knew the sentiments of People they thought as he did. That for his part he was one of the first in the late Contest and *if he could have thought of this, he never would have drawn his Sword*." Maclay replied that "there had been a Revolution in the Sentiments of the People, respecting Government, equally great as that which had happened in the Government itself," and that the people now abhorred "all the trappings and Splendor of Royalty."

Maclay and other plain republicans may have regarded the idea of endowing government officials with titles with varying degrees of amusement or scorn, but to Adams the matter involved immutable precedents that ought not be established without thoughtful consideration. To his opponents, Adams insisted that titles were essential to the successful administration of the government: "You are against Titles," he said, "but there are no People in the World so much in favour of Titles as the People of America and the Government never will be properly administered, until they are adopted in the fullest manner." Debate over the question lasted until May 14.

Ultimately, the Senate rejected Adams's proposals altogether. The decision was a defeat for Adams, but it also heightened concerns, raised by some readers of Adams's *Defense of the Constitutions*, that the vice president had abandoned his former republicanism and favored the establishment of an American monarchy and a hereditary aristocracy. Thomas Jefferson, commenting about the titles controversy to James Madison, wrote that it confirmed Benjamin Franklin's assessment of Adams: "always an honest man, often a great one, but sometimes absolutely mad." Reaction in the press was uniformly hostile. Federalists who only a short time before had supported Adams's election began to view the vice president as a political liability who might bring the new government into popular disrepute.

The controversy seems to have cast a shadow over the relationship between the president and the vice president. Washington offered Adams no support during the titles debate, writing later that "the question was moved before I arrived, without any privity or knowledge of it on my part, and urged after I was apprized of it contrary to my opinion; for I foresaw and predicted the reception it has met with, and the use that would be made of it by the adversaries of the government." Frustrated by the storm of criticism, Adams apparently made uncomplimentary remarks in private about Washington, implying that it was the president, rather than himself, who was fond of aristocratic display. Some of these intemperate remarks may have made their way to Washington's ears, and he was particularly sensitive to charges that he was conducting himself like a republican monarch. Washington's official coolness toward Adams may also have been prompted by concerns that the titles controversy had given critics of the new government fresh reasons for opposing the measures of the administration. A close friend and political confidant, David Stuart, reported to Washington that the debate over titles had rendered Adams "unpopular in the extreme" and "highly odious" in Virginia. Stuart was certain that Adams would "never get a vote from this State again."

Washington's decision not to consult with the vice president did nothing to diminish Adams's determination to support the establishment of a strong executive branch. During Adams's first term as vice president, the Senate adopted legislation creating the executive departments, establishing the foreign service, and fixing the permanent location of the nation's capital; the Senate also adopted a series of controversial measures proposed by Secretary of the Treasury Alexander Hamilton establishing tariffs, providing for the funding of the national debt and the assumption of the Revolutionary debts of the states, as well as creating a national bank and a federal excise tax. Although he remained silent during most of the debates over these measures, Adams was called upon repeatedly to use his tie-breaking vote to push legislation through the Senate. In every case, Adams supported vesting the president with broad authority and backed the measures for ordering American finance recommended by Hamilton. In all, Adams cast fifteen tie-breaking votes during the First Congress alone; five of these votes were cast in the debate over the location of the nation's capital and three in the debate over funding the national debt. During his eight years in office, Adams cast his tie-breaking vote more than any subsequent vice president.

Adams's first opportunity to determine a question in the Senate by tie-breaking vote came in the summer of 1789 on the question of whether the Senate would acknowledge a presidential power to remove, without the consent of that body, officeholders who had been previously confirmed by the Senate. The question was raised in debate over a provision of the bill establishing the department of state. To senators nervous about the accumulation of power in the hands of the president, granting him the power to remove appointees at will threatened to unhinge the balance of power between the branches of government. Adams regarded this power as essential to executive branch operations and believed that opponents were engaged in a transparent attempt to extend the Senate's authority at the president's expense. Although he remained silent during formal debate, between sessions he drew members aside, trying to persuade them to vote in favor of acknowledging the president's power to remove. When the question was called on July 16, 1789, he had enough votes. The six members from south of the Potomac, as well as Maclay, Johnson of Connecticut, and the two senators from New Hampshire, voted against admitting the power; the remaining ten voted for it. With the Senate divided 10–10, Adams cast the deciding vote in favor of acknowledging the president's authority to remove his subordinates at will. Adams later noted that this vote, among all those he cast as vice president, gave him the most pleasure, but the pleasure came at considerable political expense. His growing number of enemies accused him of using the vote to build up the power of the presidency merely because he hoped to inherit the job from Washington.

Criticism of Adams's conduct as president of the Senate continued in the press without pause through the fall recess of 1789 and into 1790. In addition to continuing accusations that he favored the establishment of an American monarchy, opponents charged that he constantly interfered in Senate debates. Adams denied the charge, asserting that he had spoken at length only once, on the issue of the removal power, and that he did not wish to involve himself in any future debate. The attacks disturbed Adams so deeply that he considered resigning, suggesting to his friend John Trumbull in March 1790 that his personal unpopularity might endanger the government, particularly if Washington died or resigned the presidency, leaving the office in his hands.

Whether Adams actually came close to resigning the vice presidency in spring 1790 is not known, but the prospect that he would succeed to the presidency by Washington's death became a real possibility a few weeks later. In the spring of 1790, Washington contracted a case of influenza. The illness apparently developed into pneumonia; Washington's condition deteriorated quickly between May 12 and May 15, and by the evening of the fifteenth his doctors were convinced that Washington was dying. His fever was very high and he was coughing blood. Abigail Adams, who seems to have been present, recorded that early in the evening Washington "was Seazd with Hicups & rattling in the throat so that Mrs Washington left his room thinking him dying." For a few hours, it was expected that Adams would soon become president, but by late evening the crisis had passed and Washington began to recover. By the end of May, he was well enough to resume his duties.

Fortunately for the country, this episode was brief and occurred at a time when national affairs were relatively quiet. The country was spared a constitutional crisis, but the incident nonetheless set important precedents. During the weeks that Washington was unable to perform his duties, the executive department heads continued to manage their business without significant direction. The immediate business of the president's office was handled by William Jackson, one of Washington's private secretaries. Adams was not called upon, and no evidence has been found to indicate that anyone in the administration or in Congress suggested turning the responsibilities of the presidency over to him—particularly while the Senate was still in session. But the possibility of an invalid president had apparently occurred to some members of Congress. Earlier in the spring, when Washington's lingering illness began to raise comment and concern, Georgia Congressman Abraham Baldwin had written that:

> Our great and good man has been unwell again this spring. . . . If his health should not get confirmed soon, we must send him out to mount Vernon to farm a-while, and let the Vice manage here; his habits require so much exercise, and he is so fond of his plantation, that I have no doubt it would soon restore him.

This situation, ultimately, did not arise, and the vice president's role in the case of the president's long-term incapacity—a matter that would come up again in the nineteenth century but that was not resolved until recently—remained undetermined during the remainder of Adams's tenure.

After Congress recessed in August 1790, Adams devoted himself to writing a series of essays on politics, entitled "Discourses on Davila," which were published serially in the *Gazette of the United States*. The essays, which constitute one of Adams's most important political works, were constructed as a series of commentaries on the work of Henrico Caterino Davila, an Italian who had been involved in the French civil wars of the sixteenth century and wrote a history of the events. By comparing the civil wars with the French Revolution, Adams intended to demonstrate that the contemporary revolution, like its predecessor, was doomed to failure because neither revolution sought to establish a truly balanced government like the one that people of the United States enjoyed under the federal Constitution. Adams also sought to refute the ideas of universal equality and human perfectibility upon which the French Revolution was based and to justify his own position in favor of titles, ceremonies, and formalities.

Adams based his *Discourses on Davila* on the argument that man was everywhere and at all times motivated mainly by a desire for distinction "to be observed, considered, esteemed, praised, beloved, and admired by his fellows." This was the motive, Adams argued, behind the accumulation of wealth and the pursuit of political and social authority and was, in fact, the basis for most of the great achievements of human history. By attempting to abolish distinctions between individuals and establish government on the false idea of universal equality, Adams contended, the French revolutionaries were stifling the most natural and vital of human desires. In a properly ordered society, the desire for public acclaim should be "gratified and encouraged, and arranged on the side of virtue." Rather than frustrate the passion for distinction, then, governments should channel men's efforts to achieve superiority into useful pursuits by rewarding men of merit and accomplishment with titles and other honors. Without distinctions to award, governments would be despised, and men would seek acclaim in other spheres. Ultimately, they would overthrow the government and replace it with one that recognized and rewarded superiority.

Public reaction to Adams's *Discourses on Davila* was hostile, as he apparently expected. Opponents denounced him as a friend to monarchy and an enemy of the rights of man and the principles of American Revolution. Critics, some of whom called Adams the "Duke of Braintree," charged that he had been seduced by aristocratic corruption during his years in Europe and converted into a reactionary. John Fenno, the editor of the *Gazette of the United States*, found himself under a hail of criticism for printing the essays and decided to stop publishing the series. This put an end to Adams's efforts to present his political ideas for public discussion for the remainder of his vice presidency.

Although Adams had made himself a focus of controversy during his first term, Federalist leaders were content to support his reelection in 1792. His critical votes for administration measures had earned him the grudging support of Hamilton, who was also determined to defeat George Clinton, an old political opponent proposed by the emerging Republican opposition as an alternative to Adams. Clinton had the support of New York, Virginia, and North Carolina; Adams could expect the support of New England and solidly federalist South Carolina. The election hinged on the vote of the Middle States, most important of which was Pennsylvania, where the Republican opposition was well organized and active in promoting Clinton's election. Under these circumstances, Hamilton urged Adams, who had withdrawn to his farm in Quincy, to return to Philadelphia. Adams, who was determined to avoid the appearance of campaigning for office, refused. Hamilton's concern increased when he learned that Republican leaders were considering dropping Clinton as their candidate in favor of Aaron Burr. He implored Adams to come to Philadelphia immediately, but the vice president was unmoved.

The burden of securing Adams's reelection fell largely to Hamilton and his associates. When the electoral votes were counted in February 1793, Washington was reelected by a unanimous vote; Adams was reelected vice president with seventy-seven electoral votes. Clinton received fifty electoral votes, including all of those from New York, Virginia, North Carolina, and Georgia, and one from Pennsylvania. Jefferson received the four votes of Kentucky, and Aaron Burr received one vote from South Carolina. Adams received all the rest, including all the votes of New England, New Jersey, Delaware, and Maryland; fourteen of fifteen from Pennsylvania; and seven of eight from South Carolina.[*]

During his second term as vice president, Adams conducted himself with caution and circumspection, avoiding the kinds of controversies that had embroiled his first term. In the process, he isolated himself from partisan politics at the very moment when the national government was dividing into Federalist and Republican camps. By the beginning of 1793, the national government was deeply divided between Federalists, who supported Hamilton's financial program and American neutrality in the European conflict caused by the French Revolution, and the Republican opposition, which was violently opposed to Hamilton's financial system and sympathetic to the principles of the French Revolution. Although Adams had long since made his views on these matter abundantly clear, he refused to give his opponents further grounds for criticism and declined to make a partisan stand with the Federalists.

The controversy came to a head in 1793, when the new French minister to the United States, Edmond Genêt, sought to invoke the French-American alliance to draw the United States into France's war against Britain. Washington received conflicting advice from his cabinet on dealing with Genêt. Jefferson argued that Genêt should be received as the legitimate representative of France, while Hamilton urged the president to decline to receive him. Both men agreed that American neutrality should be declared, but Jefferson argued that this was the responsibility of Congress, while Hamilton contended that the president was empowered to issue a neutrality proclamation. When Hamilton's subordinate, Tench Coxe, wrote to Adams seeking support for Hamilton's position, Adams refused to become involved, writing that "I have no constitutional vote in it" and adding that "I therefore protest against taking any side in it or having my name or opinion quoted about it."[**]

As Adams's reticence increased, the barrage of public criticism of him declined. As early as 1792 opponents of the administration had begun to focus their harshest blows on Hamilton rather than Adams, and by the beginning of 1794 even Washington, formerly immune to public criticism, came under attack. Adams seems to have taken a certain wry pleasure in this change. "I have held the office of libellee-general long enough," he commented; "the burden of it ought to be participated and equalized, according to modern republican principles." Yet, with his determination not to wade into the political

---

[*]Editor's note: See GEORGE CLINTON for further explanation of this election.

[**]Editor's note: See GEORGE CLINTON for further explanation of the Genêt Affair.

struggle, Adams began to feel even more irrelevant. In December 1793, he complained to Abigail that "My country has in its wisdom contrived for me the most insignificant office that was the invention of man . . . or his imagination conceived."

Adams's second term as vice president, was, in many ways, the true twilight of his career. His health, never robust, had been deteriorating since his return from Europe. He had experienced repeated bouts of illness, lost several of his teeth, and suffered increasingly from rheumatic symptoms. Repeated inflammations of the eyes at times rendered him almost blind. Abigail's health was failing as well, and Adams endured frequent separations from her when her ills confined her to the farm in Quincy while he journeyed to Philadelphia to attend the Senate. In 1794, he recorded that his routine during one of these solitary periods consisted of going to the Senate each day, seeing a few friends once a week, and going to church on Sundays. For amusement and intellectual stimulation, he turned increasingly to his books, although after the hostile reception of his *Discourses on Davila*, he no longer sought to express his political ideas in the public press. Instead, he became increasingly eccentric and reclusive and also suffered from bouts of depression, during which he tended to be particularly gloomy about the future of the country.

Adams's private pessimism about the future of the nation did not diminish his ambition to succeed Washington as president. Adams regarded his succession to the presidency as natural, due to him by seniority and long service in the second post. When he had assumed the presidency, Washington seems to have regarded the vice president as his natural successor, but as the election of 1796 approached, he studiously avoided endorsing any of the potential candidates. Thomas Jefferson was the candidate of the Republicans and Adams's principal competitor, but neither Adams nor Jefferson actively campaigned for the office. The Republicans supported Aaron Burr for the vice presidency. Federalist leaders settled on Thomas Pinckney of South Carolina for vice president, but some, including Hamilton, worked behind the scenes to secure Pinckney's election as president by making sure that he received the second votes of electors from all sections. Some southern electors could be expected to vote for Pinckney and Jefferson and thus deliver the presidency to the South Carolinian and leave Adams with the vice presidency. This possibility occurred to Adams's supporters in New England, and some of them cast their second votes for candidates other than Pinckney. When the ballots were counted, Adams received seventy-one electoral votes, while Jefferson received sixty-eight, Pinckney fifty-nine, and Burr thirty. Adams was thus elected president by only three electoral votes.

Adams was inaugurated as president on March 4, 1797. By the time Adams assumed the presidency, relations with France had reached their lowest point since the Revolution. The French government, infuriated by Jay's Treaty and the recall of James Monroe as minister, had issued decrees permitting attacks on American shipping and refused to permit Monroe's successor, Charles C. Pinckney, to remain on French soil. The ensuing diplomatic crisis with France completely dominated Adams's presidency. Although Adams managed to preserve peace with France, the effort ultimately cost him his political career. It also undermined the unity of the Federalist party and delivered the presidency to Adams's Republican opponent in the election of 1800, Thomas Jefferson.

Adams's conduct throughout the crisis in relations with France—and indeed his whole administration—was shaped by the personal, political, and intellectual isolation that had gradually overtaken him during his eight years as vice president. Although his principles were consistently Federalist, Adams had not established himself as a leader of the Federalist Party. The principal members of his cabinet—Secretary of State Timothy Pickering, Secretary of the Treasury Oliver Wolcott, and Secretary of War James McHenry—were retained from the Washington administration and were close political allies of Hamilton, to whom they looked for guidance and leadership. Adams made no effort to cultivate their loyalty to him or to build a loyal following among others in the government. He preferred to make important decisions on his own, and his failure to consult with his cabinet or other members of the government often made his decisions appear erratic and impulsive. This tendency, combined with his touchiness and vanity, alienated him from the members of his own party and led ultimately to his political downfall.

Shortly after taking office, Adams dispatched a special commission to France to reestablish cordial relations. The commission quickly ran into difficulty: French foreign minister Talleyrand saw that he could take advantage of the crisis in relations between the two countries to embarrass the Adams administration, thus helping the American friends of France in the Republican Party. He consequently sent three unofficial agents to demand payments from the commissioners before beginning negotiations. When the attempts by Talleyrand's agents (dubbed X, Y, and Z) to extort these bribes from the commissioners became known in the United States, the public was outraged. Adams, with widespread public support, announced that he would not send another minister to France without assurances that he would be received with courtesy and began preparations for war.* Congress declared the existing treaties with France void and ordered the construction of new ships for the navy and the establishment of a large provisional army. Encounters between French and American warships off the American coast and in the Caribbean, including several full-scale engagements, pushed the United States and France to the brink of war.

Having provoked the crisis, Talleyrand was prepared to appear conciliatory, by stages, in order to divide the Federalist Party between advocates of peace and war. In trying to preserve peace, Adams fell victim to this strategy. In the fall of 1798, Adams embraced reports that the French were prepared to renew negotiations. Members of the cabinet, however, argued against sending another minister to France without assurances that he would be received with honor. Adams initially agreed, but when he learned in February 1799 that the French had retracted their maritime decrees, he decided to nominate William Vans Murray as minister to France. When this decision encountered hostility in the Senate, Adams proposed sending a peace commission to France, of which Murray would be a member, as soon as the French indicated a willingness to receive them. The Senate grudgingly approved the plan, but many Federalists believed that Adams's efforts to avoid war only invited further national humiliation. Pickering, Wolcott, and McHenry privately blamed Adams for dividing the Federalist Party, arguing that this could only benefit the French and their American friends in the Republican Party. Within the government, they worked to prevent the departure of the commissioners, contending for months that the French had not provided adequate assurances that they would be received with respect.

Adams unwittingly obliged his opponents by retiring to Quincy for several months, conducting public business by correspondence, and deferring many important decisions to cabinet members. Federalist leaders, including Hamilton, met with Adams when he returned to the capital in October, imploring him to delay the mission indefinitely. Unmoved, Adams ordered the commissioners to depart for Europe. "We have succeeded," Talleyrand boasted in a confidential report to his superiors, "in dividing the party of Mr. Adams himself."

The commission opened negotiations with the French in April 1800, but the talks proceeded at a frustratingly slow pace. Talleyrand was not inclined to make Adams a hero by allowing the commissioners to return home quickly with a treaty meeting all or even most of the American demands. Instead of a definitive treaty, the two sides ultimately agreed to a modest convention, signed on October 3, 1800. In it, the parties agreed to return captured naval vessels and all captured property not yet condemned, and they effectively agreed to dissolve the alliance signed in 1778, as well as the consular convention of 1788. The new convention renewed the maritime principle of the treaty of 1778, discarded by the French in their campaign

---

*Editor's note: See ELBRIDGE GERRY for further explanation of the XYZ Affair.

against American shipping, that free ships make free goods. In this sense the convention was a diplomatic success for the Adams administration, but it came too late to save Adams's political career.

Federalist leaders meeting in May 1800 had decided to support Adams's reelection and chose Charles C. Pinckney as their candidate for vice president. Despite their hostility to Adams, Hamilton and his associates realized that supporting a war candidate would divide the party in the election and ensure the victory of Jefferson. Hamilton's reluctant support of Adams's reelection soon turned to open hostility, however, and in the closing weeks of the campaign he made a savage attack on Adams in the press that all but ensured Federalist defeat. While the Federalists quarreled, Republicans, united behind the candidacy of Thomas Jefferson, staged a well-organized and effective campaign. When the electoral votes were counted, Jefferson and the Republican vice presidential candidate, Aaron Burr, received seventy-three votes each; Adams received sixty-five, and Pinckney sixty-four. John Jay received one vote. Adams retained the support of New England, New Jersey, and Delaware, as well as five of ten votes from Maryland, seven of fifteen from Pennsylvania, and four of twelve from North Carolina. The tie between Jefferson and Burr threw the election into the House of Representatives, where Jefferson was ultimately elected.

Adams's defeat ended a career in public service that had lasted some twenty-six years. He lived for more than twenty-five more years but never again held public office. In the first years of his retirement, Adams was blamed for the defeat of the Federalists by the Hamilton wing of the party, although he continued to enjoy the esteem of many moderate New England Federalists. Although out of office, he maintained a keen interest in politics and political philosophy untinged by partisanship. After Jefferson left the presidency, the two old friends were reconciled and engaged in a lively correspondence that lasted until both men died. Abigail Adams died on October 28, 1818, depriving Adams of his closest friend. John Adams lived long enough to see his eldest son, John Quincy, elected president in 1824. John Adams's own death occurred on July 4, 1826, just a few hours after the death of Thomas Jefferson.

REFERENCES

Page Smith, *John Adams*, 2 vols. (Garden City, N.Y.: Doubleday & Co., 1963); John Ferling, *John Adams: A Life* (Knoxville, Tenn.: University of Tennessee Press, 1992); Peter Shaw, *The Character of John Adams* (Chapel Hill, N.C.: University of North Carolina Press, 1976); Joseph J. Ellis, *Passionate Sage: The Character and Legacy of John Adams* (New York: W.W. Norton & Co., 1993); Stanley Elkins and Eric McKitrick, *The Age of Federalism* (New York: Oxford University Press, 1993); Alexander DeConde, *The Quasi-War: The Politics and Diplomacy of the Undeclared War with France, 1797–1801* (New York: Charles Scribner's Sons, 1966); Edmund S. Morgan, *The Meaning of Independence: John Adams, George Washington, Thomas Jefferson* (Charlottesville, Va.: University of Virginia Press, 1976); Gordon S. Wood, *The Creation of the American Republic, 1776–1787* (Chapel Hill, N.C.: University of North Carolina Press, 1969); *The Diary and Autobiography of John Adams*, Lyman H. Betterfield et al., eds., 4 vols. (Cambridge, Mass.: Harvard University Press, 1961); *The Papers of John Adams*, Robert J. Taylor et al., eds., 6 volumes to date (Cambridge, Mass.: Harvard University Press, 1977–); *Adams Family Correspondence*, Lyman H. Butterfield et al., eds., 6 volumes to date (Cambridge, Mass.: Harvard University Press, 1963–); *New Letters of Abigail Adams, 1788–1801*, Stewart Mitchell, ed. (Boston: Houghton Mifflin, 1947); *The Adams–Jefferson Letters*, Lester J. Cappon, ed. (Chapel Hill, N.C.: University of North Carolina Press, 1959); *The Diary of William Maclay and Other Notes on Senate Debates*, Kenneth R. Bowling and Helen E. Veit, eds. (Baltimore, Md.: Johns Hopkins University Press, 1988); *The Papers of George Washington*, W.W. Abbot et al., eds., 27 vols. to date (Charlottesville, Va.: University of Virginia Press, 1983–).

JACK D. WARREN is assistant editor of *The Papers of George Washington* and a member of the faculty of the University of Virginia. He specializes in politics in the Federalist era and is the co-author of *A Covenanted People: The Religious Tradition and the Origins of American Constitutionalism* (Providence, R.I., 1987) and the author of several articles on the Early Republic.

THOMAS JEFFERSON (1743–1826)

Vice President, 1797–1801

(President John Adams)

THOMAS JEFFERSON
(Library of Congress)

By Eugene R. Sheridan

A true Renaissance man, Thomas Jefferson combined the skills of an astute political leader with the vision of a dazzling intellectual virtuoso to a degree that is unsurpassed in American history. In the course of four critical decades of public service, during which he played a key role in the disruption of the First British Empire and the emergence of the new American nation, Jefferson distinguished himself as a member of the Continental Congress, Virginia legislator and governor, minister to France, secretary of state, Republican Party leader, vice president, and president. As a political philosopher, he eloquently proclaimed in the Declaration of Independence the core values of liberty, equality, and natural rights that constitute the heart of the American experiment in self-government. As the author of the epochal Virginia Statute for Religious Freedom, he set forth the pattern of complete religious liberty through strict separation of church and state that eventually became standard throughout the United States. As a leading man of science, he wrote a pioneering work in natural history, *Notes on the State of Virginia*, was a proficient archaeologist and inventor, and served for almost two decades as president of the nation's most prestigious scientific institution, the American Philosophical Society. As the most accomplished American architect of his time, his designs for his home at Monticello, the Virginia state capitol, and the University of Virginia helped to inspire the revival of classical architecture in the new republic. As an educator, he was a strong champion of public education and the main founder of the University of Virginia. As a devoted bibliophile and accomplished linguist, he amassed an extraordinarily varied library of almost 7,000 volumes that served as the nucleus of the new Library of Congress after the destruction of the old one during the British attack on Washington in 1814. Finally, as a religious pilgrim who moved from Anglican orthodoxy to natural religion to demythologized Christianity, he was the first person in American history to engage in one of the key developments in modern biblical criticism, the quest for the historic Jesus. In view of this extraordinary record of accomplishment, President John F. Kennedy spoke only half in jest when he hailed a group of Nobel laureates in various fields as the "most extraordinary collection of talents that has ever gathered together at the White House, with the possible exception of when Thomas Jefferson dined alone."

The central theme of Jefferson's career was his fervent commitment to the establishment of a lasting republican social and political order in the United States. Jeffersonian republicanism was a dynamic blend of Lockean liberalism and civic humanism that rejected all vestiges of monarchy and hereditary privilege and sought to promote liberty, advance enlightenment, and unleash the creative energies of the American people within the framework of limited government, popular sovereignty, and an agrarian society guided by a natural aristocracy based on virtue and merit rather the birth and wealth. To ensure that government respected the natural rights of man and guaranteed to free men the fruits of their labor, Jefferson insisted that its powers must be sharply limited and made strictly accountable to the people through written constitutions, institutional checks and balances, and frequent elections. In Jefferson's view, the central theme of history was the perpetual struggle between power and liberty,

and he rarely wavered in his conviction that the government's powers had to be limited in order to make people's liberties secure.

In the end, however, Jefferson believed that the survival of republicanism in the United States depended more on the character of its people than the structure of the U.S. government. In his opinion, a republic could only survive among a virtuous people who were independent, frugal, temperate, industrious, ready to fight for their liberty, and willing when necessary to subordinate their private interests to the greater public good. Convinced that these qualities were best exemplified by farmers and planters, whose ownership of land endowed them with the personal independence he considered absolutely essential for politically responsible citizenship in a republican polity, he hoped to preserve agrarian dominance of American society indefinitely by seeking foreign markets to absorb surplus agricultural production and by supporting the westward advance of American settlement. By thus inhibiting the development of manufacturing and urbanization, which he feared would undermine republican virtue by creating increasing webs of economic and social dependence among the American people, Jefferson hoped that expansion across space would delay the corruption over time to which, according to his reading of history, republics were invariably subject.

Jefferson was born into a Virginia gentry family on April 13, 1743, the eldest son and the third of eight surviving children. He attended the College of William and Mary from 1760 to 1762 and then studied law for five years with George Wyth. Until his retirement from the legal profession in 1775, Jefferson enjoyed a successful legal practice in Virginia. Among other things, this helped him to contract an advantageous marriage in 1772 with a young widow, Martha Wales Skelton, who before her untimely death ten years later bore him six children, only two of whom, Martha and Mary, reached adulthood. Between what he inherited from his father and acquired through marriage, Jefferson was one of the wealthiest Virginians of his time, owning about 10,000 acres of land and 150 slaves, with the centerpiece of his estate being the elegant Palladian villa of Monticello, set high atop a 987-feet-high mountain overlooking the town of Charlottesville. It was the greatest irony of Jefferson's life that his career as a defender of republican liberty was based upon an economic system in which his own freedom and prosperity depended upon depriving black people of theirs.

Jefferson's belief that British efforts to reorganize the Empire after 1763 were part of a systematic conspiracy to destroy American liberties launched a political career that lasted for forty years and left a decisive mark on American history. He entered the House of Burgesses in 1769 and within a few years emerged as a strong proponent of unified colonial resistance to British imperialism. In 1774, he placed himself in the vanguard of the radical movement with the publication of *A Summary View of the Rights of British America*, a pamphlet that denied parliamentary authority over the colonies and argued that the colonies were only bound to Britain by their allegiance to the king. As a member of the Continental Congress during the final throes of the imperial crisis in 1775–1776, he made his greatest contribution to the revolutionary cause through his authorship of one of the fundamental charters of American freedom, the Declaration of Independence.

After the congressional decision for independence, Jefferson turned his attention to the task of laying secure foundations for the emerging republican order in the new nation. As a member of the Virginia House of Delegates from 1776 to 1779, he sought with only partial success to replace the traditional aristocracy of birth and wealth in his native state with a natural aristocracy of virtue and merit to guide an enlightened citizenry. In consequence of the role he played in revising the entire structure of Virginia law so as to rid it of all vestiges of monarchy and make it compatible with republican principles, Jefferson served as governor of Virginia from 1779 to 1781. Though a capable administrator, he dealt ineffectually with two British invasions of the state in 1781, and the resultant criticism led him to retire to private life in June of that year.

Jefferson returned to public service in reaction to the tragic death of his wife in 1782, which shattered his dream of spending the rest of his life at Monticello pursuing his scientific interests. Before this devastating loss, however, he had taken advantage of his first retirement from public life to write the manuscript of his first book, *Notes on the State of Virginia*, an eloquently written essay on natural history, published in 1785, in which he vigorously disputed the contention of European naturalists that human, animal, and plant life had degenerated in America because of the New World's allegedly insalubrious climate.

Resuming his legislative career on the national level, Jefferson served in the Confederation Congress from 1783 to 1784. During this period he made a profound contribution to American political and social development with a report on territorial government whose basic principles were incorporated into the more celebrated Northwest Ordinance of 1787. By providing procedures for the admission of new states into the Union on the basis of equality with the original thirteen, Jefferson sought to promote rapid settlement of the American West by farmers in order to preserve and extend the agrarian social base that he regarded as necessary for the success of the American experiment in republicanism.

Jefferson's second term in Congress was followed by his entry into diplomatic service. Between 1784 and 1789 he served Congress in Paris, first as a commissioner to negotiate commercial treaties with various European powers and then as American minister to France. This experience convinced him that the United States needed a stronger central government to achieve its foreign policy objectives, so he generally supported the Constitution of 1787; however, he criticized its lack of a bill of rights and its failure to limit the number of presidential terms. His criticisms played a small part in convincing Federalists to remedy the former omission. He left France in the fall of 1789, convinced that a new day of liberty was dawning in Europe and that France was the only nation on which the United States could rely as an effective counterweight to Britain. Even though he hoped to return to his ministerial post in Paris, he reluctantly agreed in 1790 to serve instead as George Washington's first secretary of state.

During Jefferson's tenure as secretary of state from 1790 to 1793, he became involved in a titanic struggle with Secretary of the Treasury Alexander Hamilton over the future of the American republic. In the great trinity of Hamiltonian finance—funding, assumption, and the national bank—Jefferson eventually detected a vast system of special privilege that enriched the few at the expense of the many, encouraged an unhealthy speculative spirit among the people, upset the balance of property, and corrupted the national legislature. In the Hamiltonian call for federal encouragement of a wide range of U.S. manufacturing, Jefferson perceived a grave threat to the agrarian social order he considered essential for the health of American republicanism. In the Hamiltonian insistence on loose construction of the Constitution, Jefferson espied a source of constitutional degeneration that was designed to aggrandize the powers of the central government at the expense of the states' authority and the people's liberty. In the Hamiltonian support of a pro-British foreign policy, Jefferson perceived an effort to align the United States with the forces of monarchy and aristocracy in their conflict with revolutionary France. Viewing these policies cumulatively, Jefferson detected nothing less than a concerted Federalist effort to establish a monarchical form of government in the United States along British lines.

Convinced that Federalist centralism was a mortal threat to his vision of the United States as a virtuous agrarian republic, Jefferson joined James Madison in creating the Republican Party as an effective counterweight to Federalism. After collaborating in 1791 to establish the *National Gazette* in Philadelphia to promote the Republican cause, the two Virginians followed a natural division of labor with respect to the emerging opposition: While Madison organized Republicans in the House of Representatives and articulated their position in the columns of the *National Gazette,* Jefferson opposed Hamilton in the cabinet and in a series of remarkable private communications in which he sought to persuade President Washington that the treasury secretary and his policies were undermining American republicanism. Jefferson's efforts to mobilize

opposition against Hamiltonian Federalism reached a climax early in 1793, when he secretly engineered an abortive attempt by capital Republicans to drive Hamilton from office by censuring his management of the Treasury. Although thereafter Jefferson continued to be involved in formulating Republican Party strategy, he felt so ambivalent about acting as a party leader that he retired from office on the final day of 1793, determined to remain a private citizen for the rest of his life.

The imperatives of party politics drew a reluctant Jefferson back into the political arena only three years after beginning what he fondly hoped would be a lifelong period of retirement at Monticello. Frustrated by Congress's failure to enact the program of commercial retaliation against Britain he had recommended shortly before leaving office as secretary of state, Jefferson then lost confidence in the president after Washington denounced the Democratic Societies in the wake of the Whiskey Rebellion and approved the Jay Treaty, an agreement that Jefferson viewed as a craven surrender of vital American national interests to the British. Unable to persuade Madison to stand as Republican candidate for president, Jefferson reluctantly allowed Republicans to cast him in this role after Washington announced that he would not serve a third term. Jefferson took no active part in the campaign and actually hoped that the moderate Federalist John Adams would prevail, in large part because the francophile Jefferson was disinclined to serve as president when American relations with France were rapidly deteriorating in the wake of French dissatisfaction with the Jay Treaty. In the event, Jefferson received the second-highest number of electoral votes after Adams, and because at that time electors did not cast separate votes for president and vice president, the Virginia leader won the latter office.

Jefferson was the first vice president in American history to preside over a Senate dominated by an opposing party. From 1797 to 1801, Federalists held solid majorities in the Senate, and if Jefferson viewed Federalists as covert monarchist conspirators, they regarded him as an unregenerate Jacobin fanatic who threatened their vision of the United States as an orderly, centralized, hierarchical republic. Federalists made no secret of their contempt for Jefferson, and it was not unusual for Federalist senators to make sharp verbal attacks on the Virginia leader even as he presided over the Senate. As a result of this situation, Jefferson as vice president carefully confined himself to serving as the Senate's presiding officer and made no official effort to use this office to shape that body's legislative agenda.

Federalist control of the Senate accounts in no small measure for Jefferson's pattern of attendance as vice president. Except for the first session of the Fifth Congress, which met from May 15 to July 10, 1797, Jefferson arrived in the Senate several weeks after the legislature opened, and apart from the first session of the Sixth Congress, which met from December 2, 1799, to May 14, 1800, he left a few days before it closed. In response to public criticism that he was thereby neglecting his public duty, Jefferson contended that there was no need for him to attend during the first three weeks of the legislative session because the Senate rarely considered any bills during that time. At the same time he argued that it was essential for him to leave early and enable the Senate to choose a president pro tempore because under the Presidential Succession Act of 1792 that official stood next in line for the presidency after the vice president. Although these factors were undoubtedly operative, it also seems clear that Jefferson deliberately delayed his arrival at the beginning of each legislative session so that he did not have to affix his signature as vice president to the inevitably laudatory replies that the Federalist-dominated Senate made to President Adams's opening addresses to Congress. He had fallen into this trap during the emergency legislative session called by Adams during the summer of 1797 but thereafter avoided committing the same political error.

Jefferson was involved in two dramatic episodes in senatorial history during his tenure as vice president. In the first, he presided over the Senate trial of William Blount, a Republican senator for Tennessee who had been expelled in 1797 for conspiring to establish British control over the Spanish provinces of Louisiana and West Florida

and then had been impeached by the House. Jefferson, who at this point in his career was fearful of impeachment as a tool that Federalists might abuse in the heat of partisan warfare with their Republican adversaries, privately advised Senators Henry Tazewell of Virginia and Samuel Livermore of New Hampshire that it would be preferable to have Blount tried by a jury. Jefferson's advice was disregarded, but in the end he was mollified by the Senate's decision that senators were unimpeachable civil officials.

In addition to presiding over the first impeachment trial in Senate history, Jefferson was apparently instrumental in frustrating a Federalist effort to try the noted Republican editor, William Duane, for contempt of the Senate. In 1800, Federalist senators sought to try Duane for contempt in retaliation for his unauthorized publication in the Philadelphia *Aurora* of a Senate bill that provided for the creation of a special commission to rule on the validity of disputed presidential election votes and for his depiction of it as a blatant partisan maneuver to ensure Federalist success in the forthcoming national election. With Jefferson's covert support, Duane refused to appear before the Senate for trial because of that body's refusal to allow his counsel to question its jurisdiction in this case. Changing tack, the Senate then requested President Adams to have Duane prosecuted for seditious libel under the Sedition Act, a maneuver that Jefferson himself deflected after he became president.

Jefferson's most lasting contribution as vice president was the compilation and publication of his *Manual of Parliamentary Practice for the Use of the Senate of the United States*. The orderly conduct of parliamentary business had been a central concern of Jefferson's ever since his early days as a Virginia colonial legislator. Upon taking office as vice president, he was accordingly distressed to encounter what he regarded as the excessively wide latitude the Senate had given to this officer in deciding points of order. As he noted in the introduction to his *Manual*:

The Senate have accordingly formed some rules for its own government: but these going only to few cases, they have referred to the decision of their President, without debate and without appeal, all questions of order arising either under their own rules, or where they have provided none. This places under the discretion of the President a very extensive field of decision, and one which, irregularly exercised, would have a powerful effect on the proceedings and determinations of the House.

In order to promote the orderly conduct of business in the Senate and prevent its presiding officer from acting arbitrarily, Jefferson decided to prepare a body of parliamentary precedents for the upper house to draw upon in transacting its work. To this end he compiled a collection of precedents on fifty-three points of parliamentary procedure from the history of the British Parliament, the "model which we have all studied," as he noted in the *Manual*, and published the resulting work in February 1801 just before he left office as vice president. Although intended for the Senate, Jefferson's *Manual* was later adopted by the House of Representatives as well, and even today it continues to guide the conduct of business in both houses of Congress.

While presiding over the Senate as vice president, Jefferson emerged as the chief Republican Party leader, a role that had hitherto been played by Madison. After an initial effort to cooperate with President Adams, the leader of the moderate wing of the Federalist Party, circumstances compelled Jefferson to act as the leader of the Republican opposition to the second president. Jefferson and his followers favored a more conciliatory policy toward France than the one pursued by Adams, and they viewed the Alien and Sedition Acts of 1798 as a transparent effort to crush them as a legitimate political opposition. In order to energize Republican opposition to Adams and the Federalists, Jefferson formulated legislative strategy with congressional Republicans, formed intersectional alliances with northern Republicans, and encouraged Republican journalists to keep up a drumbeat of criticism of Federalist policies. In his most dramatic move of all, he secretly drafted the Kentucky Resolutions of 1798, which denounced the Alien and Sedition Acts as unconstitutional and asserted the right of the states to nullify any law they deemed contrary to the Constitution.

Convinced that Federalist centralism imperiled the survival of republican liberty in the United States, Jefferson unhesitatingly stood as the Republican Party's standard bearer in 1800. In deference to his personal temperament and the electoral customs of the age, Jefferson refrained from campaigning openly for the presidency. However, behind the scenes, he encouraged Republican pamphleteers and journalists to articulate the party's position, circulated Republican campaign tracts, coordinated political strategy with Republican Party organizations, and enunciated a party platform emphasizing the virtues of limited government, states' rights, strict construction of the Constitution, and noninvolvement in European political affairs. After a vicious campaign, in which he was denounced as an atheist, an unworldly philosopher, and a Jacobin fanatic, Jefferson defeated Adams by a margin of seventy-three to sixty-five electoral votes. However, because Jefferson and his running mate, Aaron Burr of New York, received the same number of electoral votes, the election was finally decided in the House of Representatives, which, after thirty-six ballots and in the face of determined Federalist efforts to select Burr, at length declared Jefferson the winner.

Jefferson's two terms in office were a crucial stage in the development of the American presidency. As the first party leader to serve as the country's chief executive, Jefferson abandoned the passive patriot-king style of presidential leadership followed by George Washington and John Adams and adopted a more activist popular style of governance to reverse the Federalist centralizing policies he regarded as dangerous to republican liberty. Whereas his two predecessors viewed themselves in effect as republicanized patriot-kings governing above political parties and through cabinet ministers in pursuit of the common good, Jefferson was the first president to govern through a political party in the interests of the people. By combining the roles of chief executive and Republican Party leader, Jefferson significantly enhanced the power of the presidency by uniting the authority granted to the president by the Constitution with the popular support he derived from his party leadership.

However, like Washington and Adams, Jefferson ultimately hoped to eliminate political parties, not to function within the framework of a two-party system. He never accepted the Federalists as a legitimate political opposition, and he long sought to rid America of institutionalized conflict between contending political parties by enticing the Federalist rank and file to embrace the Republican cause. It remained for Andrew Jackson, by combining the roles of president and party leader with an acceptance of the legitimacy of the party system, to complete the transition Jefferson began.

Jefferson enjoyed a triumphal first term as president, aided in no small measure by the restoration of peace in Europe in 1801 after nearly a decade of devastating wars between revolutionary France and its antagonists. During this period, Jefferson's overriding domestic priority was to reverse Federalist centralizing policies by reducing the federal government to its proper constitutional limits and paying off the national debt. To this end, he prevailed upon Congress in 1802 to approve Secretary of the Treasury Albert Gallatin's plan to retire the national debt of $82 million in sixteen years, which also entailed eliminating all internal taxes as well as a number of federal offices and sharply reducing the size of the army, the navy, and the diplomatic corps. Whereas Hamiltonians viewed a national debt as an effective instrument for creating a strong nation-state by attaching public creditors to the central government, Jeffersonians regarded it as the source of a corrupt monied interest that encouraged dangerous speculative habits among, and imposed burdensome taxes on, the agrarian majority. Because of a tremendous upsurge in the volume of foreign trade and thus the payment of import duties, by the time he left office in 1809 Jefferson had effected a substantial reduction in the national debt and generated a surplus in the Treasury. But it was not until the time of Andrew Jackson's administration that the Jeffersonian dream of completely eliminating the national debt was briefly realized.

Despite his wish to avoid foreign entanglements, Jefferson was obliged to face two serious international crises during his first administration. In response to news of increasing Tripolitan aggression against American merchant shipping in the Mediterranean, Jefferson in May 1801 dispatched a naval squadron to protect the nation's growing commerce in that area. There ensued four years of naval warfare with Tripoli that ended in 1805 with a peace treaty by which the Tripolitan government exempted the United States from the payment of the customary tribute to protect American shipping from Barbary piracy. Although Jefferson had long opposed this practice as an affront to national honor, the United States continued to pay annual tribute to the other Barbary states of Algiers, Morocco, and Tunis until 1815.

The war with Tripoli was far overshadowed by the Louisiana Purchase, the crowning achievement of Jefferson's presidency. The Spanish retrocession of Louisiana to Napoleonic France in 1800 threatened to create a revived French empire in the New World that would endanger the United States's vitally important right to navigate the Mississippi and halt the westward sweep of American expansion along the eastern bank of this waterway. In the face of this threat to his vision of a continental "empire of liberty" in North America, Jefferson brought diplomatic pressure to bear on France to leave Louisiana in Spanish hands and at the same time sought to purchase New Orleans and the Floridas to guarantee western settlers the right of navigation on the Mississippi. Owing to diplomatic developments in Europe, however, Napoleon agreed in April 1803 to sell all of Louisiana to the United States for $15 million—a deal that doubled the size of the nation and seemingly secured for ages yet to come Jefferson's vision of the United States as a virtuous agrarian republic.

The frustrations of Jefferson's second term stood in sharp contrast to the successes of his first, largely because of his inability to cope successfully with the challenges to U.S. neutrality stemming from the renewal in 1803 of the momentous struggle for mastery in Europe between Great Britain and France. In domestic affairs Jefferson continued his policy of redirecting the flow of power from the federal government to the states.

In addition, in 1807 he prevailed upon Congress to pass legislation implementing the constitutionally authorized ban on U.S. participation in the African slave trade after that year, but he failed to win congressional approval for an imaginative plan to use surplus government revenues to finance a system of internal improvements to cement the bonds of union. Moreover, in a matter that had domestic and diplomatic ramifications, he thwarted a plot by his former vice president, Aaron Burr, to detach the West from the Union and invade Mexico.

Jefferson's very success in reducing the powers of the federal government prevented him from responding effectively to the growing British and French violations of United States neutrality that formed the central theme of his second administration. Although both nations tried to prevent American ships from trading with the other, Great Britain, with its enormous naval power, was by far the worse offender, impressing thousands of seamen on American ships, patrolling American harbors to enforce British neutrality policies, and striving to prevent American trade with the British or French West Indies. After failing to achieve a diplomatic settlement of these Anglo-American differences, Jefferson had to face the issue of peace or war in its starkest form in June 1807, when H.M.S. *Leopard* attacked the American warship *Chesapeake* off Norfolk, Virginia, and removed four alleged British deserters. In the end, however, Jefferson chose economic coercion over war. Lacking credible military or naval power, troubled by the thought that war would impede his effort to pay off the national debt, and convinced that Britain was peculiarly vulnerable to economic pressure because of her dependence on American foodstuffs, Jefferson obtained a series of Embargo Acts from Congress that interdicted all U.S. exports to foreign countries. But the Embargo generated widespread economic hardship and popular resistance at home, while failing to obtain any British or French concession on neutrality issues, and on the eve of Jefferson's departure from office in 1809 it was replaced by the Non-Intercourse Act, which allowed the United States to trade with all nations except Britain and France and set the stage for the War of 1812.

Despite widespread Republican pleas that he serve a third term, Jefferson returned to private life in March 1809, determined to follow Washington's example and thereby help to make the two-term limit on presidents a binding precedent. In one sense, the last seventeen years of Jefferson's life were richly rewarding, marked as they were by the resumption of his rich correspondence with John Adams, the sale of his library to the Library of Congress, the foundation of the University of Virginia, and the continuation of his biblical studies. In another sense, however, these were deeply troubling years for Jefferson, for, in addition to plunging deeper and deeper into a debt that was to deprive his family of Monticello after his death, he grew more and more concerned about the threats posed to his vision of the United States as a virtuous agrarian republic by increases in urbanization, manufacturing, speculation, and sectional strife after the War of 1812. However, in the end, optimism prevailed over pessimism, and in his last surviving letter, written only ten days before his death on the fiftieth anniversary of the Declaration of Independence, Jefferson proclaimed his faith that this document would "be to the world, what I believe it will be, (to some parts sooner, to others later, but finally to all,) the signal of arousing men to burst the chains under which monkish ignorance and superstition had persuaded them to bind themselves, and to secure the blessings and security of self-government."

REFERENCES

Noble Cunningham, *In Pursuit of Reason: The Life of Thomas Jefferson* (Baton Rouge, La.: Louisiana State University Press, 1987); Dumas Malone, *Jefferson and His Time*, 6 vols. (Boston: Little Brown, 1948–81); Merrill Peterson, *Thomas Jefferson and the New Nation* (New York: Oxford University Press, 1970); Robert M. Johnstone, Jr., *Jefferson and the Presidency: Leadership in the Young Republic* (Ithaca, N.Y.: Cornell University Press, 1978); *The Papers of Thomas Jefferson*, Julian P. Boyd et al., eds., 26 vols. (Princeton, N.J.: Princeton University Press, 1950–); *The Writings of Thomas Jefferson*, Paul L. Ford, ed., 10 vols. (New York: Knickerbocker Press, 1892–99); *Jefferson's Parliamentary Writings*, Wilbur S. Howell, ed. (Princeton, N.J.: Princeton University Press, 1988); Roy Swanstrom, *The United States Senate, 1787–1801* (Washington, D.C.: Government Printing Office,

1985); Stanley Elkins and Eric McKitrick, *The Age of Federalism: The American Republic, 1788–1800* (New York: Oxford University Press, 1993); Henry Adams, *History of the United States during the Administrations of Jefferson and Madison*, 9 vols. (New York: Charles Scribner's Sons, 1889–91).

EUGENE R. SHERIDAN was senior associate editor of *The Papers of Thomas Jefferson* and a member of the Princeton University History Department. He was killed in an automobile accident in the spring of 1996 as this volume was in preparation. Before coming to Princeton, he was an editorial fellow with the *Adams Family Papers* at the Massachusetts Historical Society and associate editor of *Letters of Delegates to Congress* at the Library of Congress. He was the author of *Lewis Morris, 1671–1746: A Study in Early American Politics* (Syracuse, 1981), coeditor with John Murrin of *Congress at Princeton* (Princeton, 1985), and editor of the *Papers of Lewis Morris, 1698–1746*, 3 vols. (Newark, 1991–93).

AARON BURR (1756–1836)

Vice President, 1801–1805

(President Thomas Jefferson)

AARON BURR
(Library of Congress)

By Mary-Jo Kline

Born on February 6, 1736, in a Presbyterian parsonage in Newark, New Jersey, Aaron Burr, Jr., seemed destined for a life of intellectual and moral leadership. His father was not only pastor of the town's First Presbyterian Church but also president of the fledgling College of New Jersey. His mother, Esther Edwards Burr, was the daughter of Jonathan Edwards, the famed new England theologian. Yet, at his death in a rooming house on Staten Island, New York, September 14, 1836, Burr had made his name a symbol for treachery and corruption. Even *Princetonians, 1769–1775*, his alma mater's official alumni biographical directory, describes Burr as "the traditional bête noire of American political history." While modern scholarship has softened many harsh contemporary judgments on Burr, no other American vice president led a more troubled, complicated, tumultuous, and mysterious life.

Tragedy came early to Burr. His father died in September 1757 shortly after taking his family to Princeton, where the College of New Jersey

23

had found a permanent home. The college trustees persuaded Jonathan Edwards to succeed his son-in-law, but in March 1758, Edwards died at Princeton of smallpox. Edwards's daughter fell victim to the same disease two weeks later, leaving her son and his older sister Sarah orphaned, hundreds of miles from any members of their immediate family. When their grandmother Edwards journeyed south from Stockbridge, Massachusetts, to put her husband's affairs in order and take her grandchildren home, she too died.

The Burr children lived with friends in Philadelphia until 1760, when their mother's brother Timothy was able to assume his responsibilities as their guardian. Thus Aaron and Sarah grew up in the frontier village of Stockbridge, where their uncle was a successful merchant, respected agent with native tribes, and enthusiastic speculator in western lands. Burr left the Edwards home at the age of thirteen to attend the College of New Jersey. There he displayed two traits that marked the rest of his life: an incredible capacity for hard work and self-discipline, which he displayed in his first college year, and a capacity for what Matthew Davis, his first biographer, termed "idleness, negligence and . . . dissipation," which he showed generously in his later college career.

After graduating from Princeton in 1772, Burr briefly studied for the ministry. Quickly realizing his error in judgment, he traveled to Litchfield, Connecticut, to master the law with Tapping Reeve, his sister's husband. The outbreak of the Revolution cut short Burr's professional studies, and in the spring of 1775, Burr set out for Cambridge, Massachusetts, to join Benedict Arnold's expedition to Canada. Burr remained with Arnold's rapidly shrinking army at Quebec through that winter. In June 1776, he won appointment as Israel Putnam's aide-de-camp in Washington's Army and served in the Battle of Long Island and the American evacuation of Manhattan. The next year, Burr joined William Malcolm's "additional" regiment in the Hudson Valley, wintering at Valley Forge before returning north to guard the American border against the British, their Loyalist allies, and nonpartisan outlaw brigands in the Hudson Valley. In March 1779, after nearly four years of active service, Burr succumbed to ill health and resigned his commission as a lieutenant colonel.

By 1780, Burr was strong enough to resume his legal studies, a process that took him from one mentor to another until the fall of 1781, when he applied for admission to practice in the State of New York. In January 1782, he received that license, and six months later married Theodosia Bartow Prevost, a widow ten years his senior who brought five children to their marriage. Mrs. Prevost's first husband, a Swiss-born British army officer, had died in the West Indies in the fall of 1781, and there was no shortage of gossip about a courtship that surely began before that news reached New Jersey and New York. The Burrs ignored wagging tongues and settled in Albany, where he practiced law until the British evacuation of New York City opened the way to move to the more profitable life of a lawyer in Manhattan. In November 1783, Burr took his wife, five stepchildren, and infant daughter Theodosia to the city where he would make his mark as a lawyer and politician.

New York State's anti-Loyalist statutes created a situation described by Alexander Hamilton as "so plentiful a harvest to us lawyers that we have scarcely a moment to spare from the substantial business of reaping" (to Gouverneur Morris, February 21, 1784). Mrs. Burr's many Tory kinsmen and in-laws assured her husband an ample share in this harvest, while their claims under royal land grants introduced Burr to speculating in lands on the New York and Pennsylvania frontiers. Business and legal affairs left Burr little time for public life during the Confederation period, but he did serve one term in the state assembly, 1784–1785. Tradition has it that he spoke on behalf of the abolition of slavery in that forum, but this stand is less well documented than his work as legislative spokesman for his circle of fellow speculators.

In the years following the Revolution, New York's political world was dominated by George Clinton, the state's first and only governor from 1777 to 1795 and leader of the state's Antifederalist wing in the hotly contested 1788 battle over Constitutional ratification. Burr was not counted among Clintonians at this point. His position on the adoption of the proposed federal constitution was ambivalent, and his only recorded contemporary expression of opinion on the subject came when New York finally approved the new frame of government after Virginia's ratification had already made the new government a reality: "I congratulate you on the Adoption of the New Constitution. I think it a fortunate event and the only one which could have preserved peace; after the adoption by ten States, I think it became both politic and necessary that we should also adopt it" (to Richard Oliver, July 29, 1788). To cloud his loyalties further, in early 1789 his name appeared among members of a committee supporting Judge Robert Yates against Clinton in the gubernatorial race.

By the fall of 1789, Burr and Clinton had overcome whatever differences in opinion or principle divided them earlier. Burr accepted appointment from Clinton as state attorney general, a post that made him an *ex-officio* member of the state Land Office Commission. There Burr had a hand in decisions on the construction of the roads and bridges that opened New York's frontier and in the sale of parcels of public lands.

In January 1791, a joint session of the state legislature introduced Burr to national office by naming him Philip Schuyler's successor as one of New York's United States senators in the Second Congress. During Burr's single Senate term, 1791–97, the politics of his state and nation underwent a transformation. On the national level, Alexander Hamilton's controversial Treasury Department policies created an opposition that eventually was formalized as Jefferson's Democratic-Republicans. New York's intricate partisan patterns were complicated further by the gubernatorial election of 1792. Burr was held up briefly as a candidate in opposition to George Clinton, but his chances were dashed when Chief Justice John Jay, a far more prominent and popular candidate, agreed to run against the incumbent.

When the election returns were in, however, Burr's role became more important. So many votes were challenged that neither candidate had a clear majority. The official committee of canvassers was divided along party lines and persuaded New York's two senators, Burr and Federalist Rufus King, to review a formal "Statement of the Case." Not surprisingly, Burr and King could not agree. Ignoring Burr's suggestion that they remain silent, King insisted on submitting a written opinion in favor of counting the ballots that would give Jay the governorship. Burr had no choice but to provide a written statement of his own position. When the committee of canvassers then voted on party lines to award the prize to Clinton in June 1792, Federalists coupled Burr with the canvassers as instruments of Clintonian fraud and corruption.

This embarrassment was especially irritating to Burr as his national reputation among anti-Hamiltonians had sparked talk of his nomination for vice president. Although this boom soon died, Burr was now sufficiently aware of the need to protect his national standing and published a pamphlet defending his role: *An Impartial Statement of the Controversy, Respecting the Decision of the Late Committee of Canvassers*

Burr's emergence as a national politician within the Senate is harder to document, for the upper house at the time conducted debates in secret. Most of Burr's committee appointments reveal no special pattern of expertise or interest, but one group of deliberations was especially significant—Burr's role in fighting for Albert Gallatin's right to a seat as U.S. senator from Pennsylvania in the Third Congress. The 1792 elections gave the new Republican Party a majority in the House, but Federalists still held a narrow majority in the Senate and admitting a new and able opponent like Gallatin was unthinkable. Burr and the Republicans lost their fight in early 1794, but as the controversy focused entirely on the date of Gallatin's naturalization, the Swiss-born politician simply waited another year and easily won election to the Senate again for the Fourth Congress, when no challenge to his qualifications could be raised. Gallatin easily assumed a leadership role and did not forget Burr's role in trying to gain him a seat earlier.

As the Third Congress progressed, Burr again balanced national and state ambitions and personal concerns. Sometimes these interests coincided, as in April 1794, when he moved that justices of the Supreme Court be barred from accepting "any other office or employment, emanating from and holden at the pleasure of the Executive"—a resolve that would have prevented Chief Justice John Jay from accepting nomination as special envoy to Britain. Burr himself was mentioned as a candidate for a special mission to France, but that post went to another Republican, James Monroe of Virginia. In May, Burr's wife Theodosia died after an illness of two years, leaving Burr to care for their precocious ten-year-old daughter.

The fall of 1794 found Burr marshaling forces for the state elections the following spring. In January 1795, Clinton announced that he would not seek another term. Jay, the likely Federalist candidate, was still abroad on his diplomatic mission to Britain, and his absence could give rivals a handsome advantage. Burr's hopes to head a coalition ticket were soon dashed. Even thousands of miles away, Jay was far more attractive to Federalists than Burr, and realistic Republicans realized that Burr's role in the 1792 election controversy made him an easy target in a race against Jay.

Even as an absentee campaigner, Jay won election easily in the spring of 1795, but Burr did not let him enjoy victory long. New York's Republican senator played a central role at the special Senate session called that summer to consider the newly negotiated treaty with Britain that bore Jay's name. Ratification of the treaty required a two-thirds majority, and neither side had votes to spare. James Monroe and John Taylor of Virginia, Republican Senate leaders in the Second and Third Congresses, had resigned, and their successors had not had time to establish themselves in the House. Thus Burr played a key role in holding Republican votes together and wooing Federalists to their cause. While Burr and his allies failed to break Federalist control of twenty of the thirty votes, they did force a conditional rather than an unqualified ratification of the treaty, and the issues raised on the Senate floor provided ammunition for Republicans at the state and local level for years to come.

In the Fourth Congress that fall, Burr continued to be a Republican gadfly, attacking the Federalist majority in the Senate on every front, ever mindful of the elections of 1796. Federalists now controlled the New York legislature, and Burr knew that his career in the U.S. Senate would end in March 1797. He knew, too, that Washington was unlikely to seek a third term, and the probable Federalist candidacy of John Adams opened the field for ambitious Republicans. Debate over Tennessee's admission to the Union in the spring of 1796 spotlighted his role. Congressional Federalists opposed immediate admission of the territory, for it was clear that Tennessee voters would align themselves with the South, opposing Adams in his expected race to become the second president. While the House quickly voted for Tennessee's admission, Federalist opposition in the Senate was substantial. Burr led advocates of Tennessee statehood and was a member of the House–Senate conference committee that agreed on a bill for immediate admission.

When Washington issued his formal Farewell Address in September 1796, Burr was recognized as the Republicans' vice presidential nominee, with Jefferson the party's presidential candidate. While Burr failed in this ambition (despite the votes of Tennessee's members of the electoral college), he did contribute to undermining the strategy of Hamiltonian Federalists. Members of the electoral college could not designate which of their votes were for president and which for vice president, and Hamilton hoped to persuade some Federalist electors to withhold enough votes from Adams to give the top prize to Adams's running mate, Thomas Pinckney.

Once it was clear that he himself would fare badly in the college vote, Burr wrote to Federalists and Republicans alike to ensure that Adams, not Pinckney, would win. Jefferson was left to serve as vice president, and Burr returned to New York to rebuild his personal finances and political career.

Land speculations during his years in the Senate were now on the verge of collapse and demanded Burr's attention. In April 1797 he also accepted the Republican nomination for a seat in the New York State assembly. There Burr and allies worked to secure passage of a bill that would allow aliens to buy and hold real estate in the state—a prerequisite to the success of sale of Burr's own lands abroad. In August, he played a more creditable role by resolving a dispute between Alexander Hamilton and James Monroe that had threatened to end in a duel.

It was during these years that Burr seems to have created the urban political machine linked to the Tammany Society that served him later. Republicans in New York City triumphed in the spring 1798 elections, and Burr's position of leadership was recognized when his name appeared first among the list of assembly candidates that year. To be sure, he did not neglect nonpartisan appearances, working effectively with Governor Jay in refurbishing New York's defenses in the Quasi-War with France as well as attending to the interests of his urban constituents and his business associates.

But his success was his undoing. In the spring 1799 assembly campaign, Federalists attacked Burr's assembly record, focusing on his work for legislation favoring land speculators and his role in advancing the fortunes of the Manhattan Company, a municipal water-supply scheme exploited by Burr and the Republicans to give their party its own bank. Burr and the New York City assembly ticket he headed lost badly in the election, and he returned to private business, land speculation, and plans for the 1800 national races.

Rebuilding the Republican Party in Manhattan, Burr focused on retaking the city's assembly seats. This gave the party a majority in that house large enough to counter the Federalist margin in the state senate, thus assuring the 1800 Republican presidential candidate the state's electoral college votes when the two houses met in joint session that December. Persuading Republican celebrities such as George Clinton and Horatio Gates to run for the assembly, Burr saw the ticket win in May 1800. Burr himself was returned to the assembly from upstate Orange County. Over the summer, the party came to agreement on Jefferson as presidential candidate, with Burr as his running mate.

As soon as the November elections were over, it was apparent that there might be a tie in the electoral college between Jefferson and Burr if some Republican electors did not withhold votes from Burr by voting for another candidate. Rumors, bargains, and deals were gossiped about, but no agreements were met. Soon after delegates to the electoral college cast their votes in mid-December, it was known that there was a tie. Some Federalists hoped to make a deal with Burr: if he committed himself to Federalist demands, he would receive that party's votes when the electoral deadlock was thrown into the U.S. House. Burr's old enemy Alexander Hamilton fought the bargain and campaigned for Jefferson's approval.

The electoral tie became public when the votes were counted on February 11, 1801. The House met continuously for six days until two Federalist state delegations broke the impasse by casting blank ballots: Jefferson would be president and Burr vice president. Even while Burr traveled to Washington to take his oath, he was confronted with public questions about the position he had taken when the Federalists tried to enlist him in a deal for the presidency. The question would haunt him through his vice presidency.

In the months following the inauguration of the Jefferson–Burr administration, Burr gave his chief new reasons for distrust. The questions of patronage arose quickly: How many Federalist officeholders would be turned out and which Republicans would be rewarded? Burr's own healthy interest in distributing political favors was exaggerated when Republican politicians throughout the country came to view him as a conduit for their own requests, thus forcing Burr to present the claims of dozens of men whom he had never met and whose good will meant nothing to him.

In New York, affairs were going badly. Burr's old enemy George Clinton was elected to another term as governor in May 1801, and Burr's beloved daughter Theodosia was married to Joseph Alston, a wealthy young planter who took her away to his home in South Carolina. Burr's financial interests were, as usual, troubled, and by November, he was looking for a buyer for Richmond Hill, his Manhattan estate. Burr's personal, financial, and political problems were so pressing that he missed the first weeks of the opening session of the Seventh Congress and his initiation as presiding officer of the Senate.

The New York political drama now had a new player: John Wood, a Scottish pamphleteer who began work on a *History of the Administration of John Adams* in June 1801. Burr and other Republicans helped him with his research that fall, but Wood's book proved to be so scurrilous that not even New York Republicans dared see it published. Burr became entangled in tortuous negotiations to suppress the book, and word of the matter was soon known to James Cheetham, proprietor of New York's Republican *Morning Chronicle* and now Burr's avowed enemy. By the close of the year, New York was involved in a partisan pamphlet war that would continue for two years.

Thus Burr could not join the Senate until January 15, 1802. Eleven days later, he made his first casting vote in a tie, sending the bill for repeal of the Federalist Judiciary Bill of 1801 on to its third reading. Repeal of the statute and removal of the "midnight" judges whom Adams had appointed under the measure were cornerstones of Jeffersonian policy. The next day, however, Burr gave his enemies new ammunition by casting the vote that sent the bill to a select committee—a vote that endeared him to moderates but infuriated Jeffersonian partisans.

Personal considerations led Burr to leave the Senate before the end of the session, and he traveled to South Carolina in April 1802 to be with his daughter when she gave birth to a son, Aaron Burr Alston. His enemies in New York took advantage of Burr's absence to publish the first pamphlets concerning Burr's role in suppressing Wood's *History*, and Burrites replied in kind. Burr returned to New York in June—just in time to see a new round of pamphlets examining his role in the 1801 electoral tie. Burr spent the fall desperately trying to persuade his friends and political allies of his innocence: "You are at liberty to declare from me, that all those charges and insinuations which aver or intimate that I advised or countenanced the opposition made to Mr. Jefferson pending the late election or balloting for President . . . that all such assertions are false

and groundless" (to Joseph Bloomfield, September 21, 1802). January 19, 1803, found him back in the Senate in time to witness attempts by William Marbury's attorney to obtain evidence of his client's appointment from Senate records. At the end of the session, Burr traveled south to visit his daughter and mend fences among southern politicians.

Jefferson had called the Senate together early in the fall of 1803 to consider the Louisiana Purchase treaty. As usual, Burr missed the session's opening. Indeed, his friend Senator Jonathan Dayton of New Jersey wrote him in mid-November "to loiter on your way." A constitutional amendment reforming presidential balloting procedures had been introduced, and the debates were expected to be embarrassing for Burr. Burr finally made his appearance on December 7—five days after the Senate adopted the Twelfth Amendment. All that was left for him was a flurry of correspondence concerning the etiquette of forwarding the amendment to the states for consideration.

The session was a busy one for Burr. On January 5, 1804, Congressman John Randolph introduced a resolution for the impeachment of the outspokenly partisan Federalist Associate Supreme Court Justice Samuel Chase. Articles of impeachment were not adopted until March 26, so Burr could look forward to these proceedings in the fall. As a dress rehearsal, however, Burr presided over the Senate impeachment trial of another judge, the tragically demented John Pickering. Burr had a fateful conversation with Jefferson on January 26 in which the president made it clear that George Clinton, not Aaron Burr, would be his running mate that year. Burr was given leave to absent himself from the Senate for a few weeks at the end of January, and on his return he was furious to learn that William Duane of the Jeffersonian *Aurora* had been present in the chamber in his absence. Burr's patience with newspaper editors had grown short; it was at this time that he had brought suit against James Cheetham for libel.

The libel suit, of course, was tied to Burr's last desperate political hopes. George Clinton's nomination as vice president meant that the old man could not run in the 1804 gubernatorial race, and Burr was busy restoring his reputation in New York in preparation for that race. Federalists stood aside to let Burr run against a fellow Jeffersonian, Judge Morgan Lewis, who billed himself and his followers as the "Genuine Republicans." Burr suffered a humiliating loss in May despite his flirtation with Federalists—even Federalists with sectionalist leanings.

The aftermath of the May election ended Burr's political career. Even by New York's standards, the campaign had been a bitter one, filled with vilification and innuendo. In mid-June, Burr exploded on hearing rumors of remarks Alexander Hamilton had made at his expense. Through his friend William Van Ness, Burr demanded an explanation—and Hamilton refused. For ten days, Burr's and Hamilton's friends scurried back and forth with notes and letters. On July 28, it became apparent that nothing but a duel would settle the matter of honor, and those friends then became seconds for the two principals. On June 11, Burr, Hamilton, and their entourages rowed across the Hudson to a dueling ground in Weehawken, New Jersey. Burr's bullet struck Hamilton in the abdomen, and the Federalist died two days later. A week passed, and Burr fled a murder indictment in New York, taking refuge with friends in Philadelphia before sailing to West Florida and South Carolina for the late summer and early fall.

By the time Burr returned North, New Jersey had added a murder indictment to Burr's list. On November 4, Burr was in his chair in the Senate chamber for the opening day of business—the first and only time in his vice presidential term that he had attended so promptly. Federalists were furious at the sight of Hamilton's killer presiding over the upper house, while Burr's friends in Congress busily circulated a petition letter to the governor of New Jersey asking that his state's indictment against Burr be quashed. Burr conducted business with quiet dignity. He was applauded for his conduct of the trial that led to Samuel Chase's acquittal, and no one could fault his manner or manners on February 15 when he formally notified Jefferson of his reelection to a second presidential term. Burr's enemies were less gracious: Federalists in the House blocked a vote to grant him franking privileges for his mail.

On March 2, Burr delivered his Farewell Address to the Senate—his last public appearance as an officeholder. He spoke his regard for the Senate and of his own feelings at "a final separation—a dissolution, perhaps forever, of those associations" with individual lawmakers: "It is here if any where, that our country must ultimately find the anchor of her safety; and if the Constitution is to perish, . . . its dying agonies will be seen on this floor. . . ." Senators wept after Burr walked out of the chamber that day, and New York's Samuel Latham Mitchill, a firm Clintonian, wrote his wife: "Burr is one of the best officers that ever resided over a deliberative assembly. Where he is going or how he is to get through with his difficulties I know not" (letter of March 2, 1805).

One thing Burr could not do was return to his old life. On March 22, he wrote his son-in-law: "In New-York I am to be disfranchised, and in New-Jersey hanged. Having substantial objections to both, I shall not, for the present, hazard either, but shall seek another country." That country was, inevitably, the West. Dueling was unpopular throughout the Northeast, and Burr had no future there. The Southeast tolerated duels, but that region was solidly Jeffersonian. In the West, however, Burr still had friends and a future—or so he thought.

Burr visited Ohio, Kentucky, and Tennessee in the spring and summer of 1805, gathering support for an ill-defined expedition whose objects may not have been entirely clear even to him. He climaxed the trip with a September meeting in St. Louis with his most ill-chosen collaborator, James Wilkinson, the unstable and treacherous commander of the American Army in the West. Returning to the East, Burr spent the next months organizing his supporters and even sounding out Jefferson.

Burr went west again in early August 1806, but suspicions of his motives dogged his every step. In Kentucky, he was arrested. With Henry Clay as his counsel, Burr was acquitted of charges of planning a war on Spain, but his support from prominent men such as Tennessee's Andrew Jackson was slipping away. Worse still, James Wilkinson had embarked on his own, private campaign, sending Jefferson a report of Burr's activities in the West. The report included an incriminating cipher letter that had, in fact, been written to Wilkinson by Jonathan Dayton. Burr moved south to the Mississippi frontier, unaware that Jefferson had issued a proclamation warning "all faithful citizens" of a brewing conspiracy to force war with Spain. By the time Burr saw Jefferson's proclamation in a newspaper in a small town north of modern Natchez on January 10, Wilkinson had begun to arrest Burr's associates in New Orleans. Burr was arrested again in Mississippi—and again tried and acquitted. Fearing for his safety at Wilkinson's hands, Burr fled, reemerging to be arrested in what is today modern Wakefield County, Alabama, at the end of January.

Burr was taken to Richmond, Virginia, for trial by the U.S. Circuit Court for Virginia, with Chief Justice John Marshall presiding. Proceedings began in May and ended with Burr's acquittal—and the threat of further legal proceedings in the West. For Burr, "another country" now meant a nation an ocean's distance away. After bidding farewell to his daughter and her family, Burr sailed to England in June 1808. He remained abroad for nearly four years, dividing most of his time between England and France. He approached the British Crown and the French Empire with schemes to liberate Spain's American colonies, but to no avail, and he returned to New York City in June 1812 with no prospects, no plans. He ended the year with almost no hope.

In July, Burr learned that his only grandchild, Theodosia's son, Aaron Burr Alston, had died. Grief stricken, Theodosia planned a trip north to be with her father. Her ship sailed north in December 1812—and was never heard from again. Nearly fifty-seven, Burr had no money, no career, few friends, and no immediate family. Yet he went on, rebuilding his law practice from scratch, following the course of New York's courts from Manhattan to Albany to Utica and back. He dabbled in schemes to free Spain's last colonies in America and embarked on a twenty-year campaign to secure his pension as a Revolutionary War veteran.

Eventually Burr found young politicians such as Martin Van Buren willing to become known as his friends. He never again exerted power, but the stain of his old disgrace faded, in part because new scandals replaced it. In 1833, he took a second wife, the notorious and wealthy Eliza Bowen Jumel. The Burrs separated by the end of the year, and Eliza Burr sued for divorce the following summer. By then her husband had been incapacitated by a stroke, and Burr spent the next two years in a boardinghouse kept by the daughter of an old friend. In 1835, he put the finishing touches to his will, including a rakish codicil that provided a legacy for two little girls whom he acknowledged as his "Two Daughters." When a friend chided him for taking on the responsibility of children whom he knew were not his own, Burr is said to have replied: "Sir, when a lady does me the honor to name me the father of her child, I trust I shall always be too gallant to show myself ungrateful for the favor!" When his health deteriorated in 1836, he was moved to Staten Island, where his Edwards kin could supervise his care. On September 14, 1836, he died. He was buried next to his parents in the Princeton Cemetery.

Burr's legacy to the country was an undisguised relish for partisan warfare and a genius for machine politics, tastes that went unappreciated by such people as Jefferson and Madison and Hamilton. Yet, the vice presidency seemed to bring out the best in Burr: There he put aside partisan interest for impartial statesmanship. Presiding over the Senate while under two indictments for murder, Burr performed with a composure and courage that even his enemies had to admire. Whatever his attitude toward other public offices, Burr held the vice presidency as a trust, one that he discharged with dignity and extraordinary decency.

REFERENCES

Political Correspondence and Public Papers of Aaron Burr, Mary-Jo Kline and Joanne Wood Ryan, eds., 2 vols. (Princeton: Princeton University Press, 1983); Milton Lomask, *Aaron Burr* (New York: Farrar, Straus, Giroux, 1979 and 1982).

MARY-JO KLINE is Curator, Special Collections, of the John Hay Library at Brown University. She earned a Ph.D. in American history from Columbia University before embarking on a career in documentary editing. After serving as associate editor of the John Jay papers and the papers of John Adams, she directed the papers of Aaron Burr project at the New-York Historical Society. Her two-volume edition of *The Political Corre-spondence and Public Papers of Aaron Burr* was published by Princeton University Press in 1983. She is the author of *A Guide to Documentary Editing* (Johns Hopkins Press), which was originally published in 1987 and appeared in a revised edition in 1997.

*G*EORGE *CLINTON* (1739–1812)

Vice President, 1805–1812

(Presidents Thomas Jefferson and James Madison)

GEORGE CLINTON
(Library of Congress)

By L. Edward Purcell

George Clinton was elected to the vice presidency when the office still seemed to have significant potential for power—his immediate predecessor had, after all, nearly become president by virtue of a defect in the electoral system—and Clinton was regarded by his contemporaries as one of the first among national political leaders. At the time of his election, it was still not clear just what the vice presidency meant politically: was it a way station for the heir presumptive to the presidency, or was it doomed to become an empty office? Although he definitely played second fiddle to President Thomas Jefferson during the election of 1804 (the first to be conducted under the amended electoral proce-

dures that specified a separate vice-presidential candidate), the following campaign in 1808 found an aged Clinton nominated simultaneously as Madison's running mate *and* as a rival candidate for the presidency itself.

Clinton was elected vice president at the end of his career when he was old and much diminished in his capacities, and he performed indifferently, especially during his second term. In his younger and middle years, however, Clinton had been a larger-than-life figure whose leadership spanned the events of the imperial crisis with Great Britain, the American Revolution, the Confederation period, the struggle over the Constitution and the founding of the new nation, and the development of a working government and party system during the Early Republic.

During the 1780s, Clinton was one of America's most vigorous governors and among the very first during the Revolution to base political power on the democratic mass of freehold voters, repeatedly dealing his aristocratic opponents in New York frustrating and mortifying electoral defeats. He was a dedicated democrat as well as an iron-bound conservative. He was steadfastly practical in his approach to politics and government and almost never uttered or wrote an inspired thought (at least none that have survived). In part because of his unphilosophical bent and inarticulateness, he has not been much remembered as one of the important figures present at the creation of the American nation. Moreover, his intense focus on his native state as well as his strongly held opinions about the proper scope of government put him among the foremost Antifederalists during the contest for ratification of the new U.S. Constitution, and that was a position that did not play well afterward among makers of historical reputations: it was against George Clinton that Alexander Hamilton, James Madison, and John Jay directed their "Federalist Papers."

Clinton was born in the village of New Britain in Ulster County, New York, to Charles and Elizabeth Clinton, a Scotch-Irish immigrant couple who had landed in America in 1729 after a tragically disastrous voyage during which two of their three children died. They made a new life in America, however, and gained a modest measure of financial success and local prominence. George's siblings—he was the youngest of four children born in the New World—included his brother James, who became an important Revolutionary War general and married into the DeWitt clan of New York, a union that produced George's political heir, DeWitt Clinton.

Ulster County, which for many years formed George's political base, was a region of small freehold farms, populated mostly by Presbyterian Scotch-Irish farmers who gave definition to the classic American stereotype of agrarian virtue: the yeomanry. They owned and worked their own land, with few slaves, and they were not usually tenants or beholden to patroons or powerful families, as was the case in much of the colony of New York east of the Hudson River, where the power of the manor still held sway.

Clinton received a poor education and never really mastered language skills—he was at best a mediocre writer and often called on aides or his nephew DeWitt to draft official messages—although he was competent in mathematics and a good practical surveyor. During the Seven Years War, he served aboard a privateer for a ten-month voyage against the French and then as a lieutenant in his brother's militia company on Lord Jeffery Amherst's expedition against Montreal in 1760.

Late in the same year, Clinton moved to New York City and entered the law office of famous attorney William Smith, the younger. After three years of Smith's legal tutelage, Clinton returned to Ulster County and took up the practice of law with a side occupation of land surveying.

Five years later (1768), George Clinton was elected to a seat in the New York Assembly as a representative of Ulster. He was seldom out of public office for the rest of his life, establishing early on in his career that he could win a majority of the voters in almost any contest. For a man of his modest background, this meant overcoming a big challenge. For decades before the Revolution, officeholding in New York was at the disposal of the big, rich, and quarreling but powerful political families; the Livingstons, for example, were pitted against the De Lanceys during the 1760s. There was also an ongoing political split between New York City with its associated counties to the southeast and the northern counties. To some extent the north–south political polarity also reflected the divisions between merchants and agriculturalists and between urban and rural interests. For all of his life, George Clinton was the champion of rural, west-of-the-Hudson farming constituencies. He was disliked by the aristocratic family politicians and seldom won support in New York City or its surrounding counties.

One of the hallmark's of George Clinton's political life was his long-term, often shifting relationship with other powerful figures of the New York and national scene. He initially was an ally of the immensely wealthy Philip Schuyler, although he eventually came to be on the opposite side from Schuyler and Schuyler's son-in-law, Alexander Hamilton. For years, Clinton was alternately allied with and then opposed to Aaron Burr, whose main political strength was in New York City. Clinton almost always, however, could be found on the opposite side of the fence from the aristocratic John Jay.

In 1770, Clinton married Cornelia Tappen, who brought with her a close alliance with the old-line Dutch interests in New York and a connection to the Livingston family. The couple moved to New Windsor in the Hudson Highlands, and their daughter, Catherine (the first of five Clinton children), was born by the end of the year. Catherine eventually married Pierre Van Cortlandt, which forged another important political link for her father.

George Clinton provided his family a living by legal work and the income from ownership of a local mill, but most of his time and energies were consumed by the New York Provincial Assembly, which sat continuously from 1769 until April 1775, with only a short period of prorogation in 1774. Thus, Clinton was involved in and became a leader of the struggle between the assembly and New York's colonial governor and the British government in general. When the official assembly was dissolved in 1775 and New Yorkers moved to set up an extralegal Provincial Convention, Clinton was named as Ulster's representative. He was selected immediately by the convention as one of New York's delegates to the Second Continental Congress, and he attended sessions of the congress in Philadelphia from May to August. At the end of the year, Clinton was commissioned by the New York Provisional Assembly as a brigadier general of militia.

George Clinton took advantage of the dislocations and changes set loose by the revolutionary movement to transform himself from a small-town lawyer and surveyor into a man with powerful political and military positions. The idea that the American Revolution was a double revolution—one internally of the lower socioeconomic colonial classes against the ruling upper classes as well as an external revolution of all the colonies against Great Britain—has been a matter of tiresome historical debate for generations, but the case of George Clinton fits the model quite snugly. While he might have become someone of importance without the Revolution, he certainly would never have attained the heights of office and power that he did, especially in a place like New York, which was dominated by upper-class families. Clinton was a man of ability who was standing on the threshold as the Revolution weakened or swept away the old structures.

From March to May 1776 and again during parts of June and July, Clinton returned to the Continental Congress. During these stints as a legislator (a role he never much took to), Clinton established a firm and lasting friendship with George Washington. Of course, this personal bond, which developed over the years of fighting the British and subsequently as the two men invested together in frontier lands, turned out to be of immense importance to Clinton. Washington genuinely liked Clinton and on more than one occasion swept aside what appeared to be sharp political differences for the sake of friendship. Washington was the most important American alive, and Clinton could always call on him for help and support.

Unfortunately for Clinton's place in history, he left Congress to return to his military duties in New York in the summer of 1776 before signing the Declaration of Independence, so he could never claim membership in the august group of "The Signers."

Clinton was charged with defending the Highlands of the Hudson River against a British offensive. This was one of the key assignments of the war in the north because the British held New York City from 1776 on and if they could gain control of the up-river country the northern colonies would be split. Early in 1777, Clinton received a full commission from Congress as a brigadier general in the Continental Army, a rank of much higher standing than his state militia commission, and he set up defenses at Fort Montgomery, just below present-day West Point.

During the same period, Clinton was technically a member, but seldom attended, the drawn-out New York convention called to write a state constitution. Finally, the constitution was proclaimed in April 1777, and the first election for governor was set in motion. Because New York City and much of the southern part of the state were in the hands of the British or Loyalists and because there were no political parties to help organize the election, the entire affair boiled down to the personalities of the many candidates. Philip Schuyler, for example, was the leading candidate of the traditional officeholding New York aristocracy. He was serving as a major general in the Continental Army (a highly unpopular one with his New England troops), had important family ties, and was immensely wealthy, so most observers at the time thought he was a shoo-in and that Clinton would do well to stand only for the lieutenant governor's post.

Schuyler and his friends were shocked when Clinton won the governorship easily, taking 49 percent of the ballots to Schuyler's 32 percent (John Scott Morin and John Jay split the remaining votes).

Schuyler was relatively gracious about Clinton's victory, however. He wrote to Jay that: "Gen. Clinton's having the chair of Government will not cause any divisions amongst the friends of America. Alto' his family and connections do not entitle him to so distinguished a predominance; yet he is virtuous and loves his country, has abilities and is brave." Schuyler might have been less magnanimous if he had known that this was only the first in seven gubernatorial elections that Clinton would win in New York and that Schuyler's side of the political division in the state would never unseat the plebeian Clinton. The fact that the election was conducted for the first time by secret ballot, thus freeing tenants and debtors to vote as they wished, probably played an important part in Clinton's win, as did a sizable soldier vote.

Clinton took office in July 1777 and established himself at his in-law's house in Kingston, New York, which was the temporary capital of the new state government. Most of his time, however, was spent at his military post on the Hudson. The British had launched a grand invasion from Canada led by "Gentleman Johnny" Burgoyne and headed toward Albany and points south. The British commander in New York, Sir Henry Clinton (probably a distant relative of the new rebel governor), moved up the Hudson from the south with the goal of linking with Burgoyne. Along the way, Sir Henry attacked Fort Montgomery and easily ousted the American garrison. Governor George Clinton barely escaped capture, and the British took control of the key river position, although with the defeat of Burgoyne at Saratoga, they failed in their grand plan.

In fact, the defeat at Fort Montgomery was the highlight of George Clinton's military career. Washington continued to praise him and express every confidence in his abilities despite his defeat, and for the rest of his life, Clinton was hailed as a Revolutionary War hero, a reputation that bolstered his political potency. As E. Wilder Spaulding, one of his biographers, wrote: "Democracies are lavish in the honors they bestow on their war heroes."

Clinton's service as wartime governor was much more effective than his generalship. He did an excellent job of organizing troops and supplies for a long and difficult period, during which the British held the key port of New York City as their main troop base in the North and the pivot of several key campaigns, including the seizure of Philadelphia and Charleston. When the British raided Kingston, burning many of Clinton's official papers in the process, the state government repaired to Poughkeepsie, where Clinton established a new family home and official residence.

Clinton's energy level during the long, drawn-out final years of the Revolution was extraordinary. He seldom flagged in his efforts to help keep the army intact, and he supported Washington's difficult task of holding on at Newburgh, New York, to an ill-used and unpaid force that seemed often to be on the verge of revolt or dissolution. It was a sweet triumph when Clinton rode side-by-side with Commander-in-Chief Washington into New York in November 1783 to reclaim the city from the British. The state government of New York moved back into that city, and the Clintons took over the spacious home of an ousted Loyalist, remaining in the city until a new state capital was established in Albany in 1801. Clinton purchased a farm in the nearby rural community of Greenwich and spent much of his limited leisure time there.

Although he was intensely patriotic during the Revolution and never for a moment stinted in his support of the war effort, toward the end of the conflict, Clinton began to consider the best balance of powers between the individual states and the central government. In this, he confronted the most fundamental question in American history, one that has proved constantly since the 1780s to be the basis for the essential political division in the country between those who favor a strong, active central government and those who want power dispersed and reserved locally.

At first, Clinton leaned toward a stronger central government because his wartime experiences showed him the defects of the congressional and confederation systems, but soon the practical issues he faced as New York's governor prompted him to change his mind. For example, when struggling to feed and clothe the army during the last years of the war, the idea of a national import tax (known as the impost) seemed like a good way to fund the operations of both the army and Congress. When the great commercial port city of New York was restored to his state, however, Clinton began to see that there would be tremendous local advantages to collecting an impost but keeping the money at home. Also, apart from the financial question, Clinton probably came to believe in the idea that each state should chart its own destiny and decide its own affairs, although abstractions did not often play a big role in George Clinton's political decisions. Whatever the philosophical underpinnings of his position, during the months after the ratification of the peace treaty, Clinton became more and more wedded to the defense of *local* New York State interests and less and less interested in supporting the concerns of a central, national corporate government.

This set of beliefs and attitudes coalesced nationally as what later historians labeled AntifedeHalism (although Clinton and his contemporaries did not use the term). At the time Antifederalism made great sense to a large number of Americans and many of their political leaders, and it reflected a reasoned position in defense of hard-won democracy and liberty. Many Antifederalists were loath to give up the precious freedoms won from Britain to a new central government, which they feared would be captured by aristocratic, perhaps even monarchical, elements who would not understand or care for local or state concerns. The concept that the states had rights that were more important than the nation as a whole was not on the fringe of American political thought in Clinton's day but rather near the center.

Unfortunately for Clinton's historical reputation, the states' rights, Antifederalist position was coopted by the slaveholding states before the Civil War and by southern racial discriminators for several generations after, and it was thus largely discredited. In Clinton's own time, however, he stood staunchly for what we today fondly call the Jeffersonian tradition of a limited state and rural virtue.

Clinton was easily reelected as governor for a series of three-year terms in 1780, 1783, and 1786. As chief executive of New York State, Clinton confronted a series of issues that only reinforced his adherence to the states' rights, Antifederalist position. The long-festering fight with the renegade Vermonters, who had the effrontary to rebel against New York just as New York had rebelled against Britain, was a hot button for Clinton and many other New Yorkers. The Vermonters nearly succeeded in gaining recognition from Congress in 1778 and 1779, and they came close to statehood in 1781. Only Clinton's most strenuous efforts blocked what he understood to be a dire threat to the well-being of his state, and the pro-Vermont role of Congress in all these episodes helped form his anti–central-government stance.

He also was at odds with the Confederation Congress over the treatment of Loyalists and their property, the renewed question of approving a national impost tax, and claims and rights to western lands. Clinton's fiscal conservatism and rejection of national interests in favor of local interests consolidated New York's natural economic advantages and made him an immensely popular figure in New York: Indeed, there was always a surplus of revenue over expenses and never a general property tax in the state during all of Clinton's administrations, and he financed government from the state impost and land sales. It was ironic, however, that Clinton's chief rivals in New York for local power were also the most vocal and effective advocates of the pronationalist position. By the mid-1780s, it was clear that Alexander Hamilton was going to lead the anti-Clinton forces in the state and was likely to have a major role in resolving the national crisis of government that was building rapidly.

The pressures came to a head in 1787 after Daniel Shays's rebellion, and the proposed new national constitution and the effort to achieve ratification produced some of the defining moments in American history.*

Both opponents and advocates of the proposed constitution knew that ratification by New York would be crucial to the success of the new plan of government. The ratification process called for approval by only eleven of the thirteen states, but without the assent of the large states, such as New York, the chances for failure were good. Clinton had generally opposed the participation of New York's representatives at the constitutional convention, but it was not until the fight over ratification that he came to the forefront of the Antifederalists.

The contest was fought as a war of words in New York. The Antifederalist side was taken in the papers by a series of letters published under the name *Cato* which were perhaps written by Clinton himself. Cato's letters touched on both principles and practical matters, all condemning the proposed constitution and urging delay or rejection. In response, Hamilton, James Madison, and John Jay wrote a series of beautifully articulate and well-reasoned essays that have come to be labeled as the "Federalist Papers" that remain major texts of American political thought.

In June 1788, elected delegates met at Poughkeepsie to debate and vote on ratification. Clinton was chosen as president and presided over an initial forty-six to nineteen Antifederalist majority. Personally, however, he was circum-spect and surprisingly did not take the lead against the Constitution, preferring apparently to wait to see what would happen. To the great consternation of the Antifederalist forces, the supposed majority against ratification slipped away and the proratifiers won by a slim margin. The struggle polarized politics in the state and became the basis for party organization and faction battles for years to come. The defeat damaged Clinton, and he never quite enjoyed the same state power and reputation again.

"Paradoxically," wrote Clinton biographer Spaulding, "it was Governor Clinton's provincialism and his stubborn championship of the rights of his state that made him a national figure." Even though he had lost at home, his stand against the Constitution made him a logical rallying point for Antifederalists in other states. As the first national election under the new plan of government approached, several influential voices, including Patrick Henry of Virginia and a caucus of the Federal Republican Society, urged that Clinton be a candidate for the vice presidency. Washington was the unanimous choice for president, but the vice presidency might well be contested. In fact, all the Federalist forces, lead by Hamilton, threw their support behind John Adams, who was elected with no serious opposition, and Clinton received no electoral votes. He might have received the approval of at least some of the New York electors, but a dispute of his own making stymied selection of electors, and New York failed to cast any electoral votes at all during the first presidential election.

Historians debate when and where political parties were born in the United States, but it seems clear that the conflicts over the Constitution and the way the new federal government was to be conducted were the catalysts for new forms of political organization and allegiance, especially in places such as Clinton's New York. However, it is misleading (and somewhat bewildering to late twentieth century Americans) to describe the political alliances of the 1790s and early 1800s as parties in the modern sense. Political campaigns

---

*Editor's note: See ELBRIDGE GERRY for further explanation of Shays's Rebellion.

revolved much more around individuals than nascent parties, and there was a great deal of crossover and shifting back and forth in ways that seem irrationally undisciplined to anyone accustomed to the two-party system as it eventually developed. There were, for example, few formal party structures that politicians could rely on year in and year out to assist in election to office. In general, however, the "Clinton Party" was a consistent factor in New York politics throughout George Clinton's career and the career of his nephew, DeWitt Clinton, who became his uncle's secretary in 1788 and eventually took over the direction of the faction. Antifederalists never really became organized as a formal party, but many of Antifederalist bent—such as George Clinton himself—eventually found their way into the fold of the party that formed around Jefferson's and Madison's leadership, a party usually referred to as the Jeffersonian Republicans or the Democratic-Republicans. Clinton was a natural for the Republicans with his history of vocal opposition to a strong central government and his support for a vision—held in common with Jefferson—of a democratic, agrarian society. The Republicans also catered to Clinton as a way to cement the New York–Virginia coalition that was potentially strong enough to control national presidential elections.

Clinton was reelected for a fifth term as governor in 1789, but the opposition of Hamilton and Aaron Burr, a New York City lawyer who was intensely ambitious for high office, made it a much closer race than the four previous. The Hamilton-led Federalists won control of the New York Assembly and Senate, and Hamilton looked forward to exercising considerable power. The former aide to the commander in chief was somewhat chagrined, therefore, that when George Washington arrived in New York City to assume the presidency, the new chief executive chose to dine on his first night privately with his old friend and business partner George Clinton rather than Hamilton or any of the leading Federalists of the city.

The next election for governor proved nearly to be Clinton's undoing. The Federalists selected John Jay as their candidate (Burr was also in the field), and the campaign was particularly bitter and hard fought. Clinton, as head of the state land office, was accused of complicity in a huge recent land-speculating scandal and of misusing his position on the Board of Appointment to dispense patronage too liberally. The race was exceedingly close, and it was only after disputed ballots from three counties were thrown out that Clinton could claim a victory. There was widespread public belief that he had stolen the election and that a more honorable man would have conceded to Jay.

Within months, Clinton's attention turned to the upcoming second national election. It was a foregone conclusion that Washington would be reelected for another term, but it was not so clear that Adams would be supported again for vice president. There was no standard nominating procedure at this stage of U.S. national politics, so the field appeared at times to be wide open. Aaron Burr was the first to have his name put forward, but his support proved to be thinly based. Clinton was a much more popular choice among antigovernment politicos in the important states, based on his prominence as an Antifederalist spokesman. Hamilton, who had emerged as the most influential member of Washington's administration and the leader of the national Federalists, would have been happy to rid himself of Adams, but in the face of a Clinton candidacy, Hamilton had to back the incumbent vice president. Adams reclaimed his office but by a diminished majority in the electoral college, receiving seventy-seven votes to Clinton's fifty.[*]

During the following year, Clinton was personally involved in the famous episode of Citizen Genêt. The revolution in France had unleashed wild forces in Europe and a flood of reaction in the United States. Federalists were aghast at the excesses of the revolutionaries, but many Jeffersonian Republicans were enthused by the vision of an ancient monarchy following America's

---

[*]Editor's note: See JOHN ADAMS for further explanation of this election.

revolutionary lead. In 1793, the French revolutionary government sent Edmond Genêt to the United States as an emissary. He intended to galvanize the pro-French forces in the United States, but he managed instead to insult George Washington and to make a complete fool of himself. Worse for him, even as his mission dissolved, a factional change in Paris resulted in a call for his return. Suspecting it was an invitation to his own beheading, Genêt wisely sought asylum in the United States. Meanwhile, during a visit to New York, he had fallen in love with Clinton's daughter Cornelia. Clinton grumbled, but the couple were married in late 1794 and settled on Long Island.*

Clinton himself had begun to slow down a good deal, and he apparently had lost some of his relish for the rough and tumble of New York politics. As the 1795 election for governor approached, he decided to retire from office. The voters of the state had known no one else as governor since the Revolution, but they turned to Clinton's longtime opponent John Jay, electing him to office easily. Clinton withdrew to his Greenwich farm and by all signs appeared to be done with officeholding.

This was misleading. Within five years, Clinton was back in office, first as a member of the assembly and then once again as governor. The circumstances were noticeably different, however, from his previous eighteen-year stretch in the governor's chair. The power structure in New York State had shifted toward younger men such as DeWitt Clinton and Aaron Burr, although Hamilton remained at the head of the Federalists. Burr and his associates (known at the time as the "Martling Men," in honor of their favorite tavern, although officially organized as the Society of Tammany) had succeeded in converting New York City from a Federalist stronghold to the Republican column; however, Burr was never steady in his political allegiances, except to himself, and he was capable of switching sides or making allies of those who had been foes only yesterday.

Burr and the Clinton factions were soon to fall out, but in 1800, Burr convinced George Clinton to allow himself to be put on the ballot for a Republican seat in the state assembly. The plan was to capture the state for the Republicans and thus assure New York's electoral votes for a national Republican ticket of Jefferson and Burr. Clinton was elected and the Republicans won a majority, but soon thereafter politics in the state and at the national level lost all semblance of order.

The year must have been full of confusion and agitation for Clinton. In March, his wife Cornelia died after a lingering illness, leaving him to rely more and more on the personal support of his daughters. He stood for the assembly in the spring and then was briefly in contention for the national Republican nomination for vice president with Jefferson. The movement to put Clinton on the ticket dissolved, and Burr claimed the prize. In November, however, Clinton was nominated by the Republican caucus of the New York Assembly as a candidate for governor. With the election in the following spring, Clinton became governor for the seventh time.

Meanwhile, Burr and Jefferson had won a great national victory over the Federalists but had tied in the electoral college voting. The major defect of the new Constitution's electoral system was revealed: the provision that the second-place finisher would become vice president did not anticipate nor could it deal with a tie. It would seem a simple step for Burr to have withdrawn in Jefferson's favor, but Burr demurred and allowed the contested election to be thrown into the U.S. House of Representatives, which finally selected Jefferson as president. When the smoke cleared, the Clinton faction and the Burr faction in New York were irretrievably split, and Burr had in effect been pushed out of the fold by Jefferson's national Republican supporters.

Clinton served out his final term as governor but declined to run again, which had momentous consequences for Burr, Hamilton, and the nation. Although serving as vice president, Burr

---

*Editor's note: See JOHN ADAMS for further explanation of the Genêt Affair.

realized he would be ignored in the future by the Republicans, so he ran to replace Clinton as governor of New York. He lost badly to the Clinton-faction candidate, Chief Justice Morgan Lewis, but came to blame Hamilton for his defeat. The result was the infamous duel in Weehawken, New Jersey, in July 1804. With a single exchange of shots, two of the great players in the drama of George Clinton's political life were removed: Hamilton was dead and Burr was banished. This was the curtain raiser on the final act of Clinton's career and his national service as vice president.

As the 1804 election approached, the Republicans looked for a strong candidate to replace Burr and bolster Jefferson's electoral total. The old idea of a New York–Virginia power connection was still in play, so even though George Clinton gave more and more the impression of an aging hero, well past his prime, he was still an attractive vote-getter and highly recognizable in other states for his longtime stand on limited government. Moreover, the 1804 election would be conducted for the first time under the provisions of the Twelfth Amendment, which was passed to prevent a recurrence of the Jefferson–Burr electoral tie. The new procedure called for separate balloting for president and vice president, and it began what over the long haul proved to be the diminution of the vice presidency. It is little remembered, however, that the amendment also required electors to cast ballots for presidential and vice-presidential candidate "one of whom, at least, shall not be an inhabitant of the same State with themselves." This provision meant that if Virginia was not to waste some of its electoral votes, then a non-Virginian would have to be nominated as Jefferson's running mate. Clinton seemed the obvious choice, and he was nominated officially at a caucus of the Republican congressional continent.

Jefferson and Clinton easily defeated their Federalist opposition of Charles Cotesworth Pinckney and Rufus King by 162 electoral votes to 14.

In general, George Clinton's time as vice president was not happy. He was sixty-five when elected—ascension to the top office seemed unlikely at his age—and he gave the appearance in public of mental torpor, if not downright deterioration, although on occasion he could be roused to vigor. He lived most of the time in Poughkeepsie, where he had moved after his wife's death, but beginning in December 1805, Clinton traveled to Washington when the Senate was in session with his daughter, Maria, boarding with John Beckley, Thomas Jefferson's political campaign manager. After Beckley's death in 1807, the Clintons lived in a variety of boarding-houses.

Clinton had a hard time with the Senate, which one of his biographers described as "a tiny assemblage of thirty-four mediocrities." He had never been much inclined toward the pace of legislative deliberation, having avoided service as a delegate during most of his career in favor of executive office, and he was apparently too old to learn either the substance or the subtleties of the Senate presiding officer's role. He also suffered by comparison to his immediate predecessor, Burr, who, whatever his defects of character, had been a superb president of the Senate.

The tenor of the complaints about Clinton's shortcomings can be heard in a letter from John Quincy Adams to his father, who had of course been the first presiding officer of the Senate, written in early 1805 during Clinton's first session:

> Mr. Clinton is totally ignorant of all the most common forms of proceeding in the Senate, and yet by the rules he is to decide every question of order without debate and without appeal. His judgement is neither quick nor strong; so there is no more dependence upon the correctness of his determinations from his understanding than from his experience.

Clinton cast tie-breaking votes to pass a bill postponing the abolition of the slave trade and to confirm General John Armstrong as a negotiator with Spain. Otherwise, he bumbled along during the first session and left for New York in March well before adjournment. This was the pattern he followed throughout his vice presidency. As the end of Jefferson's second term approached, however, circumstances allowed George Clinton to take an important political role one last time.

Clinton had been circumspect in general about criticizing Jefferson or the Republican Party, but with the eclipse of the Federalists after Jefferson's election and Hamilton's death, there were fewer reasons to keep peace within the Republicans' own house. Clinton was irritated with Jefferson's failure to take the British military threat to New York seriously, and he especially disagreed with Jefferson's embargo scheme. By 1807, the vice president had become a vocal critic of the administration.

So it was that antiadministration elements within the Republican Party, who wanted to mount a challenge to Secretary of State James Madison's "inheritance" of the presidency, looked to Clinton in 1808. There were sharp divisions within the Virginia section of the party, with many pushing for the candidacy of James Monroe in place of Madison. The lack of an established nomination process lead to a very confused situation. Knowing that they controlled the majority of the members of congress, Republican supporters of Madison called a congressional caucus in January. The caucus was poorly attended, but after a quick endorsement of Madison, the members present nominated Clinton as the party's vice-presidential candidate. They had failed, however, to consult Clinton beforehand and acted without his knowledge or approval. Clinton was offended by the caucus's behavior and refused ever to accept the nomination at its hands.

Many of Clinton's friends and allies proceeded then to put his name forward for the presidency, employing the usual technique of ballyhooing him in the papers and writing letters to leading politicians in the states. The hope was to make Clinton the fountainhead of anti-Madison Republicanism. The Federalists, meeting in what some historians consider the first political convention, came within a whisker of nominating Clinton as their candidate as well!

The result of all this maneuvering was that Clinton ran as both the Republican vice-presidential candidate hitched to Madison *and* as a presidential candidate in opposition to Madison. Not many appeared to take Clinton's chance for election as president too seriously, but he was a bona fide candidate by the standards of the time.

The tally of electoral votes gave Madison an easy victory of 122 to 47 over the Federalist Charles Cotesworth Pinckney, but George Clinton received 6 electoral votes for president. Of the vice-presidential votes, cast separately, he won in ten states with 113 electoral votes in total to 47 for Rufus King, the Federalist vice-presidential candidate.

Clinton's second vice-presidential term began with his calculated snub to the new president—Clinton delayed his arrival in Washington City until after Madison's inauguration in March 1809. In fact, he didn't arrive in the capital to take the oath of office until May.

In general, Clinton's second term was plagued by misfortune and increasing illness. His daughter Cornelia Genêt died in 1810, a significant blow to Clinton, and he himself suffered from a variety of ailments. His one important act, however, was to cast a deciding vote in 1811 defeating the attempt to recharter the National Bank. President Madison and Secretary of the Treasury Albert Gallatin supported the bank, but a significant number of Republicans were against it. Clinton's speech explaining his vote (apparently drafted by Henry Clay) condemned the prevailing broad interpretation of the Constitution that justified chartering a National Bank. Clinton, thus, remained loyal to the narrow Antifederalist position he had held for so long, and it must have been an additional measure of satisfaction to give a blow to the pet project of his old nemesis, Alexander Hamilton.

Clinton attended his last session of the Senate in the spring of 1812, but he was repeatedly ill and often unable to preside. He died on April 20 and was buried in the Congressional Cemetery—the first president or vice president to die in office—with great ceremony. In 1908, his coffin was removed from Washington, and George Clinton was laid to rest at Kingston, New York. The inscription on his tomb says in part: "While he lived, his virtue, wisdom, and valor were the pride, the ornament and the security of his country. . . ."

REFERENCES

E. Wilder Spaulding, *His Excellency George Clinton: Critic of the Constitution* (New York: Macmillan, 1938); John P. Kaminski, *George Clinton: Yeoman Politician of the New Republic* (Madison, Wisc.: Madison House, 1993); Gilbert D.B. Hasbrouck, "Governor George Clinton," *Quarterly Journal of the New York State Historical Association*, 1 (July 1920), 143–164; *Public Papers of George Clinton*, Harold Hastings, ed. (New York and Albany, 1899–1911).

L. EDWARD PURCELL, a historian, is the author, coauthor, or editor of 15 books, including Facts On File's *Who Was Who in the American Revolution* and *Encyclopedia of Battles in North America*. Purcell holds history degrees from Simpson College and the University of Iowa. He was previously editor in chief of publications at the Iowa State Historical Society. He has taught history at several colleges and universities, most recently at Drake University in Des Moines, Iowa, and his journalism has been nationally syndicated.

ELBRIDGE GERRY (1744–1814)

Vice President, 1813–1814

(President James Madison)

ELBRIDGE GERRY
(Library of Congress)

By Sarah J. Purcell

Elbridge Gerry was a public-minded "Founding Father" whose term as vice president capped a long and illustrious political career spent fighting for the security of the new American nation. Gerry's involvement in nearly every major political event between 1775 and 1812 is little remembered, and his main public legacy remains the dubious political practice of "gerrymandering," which is named after him. Contemporaries, as well as some historians since, characterized Elbridge Gerry as a man of contradictions, but he was consistently motivated by a desire to do what he thought was right to create the most virtuous, moral, and stable American nation possible.

Gerry spent the last two years of his life as James Madison's vice president. His election as vice president was ironic, given his vocal opposition during the 1787 Constitutional Convention to creating such an office. At the convention, Gerry had spoken against establishing the office of vice president as a violation of the separation of powers, stating: "We might as well put the President himself at the head of the Legislature."

Although a renowned antiparty politician for most of his career, Gerry had become an ardent

Jeffersonian Republican by the 1810s, when he became convinced that the Federalists increasingly represented a threat to the new nation. By the time he was elected vice president in 1812, Gerry had lost most of the tremendous political influence he had once possessed, yet he proved to be a strong presiding officer in the Senate. Gerry's own term as vice president demonstrated his trademark adaptability when faced with an opportunity to help his country.

Elbridge Gerry was born January 17, 1744, in Marblehead, Massachusetts, to Thomas and Elizabeth Gerry. Elbridge's parents participated in the economic expansion that began in the 1730s and that turned Marblehead into one of the most important ports in New England, vital to both the fishing industry and to colonial trade with Britain and the West Indies. Thomas Gerry was a merchant seaman from Devonshire, England, who married Elizabeth Greenleaf, the daughter of a Boston merchant, before moving to Marblehead to raise twelve children and build a thriving merchant house and retail business. By the 1770s, Thomas Gerry ranked as one of the wealthiest men in the region.

Befitting his station as son of a wealthy, prominent family, Elbridge was educated by tutors in Marblehead and then sent to Harvard College in 1758 at the age of fourteen. He was ranked twenty-ninth in a class of fifty-two on entrance, a standing determined by the student's social prominence, not his academic merit. Gerry received a thorough education in classical political theory, and he graduated from Harvard in 1762, staying to study for an M.A. until 1765. Gerry exited Harvard in the year the Stamp Act inaugurated the full-scale British-American crisis in Massachusetts, ready to take up his role as a gentleman dedicated to public service.

Elbridge returned to Marblehead, entered the family mercantile business with his brothers Thomas and John, and set about becoming a prominent citizen of the town in his own right. Although he had no formal legal training, Gerry performed legal duties for the business. A handsome man, Elbridge Gerry became a popular guest at social occasions. As Gerry sought to become more cosmopolitan and refined, he joined a prestigious Marblehead political club and made the acquaintance of prominent men from other colonies on his business travels.

Gerry entered politics when he was appointed with his brother to the Marblehead patriot Committee of Inspection following the Boston Massacre in January 1770. The committee was charged to pressure local merchants and inhabitants to observe the American boycott against specified British goods. Gerry was committed to political opposition to Britain's unfair taxation, but he was obviously also concerned about the economic effects of harsh British legislation on his merchant community. He expressed a desire to fight what he viewed as corrupt governmental power on a local and colonial level, a desire that shaped much of his subsequent career.

As the crisis with Great Britain worsened, Gerry joined the extensive network of correspondents and committees who formed the backbone of American Revolutionary politics. This marked the beginning of Gerry's lifelong career as an ardent letter writer who debated theories of politics, society, and diplomacy with a wide variety of other public figures. Gerry's most faithful prominent correspondents included Samuel Adams, Rufus King, John Adams, Abigail Adams, Thomas Jefferson, Mercy Otis Warren, and James Warren. Gerry eventually served on both the Marblehead and Massachusetts Committees of Correspondence.

One of Marblehead's strongest patriots, Gerry headed a town-meeting committee that strongly assented to the Boston Town Meeting's 1772 circular letter that roundly condemned parliamentary action against the colonies.

Over the objection of some Marblehead moderates who found Gerry's Revolutionary politics too radical, Elbridge Gerry was elected to the Massachusetts General Court in 1773. In the Massachusetts legislature, Gerry advocated stronger boycotts and the formation of a colonial militia. Thus began Gerry's lifelong advocacy for state militias to hedge against what he considered the frightening prospect of a standing army.

The year 1773 brought smallpox to Massachusetts, and Elbridge Gerry was tangled up in the social and political ramifications of the epidemic. His brother John was one of a group of Marbleheaders who constructed Essex Hospital, a private hospital on Cat Island to provide inoculation, and Elbridge Gerry became one of the proprietors when the hospital opened. Because of uncertainty about how smallpox was spread, the public was fearful and opposed the hospital. In January 1774, rioters attacked the island and burned down the hospital, an incident subsequently referred to as the "Smallpox War." The violence shocked Gerry and reinforced his belief that the passions of the common man had to be controlled and channeled for the public good. Gerry resigned from the Marblehead Committee of Correspondence in protest.

Gerry reentered public affairs later in 1774 when he spearheaded Marbleheaders' resistance to the closing of the Port of Boston by the British and took over local relief efforts. He was unanimously nominated as a potential local Marblehead representative to the first meeting of the Continental Congress in September, but when only colonywide representatives were sent to Congress he attended the Essex County convention instead. Gerry was publicly hailed as a leading member of the convention, which resolved the most strenuous resistance to British punishments of Boston, and after the convention he began to consult with local leaders from around Massachusetts to coordinate anti-British actions.

After General Thomas Gage dissolved the Massachusetts legislature in October, Gerry helped to form the alternative Provincial Congress and was elected as a Marblehead representative. The Provincial Congress was an extralegal body that would evolve into the new Revolutionary legislature of the state of Massachusetts. As a member of the Provincial Congress, Gerry served on many important committees, but he particularly concerned himself with encouraging statewide military preparations. Gerry began to coordinate the collection of weapons and ammunition and soon began to organize military supplies of all kinds. As he became more prominent throughout Massachusetts, Gerry continued to be concerned with issues in Marblehead, in-

cluding the formation of a corps of minutemen and local protests against British curtailing of fishing rights.

As the leader of the Provincial committee in control of military supplies, Elbridge Gerry played a role in the dramatic events at Lexington and Concord on April 19, 1775, that marked the beginning of the Revolutionary War. Gerry's committee was in charge of the weapons stored in Concord, the seizure of which was one of the British soldiers' primary objectives in their foray out of Boston. Gerry and several of his fellow committee members narrowly escaped capture by the British on their march to Concord by fleeing from the Black Horse Tavern in Menotomy in their nightclothes to hide in a cornfield. After the battles of Lexington and Concord, Gerry collected, from minutemen and witnesses, depositions for the Provincial Congress that were published in pamphlets and in newspapers around the country.

Although he despised arbitrary military power, Gerry was quickly convinced by his involvement at Lexington and Concord that the Revolutionary War was a necessary defense against tyranny. As a politician and as a merchant, Gerry continued to coordinate military supplies and funding, and he continued to be interested in the workings of militia and Continental army and navy forces.

Gerry soon came to realize that reconciliation with Britain would be impossible, and late in 1775 he became an early and strong proponent of American independence. In January 1776, after a fight against a more conservative Provincial Massachusetts faction lead by John Hancock (whom he despised for playing on popular passions), Gerry was elected to the Continental Congress, and he immediately helped the Massachusetts delegation take the lead on the question of independence. Gerry felt that independence was the only way for Americans to guard their virtue and morality from contamination by the corrupt British Empire. Gerry's leadership paid off, and on July 2, Congress voted for independence. Gerry was proud to sign the Declaration of Independence.

Gerry continued his interest in military matters as a member of Congress. He chaired a committee that oversaw supply of the Continental Army and investigated the quartermaster department, and he traveled with a committee to inspect several of Washington's encampments. Gerry also directed his brother to use the family's merchant fleets to trade with the army's commissary agents and with Joseph Gardoqui and Sons, a company of Spanish traders who were secretly sending funds to help the American cause. Enlistments were a constant problem for the army, and Gerry advocated extending the term of service for the entire war (a much more extreme position than Congress would ever endorse).

Gerry's name was linked with the Conway Cabal, a movement by some members of Congress in 1777 to replace George Washington as commander of the Continental Army with Horatio Gates, the hero of Saratoga. While Gerry was a great supporter of Gates's victory, there is no conclusive evidence that Gerry actually conspired to oust Washington.

Alongside military matters, Gerry became interested in finance. He openly advocated price controls after 1777 and was constantly concerned with bolstering the stability of paper currency. Much of Gerry's considerable personal fortune was invested in paper money and government securities during the war; yet he was in favor of limits on profiteering and attended several price-fixing conventions around the country. He also pushed to have fishing rights included in the economic demands placed on the British in peace negotiations.

Although Gerry was in favor of a central government to coordinate financial and military actions and was a proponent of the Articles of Confederation, he remained a strong advocate in Congress for the interests of Massachusetts. In 1780, Gerry objected to a committee recommendation for the requisitioning of supplies from the states because he felt the bill particularly hurt Massachusetts. When Gerry called for reconsideration of part of the bill, he became incensed when he was ruled out of order. He returned to Massachusetts and vacated his Congressional seat until 1783, despite the fact that he was frequently reelected. Under the current election system, which allowed candidates to run for more than one office at a time, he had also been elected to both houses of the Massachusetts legislature, and he served as a member of the state house of representatives, where he continued to oppose John Hancock.

Once the Revolutionary War was over, Gerry's support for a national military force ended. He strenuously opposed the maintenance of any peacetime standing army (such as the one proposed by Alexander Hamilton) as the potential tool of arbitrary governmental power, and he continued to be a supporter of the state militias' right to keep the peace once he reentered Congress in 1783. Another institution that Gerry despised was the Society of Cincinnati, founded in 1783 as an hereditary honorary association of officers of the Continental Army. Gerry contended that members of the society, including George Washington, were susceptible to becoming military dictators and represented a dangerous aristocratic element that was detrimental to society.

Gerry opposed the Impost of 1783, a national tariff designed to grant more independent revenue to the federal government, which was financially dependent upon the states under the Articles of Confederation. In Gerry's mind, the states needed to be able to check any power held by a few individuals in the central government, and he was even wary of letting the Confederation government regulate foreign commerce, although in one of his many seeming contradictions, Gerry did favor federal assumption of each state's war debts.

When the question of where to locate the newly planned national capital arose in 1783, Gerry led two congressional committees to review proposed locations. Gerry balanced sectional and economic conflicts to favor a location on the Potomac River.

Ineligible for reelection to Congress in 1785 according to the Articles of Confederation, Gerry returned to the Massachusetts house of representatives. During 1785, Gerry opposed the efforts of Governor James Bowdoin and others in the state who began to call for a stronger national government. In 1786, he refused to attend the Annapolis Convention, a meeting called to discuss measures for bolstering national power.

Gerry's years as an unmarried ladies' man came to an end in 1786. He had courted Katherine Hunt of Watertown, Massachusetts, during his early years in Congress, but her illiteracy had stood in the way of his continuing their romance through correspondence, and he never proposed to her. Instead, Gerry married the intelligent and beautiful Ann Thompson, daughter of a prominent New York merchant family who was twenty-one years his junior.

Gerry had always cultivated good taste and public approval as a learned gentleman; in 1781 he had been elected to membership in the American Academy of Arts and Sciences. Marriage marked the beginning of his effort to be even more gentlemanly and refined as Gerry became an Anglican, shifted his investments into land and farming, bought a large estate in Cambridge (which he named Elmwood), and settled into polite society. Elbridge and Ann never again lived in the provincial fishing town of Marblehead.

Gerry was an extremely devoted husband and father. Ann bore ten children, nine of whom survived. Elbridge encouraged the education of both his sons and daughters, and he carried on tender correspondences with them when his political commitments took him away from home. Once he was married, Gerry expressed a constant desire for a comfortable home life, and he never ceased worrying about how his public commitments affected his family. Although Elbridge frequently worried about Ann's poor health, she was to live until 1849, making her the last surviving widow of a signer of the Declaration of Independence.

The year 1786 brought not only marriage for Gerry but also the signal event that frightened him into support for a stronger national government: Shays's Rebellion. In September, Daniel Shays, a poor Revolutionary war veteran, led a group of disgruntled debtors from western Massachusetts in a mob action to close down the county courts that were foreclosing on their mortgages. Though they were put down by the Massachusetts militia under Benjamin Lincoln (whom Gerry supported), the rebels shocked elitists like Gerry and caused even more consternation the following year when they began to be elected to offices in state government. Gerry saw the democratic threat he had been aware of since the Smallpox War horribly realized as the "rabble" became successful in the newly opened field of electoral politics.[*]

Convinced that an excess of either aristocracy, as embodied in the Society of Cincinnati, or of democracy, as in Shays's Rebellion, would lead to the downfall of the republic, Gerry now became persuaded that a stronger national government would help ensure stability. Gerry began his stint as a delegate to the Constitutional Convention in May 1787 still committed to states' rights but willing to consider more centralization of power in the interest of preserving a republican nation. Gerry's middling opinions shaped the ideas about separation of powers and checks and balances that he put forth throughout the convention.

Gerry was bothered by several points in the initial Virginia Plan offered by Edmund Randolph early in the convention. The plan called for a "National legislature" based on population, with a popularly elected lower house that would elect the upper house, a chief executive elected by the legislature, and a federal court system. Gerry thought the term "National legislature" to be too sweeping, opposed direct election of the lower house, and wanted the executive to have a council. One of Gerry's greatest concerns was about how the chief executive should be elected, and his constant efforts to oppose direct election in order to assure the merit of the candidates eventually led to a compromise between direct and legislative election and the creation of the electoral college.

After William Paterson introduced the New Jersey Plan, a scheme much closer to the Articles of Confederation and more favorable to small

---

[*]Editor's note: See GEORGE CLINTON for further explanation of Shays's Rebellion.

states and to the South than the Virginia Plan, Gerry was appointed head of a committee to work out a compromise. The "Great Compromise" that Gerry's committee produced became the new working plan for the convention, but as he worked on the document, Gerry's personal apprehension about the entire project began to increase, as did his old worries about militarism and aristocracy. By late July, when a draft of the document was drawn up, Gerry had become skeptical of the prospects of working out any satisfactory national government. Gerry could not accept a modern definition of federalism under which ultimate sovereignty resides in the people but where the federal and state governments share the power to govern.

Gerry particularly thought the Senate was being given too many powers. He opposed the creation of the vice presidency, and he thought having the vice president preside over the Senate was a direct violation of the separation of powers so necessary to the health of any republican government. Gerry felt it would be too easy for the president to impose the will of the executive branch on Congress through the vice president, and he feared that such corruption might unalterably weaken the republic.

By the end of the convention, in a highly controversial and exceptional move, Gerry decided not to sign the Constitution. A month later, Gerry wrote a public letter explaining his Antifederalism; his reasons included the lack of a bill of rights and the possible damage to the independence of the states. The letter brought public scorn from the staunch Federalists in Massachusetts, but the state ratifying convention invited Gerry to appear and explain his position. Gerry was angered by the conduct of the convention, however, and when he left the proceedings he forever severed ties with some of his closest political friends, including Rufus King and Francis Dana. In the end, the Federalists prevailed.

Once the Constitution was ratified in 1789, Gerry decided to support the new federal government in the interest of national unity and stability. He reluctantly stood for election to Congress. Gerry was committed to no party but was sympathetic to many national Federalist positions,

although he was never overly fond of George Washington and feared that some, such as Alexander Hamilton, still harbored monarchical tendencies.

Though he still clung to the ideas of states' rights, Gerry supported the Bank of the United States and invested his personal funds in the bank. He continued to advocate federal repayment of all war debts, but he opposed the creation of a strong Treasury Department. Separation of powers continued to interest Gerry, who demanded particularly strict limits between the executive and the legislative branches, as in 1789 when he voted in Congress to oppose the presidential removal of Theodore Sedgwick as secretary of state. When the Bill of Rights was adopted, Gerry especially advocated the independence of the state militias, and he continued to object to centralized military force.

Gerry left the Congress in 1793. He was mentioned by several political backers as a candidate for governor of Massachusetts in 1794, but his middling politics satisfied those on neither side of the increasingly well-defined political split between Federalists and Jeffersonian Republicans. In 1796, Gerry became a presidential elector, and he supported John Adams for president despite Adams's strong Federalism.

Gerry had maintained his close personal ties to John Adams during Adams's vice presidency, and he continued the relationship after Adams became president. As an antiparty politician, Gerry particularly felt that Jefferson's "opposition" vice presidency during the Federalist administration could be a successful test of party cooperation. Gerry probably also hoped that having a president and vice president of different parties would provide another check on the potential growth in the power of the presidency that he so feared. Gerry corresponded with both Jefferson and Adams about his hopes that the president and vice president would rise above party spirit, and he even told Adams that he should try to garner Jefferson's cooperation as vice president by assuring him that he would someday become president. In reality, the party split between president and vice president during the Adams–Jefferson administration drove the parties farther apart.

Gerry faced his own political test during the XYZ Affair, a major diplomatic crisis between the United States and France in which he played a prominent role. In 1797, President John Adams, over the objections of his own Federalist cabinet members, appointed Gerry to accompany Charles Coatsworth Pinckney and John Marshall to France to try to negotiate a peaceful solution to the increasing friction with France. France had stepped up harassment of American shipping in the wake of the Jay Treaty, which abrogated the Franco-American alliance and which France considered to be far too pro-British.

Gerry arrived in France after Pinckney and Marshall firmly resolved to uphold U.S. neutrality toward France and to prevent a full-scale war. French Foreign Minister Charles Maurice de Tallyrand-Périgord, whom Gerry had met in America during the Revolutionary War, sent four associates to make demands upon the American negotiators. Tallyrand's representatives, three of whom were identified in America only as X, Y, and Z, insisted that in order to avoid a war, the Americans would have to pay bribes and loans to the French. For several months, the Americans resisted the demands for payment, and eventually negotiations broke down.

Pinckney and Marshall left Paris in April 1798, but Gerry stayed behind at the demand of Tallyrand. When the XYZ "dispatches" were published to great public outcry in the United States, Gerry smoothed over the controversy in France by substantiating Tallyrand's claim that the agents had acted independently, while at the same time Gerry assured John Adams that Tallyrand was at fault. Gerry's frequent requests for a passport to leave France were not granted until August. France never declared full-scale war on the United States, but its harassment increased after the breakdown of the negotiations.[*]

Gerry acquired a bad reputation from the affair, based largely on the hostile impressions of him recorded by John Marshall in a journal that he later made public. Gerry argued, counter to Marshall's charges and to attacks on him by Timothy Pickering, that he had not taken advantage of his personal relationship with Tallyrand, but rather that he had always sought to include the other two Americans in their talks and to defend American neutrality. Contrary to the picture of Gerry painted by the Federalists upon his return, the evidence bears out his claim that he sought no personal advantage by remaining in France, but rather saw his remaining there as the only chance to preserve peace. Upon his return to Boston, Gerry was snubbed by the Federalists, who became increasingly militant toward France. Particularly bothersome to Gerry were vicious personal attacks on his family that included threats and burnt effigies on the front lawn of Elmwood. Gerry was not publicly vindicated until his correspondence with Tallyrand was published in 1799.

While Gerry remained personally loyal to John Adams in the aftermath of the affair, he was slowly drawn toward the Jeffersonians. In the wake of the XYZ Affair, the Federalists became even more publicly identified as pro-British and the Jeffersonian Republicans as pro-French. Gerry did not embrace France, but he did want peace, and he thought the British were dangerous. Jefferson personally urged Gerry to be the Republican candidate for the Massachusetts governorship in 1800, on a platform of peace with France. Gerry lost the election, but he received a record number of votes against the Federalists and even won a majority of votes in Boston.

Still hoping that neutrality would dull the political forces that threatened to rip the country apart, Gerry supported Adams's presidential race in 1800 hoping that Jefferson would again come in second and be reelected as vice president. When Jefferson beat Adams for the presidency in the election, the Federalist Party was taken over by the Hamiltonian Federalists, whom Gerry viewed as dangerous militants and possible monarchists.

---

[*]Editor's note: See JOHN ADAMS for further explanation of the XYZ Affair.

Elbridge Gerry then abandoned his antiparty status and became a Jeffersonian Republican because he thought it the only way left to protect America's virtue. Gerry ran as the Republican candidate for Massachusetts governor from 1801 to 1803. Each race was unsuccessful but showed an increase in Republican votes.

For a time, it seemed Gerry was finally to have the tranquil private life away from demanding public service that he had craved for so long. Not yet ready to embrace all the machinations of modern party politics, Gerry left the governing to others during Jefferson's first administration. Elbridge and Ann raised their children at Elmwood, and Elbridge sought to straighten out financial troubles caused by the shoddy handling of the family businesses by his brother Samuel.

During the Embargo Crisis in 1809, when the Jeffersonians blocked all exports to protest foreign interference with American trade, Gerry became more convinced than ever that the Federalists were plotting with the British to undo the republic. The danger he perceived convinced Gerry to reenter public life. He agreed to stand for governor in 1809 after the Republican candidate died. When Gerry ran again in 1810, he won. Although he had embraced party politics, Gerry still sought political middle ground during his first administration as governor.

Gerry's second term as governor of Massachusetts in 1811 was far more partisan. Gerry lost patience with the Federalists, who were viciously attacking President Madison, and he purged Federalists from public office in Massachusetts wherever possible. Gerry appointed a particularly high number of Republicans to the state judiciary and ended the Federalist hold on the Corporation of Harvard University. Gerry also investigated and prosecuted a record number of Federalist newspapers for libel.

It was during Gerry's second term early in 1812 when the term "gerrymander" was born. The Republican state legislature redistricted the state along heavily Republican lines, and the Federalists were none too pleased. Although Gerry himself always claimed that he protested the redistricting, he was targeted by the Federalists as the culprit. A Federalist cartoonist, Elkanah Tis-

dale, drew Gerry's head atop a map of the new district of Essex County. The caption drew attention to the cartoon district's resemblance to a salamander, and the name "gerrymander" stuck to the practice of partisan redistricting.

Gerry was nominated as the Republican candidate for vice president in 1812 after John Langdon of New Hampshire declined the nomination. The election was fought mainly over the War of 1812, and supporters hoped that Gerry's reputation as a supporter of Madison and of the Revolutionary military would counteract some antiwar Republicans. Although he had always opposed arbitrary military power, Gerry viewed the War of 1812 as a fight necessary to save the American republic. Republican handlers also supported Gerry's nomination because his age (sixty-eight) would prevent him from threatening James Monroe as Madison's presidential heir apparent and because they hoped he would draw support away from the Federalists in New England. Madison and Gerry defeated the Federalist ticket led by DeWitt Clinton, and Gerry was inaugurated as vice president on March 4, 1813.

The war added new fuel to Gerry's partisan fire during his vice presidency. In his first inaugural address, Gerry claimed that the war would decide "whether the republican system adopted by the people is imbecile and transient, or whether it has force and duration worthy of the enterprise." Gerry was not alone in considering the War of 1812 a test of the strength of the American Revolution.

Gerry did not perform many important political functions as vice president, but he did take his role as presiding officer of the Senate very seriously. Gerry shaped the office by refusing to abide by the tradition that the vice president would allow another presiding officer to be named in case both the president and vice president both died while Congress was not in session over the summer. In June 1813, Gerry was unwell and President Madison was gravely ill, yet Gerry would not resign his senatorial leadership for fear that if he died, William B. Giles, a political enemy, might become presiding officer and hurt the war effort.

Gerry was concerned with preserving the integrity of the Republican Party and of the office of vice president. During the 1814 session of the Senate, Gerry discovered that a stenographer whom the Senate had appointed to record its debates was publishing antiadministration articles in Washington, D.C., newspapers. After suspecting that the entire affair consisted of a plot just to embarrass him, Gerry avoided scandal and refused to dismiss the man.

During his vice presidency, Elbridge Gerry took an active part in the Washington, D.C., social scene. While his wife remained at home in Massachusetts, he accompanied the famous and fashionable Madame Bonaparte, the daughter of a Maryland merchant family and the wife of Jerome Bonaparte, to many public functions. Gerry spent much of the remainder of his time in office trying to secure patronage positions for members of his family who were beginning to suffer financially.

Gerry became ill, probably from a stroke, during the summer of 1813. He recovered from the initial attack, but at the age of seventy he did not regain his full strength. On November 23, 1814, Gerry was afflicted again in the Senate chamber, and he died later that day. Gerry was buried in the Congressional Cemetery in Washington, D.C., where a monument to his vice presidential years marks his grave. Senator Christopher Gore proposed that Gerry's wife be paid his full vice-presidential salary for life, but the proposal was rejected by Republicans who feared setting a precedent for Federalist pensions.

Elbridge Gerry was in many ways an important Founding Father of the United States—revolutionary, signer of the Declaration of Independence, member of the Constitutional Convention, diplomat, congressman, and governor. Although he was accused of vacillating over the course of his political career, he worked tirelessly on behalf of measures he thought would be best for the nation. It was fitting that Gerry died still in the service of his country as vice president. Abigail Adams provided a just eulogy for Gerry in a letter to her sister Elizabeth Peabody on December 12, 1814:

> Alas, the last compatriot is gone . . . A Friend who was neither warped nor shaken by change of time or fortune . . . Faction may rave & Party spirit slander, but an honester man he has not left behind nor a more sincere disinterested Friend of his Country.

REFERENCES

George Billias, *Elbridge Gerry: Founding Father and Republican Statesman* (New York: McGraw Hill, 1976); James T. Austin, *The Life of Elbridge Gerry*, 2 vols. (Boston: Wells and Lilly, 1828–29); Samuel Eliot Morison, "Elbridge Gerry, Gentleman-Democrat," *New England Quarterly*, II (1929), 6–33; *A Study in Dissent: The Warren-Gerry Correspondence, 1776–1792*, C. Harvey Gardiner, ed. (Carbondale, Ill.: Southern Illinois University Press, 1968); *Elbridge Gerry's Letterbook, Paris 1797–1798*, Russell W. Knight, ed. (Salem, Mass.: The Essex Institute, 1966).

SARAH J. PURCELL teaches American history at Central Michigan University. She earned history degrees from Grinnell College and Brown University, specializing in the era of the Revolution and the Early Republic. During 1996–97, she was a fellow at the John Carter Brown Library. She is a contributing editor for the forthcoming *Military Women World Wide,* and her scholarly work has appeared in *The Journal of Church and State.* She has also written several entries for the new *American National Biography* series and *The Encyclopedia of New England Culture.*

DANIEL D. TOMPKINS (1774–1825)

Vice President, 1817–1825

(President James Monroe)

DANIEL D. TOMPKINS
(Library of Congress)

By Gaspare J. Saladino

Daniel D. Tompkins was the sixth vice president. At about age twenty-six, Tompkins entered public life, and before his thirtieth birthday he became a New York State supreme court justice, a remarkable achievement for a farmer's son. In 1807, "The Farmer's Boy" was elected governor of New York, holding that position for ten years. A democrat, republican, humanitarian, and patriot, Tompkins achieved unparalleled popularity, especially during the War of 1812 when he was America's finest war governor. His splendid war record brought him national attention, and he was considered for the presidency. An ambitious man, Tompkins took his presidential candidacy seriously, but astute politicians recognized that he lacked widespread support.

Therefore, Tompkins settled for the vice presidency, a dead-end office in which his reputation suffered badly. His financial problems and related intemperance caused him to neglect his duty as president of the Senate and made his vice-presidential years the unhappiest of his life. Notwithstanding, he was courted by presidential candidates who recognized his enormous popularity in the important state of New York. They took his presidential aspirations in earnest, or at least did not openly disparage them. His enemies—often wealthy aristocrats with personal grudges—mercilessly belittled him, however. Tompkins ended his vice presidency aware that his political career was over, even though he was but fifty years old.

Tompkins was born on June 21, 1774, in Scarsdale, Westchester County, New York, the son of Jonathan Griffin Tompkins and Sarah Ann Hyatt. His father was descended from English settlers, his mother from Scottish. The elder Tompkins, a farmer and Revolutionary patriot, became a county judge and state assemblyman. Daniel Tompkins entered Columbia College as a sophomore in 1792, and three years later he was valedictorian. In his senior year, he entered the New York City office of attorney Peter Jay Munro and in 1797 was admitted to the bar. That same year he married Hannah Minthorne, daughter of Mangle Minthorne, a wealthy New York City merchant from the city's Seventh Ward. The Tompkinses had seven children.

Tompkins was part of "The Little Band," young intellectuals who met at the home of New York City lawyer Aaron Burr, a powerful Republican leader. In the spring 1800 state elections, Burr controlled the city's General Republican Committee and turned his "Little Band" into campaign workers. Tompkins operated in the Seventh Ward. The Republicans elected their entire slate of candidates to the state assembly, giving them a majority in that body. Later that year, the assembly and the senate gave the state's twelve electoral votes to Thomas Jefferson and Burr for president and vice president, respectively. New York's electoral votes were critical to Jefferson's ultimate election.

The election brought Tompkins to the attention of President Jefferson, who appointed him a commissioner of bankruptcy under the Bankruptcy Act of 1800. Burr engineered Tompkins's election to the state constitutional convention of 1801, Tompkins's first elective office, where he distinguished himself by his independence. In 1802, Tompkins was elected a New York City assembly delegate, serving for several months the next year; he resigned in 1804 to become an associate justice of the state Supreme Court and in the same year was elected to (but resigned from) the U.S. House of Representatives. In 1805, he declined appointment as judge of the U.S. District Court for New York because he earned more as a state judge. These were the first of several federal positions that Tompkins turned down in favor of a state office, a not uncommon practice among New York politicians. In these years, Tompkins also became a Mason, a founder of the New York Academy of Fine Arts, an organizer of the New-York Historical Society, a member of the New York Manumission Society, and a founder of a free school for poor children.

His judicial position boosted Tompkins's public career. As he rode circuit, he became acquainted with voters and developed a statewide reputation as an honest judge who rendered accurate judicial decisions and delivered eloquent charges and addresses. According to Jabez Hammond, a Republican politician and a New York historian, Tompkins (as a judge) was "extremely prepossessing, his manners highly popular, and his address . . . every way pleasing." Mordecai Noah, a Republican newspaper editor, asserted that Tompkins also had "the faculty of attaching every person to him who once knew him."

In 1807, DeWitt Clinton, leader of the Clintonian wing of the Republican Party and a nephew of U.S. vice president George Clinton, wanted to unseat Governor Morgan Lewis, a leader of the party's Livingston wing who was also favored by Federalists. DeWitt Clinton wanted to be governor (as his uncle had been), but his aristocratic background made that difficult. Therefore, he convinced the Republicans in the state legislature to nominate Tompkins, thinking that he could "mould" him. Tompkins won by more than 4,000 votes in an election that was described as a Tompkins crusade to frustrate "a combination of rich families."

Tompkins was inaugurated governor in July 1807 and moved his family to Albany, the state capital, a few months later. He was reelected in 1810, 1813, and 1816. During his first administration (1807–10), he diligently enforced the embargo against Great Britain levied by Congress, although he was reluctant, despite

President Jefferson's entreaties, to use force to do so. Nevertheless, Tompkins's support was "highly consolatory" to Jefferson. His actions marked the beginning of an alliance with the Virginia Dynasty, to which he was drawn both by political philosophy and expediency. He also began to distance himself from DeWitt Clinton, an opponent of the embargo. His breach with Clinton widened during the presidential election of 1808 when he backed James Madison against George Clinton. With little aid from the federal government or state legislature, Tompkins prepared for war with Great Britain by raising and equipping the militia and constructing arsenals and fortifications.

His war preparations did not diminish his Jeffersonian humanitarianism. In his state papers—praised for their brevity, vigor, and eloquence—Tompkins stressed the pivotal role of education in a democracy, advocated the improved treatment of the insane, sought to restrict capital punishment, pardoned criminals to relieve overcrowding in prisons, and opposed whipping and other humiliating punishments. He developed most of these ideas, as his college essays attest, when he was young.

In 1810, the Republicans again nominated Tompkins for governor. He defeated Federalist Jonas Platt of Herkimer by more than 6,000 votes. DeWitt Clinton was elected lieutenant governor despite the opposition of Tompkins and the "Martling-Men" of Tammany. ("Martling" was the name of the New York City tavern where they met.) The Tammany faction had recently become a significant political force, one that would back Tompkins for his entire political career and would try to drive the aristocratic and despised Clinton from power.

Harshly critical of Great Britain, Tompkins continued his war preparations and was so effective that in 1811 it was rumored that he would become secretary of war in Madison's administration "with a reversion of the presidency, when Monroe and Madison have done with it."

In 1811, Congress failed to renew the charter of the Bank of the United States, and to fill the void New York investors, mostly Federalists, sought to incorporate the Bank of America. In January 1812, Federalists, aided by some Republicans, introduced and pushed for an incorporation bill in the New York legislature. Tompkins told the legislature that the state already had too many banks; too much wealth was amassed and concentrated in bank stock, and bankers were not accountable to the public. Nevertheless, the assembly adopted the bank bill, and in March Tompkins prorogued the legislature to prevent the senate from acting. Seeking Federalist support for the presidency, DeWitt Clinton equivocated on the bank bill. His brother-in-law remarked: "Our Governor has prorogued our Assembly. Farmer's boys are apt to use power when in power as perhaps Gentlemen's sons." Some Clintonians charged the prorogation was really an attempt to prevent the legislature from endorsing Clinton for the presidency before a congressional caucus could nominate Madison.

About a week after the legislature convened on May 21, 1812, Republicans nominated Clinton to run for president against Madison, who had been unanimously nominated by congressional Republicans on May 18. (The legislature also incorporated the Bank of America.) Tompkins supported Madison. In June, war was declared against Great Britain. Tompkins called out the militia, ordered men and equipment to New York's northern and western frontiers, helped to defend New York City, erected more arsenals and magazines, made inspection tours, and tried to rouse a deeply divided public. However, he was hampered by the Federalist-dominated assembly which, for example, refused to vote funds for the militia.

In November 1812, Madison was reelected president, although New York's electoral votes went to DeWitt Clinton, the favorite of peace Republicans and Federalists. In February 1813, Republicans in the New York legislature unanimously nominated Tompkins for governor and refused, to Tompkins's delight, to renominate Clinton for lieutenant governor. State Senator Martin Van Buren led the fight against Clinton and joined Tompkins as a leader of the state's Republican party. Clinton's courting of Federalists was anathema to these two loyal party men. Federalists nominated "The Great Patroon," the wealthy Stephen Van Rensselaer, for governor.

Described as Madison's "tool," Tompkins was attacked for calling out the militia and proroguing the legislature, but the bitter campaign's main theme was support for the war, and a vote for Tompkins was a vote for the war. In the spring elections, Tompkins defeated Van Rensselaer by more than 3,600 votes. His greatest support came from the militarily vulnerable southern and western districts. The Madison administration rejoiced in Tompkins's victory because it destroyed the prospects of a northern confederacy; New York was not likely now to join violently antiwar New England. By late 1813 and early 1814, Tompkins was being boosted for the presidency, but most knowledgeable politicians dismissed him.

In August 1814, Washington, D.C., was burned, and a British invasion of New York City seemed imminent. Although the city's defenses needed improvement, its banks refused to lend money for that purpose solely on the security of U.S. Treasury notes. Encouraged by prominent New Yorkers, including U.S. Senator Rufus King (a Federalist), Tompkins personally endorsed these notes. In September, he called a special session of the legislature, which, under the leadership of Van Buren (a loyal ally of Tompkins), hiked the militia's pay, raised twenty companies to protect New York City, and provided for fortifications in the area of the city. In later years, King praised Tompkins for "performing the duties of almost every Department" in prosecuting the war.

On September 28, 1814, Madison offered Tompkins the position of secretary of state, "then regarded as the stepping stone to the Presidency." Tompkins declined, stating that he could serve the the war effort better as governor of New York. Moreover, he believed it was unwise to leave New York because, in his absence, his unauthorized defense expenditures might be used against him by his political enemies. According to Van Buren, who praised Tompkins's genuine patriotism, his declining the office and "the subsequent selection of Mr. Monroe, in all probability controuled the question of succession to Mr. Madison." Tammany leader Matthew L. Davis disagreed; if Tompkins wanted the nomination, he needed some "warm, open, and active friends" in Washington or else he would "be *led off the course as a distanced poney; or not in a condition to run the heats.*"

Madison was disappointed and angry, but in October 1814 he gave Tompkins command of the Third Military District, embracing southern New York and much of New Jersey. Colonel Washington Irving, a recent addition to Tompkins's staff, was overjoyed; the governor was "absolutely one of the worthiest men" he ever knew. He had "good sense and ready talent" and "nerve to put into immediate execution any measure that he is satisfied is correct." Taking command immediately, Tompkins made inspection tours, improved the city's and district's defenses, and organized and disciplined 25,000 troops. In December the United States and Great Britain signed the Treaty of Ghent, and in February 1815 the U.S. Senate ratified it. Tompkins relinquished his command in April. Jabez Hammond wrote:

> The popularity and influence of Gov. Tompkins may be said now to have been at its zenith. In New-York he was all but idolized by a formidable and well organized political party, who held strong majorities in both branches of the legislature; abroad he was esteemed and respected, and at Washington the national cabinet had virtually declared him their candidate for the next national executive vacancy.

A confident Tompkins moved against DeWitt Clinton in 1815. Although he refused to break a tie in the five-member Council of Appointment, he convinced the two Clinton supporters to oust Clinton as New York City mayor. He wanted to maintain party harmony so that his presidential chances would not be hurt. One politician noted: "The Governor is every man's friend & he is so ardent in his pursuit of popularity, that he will not venture to lose an atom of it." Tompkins also attacked Clinton's campaign to build the popular Erie Canal. Because the anglophobic Tompkins believed that the Treaty of Ghent (1815) was only a truce, he wanted state money to be spent in preparing for another war, not on the canal.

In February 1816, the Republicans in the state legislature nominated Tompkins for the presidency and instructed the state's congressional delegates to support him. The delegates were already working for him, even though they were not optimistic. Tompkins had no support in the South. The same month, the Republican legislative caucus also backed him for governor. Tompkins did not want the nomination, but ever loyal to the party, he accepted. He preferred a presidential nomination, being among those politicians who thought that the next president should come from a state other than Virginia. When he realized he could not be nominated, Tompkins agreed to accept a vice-presidential nomination on a ticket with either Secretary of the Treasury William Crawford of Georgia or Secretary of State James Monroe of Virginia. In March, the Republican congressional caucus gave Monroe sixty-five votes to fifty-four for Crawford for the presidential nomination and Tompkins eighty-five votes to thirty for Pennsylvanian Simon Snyder for the vice-presidential nomination. The vice presidency, however, was not a path to the presidency. The Virginia Dynasty used it to obtain support outside the South.

In the spring 1816 gubernatorial election, Tompkins defeated Federalist Rufus King by almost 7,000 votes after a bruising campaign in which the war and Tompkins's conduct of it were the main issues. His greatest support came from western New York, whose protection had been one of his wartime concerns. Monroe and Tompkins were elected in November 1816, each receiving 183 of 217 electoral votes. In January 1817, Tompkins—reiterating a plea that he made to the state legislature in 1812—recommended (in a special message) that the state legislature expunge "the reproach of slavery" from the statute book by 1827. The legislature responded on March 31 by emancipating all African Americans born before July 4, 1779, as of July 4, 1827. On February 12, 1817, Congress counted the electoral votes and declared Monroe and Tompkins elected. Tompkins resigned as governor on February 24.

Monroe and Tompkins were inaugurated on March 4, 1817. As president of the U.S. Senate, Tompkins had a poor attendance record. In his two vice-presidential terms, he never presided over an entire session of the Senate, and he missed two of eight sessions (plus a brief special session). The two missed sessions were the last ones in each of his terms. Sometimes Tompkins did not even leave his Washington boardinghouse to preside, once lamenting that "there is nothing for him to do here, and any other man may preside in the Senate as well as he." As presiding officer, he was cordial and conciliatory, although Delaware Congressman Louis McLane found him awkward in the chair.

Tompkins's profound financial problems (personal and official) and his related intemperance prompted his poor attendance. During the war and after, the "Farmer's Boy" purchased land on Staten Island, built a mansion, and developed Tompkinsville on the island's northeastern end directly opposite lower Manhattan. With others, he undertook projects that connected Tompkinsville by steam ferry with Manhattan and joined the northern and southern ends of Staten Island by turnpike. These grandiose schemes, common to America's budding entrepreneurs, ran him into debt.

As war governor, Tompkins expended about $4 million of state and federal money, as well as money he raised. Unfortunately, according to Jabez Hammond, Tompkins "was irregular and unmethodical in business; not systematical in keeping his accounts; employed too many agents; mingled his own private funds with those of the public; was naturally careless about money, and sometimes profuse in his expenses." The accounts of the New York comptroller showed in 1816 that Tompkins had not legally accounted for $120,000 in state funds. In 1819, a legislatively appointed commission recommended that Tompkins be paid a premium of $120,000 on money he had raised, thereby offsetting what he owed. The legislature passed a bill approving the premium. But Tompkins claimed the state owed him $130,000. Clintonian comptroller Archibald McIntyre rejected this claim, and the issue became a political football before it was resolved. Although Tompkins tried repeatedly to settle his federal accounts, the government's system of accountability for many years after the war was in a chaotic condition. It was several years before he was even told whether or not he owed or was owed money.

An embittered and disillusioned Tompkins probably started to drink heavily at this time. Van Buren visited him early in 1820 and discovered that Tompkins's "habit of intemperance" had started. He explained that Tompkins's "feelings had not been callous or his resolution strong enough to enable him to bear up against the injustice, the ingratitude and the calumny of which he was now made the victim." Hammond speculated that Tompkins drank "in order to allay nervous irritability and excitement." A less sympathetic Clintonian described Tompkins as "a degraded sot."

In his first vice-presidential term, Tompkins cast two of his five tie-breaking votes as the Senate's president. On January 21, 1819, he voted against an amendment to strike out a clause in a military appropriations bill, requiring the army to give extra pay to noncommissioned officers and soldiers employed in military road construction and repair. In a message (the only extant one for his casting votes), he defended the clause's constitutionality, declaring that Congress continuously gave the president the power to build and repair military roads, a power that he had exercised for years. "When they give to the Executive plenary powers to effect any certain and legal public object, the right to employ all lawful means to accomplish that object is necessarily implied and conferred." On February 10, 1819, Tompkins voted negatively on a motion to postpone a bill providing for an equestrian statue of George Washington.

On January 24, 1820, Tompkins wrote his wife that he was much occupied in the Senate: "The question of slavery in Missouri has been debated for 12 days past with great animation and at great length." During the history-making debate, the "gallant" Tompkins permitted some women to sit on the floor in seats usually reserved for dignitaries. To the dismay of the senators, others followed them to the floor. The next day Tompkins affixed a note to the Senate's door "excluding all ladies" not introduced by a senator. Senator Rufus King was unhappy with Tompkins for another reason; he thought Tompkins questioned whether Congress could exclude slavery from Missouri as a condition for statehood. King apparently believed that Tompkins's hankering for the presidency made him curry favor with the South. A Clintonian was more candid, describing Tompkins as "that miserable Sycophant who betrayed us to the Lords of the South, to enable him to subserve his own purposes."

Led by Van Buren, the Republican Party's "Bucktails" (named for a Tammany insignia, a deer tail worn in a hat; formerly the Martling-Men) nominated Tompkins on January 16, 1820 to run for governor against Governor DeWitt Clinton, who had won a special election in 1817 after Tompkins resigned. Upon Tompkins's return to Albany in February, he hesitantly accepted the nomination because he realized that the campaign, centering on his wartime accounts, would be vicious. The election drew national attention because politicians believed that Tompkins and Clinton would be presidential candidates in 1824.

Beginning in February 1820 the Bucktails sought an alliance with Federalist Rufus King, who was indebted to them. Led by Van Buren and Tompkins, the Bucktails had engineered King's reelection as U.S. senator the previous month, against Clinton's opposition, but King was disturbed by the state of Tompkins's wartime accounts and his alleged attitude on Missouri statehood. Tompkins wrote King's son in March that Congress possessed the constitutional authority to require the exclusion of slavery as a condition for Missouri statehood. This reply satisfied King, but he still did not openly favor Tompkins. Clinton was elected narrowly—47,447 to 45,990. Most Federalists voted against Tompkins, who had long been their chief foe. The most damaging vote against Tompkins came from western New York, which repaid Clinton for supporting the Erie Canal. Tammany got an astonishing 59 percent of Federalist New York City's vote for Tompkins. Later in the year the Bucktail-controlled legislature, led by Van Buren, passed an act balancing the wartime accounts of Tompkins, who had released his claims against the state.

In 1820, the congressional caucus did not even bother to renominate Monroe and Tompkins. In mid-November, after the presidential election, Massachusetts Congressman Daniel Webster hatched a plot whereby he and others would cast their electoral votes for Secretary of State John Quincy Adams of Massachusetts instead of Tompkins. Their purpose was not to defeat Tompkins, but only to lay groundwork for Adams's run for the presidency in 1824. Adams rejected the scheme, urging his adherents to vote for Tompkins. Adams refused to antagonize Tompkins, who was so popular in New York; moreover, Tompkins was an enemy of Clinton, a man whose presidential aspirations Adams feared more.

Congress counted the electoral votes in February 1821 and declared Monroe and Tompkins elected. The former received 231 of 232 votes cast, the latter 218 votes. William Plumer, Sr., a New Hampshire elector who cast the only vote against Monroe in December 1820 and who also voted against Tompkins, explained that Tompkins

> whose duty consists in presiding over the senate—for which he receives annually a salary of five thousand dollars; during the last three years he was absent from the senate during their session nearly three fourths of the time, & thereby occasioned an extra-expense to the nation of nearly twenty five hundred dollars. He has not that weight of character which his office requires—the fact is he is grossly intemperate. I cannot vote for him to be again Vice President.

Because Tompkins failed to attend the previous congressional session, Monroe sent a messenger to New York to inform him of his reelection. Tompkins took the oath of office on March 3, 1821, and again on March 5, upon learning that Monroe would take the oath that day.

Before Tompkins was on hand for the first session of his second term in December, he was Staten Island's sole delegate to the New York constitutional convention, called to revise the state constitution of 1777. The calling of the convention by popular referendum was a manifestation of the democratic fervor sweeping the state. The Bucktails, the Republican Party's more democratic wing, elected 110 of the 126 delegates. On August 28, Tompkins was elected president. He excused himself once for ill health,

but apparently attended the convention almost every day until it adjourned on November 20, demonstrating his keen interest in democratic reform and state government. He was delighted to see the abolition of the "aristocratic" and "partisan" Council of Revision, a body composed of the governor, the chancellor, and supreme court judges, that could veto laws. But he opposed the convention's decision to give the governor sole veto power. Tompkins successfully argued for the abolition of the Council of Appointment and the placing of its power in the hands of the executive and legislature. He supported universal manhood suffrage, which the convention did not accept, although it extended the suffrage to more men. Early the next year the voters overwhelmingly accepted the new constitution.

On December 28, 1821, Tompkins began to preside over the U.S. Senate, remaining until about February 1, 1822. Upon arriving in Washington, he was refused admittance into the congressional mess at Strother's boardinghouse, according to Louis McLane, because "he bears the most evident and conclusive marks of a sot." A friend of General Andrew Jackson of Tennessee, a candidate for the presidency in 1824, wrote him that Tompkins was "several times so drunk in the chair that he could with difficulty put the question." In mid-January 1822, Tompkins, hounded by his creditors, placed in trust for their benefit all his real and personal property. His Washington stay was enlivened by a dispute over the appointment of a new Albany postmaster. The postmaster general wanted to appoint a Clintonian Federalist but was opposed by Tompkins and New York senators Van Buren and King, all political enemies of DeWitt Clinton. Monroe refused to interfere, and the postmaster general prevailed. Tompkins was once so angry that he used "violent language" against the president. On January 30, he cast a vote (his third) to keep the revenue officer at Natchez, Mississippi, who a proposed bill sought to remove. Two days later Tompkins informed King officially that his poor health forced him to leave Washington.

The longtime failure of the federal government, despite Tompkins's many efforts, to settle his wartime accounts compounded his problems. His plight became more desperate in April 1822 when Congress placed a rider on an appropriations bill stating that any person in arrears would have his salary withheld until his accounts were settled. Such a person, however, could demand prompt action from the Treasury. By this time, the Treasury had finally certified that he owed the government about $11,000. In June 1822, Tompkins went to the federal district court in New York, claiming that the government owed him money. Rufus King and many others testified for him. Tompkins spoke of ten years of "fears, anxieties, perplexities, sorrows, sicknesses, blighted prospects, and wounded feelings." The jury concluded that the government owed him about $137,000.

Tompkins returned to the Senate in December 1822 in such good spirits and health that, for the first and perhaps only time, he brought along his wife. A correspondent of Kentucky Congressman Henry Clay thought Tompkins still wanted to be president. Tompkins pursued the settlement of his accounts. In January 1823, a select committee of the House of Representatives backed most of his claims. The House and Senate adopted a bill in February, authorizing the Treasury and the president to adjust and settle his accounts and claims. The bill also repealed the rider to an earlier law that had cut off his salary. In late November 1823, Monroe informed Congress that the Treasury had certified that Tompkins was owed $35,190. Before year's end, both houses adopted a bill appropriating that sum. In the House one of the bill's sponsors was Henry Clay, a candidate for the presidential nomination in 1824, who well understood Tompkins's "controuling influence" in New York. Earlier in the year Clay wrote a New York correspondent that he "cherished the greatest respect" for Tompkins. Secretary of War John C. Calhoun of South Carolina, another presidential candidate, also considered Tompkins's backing critical; in October 1823 he told a New York supporter that it was necessary Tompkins should "heartily acquiesce" in Calhoun's choice of a New York vice-presidential candidate. Calhoun hoped that Tompkins would not depart from "the 8 year rule" and seek a third term. Calhoun need not have worried because, according to New Hampshire congressman William Plumer, Jr., no one wanted Tompkins, "much fallen both in fortune & in fame," to serve again.

On January 21, 1824, Tompkins began to preside over the Senate for the last time, remaining in the chair until May 20, his longest continuous service. John Quincy Adams visited Tompkins on January 25 and recorded in his diary that the vice president

> told me that he had recovered his health, with the exception of sleepless nights, and that he was relieved from all his embarrassments; that he had no intention of being a candidate for election to the Presidency or for re-election as Vice-President. All he wanted was justice . . . quiet and retirement.

In April, Monroe recommended that Tompkins be awarded more money on his accounts, and in May the two houses approved an appropriation of $60,239, bringing the amount due Tompkins to over $95,000. During these same months, Tompkins cast his fourth and fifth votes. On April 22, he approved a motion to adjourn rather than to consider further a bill for surveying roads and canals.

On May 17, he accepted a Senate amendment to a tariff bill that provided for a 25 percent ad valorem duty on woolen manufactures.

On May 20, 1824, the last day Tompkins presided, his public career ended. He retired to Tompkinsville and took no part in the presidential election of 1824. Before long, he began to drink heavily again, and he died on June 11, 1825, still in debt. With much ceremony, "The Farmer's Boy" was buried in his wife's family vault in lower Manhattan's fashionable St. Mark's-in-the-Bowery.

REFERENCES

Ray W. Irwin, *Daniel D. Tompkins: Governor of New York and Vice President of the United States* (New York: New-York Historical Society, 1968); Ray W. Irwin and Edna L. Jacobsen, eds., *A Columbia College Student in the Eighteenth Century: Essays by Daniel D. Tompkins, Class of 1795 . . .* (New York: Columbia University Press, 1940); Jabez Hammond, *A*

History of Political Parties in the State of New-York . . . , 4th ed., 3 vols. (Syracuse, N.Y.: Hall, Mills, and Company, 1852); John Niven, *Martin Van Buren: The Romantic Age of American Politics* (New York: Oxford University Press, 1983); Alvin Kass, *Politics in New York State, 1800–1830* (Syracuse, N.Y.: Syracuse University Press, 1965); Jerome Mushkat, *Tammany: The Evolution of a Political Machine, 1789–1865* (Syracuse, N.Y.: Syracuse University Press, 1971); and J.C.A. Stagg, *Mr. Madison's War: Politics, Diplomacy, Warfare in the Early Republic, 1783–1830* (Princeton, N.J.: Princeton University Press, 1983).

———————

GASPARE J. SALADINO is coeditor of *The Documentary History of the Ratification of the Constitution* (twelve volumes to date) at the University of Wisconsin-Madison. He earned his B.A. at Brooklyn College and his M.A. and Ph.D. degrees at the University of Wisconsin-Madison. He has taught at the State University of New York at Albany and has been a fellow at the Adams Papers at the Massachusetts Historical Society. His publications include several articles on the ratification of the Constitution in New York and Delaware, the evolution of liberties in Delaware, and the historiography of the Bill of Rights and the era of the founding of the republic.

JOHN CALDWELL CALHOUN (1782–1850)

Vice President, 1825–1832

(Presidents John Quincy Adams and Andrew Jackson)

JOHN CALDWELL CALHOUN
(Library of Congress)

By Mark G. Malvasi

The 1820s and 1830s marked a transition in American political history from the patrician republic of the eighteenth century to the spirited, disorderly, turbulent, and volatile democratic republic of the nineteenth. With the election of 1800, the so-called First American Party System, composed of Federalists and Democratic-Republicans, began to disintegrate. By 1820, the Federalist Party of Alexander Hamilton and John Adams had all but withered away and presented no opposition at the national level to the Democratic-Republican Party of Thomas Jefferson and James Madison.

Yet, having eliminated the Federalists as a force in national politics, the Democratic-Republican Party itself began to dissolve into factions. No opponent contested James Monroe's reelection in the perfunctory campaign of 1820. But four years later, in 1824, no fewer than five candidates sought the presidency: William H. Crawford of Georgia, John Quincy Adams of Massachusetts, Henry Clay of Kentucky, and Andrew Jackson of Tennessee.

The fifth candidate for president in 1824 was John Caldwell Calhoun of South Carolina. Calhoun was born at Long Canes settlement, near

Abbeville, South Carolina, on March 18, 1782. His father, Patrick Calhoun, rose to prominence as a planter, slaveholder, and Indian fighter, and later represented the Abbeville district in the state legislature. Although he died in 1795 when John was but a boy of thirteen, Patrick Calhoun exercised a remarkable influence on the formation of his son's temperament and world view.

A stern Scotch-Irish Presbyterian, Patrick Calhoun taught his son that life was a perpetual struggle against evil. To do God's will on earth required discipline, strength, perseverance, and courage. He also instilled in young John an abiding love of liberty and an unqualified hatred of tyranny. For Patrick Calhoun, the obligations to God, family, neighborhood, and country defined the parameters of private and public life. Calhoun fully absorbed his father's convictions.

Although only forty-two years old in 1824, Calhoun had already enjoyed a distinguished political career. He entered public life with his election to the South Carolina House of Representatives in 1808. He then served as a member of the United States House of Representatives from 1811 until 1817. There Calhoun became one of the leaders of the "War Hawks," who supported James Madison in his fight to defend the republic against British commercial restrictions and political insults.

The War of 1812 was unpopular among the maritime and mercantile interests of the Northeast and proved a near catastrophe for the United States. But by the time it ended in 1815, Calhoun, "the young Hercules who carried the war on his shoulders," had emerged as one of the dominant figures in the Democratic-Republican Party and in Congress.

The American experiment in republican government faltered badly during the years 1812 to 1815. After the war, Calhoun advanced a strategy of national development to revitalize it. He proposed that the federal government, operating within the strict limits imposed on it by the Constitution, moderately expand the army and the navy, restore the national bank, and undertake a vigorous program of internal improvements. By these means, Calhoun hoped to rectify the glaring inadequacies he saw in the organization of the

military; the condition of U.S. roads, bridges, and waterways; and the financial structure of the nation. Most important, he sought to strengthen and preserve the Union.

These activities earned Calhoun a reputation as a nationalist. This view has remained powerful enough among historians to make it conventional practice to divide Calhoun's career broadly into "nationalist" and "sectionalist" phases that seem to contradict one another, but Calhoun's principles changed little, if at all, over the course of his long career. If sentiment made Calhoun a nationalist, circumstances soon made him a sectionalist.

Against the advice of political friends and colleagues who believed that he was damaging his future prospects, Calhoun resigned his seat in the House of Representatives to become the secretary of war, a post he occupied from 1817 until 1825, throughout the eight years of Monroe's presidency. During Calhoun's tenure, the War Department was the largest and most diverse federal agency. The secretary of war not only supervised the military, but administered Indian affairs as well. Calhoun was an efficient and scrupulous executive, eliminating bureaucratic confusion in the War Department and fashioning a system of management that won him acclaim at home and abroad.

Confident of his abilities and his principles, Calhoun entered the race to succeed Monroe, but when it became apparent that he did not have extensive support in the North and that he had to compete with Crawford and Jackson in the South, Calhoun withdrew and agreed to accept the vice presidency.

As it happened, no candidate in the presidential election of 1824 won the required majority of electoral votes. Of the 261 electoral votes cast, Jackson won 99, Adams 84, Crawford 41, and Clay 37. Jackson prevailed in a contest with Adams for the popular vote, accumulating 153,544 votes to 108,740 for Adams. By this reckoning, Andrew Jackson should have become president, but because no candidate had garnered a numerical majority of electoral votes, the House of Representatives, with one vote for each delegation, had to choose the president from among the three leading candidates: Jackson, Adams, and Crawford.

Thus eliminated, Clay could broker a deal that would bring victory to one candidate in return for certain considerations. After long deliberation, Clay awarded his support to Adams. His decision was logical because both he and Adams favored a similar domestic policy, including a vigorous federal program to promote internal improvements and economic growth.

On February 9, 1825, Adams, who had carried just seven states in the election, received thirteen of the twenty-four votes cast in the House and won the presidency by a bare electoral majority. To Jackson and his supporters, the outcome reflected not only the extent of Clay's sinister influence on American politics but an audacious veto of the popular will. When Adams imprudently appointed Clay as his secretary of state, the Jacksonians clamored that their man had been robbed of the presidency by a "corrupt bargain."

There is no hard evidence to confirm that Adams entered into any sort of formal arrangement with Clay. The charge, nevertheless, gained credence among many voters who, as a consequence, expressed their sympathy for Jackson and their suspicion of Adams. Calhoun, meanwhile, had easily been elected vice president. The editor of Calhoun's papers, Clyde N. Wilson, has maintained that ". . . Calhoun was Vice-President because of his importance, not important because he was Vice-President." Indeed, Calhoun received more electoral votes than any of the presidential candidates. He was an independent agent who rose to the vice presidency of his own accord, not as the representative of a political party or the ally of a presidential nominee.

Owing nothing personally or politically to Adams, Calhoun thus felt no obligation to embrace his policies. Even before he took office on March 4, 1825, Calhoun began to disengage himself from the administration and to associate more intimately with the Jacksonian opposition. Nearly a month before the inauguration, President-elect Adams already sensed what he erroneously characterized as Calhoun's betrayal. Writing in his diary on February 11, 1825, Adams

noted that Calhoun's sinister purpose was ". . . to bring in General Jackson as the next President. . . . To this end, the Administration must be rendered unpopular and odious; whatever its acts and measures may be. . . ."

During the first year of Adams's term, a lively debate about the nature and extent of the powers and duties of the vice president as the presiding officer of the Senate illustrated the growing estrangement between Calhoun and Adams. Under the leadership of John Randolph of Virginia, Adams's opponents in the Senate tried to embarrass him and to undermine his ability to govern. For hours at a time, Randolph lectured his fellow senators on the subtleties of the Constitution and denounced Adams and Clay for the chicanery they had perpetrated in the recent election. Calhoun refused to call Randolph to order. Adams's supporters accused Calhoun, by his willful inaction, of harming the government.

In a speech that he delivered on April 15, 1826, Calhoun defended himself against these charges, arguing that under the rules of the Senate, "the right to call to order, on questions touching the latitude or freedom of debate" belonged to the senators themselves and not to the presiding officer. A few weeks later, on May 1, a correspondent to the *Washington National Journal*, an administration newspaper, writing under the name "Patrick Henry," assailed Calhoun's judgment and demeanor. He characterized Calhoun's conduct as unseemly, insulting, and malicious.

On May 20, Calhoun replied using the pseudonym "Onslow," after a celebrated Speaker of the British House of Commons. He thereby inaugurated an exchange that continued for six months and revealed not merely a disagreement about an arcane question of parliamentary order, but also a conflict about the fundamental principles of republican government and the very nature of political power.

Contemporaries and scholars have long disputed the identity of Calhoun's antagonist. Duff Green, a political associate of Calhoun and the editor of the Jacksonian *United States' Telegraph*, believed that the author of the "Patrick Henry" letters was none other than President Adams himself. In his biography of Calhoun, Charles M. Wiltse arrived at the same conclusion, but Calhoun's most recent biographer, Irving H. Bartlett, revived an older argument, dating from at least 1888, that identifies "Patrick Henry" as Philip Ricard Fendall, a clerk in the State Department who sought to vindicate Adams.

Clyde N. Wilson, the editor of *The Papers of John C. Calhoun*, has also been reluctant to ascribe the "Patrick Henry" letters definitively to Adams's pen, asserting the impossibility of establishing the author's identity with confidence. Nevertheless, he deduced that, like Adams, "Patrick Henry" was learned, sympathetic to the Federalist heritage of New England, and "personally involved in the issues" under review. The letters, according to Wilson, represent Adams's opinions and beliefs, whether he composed them himself, supervised their composition, or had no involvement with them at all.

Apart from partisan bickering and personal recrimination, the debate between "Patrick Henry" and "Onslow" offered a sophisticated exposition of two conflicting definitions of power in a republic. For "Patrick Henry," Calhoun had erred by not exercising the full prerogatives of his office. It was a dereliction of duty, "Patrick Henry" charged, for the vice president to refuse to control the proceedings of the Senate, to discipline unruly members, to silence critics of the administration, and to organize committees friendly to the president. The principal at stake, beyond the immediate occasion of the dispute, was the conviction that government officials not only had the authority but the obligation to use the powers inherent in their office.

Calhoun demurred. He embraced the Jeffersonian suspicion of power and feared political consolidation and governmental initiative. If "Patrick Henry" urged the fullest discharge of the powers of office, Calhoun alternately warned that their application in all cases must be undertaken with prudence and caution. In his view, political power flowed from the sovereignty of the people, and legitimate authority rested on the consent of the governed. Except in extraordinary circumstances, virtuous representatives of the people would thus not evade or ignore the customary limitations imposed on their actions. They would instead hesitate to use even the powers vested in their office and would never assume additional powers that remained equivocal or dubious.

The exchange between "Patrick Henry" and "Onslow" represented another chapter in the continuing debate that had originated in the 1790s about the tenets of republican government. Calhoun remained convinced that, like the Founding Fathers, he defended the cherished liberty of the people against the encroaching power of the state—an enterprise that guided and sustained his political career from beginning to end.

On June 4, 1826, Calhoun wrote to Andrew Jackson that

an issue has been fairly made . . . between *power* and *liberty;* and it must be determined in the next three years, whether the real governing principle in our political system be the power and patronage of the Executive, or the voice of the people. For it can scarcely be doubted, that . . . those now in power act on a scheme resting on the supposition, that such is the force of Executive influence, that they, who wield it, can mould [sic] the publick [sic] voice at pleasure by an artful management of the patronage of office.

In this estimation, events proved Calhoun incorrect. Whatever patronage Adams may have disbursed, it was not enough to save his presidency, which was doomed to frustration and failure from the outset. By 1825, an opposition party was rapidly coalescing around the figure of his arch rival, Andrew Jackson, whose supporters openly defied the administration and bided their time, awaiting the election of 1828. In the process, they began to assemble one of the most enduring popular organizations in modern U.S. political history: the Democratic Party.

Policies and issues were not very important in the bitter campaign of 1828. The race was largely a personal contest between Adams and Jackson. When the returns came in, Jackson, who portrayed himself as a "man of the people," had won by a comfortable margin. The electoral vote was 178 for Jackson to 83 for Adams, and the popular vote was approximately 647,276 to 508,064. Adams carried New England and had some support in Illinois, New York, New Jersey, Delaware, and Maryland. The rest of the country belonged to Jackson. With his rise to power, the age of democracy was born.

Principle more than expedience inspired Calhoun to attach himself to Jackson. He believed, naively as it turned out, that Jackson would prove a better friend of liberty than Adams. Adams's election by the House of Representatives in 1824 seemed to Calhoun a terrible affront to the integrity of republican institutions and a callous disregard for the will of the people. He feared above all the substitution of rule by political parties for government according to constitutional regulation. Apprehensive about the manifest indifference to the Constitution and the growing consolidation of political power, Calhoun, quite sensibly from his perspective, rallied to Andrew Jackson.

Once again, Calhoun's nomination and re-election to the vice presidency were virtually uncontested. He brought a distinguished record of statesmanship and public service to the Democratic ticket, for even in 1828 Jackson's fame rested on his military exploits, not on his political accomplishments. Calhoun knew that to satisfy his political ambitions he needed Jackson, but Jackson, if only for the moment, also needed Calhoun.

The Jacksonian coalition was composed of diverse elements that had no common purpose except the attainment of political victory. Only after coming to power did this coalition acquire a program, an ideology, and an identity. Throughout the eight years of Jackson's tenure, however, the Democratic Party remained largely his personal organization. He seldom forgot a friend or forgave an enemy. The compass and nature of personal dominion was especially apparent in his choice of advisors. He pieced together his cabinet from among old friends, political cronies, and men to whom he owed favors. With a few notable exceptions they were impotent and weak, and Jackson knew it.

Except for Secretary of State Martin Van Buren, Jackson relied not on his cabinet but on an influential though informal coterie of politicians and journalists known as the Kitchen Cabinet. One member of the official cabinet who, besides Van Buren, stood close to Jackson's inner circle was Secretary of War John H. Eaton. Eaton was at the center of a scandal that aroused Jackson's intense loyalty and intense scorn, divided his cabinet, and at last destroyed his cordial relations with Calhoun.

Peggy O'Neill Timberlake was the daughter of an Irish innkeeper in Washington. Her first husband had allegedly committed suicide, evidently distraught over his wife's love affair with John Eaton, then a senator from Tennessee. Eaton's marriage to her, which took place at Jackson's insistence on January 1, 1829, scarcely made an honest woman of Peggy in the eyes of the proper ladies of Washington society. Floride Calhoun, the wife of the vice president, was particularly adamant, publicly snubbing Mrs. Eaton. The wives of most of the other cabinet members followed suit.

But Jackson sympathized with the Eatons, for their plight reminded him of the accusations of adultery and bigamy that had tormented his beloved wife Rachel, who had died shortly before the inauguration. Jackson pronounced Peggy as "chaste as a virgin." Among the members of Jackson's cabinet, only Van Buren, a widower, was free to lavish on Peggy the attention that Jackson thought she merited. Van Buren's graciousness endeared him to Jackson, who now took him ever more fully into his confidence.

Van Buren had quickly surmised that Jackson, as a matter of honor, would never abandon Peggy Eaton. Initially, Jackson believed that the "Eaton Affair" was the work of Henry Clay, but when the wives of his cabinet members disclaimed any knowledge of Clay, Jackson began the search for other villains. Eventually, following a bizarre exchange of accusations, Jackson settled on the vice president and his wife as the principal culprits.

Floride Calhoun was the most outspoken critic of Mrs. Eaton, but Calhoun himself neither instigated nor participated in any plot to embarrass her or to discredit Jackson. Nevertheless, Jackson was outraged with Calhoun, who suffered most from what Van Buren dubbed "the Eaton Malaria." Calhoun had already aroused Jackson's ire, and from Jackson's point of view, the "Eaton Affair" presented yet another reason to distrust him.

On May 13, 1830, in the midst of the controversy over Peggy Eaton, Jackson challenged Calhoun to explain whether, while secretary of war, he had favored an investigation of Jackson's attack on the Spanish government of Florida in 1818 and Jackson's subsequent execution of two British subjects. Calhoun, like President Monroe, believed that on the occasion in question Jackson had exceeded his orders and his authority. Only John Quincy Adams, who was secretary of state at the time and who sought to annex Florida, exonerated Jackson.

Rumors had circulated for years that Calhoun had opposed Jackson, but because the political fortunes of the two men seemed for a time to be intimately intertwined, Jackson chose to ignore them. The dispute resumed when a letter that William H. Crawford had written to Major William Lewis, an old friend of Jackson and a member of the Kitchen Cabinet, came to Jackson's attention. In this letter, Crawford, a fierce political rival of Calhoun, maintained that Calhoun was duplicitous. In cabinet he had been adamant not only to probe Jackson's conduct but to punish him. In public, however, Calhoun had long taken credit for defending Jackson and had implied that Crawford was Jackson's main adversary.

At Crawford's revelations, Jackson's anger exploded. He convinced himself that Calhoun was intent on destroying his administration and positioning himself to win the presidency in 1832. He demanded an explanation and an apology. Calhoun declared that his conduct was above reproach and, in turn, defied Jackson to do the "impossible" and prove that he had not disobeyed orders during the Florida campaign.

Behind the scheme to implicate and discredit Calhoun lay Martin Van Buren. Van Buren had first suggested to Jackson the possibility that Calhoun and his wife were responsible for the insults leveled against Peggy Eaton. He had also encouraged Major Lewis to solicit the letter from Crawford that identified Calhoun as the most stubborn and ruthless critic of Jackson in Monroe's cabinet. Van Buren, of course, intended to provoke a confrontation between the president and the vice president that would prompt Jackson to dismiss Calhoun and exalt Van Buren. "Van Buren glides along as smoothly as oil and as silently as a cat," wrote Amos Kendall, one of Jackson's closest advisers. "He has the entire confidence of the President and all his personal friends while Calhoun is fast losing it."

Van Buren had little difficulty in persuading Jackson that Calhoun had masterminded a conspiracy to disgrace his presidency. Jackson's administration, and, indeed, the emerging Democratic Party, thus became divided between the partisans of Van Buren and of Calhoun. Much of United States political history during the early 1830s turned on the growing rivalry between these two men as each jockeyed for position as Jackson's successor.

In this contest, Van Buren had most of the advantages, foremost among which was his skill at political manipulation and maneuvering. Calhoun bested him in acuity of intellect but operated from an increasingly obsolete set of assumptions about the character of American politics. Never at ease with mass politics, Calhoun found it impossible, as his most recent biographer, Irving Bartlett, concluded, "to speak to the democratic spirit of the age." No such inhibitions troubled Van Buren. By the end of 1832, Jackson had designated Van Buren as his heir apparent.

But it was not political ambition alone that motivated Van Buren. It was also the deepening antagonism between the North and the South. Van Buren represented the progressive, commercial, democratic, and capitalist interests of the North. Calhoun stood for the more traditional, agrarian, republican, and slaveholding South. Once more, the very meaning and prospects of the United States were in dispute.

As his political isolation deepened and as his apprehension about the future of the republic escalated, Calhoun became more completely the spokesman for southern interests and states' rights. The final drama of his vice presidency, and one of the most critical episodes of his political career, began to unfold in 1828 with the passage of another tariff that once again, as in 1824, raised duties on imports.

In 1816, Calhoun, then a member of the House of Representatives, had voted in favor of a tariff as a temporary measure to protect domestic industry from foreign competition, even though it artificially raised the price of manufactured products for southerners. In the spirit of compromise and reconciliation, Calhoun had argued that justice demanded concessions be made to the manufacturing and commercial communities of the Northeast that had suffered under the burdens of a trade embargo in the years before the War of 1812. But, by 1828, Calhoun feared that the tariff had become a permanent means for the government to subsidize industrialists indirectly at the expense of farmers and consumers. This development he found intolerable.

While still vice president, Calhoun anonymously drafted a pamphlet entitled the "South Carolina Exposition and Protest," in which he argued that the tariff was unconstitutional and pernicious. Legally, Congress could impose a tariff to raise revenue but not to promote one interest, in this case domestic manufacturing, at the expense of any other. The Tariff of 1828, the so-called Tariff of Abominations, was, therefore, "unconstitutional, unequal, and oppressive." Such legislation, Calhoun warned, would divide citizens into two antagonistic classes with interests as distinct and hostile as those of two separate nations. The tariff made southerners "the serfs of the system—out of whose labor is raised, not only the money paid into the Treasury, but funds out of which are drawn the rich rewards of the manufacturer and his associates in interest." The results of such policies were wholly predictable: the appearance of political envy, the development of class conflict, and the end of national unity.

In the "Exposition and Protest," Calhoun did not merely identify the problem but also proposed a remedy. He preferred to call his doctrine interposition, although it became more commonly known as nullification. Before the adoption of the Constitution, Calhoun explained, the states were independent and sovereign. They had created the federal government and had endowed it with strictly limited powers. The federal government possessed only the authority that the sovereign states had consented to surrender. A state, therefore, had the right to "interpose" its original sovereignty against the "despotism of the many." The citizens of a state could summon a state convention and nullify any act of Congress that exceeded the authority granted the federal government under the Constitution.

Calhoun believed that when conventional politics failed to redress the grievances of a minority, some relief had to be found. The doctrine of interposition provided it. In propounding this theory, Calhoun argued that the ability to check federal power was essential to preserving constitutional government. On October 30, 1830, he had written to his friend Samuel D. Ingham of Pennsylvania that: "To protect the subject against the Government is in fact the only object & value of the Constitution. The government needs no constitution. It is the governed, that needs its protection."

In Calhoun's view, the purpose of a constitution was to restrain government, as it was the purpose of the law to restrain individuals. He assessed the merit of any constitution according to the degree to which it incorporated this principle of restraint. The ultimate recourse, he maintained, was the state veto of a federal law. That action, Calhoun thought, was much less dangerous than the power of an unrestrained federal government. Nor could the states, in his estimation, rely on the Supreme Court to protect them or to resolve constitutional conflicts. For "it is not possible to distinguish, practically, between a government having all power," he wrote, "and one having the right to take what power it pleases."

The doctrine of interposition, as Calhoun proposed it, offered a peaceful remedy to constitutional disputes that superseded the resort to coercion, violence, revolution, and bloodshed on the one hand and despotic government on the other. Interposition was one more qualification on majority rule and one more defense of the ideal that government rested on the consent of the governed, which, Calhoun affirmed, had been the founding principle of the American republic.

After Congress not only failed to enact significant tariff reform but passed a new tariff bill in 1832 that contained no significant reduction in rates, events in South Carolina moved quickly. On November 24, 1832, a special convention met in the state capital, Columbia, and enacted an Ordinance of Nullification that declared the Tariffs of 1828 and 1832 unconstitutional and, therefore, null and void in South Carolina. The federal collection of duties was forbidden after February 1, 1833, unless Congress lowered the tariff rate to 12 percent. Any attempt on the part of federal authorities to coerce the state into obedience would be "inconsistent with the longer continuance of South Carolina in the Union."

At the same time, Calhoun resigned the vice presidency to accept a seat in the Senate, to which the South Carolina legislature elected him on December 12, 1832. Amid rumors of his imminent arrest, he hastened to Washington not only to defend the interests of his state but also to moderate public opinion and, if possible, to defuse the crisis. By the time Calhoun arrived, Jackson had already declared the actions of South Carolina to be treasonous. Jackson's "Nullification Proclamation" of December 10, 1832, repudiated nullification as "endangering the integrity of the Union." The power to nullify a law of Congress was, Jackson declared, "incompatible with the existence of the Union, contradicted expressly by the letter of the Constitution, unauthorized by its spirit, inconsistent with every principle on which it was founded and destructive of the great object for which it was formed."

Although he admonished the South Carolina nullifiers, Jackson also urged Congress to lower the tariff and to limit protection to articles essential to national defense. However, he did secure passage of the "Force Bill" early in 1833, which authorized the collection of import duties in cash from all ships entering American harbors and the use of the state militia and the federal armed services to enforce the ordinance.

Infuriated by the arrogance of the Force Bill, many South Carolinians were eager for secession, but Calhoun opposed what he called that "most fatal of steps." Writing to leading advocates of nullification in late January 1833, Calhoun urged

that "we must not think of secession but in the last extremity. . . . A year would make an immense difference in our fortunes. . . . I feel confident, we want only time to ensure victory." Some nullifiers thought that Calhoun had surrendered. They believed that the choice of nullification rather than submission implied secession in the event of failure. Having taken their state to the brink of secession, and perhaps of civil war, they were not prepared to give up the fight.

To Calhoun, suspension of the Ordinance of Nullification represented a strategic retreat designed to prevent secession and civil war, rather than an abandonment of the principle of interposition itself. He always considered nullification as a way to protect the South and to preserve the Union. To leave the Union because nullification had failed—and perhaps only for the moment—was to sacrifice the reason for having waged the struggle in the first place: the assertion of the right of a state to protect itself against the unlawful encroachment of the federal government.

Calhoun was one of the most ardent and determined southern sectionalists, but throughout his career, his love of the Union almost balanced his fear for the South. He proposed the doctrine of nullification because he wished to save his nation and his section and because he understood the dangers that threatened to destroy both.

In this instance, Calhoun's wisdom, prudence, and moderation prevailed. As the "fatal first" of February approached, he delayed the enforcement of the Ordinance of Nullification at least until Congress had completed its deliberations. In early February, Calhoun agreed to cooperate with Henry Clay on a compromise tariff. On February 13, 1833, Clay introduced his tariff bill into the Senate, and Calhoun spoke in favor of it. On February 26, Clay's measure passed the House of Representatives, and on March 1 the Senate concurred.

Although the new rates were considerably higher than those demanded in the Ordinance of Nullification, South Carolinians welcomed the compromise tariff with a mixture of relief and disappointment. When the South Carolina legislature reconvened on March 11, 1833, it repealed the ordinance and accepted the compromise tariff. In a symbolic gesture of defiance, the legislature nullified the Force Bill, thus demonstrating that nullification remained a legal and viable option.

In a speech delivered against the Force Bill on February 15 and 16, 1833, Calhoun was careful to distinguish between a majority of consenting citizens and a powerful coalition of interests backed by force. He concluded that "the government of the absolute majority, instead of the government of the people, is but the government of the strongest interests, and when not efficiently checked, is the most tyrannical and oppressive that can be devised." South Carolinians, he maintained, had merely invoked the reserved powers of a state to effect a temporary suspension of a law widely agreed to be unconstitutional and to prevent so unprecedented an assertion of federal power as the Force Bill.

He continued, asking his colleagues in the Senate: "Does any man in his senses believe, that this beautiful structure—this harmonious aggregate of states, produced by the joint consent of all can be preserved by force?" He answered his own question, saying that the mere introduction of force ". . . will be certain destruction to this Federal Union. . . . Force may, indeed, hold the parts together, but such a union would be the bond between master and slave: a union of exaction on one side, and of unqualified *obedience* on the other." Calhoun argued that the Force Bill defied the principles of republican government. It implied despotism instead of consent. The Force Bill, as he understood it, imposed unquestioning obedience at the expense of enlightened self-government.

Nullification never became the kind of constitutional remedy that Calhoun hoped it would be. It was a theoretical, but not yet a very practical, alternative to the consolidation of federal power that he recognized was embodied in legislation like the Force Bill. Calhoun nevertheless always regarded the episode as the finest moment of his political career. Sacrificing ambition, status, and his immediate prospects for presidency, he had cast his lot with a small but gallant state that unflinchingly defended the cause of republican self-government. Their actions had proved, he later wrote, that nullification was a principled,

conservative, peaceful, constitutional, and efficient means to preserve the legitimate rights of a free people.

After 1832, save for a brief period from 1843 to 1845, Calhoun remained in the Senate. There, for the most part, he operated independently of either the Democratic or the Whig parties that constituted the "Second American Party System." He condemned the Democrats as unscrupulous and unprincipled but at the same time denounced the Whigs as self-seeking and shortsighted. Having regained some of the national esteem that he had lost as a result of his defense of nullification, Calhoun launched his last serious effort to attain the presidency in March 1843, but in February 1844 he withdrew his name from consideration.

In March 1844, President John Tyler appointed Calhoun secretary of state to succeed Abel P. Upshur, who had been killed on February 28 when a gun exploded aboard the USS *Princeton* during an inspection tour. Although his tenure at the State Department was brief, Calhoun initiated negotiations that led to the acquisition of the Oregon Territory from the British. He also fashioned a treaty for the annexation of Texas, but the Senate did not ratify it.

In 1845, when James K. Polk failed to reappoint him to his post in the State Department, Calhoun returned to the Senate and retained his seat until his death on March 31, 1850, becoming an outspoken and eloquent critic of the war with Mexico that began in 1846. Drawing on his long experience in public life and relying on the principles that had sustained him in many partisan battles, Calhoun asserted that Polk had illegally brought the United States into war, for he had not first received the consent of the Senate to sanction his course of action. He detected in Polk's declaration of war the same sort of executive usurpation of power that he had combated in Adams and Jackson. Calhoun lamented that "Mexico is to us forbidden fruit; the penalty of eating it [is] to subject our institutions to political death."

Calhoun devoted the last years of his life to encouraging southern unity against the mounting northern hostility to slavery. He believed that a unified South could operate as a restraint on federal power and thus hold at bay the forces of national dissolution. Although disappointed in this quest, Calhoun explored its ramifications in his most systematic and theoretical work on politics, *A Disquisition on Government.*

Elaborating on ideas that he had articulated in the "Onslow Letters," the "South Carolina Exposition and Protest," many of his major speeches, and his public and private correspondence, especially the "Fort Hill Address" of 1831, Calhoun formulated the theory of the concurrent majority. According to this concept, the majority was prevented from undertaking certain actions or implementing certain policies without the willing agreement of the minority. To Calhoun, the concurrent majority did not represent an impediment to the operation of majority rule or weaken the power of the general government; instead, he regarded it as the logical fulfillment of the democratic ideal of government by consent, in which the vital interests of a minority group or section remained inviolate.

Most of Calhoun's political aspirations ended in frustration. He never attained the presidency, which he ardently desired, but he was no political opportunist. He repeatedly declined to advance his career at the expense of the country and thus sacrificed ambition in defense of all that he cherished.

Events also ruined Calhoun's hopes for the future of the republic. During his lifetime, he never effected southern unity. When national division at last came a decade after his death, his doctrine of state interposition could not prevent secession and civil war, which rent asunder the Union that he loved and desired above all else to save.

Yet, his private disappointments and public defeats notwithstanding, Calhoun identified the enduring dilemma of American politics: the tension between centralized power and republican self-government, between unbounded majority rule and ordered political liberty. Interpretations of Calhoun's character and accomplishments have ranged from enmity to misunderstanding to admiration, but in the end, Calhoun can neither be evaded nor ignored. Indeed, Vernon L. Parrington long ago recognized as much when he wrote in *Main Currents in American Thought:* "Whatever road one travels one comes at last upon the austere figure of Calhoun, commanding every highway of the southern mind." However scholars may judge him, American political history offers few examples of statesmen whose legacy has continued to generate such vital interest or to excite such passionate controversy as that of John C. Calhoun.

REFERENCES

Irving H. Bartlett, *John C. Calhoun: A Biography* (New York: W.W. Norton & Company, 1993); John C. Calhoun, *A Disquisition on Government* (Indianapolis, Ind.: Bobbs-Merrill, 1953); *John C. Calhoun*, Margaret Coit, ed. (Englewood Cliffs, N.J.: Prentice-Hall, 1970); *John C. Calhoun: A Profile*, John L. Thomas, ed. (New York: Hill & Wang, 1968); Margaret L. Coit, *John C. Calhoun: American Portrait* (Boston: Houghton Mifflin, 1950); *Correspondence of John C. Calhoun*, J. Franklin Jameson, ed., *American Historical Association Annual Report for 1899* (Washington, D.C.: Government Printing Office, 1900); Richard N. Current, *John C. Calhoun* (New York: Washington Square Press, 1963); Richard Hofstader, "John C. Calhoun: The Marx of the Master Class," *The American Political Tradition and the Men Who Made It* (New York: Alfred A. Knopf, 1948); John S. Jenkins, *The Life of John C. Calhoun* (Auburn, N.Y.: James M. Alden, 1850); Ralph Lerner, "Calhoun's New Science of Politics," *American Political Science Review*, 57 (December 1963), 918–932; William M. Meigs, *The Life of John C. Calhoun* (New York: Neale, 1917); John Niven, *John C. Calhoun and the Price of Union* (Baton Rouge: Louisiana State University Press, 1988); Vernon L. Parrington, *Main Currents in American Thought* (New York: Harcourt, Brace and Company, 1927), 2: 69–82; Merrill D. Peterson, *The Great Triumvirate: Webster, Clay, and Calhoun* (New York: Oxford University Press, 1987); August O. Spain, *The Political Theory of John C. Calhoun* (New York: Octagon Books, 1951); Arthur Styron, *The Cast-Iron Man: John C. Calhoun and American Democracy* (New York: Longmans, Green, 1935); *The Essential Calhoun: Selections from Writings, Speeches, and Letters*, Clyde N. Wilson, ed. (New Brunswick, N.J.: Transaction Publishers 1992); *The Papers of John C. Calhoun*, Robert L. Meriwether, W. Edwin Hemphill, and Clyde N. Wilson, eds., 22 vols. to date (Columbia: University of South Carolina Press, 1959–); *The Works of John C. Calhoun*, Richard K. Cralle, ed., 6 vols. (Columbia, S.C.: A.S. Johnston, 1851; New York: A. Appleton, 1853, 1857); Charles M. Wiltse, *John C. Calhoun*, 3 vols., *Nationalist, 1782–1828; Nullifier, 1829–1839; Sectionalist, 1840–1850* (Indianapolis, Ind.: Bobbs-Merrill, 1944–1951).

MARK G. MALVASI received his B.A. from Hiram College in 1980, his M.A. in history from the University of Chicago in 1981, and his Ph.D. from the University of Rochester in 1991. He has taught history at the University of Rochester, the University of Puget Sound, and the University of Alabama. He joined the faculty of Randolph-Macon College in Ashland, Virginia, in 1992. He has written for such journals as Chronicles: *A Magazine of American Culture; Crisis: A Journal of Catholic Lay Opinion; Southern Partisan;* and *The Journal of the Early Republic.* His manuscript, *The Unregenerate South: The Agrarian Thought of John Crowe Ransom, Allent Tate, and Donald Davidson,* was published by Louisiana State University Press in 1997.

Martin Van Buren (1782–1862)

Vice President, 1833–1837

(Second Term of President Andrew Jackson)

MARTIN VAN BUREN
(Library of Congress)

By Charles H. Schoenleber

Martin Van Buren is often viewed as a political manipulator or intriguer, as "The Little Magician" or "The Red Fox of Kinderhook." Such stereotyping, however, does severe injustice to Van Buren's political skill. He was an excellent judge of people and was a political innovator throughout his career. He carefully brought together an able group of New Yorkers to form the Albany Regency that dominated state politics for more than two decades. Van Buren plotted strategy, expertly timed political moves, and adroitly employed patronage. He was in large part responsible for reinvigorating the Vir-

ginia–New York coalition that put Andrew Jackson into the White House in 1828. He provided Jackson with cogent political advice and then served one term as president.

Politics to Van Buren was much more than just organization and campaigning. He believed that an active and competitive two-party system was essential to the nation's future. He saw the United States perpetually divided between the competing interest groups that originally backed Thomas Jefferson and Alexander Hamilton. The sharp contest over these differing political visions had to be maintained. Hence the two parties had to maintain their distinctiveness and ideological purity. Party loyalty and regularity were very important for Van Buren.

Van Buren himself was always a Jeffersonian Republican. He advocated states' rights and a limited federal government, but he also firmly believed in a strong Union. He supported the interests of the farmers and workers but was no agrarian or urban radical. Government had to encourage business, commerce, and manufacturing because they were essential to national economic growth, but all Americans—all regions of the country—must share in this increased prosperity.

Van Buren's lack of formal education gave him a feeling of inadequacy. To compensate, he always worked harder and was better prepared than his opponents. He was a stylish dresser, in part to show his importance. Van Buren did not let politics lead to personal hatreds. Differences were based on principle and issues and did not preclude civil social relations with his opponents.

From the mid-1820s onward, Van Buren had his eyes on the presidency. He swung his political forces into the Jacksonian camp, served as Jackson's secretary of state, and isolated his rival, John C. Calhoun. Being eighth vice president was the last step before the presidency. When Jackson selected him for the job, the Old Hero anointed his heir—a first for the vice presidency in American politics. Van Buren's role as one of Jackson's key political advisers and second in command in the Democratic Party was another first for that office. In what was often considered a dead-end job, Van Buren wielded substantial political power and crucial influence in Jackson's administration.

Van Buren was born in Kinderhook, New York, on December 5, 1782. His parents, of Dutch ancestry, operated a farm and tavern that provided a modest living for their large family. Van Buren attended the local one-room school until age fifteen and then read law with the respected Kinderhook lawyer Francis Sylvester. While clerking in the law office and working in a store for his board, the seventeen-year-old Van Buren attended the Jeffersonian Republican congressional district convention in Troy in 1800. So far, Van Buren had benefited significantly from the encouragement of the leading Federalist gen-

tlemen in Columbia County; yet he became increasingly active in the Republican Party organization.

With a loan from Republican Congressman John P. Van Ness, Van Buren moved to New York City in 1802 and clerked for Van Ness's lawyer brother. He observed firsthand the Aaron Burr–DeWitt Clinton infighting in the Republican Party as he completed his legal studies. Admitted to the bar in November 1803, he returned to Kinderhook and began a law partnership with his half-brother James Van Alen. In April 1804, in his first chance to vote, Van Buren broke with the Federalist elite in Columbia County and the Burrite Van Nesses to vote for the Clintonian candidate for governor. In the courtroom, he also challenged the elite by often representing small farmers and tenants in cases involving the Livingston family's claims under old British grants to much of the land in Columbia County.

On February 21, 1807, Van Buren married Hannah Hoes in a private and small (to save money) ceremony. The next year their first of four sons was born. As an increasingly popular and prosperous lawyer who was active in the Republican Party, he was appointed county surrogate (replacing his half-brother and partner) on March 20, 1808. The office provided Van Buren with a small income, but of more importance, it increased his prestige in the county and offered him increased opportunities to meet the voters.

In 1808, Van Buren supported New York's George Clinton for the presidency over James Madison. Recognizing his mistake, Van Buren retreated temporarily from politics to practice law. In 1812, he reluctantly agreed to run for the state senate and then vigorously campaigned and defeated Edward P. Livingston by 200 votes of the 40,000 cast. As victor over a Livingston-Federalist coalition, Van Buren became the defender of the party and Republican leader in the Middle Senate District. He, nevertheless, supported New York's favorite son, DeWitt Clinton, over Madison in 1812. Soon disillusioned with Clinton's willingness to sacrifice party principles and loyalty for personal gain, Van Buren joined Governor Daniel D. Tompkins and state Supreme Court Justice Ambrose Spencer in working to overthrow Clinton.

Van Buren promoted a vigorous military policy in the state senate and ably aided Governor Tompkins's efforts to ensure that New York could defend itself during the War of 1812. Because Van Buren refused to support Spencer's candidate for the U.S. Senate, the justice tried to block Van Buren's appointment as state attorney general. Governor Tompkins, however, broke a tie vote in the Council of Appointment by voting for Van Buren on February 17, 1815.

Van Buren now moved his lucrative practice to Albany and supplemented his income by speculating in land and lending small amounts of money. Reelected to the state senate in April 1816, Van Buren struggled against a reunited Spencer-Clinton coalition. Heading the opposition to Clinton known as the Bucktails, Van Buren nevertheless supported Clinton's cherished project, the Erie Canal. He made an impassioned speech in the senate on behalf of the project, underscoring the canal's economic benefits to the state. While he was in the midst of building a powerful political machine known as the Albany Regency, Van Buren's wife died on February 5, 1819. He was distraught and ill but soon plunged back into the political maelstrom. Joining with the Rufus King Federalists, the Bucktails elected one of their members to the canal board. Governor Clinton retaliated by using his control of the Council of Appointment to remove Van Buren from the attorney generalship. The Council of Appointment then considered putting Van Buren on the supreme court, but Clinton blocked "that prince of villains" from being shunted aside to the high court. In 1820, Van Buren lacked the strength to block Clinton's reelection, but the Bucktails gained control of both houses of the legislature. Van Buren and his supporters pushed for a state constitutional convention in 1820 and 1821 against Clintonian opposition. In the latter year, they used their control of the Council of Appointment to remove all Clintonians from office. On February 6, 1821, the Bucktails also elected their leader to the U.S. Senate. Before heading off to Washington, Van Buren—a convention delegate from Otsego County, where he owned land—smoothed over the differences between the radicals among the Bucktails and the more conservative King supporters in the state constitutional convention by guiding the delegates in crafting a moderate constitution for New York.

In going to Washington, Van Buren was determined to make New York once again central in national politics. He hoped to revitalize the New York–Virginia coalition that had propelled Jefferson to the presidency. With control of New York assured by the Bucktail sweep of the state elections in April 1821, Van Buren arrived in Washington in November. He immediately worked to defeat the incumbent Speaker of the House of Representatives, John W. Taylor, a New Yorker too closely associated with Clinton. Van Buren also succeeded in putting Philip P. Barbour of Virginia in the chair and in the process established a working friendship with Thomas Ritchie, the editor of the Richmond *Enquirer* and one of the leaders of the conservative and states' rights Old Republican Richmond Junto political faction. However, he was unable to block the appointment of Federalist Solomon Van Rensselaer as postmaster of Albany.

When Van Buren returned to the nation's capital from New York in November 1822, he came with a secure base of support. His choice for governor had easily won, and the Albany Regency controlled both houses of the legislature. Now Van Buren turned his attention to presidential politics. He had already decided privately to support William H. Crawford of Georgia for the Republican nomination. Crawford was attractive to Van Buren as a conservative, an advocate of states' rights, and a loyal party member. But Crawford was a southerner and had to be carefully sold to New Yorkers. Once Congress adjourned in March 1823, Van Buren returned to New York and immediately faced newspaper attacks on nominations made in party caucuses that they stated were undemocratic. Soon a People's Party coalesced out of the opponents of the Albany Regency. The party carried New York County in the November legislative elections. Faced with revolt in New York, Van Buren attended the Republican congressional caucus on February 14, 1824. Half of the attendees were New Yorkers and Virginians.

Crawford received the nomination as Van Buren planned, but the nomination was tainted by the scant turnout. Crawford was also seriously ill. Back in New York, the Regency blundered by firing Clinton from his job as unpaid president of the canal board. When the People's Party nominated Clinton for governor, he won easily, and the People's Party captured the New York House of Representatives. Van Buren and the Regency were able to capture only four of New York's thirty-six electoral votes for Crawford. Van Buren learned that even the best party organization was ineffective against an aroused public. He had to find a new presidential candidate who possessed traditional Republican views, was acceptable to the New York–Virginia coalition, and had broad popularity.

Crawford had no chance for victory once the presidential election of 1824 was thrown into the House of Representatives. Van Buren excelled in putting together majority coalitions in caucuses or legislative bodies, but he remained on the sidelines in the struggle between John Quincy Adams and Andrew Jackson. He still supported Crawford and had not as yet decided whom next to support.

In November 1825, the Regency overwhelmed its opposition in the state elections. Adams's first annual message supporting a grand system of federally financed internal improvements gave Van Buren the issue to begin to swing the New York Republicans into the Jacksonian camp. New York had built its Erie Canal and consequently opposed federal funding of competing ventures in other states. Van Buren and the Regency also advocated a limited national government, which made opposition to Adams also a matter of remaining true to Republican ideals. Van Buren, however, faced a major problem. In New York the Clintonians had been the original supporters of Jackson. Van Buren decided that he needed a rapprochement with Clinton. He maneuvered the nomination of a weak Regency gubernatorial candidate, which gave Clinton a narrow victory in November 1826. The legislature, remaining solidly in Regency hands, reelected Van Buren to the Senate on February 6, 1827.

Van Buren toured the seaboard south after the Senate adjourned in March 1827. He met with Crawford, and both men agreed that Jackson was the logical choice to support for the presidency. Crawford also shared his fierce hatred of Vice President John C. Calhoun with the visiting New Yorker. Now a comparatively wealthy man, Van Buren sold his house in Albany; Washington henceforth would be his stage. His position, however, was precarious: Jackson was intensely suspicious of Van Buren, whom he believed to be overly ambitious and an intriguer. Jackson also admired Clinton. In New York, Van Buren's Regency was being vigorously challenged by a growing Anti-Masonic movement. Van Buren also was being forced to finesse the tariff issue by taking a position that would neither alienate protectionist sentiment in New York nor his Richmond Junto allies who were free traders.

Van Buren skillfully managed to win Jackson's favor and maintain intact the New York–Virginia coalition. In 1827, Van Buren saw to it that most of the Republican newspapers in New York simultaneously came out in favor of the Old Hero. When Congress met, Van Buren used his persuasive powers to get Andrew Stevenson of Virginia elected speaker: Stevenson, Van Buren believed, would bind together all the opponents of Adams in the House into an effective opposition. Next, Van Buren worked for passage of a tariff bill that would both strengthen the Regency and elect Jackson. As Van Buren shrewdly calculated, the South would be dissatisfied with higher rates but, because of its dislike of Adams, would have to support Jackson's candidacy. The bill, therefore, was designed primarily to win northern support for Jackson without unduly offending the South. Van Buren's maneuvering on the tariff bill turned Calhoun against the New Yorker. With the death of Clinton, Calhoun realized that Van Buren was his chief rival to succeed Jackson as president. Calhoun now began to calculate how he could thwart his rival.

Van Buren's actions in Congress had helped Jackson defeat Adams. In New York, Jackson's margin of victory was slim, winning by some 5,000 votes, translating into 20 of the Empire

State's 36 electoral votes. To bolster Jackson's victory and extend his influence, Van Buren ran for governor. Although he faced both National Republican and Anti-Masonic candidates, Van Buren won by 30,000 votes, and the Regency carried both houses of the legislature. In his message to the legislature, the new governor recommended a progressive program that included establishing a safety fund to regulate the banks within the state, election reform, and reform of the corrupt auction system for goods imported into New York City.

In early January 1829, President-elect Jackson offered Van Buren the cabinet position of secretary of state. Van Buren accepted but remained in New York to wind up his gubernatorial responsibilities. He resigned on March 12, serving a mere forty-three days as New York's chief executive. Jackson, who had hoped for Van Buren's able counsel, expected the New Yorker in Washington by inauguration day, but he was not able to leave Albany until March 17.

When Van Buren arrived in Washington, he had to be concerned over how much input he would have in the new administration. In his absence, the president had appointed ministers to England and France without even notifying his secretary of state. Jackson's close Tennessee friend John H. Eaton was in the cabinet as secretary of war. The other cabinet members were undistinguished, but Tennessean William B. Lewis was a powerful adviser to Jackson.

Van Buren was also immediately forced to wage an unsuccessful battle to prevent Jackson from appointing Samuel Swartwout, a man abhorrent to Van Buren's Tammany Hall allies, to the important patronage position of customs collector of the Port of New York. In the midst of this uncertainty, Van Buren came to see his role in the administration as a steadying influence on the president. By giving Jackson careful and cautious advice, he could curb some of the president's impulsiveness. Van Buren was also alert to Vice President Calhoun's power and influence in Washington. Calhoun had a hand in Swartwout's appointment, and his newspaper voice, Duff Green's *United States Telegraph*, was hard at work promoting the vice president.

Van Buren quickly eclipsed Calhoun. The secretary and the president became warm friends, sharing evening rides into the country. The two men agreed on public policy, and the president incorporated Van Buren's suggestions into his first annual message. Calhoun even attributed Jackson's new opposition to federally financed internal improvements to the secretary of state's influence. Both Van Buren and Jackson were looking for ways to isolate the vice president. Jackson disliked Calhoun's blatant attempt to anoint himself Jackson's heir; Van Buren, of course, hoped to be the next president.

A series of interrelated events in 1830 undid Calhoun and assured Van Buren of the succession. One involved Peggy O'Neal Eaton, the wife of the secretary of war. Most of social Washington, including the vice president's wife and all of the cabinet except Van Buren, snubbed Peggy. Van Buren, a widower, went out of his way to greet Peggy and thereby endeared himself to the president, who championed the unjustly abused Peggy.[*] Jackson, Van Buren, and the circle of advisers around the president, known as the Kitchen Cabinet, forced Calhoun to respond to the president's toast supporting the Union at the Jefferson Day Dinner on April 13. Jackson also took a slap at Calhoun and Kentucky Senator Henry Clay by vetoing the Maysville Road Bill. Van Buren had helped draft the veto message that put the administration firmly in the camp of the Old Republicans. The secretary of state thereby solidified his support with conservative and states' rights southerners such as the Richmond Junto, while painting the vice president as an extremist whose views threatened the Union and pure Republican principles.

To end the controversy over Peggy Eaton and to purge the cabinet of Calhoun's influence, Van Buren convinced Jackson to accept his resignation as secretary of state and to demand that of the

---

[*]See JOHN CALDWELL CALHOUN for further explanation of the Peggy Eaton affair.

other members. The cabinet reorganization occurred in April 1831. Van Buren virtually selected the new secretary of state and was rewarded by being named minister to Great Britain. He sailed for the Court of St. James on August 16.

Van Buren was well qualified for his diplomatic post. Although he had spent much of his time as secretary of state advising Jackson on political matters, he had not neglected his foreign policy duties. He skillfully directed negotiations with Britain that allowed the United States its first unrestricted trade with the West Indies since independence. In London, Van Buren was on the most cordial terms with Lord Palmerston, the British foreign minister. On December 17, 1831, Jackson wrote Van Buren that he could not close his letter, although it was getting late, without confiding a subject that was constantly on his mind. The president continued:

> If I am reelected, and you are not called to the vice presidency, I wish you to return to this country in two years from now, if it comports with your views & your wishes. I think your presence here about that time will be necessary. The opposition would if they durst try to reject your nomination as minister, but they dare not, they begin to know if they did, that the people in mass would take you up & elect you vice president without a nomination; was it not for this, it is said Clay, Calhoun & Co would try it.

On February 20, 1832, Van Buren received the news that his nomination as ambassador to Great Britain had been rejected by the Senate, with Vice President Calhoun breaking a contrived tie vote. Jackson wanted Van Buren to return immediately to help him battle Calhoun and Clay. The rejected minister, however, decided to stay in London until after the Democratic convention. A quick return, Van Buren reasoned, would make it appear that he was grasping for the vice presidency. In his absence, the Regency and the Kitchen Cabinet directed his campaign for that office. He won the Democratic Party nomination on the first ballot, with 208 votes to 75 for two opponents.

When Van Buren arrived in New York City from Britain, he was met with an urgent letter from Jackson stating that the president was working on a veto message to the bill rechartering the Bank of the United States and wanted Van Buren's advice on it as soon as possible. Van Buren arrived in Washington on the evening of July 8. He had always believed that banks were essential to the growth of the United States economy, but also that their abuses had to be restrained. He read the veto message and heartily approved. The next day, Jackson drove Van Buren to the Capitol, where the New Yorker lobbied Congress to sustain the veto and to pass a compromise tariff bill. Congress was unable to muster the votes needed to override, and it soon passed the tariff bill. Once Congress adjourned, Van Buren returned to New York to campaign. He personally canvassed the state and adroitly stated his political views in reply to a series of antitariff resolutions adopted by a public meeting in Shocco Springs, North Carolina. Van Buren asserted that Congress had the power to regulate commerce, that a tariff should not benefit one part of the Union at the expense of the others, and that with the rapid repayment of the national debt, tariff rates could soon go down. He opposed federally funded internal improvements of a local nature and stated that even national projects must be postponed until the debt was liquidated. He also defended the bank veto and denounced nullification as a threat to the Union. The Jackson–Van Buren ticket carried all of New York's thirty-six electoral votes.

Between the election and the inauguration, Congress met and the crisis caused by South Carolina's attempt to nullify the tariff simmered. Van Buren remained in New York to solidify the Regency's control over the state. He attended a mass meeting in Albany on January 24, 1833, called to debate the tariff. In the next few days, he drafted a report that argued that nullification threatened the Union and was just as dangerous as Federalist extremism had been at the Hartford Convention; that Jackson as president had to stand firm against disunion in his Nullification Proclamation; but also that tariff rates should be reduced to bring about reconciliation. Circulation of Van Buren's views did much to calm the fears among Old Republican states' righters in the

South. Van Buren also worked through New York Senator (and Regency stalwart) Silas Wright to push through Congress a compromise tariff acceptable to southerners. He also hoped that Jackson's Force Bill would quietly die in Congress. Both measures, however, became law on March 2, and Van Buren's political enemies—Calhoun and Clay—used them to attack the vice president-elect.

On March 4, 1833, Van Buren was sworn in as the eighth vice president of the United States, the first vice president to be elected into the office as the anointed heir of the current president. He was also the first vice president to be a close and very important adviser to the president. Essentially, Van Buren continued to serve Jackson as he had done as secretary of state, replacing the conducting of foreign affairs with presiding over the Senate. Van Buren also continued to head the Albany Regency.

Van Buren, nevertheless, was in an awkward position: While advising the president, he had to avoid alienating Jackson without being reduced to being a mere yes-man because he needed Jackson's support to be elected the next president but could be hurt politically by any rash measures adopted by the current administration. Van Buren also had to avoid the appearance of orchestrating administration policy in such a way as to secure his election to the presidency or to benefit his home state.

The first test of Van Buren's political skill as vice president involved the future of government funds in the Bank of the United States. Jackson and his Kitchen Cabinet advisers Amos Kendall, Roger B. Taney, and Francis Preston Blair favored the immediate removal of government deposits from the "monster" bank. Van Buren was more cautious: He supported removal but only if the public had been prepared for such a move. He also clearly realized the power held by the bank and the economic chaos that removal of the deposits might cause. He hoped to delay removal until the next Congress met. Jackson had not made a final decision when Van Buren left Washington for New York. The president planned a northern tour and consequently the two men would soon meet again in New York City.

Jackson's reception in the city was a triumph, and Van Buren accompanied him on his tour of New England; while together they discussed removal of the deposits. Van Buren eventually supported removal as early as September when convinced that Kendall's plan of gradually withdrawing government funds from the Bank of the United States and then depositing them in state banks contained the safeguards necessary to protect the government's money. Still the vice president preferred a cautious approach. He did not want to alienate Congress or to panic the banking community with precipitous action. Jackson almost misread Van Buren's caution as disloyalty, prompting careful fence-mending on the part of the vice president. The president wanted Van Buren back in Washington by October, when the removals would begin; instead Van Buren remained in New York, traveling throughout the state with author Washington Irving. The vice president had convinced Jackson that his absence would hinder the opposition's attempts to paint removal as a grab by New York banks for supremacy.

Van Buren's tour was cut short when Jackson—faced with a cabinet crisis—summoned his vice president to Washington. Van Buren, nevertheless, remained in New York City, where he could easily give timely advice without providing the opposition with the opportunity to picture Jackson as the hapless tool of the Little Magician. He also served the president by persuading his former law partner Benjamin F. Butler to fill the vacant post of attorney general.

Jackson looked to Van Buren for more than advice. The two men were also close friends. When the vice president arrived in Washington, Jackson was heartened. Following precedent, Van Buren was absent from the capital when Congress convened on December 2, 1833. Although as presiding officer of the Senate the vice president had the power to appoint the committees, vice presidents in the past had remained absent until the president pro tempore had made the appointments. The current president pro tempore, Hugh Lawson White of Tennessee, was reluctant to appoint the committees, hoping to avoid alienating either the administration or its opponents. Tennessee Senator Felix Grundy then struck a deal with Senator Daniel Webster of

Massachusetts to delay the appointments until Van Buren arrived. Webster offered to join the Jacksonians in opposing the Clay–Calhoun coalition in the Senate. Van Buren arrived in Washington late on December 14. The next morning he discussed with the president Webster's offer. Van Buren totally rejected amalgamation. He had long believed that the nation needed two parties opposed to each other on key issues of public policy. Amalgamation with Webster would undermine what had been his life's work. Not lost on Van Buren were the implications that a Webster–Jackson alliance might have on his own chance to be president. Jackson agreed with Van Buren, and Webster rejoined the opposition.

Van Buren took his seat in the Senate chair on December 16. In a short speech, he asked that body's indulgence as he reacquainted himself with the Senate's procedures. As presiding officer he had to listen to Whig attacks on the administration's policy of removing the deposits from the Bank of the United States. Clay denounced Van Buren for destroying the bank for the benefit of New York bankers.

The bank began to call in loans, causing a tremendous disruption in the U.S. economy. Petitions flooded Congress demanding reversal of the administration policy. Van Buren drafted resolutions for the New York legislature to adopt the support of removal.

On March 7, 1834, Webster read a petition from the mechanics of Philadelphia, castigating removal. Clay then rose and asked Van Buren to intercede personally with the president to end the nation's anguish. Van Buren carefully vacated the chair, walked up to Clay, and upstaged the Kentuckian by asking for a pinch of snuff.

On the March 17, Van Buren presented a petition from a public meeting in York County, Pennsylvania, opposing recharter of the bank and supporting removal of the deposits. After some debate, Clay moved that the petition should not be received. The vice president then addressed the Senate at length. Van Buren defended his practice of presenting all petitions sent to him to the Senate, withholding only those few that were blatantly disrespectful to that body. He did not consider the York County plea to be such and submitted it because the subject was already before the Senate. Clay's motion not to receive the petition was carried 24 to 21 and, continuing the assault on the administration, the Kentuckian soon pushed through the Senate a measure to censure Jackson for unconstitutionally removing the deposits. The censure passed. Van Buren helped Jackson draft a protest, but Clay kept the protest from being entered into the journal.

Presiding over the "Panic Session" of the Senate exhausted Van Buren, but the vice president continued to entertain as was expected of his office. He also provided timely advice to prevent any rash or politically embarrassing administration action in the crisis that arose over settlement of spoliation claims against the French. Van Buren also selected John Forsyth of Georgia to replace Louis McLane, who had left the State Department.

In November 1834, the Albany Regency won a landslide victory in the state elections. With his home-state political base secure, Van Buren was virtually assured of being the Democratic presidential nominee in 1836, but he continued to need Jackson's support. The crisis with France over its refusal to pay spoliation claims due Americans still festered. Jackson was determined to act decisively, even threatening to use force. Seeing the political damage that the crisis could do to the administration, Van Buren urged caution. He eventually found a formula to diffuse the crisis, but it took the vice president's considerable persuasive powers to convince Jackson, Forsyth, and the Kitchen Cabinet to risk a compromise solution.

In contrast, presiding over the Senate during the second session of the Twenty-third Congress was uneventful. Van Buren was in the chair on the opening day, December 1, 1834, and left the evening of March 3, 1835, the last day in the session.

The 1836 presidential campaign began early for Van Buren. The Whigs attacked the vice president as an eastern political schemer who was unfit to be president. Van Buren had to struggle to hold together the New York–Virginia alliance that had propelled Jackson to the presidency in 1828. The Democratic Party convention met in Baltimore in May 1835 and nominated Van Buren. In replying to the committee informing him of his nomination, Van Buren promised to follow "generally in the footsteps of President Jackson" if elected.

While directing his presidential campaign, Van Buren presided over the Senate at its 1835–1836 session. He was in the chair as the Twenty-fourth Congress opened on December 7, 1835. On February 13, 1836, Van Buren ruled that Thomas Hart Benton, a Democratic senator from Missouri, was not out of order in what the Whigs believed was a personal attack on Senator Calhoun. Voting 24 to 21, the Senate rebuked the vice president by affirming that the ruling was incorrect. On May 21, Van Buren broke a tie by voting against a bill to extend the charters of certain banks in the District of Columbia. However, he faced a potentially embarrassing decision on June 2. The Senate tied 18 to 18 on whether to order the engrossing and third reading of a bill designed to prevent abolitionist literature from being sent through the mails into the southern states. The vice president voted yes, but the Senate rejected the bill 25 to 19 six days later. This issue could easily split the North–South Democratic coalition that Van Buren had labored for years to build.

Although Van Buren remained in the senate chair until June 30, the fifth to last day of the session, he was actively directing his presidential campaign throughout this period. He publicized his opposition to the distribution of surplus federal revenue to the states and his support of Jackson's Specie Circular of July 1836 that ordered federal land offices to accept only gold and silver coin in payment for public lands. His political skill yielded a narrow 28,000-vote victory over four regional Whig candidates. Van Buren had 170 electoral votes to 124 for his combined opposition.

The president-elect was still vice president and presiding officer over the Senate for the short session of the Twenty-fourth Congress. He was in the chair as the session opened on December 5, 1836. Van Buren cast another tie-breaking vote on December 21. This time the issue was procedural: Van Buren voted to refer Calhoun's bill on extending an 1836 act regulating deposits of money in the Treasury to the Finance Committee, rather than making

it the order of the day the following Monday. On January 28, 1837, Van Buren made a short farewell speech and retired from the chair. Senator Benton asked for unanimous consent to a resolution thanking the vice president for the "impartiality, dignity, and ability" with which he presided over the Senate. Calhoun objected in another swipe at his arch rival but withdrew his objection, allowing Benton's resolution to pass.

On March 4, 1837, Van Buren became president. His administration was mostly a continuation of Jackson's presidency. Van Buren had been a key adviser during Jackson's eight-year tenure; now Van Buren was his own chief adviser. The new president kept Jackson's cabinet, only filling the vacant position of secretary of war with Joel Poinsett. He inherited a costly and politically embarrassing war with the Seminole Indians in Florida that would not end. Likewise, Jackson's Indian policy finally culminated with the removal of the Cherokee under Van Buren. His opponents seized the issue to condemn the mistreatment of the tribes, which cost the administration political support, especially in the Northeast.

As one of his last acts in office, Jackson had recognized Texas independence. Van Buren faced strong protests from Mexico as a result. United States annexation of Texas would not only eventually cause war with Mexico, but it was also a sectional issue that could tear asunder the Democratic coalition. Van Buren handled the explosive Texas issue by ignoring it until it disappeared, at least for the time being.

In other areas of foreign policy, the administration had remarkable success. The president skillfully resolved crises with Britain over Americans aiding Canadian rebels and over the disputed Maine–New Brunswick border. Eventually Van Buren also replaced members of his cabinet as resignations occurred.

Foreign policy, Indian affairs, and cabinet appointments turned out to be minor concerns for the administration. The economy came to dominate Van Buren's presidency and eventually brought it down. On March 17, 1837, an economic panic began with the failure of a New York City commercial house. Economic misery would last for the rest of Van Buren's term. The president decided to retain the Specie Circular to prevent banks from paying debts in depreciated paper money. On May 16, Van Buren called a special session of Congress for September. Van Buren decided to ask Congress to establish an Independent Treasury so that the government would not have to entrust its funds to private banks. He also needed congressional permission to withdraw government funds from the deposit banks and issue short-term treasury notes to cover the deficit in the Treasury.

The Independent Treasury proposal split the Democrats. Conservative and probusiness Democrats refused to support it. Van Buren stubbornly clung to his proposal. It failed in Congress during three sessions before the economy rebounded slightly in May 1838 when New York banks resumed specie payments. In the summer of 1838 Van Buren toured the North, breaking all precedent by making campaign speeches. The president and Senator Calhoun also made peace, allowing the South Carolinian to bring his supporters back into the Democratic fold. When Congress met in December 1839, Van Buren again pushed the Independent Treasury. With Calhoun's help, the bill passed and Van Buren signed it into law on the Fourth of July 1840. By then the Whigs were campaigning furiously to put William Henry Harrison into the White House. Van Buren valiantly fought back, but he could not overcome the burden that depression placed on his administration. Harrison had 234 electoral votes to the incumbent's 60.

Before retiring from office, Van Buren entertained president-elect Harrison; then he moved back to Kinderhook, taking up residence at Lindenwald, the first permanent home that he owned. He immediately contemplated a run for the presidency in 1844. Between February and July 1842, he toured the South and West in a private journey that soon became a campaign swing. With Harrison dead and President John Tyler feuding with the Whigs in Congress, Van Buren quickly built an organization to win back the presidency. His principal rival Calhoun blundered himself out of contention for the Democratic nomination, so Van Buren expected to face his Whig rival Henry Clay in 1844. On April 27, Van Buren published his "Hammet Letter," in which he opposed the annexation of Texas. (Clay published his opposition on the same day.) Van Buren's stance on Texas cost him the Democratic nomination. Unable to obtain the necessary two-thirds majority needed for the nomination, he withdrew in favor of James K. Polk, who defeated Clay for the presidency.

Polk soon alienated Van Buren and much of the Democratic Party in New York. Disagreements over cabinet appointments and patronage joined with opposition to the extension of slavery into the territory conquered from Mexico propelled Van Buren to leadership of the "Barnburner" faction within the New York Democratic Party. They wanted Van Buren as the Democratic presidential candidate in 1848; instead they ran Van Buren as the unsuccessful Free Soil Party candidate. In 1852, Van Buren returned to the Democratic fold and supported Franklin Pierce for the presidency. As the nation drifted toward secession and civil war, Van Buren became increasingly disillusioned. At seventy-nine, he died at Lindenwald on July 24, 1862.

REFERENCES

John Niven, *Martin Van Buren: The Romantic Age of American Politics* (New York and Oxford, England: Oxford University Press, 1983); Robert V. Remini, *Martin Van Buren and the Making of the Democratic Party* (New York: Columbia University Press, 1959); Major L. Wilson, *The Presidency of Martin Van Buren* (Lawrence, Kans.: University Press of Kansas, 1984); *The Autobiography of Martin Van Buren*, John C. Fitzpatrick, ed., *Annual Report of the American Historical Association for the Year 1918* (Washington, D.C.: Government Printing Office, 1920).

CHARLES H. SCHOENLEBER holds a Ph.D. from the University of Wisconsin, Madison. After teaching at the University of Wyoming, he joined the Documentary History of the Ratification of the Constitution project in Madison in 1987. His research interest is the politics of Indian removal, especially in the southern states.

RICHARD MENTOR JOHNSON
(Library of Congress)

By Lindsey Apple

Richard Mentor Johnson, the ninth vice president of the United States, was certainly one of the most colorful men to serve in that position. A frontier entrepreneur, Indian fighter, and military hero, he shared many of the personal characteristics that made Andrew Jackson so popular with Americans and assured his own intimate friendship with General Jackson. Plainspoken, of a democratic manner, loyal to friends, and disinterested in dress or genteel manners, Richard Mentor Johnson embodied the frontier politician. Because he championed causes

popular with the common man he also became the candidate of the northeastern worker, including the radical "locofoco" faction. He also encouraged the development of educational institutions of many types across the nation and on a personal level sought to educate disenfranchised elements of the American people—the American Indian, women, and even African American slaves.

Like many vice presidents, however, Johnson's election to the office marked the end of his political career rather than a stepping stone to the presidency. Noted as a potential presidential candidate throughout the 1830s, he was nearly forgotten, or dismissed, soon after his term as vice president. That says as much about the United States and its people as it does about Johnson. His political career reflects the rapidly changing nature of American political life; the homespun frontiersmen became a caricature as the country became more complex. Johnson's historical reputation says a great deal about American social values and attitudes, particularly those regarding race.

Richard Mentor Johnson was born in a hastily constructed fortress near Louisville, Kentucky, when that region was the American West. In the fall of 1779 his parents, Robert and Jemima Suggett Johnson, moved their growing family from Orange County, Virginia, to the Beargrass Creek settlement. While Robert Johnson was off fighting Indians with George Rogers Clark, Jemima awaited the birth of their fifth child, the future vice president. The family then moved to Bryan Station in the Bluegrass region, where the entire family became involved in the Indian wars. At the siege of Bryan Station, Richard's older brother James, at the age of eight, dashed across the roofs of the cabins dousing fire arrows launched by the attacking Indians. On the frontier, women also played an active role. His mother led a group of women to get water for the fort, and older sister Betsy pulled a flaming arrow from the cradle where Richard slept. Such stories may have been embellished over time or for political purposes, but they are the means by which families shape an identity and politicians create careers.

The Johnson family quickly developed that identity. Robert Johnson built a fortified homestead on a 2,000-acre tract of land purchased from Virginia patriot Patrick Henry. The tract was located at the Great Crossings, a buffalo trace on North Elkhorn Creek. The family farmed the land, but they also created commercial and manufacturing ventures as diverse as hemp factories, general stores, stage lines, and steamboat construction. Richard Johnson later operated a tavern and a spa where wealthy southerners came to spend their summers.

Like many frontier families, the Johnsons had journeyed west to prosper economically, and they pursued that goal relentlessly, seeing no contradiction in mixing economic gain with their political, cultural, and even religious activities. Quite common among frontier folk, such mixing of goals gave Johnson's political rivals, and later historians, significant ammunition to use against him.

Johnson's father was an influential member of the legislature that created the first Kentucky state constitution. Family members were also leaders in the affairs of the Baptist Church, served on the boards of Transylvania College and Georgetown College, and became leaders in the judicial, legislative, and cultural affairs of the region. Some have argued that Scott County was created by the state legislature virtually as a Johnson fiefdom. Their political and economic empire became the base from which three of Robert Johnson's sons won election to national office.

The education of Richard Mentor Johnson is shrouded in the mystery of the frontier. After attending a local common school, he is believed to have attended Transylvania College briefly. He then studied law with George Nicholas and James Brown, men who trained a generation of Kentucky leadership. Admitted to the bar in 1802, he practiced law at Great Crossings. Johnson was not well read, nor could he be considered an intellectual. His abilities were of a more practical nature. He saw business opportunities everywhere, enjoyed politics, and was said to have a "natural aptitude" for military affairs. Throughout his career he combined the three areas, usually to his advantage.

Johnson served in the United States House of Representatives from 1807 to 1819, except for two years when he fought in the War of 1812 and recovered from wounds received at the Battle of the Thames. In 1819, the Kentucky legislature named him to the U.S. Senate, where he remained until defeated ten years later. He then returned to the House of Representatives, where he served until chosen as vice president in 1837. Thus, he had significant experience in the legislative branch of government before he became the presiding officer of the Senate.

Johnson's rise to political prominence rested on a number of factors. Modern historians have been inclined to dismiss his importance by questioning aspects of his political power and his personal life. There is certainly evidence to support such attacks, but the issues are far more complex. Some argue that his fame rested on an undeserved military reputation. Johnson was, before the War of 1812, one of the War Hawks, a group of congressmen who believed that he United States should stand up to the British. Once war was declared, Richard M. Johnson left Congress to raise a regiment from Kentucky, which he led north to join the army of General William Henry Harrison. At the Battle of the Thames, Johnson, with help from others, devised a plan to expel British General Henry Proctor and his Indian ally Tecumseh from a strategic position along the Thames River. James Johnson, Richard's brother, attacked the British forces of General Proctor. Richard Johnson led twenty men in a suicide mission, called the "forlorn hope," to discover the position of Tecumseh and his warriors. Fifteen of the twenty were killed immediately, and four others were wounded. Johnson, shot through the hip and thigh, managed to remain on his horse to direct the force that then attacked the warriors. Though receiving several additional wounds and having his horse shot out from under him, Johnson was able to kill an Indian who charged at him. Later, he claimed that his dead adversary resembled Tecumseh. Political supporters proclaimed Richard Johnson the "hero of the Thames" and the slayer of Tecumseh. He would later campaign under the slogan "Rumpsey, Dumpsey, who shot Tecumseh!"

Political detractors and historians have argued that he probably did not kill the Indian chief. Historians also argued that his actions were foolhardy. Whether he killed Tecumseh is a mute point; the chieftain was killed in the battle. Moreover, foolhardy or no, such actions were seen as signs of manliness, and Richard M. Johnson was a legitimate hero in his day. Even the Congress presented him with a ceremonial sword when, recovered from five separate wounds, he returned to Washington. A severe limp spoke to his patriotism thereafter wherever he campaigned.

In addition to military heroism, Johnson's political success rested on his family's economic power and his ability to use his political position to enhance the region in which he lived. In Kentucky there was no secret ballot after 1799. The "voice vote" meant that few men could afford to vote against the Johnsons. Conversely, the Johnsons were also the subject of local admiration. They had accomplished what most people came west hoping to achieve. Richard Johnson also brought national attention to the area. Famous visitors frequently journeyed through Kentucky to pay their respects to Johnson and to Henry Clay, 15 miles away in Lexington: In 1819, President James Monroe visited Johnson's farm; in 1825, the Revolutionary War hero Lafayette was entertained by Johnson, who invited most of Central Kentucky to participate. Johnson also used his political position to create government spending in the West and to secure contracts for western businessmen.

One such venture nearly bankrupted the Johnson family and damaged the reputations of President Monroe and Secretary of War John C. Calhoun. It might be argued that the affair permanently shaped Johnson's reputation. In 1818, Calhoun sought to establish a line of fortresses up the Missouri River to the Yellowstone, thereby strengthening control of a vast new frontier. Johnson, the chairman of the House Committee on Military Affairs and a friend of Calhoun, used his influence to secure contracts to supply the materials for the new fortresses. The Johnsons began to collect the supplies and built four steamboats to carry them, drawing frequent advances from the government. The project was a disaster. The Johnsons sensed the commercial value of steam transportation but knew too little about the technology and made bad decisions. The steamboats could not navigate the shallow water. They were also confronted by the financial panic that began in 1819. Creditors began to call in notes owed by the Johnsons or guaranteed by them. The venture cost the United States government approximately $266,000. Richard Remini calls the Yellowstone affair a "colossal boondoggle." "Honest men," he argues, "shook their heads in disbelief when they heard about it."

In fact, there was nothing illegal by nineteenth-century standards about the venture, and the courts later accepted James Johnson's financial accounting of the incident. The War Department also continued to award the Johnsons contracts to provision military bases at New Orleans, Natchitoches, St. Louis, and elsewhere. Moreover, the Johnsons hardly profited from the venture: Local court records indicate that they sold large parcels of land to meet their obligations. Historians have been inclined to evaluate the incident by twentieth-century standards, but the *Argus of Western America*, a major western newspaper of the time, praised the Johnsons for bringing so much currency into the specie-starved West.

Johnson also won the support of many individuals and communities by his consistent support of pensions for veterans and their widows and orphans. He seemed to have the interests of the common man uppermost in his thought. He fought against imprisonment for debt on both the state and national level and opposed an effort to stop the transportation of mail on Sunday because, in a nation as mobile as the United States, citizens needed to maintain contact with their relatives. Johnson also opposed the National Bank, believing it, erroneously or otherwise, to be a tool of the wealthy, and encouraged internal improvements as a means to develop the western territories.

Richard Johnson's political prominence also rested on his intimate friendship with Andrew Jackson. Jackson held virtually all veterans in high esteem, but Johnson had exhibited the kind of courage the general most admired: he had been wounded in defense of his country. Johnson also had been the sole member of the committee on military affairs to support Jackson when charges were brought in 1819 regarding Jackson's conduct in the Seminole Wars. Again in 1824, Johnson argued that Henry Clay's "corrupt bargain" with John Quincy Adams was no way to treat a true patriot.

Johnson was also led into the Democratic Party by events in Kentucky. The economic Panic of 1819 created great suffering in Kentucky. One of the main causes for the failure of the Yellowstone expedition, the panic nearly destroyed the Johnson family. Like many Kentuckians, the Johnsons were inclined to blame the Bank of the United States. Richard Johnson voluntarily left Congress in 1819 to run for election to the state legislature, where he supported government relief for those who were losing their property because of the financial collapse. Known as the Relief/Antirelief controversy in Kentucky, the struggle colored Kentucky politics for years. Jasper B. Shannon and Ruth McQuown note in their study of Kentucky elections that areas that supported the Relief candidates became Jacksonian Democrats and those who opposed relief to debtors became Whigs. Richard Johnson joined fellow Kentuckians Amos Kendall, Francis Preston Blair, and others in the Democratic Party. The fact that Johnson controlled the party in Kentucky, a very important state at the time, no doubt endeared him to Jackson and his political supporters as well.

When Jackson was elected president in 1828, Johnson exhibited the loyalty that characterized his political life: He signed a report condemning the Bank of the United States, an issue central to Jackson's thinking; supported the president's tariff policies despite his long friendship and political alliance with John C. Calhoun; and even supported the president's opposition to internal improvements, though he felt them essential to economic development in his home state.

Jackson had stated his intention to serve only one term. Johnson was mentioned as a possible presidential candidate of the Democratic Party because of his party loyalty and his popularity. He had the misfortune, however, to be pitted against one of the shrewdest politicians in antebellum America. Martin Van Buren, the political boss of New York, was known as the Little Magician because of his ability to manipulate people and conditions to his advantage. Moreover, conditions favored the magician. The United States was no longer a frontier republic. The number of states had more than doubled by 1832, and the population was growing even faster. Seven out of ten Americans were still farmers, but commerce and manufacturing were growing, spurred by population growth and the building of canals and railroads. The role government should play was being questioned, and the issue began to divide the commercial North from the rural South. The issue of slavery also led to sharp differences. It was a difficult time for any politician. Caucuses, party conventions, and outright manipulation became the means to build an electoral majority in an age when support of principles was almost a guarantee of the animosity of half the nation.

During Jackson's first term, Martin Van Buren used his charm and his manipulative abilities to endear himself to Andrew Jackson. Calhoun, Johnson, and other presidential hopefuls were no match for the wily New Yorker. Johnson was described by his contemporaries as mild mannered and pleasant, open and honest in his dealings. One prominent Washington hostess described him as "the most tender-hearted, mild, affectionate and benevolent of men." Intensely loyal to friends and political allies, he was more inclined to compromise, to seek consensus. Fair minded and lacking strong prejudices, he often sacrificed his own interests to secure harmony and the interests of his region for that of the nation. A border-state politician, he seemed, perhaps like his rival and fellow Kentuckian Henry Clay, to recognize that the issues that increasingly separated North from South were more complex than either region admitted. Such qualities had served him well in the past; they were handicaps in the new politics of Martin Van Buren.

Johnson played the role of mediator in Jackson's administration. When a group of western congressmen urged Johnson to speak to the president in favor of internal improvements, he agreed; however, he confronted not only Jackson but a whispering Van Buren, who had carefully nurtured Jackson's opposition to internal improvements. Johnson also became involved in the Peggy Eaton affair when he tried to serve as mediator. Mrs. Eaton was married to one of Jackson's cabinet members, but her life before that marriage had been somewhat scandalous.

When the other ladies of the cabinet snubbed her, President Jackson was furious. He blamed his vice president, John C. Calhoun. Johnson, a friend of Jackson and Calhoun, attempted to mediate. Van Buren championed Mrs. Eaton, thereby increasing his standing with Jackson.[*]

Such conduct won Van Buren the support of Jackson and the distrust of many others. Some have argued that Jackson chose to accept a second term because he realized the nation would not accept Van Buren as his successor. Johnson was mentioned as a presidential candidate for the 1832 campaign until Jackson decided to run again, and as a vice-presidential candidate until Jackson handpicked Van Buren as his running mate. Johnson supported the ticket, stumping the country on its behalf, but his position with the president waned as Van Buren's influence grew.

In 1836, Jackson chose Van Buren to run for president. To assuage Johnson's disappointment at not getting the nomination for the presidency and, to a degree, Jackson's sense of guilt for his own disloyalty, Johnson was offered the position of vice president. Jackson's support proved sufficient for Van Buren but less so for Johnson. By 1836, the issues of slavery and race were hardening attitudes across the United States. Within the Democratic Party, the Virginians wanted their own native son, William Cabell Rives, to be chosen as the candidate, and they were willing to play the race card to defeat Johnson.

Richard Johnson never married, but he maintained a long term relationship with Julia Chinn, one of his slaves. She lived in his house, ran his farm in his absence, and even accompanied him to Washington. She was, in short, his wife in every way but the legal sense. When apart they corresponded regularly, his letters suggesting that he held her opinions in high regard. They also had two daughters, Adeline and Imogene, whom Johnson educated and, if his correspondence is any indication, adored and respected. Rev. Thomas Henderson, the girls' tutor, claimed Johnson insisted that they were to be educated as

[*]Editor's note: See JOHN CALHOUN for further explanation of the Peggy Eaton affair.

well as any woman of the time. Adeline, for example, played the piano for General Lafayette when he visited Colonel Johnson in 1825. Johnson also arranged marriages for his daughters to white men and provided them with substantial farms.

In the 1820s, little of this seemed to matter. John Niven, Van Buren's biographer, notes that Johnson's family was accepted by "the easy-going society of the West." Even the good folk of the Great Crossings Baptist Church accepted them, and only an occasional comment on their octoroon mother called attention to Johnson's domestic life. President Jackson knew of it. Henry Clay was aware of it. In 1836, however, it became a major issue. The South declared Johnson unacceptable as a candidate, and even within his own party, the attacks were cruel, scurrilous assaults. The Whigs continued the assault when, with Jackson's support, Johnson prevailed at the convention. Johnson refused to respond to the charges. Julia Chinn had died in 1833, the victim of a cholera epidemic, and Johnson refused to deny their relationship. The attacks were so harsh that some have argued that Adeline grew ill because of them. She died just prior to her father's election. Johnson proclaimed her a "lovely and innocent child . . . a source of inexhaustible happiness and comfort to me. She was a firm and great prop to my happiness here—but she is gone where sorrow and sighing can never disturb her peaceful and quiet bosom." Johnson won the nomination and the vice presidency, but his family and his chance for higher elective office had been destroyed.

Ironically, it was not miscegenation that bothered southerners. Indeed, the mixing of the races was quite common on southern plantations. George Prentice, the Whig editor of the Louisville (Kentucky) *Journal,* and, according to one author, no stranger to "blood pollution" himself, captured the real issue and the hypocrisy when he wrote:

> If Col. Johnson had the decency and decorum to seek to hide his ignominy from the world, we would refrain from lifting the curtain. His chief sin against society is the publicity and barefaced-

ness of his conduct, he scorns all secrecy, all concealment, all disguise.

Even for political gain Johnson would not deny his "wife" and daughters. Future generations of the family and society in general did seek to conceal his relationships, however. Members of his white family tried to forget, perhaps even destroying some of his papers. The local newspapers cooperated in hiding such a "blight" upon the community, and Johnson's biographer, Leland Meyer, handled the matter very discreetly. Historians relegated Johnson to a footnote that usually referred to his domestic arrangement. In the late nineteenth century, the United States, not just the South, wished to conceal its hypocrisy on racial issues.

Johnson won 147 electoral votes in the election of 1836, just short of the required majority, and the election was thrown into the Senate. Johnson became the only vice president to be elected by the Senate. The vote was 33 to 16.

Like many who held the office, Johnson found the vice presidency frustrating. As presiding officer in the Senate, the major issues of the day passed before him, but he was not at liberty to speak on them. For men who actively participated in the affairs of state, the inactivity was difficult. Perhaps the harshness of campaign rhetoric and the human cost sapped his energies. A biographer of Franklin Pierce claimed that Johnson presided over the Senate in a careless and inefficient manner. He was more inclined to leave the chair "to lounge around" or to stand and chat near one of the four fireplaces that warmed the Senate chambers. Johnson spent a lot of his time seeking support for his Choctaw academy and actually left the chair for an entire summer, apparently preferring to operate his tavern and spa at the Blue Springs.

Despite their rivalry during the Jackson years, Johnson and President Van Buren remained on cordial terms. Though never one of his major advisers, Johnson supported the president's legislative program as the presiding officer of the Senate. Historians have made much of his role as a compromiser or peacemaker. One implied that his tolerance of differing views may have resulted from "a fuzzy timidity" rather than from any liberal spirit. That seems too harsh for one who exhibited a personal tolerance in so many areas. It should also be noted that another famous Kentuckian of the era made a reputation as a compromiser and "pacificator" too.

Johnson's moderating skills and his easy, gregarious manner made him an excellent choice for the presiding officer of the Senate. The nation faced a number of divisive issues during Johnson's term of office. A financial panic brought on in part by the debates over national monetary policy and the government's efforts to shape it accompanied Van Buren's inauguration. The Senate debated the issues of responsibility for economic collapse and the solutions. Disassociation from private banks and the development of an independent treasury highlighted the discussions of nearly the entire four years, and the debates became quite heated at times. There was also the issue of federal land policy and also the annexation of Texas, issues on the periphery of a larger one that would dominate political debate for more than a quarter of a century—slavery and its place in American life.

Such issues created party and personal divisions. Senatorial privileges were demanded and the rulings of the chair carefully assessed. As presiding officer, Johnson recognized senators seeking the right to address the body. A perusal of the *Congressional Globe* suggests that it was more than perfunctory courtesy when, at the end of his term, several senators, including Clay, spoke to his impartiality and fairness. Though most vice presidents extol the virtues of the Senate, Johnson's service in that body made him particularly respectful of its function. He claimed to have attempted to give to each senator the respect due "the representative of a sovereign and independent state."

The presiding officer of the Senate also has the duty to break the deadlock when votes on an issue are evenly divided. Johnson cast fourteen tie-breaking votes, the fourth highest in U.S. history. On March 25, 1840, he cast three deciding votes that secured the passage of a treaty. It was fitting, given his interest in Native Americans, that the treaty was one signed between the government and the Six

Nations, a confederation of tribes. It was equally appropriate that several of his deciding votes were for the relief of individuals.

The role of Richard M. Johnson was, however, far more important in the politics that led to office than in the exercising of it. By 1840, Johnson was considered a major liability to the Democratic Party. He had cost the party the support of the South. He had even failed to carry his own state, proving far less effective in the West, supposedly the area where he could add most to the ticket. Party leaders encouraged the selection of another candidate: Andrew Jackson urged Van Buren to drop Johnson and run with James K. Polk of Tennessee. Amos Kendall, a former ally, accused Johnson of having taken a second slave mistress. Ironically, he had also lost his appeal in the North. The locofocos announced their opposition to any slaveholder.

Van Buren remained neutral, at least in public, and the Democratic convention decided to let the states support their own candidate for vice president. As the campaign progressed, however, Johnson became the major candidate when James K. Polk withdrew. Whether an asset or a detriment to the campaign, it mattered little. Feelings ran high against Van Buren, and the Whigs, who had argued that Johnson's military record did not mean political ability, nominated their own military hero, William Henry Harrison. The Democrats lost the election.

Defeated for national office, Johnson returned to his home in Kentucky, where he took an interest in local affairs. He represented Scott County in the Kentucky legislature from 1841 to 1843. He then retired from politics for a few years but traveled throughout the country as if he intended to be a candidate for national office again. Mentioned briefly for office in 1844, Johnson played only a spoiler's role in politics. In 1848, he again served in the state legislature and was briefly a candidate for state governor before his death in 1850.

Most of his energies after 1841 involved his life long interest, education. Except for the Choctaw Academy, historians have virtually ignored his support of education. Johnson served for many years as a trustee of Georgetown College and encouraged other Baptist efforts to establish academies and schools. After the War of 1812, he also encouraged the government to create military academies throughout the nation, and he was an organizer of Columbian College, the predecessor to George Washington University.

Some of Johnson's ideas about education were decidedly progressive, albeit limited. As early as 1819 he had attempted to establish a school for Indian youths. His Choctaw Academy educated hundreds of young men from a variety of tribes. Ella Drake criticizes him in an article in the *Register of the Kentucky Historical Society* for seeking a profit and saving money at the expense of education at the academy. As noted earlier, frontiersmen sought economic gain through political, cultural, and religious offices far too openly for modern taste. Though the educational opportunities seemed limited at the academy, they were limited in most Kentucky schools. Johnson's nephews and other local white youth attended the Choctaw Academy, which would suggest that it was not considered substandard at the time. Moreover, most people in the 1820s and 1830s were far more interested in removing the tribes to the west than in educating them.

Johnson also insisted that the school superintendent educate Adeline and Imogene, as well as several promising slaves. In an uncharacteristically quiet way, Johnson spoke to his neighbors about the abilities of Native Americans, women, and African Americans. At the Choctaw Academy, red, white, and black Americans were educated together, and even gender was overlooked.

Richard Mentor Johnson died on November 19, 1850, in Frankfort, Kentucky, where he was serving in the state legislature. Though his term as vice president lacks distinction, Johnson's life should stand as an indication of the dangers of generalization in the study of history. It also speaks to the speed of change in American life.

REFERENCES

Leland Winfield Meyer, *The Life and Times of Colonel Richard M. Johnson of Kentucky* (New York: Columbia University Press, 1932); Lindsey Apple, Frederick A. Johnson, Ann Bolton Bevins, eds., *Scott County Kentucky: A History* (Georgetown, Ky.: Scott County Historical Society, 1993); Robert Bolt, "Vice President Richard M. Johnson of Kentucky: Hero of the Thames—Or the Great Amalgamator?" *The Register of the Kentucky Historical Society*, 75 (July 1977), 191–203; Ella Wells Drake, "Choctaw Academy: Richard M. Johnson and the Business of Indian Education," *The Register of the Kentucky Historical Society*, 91 (Summer 1993), 260–297.

LINDSEY APPLE is professor of history at Georgetown College, Georgetown, Kentucky. He is an editor and an author of *Scott County Kentucky: A History* (Georgetown, 1993). A biography of Susan Clay Sawitzky, a great-granddaughter of Henry Clay, entitled *Never Excelled: Tradition and Modernity in the Life of a Southern Lady*, is forthcoming from Kent State University Press. He has written articles for the *Register of the Kentucky Historical Society*, *The Filson Club Quarterly*, *Border States*, *The Kentucky Encyclopedia*, and a sketch on James Johnson for the *American National Biography*.

*J*OHN *TYLER* (1790–1842)

Vice President, March 4–April 4, 1841

(President William Henry Harrison)

JOHN TYLER
(Library of Congress)

By M. Boyd Coyner, Jr.

With the death of William Henry Harrison on April 4, 1841, John Tyler became not only the first vice president to succeed to the presidency, but also the vice president with the shortest tenure in that office and, only six days past his fifty-first birthday, the youngest chief executive up to that date. As the first accidental president, he set the precedent for his successors by his insistence that he was no mere acting president but fully president, by title as well as in privilege and function. Unfortunately for Tyler, he also set a pattern for his three nineteenth-century successors as accidental presidents by failing to win renomination to succeed himself.

It is highly unlikely that Tyler, because of the political dogmas to which he so strictly adhered, would have come to the presidency by any route other than that which brought him to the White House. His early political successes came quickly enough; he inherited position and sufficient fortune to place him among the plantation elite of the James River bottoms in Virginia. Born in Charles City County, in Virginia's Tidewater, less than a year after George Washington's first inauguration, with the exception of a dozen years in nearby Gloucester County and the colonial capital of Williamsburg, his permanent residence for the other six decades of his life was in his native

Charles City, one of the oldest counties in that oldest section of that Oldest Dominion. He became both exemplar of and spokesman for the dominant rural squirearchy, representing and embodying the strictest sect of Old-School Republicanism. His father, Judge John Tyler, had served in the Virginia legislature, was elected to a maximum-possible three terms as governor, served for many years as judge of the general court of Virginia, and at his death was judge of the federal district court of eastern Virginia. Through both his parents and by an early marriage to Letitia Christian of a neighboring county, Tyler was well connected with the plantation elite of the James–York Peninsula.

Tyler himself possessed talents that would enable him to translate the advantages of birth and position into political leadership very early in life. Discounting the partisan vitriol of his enemies, by general accounts this six-foot Virginian was thought to be attractive in appearance, even handsome to some, amiable and cordial in manner, endowed with a good mind, and an able speaker. Charles Dickens, not inclined to be overly kind to things American, met Tyler during his presidency and wrote of him that "the expression on his face was mild and pleasant, and his manner was remarkably unaffected, gentlemanly, and agreeable. I thought that, in his carriage and demeanor, he became his position singularly well."

A graduate of William and Mary College at the age of seventeen, admitted to the bar at twenty, he was barely twenty-one when he won a seat in the Virginia House of Delegates in 1811. He served five successive terms in that body, during which time he was elected to the executive council of state. From the Virginia House he was elevated in 1816 to the U.S. House of Representatives at the age of twenty-six. He resigned from the federal House in 1821, was returned to Virginia's lower house in 1823, and resigned in 1825 to assume the governorship of the state. He resigned from the governorship to take a seat in the U.S. Senate, where he remained until his resignation in 1836.

During this first quarter-century of his political career, Tyler was a thoroughgoing and consistent champion of Old Republicanism of the very starched variety. His convictions well illustrate the minds of those popular and legislative majorities who chose him to be their spokesman. Tyler would have nothing of an "American system" and spoke and voted against those chief agencies of economic nationalism: the National Bank, protective tariffs, and federal subsidies for roads and canals. In the Missouri Crisis of 1819–20, he insisted that the federal government had no right to exclude slavery from the territories. In Virginia he opposed reformers' efforts to bring a greater degree of democracy to the commonwealth.

In 1811, when only twenty-one, the young legislator introduced resolutions of censure directed against Virginia's two senators for defying legislative instructions to vote against recharter of the First National Bank. He served on a committee to investigate the Second Bank in 1818, concurred with the committee report denouncing the bank's practice, and in a lengthy speech declared that the bank had been unconstitutional in the first place, and because it had so grossly violated its charter, the charter should be annulled. He voted against recharter of the Second Bank as a senator in 1832, and joined the successful effort to sustain Andrew Jackson's veto of the recharter bill.

In 1816, a month after taking his seat in the House of Representatives, Tyler joined a majority of Virginians east of the Blue Ridge in opposing John C. Calhoun's Bonus Bill, by which the federal government was to provide a fixed annual subsidy to construct roads and canals. The federal government had no authority for such endeavors, Tyler maintained, and the Richmond *Enquirer* published a letter from the congressman to his constituents in which he said that the state of Virginia was not "in so poor a condition as to require a *charitable* donation from Congress." In his first speech as a senator, he denounced a proposed appropriation to extend the Cumberland Road; it was unconstitutional, and bad policy to boot, according to Tyler. Among many objections, he deplored the federal patronage that would be created. As governor, he had denounced such appropriations as bribes. In opposing the Maysville Road Bill in 1830, he warned of a dangerous expansion of a national authority, and expressed the concept of "federal republicanism" so characteristic of gentlemen of his stripe:

> I have no such word (as national) in my political vocabulary. A nation of twenty-four nations is an idea which I cannot realize. A confederacy may embrace many nations; but by what process twenty-four can be converted into one, I am still to learn.

This doctrine was the basis for Tyler's Senate denunciation of Jackson's Force Bill on February 6, 1833.

With all the invective hurled against bank and federal subsidies, it was the protective tariff that most excited—and unified—southerners of the middle and lower regions (those that later would join the Confederacy, that is) during the 1820s and early 1830s. Protectionism was indeed a levy on exporters of southern staples to benefit a manufacturing interest concentrated in the free states, and demands for higher levies came with the depression that followed the Panic of 1819. Tyler was in the House of Representatives in 1820 when the first depression-era demands reached the Congress, and he became a major spokesman of the antitariff forces. Not only was a protective tariff clearly unconstitutional, but it was also an unjust levy by one section of the Union on another. Tyler warned of a cyclical pattern of tariff hikes as one set of manufacturers after another, who could not compete in the free marketplace, were "protected" into being; as Jefferson before him, Tyler believed that the seemingly endless supply of land in the United States destined the country to be primarily agricultural; the artificial encouragement of manufacturing "would subvert the order of Heaven itself." The iniquitous Tariff of Abominations of 1828 was "a curse on the whole South." Even the Tariff of 1832 that, by lowering a number of nonprotective duties, won the support of a majority of Virginia's house delegation, was unacceptable to Tyler. He delivered a three-day assault on the bill, denouncing it, among many reasons, for raising consumers' prices. "It cripples the farming interest of the Union," he charged, not without justice for those who exported their produce, with no concurrent benefits from the growth of towns and cities as home markets for their foodstuffs. It was this tariff that South Carolina was to nullify in November 1832.

The Missouri Crisis erupted during Tyler's second term in the House, and he became a spokesman for the more intransigent segment of southerners. He took an unyielding stand on the right of slaveholders to take their slaves into federal territories; this was to characterize him for the rest of his life. He was among those southerners who professed slavery to be an evil, a profession shared by virtually all who spoke during the Missouri debates, as well as by the Virginians of the notable antislavery debates in the legislature a dozen years later. Tyler and a great majority of his fellow southerners were adamantly hostile, however, to what seemed to them as dangerous outside meddling with the institution. Tyler's speech of February 17, 1820, was as clear an exposition as the House would hear of the widely held southern argument by which they could profess hostility to the institution at the same time that they urged its expansion into new territories. This was the "diffusion" argument, whereby it was maintained that, by spreading slaves more thinly over the territories, the concentration of bondsmen and bondswomen in the older slave states would be alleviated, thus allowing them to think more readily of some form of emancipation. With the importation of slaves made illegal, there would be no new slaves; they would simply be "diffused."

Tyler correctly pointed to the fact that gradual emancipation had been begun where there were the fewest slaves. "What enabled New York, Pennsylvania, and other states to adopt the language of universal emancipation?" Tyler questioned rhetorically. "Rely on it, nothing but the paucity of the number of their slaves. That which would have been criminal in these states not to have done would be an act of political suicide in Georgia or South Carolina." When the Missouri Compromise was presented to the House in segments, Tyler joined a unanimous southern delegation to remove the antislave restriction on Missouri. He was, however, with a majority of his fellow Virginians, and roughly half the slave-state delegation, in rejecting the ban on slavery in the remainder of the Louisiana Purchase territory above the 36°30′ parallel. It was an unconstitutional restriction, Tyler believed, and in later years he was to write that the South, by yielding on this point in 1820, had brought upon itself much of its subsequent difficulties.

Tyler also, as spokesman for the plantation elite, opposed efforts to push Virginia in the direction of white male democracy. As a member of the legislature in 1825 he had opposed demands for a convention to reform the constitution of 1776. During his years as senator, he rather reluctantly served in that "assembly of notables" that was the constitutional convention of 1829–30; he did not care to antagonize western reformers or eastern conservatives lest he lose support in his struggle against federal encroachment. He took little part in the proceeding but voted with the conservatives to retain a property qualification for suffrage, against making white population the sole basis for representation in the legislature, and against popular election of the governors. Tyler had, in the federal House in 1818, taken a procreditor stand in opposing a federal bankruptcy law.

Tyler's legislative elections to both the governorship and the Senate demonstrated quite clearly the political direction in which the state seemed to be moving. When first elected to the U.S. House in 1816, his Old Republicanism had put him in a rather small minority within the Virginia delegation, let alone in the rest of the country. Missouri and the depression-born tariffs had pushed Virginia and much of the middle and lower South in the direction of strict construction and states' rights, on many issues at least. Reconciling such views within the nation at large was to become increasingly difficult, however. With the development of a national two-party system—Andrew Jackson versus his opposition, more or less—the dilemma for ambitious political leaders was to choose that party most congenial to their principles and to their desire for political

preferment. What proved to be Tyler's wrong choice of national party led, after his accidental election to the White House, to his sixteen-year elimination from the political scene, both in the state and in the nation.

Tyler was born when Virginia was by far the most populous state, and during his first thirty-five years he would only have had a boyhood memory of the only four years in which a Virginian did not occupy the presidency. "The Virginia Dynasty" came to an abrupt end, however, with the completion of James Monroe's second term in 1825. Tyler, with a large majority of Virginians, supported that most logical heir of The Dynasty, William H. Crawford of Georgia. When Crawford came in third in a field of four candidates and a second Adams from Massachusetts was chosen president in the House, it was indeed the end of an era—not only so, but President Adams's expansive nationalism created a virtually one-party region in presidential balloting among the states that would one day join the Confederacy. The only question was the most propitious means of sending the president back to his native state. Adams suffered dearly at the hands of southerners. He was to have ample opportunities for vengeance, not least of which was his memorable diary. On the day of Harrison's death, attempting to absorb the idea of a Tyler presidency, he said of the new chief executive that he was "a political sectarian of the slave-driving, Virginia, Jeffersonian school . . ." and other such niceties.

Tyler was a rather reluctant latecomer to the coalition that put Jackson in the White House in 1828; it was a choice of evils for that Virginian. Tyler was most definitely not among those Virginians, led by Thomas Ritchie, editor of the Richmond *Enquirer*, who forged an alliance with Martin Van Buren of New York, an alliance that did much to secure Jackson's victory. Tyler was, rather, friendly to the interest of Calhoun, Jackson's vice president, erstwhile nationalist; Calhoun had, in fact, suggested Tyler's name to Jackson as secretary of state. When Calhoun fell from the president's favor and Van Buren emerged as heir apparent, Tyler was in a faction of very restless Jacksonians in his state. The Hero of New Orleans was enormously popular among Virginia voters; he won staggering majorities in Virginia and in the other states of the middle and lower South in both 1828 and 1832—with the exception of South Carolina in 1832. Tyler could not quarrel with Jackson's vetoes of the bank and the Maysville Road. What the cryptic Calhounites needed was an issue that would arouse the voters, and Jackson obliged them with his Nullification Proclamation.

It is difficult to find a political leader in Virginia who openly espoused the doctrine of nullification, and not many more to justify fully South Carolina's use of it in late 1832. Certainly Tyler did not endorse the doctrine, although he thought South Carolina and the rest of the South to be much injured by the tariffs. But Jackson's proclamation was another matter. The president denied the right of peaceful secession, that sword in the attic for many a southerner, and his Force Bill threatened military coercion to enforce federal law in South Carolina. For a time it looked as if east Virginia would desert the president *en masse*. Tyler talked of the imminence of civil war and urged Virginians to stand fast in the defense of their principles. In his speech denouncing the Force Bill delivered in the Senate in February 1833, Tyler scoffed at the idea of an American "nation." Each individual state was a nation and, acting together, they had created a confederacy, the United States of America. A state convention had taken Virginia into the union, and a state convention called for that purpose could take her out. Southerners would defend themselves against such a "consolidated despotism" as Jackson threatened.

It was in the midst of this crisis that Tyler was reelected to the Senate. His first election, in 1827, had been made possible by the support of a solid base of the National Republican minority, plus those states' righters who thought the Ritchie faction's candidate, the irascible John Randolph, was a bit too much. In his second election, Tyler's support came from National Republicans (Henry Clay himself urged a supporter in the Virginia legislature to cast his vote for Tyler) and the extreme states' righters. It was a coalition of opposites—they had little in common save opposition to President Jackson—but it was an alliance Tyler worked to maintain until it proved, in his presidency, impossible to hold together. Tyler later claimed that it was he who suggested the Compromise Tariff of 1833 to Clay, a law that lowered the tariff significantly over a period of nine years. Whoever suggested it, the crisis was resolved; whatever threat of civil war there might have been was defused.

Following the crisis, Ritchie and a large number of east Virginians returned to Jackson's Democratic Party. Another group, which might be loosely called the extreme states' righters, possibly rivaling in numbers the Jacksonians in east Virginia—at first—left the Democratic Party. Jackson once again obliged them with an issue, the issue through which southerners such as Tyler could cement a political union with National Republicanism, arguably the least logical alliance in the history of American parties.

It was in Tyler's second term in the Senate that President Jackson, in an effort to weaken the dying Second Bank, determined to make no further deposits of federal money in the institution. To Tyler and others of his faction, this was executive usurpation. In a long and vigorous speech in the Senate delivered in February 1834, Tyler denounced the president's action as a violation of the bank's charter; it was a "flagrant assumption of power" by the chief executive. Tyler joined Clay and Calhoun in passing senate resolutions of censure: the president had assumed an "authority and power not conferred by the Constitution and laws." So was born the Whig Party, with a common purpose of curbing executive usurpation.

In the meanwhile, in Richmond, a Whig majority in the legislature celebrated its success by instructing Virginia's two senators to vote for the censure, as if they needed such instruction. Unfortunately for Tyler and the Whigs, Democrats won control of the legislature in 1835, and that body instructed the Virginia senators to expunge the censure from the record. Much to the chagrin of many Whigs, and particularly distressing to the other Whig senator who kept his seat, Tyler resigned from the Senate rather than obey the instructions. His decision was in keeping with previously expressed opinions as to the right of instruction. It was a decision also in keeping with his theories of state sovereignty; by right of legislative instruction, it was almost as if senators were ambassadors from sovereign entities. However consistent he may have been, Tyler's resignation from the Senate in February 1836 was the worst political defeat he had suffered. He was a casualty of the two-party system that now embraced Virginia, the South, and indeed the nation at large. There was, however, consolation for the Virginian when, later in 1836, he was nominated for the vice presidency to run with Hugh Lawson White on a Southern Whig ticket.

White carried only two states, but Jackson's astonishing majorities in the middle and lower South in 1828 and 1832 shrank to a bare popular majority for Van Buren, Jackson's hand-picked successor. Virginia and other states of the future Confederacy had for the first time given a majority of their popular and electoral votes to a northern candidate, but the region had also for the first time been almost evenly split in its political allegiance. Tyler had, in fact, run better than White. Maryland chose electors for the northern and western Whig candidate, William Henry Harrison, but those electors cast votes for John Tyler as vice president. South Carolina went its independent way, choosing electors for Willie P. Magnum as an expression of gratitude for support in its crisis, and the same electors voted for Tyler as vice president, for services he had rendered.

Even historians most inclined to give Tyler a sympathetic hearing have been known to fault him for not following Calhoun and other states' rights Whigs back to the Democratic Party in the late 1830s. On the other hand, *if* he had not been catapulted into the presidency in 1841, one can well imagine Tyler finding reasons to support Whig candidates so long as they supported him in return. He was elected as a Whig to the Virginia House in 1838, and that amorphous party chose their ex-senator as Speaker. Tyler spoke well of Clay—they were friends of long standing—and of Clay's distribution bill, then being debated in Congress. Clay himself contributed to Tyler's decision not to switch parties. In the 1830s, the Kentuckian was positioning himself to win Whigs

of both North and South in his run for the presidency in 1840. Without repudiating any of his economic nationalism, he declared himself ready to postpone its chief measures: state activity lessened the demand for federal aid to transportation systems. The Compromise Tariff of 1833, his own work, had put that issue at rest for at least nine years; the voters were evidently not ready to support a bank recharter at that time. Not only that, Clay professed to see the greatest threat to the Union in the abolition movement.

It was hardly surprising that southern Whigs flocked to his support and Tyler was in the forefront. So great was Tyler's commitment to Clay that it was said that he wept when the Whigs rejected the Kentuckian in their nominating convention, passing him over in favor of their military hero, William Henry Harrison of Indiana. Under those circumstances, as it turned out, John Tyler was as "available" a vice-presidential candidate as there had ever been: he was both a prime supporter of the defeated candidate, and his nomination would be a gesture to the southern states' righters who had not deserted to the Democrats.

It was a measure of the hype and buncombe of the presidential election of 1840 that the Whigs, with great acumen, did not present a platform to the voters. It was all "Log Cabin and Hard Cider," "Tippecanoe and Tyler Too," while the issues that so often bedeviled the politicians were laid to rest for the duration. It had some of the stuff of modern politics, and indeed something of modern political organization was emerging, encouraging, and responding to the popular excitement. The number of Americans who went to the polls in 1840 represented a two-thirds increase over the number of voters in 1836; in the middle and lower South, the increase was a whopping 80 percent. With a presidential candidate known to the general public as a slaughterer of Indians, and for the alleged simplicity of his lifestyle, and with southerners such as Tyler not only still in the party but recognized on the ticket, the middle and lower South gave "Tip and Tyler" the largest popular and electoral majorities any Whig presidential candidate ever received.

Tyler's services as vice president, with the possible exception of Andrew Johnson, were the least eventful in a long succession of uneventful vice presidencies. After being sworn in, in the presence of the accustomed dignitaries assembled in the senate chamber, Tyler delivered a brief homily containing a reference to the senators assembled before him as "the immediate representatives of the States, by whose sovereign will the Government has been spoken into existence." The gathering adjourned shortly thereafter to accompany Harrison to the east portico of the Capitol, where he took his oath of office and delivered his lengthy inaugural address. As vice president, Tyler then chaired a session of the Senate that approved with unanimity President Harrison's choice of cabinet officers. The Virginian was now free to return to his home in Williamsburg; with the paucity of vice-presidential functions, he had every right to anticipate four years of relative independence, couched in obscurity. Within weeks, loud knocks on his door at 5:30 of a Monday morning introduced messengers from Washington informing Tyler that the president was dead. Geographical propinquity and the railroad made it possible that only a fifty-three-hour interval separated the death of one president and the accession of another.

If George Washington was called upon to set all manner of precedents in the conduct of the presidency, John Tyler was called upon by fate to blaze a path for subsequent vice presidents succeeding to the presidency. Fifty-two years had elapsed under the federal constitution with no death or other removal of a president. However, since Tyler's accidental accession in 1841, four assassinations, three deaths by natural causes (wild fancy has supposed that two of them were by assassinations), and one resignation have meant that at no time since 1841 has there been an interval of uninterrupted presidential administrations half so long as that first half-century.

Tyler's presidency is, of course, the period of his life most familiar to historians and to the general reader; naturally enough, these years have been most subjected to scholarly scrutiny. He managed to become "the President without a Party"; his tiny "Corporal's Guard" of loyal supporters in Congress constitute a sort of record for minimal allegiance. The generality of historians of the United States, it would be fair to say, have assigned to his role as president a ranking of below average at best. A few specialized studies of his presidency have reminded us that, despite Tyler's failure to generate a coalition to support his reelection in 1844, third party or otherwise, his vetoes, like Jackson's before him, sustained by Congress, helped set the course of American political life. Certainly, if Jackson's veto killed the Second National Bank, Tyler's vetoes aborted the birth of a third. Likewise in diplomatic matters of foreign policy, where the chief executive has more freedom to initiate policy, very significant and positive achievements resulted, and, for weal or woe, Tyler himself and his administrators did much to initiate the process by which Texas was annexed during the closing days of his administration.

First of all, as indicated earlier, there was the question as to whether he were a mere acting president. After Harrison's death, the Harrison cabinet first addressed Tyler as vice president. Some in both parties considered him as caretaker, a regent, officially the Acting President, "His Accidency" in scorn. Some among modern historians have questioned the soundness of Tyler's argument, but Tyler insisted upon the title and full function as president, equal to any other president, and it was accorded to him and to his successors. In the words of one modern historian, it was "a constitutional coup."

As to the possibility of chartering a Third National Bank or some reasonable facsimile thereof, it is certainly possible the gridlock between president and Congress could be attributed to either or both of the parties to the conflict. Tyler has been said to have planned from the beginning of his administration to use the bank or anything else to gain renomination in 1844. Senator Clay, most assuredly embittered by Harrison's nomination in 1840, at first consoled himself with Harrison's pledge to serve but a single term. Clay was the unquestioned leader of the Whig majorities in Congress, and a majority of Harrison's cabinet were active in his interest. Harrison, in fact, had felt called upon to remind the Kentuckian that it was he, Harrison, who was president. The accession of Tyler meant the replacement of the oldest president before Ronald Reagan by the youngest in the first half-century under the Constitution. Something, at any rate, led the Kentuckian to conclude that his earlier talk of no popular demand for a bank was untrue as of 1841. There was no difficulty in persuading the Whig Congress to ratify Clay's decision.

Tyler most probably decided early on to veto this would-be Third Bank, although ten days elapsed between the time Tyler received the bill and the submission of his veto. Everything in Tyler's career justified his claim that his opposition to a national bank on constitutional grounds "has been uniformly proclaimed." Tyler's veto brought such jubilation among Democrats that the president here, and afterwards, entertained the forlorn hope that they might accept him as their leader; Democrats might contribute mightily to sustaining his vetoes and afterward rejoice at the defeat of the bank, but they had their own chieftains who would profit from the issue. From Whigs came a storm of protest, although many of their leaders were conciliatory, hoping to tailor a new bill to satisfy the president's constitutional scruples. In the Senate they had been able to muster only a one-vote majority to override Tyler's veto.

The second bank fight presents more ambiguities. The Whigs did construct a proposal—a Fiscal Corporation—more in keeping with the president's sensitivities; the president gave evidence of vacillating before making his final decision. The sincerity of Clay's overtures has been questioned, as has the degree of Tyler's approval on first being presented the outlines of the Fiscal Corporation. Of many accommodations in the new bill, perhaps the most striking example was the claim that this "Corporation was to be established by Congress in its duly recognized authority as the legislature of the District of Columbia." Just as state governments were chartering a great multitude of state banks, so might Congress establish a bank in the district. In Tyler's veto was the rejoinder that because Con-

gress was creating a bank designed to do business in all of the states, it was acting in its capacity as a national legislature. However much he may have vacillated, the president did finally veto the Fiscal Corporation, and it was this veto that brought down the full fury of Whig vituperation upon Tyler, a venom scarcely matched in American political history. The Lexington *Kentucky Intelligencer* caught the savagery of it: "If a God-directed thunderbolt were to strike and annihilate the traitor, all would say that 'Heaven is just.'" Four days after the House received Tyler's veto, a caucus of fifty or so Whig members met and formally drummed the president out of their party.

To be sure, Tyler's "victory" was a negative one, and it cost him the party that had brought him to the presidency, but a National Bank similar to the first or second, or of either of the two Whig proposals, rather quickly left the center stage of American political debate. The Whig platform of 1844 made no mention of a national bank. It was not only that Tyler had aborted the birth of a Third National Bank, but the erosion of interest in such an institution suggests that, on this one issue, at least, Tyler spoke with the voice of the people. How much happier would he have been as a Democrat.

Tyler's six vetoes were two more than those of Andrew Jackson. Counting pocket vetoes, Jackson in his two terms had the advantage. Between the two of them, they submitted more than two-thirds of all presidential vetoes from the beginning of the Republic through Tyler's administration. Tyler was the first president to have a veto overridden—that of a naval appropriation bill—but on the larger issues, Democratic minorities plus the minuscule Corporal's Guard were numerous enough to sustain him.

Another significant issue on which Tyler used his veto to influence the course of political history was to intertwined issues of the tariffs and Clay's pet project of distribution. The two issues meshed nicely in Clay's arsenal of economic nationalism. By distributing to the states federal money derived from the sale of public lands, not only were many states happy to receive federal subsidies, but by giving money to the states the federal government could more readily justify higher tariffs to meet its expenses. Tyler had kind words to say of distribution in the late 1830s, but times were hard in the early 1840s. The federal government was spending more money than it was taking in, and President Tyler did abhor a national debt; frugality was an essence of Old Republicanism. This arch antiprotectionist did agree that the tariff needed to be raised above levels set by the Compromise Tariff of 1833, but that was a tariff for revenue only. Tyler would not hear of raising the tariff while at the same time giving money to the states. Twice he vetoed Whig bills that combined distribution with and increase in the tariff. This did nothing to alleviate Whig hostility, especially as Democrats were able to sustain the vetoes. Tyler signed into law a tariff bill in 1842, one that raised duties above the Compromise Tariff level, and for that he was denounced by some Democrats, for whom any rise in the level of protection was anathema.

On one significant issue Tyler could agree with the Whig leadership in Congress, one that came up before Tyler was drummed out of the party. Harrison's predecessor in the White House, the Democrat Van Buren and his party, had ceased depositing money in state banks because political favoritism was too likely to affect the choice of state banks as repositories. Federal money was then put in what amounted to a government vault, the Subtreasury, the system itself being known as the Independent Treasury. Tyler, by contrast, and the Whig majorities preferred to keep federal money in state banks. It seeded their capital, thus making credit more available, and in general strengthened the state institutions. The Whig majorities readily produced a bill to repeal the Subtreasury, and Tyler signed it into law at almost the same moment he vetoed the first bank bill. Democratic dismay over the former was tempered by their jubilation over the latter, a mirror opposite of the Whig reaction. On neither the tariff nor the Subtreasury did Tyler's approval have any permanent effect: Democrats returned to power after Tyler's single term, and they lowered the tariff and reinstituted the Independent Treasury. Tariffs stayed low until southern secession, and the Independent Treasury survived the Civil War by some decades.

It was in the realm of foreign affairs that the achievements of the Tyler administration were positive—in the sense that they were not accomplished by the veto, and, in significant areas, in the sense that the achievements have rated general applause from the community of historians.

When Harrison's cabinet resigned after Tyler's bank vetoes, one stayed on: Secretary of State Daniel Webster. Webster was engaged in delicate negotiations with the British concerning a number of issues, the most dangerous of which was the disputed boundary between Maine and New Brunswick. War had been threatened in the disputed area in 1839, and there was fear of renewed violence at any time. Frederick Merk, in a volume cited below, has credited Tyler himself and other members of his administration with an innovative use of propaganda to persuade the residents of Maine to abandon an obstinate resistance to compromise and to accept the treaty settlement, which was, in effect, splitting the difference. The Webster-Ashburton Treaty of 1842 settled more than the Maine boundary, but the resolution of that dispute was its most signal accomplishment. President Tyler also dispatched Caleb Cushing of Massachusetts to China to negotiate a commercial treaty. The resulting Treat of Wanghia (1844) gained for the United States access to ports already opened to the British, most-favored-nation privileges, and rights of extraterritoriality. Cushing's treaty, as Webster's before it, won approval in the Senate.

Tyler's efforts to annex Texas were manifestly a part of his effort to win a presidential nomination in 1844, and that resulted in part from a desire to see the addition of new slave territory to the United States. He defended the expansion of slavery with the "diffusion" argument he had expounded in the Missouri Crisis two decades earlier. Unquestionably Tyler deserves much credit for bringing Texas annexation to the center stage of national politics. In so doing he helped break the sectional equilibrium that made possible the national two-party system of Whig versus Democrat, which in so many ways transcended sectional boundaries. As late as the votes in Congress on Texas annexation in early 1845, members of Congress voted in great degrees as party members, not as southerners or northerners. It was the right to take slaves to federal territories versus the right to exclude slavery from the territories that brought the sections to the brink of disunion. Agitating the Texas question in the 1840s was a huge step in the process by which parties were ultimately sectionalized.

James Knox Polk, the Democratic nominee in 1844, temporarily nationalized the annexation issue by promising Oregon to the free states and Texas to the slave. Tyler also had interests in Oregon. Webster and Ashburton had wrestled with the border question. Tyler insisted on the forty-ninth parallel as the line of division between the United States and Canada, as did Polk in 1846, but the British were not ready to deal in 1842 as they were with the bellicose Polk in 1846. Tyler also favored the construction of U.S. forts to protect settlers on the way to Oregon, the U.S. portion of which was to be organized as free territory in 1846, but what Tyler might have wanted to do does not justify what he did: push for Texas annexation with no compensating territory for the free states.

The chief difficulty for Tyler and his lieutenants—and some of his nominal lieutenants acted as if they were the generals—was to win the support of enough northern senators to give the two-thirds majority necessary to ratify a treaty of annexation. Other than elaborations of the diffusion argument, the principal tactic was to play the British card. Once again the engines of propaganda rolled: without Texas annexation, the United States might awaken one fine day and find John Bull ensconced on its southwestern frontier. For southern audiences, the British threat had a more sinister element: John Bull was plotting to abolish slavery in Texas. Tyler himself refused to endorse the charge that Britain was plotting to emancipate the Texas slaves—refused, in fact, until British Foreign Secretary Lord Aberdeen declared in the House of Lords in August 1843 that Her Majesty's government hoped to persuade Mexico to recognize the independence of the Republic of Texas in exchange for the abolition of slavery in the latter. The aging Democratic chieftain An-

drew Jackson was enlisted in the cause of annexation; on the other hand, Tyler's appointment of Calhoun as secretary of state did nothing to win northern support for the project. Calhoun, far more than Tyler, pursued southern ends, with less concern for parties and sectional adjustment. For the secretary of state, if the South were united, the North would have to accommodate it—or else. With Tyler there was always the hope that Texas might be his guarantee of a presidential nomination in 1844.

With Calhoun managing the State Department, a treaty of annexation was agreed to by representatives of two republics, Texas and the United States, and submitted to the Senate in April 1844. It was a disaster for the annexationists: more than two-thirds of the senators voted *against* the treaty. It was a vote both partisan and sectional, but more partisan than sectional. Of twelve northern Democrats, five joined all the southern Democrats in favor; a Mississippian was the only Whig to vote for annexation. With the hindsight of so many votes during the Tyler administration, it was demonstrated with great clarity to which party the president should have adhered. In Tyler's mind, those same figures might have illustrated the possibilities of his political advancement, as well as the possibilities for Texas annexation.

Any hope that Texas might further the president's ambitions rested on the assumption that the major party nominees would continue the eight-year practice of excluding Texas annexation from partisan controversy, and as candidates began to jockey for position in early 1844, the exclusion of Texas seemed a strong likelihood. The strongest candidates for each party, Clay for the Whigs and Van Buren for the Democrats, gave every indication that Texas would not be an issue, and what an opportunity that would be for President Tyler! That enthusiastic unanimity among southern Democratic senators! That near-half of northern Democrats voting for a Tyler treaty! Perhaps even southern Whigs might be persuaded to see their true sectional interest. With a solid southern base and a strong northern minority—James Buchanan's winning combination in 1856—the presidency itself was a possibility. But it was to be others who reaped where Tyler had sown.

The principal results of Tyler's Texas policy among southern Democrats, as it turned out, were, first, to rouse their enthusiasm for, and excite their hopes that, Texas might be had. It was not long before that translated itself into a determination not to support a Democratic candidate who would not declare himself for Texas annexation.

It is perhaps idle to speculate on what might have been—for Tyler *and* the nation—if the majority of delegates to the Democratic convention, a majority Van Buren possessed, had been sufficient to nominate. Then there would indeed have been a third-party, pro-Texas Tyler candidacy that might well have drawn large numbers of southern defectors from the Democratic candidate—large enough numbers to throw the election to Tyler's nemesis, Whig candidate Henry Clay, but enough defectors to pull the Democratic Party southward in the near future. But a majority of the delegates was not enough; Van Buren needed two-thirds, and that he could not get. The convention finally turned to Polk of Tennessee, whose broad-scale annexationism reduced a Tyler candidacy to irrelevancy. Tyler's friends had engineered a convention in Baltimore in late May 1844, timed to coincide with the Democratic convention. That meant that Tyler was informed of his nomination exactly one day before the exhausted Democrats turned unanimously to Polk. Even so, the Tyler candidacy worried the Democrats to the extent that considerable effort was expended to persuade Tyler to withdraw. Tyler did finally bow out, but not until August 20 was his decision made public.

With all the correct stands on major issues, Polk rolled up the largest Democratic majority of popular votes in the middle and lower South in the twenty years between Jackson and Franklin Pierce. His support elsewhere was thin enough to make him, by a gnat's eyelash, a plurality winner in the nation at large.

Through forces over which Tyler had little control but which received his eager support, Texas annexation was accomplished in the last days of his presidency. Winning a two-thirds majority for a treaty of annexation in the Whig-controlled Senate was an impossibility, so the measure was achieved through joint resolutions of the houses, requiring only a majority in each. It was a party triumph. Every Democratic senator, North and South, voted for annexation; their narrow victory in the face of a slim Whig majority was made possible by the support of annexation by three of fifteen southern Whigs. The Democratic-controlled House concurred by a heavily partisan vote. Those majorities were the sort of figures of which Tyler might once have dreamed. In the meantime, Tyler had made a belated return to the Democratic Party. He voted for Polk in 1844 and thereafter supported Democratic candidates for as long as he lived—which meant Southern Democrat John C. Breckinridge in 1860.

Some among modern historians of the South have given Tyler an eminence in history scarcely imagined by either his contemporaries or previous historians. A recent two-volume history of the South by William J. Cooper, Jr., and Thomas E. Terrill contains this startling assessment: "Usually dismissed as an unimportant president, John Tyler was in fact of enormous importance. Between 1815 and 1860 only Andrew Jackson and John C. Calhoun had more influence on southern politics, and a legitimate argument can be made that Tyler ranked with the other two." Tyler is granted this extraordinary ranking because he deliberately used the issue to stir southern passions on slavery: "Texas could cause such a thunderous reaction because it touched the raw nerve of southern politics." And again, "Texas obliterated economics. The Texas issue proved again that in the South nothing could withstand the force of a political issue closely connected with slavery and liberty." Thus can yesterday's image of a hapless and beleaguered president, with no claim to any major significance, be transformed, not into a great president, but one of the greatest significance in stirring up the worst in the southern psyche.

In an entirely different vein, several recent studies of Tyler's presidency, concerned more with conventional "successes" and "failures," have rather balanced the two concerning both

Tyler and his administration. Norma Lois Peterson, in a volume listed below, wrote of Tyler's presidency that it "was flawed as, to a greater or lesser extent, all presidencies are, but it was not a failure. On numerous occasions he demonstrated exemplary executive skill and common sense." One wonders if Peterson and professors Cooper and Terrill are describing the same human being.

Tyler left the White House to take up permanent residence in his new home, called Sherwood Forest, located in his native county of Charles City. In the years of his involuntary political exile, he did have the leisure to enjoy his many children and his young second wife, to whom he had been married for less than a year when he retired from the presidency. Tyler was a genuinely good husband and a good father; there is much to suggest it and nothing to suggest otherwise. He had married his first wife, Letitia Christian, on his twenty-third birthday. She bore him several children who survived infancy, including two sons who would become officials of the Confederate government. She was admirably suited by nature and social custom to fulfill the role of hostess in the governor's mansion when her husband was its occupant. She suffered a stroke before Tyler entered the White House, was paralyzed, and died less than a year and a half after the beginning of Tyler's presidency. Within two years, President Tyler was married for the second time—to Julia Gardiner whose father had been killed by the same tragic *Princeton* explosion that had also killed two members of Tyler's cabinet.

Tyler was fifty-four and Julia twenty-four when they were married less than a year before leaving the White House. Despite the difference in their ages, they obviously cared much for each other; they richly deserved that cliché, "they had a happy marriage." Robert Seager, by an intelligent and resourceful use of correspondence and other sources, leaves us little room to doubt. In a recent doctoral dissertation, Julia is portrayed as an independent figure in her own right, especially in the years after her husband's death. Julia bore her husband seven children, the youngest born when the father was seventy. Julia's oldest son, David Gardiner, named for her father, served, like his father, in the House of Representatives and as a judge of a Virginia circuit court. Another of Julia's sons, Lyon G. Tyler, became a historian and was for many years president of the College of William and Mary. He edited and published a great number of family manuscripts, most of them relating to his father, and conducted during his lifetime a spirited defense of his father's career.

Ex-president Tyler was returned to public life during the secession crisis. At the age of seventy, Tyler was sent by his native state as a delegate to the Washington Peace Conference in January 1861 when the lower South was in the process of withdrawing from Union. Tyler had no great hopes for this last-gasp search for some form of compromise that might prevent secession and civil war. As the attendant ex-president, Tyler was made president of the conference. He and the Virginia delegation voted against the recommendation of the conference—they proposed the revival of that 36°30' line—and he returned to Virginia ready for secession.

REFERENCES

The Letters and Times of John Tyler, Lyon G. Tyler, ed., 3 vols. (1884–96: reprint, New York: DaCapo Press, 1970); Oliver P. Chitwood, *John Tyler, Champion of the Old South* (New York: Appleton-Century, 1939); Robert Seager II, *And Tyler Too: A Biography of John and Julia Gardiner Tyler* (New York: McGraw-Hill, 1963); Norma Lois Peterson, *The Presidencies of William Henry Harrison and John Tyler* (Lawrence, Kans.: University Press of Kansas, 1989); Frederick Merk, *Fruits of Propaganda in the Tyler Administration* (Cambridge, Mass.: Harvard University Press, 1971); Robert J. Morgan, *A Whig Embattled: The Presidency Under John Tyler* (Lincoln: University of Nebraska Press, 1954); Theodore Delaney, "Julia Gardiner Tyler" (Ph.D. diss., College of William and Mary, 1995).

M. BOYD COYNER, JR., is a native of Lynchburg, Virginia, and received his B.A., M.A., and Ph.D. degrees from the University of Virginia. He taught history at Southwestern at Memphis (now Rhodes College), Hampden-Sydney College, and the College of William and Mary, where he is now professor emeritus. He has taught many advanced undergraduate and graduate courses in various aspects of the Old South and slavery.

GEORGE MIFFLIN DALLAS (1792–1864)

Vice President, 1845–1849

(President James K. Polk)

GEORGE MIFFLIN DALLAS
(Library of Congress)

By John M. Belohlavek

George Mifflin Dallas, the scion of a powerful Philadelphia family, pursued Jeffersonian politics with a Federalist mindset. Born of patrician cultural tastes and political values, he would seem to have been more comfortable as a Whig rather than a Jacksonian. Yet, Dallas hoisted the banner of "Old Hickory" and became a force in Pennsylvania politics for over a generation as United States senator, minister to two countries, and vice president under James K. Polk. Controversy marked his tenure in the Polk administration, including a heated tariff debate, the question of slavery in the territories, and the explosive expansionism of the Mexican War. Although he played an outspoken and sometimes courageous role as vice president, the coyly ambitious Dallas received neither the recognition he desired nor the party's nomination he awaited.

Dallas benefited greatly from the mentoring of his father, Alexander. The elder Dallas, a lawyer-politician, achieved social prominence and political stature that culminated in his appointment as secretary of the treasury under James

Madison. Alexander named his second son, George Mifflin, born July 10, 1792, after Democratic-Republican friend and ally, Governor Thomas Mifflin. The Dallas family enjoyed an elegant lifestyle, with a mansion on Fourth Street and a country house ("Devon") on the Schuykill River. Young George received an appropriate education—Quaker preparatory schools and Princeton University, where he became valedictorian of the class of 1810. He began his legal studies soon thereafter, but they were fortuitously interrupted by the War of 1812.

Early in 1813, Albert Gallatin received an appointment to travel to Russia to seek the czar's mediation to end a conflict with Great Britain over international shipping rights. George Dallas prevailed upon the old family friend to take him along as his private secretary. The two-year sojourn in Russia, England, and the Netherlands matured Dallas and prepared him to take on new responsibilities at home. Upon his return in October 1814, he began a brief stint in Washington in a minor treasury post before moving on to private legal practice in Philadelphia with Charles J. Ingersoll. His marriage to Sophia Chew Nicklin, the daughter of a prominent businessman, in 1817 boosted the career of the aspiring young barrister. Happily united for almost fifty years, George was a devoted husband and father of eight children.

The vacuum in the Era of Good Feelings created by the death and retirement of a number of leading figures—including his father—allowed Dallas to move quickly into a position of leadership in the chaotic world of Keystone State politics. In 1817, Dallas played a pivotal role in forming a cadre of economic nationalists dubbed the "family party" because of their marital connections. These "New School" Republicans included Samuel Ingham, William Wilkins, Richard Bache, and Thomas Sergeant. They provided a leadership core from Philadelphia but relied heavily upon the Scotch-Irish vote of the West. The family party successfully elected two governors and then transferred its energies to the presidential campaign of John C. Calhoun in 1824. When this effort foundered badly, Dallas salvaged the situation by leading the family party

in an eleventh-hour endorsement of frontier hero Andrew Jackson. Calhoun no doubt felt abandoned, but Dallas had changed direction at a propitious moment: in November Jackson overwhelmed all opponents in the Keystone state.

The election of 1824 indicated clearly that Dallas was not a prisoner of ideology. A member of the silk-stocking gentry and a spokesman for eastern Pennsylvania economic interests, Dallas had virtually nothing in common with the mechanics, small farmers, and coonskin-clad pioneers who comprised the bulk of the surging movement for Old Hickory. Personal relationships and private ambitions, not party principles, determined the Philadelphian's allegiances. On issues such as slavery, Dallas could fall back upon his genuine devotion to the permanence of the Union and the inviolability of the Constitution. With such matters as the national bank, protective tariffs, and internal improvements, however, he appeared hopelessly out of step with his Jacksonian compatriots.

During the next four years, Dallas and the family party battled the "Amalgamators," led by former Federalist James Buchanan, for control of the nascent Democratic Party. When Jackson soared to victory over John Quincy Adams in 1828, family-party favorite John C. Calhoun continued in the vice presidency. Such alliances boded well for Dallas—at least temporarily. Deserting his post as mayor of Philadelphia, Dallas accepted the position of district attorney for the eastern district of Pennsylvania and then was elected to the U.S. Senate in 1831. Meanwhile, Ingham received a cabinet slot as secretary of the treasury, and Dallas's brother-in-law, William Wilkins, was chosen by the legislature as the other U.S. senator. The family party had reached the zenith of its power and influence.

After almost a decade of dominating state politics, the family party then fell victim to greed, ambition, and internecine struggles. When Calhoun embraced nullification, Dallas could not distance himself quickly enough from the Carolinian. Although the Philadelphian hoped somehow to weather the political gales, the forces of Jackson, Calhoun, and National Republican aspirant Henry Clay formed a whirlwind that enveloped and blew away the once-powerful family party.

If Dallas envisioned reaching a new accord with President Jackson, the recharter of the Bank of the United States in 1832 doomed those prospects. The freshman senator had been chosen—against his will—to champion the Philadelphia-based institution in Congress. Dallas understood that the bank was being used as an issue in the upcoming presidential campaign, and his advocacy of the bill would be seen as a decidedly anti-Jackson move. As a promoter of the interests of his state, however, he felt he had no choice but to sponsor the bank. Although the recharter passed through both houses of a Democratically controlled Congress, Jackson registered his famous veto on July 10. Dallas's endorsement of the bank, combined with his support in the Senate for federally funded internal improvements and a protective tariff, marked him as a true Pennsylvanian—but such allegiances seemed too often incompatible with the program of the president. The disillusioned and discredited senator decided not to seek reelection and returned to private life in 1833.

Dallas's retirement was brief. Appointed attorney general for the commonwealth in October, he remained there for the next three years, battling for penal reform and opposing the anti-Masonic witch hunt that enveloped the state. When New Yorker Martin Van Buren captured the White House in 1836 (and the votes of Pennsylvania as well), he sought to end Jacksonian factionalism. Accordingly, he offered the post of minister to Russia to Dallas in February 1837. The Philadelphian agreed to this self-exile, following his likewise errant relative, Wilkins, to St. Petersburg.

For the next two-and-a-half years, Dallas struggled to survive at the Court of Nicholas I as an underpaid diplomat representing a second-rate power. Because he was paid only $9,000 a year and had taken his family with him, poverty compounded his rapidly rising disaffection with the mission. Dallas bemoaned the constant round of parties and balls, which he found unexciting, and the society, which he found oppressive. Dallas did develop, however, a personal fondness for Czar Nicholas I, a man he respected, admired, and warmly compared to Peter the Great.

Tedious diplomatic disputes did little to relieve Dallas's boredom, although at times they threatened Russo-American tranquility. For example, American violations of Russian fishing and trade restrictions off the Alaskan coast resulted in a reaffirmation of czarist sovereignty but no change in the activities of Yankee sea captains.

Dallas realized, however, that he could accomplish little personally or professionally by remaining in St. Petersburg. He departed Russia in July 1839, following an undistinguished stint in which he did penance for his sins against the national party.

In the autumn of 1839, Dallas returned to Philadelphia to practice law. For the next four years, he held no elective or appointive public office but remained an active and eager—if not powerful—force in the national and state Democratic Party. Dallas supported energetically a variety of candidates for the 1844 presidential contest. He also commented on a number of issues, including the independent treasury, the national bank, and Texas annexation. His views of this last problem of widespread concern would be a primary factor in catapulting him into the vice presidency.

The Dallas faction of the Pennsylvania Democratic Party now constituted a narrow, isolated clique and was, outside the confines of Philadelphia, politically ineffectual. The blows the old family party had sustained at the hands of Jackson, combined with the successive exiles of Wilkins and Dallas to Russia, severely wounded the organization. For the next two decades Dallas attempted to recapture the political magic of the 1820s and failed because he burdened himself by a tendency to commit on too many pressing state and national issues. James Buchanan, ever evasive and thus increasingly acceptable to the electorate, emerged in sharp contrast; from his lofty perch as U.S. senator, he controlled the state party.

Despite Dallas's minority status in the state party, he retained influence in Washington. Van Buren offered him the attorney generalship in 1839, but the Philadelphian declined. (Van Buren, of course, failed in his reelection bid in 1840, losing Pennsylvania and the nation to William Henry Harrison.) When the ambitious Buchanan threw his hat in the ring in an ill-timed bid for the 1844 nomination, Dallas remained loyal to Van Buren. He hoped to parlay his support for the Little Magician's comeback into a resurgence of control of the state Democracy.

Unfortunately for Van Buren, Texas stood in his path. The Lone Star Republic, independent since 1836, desired to become a state. A sizable body of congressmen, mostly expansionist-minded southerners, but also many Yankees like Dallas—wanted immediate annexation. This group became increasingly skeptical about Van Buren's position on Texas and flirted with a variety of alternative candidates in the winter of 1843–44. When Van Buren opposed the Tyler–Calhoun annexation treaty in April 1844, the pro-Texas cadre began its search in earnest. Led by Senator Robert John Walker of Mississippi, the group first blocked Van Buren's candidacy in the May convention by passing a two-thirds rule for nomination. They then proceeded to weigh the merits of Senators Lewis Cass of Michigan, Richard Johnson of Kentucky, James Buchanan, and President John Tyler. Nine ballots produced a compromise choice on May 28 in Texas annexationist and former Speaker of the House James K. Polk.

In an effort to assuage the Van Buren forces, Walker placed loyal New Yorker Silas Wright in nomination as vice president. The selection carried easily on the first ballot, but an offended Wright would not be co-opted and refused a spot on the ticket. On May 30, the disappointed convention returned to its task with the goal of attempting to balance the team with the choice of a northeastern candidate. The Maine delegation offered Buchanan's name but withdrew it under his own instructions. Levi Woodbury of New Hampshire, Marcus Morton of Massachusetts, and Governor John Fairfield of Maine comprised a band of nominated New Englanders, while westerners pushed Lewis Cass and Richard Johnson. Fairfield emerged as the solid leader (106 votes) on the first ballot but fell short of a majority.

George M. Dallas lurked in the shadows. He had the support of some Pennsylvania delegates and had garnered thirteen votes. Walker, Dallas's nephew by marriage, immediately gained the floor and argued that his uncle's views were in accord with Polk's in opposition to the recharter of the national bank and in favor of Texas annexation. Additionally, Dallas had the respect of northern commercial interests and could influence a significant portion of Pennsylvania. The speech was magic. On the second ballot the delegates stampeded to Dallas, who won with a resounding 220–30 margin over Fairfield.

The selection of Dallas received widespread—though hardly uniform—support among Democrats. Many argued that he was more acceptable than Silas Wright, seemed solid on Texas, and insured Pennsylvania for the Jacksonians. Buchanan backers voiced predictably less enthusiasm. The Whigs, countering with the venerable Henry Clay of Kentucky and Theodore Frelinghuysen of New Jersey, seemed genuinely delighted over a seemingly lacklustre Democratic team. Philadelphia Whig aristocrat Sidney George Fisher offered a hyperbolic analysis of the ticket:

> Polk is a fourth rate partizan politician, of ordinary abilities, no eminence or reputation and chiefly distinguished for being a successful stump orator in Tennessee. . . . Mr. Dallas is a gentleman by birth and education (but) . . . a reckless partizan totally devoid of principle and capable of upholding or relinquishing opinions whenever his own or his party's interests require it. His talents are very moderate, his acquirements scanty, he has an inferior position at the bar, and no one would give a dollar for his opinion. . . .

Dallas reacted to his nomination with amazement and some indifference. He realized that he was being used by his party, not having been chosen for his political record or his abilities, but because he happened to agree with Polk on the major national issue of the day—Texas—and because he came from Pennsylvania. Dallas also recognized the political feebleness of the vice presidency but would endure it for the good of the party and his country. He described his position to Polk as "a bobtail annexed to the great kite."

The campaign of 1844 focused upon both issues and personalities. While the party press of the nineteenth century commonly employed character assassination, Texas, the bank, and the tariff presented problems that had to be discussed or properly evaded Dallas, in trying to capture Pennsylvania for the Democrats, had to deal with all three. He had made his position on Texas clear long before the convention and, while annexation certainly became an issue in some quarters, it received considerably less attention in Pennsylvania. The bank and the tariff constituted different matters, however. Dallas's support for recharter in 1832 haunted him, but he blamed his position at that time on instructions from the legislature. The Democrats opposed the bank in the 1844 platform as unconstitutional and inexpedient. Dallas agreed, declaring: "The principles and policies of Andrew Jackson are of more value to the United States than the Bank in its purest form." Dallas spoke aggressively about the tariff, but had to convince many doubting Pennsylvanians about Polk's reliability on the issue. In July, Dallas wrangled a document from the reluctant Polk (the Kane letter) and then offered a middle position between tariffing for protection and revenue. Polk proffered a half loaf, but it satisfied many skeptical Democrats.

Dallas also feared the divisiveness of the immigrant issue and abolitionism on the party. He personally was a fellow traveler of nativists in his anti-Catholicism, and he viewed abolitionists as fanatics and threats to the Constitution. He recognized, however, that any opinions on these issues would damage the Democrats in both Pennsylvania and the nation. His concern was justified.

Polk and Dallas triumphed, albeit with a popular vote margin of just 37,000 out of 2.7 million ballots cast across the country. The decision in Pennsylvania was just as narrow; a 6,382 vote plurality out of a total of 328,000 votes. Even the 170–105 electoral majority was misleading: the switch of either New York or Pennsylvania from the Democratic to Whig column would have given the election to Clay. Dallas had apparently justified his place on the ticket.

The first two years of the Polk administration were significant for the nation and the political career of Vice President George M. Dallas. During this period, Dallas displayed unusual ambition and made conscious efforts toward reaching the White House. In his way stood the personage of James Buchanan and a host of dangerous issues. A wrong vote, for example, on the tariff would alienate a substantial portion of his Pennsylvania base. Ultimately, Dallas failed to win control of the state Democratic Party or to rally the support of the general populace to his side. The events of 1845–46 forever doomed Dallas's chances of attaining the presidency.

Although Polk was an unknown quantity to Dallas, the Philadelphian hoped to be a powerful influence in the new administration. Dallas told Robert J. Walker:

> I have become Vice President willy-nilly, and anticipate the necessity of enduring heavy and painful and protracted sacrifices, as the consequence. Well!—I am not, in the bargain, disposed to be considered a cypher! Contrary, I am resolved that no one shall be taken from Pennsylvania in a cabinet office who is notoriously hostile to the Vice President. If such a choice be made, my relations with the administration are at once at an end.

Dallas's intentions received a prompt challenge in February 1845 with the appointment of Buchanan as secretary of state. The vice president deemed this "a most dangerous choice." Instead of sulking, however, or breaking the bond with Polk, Dallas redoubled his efforts. Polk selected Walker as his secretary of the treasury in March as a balm to the wounded Dallas men. Fearful of factionalism, the president warned his administration that he expected cooperation with his principles and policies and would promptly accept the resignation of anyone who demonstrated White House ambitions for 1848. While the choice of Buchanan was a transparent effort to balance the factions in Pennsylvania and placate both sides, it only served to heighten existing tensions and frictions. Unfortunately, too, Keystone factionalism represented the plight of the party throughout much of the nation.

After the inauguration on March 4, 1845, the battle for power began in earnest between Dallas and Buchanan. The struggle revealed itself most immediately in patronage contests: When Polk attempted to compromise or adopt a neutral course, he angered everyone. The embattled chief executive could do nothing right. Polk tried to mollify Dallas in August, writing that he would be gratified to confer with him on policy matters and benefit from his sage counsel. The president promised additional patronage but delivered little. By the end of the summer, Dallas had been defeated. His loss resulted from a combination of intertwined factors: he commanded a small faction with a narrow geographical base, he was not influential with the state administration in Harrisburg, his efforts to become a confidant of Polk had failed, and he was typically unaggressive in demanding patronage posts for his compatriots. By October 1846, Polk confessed that he had given too many appointments to Buchanan and that severe damage resulted. The admission came too late; the wounds inflicted in the patronage wars in Pennsylvania never totally healed.

While Dallas's political future suffered a setback in 1845, he remained eager to fulfill his role as presiding officer of the Senate. An avowed expansionist on the Oregon issue, Dallas played a key role in selecting fellow extremists to the Foreign Relations Committee in the March session of Congress. The "All Oregon" men held their positions when the regular session met in December in spite of a rebellion by the Whigs and a handful of moderate Democrats. Nevertheless, an angry Dallas lamented:

> Parties are in a wretched condition in both houses of Congress and are likely to get worse and worse. It can hardly be said that the administration has a majority in the Representative chamber. In the Senate on all measures beyond mere form, it is in a decided minority. The Triumverate of [Thomas H.] Benton, [John C.] Calhoun, and [Daniel] Webster—of men whose greatness has been achieved by hostility to each other—is too powerful to be resisted by [Lewis] Cass, [William] Allen and [John] Dix.

The party had been prostrated by factional patronage disputes and the Oregon issue; yet, Dallas served the administration well in the Senate, and the vice president had taken advantage of every opportunity to ingratiate himself with the president. When Buchanan and Polk fell out over a Supreme Court nomination in late 1845, Dallas's stock rose appreciably. The vice president told Richard Rush in December:

> My relations with the President are just now of the kindest and most confidential nature. How long to continue so I cannot venture to guess as the foible of instability on some matters is, I fear radical.

Dallas realized, however, that his relationship with Polk was tenuous at best and might be sundered by the slightest incident. He never became a true confidant of the Tennessean. Sometimes, Dallas believed the president sought his exclusive advice on important matters of state (he did not), while at other times Polk irritated him by "making mountains out of mole hills." Nevertheless, Dallas demonstrated unswerving loyalty to his chief and to the party.

Dallas was an important man in the plans of the Polk administration. Senators loyal to the president formed a minority and the deciding vote of the vice president in the Senate could be crucial on a number of issues. Therefore, in late 1846 and early 1847, Polk carefully cultivated Dallas and won his support but without deliberately placing him in a position of power or authority within the administration.

The tariff loomed in 1846 as an issue where the vice president's vote might be crucial. Polk considered the reduction of tariff duties as the most important domestic measure of his administration, but home industry—for example, Pennsylvania coal and iron interests—feared the collapse of all American production. In Harrisburg, panicky legislators urged national representatives and senators to oppose any tariff reduction. Meanwhile, Democratic committees and conventions throughout the state denounced this attempt to destroy the protective system. On April 14, James McKay reported the tariff bill out of committee to the House of Representatives. During the last two weeks of June, the committee of the whole intensely debated the measure. Pennsylvania congressmen spoke loudly against the bill, but to no avail. The House approved the revisions (114–95) on July 3. David Wilmot, the only Pennsylvania representative to vote for the reductions, represented a northern agricultural district. He viewed the Tariff of 1842 as oppressive to American industry. On July 6, the Senate received the bill and promptly began two weeks of debate. While Pennsylvania broadly opposed revision, the Baltimore convention (at which Dallas had been nominated) and the Polk administration had pledged alteration. If Dallas remained loyal to his party and sacrificed his state's interests, he would be committing political suicide.

Fully aware of the situation in which he might be placed, the vice president thought out his position carefully. He believed that the convention's resolutions committed him to represent the whole of the American people as well as the executive branch of government. He would study the situation daily, and if he judged that the nation and the party would benefit from a lower tariff, then this state would have to suffer. Dallas worked mightily through mid-July in a futile effort to arrange a compromise and avoid personal disaster. He failed. The pressure mounted as Senator William Haywood of North Carolina resigned on July 25 rather than vote for the bill, as instructed by his legislature. Whig Senator Spencer Jarnagin of Tennessee refused to cast his ballot, leaving the chamber deadlocked in a 27–27 tie (twenty-seven Democrats in favor, twenty-four Whigs and three Democrats opposed). Dallas had prepared carefully for this dreaded moment. He told the senators that he had analyzed the vote and determined it was not on a sectional basis. The will of the House had expressed a desire to change the system as well. Certain provisions clearly offended him, but this tariff provided greater equality and justice than the Tariff of 1842. Because of the obvious sentiments of his native state, Dallas's decision was more difficult and painful. But as a representative of all the people, he was obliged to vote for the tariff. Before he could cast his ballot, however, Jarnagin changed his mind, and following the wishes of his Democratic legislature, voted for the measure. The Tariff of 1846—the so-called Walker Tariff—become law on July 30.

Dallas knew full well that his stand placed him in an unenviable position in Pennsylvania. Fearful of violence against his family, he told his wife Sophy to "pack up and bring the whole brood to Washington" if rioting commenced. The predictions of reaction were all too real. A crowd hanged Dallas in effigy from the telegraph wires of a main street in Philadelphia, and Whig newspapers branded Dallas "a scourge of mankind," "treacherous," and an "assassin." Democratic editors in Pennsylvania had difficulty defending the vice president, but those outside the state praised his self-sacrifice for placing the value of the nation over his local interests.

The tariff evinced strong political and economic feelings, however, in the commonwealth. Even though unbiased sources noted that the real reduction on coal and iron was 25 percent (from 40 percent to 30 percent duty rate—maintaining a strong protectionist level), anger flowed unabated. Dallas had taken an active part in convincing Pennsylvanians that "Polk, Dallas, and the Tariff of '42" would provide a safeguard for their industries. Since he knew that the Baltimore convention had promised reductions, Dallas engaged knowingly in deceiving his state during the campaign. Democrats trumpeted tariff reform in the South and West and played it down in the North. The vice president had been instrumental in this campaign, which was at best equivocal and at worst fraudulent.

Dallas realized that Pennsylvania industry would not be destroyed by his tariff vote. Yet, he engaged in a political trade-off: the sacrifice of support in his native state for that of southern and western Democrats. Dallas believed in the Union and the Democratic Party and could vote in good conscience for a measure he deemed to be for the betterment of both. The vice president would rely on his stand on the tariff as well as views on foreign affairs to carry him to the White House in 1848. However, just as his tariff vote ruined him in Pennsylvania, so did his extreme views on Oregon and the Mexican War blunt his campaign efforts in the rest of the nation. He clung to a precarious position in 1846.

As an expansionist and exponent of American Manifest Destiny, Dallas espoused an aggressive foreign policy. He viewed the Monroe Doctrine with favor and the Western Hemisphere as a U.S. preserve. Great Britain posed a particular obstacle to United States goals, especially in Oregon, Texas, and Cuba. Perennially anxious about the "pearl of the Antilles," he feared that Britain would pluck Cuba before the "pear would ripen and fall into our lap." The vice president judged that $100 million was not too great a price to pay Spain for the island.

Oregon had been an Anglo–American problem since the 1790s. Although other European powers had been squeezed out and Britain and the United States now jointly occupied the territory, the two nations could not agree on a boundary. In 1845, British Minister Richard Packenham rejected an American offer to set the boundary betwen Oregon and Canada at 49° north latitude, which had given the United States control of the vital Columbia River. The threat of war with Great Britain loomed large, and Dallas did not recoil from it. His fears rested less with the damage that the British navy would likely inflict on the eastern seaboard and more to the danger caused by a division of effort if the United States engaged Mexico simultaneously at the Rio Grande. Nonetheless, for Dallas, settlement at 49° would be a national disgrace. An even worse fate—disunion—would befall the country, however, if the administration sacrificed the Columbia River.

By April 1846, a less-jingoistic Dallas counseled diplomacy. Although his private position had not changed on the justice of claiming the boundry as far north as 54°40′, he recognized that negotiation must be allowed to take its course before more extreme measures could be adopted. Dallas believed that Prime Minister Robert Peel's experiment with free trade would force an English compromise. He was correct. London offered to settle the boundary at 49° and Polk accepted. Although Oregon "ultras" screamed foul, the Senate approved the agreement on June 15. A realistic Dallas concurred with the treaty—war with Mexico had been declared on May 13. Throughout the Oregon crisis of 1845–46, Dallas shared his views with the president, but there is no evidence that he affected policy in any meaningful way.

The caution that Dallas displayed toward Britain evaporated in regard to Mexico. He respected and feared English power but viewed the Mexicans with racist contempt and disdain. He envisioned a war with Mexico as an opportunity to gain territory, as well as to unify the nation and the Democratic Party. Just as his early extreme views on Oregon had endeared him to westerners, he combined his advocacy of the annexation of California and New Mexico with the demand for the cession of a strip of land across the Isthmus of Tehuantepec for a U.S. canal or railroad. By February 1848, the vice president had moved to the land-hungry position of the "All Mexico movement" and conceded that the United States "might be assigned to it by the resistless force of events—guardianship of a crowded and confederated continent."

Once again, Dallas's extremism collided with Polk's realism. In February 1848, the president accepted a treaty negotiated by diplomat Nicholas Trist that gave the United States *only* California and the Southwest. Dallas lamented the signing but continued to hope for further territorial concessions, noting in 1855, "the door of peaceful annexation ought never to be shut."

Dallas's presidential hopes expired with the demise of radical expansionism. The vice president, however, challenged his more powerful rivals—especially Cass and Buchanan—for the nomination. Dallas clubs, formed as early as 1845, held a series of dinners and rallies for the vice president. Five thousand people appeared at a fete on December 1, 1847, at the Chinese Museum in Philadelphia. The campaign established the *Daily Keystone* to promote the candidate properly.

Dallas also found an issue—slavery in the territories—to assist in defining his philosophy of government. The debate over the ill-fated Wilmot Proviso of 1846, which demanded no slavery in the territories gained from the Mexican War, ripped the Democratic Party asunder. On September 18, 1847, in Pittsburgh, Dallas promulgated the doctrine of *popular sovereignty*—an ambiguous posture that allowed each territory to decide its own fate on slavery at some undetermined time in the future. While the vice president intended his sentiments to appeal to radicals on both sides of the issue, the concept received a weak response in the press.

In March 1848, the Buchanan forces captured the majority of the delegates at the Pennsylvania state convention. With the May national gathering in Baltimore only weeks away, Dallas's candidacy seemed at an end. His own state had committed for "Old Buck." The Northeast seemed alienated by his opposition to the protective tariff, his stand against the Wilmot Proviso, and his alignment with the South. The West was not opposed to him, but it backed sectional favorite Lewis Cass of Michigan, and the South factionalized over a number of candidates.

Dallas's only hope was a repeat of 1844: a failure of the front-runners to achieve the two-thirds necessary for nomination. The possibility evaporated as Cass, who had embraced Dallas's popular sovereignty position in January, moved to an easy fourth-ballot victory. November, however, brought dispair for the Democrats as Cass lost both Pennsylvania and the national election to Mexican War hero Zachary Taylor.

Dallas, more disappointed over the fate of the party than his personal failures, now turned his attentions to Congress, the Wilmot Proviso, and his future in the Democratic Party. As a lame duck, the vice president could now be more outspoken and corrosive in his comments on events and personalities. Dallas feared the passage of the Wilmot Proviso, a measure he was convinced the great but misguided Calhoun would use to promote disunion. A firm believer in the sanctity of the nation, Dallas balanced his concerns about the proviso with a naive optimism that president-elect "Old Rough and Ready" had the tools to hold the country together. This view quickly disappeared in March 1849 after Dallas met with the general.

Meanwhile, relations between the vice president and Polk virtually collapsed. Tardy presidential dinner invitations angered the sensitive Philadelphian, and when Polk invited Dallas to visit Nashville in the fall, he refused. "Bah!" he commented pointedly in a letter to his wife. Dallas took simple pleasure in presidential embarrassment. He appeared almost gleeful when the first attempted use of gaslights in the White House in January 1849 resulted in powerful odors and a mass exodus to the front lawn. Dallas also confided to his diary the devious similarities in character between Polk and English King Charles I, who was deposed and executed in the seventeenth century. Unless he had an eleventh-hour rehabilitation, it is unlikely that Dallas shed any tears over Polk's untimely death in June 1849.

The experiences and disappointments of the campaign and the election of 1848 removed the excitement and enjoyment from many of Dallas's official duties. He now wanted to escape Washington for the pleasures of family and career in Philadelphia. Sophy disliked the capital and chose not to stay there, although she visited often. Consequently, Dallas lived a rather Spartan life in Washington, first residing with Lewis Cass and then taking rooms on Capitol Hill. He dined out frequently with Secretary Robert John Walker. In an effort to support his family comfortably, he continued his law practice, taking on sometimes controversial cases (such as high-profile divorces) for lucrative fees. Although his name was already bantered about for the 1852 nomination, a bitter Dallas embraced the idea of retirement. He autobiographically confided to his diary: "Truth, courage, candour, wisdom, firmness, honor, and religion. Many by accident now and then [may] be serviceable, but a steady perseverance in them leads invariably to private life."

Between 1849 and 1856 George Dallas experienced the private life that he clearly viewed as a mixed blessing. He rebuilt his law practice with such profitable business cases as railroad mergers and argued before both state and national courts. Never far from politics, however, the Philadelphian offered his views on the leading issues of the day. The Compromise of 1850, for example, angered Dallas because it allowed Congress to legislate on slavery in the territories. This topic, he determined, presented a Pandora's box of problems. Once opened, the lid could never be closed on the antislavery forces. For Dallas, constitutional guarantees protected the institution, and legislative directives would lead to disunion. An amendment should be passed that would guarantee the rights of the states to slavery and thus forever end the divisive debates.

Undoubtedly, Dallas's position in defense of southern rights, the Fugitive Slave Law of 1850, and the purchase of Cuba are what marked him as a "Doughface Democrat"—a Yankee sympathetic to the cause of the South. In 1852, the nation elected a man of exactly such principles in Franklin Pierce of New Hampshire. As a loyal Democrat, Dallas campaigned for Pierce, but he grew disillusioned as the administration blundered badly in both foreign and domestic affairs. That much-abused president sought to eliminate potential rivals for the 1856 nomination, and Dallas marginally fell into this camp. Consequently, in January 1856, Pierce named Dallas minister to Great Britain to replace the retiring James Buchanan.

Dallas accepted the British mission, abandoning all fleeting hope of becoming president, but commencing the most active and exciting segment of his long public career. Dallas arrived with his family in London in mid-March 1856 to face several festering Anglo-American problems. Prime Minister Palmerston and Foreign Secretary Clarendon demanded redress for the so-called Crampton Affair.

In December 1855, Washington had asked for the recall of British Minister John Crampton for recruiting Americans for the British army in the Crimea. When Clarendon refused to do so, Crampton and several English consuls were dismissed in May 1856.

Much to Dallas's amazement, Palmerston and Parliament acted with restraint. Crampton would be sacrificed in the interests of promoting the resolution of a larger issue—Anglo–American accord in Central America. Both nations had been competing for influence in the area since the 1820s. Economic and military power had given the British the edge; they held British Honduras, the Bay Islands off the coast of Honduras, and the Mosquito Coast of Nicaragua. An American bid for canal or railroad transit increased, however, in 1855 when adventurer William Walker gained control of Nicaragua. The Clayton-Bulwer Treaty of 1850 had promised that neither Britain nor the United States would further colonize

Central America, but members of Congress remained angry over the strong preexisting English presence.

Dallas attempted to negotiate the British out of Central America, and he partially succeeded. The Dallas-Clarendon Convention of October 1856 ended British ownership of the Bay Islands and protection of the Mosquito Coast and provided restrictions on the borders of British Honduras. Unfortunately, southern senators reacted strongly to a provision that prohibited slavery in the Bay Islands. Senate amendments that dealt with slavery and other issues doomed the convention. Clarendon refused to compromise on such points and allowed the treaty to die a quiet death in April 1857.

A frustrated Dallas continued his ministry, however, under newly inaugurated President James Buchanan. With an old enemy now in the White House and his ineffectual former roommate Lewis Cass as secretary of state, Dallas had little influence on policy. Nonetheless, he performed well in a crisis. Most notably, Dallas helped resolve to U.S. satisfaction a nettlesome point of law that allowed the English to visit and search United States vessels on the high seas—often slavers flying the U.S. flag.

In 1860, a disconsolate Dallas observed from afar as "Black Republican" Abraham Lincoln triumphed in November and South Carolina seceded in December. With relief, Dallas turned over the legation to Charles Francis Adams in May 1861 and sailed for Philadelphia. Although now withdrawn from public life, he staunchly defended the republic and leveled blistering attacks on secessionist agitators. The next three years would be spent practicing law and holding a sinecure appointment as president of the Atlantic and Great Western Railroad. He quietly cast his ballot for George B. McClellan for president in 1864. Until his death of a heart attack on December 31, George M. Dallas remained loyal—as he always had been—to the Democratic Party, the Union, and the Constitution.

REFERENCES

John M. Belohlavek, *George Mifflin Dallas: Jacksonian Patrician* (University Park, Pa.: Penn State University Press, 1977);

Bruce Ambacher, "George M. Dallas and the Family Party" (Ph.D. diss., Temple University, 1970); Philip S. Klein, *Pennsylvania Politics, 1817–1832: A Game Without Rules* (Philadelphia: Historical Society of Pennsylvania, 1940); Charles M. Snyder, *The Jacksonian Heritage: Pennsylvania Politics, 1833–1848* (Harrisburg: Pennsylvania Historical and Museum Commission, 1958); John F. Coleman, *The Distruption of the Pennsylvania Democracy, 1848–1860* (Harrisburg: Pennsylvania Historical and Museum Commission, 1975); Philip S. Klein, *President James Buchanan* (University Park, Pa.: Penn State University Press, 1962); Paul Bergeron, *The Presidency of James K. Polk* (Lawrence: University of Kansas Press, 1987); Charles Sellers, *James K. Polk: Continentalist, 1843–1846* (Princeton, N.J.: Princeton University Press, 1966); Norman Saul, *Distant Friends: The United States and Russia, 1763–1867* (Lawrence: University of Kansas Press, 1991); Mary Williams, *Anglo-American Isthmian Diplomacy, 1815–1915* (New York: Russell and Russell, 1914).

JOHN M. BELOHLAVEK is professor of history at the University of South Florida. He is the author of a number of works on Jacksonian diplomacy, including *George Mifflin Dallas: Jacksonian Patrician* and *"Let the Eagle Soar!": The Foreign Policy of Andrew Jackson*. Professor Belohlavek is currently at work on a biography of nineteenth-century politician and diplomat Caleb Cushing.

MILLARD FILLMORE (1800–1874)

Vice President, 1849–1850

(President Zachary Taylor)

MILLARD FILLMORE
(Library of Congress)

By Dieter C. Ullrich

Millard Fillmore has become somewhat of an enigma in the history of American politics. Prolific critics and political enemies of his generation labeled him as an ineffective, self-serving politician who lacked insight and political finesse. Modern historians, on the other hand, have characterized Fillmore as an energetic and modest individual whose perseverance and self-sacrifice lifted him into the forefront of antebellum politics. In recent years, with the added discovery of unpublished personal correspondence, Fillmore's role has been reevaluated and his impact on American history more fully recognized.

The vice presidency of Millard Fillmore lasted a mere fifteen months, but his brief term was both eventful and controversial. Two major, related issues troubled Fillmore as vice president and during his later role as successor to President Zachary Taylor: the chronic controversy over slavery and the territorial expansion in the American West. The dilemma over slavery had plagued the United States since the Constitutional Convention of 1787, but the new territories acquired following the war with Mexico threatened the equilibrium of antislave and pro-slave representation in the Senate. Fillmore's role as vice president was decisive, particularly in the debates that devised the

Compromise of 1850. President Zachary Taylor's untimely death on July 9, 1850, ended Fillmore's brief reign as vice president and placed him in the seat of chief executive. He became the second vice president to attain America's highest office due to a presiding president's death.

Millard Fillmore was born in a wilderness cabin on January 7, 1800, in the township of Locke (now Summerhill), Cayuga County, in the Finger Lakes region of New York State. He was the first son born to Nathaniel and Phoebe Fillmore and was given his mother's maiden name of Millard. His parents were originally from Bennington, Vermont, and were among many of the recent migrants to settle in central New York. Millard's father and his uncle Calvin purchased the land, sight unseen, in 1799 and moved there soon afterward. Their expectations of finding fertile lands for farming proved to be unfulfilled. What awaited the Fillmore family were clay fields, poor crops, and bitter weather. Eventually, poverty and a defective land title caused the family to relocate to a tenant farm in Sempronius (now Niles), New York.

Millard spent most of his youth working on his father's farm in Sempronius. As a boy, he experienced the hard and tedious labors of a frontier farmer. By the time he was a teenager, he had matured enough to manage his father's farm effectively. Millard's father had higher expectations for and him, and he encouraged his son to pursue a more profitable trade than farming. Lacking the funds to educate Millard in a learned profession, his father decided to apprentice him to a cloth dresser in 1814. After four months, Millard returned home disheartened and confused. His father encouraged him to try again and apprenticed Millard the following year to a cloth dresser and wool carder in nearby New Hope, New York. During his apprenticeship Millard recognized his limited education. Unable to read or write well, he found his ignorance to be a great handicap. At age seventeen, Millard bought membership in a circulating library in New Hope, purchased a dictionary, and diligently studied while working the carding machine at the mill. In 1818, when times at the mill were slow, he enrolled in an academy in New Hope, where he continued to enhance his education while he apprenticed.

The next year brought many surprises and changes for Millard. While attending the academy in New Hope he met a young lady named Abigail Powers, the daughter of a minister, Reverend Lemuel Powers, and the younger sister of a local judge. Millard began to court Abigail by winter 1819, but, recognizing that he was not of the proper stature to marry, he chose to wait before asking for her hand. During that period, Millard's father sold his tenancy in Locke and relocated to Montville, New York, where he became a tenant to a distinguished county judge, Walter Wood. Seeing an opportunity to advance his son's career, Nathaniel persuaded the judge to try Millard for a couple of months as a clerk in his law office. Millard was overjoyed by the opportunity and worked hard during those two months. After his trial period ended, the judge offered him advice and assistance: He told Millard to study law and offered to employ him as a clerk while he did so. Millard found the opportunity irresistible and so began his career in the field of law.

In 1820, after a disagreement with the judge, Fillmore moved to his father's new farm in Aurora, New York, with hopes of revitalizing his plans to become an attorney. In nearby Buffalo, he continued working as a law clerk and taught school on a seasonal basis. Teaching paid his expenses and clerking allowed him to acquaint himself with prominent attorneys in the region. Although he had not completed the several years of course study usually required, he was admitted to the Erie County bar in 1823. His cultivation of key members of the bar and his upstanding image in the Buffalo community hurried along his admittance. He was offered a position at one of the more prestigious firms where he had studied and clerked, but he chose instead to open a small law office in East Aurora.

Fillmore's law office became successful in a few short years, as his practice rapidly grew with western New York's agricultural and industrial development. His early professional labors focused on local land titles, mortgages, and debt collections in the East Aurora and Buffalo region. By late 1825, he was confident about his future and decided that it was now the proper time to marry the woman he had courted for more than five years. On February 5, 1826, in Moravia, Abigail Powers and Millard Fillmore were joined in matrimony.

Fillmore became actively involved in local and state politics soon after his marriage. Prior to 1826, Fillmore had been affiliated with the National Republicans, though he was never motivated to participate in the leadership of the party, but his desire to seek political reform in New York State drew him into the Anti-Masonic movement of the late 1820s and early 1830s. After the mysterious abduction and disappearance of William Morgan, a Mason known to be publishing a book criticizing the order, Fillmore joined the reform movement. He was further influenced by the writings of Thurlow Weed, who was then the editor of an Anti-Masonic paper in Rochester and the chief promoter of the Anti-Masonic movement.

In spring 1828, he served as an Anti-Masonic delegate during the Erie County National Republican convention and supported John Quincy Adams for the presidency. As the months progressed toward the elections, Fillmore became more and more entwined in both the Anti-Masonic movement's political leadership and Weed's plans for a third political party. When the Anti-Masonic Party materialized, the leaders of the new party declared Fillmore a candidate for the state assembly in September.

He had his doubts about his success as a candidate: He was considered an underdog to the Democrat contenders, who were riding on the popularity of the Andrew Jackson–Martin Van Buren presidential ticket. On election day, Fillmore was surprised to find that he had won, receiving more votes in Erie County than any other candidate. His election to the state assembly was the beginning of his long career in politics.

Fillmore's first term as a state assemblyman was unimpressive as he lacked confidence and experience for the position. In his succeeding terms, however, he began to show more conviction and a growing desire to engage in political discussions and debates. Between 1830 and 1831, he supported the building of branch canals

to extend the Erie Canal's waterways, fought against statewide banking monopolies, and made efforts to secure the abolition of imprisonment for debt in New York State. He also began to make significant strides toward organizing the Anti-Masonic Party's leadership within the state. In a short amount of time, Fillmore had become a major force in the New York political arena.

He and Abigail moved to the village of Buffalo in 1830, where Fillmore accepted a partnership in Joseph Cleary's prestigious law firm. Though their partnership would dissolve within a few years, Fillmore gained a sure foothold for his legal practice. To become better community members and to increase his popularity, he and Abigail joined various village social and religious groups. The most significant group in which he and his wife became active was the new Unitarian Church, where they would be lifelong members and faithful supporters. Fillmore was now more socially active, attending formal dinners, dances, and other events. His integrity and growing popularity marked him as a likely candidate for the United States Congress.

Withholding his name from nomination for a fourth term in the state legislature, he decided to run as his district's Anti-Masonic Party candidate for the United States House of Representatives. His allegiance to the Anti-Masonic movement faded during the campaign as Fillmore foresaw the party's eventual demise. Nonetheless, he was elected to the Twenty-third Congress in 1832, receiving a solid majority of his district's vote. He arrived in Washington in 1833, supporting the concept of forming a new political party that would unite the fractured National Republicans and Anti-Masons.

In his first congressional year, Fillmore acquainted himself with the federal structure of government and the key politicians in both the House and the Senate. His activities on the House floor were minimal as he focused his concerns on the birth of a new party. Fillmore had supported his Anti-Masonic colleagues on major issues brought before the Congress but was tactfully disengaging himself from the party. By his second year in office, he decided not to resolve the vast differences between the National Republicans and

Anti-Masons but to cross party lines, so in August 1834, he withdrew his name from the Anti-Masonic ticket and threw in his lot with the upstart Whig Party. The Whigs offered him the nomination to run for his current congressional seat, but Fillmore declined. Recognizing that the Anti-Masonic Party still controlled his congressional district, he decided to retire temporarily from politics and wait for a more opportune moment.

The opportunity to reclaim his congressional seat came in fall 1836, when Fillmore was offered and accepted the Whig nomination. He was highly optimistic about his chances for victory, and after a well-prepared campaign he regained his old House seat. The Whig Party, however, did not fare as well as Fillmore. The party's popularity continued to increase in 1835 and early 1836, but after a series of setbacks and internal disputes the Whigs popularity began to wane. The Whigs lost the presidential election of 1836 and suffered their worst defeat in New York State in sixteen years. Being one of the few Whig stars in New York, Fillmore was thrust into the forefront of his adopted party.

Fillmore served three consecutive terms in the House of Representatives between 1836 and 1842. While in Congress he quickly acquired recognition as an influential leader within the Whig Party and gained his colleagues' respect. Fillmore became a key player in the National Bank's demise and in the protectionist movement that designed the Whig tariff of 1842. When the Whig Party won control of the House of Representatives in 1840, Fillmore ran second in votes behind Henry Clay to receive the coveted Speakership. As was House custom, the runner-up was offered the powerful Ways and Means Committee chairmanship. Fillmore gladly accepted the appointment and effectively governed the committee from 1840 to 1842. In July 1842, he declined his district's renomination as representative and publicly announced that he would retire to "family and fireside."

In reality, Fillmore stepped down to seek other opportunities that would further enhance his political career, much as he had done in 1835. While still in the House of Representatives, he had had thoughts of seeking a U.S. Senate seat, but the two incumbent New York senators were well entrenched in their positions. A year after his departure from Congress, he was called upon by the Whigs to consider a nomination as Henry Clay's running mate for the presidency. In the spring of 1844, Fillmore met with other prominent Whigs in New York and agreed to take part in the Whig convention to be held in Baltimore. Just prior to the convention, the leading Whig candidate for governor of New York, Willis Hall, fell ill and became physically unable to run an effective campaign. The Whig Party's elite, particularly Thurlow Weed, realized that the party's best hope lay with Millard Fillmore for governor. Weed asked him to run for the governorship, but Fillmore declined the offer and continued to press for the vice presidential nomination. Weed and other members of the party elite withdrew their support, and Fillmore lost the nomination to Theodore Frelinghuysen on the third ballot.

Distraught over the loss, Fillmore returned to Buffalo and quietly withdrew from the presidential campaign of 1844. He continued to support the Whig ticket of Clay-Frelinghuysen, but his pride was deeply hurt by the loss of the nomination. Meanwhile, Weed and his supporters continued to encourage Fillmore to run for the New York governorship. Fillmore resisted the offer for a while longer, but after prolonged encouragement he reluctantly agreed to run for office. His spirits began to rise as he launched a gubernatorial campaign that concentrated on the growing abolitionist and nativist movements in western New York. His campaign focused on uniting the antislavery and antiforeigner vote within the Whig Party. The immigrant and Catholic vote in New York's urban areas led to his slim defeat to Silas Wright. By the end of 1844, he had lost two major campaigns and was bitterly disappointed in the Whigs' inability to embody nativist and abolitionist interests within the party's platform.

For the next three years, Fillmore withdrew from the political scene and concentrated on the home life he had promised himself in 1842. His retirement from politics, however, was at most partial; he continued to be involved in the Whig Party's reunification and restructuring in the mid-1840s. In 1846, he was appointed to the chancellorship of the University of Buffalo, a college he helped to found earlier in the same year. During the Mexican War, Fillmore publicly spoke out against the conflict as a southern conspiracy to encourage the spread of slavery. He also became more outspoken on the controversial issue of immigrants and Catholics infiltrating the American political system. Fillmore patiently waited in the wings for a challenge that would stimulate his aspirations to reenter politics.

That challenge came by fall 1847 when he was approached by friends in the Whig Party to run for state comptroller. Without much hesitation, he decided to forsake retirement and campaigned for the office. On election day Fillmore won with astonishing numbers, beating his opponent by the largest plurality ever recorded by a Whig candidate against a Democrat.

Fillmore took office as comptroller on January 1, 1848. His term was productive but short lived. In a little more than a year, he developed successful programs that fostered internal improvement projects, revised state banking methods, and devised a currency program that would later be adopted in the National Banking Act of 1863. With renewed confidence in himself and in the Whig Party, Fillmore sought to reassert his efforts to claim the coveted vice presidency.

By early 1848, he had patched up old quarrels with the still influential Thurlow Weed and had become an active participant in the Whig presidential nomination process. The Whig national convention in Philadelphia began with serious divisions between northern abolitionists, southern slaveholders, and western expansionists. The party's leading contenders for the presidential nomination were the aging Henry Clay and Mexican War hero Zachary Taylor. Northern abolitionists promoted Clay's nomination; southern and western segments preferred Taylor, who was a slaveholder from Louisiana. To appease the abolitionists and prevent a fatal breach in the party, an antislavery candidate for the vice presidency had to be selected. Southern and western contingencies favored the nomination of Abbot Lawrence, who was a Massachusetts cotton manufacturer. Clay opposed Lawrence's nomination by declaring that the Whig Party would not "have cotton on both ends of the ticket." The convention was in a deadlock when

John A. Collier, the New York delegation's most prominent member, put Fillmore's name in contention. The peace offering worked, and on June 9, Fillmore was nominated on the second ballot. He had finally attained the nomination he was denied four years earlier.

The ensuing presidential election, like most in the years preceding the Civil War, focused on slavery and the new territories. The presidential campaign was intensely fought and was at times dirty. The Democrats openly attacked Fillmore in the southern states as being a hard-line abolitionist, though his stance regarding antislavery was at most middle ground. Fillmore agreed that slavery was an evil but that the slave states had the "constitutional right to enjoy it." Throughout the campaign, Fillmore wisely refused to address the controversial issues of slavery and nativism, fearing it might hinder the Whig Party at the polls. His passive and impartial approach during the campaign succeeded as the Whigs claimed a narrow victory on November 7, 1848.

Fillmore resigned as New York State comptroller on January 1 but continued to perform his official duties until February 20. As inauguration day grew near, the many perplexities over the western territories became more profound and complex. Gold had been discovered in California, and thousands of Americans began to migrate to the West Coast. Tensions had reached a boiling point in Texas as residents in the state's western region sought sovereignty as a territory free from slavery, and reports of anarchy and lawlessness in the West caused great concern and demands for a strong civil government. Congress balked at the issues in the western territories and continued to divide itself into pro- and antislavery movements. The seemingly perpetual argument over slavery in the territories and the proposals for statehood plagued the Thirtieth Congress until its final days in March. The stage had been set for the newly elected Taylor administration, with Vice President Fillmore playing a major role in forthcoming debates.

On May 5, 1849, Millard Fillmore was sworn in by Chief Justice Roger B. Taney as the vice president of the United States. Soon after, he addressed the Senate as their presiding officer, briefly explaining the administration's plans and his personal hopes that "the glorious Union may endure forever." Fillmore's aspirations of unity were dashed, however, when Congress reassembled in December.

The inherited dilemma over California and the other western territories created a division among congressional members who either supported or opposed the spread of slavery. A huge gulf separated the two groups that led to dissension within the ranks of both the Democratic and the Whig parties. Southern legislators had passed resolutions defending the constitutional rights of the slave states and voiced a strong resistance to plans that might restrict the growth of slavery in the territories. Some pro-slavery extremists went as far as to threaten to hold a convention in Mississippi to discuss alternatives to an unfavorable administration decision. Exacerbating hostilities between camps, President Taylor chose unpopular cabinet members and supported a plan that called for free homesteads and the nonextension of slavery into the territories. By the end of 1849, there appeared to be no end to the bitter stalemate that existed in both houses of Congress.

Besides the numerous distractions in the Senate, Fillmore was confronted by a climactic change of power in his home state. Weed had once again turned on Fillmore and allied himself with William Henry Seward, the former governor and newly elected senator from New York. Conspiring against Fillmore, Weed and Seward strove to obtain control of the Whig Party in New York State. Seward gained the confidence of President Taylor, and his political advisers encouraged the administration to secure key appointments in New York State, which in turn greatly enhanced Weed and Seward's position. A determined struggle between Seward and Fillmore to control the New York Whig Party ensued, turning into a political battle that occupied Fillmore throughout his vice presidency and, later, his presidency.

In early 1850, the national issues were again joined when California sought statehood by approving a state constitution that prohibited slavery. President Taylor urged Congress to admit California as a free state and organize New Mexico and Utah as free territories apart from slaveholding Texas. The issues were thrown onto the floor of Congress, where they met with violent opposition from both southern Democrats and Whigs. The evenly split Senate could not agree on admitting California and the new territories as free. The southern legislators declared that if a free California was permitted to enter the Union and new free territories were created, the historical balance of pro-slave and antislave representatives in the Senate would tip toward the northern faction. Various alternative plans were placed before the House and the Senate, but "the great compromiser," Henry Clay, introduced a plan he hoped would ease sectional differences and retain the balance.

Much as he had done during the Missouri Compromise, Clay envisioned a scheme that would extinguish the flames of disunion by accommodating both the antislavery and pro-slavery factions. With the assistance of Stephen Douglas and Alexander Stephens, Clay devised a compromise that would prohibit the slave trade in the District of Columbia, create a stricter fugitive slave law, and incorporate a far-reaching "Omnibus Bill" that would resolve the complicated issues of the new territories. The "Omnibus Bill" proposed the admittance of California as a free state, addressed the Texas debt and boundary issue, and deferred the decision of slavery to the territories prior to their applying for statehood. In effect, the compromise pleased the abolitionists by admitting California as a free state and forbidding slave trade in the nation's capital. It also attempted to satisfy southern demands for an enforceable slave law and the premise that slavery could be expanded into the new territories by self-determination.

Throughout the vigorous and heated debates, Vice President Fillmore maintained order in the rambunctious Senate, a difficult task because fierce rivalries led to personal attacks and confrontations upon the Senate floor. In an effort to curtail the contention and defamation, Fillmore threatened to exercise his power to call members to order. On April 17, Fillmore had an opportunity to use this authority when Senator Henry S. Foote tried to intimidate fellow Democrat Thomas H. Benton by brandishing a pistol on the Senate floor, but Fillmore merely acknowledged the event and did not exercise his power to punish Foote. The press criticized the vice president for not preventing the incident or disciplining Foote. Fillmore, recognizing the adverse publicity of enforcing discipline on the outlandish Foote, prudently chose to ignore the senator's absurd act. His reasoning proved correct as the debates over compromise continued at a more respectable tone, and Foote's reputation was considerably damaged.

During spring and early summer 1850, Vice President Fillmore remained indecisive and publicly voiced no commitment to either the president's plan nor the solution proposed by Clay and Douglas. Fillmore initially told the president that he favored the administration's plans to admit California as a free state. However, the influence of Senators Daniel Webster and Henry Clay converted the vice president to the practicality of compromise. Aiding in Fillmore's conversion was his distress over Taylor's political appointments in New York and the president's failure to grant him an active role in his administration. By early July, Fillmore formally reversed his stance by informing Taylor that if he were called upon to give a deciding vote in the Senate, he would favor the bill embodying compromise. Fate intervened and the opportunity to cast the deciding vote never came.

On the evening of July 9, Fillmore learned that President Taylor had succumbed to a sudden illness and had passed away. By noon the next day, Fillmore was sworn into office by Circuit Court Justice William Cranch in a simple ceremony in the Hall of Representatives. Almost immediately after taking office, Fillmore began to restructure the executive branch by accepting the resignations of Taylor's cabinet and appointing pro-compromise leaders. He chose Webster as his secretary of state and fellow compromise proponent John J. Crittenden as attorney general. In a message to Congress on August 6, Fillmore urged the indemnification of Texas for the surrender of her claim to New Mexico and encouraged compromise. The message persuaded the middle of the road southern Whigs

and northern Democrats that compromise was to be supported by the new administration.

By the end of summer, both houses of Congress voted upon and passed all the acts that constituted the Compromise of 1850. On September 9, Fillmore signed acts that admitted California as the thirty-first state and established the territories of New Mexico and Utah. Nine days later, he signed the Fugitive Slave Act, and on September 20, he abolished the slave trade in the District of Columbia. The Fillmore administration had helped break the stalemate in Congress, and so disunion was temporarily averted.

The subsequent presidential years of Millard Fillmore focused upon the implementation of the acts of the Compromise of 1850, the containing of overzealous expansionists, and the promotion of economic development. His actions to enforce strictly the Compromise of 1850 isolated him from both pro-slavery and antislavery factions. In early 1851, Fillmore issued a proclamation that defended the Fugitive Slave Act's provisions by calling for the capture and return of a runaway slave. Northern Whigs and abolitionists were astounded by the proclamation and began a public campaign to criticize his administration. The president separated himself from pro-slavery expansionists by issuing proclamations against U.S. citizens' participation in military expeditions to Cuba and Mexico. By issuing these proclamations, Fillmore helped stifle southern hopes for expanding slavery into other militarily acquired territories. In an effort to promote economic development, the Fillmore administration arranged federal grants for railroad construction, expanded international trade, and advocated internal improvements to both roadways and waterways. It was under Fillmore's authority that Commodore Matthew C. Perry voyaged to Japan to open an American trade route to the Pacific rim.

Fillmore's diligence and determination to keep the peace and preserve the Union were successful but at the cost of his political career. The contest for the Whig nomination for the presidency in 1852 brought forth two contenders for Fillmore's job: New England favorite Daniel Webster and General Winfield Scott, the choice of extreme abolitionists. Fillmore had considerable support from the southern Whigs and received the endorsement of Henry Clay. He sought the nomination on a platform supporting the Compromise of 1850 as a final settlement on the slavery issue. Webster and Fillmore could not find a common ground and after a tight battle, which took fifty-three ballots to decide, Scott won the party's nomination. The controversy over slavery eventually tore the Whig Party apart, and the Democratic candidate, Franklin Pierce, won the presidential election in a landslide victory.

Fillmore's final months as president were politically uneventful. He concluded his presidency by appropriating funds for the repair and maintenance of the Library of Congress, which had been damaged by fire in December of 1851. He signed an act to establish the Territory of Washington on March 2. And on his last day as president, possibly recalling the financial hardships he had as vice president, he signed an act raising the salary of the vice president from $5,000 to $8,000. On March 4, 1853, Fillmore's presidential term ended after thirty-two months.

Fillmore returned to Buffalo alone and anguished. His beloved spouse, Abigail, had died in Washington from complications related to a severe cold she contracted while participating in Pierce's inauguration. Fillmore sought retirement from politics, but after a few brief months loneliness and political aspirations drove him to begin a series of speaking engagements. During the spring and summer of 1854, he toured southern and midwestern states, hoping to resurrect the Whig Party. His efforts failed hopelessly as the Whigs splintered into different sectional groups, including the upstart Republican Party and the Know-Nothing (or American) Party. Fillmore was favored by the pro-Protestant, nativist Know-Nothings, who sought to unite former Whigs with a xenophobia directed against Catholic immigrants. In early 1856, while visiting Europe, Fillmore was surprised to learn that he had received the Know-Nothing nomination for the presidency. He reluctantly accepted the nomination and began a campaign that stressed the significance of the Union and the necessity of compromise. The election was an embarrassing defeat;

he collected only 8 electoral votes and ran a distant third behind Democrat James Buchanan and Republican John C. Frémont.

Following the elections, Fillmore finally recognized the inevitable and retired from national politics. In February 1858, he married Catherine C. McIntosh, the childless widow of an affluent merchant from Troy, New York. He and his wife continued to reside in Buffalo, where they became very active in community projects and organizations.

Former President Fillmore became the founder of the Buffalo and Erie County Historical Society, Buffalo General Hospital, and the Buffalo Club. He was a major supporter of the local Society for the Prevention of Cruelty to Animals and was later named the vice president of the society. He contributed large endowments to the local library and created a fund on which the Buffalo Fine Arts Academy was founded. He also donated his personal time to speak at numerous charities and events promoting needy causes.

During the Civil War, Fillmore organized pro-Union demonstrations in Buffalo, encouraged the enlistment of men, created a fund to assist local families of volunteers, and was elected the chairman of the Buffalo Committee for Public Defense. Though Fillmore never approved the Republican Party's conduct of the war, he unselfishly supported the Union cause throughout. When the war concluded, he was given the solemn honor of escorting Abraham Lincoln's body from Batavia to Buffalo following the president's assassination. After the war, Fillmore chaired an organization to erect a monument to the soldiers and sailors of Erie County.

On February 13, 1874, Fillmore suffered a stroke that left the left side of his body paralyzed. Two weeks later, he had a second stroke, and his health deteriorated rapidly. On March 8, at the age of seventy-four, Fillmore died. He was buried two days later at Forest Lawn Cemetery in Buffalo, New York.

The vice presidency of Millard Fillmore proved to be the prologue of his presidency. His quiet restraint during the debates over compromise and his tactful methods of guiding the Senate displayed remarkable insight and prudence. When he ascended to the presidency on Zachary Taylor's death, he totally committed his administration to endorsing and implementing the acts that embodied the Compromise of 1850. Unfortunately, the vast differences between pro- and antislave powers proved to be irreconcilable. Fillmore's efforts to promote compromise and preserve the Union isolated him from both his party and the political mainstream. His determined unwillingness to alter his stance on compromise, slavery, and nativism doomed his later presidential candidacy in 1856. The overwhelming defeat and his inability to conform to popular political ideologies led him into retirement, where he demonstrated his generosity, kindness and devotion to the community.

REFERENCES

Elbert B. Smith, *The Presidencies of Zachary Taylor and Millard Fillmore* (Lawrence: University Press of Kansas, 1988); Robert J. Rayback, *Millard Fillmore: Biography of a President* (Buffalo, N.Y.: Publications of the Buffalo Historical Society, 1959); primary source information can be found in the "Millard Fillmore Papers," Vols. I and II, ed. by Frank H. Severance, in the *Buffalo Historical Society Publications*, Vols. X and XI (1907); collections of manuscript letters are located at the Buffalo Historical Society and the State University of New York at Oswego.

DIETER ULLRICH is a special collections librarian and archivist at the University of Tennessee at Martin. He holds graduate degrees in both history and library science and worked with the Millard Fillmore papers while an assistant special collections librarian at the State University of New York at Oswego. Currently, Mr. Ullrich resides in Mayfield, Kentucky, with his wife Kara.

WILLIAM RUFUS DE VANE KING (1786–1853)

Vice President, 1853

(President Franklin Pierce)

WILLIAM RUFUS DE VANE KING
(Library of Congress)

By Daniel Fate Brooks

William Rufus de Vane King, the second son of William King and Margaret de Vane, was born April 7, 1786, on his family's plantation near Craddock Creek in Sampson County, North Carolina. His father, a planter of Irish descent, was listed in 1790 as owning thirty-one slaves and substantial lands in both North Carolina and Tennessee. The elder King was a justice of the peace, a North Carolina state legislator, and a delegate to the convention that ratified the U.S. Constitution. His son, William R. King, attended the Grove Academy near

Kenansville and Fayetteville Academy, and at age thirteen became a student in the Preparatory School of the University of North Carolina. He enrolled in the university in 1801 and later became a member of the Philanthropic Society, a distinguished campus literary club. In 1804, at the end of his junior year, he left Chapel Hill and moved to Fayetteville, where he read law in William Duffy's office. After admission to the bar in 1805, King relocated to Clinton, the county seat of his home county, and opened a law office.

In 1808, King, then age twenty-two, was elected to the North Carolina House of Commons as a Jeffersonian Republican from Sampson County. He was chosen the fifth circuit's solicitor in 1809 and was elected to Congress from the Wilmington District in 1810. Once in Washington, he quickly became a defender of the Madison administration and aligned himself with John C. Calhoun and Henry Clay and the young War Hawks' cause. He firmly believed in the use of tariffs to promote American manufacturing and favored involvement in the War of 1812. Reelected without opposition in 1813 and 1815, he continued to support nationalistic programs.

In spring 1816, King resigned his congressional seat to become secretary of the legation to William Pinckney of Maryland, the newly appointed minister to the Court of Naples and the Two Sicilies, and the Court of Russia. During his tenure first in Naples and later in St. Petersburg, King recorded that he traveled extensively and observed social customs, "a desire fostered from the very early period of my life." No doubt the young diplomat greatly profited from this experience. Later in his public career, this mission was cited by the *Illustrated News* of New York as one that "amply improved those abilities that have since been so well tested."

King returned to North Carolina in fall 1817 and was soon persuaded to follow his older brother, Thomas, to the newly opened Alabama Territory. "Alabama Fever" had swept the seaboard states, beckoning planters and plainfolk alike to the newly tamed wilderness. By early 1818, King had relocated on the Alabama River in a fertile region known as the Alabama Black Belt. In a short time he amassed vast acreage, built his home "Chestnut Hill," and by 1820 had assembled the second-largest slave force in Dallas County. In addition to planting interests, he purchased lands in and around the river port of Moore's Bluff and became a partner in the land company that founded the city of Selma. King is credited with naming the city in honor of Ossian's poem, "Songs of Selma."

Recognized by Alabama settlers as a proven leader, King was elected to represent Dallas County in Alabama's Constitutional Convention in 1819 and was named to the subcommittee that drafted the state constitution. During convention debates, King constantly supported a conservative constitution instead of one characterized by lenient democracy. When the first general assembly convened in the fall of 1819, he and John Williams Walker of Madison County were almost unanimously elected as Alabama's first two United States senators. As the representative of south Alabama, King drew a short term but was reelected in 1822 to a full six-year term after defeating U.S. District Attorney William Crawford of Mobile by a vote of 38 to 35. In both the elections of 1828 and 1834, King, then a Democrat, won his Senate seat without opposition and in 1840 was victorious over Whig candidate former Governor John Gayle.

By the third of his first four terms as senator, King emerged as a leader in the causes of generous land legislation, tariff reform, and banking. On land questions he supported Jeffersonian principles by declaring that without more reasonable prices and better purchasing terms, the country would be controlled by the monied aristocracy. As chairman of the Public Land committee and a long-time proponent of policies that favored settlers, King led the efforts to oppose Henry Clay's distribution bill, which would allow states to receive proceeds from public-land sales.

On tariff issues, King remained a moderate, even though he rejected the tariffs of 1816, 1824, and 1828. He was a foe of nullification as well as of Jackson's Force Bill, but as a Unionist, he limited his criticism of South Carolina to "most unfortunate" and "an embarrassment to the country." Considering first the good of the Union, King finally accepted the Tariff of 1832 and even supported Clay's tariff bill of 1833 as a restoration of peace.

In 1832, King opposed a bill that would allow the Bank of the United States to be rechartered, which he viewed as partisan legislation and an action that provided no measures to correct abuses. He remained a strong advocate and a leader in the Democratic Party and, with few exceptions, a supporter of Jackson. During the Democratic Convention in Baltimore in 1832, King reported for the Committee on Rules and proposed the rule that provided for a two-thirds vote to nominate a candidate. This rule was used by the party until its repeal in 1936.

Throughout his career, King was respectfully addressed as Colonel King, a title given him by endearing admirers from whom he commanded confidence. He was described as about "six feet high, remarkably erect in figure, well proportioned and impressive even to strangers." One surviving image of King portrays the secretary of legation as a Byronic youth, while later portraits show him as a handsome statesman whose aquiline nose and high cheekbones suggest the Huguenot blood of his mother's family. Seen as "brave and chivalrous" in character, King was remembered by his contemporaries as possessing "manners as courtly as Chesterfield's." He was described as "lavishly hospitable" and "courteous to the humblest," qualities that "marked a finished gentleman."

About 1834, King met and developed a friendship with James Buchanan of Pennsylvania. The two men shared most political sentiments, and both remained lifelong bachelors. In time their relationship became more intimate, and by 1836 the two senators shared a residence in Washington. Soon the usual talk about King's traits as a "southern gentleman" generated amusement from northerners and caused others to joke about the two and refer to them as "the Siamese Twins."

Despite the gossip, King continued to focus his attention on governmental affairs. Concerned about the personal suffering resulting from the Panic of 1837 and its threat to the Democratic Party's future, he became a proponent of the Independent Treasury System. During the discussions on the distribution of abolitionist material in the southern states, King remained a moderate, taking a position supporting the view that petitions from distributors should be received by the Senate and rejected.

By 1838, interest was already focused on the Democratic Convention of 1840. While Martin Van Buren was almost certain to be the presidential nominee, there were several likely contenders for the vice-presidential nomination. Included in the list were John Forsyth of Georgia, Richard Mentor Johnson of Kentucky, James K. Polk of Tennessee,

and William Rufus King. While the Democratic press in Alabama pushed King's name at home, Buchanan was active in gaining support for him in Pennsylvania. These efforts proved to be popular among Buchanan partisans because the advancement of King would likely deprive Polk of the nomination and eliminate him as a threat to Buchanan's candidacy in 1844. King had previously assured his roommate that should he become vice president, he would not seek the presidency and would endorse Buchanan's nomination.

Using campaign material furnished by Buchanan, some Pennsylvania newspapers praised the Alabama senator for his proven leadership and his "unwavering devotion to the pure and patriotic principles of the Democratic creed." Although King received scattered support in New Hampshire, Indiana, and Virginia, he failed to get North Carolina's endorsement. Disappointed by his native state's rejection, King withdrew from the race, gave his support to Johnson, and eventually endorsed the Democratic ticket.

Interest in the Democratic nomination for 1844 began almost immediately. As early as 1842, newspapers in Alabama and other states advocated a Buchanan-King ticket, but as time passed, optimism about its success waned. Party leaders considered Polk and King to be the leading vice-presidential contenders, but only as long as Van Buren was the presidential nominee. In December 1843, King wrote his niece Catherine Ellis that even though Buchanan was no longer a contender, he remained optimistic about his own success.

By early January 1844, defaming comments about the intimacy of King and Buchanan again circulated around Washington. Andrew Jackson, who favored his fellow Tennessean, James K. Polk, spoke of King as "Miss Nancy," while the Tennessean Aaron V. Brown, a former law partner of Polk, referred to King as "Mrs. B." and "Buchanan's wife." In a scathing letter to Polk's wife, Sarah, dated January 14, 1844, Brown wrote:

> Mr. Buchanan looks gloomy and dissatisfied &
> so did his better half until a private flattery and
> a certain newspaper puff which you doubtless

noticed, excited hopes that by getting a *divorce* she might set up again in the world to some tolerable advantage.

Referring to King as "Aunt Nancy," Brown went on to say that he "may now be seen everyday, triged [sic] out in her best clothes & smirking about in hopes of securing better terms than with her former companion."

Once again King's chances of receiving the nomination began to fade. In a letter to his niece, he wrote that he was resigned to surrender the vice presidency "without one feeling of regret." However, by April 1844, King was asked by President John Tyler to accept an appointment as minister to France. Tyler instructed him to strengthen "subsisting relations" but left the method for accomplishment entirely up to King. After King resigned his Senate seat and accepted the post, he wrote a letter in May to Buchanan expressing his reluctance on leaving him:

I am selfish enough to hope you will not be able to procure an associate who will cause you to feel no regret at our separation. For myself, I shall feel lonely in the midst of Paris, for there I shall have no friend with whom I can commune as with my own thoughts.

As King developed plans to go abroad, he made sure that he surrounded himself with family. Together with his widowed niece Catherine Ellis, two nephews, William T. King and Alfred Beck, and his trusted body servant, John Bell, he sailed from New York to Havre in June 1844. Arriving in Paris, he quickly received an audience with King Louis Philippe and began tedious negotiations regarding U.S.–French relations over the annexation of Texas, the settlement of the Oregon boundary, and problems with Mexico. Despite several diplomatic differences with French foreign minister François Guizot, King ably expressed the U.S. position and assured the monarch that a French alliance with England in Lord Aberdeen's proposed plan of intervention in the Texas annexation was unwise. Through the "lavish entertaining" hosted by his niece and his own diplomatic skills, King was successful in permitting the United States to annex Texas without

fear of foreign interference and gained French neutrality in the Oregon question and the Mexican War.

Completing his mission, King resigned his diplomatic post and returned to Alabama in November 1846. After being virtually cut off from politics for more than two years, he quickly began a campaign to regain his Senate seat. In his absence, Dixon Hall Lewis, states' rights advocate and former House member, had been appointed by his brother-in-law, Governor Benjamin Fitzpatrick, to fill the vacancy. In 1847, Lewis ran for a full term with King as his challenger. Contrary to early expectations, King soon found the almost 500-pound Lewis to be no easy opponent. The race, described by the press as "a meeting of the giants," created a deadlock in the Alabama legislature. With Whigs remaining loyal to their candidate, Arthur F. Hopkins, King's constituency refused to accept Lewis. After two days of balloting, King, unable to secure a majority of votes, withdrew from the race, and Lewis was elected. The loss marked King's only defeat in a state election.

Disappointed and concerned about the division that now existed in the state party, King focused his attention on the 1848 vice-presidential nomination. While Lewis and other Calhoun supporters failed to endorse him because of his moderate views, Unionists in the North and South once again looked to a Buchanan-King ticket. In February 1848, the Alabama Convention unanimously nominated King for vice president, but only after states' rights leader William Lowndes Yancey attached some extreme resolutions regarding slavery. King supporters reluctantly accepted the resolutions without knowing that Yancey had planned an unsuccessful walkout to ruin their candidate.

During the Democratic national convention of 1848, Lewis Cass was nominated for the presidency. Vice-presidential nominees included William O. Butler, John A. Quitman, John Y. Mason, Jefferson Davis, J.J. McKay, and William Rufus King. When the first vote was counted, King was in third place, with only twenty-six scattered votes, the majority of which came from Alabama and Pennsylvania. General Butler won the nomination, and King received fewer Alabama votes because Yancey had defected from the state delegation and cast his ballot for Quitman. This action signaled an even more decisive split in the Alabama party.

Despite his defeat by Dixon Hall Lewis, King soon found himself back in Washington. In June 1848, Arthur P. Bagby resigned from the Senate to become minister to Russia, and King was appointed by Governor Reuben Chapman to Bagby's seat. The following year, King was reelected to a full term but only after making some concessions to Yancey and his supporters.

With the sudden death of President Zachary Taylor in the summer of 1850, King was again selected president pro tempore of the Senate. He had held this position from 1836 to 1841 and was recognized as the leading authority on senate rules. King readily accepted the duties of presiding officer and acknowledged this as his opportunity to calm the emotions of both North and South and hopefully bring about some compromise to save the Union.

Sectional controversy and the problems with slavery and westward expansion dominated King's last years as a statesman. Realizing that the best hope of the South lay in unity, King wrote that he pleaded with "the patriotic men of every section to meet on grounds of compromise." However, in the following months, lack of cooperation among the southern representation gave more encouragement to the abolitionists and made it increasingly difficult for King to remain a moderate. When California sought admission to the Union, William R. King served as a member of the select committee of thirteen that drafted the Compromise of 1850. He is credited not only with aiding its passage but also with bringing about its acceptance by southern rights enthusiasts. Although he acknowledged that southerners had legitimate complaints about some provisions, he remained an ardent defender of any measure that threatened the good of the Union.

During the next year, King served on various Senate committees, chairing the Committee on Foreign Relations and being credited with responsibility for the passage of the Clayton–Bulwer Treaty. However, most of his energies were spent working to reunite Alabama Democrats, settling dissension in the national party, and steering younger U.S. politicians on a more moderate course. By 1852, King was the last of the Senate leaders of his generation. Calhoun, Clay, and Webster were dead, and Thomas Hart Benton had been defeated. At times it seemed that only he and Buchanan shared a devotion to the Union.

In January 1852, the Alabama Democratic convention endorsed King for vice president, with a resolution proclaiming him "the distinguished, long tried, and ever faithful Senator." At the national Democratic convention in Baltimore the following June, King was the leading contender for the second office, while Buchanan, Lewis Cass of Michigan, William Learned Marcy of New York, and "the little giant," Stephen A. Douglas of Illinois, vied for the presidential nomination. After a grueling battle, Buchanan's name jumped to the top with 104 votes. Needing a majority, Buchanan supporters begged Marcy's New York delegation for their votes, but to no avail. Finally, Buchanan's poll declined, and his bid failed. Two votes later, on the forty-sixth ballot, Marcy's score began to rise, and New York came to Buchanan begging for his support. Pennsylvania partisans, however, had already decided their next move: Buchanan would back General Franklin Pierce of New Hampshire, a dark-horse candidate who was satisfactory to both North and South.

To reward Buchanan and his friends for their endorsement, Pierce supporters allowed them to select William Rufus King as the vice-presidential candidate. On the second ballot, the sixty-six year old Alabamian received the nomination with 282 votes. In a letter to Pierce, one supporter wrote: "I think we did right putting King on the ticket. You know he is Buchanan's bosom friend, and [therefore] a great powerful interest is consolidated."

King had at last reached his ambition and triumphed with a landslide victory. He was pleased with the nomination, but in a letter to Buchanan dated June 12, 1852, King confided disappointment that his friend was not the presidential nominee. Two days later, Buchanan wrote a clergyman and expressed little regret in his own defeat but pledged his "cordial support to Pierce & King; because they are the nominees of the convention & to the latter because I love and respect the man."

In regard to Pierce, King now felt that, next to Buchanan, he was more acceptable to the South than the other candidates. During the campaign, King, who complained of a "distressing cough," rarely gave speeches but spent most of his time writing letters, assuring southerners that the forty-eight-year-old Pierce was indeed a leader they could count on.

In two earlier elections, the Whigs were successful in electing an aging war hero as president. The party elected Harrison in 1840 and Taylor in 1848; therefore General Winfield Scott of Mexican War fame appeared to be a hopeful choice for the Whigs. With "Old Fuss and Feathers" as the presidential nominee, the Whigs looked to balance their ticket with a younger man, William A. Graham of North Carolina.

The Democrats now had the task of maintaining party unity and guarding against dissension and outside intrusion. In fall 1852, the Free Soil Party, under the slogan "Free Soil, Free Speech, Free Labor, and Free Men," threatened to split Buchanan's supporters with the nomination of John P. Hale for president. Building their platform on the belief that "slavery is a sin against God and a crime against man," the Free Soilers cited Harriet Beecher Stowe's newly published novel, *Uncle Tom's Cabin* which threatened to upset Pennsylvanian's solid Democratic vote. Determined to settle the challenge, Buchanan defended the Democrats and the Compromise of 1850 by offering the question of who would maintain the security of the Compromise of 1850, Pierce and King or the Whigs.

In the weeks before the election, King's cough had turned into a more serious problem. Throughout the fall, he had to decline invitations to events held in his honor. However, when election results were announced, he was elated to learn that the Democrats had carried all but four states with 85.8 percent of the electoral vote. For King the election of Pierce was important "for the protection of southern rights and the preservation of the Union." In a letter dated November 17, 1852, King wrote from Selma: "I am satisfied that the triumphant success of the Democrats has not prostrated the Whig Party but has to a great extent annihilated freesoilism, so that in the future we shall only have to contend against the insane movements of the Abolitionists." Plagued by his bad health and considering a resignation, King continued: "My health is not good. I am troubled by a distressing cough, and if I consulted my own wishes I would not hesitate to resign my senate seat and spend the next winter in Alabama."

Disregarding his health, King left home and returned to Washington. By December 1852, the *Congressional Globe* reported that he had found it necessary to resign as president pro tempore and as senator from Alabama. King had been diagnosed with consumption. Earlier in the year, he had written that he wanted to "seek some quiet watering place in the mountains" where he could find "pure air and rest." However, because it was winter and his doctors had prescribed a warm climate, it was even more difficult to locate ideal conditions in the United States.

Following the advice of his physician, King left Washington on January 15, 1853, bound for Cuba. After stopping in Key West, he arrived in Havana on January 30. Sixteen days later, he moved east into Mantanzas to Ariadne, a sugar plantation near the town of LaCumbre. There he took advantage of the heat in the sugar mill, which he hoped would provide relief from his respiratory ailments.

As weeks passed, however, King's health did not improve, and it became evident that he would be unable to return to Washington for the inauguration. If he was to be sworn in as vice president, Congress would need to work quickly and make a provision for him to be inaugurated in Cuba. On March 2, 1853, a special act was passed that permitted the U.S. Consul General William Sharkey to administer to King the oath of office in "Havana or another place on the Island."

Cuba in the early spring was an exotic place in comparison to cold and windy Washington. On March 24, 1853, the day of King's ceremony, one witness described the elements of the setting:

"The clear sky of the tropics over our heads, the emerald carpet of Cuba at our feet, and the delicious breeze of coolness over us." The 300-foot peak overlooking the sea of Ariadne Plantation was indeed an impressive place for this unusual inauguration. As King was sworn in as vice president, he could view not only the coast, but a valley with a winding stream, colorful fields, and brown mountain peaks. Following the ceremony, a large open carriage accompanied by more than a dozen Americans on horseback, took the ailing vice president back to his quarters. William Rufus King had gained the distinction of being the first and only United States executive official to take the oath of office on foreign soil.

In the days that followed, King's health steadily worsened. No longer did he resemble the handsome statesman of his earlier likenesses. He was now the subject of his completed inaugural portrait: a sickly old gentleman prophetically holding his Book of Common Prayer. Realizing that death was near, he wanted to go home to his plantation. In a letter to Secretary of State William Marcy dated March 26, 1853, Consul General Sharkey wrote of King's condition: "He is very feeble and thus would seem to be but little ground to hope for a recovery. He proposes to leave the Island on the 6th of April for Mobile on the U.S. Steamer *Fulton*." King departed Cuba on April 7, his sixty-seventh birthday. As he crossed the Gulf of Mexico, he confessed to an Episcopal priest his desire to die among his family.

After a five-day voyage of some 500 miles, the *Fulton* arrived in Mobile. *The Mobile Press Register* reported that "an immense assemblage of citizens" waited at the Government Street wharf to greet their beloved leader, but instead of cheers, sadness hung over the crowd as two ship's officers helped the "feeble and attenuated" vice president from the ship and into his carriage. King was not quite home. He remained in Mobile for a few days' rest before he boarded the river packet *Royal St. John* for his final trip. Running full steam from Mobile to King's landing, the boat broke all previous records for speed on the Alabama River.

As King traveled from the river to Chestnut Hill, he reportedly remarked that his fields never looked greener. At 6:00 P.M. the following after-noon of April 18, 1853, William R. King died in the front room of his one-story house, surrounded by his family and faithful servants. He had been an elected official for forty-five years and vice president for less than a month.

In the days and years that followed the death of Vice President William Rufus de Vane King, his countrymen recognized that here was no ordinary man. With a life, lifestyle, and political views distinctively different from some of his more distinguished and more colorful contemporaries, King significantly contributed to his state's development and his nation's preservation. Although he never formally served as vice president, he had served his country well.

REFERENCES

Walter Jackson, *Alabama's First United States Vice President, William Rufus King* (Decatur, Ala.: Decatur Printing Co., 1952); Henry Poellnitz Johnston, Sr., *William R. King and His Kin* (Birmingham, Ala.: Featon Press, 1975); William Rufus de Vane King Papers (Alabama Department of Archives and History, Montgomery); William Rufus de Vane King Papers (Southern Historical Collection, University of North Carolina Library, Chapel Hill); "Lives of General Franklin Pierce and William R. King, Democratic Candidates for President and Vice President" (Boston, Mass.: George Roberts, 1852); John M. Martin, "William Rufus King and the Compromise of 1850," *The North Carolina Historical Review*, 39, 4 (Autumn 1962), 500–518; John M. Martin, "William R. King and the Vice-Presidency," *The Alabama Review*, 16, 1 (January 1963), 35–54; John M. Martin, "William R. King: Jacksonian Senator," *The Alabama Review*, 18, 4 (October 1965), 243–267; John M. Martin, "William Rufus King, Southern Moderate and Champion of the Southern Cause" (Ph.D. diss., University of North Carolina, Chapel Hill, 1956); Lewy Dorman, *Party Politics in Alabama from 1850 through 1860* (Wetumpka, Ala.: Wetumpka Printing Company, 1935); William Garrett, *Reminiscences of Public Men in Alabama* (Atlanta, Ga.: Plantation Publishing, 1872); *Gleason's Pictorial*, 3, 23 (December 4, 1852); *Illustrated News*, 1, 12 (March 19, 1853); Philip Shriver Klein, *President James Buchanan* (University Park, Pa.: Pennsylvania State University Press, 1962).

DANIEL FATE BROOKS is a native of the Alabama Black Belt and author of a larger manuscript on William Rufus King. He now lives in Birmingham, where he is director of Arlington (a museum of decorative arts).

JOHN CABELL BRECKINRIDGE (1821–1875)

Vice President, 1857–1861

(President James Buchanan)

JOHN CABELL BRECKINRIDGE
(Library of Congress)

By John Marshall Prewitt

If Hollywood ever decided to make an action film of the life of a vice president of the United States (among those who never became president), the choice might likely fall on John C. Breckinridge. It is difficult to imagine the public buying tickets to see any other vice president's story, with the possible exception of Aaron Burr.

The various periods of Breckinridge's life are each worthy of a tale to be told, except for one—the period of his vice presidency. For three-

and-a-half years of his term of office, President Buchanan ignored him, other than to ask advice on a handful of appointments to offices that might affect Kentucky. There is really nothing very unusual about a president ignoring a vice president. Many vice presidents have had no duties or functions but to preside over the Senate and to keep informed of the president's state of health.

Finally, near the end of his vice-presidential term, a summons to the White House came to

Breckinridge. The great political and national crisis of 1860 was in full bloom, with the country starting to pull asunder in preparation for civil war. Buchanan could not solve the problem. Breckinridge's biographer, William C. Davis, has described Breckinridge's expectations when the interview began. Buchanan told his staff to leave them undisturbed and then, with great ceremony, unlocked a desk drawer and pulled out a manuscript. The president looked gravely at Breckinridge and asked his opinion about issuing a proclamation for a day of humiliation and prayer.

According to Davis:

> The vice president sat in mute shock, fighting with his facial muscles to conceal the anger and frustration that he felt. He listened quietly, respectfully, made a few complimentary remarks, and then smiled and bowed his way out. In time he would be able to laugh over the incident, repeating it to friends with "inimitable narration," but now it was one more example of the stupidity and disarranged priorities on all sides that led the country into its difficulty, and a hallmark of Buchanan's singular incapacity for his office.

To a man as active as Breckinridge, of all the periods of his life, his term as vice president must have been the most restricting and unrewarding.

John C. Breckinridge was born into a political family. His paternal grandfather, John Breckinridge, was a Virginia lawyer who moved near Lexington, Kentucky, in 1793, was appointed Kentucky's attorney general, but preferred the legislative branch, where he became speaker of the Kentucky House of Representatives. In 1800, the grandfather was elected U.S. Senator. His consistent backing of friend President Thomas Jefferson's policies brought him appointment as Jefferson's attorney general. His career was cut short by his death in 1806 at the age of forty-six. He left a substantial estate, mostly in the form of his Fayette County, Kentucky, farm, which was called "Cabell's Dale."

John Breckinridge's widow was Mary Hopkins Cabell, known to her descendants as "Grandma Blackcap" for her ever-present head covering. One of the prominent Cabells of Virginia, she survived her husband by fifty-two years to become the dowager empress of the Breckinridge family.

John and Mary Breckinridge's son (John C. Breckinridge's father) was Joseph Cabell Breckinridge. He graduated from Princeton in 1810 and a year later married Mary Clay Smith, daughter of the college president, Dr. Samuel Stanhope Smith (whose own father-in-law was the illustrious Rev. John Witherspoon, a signer of the Declaration of Independence and previous president of Princeton, known in his day as the College of New Jersey). Cabell Breckinridge, as he was known, served in the War of 1812 and then returned to Lexington to practice law. In due course, he too was elected to the Kentucky legislature and became speaker of its house, followed by an appointment as Kentucky's secretary of state. At age thirty-four he, like his father, was cut off in his prime by death.

The future vice president, John Cabell Breckinridge, was born January 16, 1821, in Lexington. He was only two years old when his father died, and there was apparently an overwhelming influence of women in Breckinridge's early childhood. His father had not had time to build an estate and left a considerable debt; consequently, the widow and children had to go live with Grandma Blackcap at Cabell's Dale.

Breckinridge found himself living with six women. His grandmother, his mother, and four sisters. A little boy living in such a house should, by folk sociology, turn out to be a sissy. Also, the grandmother and mother were both demanding women. The difficulty of two aristocratic and haughty women, used to running their own houses and trying to occupy one together, is obvious. Eventually, after a domestic uproar in 1832 when Breckinridge was nine years old, his mother and family left Cabell's Dale and went to live with her daughter Frances, now married to John Clarke Young, a Presbyterian clergyman and president of Centre College in Danville, Kentucky.

Breckinridge was sent to Pisgah Academy in Woodford County, Kentucky, and later enrolled at Centre College. He continued to live with his sister and her husband when his mother departed to Lexington in 1835 when her daughter Mary Satterwhite died; she spent the next ten years rearing the Satterwhite children.

Presbyterian religious influence appears to have been strong on Breckinridge. His great grandfather, John Witherspoon, was not only the president of Princeton but also the first moderator of the Presbyterian national assembly. His uncles included a chaplain of the U.S. House of Representatives, a nationally known Presbyterian minister, and the Presbyterian president of Centre College.

One of Breckinridge's biographers, Frank H. Heck, points out that although he joined the Presbyterian Church in Danville, he requested that his membership be suspended in 1840 on the grounds that he no longer felt worthy to be a communicant. He was never after an active churchman. Breckinridge followed this incident by joining the Masons, which some considered a religious organization with teachings adverse to Presbyterian Calvinism. The present generation of Americans can scarcely conceive of the church's influence in the times of which we write. Today, a Presbyterian would most likely just quit going to church without feeling any necessity for justification, but in Breckinridge's youth, to be blackballed by your church—any church—was to risk disapproval, even shunning, by the entire community.

Being sent away to school freed Breckinridge from feminine influences, and he was universally popular with his schoolmates. He became a capable athlete and a believer in a daily exercise program. Going further, he adopted "daily regularity in a particular habit," which he applied to all of his activities. It may be that this foreshadowed his later successful adaptation to the routine of military life.

After graduating from Centre, Breckinridge studied law at Princeton and Transylvania University in Lexington, and then under Judge William Owsley. He was admitted to the bar in 1841.

Then an unusual event occurred. This recent graduate, only twenty years old, was asked to deliver the main address at the state Fourth of July celebration at the capitol in Frankfort. Breckinridge's natural flare for oratory was apparently recognized by his schools, classmates, and Judge Owsley, who may have influenced the choice of Breckinridge as the speaker for the occasion. The speech was successful and gained him a considerable measure of favorable notice.

In his oration, Breckinridge mentioned "unlawful dominion over the bodies of men," which seemed to hint at his abhorrence of slavery. His attitudes were probably influenced by his uncle, Rev. Robert J. Breckinridge, an emancipationist of whom he was very fond. His uncle was associated with the American Colonization Society, a group that promoted the founding of the African nation of Liberia as a haven for freed American slaves. Breckinridge's family also all approved the Kentucky slave law of 1833 that prohibited further import of slaves into the state. There was a distinct limit, however, to the range of Breckinridge's thinking on the slavery issue: Although he used the word "unlawful" in his July Fourth speech, for him abolition was the confiscation of property by the government and was constitutionally out of the question, even though he might have viewed slavery as intrinsically evil.

Despite his notable beginnings as a Kentucky lawyer, Breckinridge and his cousin Thomas Bullock soon departed for what they hoped would be greener pastures when they set up a law office in the developing frontier town of Burlington, Iowa. He dabbled there in local politics, abandoning his early Whig sympathies and becoming a Jackson-style Democrat. There does not appear to be any reason of principle behind this change, perhaps only expediency. Two years later, he returned to Kentucky for a visit and met and married Mary Cyrene Burch, which ended the Iowa venture. The new family settled in Georgetown, Kentucky, and Breckinridge formed a new law partnership with another cousin, Samuel R. Bullock. Breckinridge handled the Georgetown office, and Bullock saw to Lexington.

In the 1844 presidential election campaign, Breckinridge made speeches for Democrat James K. Polk, developing such a reputation that he was asked to address a Polk rally in Nashville (he was unable to attend). The speeches had the effect of making him well known in the Bluegrass section of the state.

In 1846, Breckinridge moved to Lexington and the firm's Georgetown office was closed. By this time two sons had been born to the family.

In the same year, war was declared against Mexico. When the battle of Buena Vista produced a number of casualties among Kentuckians, the legislature ordered that the bodies be brought home for reburial, and Breckinridge was chosen to be the main speaker at the ceremony. To 15,000 or 20,000 people, a crowd of unusual size for the time, at Frankfort Cemetery, Breckinridge delivered the address that established his statewide reputation and eventually led him to the vice presidency.

Soon after the memorial ceremony, Breckinridge received a commission and within months was on his way to Vera Cruz and a march to Mexico City as a major of the Third Kentucky Volunteers. Not a shot was fired on the Third during the balance of the war, and eight and a half months after they left home, the peace treaty had been signed and Breckinridge and his men were back home.

In 1849, Breckinridge was elected to the Kentucky House of Representatives on the Democratic ticket. (About this time in Lexington, he met Abraham Lincoln, the husband of Breckinridge's childhood playmate, Mary Todd.) Most members of the Kentucky legislature went to the capital and were seldom heard from again. Fearing to offend even one voter, they introduced no legislation and tried to avoid voting on anything controversial. Not so with John C. Breckinridge: His legislative record is too voluminous to detail, but it covered a vast number of subjects, particularly so-called internal improvements such as railroads. State financing of public works was a controversial subject at a time when many advocated a laissez-faire state wherein improvements, if any, should be paid for by private enterprise or at the local government level. Breckinridge also spoke out for states' rights and the Union, two principles that were soon proved in actual practice to be mutually exclusive.

Because of his financial situation, Breckinridge turned down a second term in the Kentucky legislature, but in 1851, he was elected to the U.S. Congress in a hard-fought campaign against an elderly Whig candidate, war hero and elder statesman General Leslie Combs. The election was lost in other counties until the final vote from Owen County was received, giving Breckinridge a majority. Thus, his newly born son John Witherspoon Breckinridge acquired from his father the nickname "Owen," which stayed with him all his life.

Breckinridge's first biographer, Lucille Stillwell, reported that prior to the election, a committee came to Breckinridge from Owen County, asking how great a majority in that county would certainly elect him. He named a thousand. Owen County gave him 1,500 votes out of a voting population of less than 2,000. This was typical of Kentucky politics, and county political machines of this type exist to this day. The trick is to control all the voting-booth officials, if necessary by having some of your supporters register as members of the opposing party. They then report whatever voting result is required. If a voter does not come to the polls, an official will cast his vote. Kentuckians took the attitude that if a candidate could not protect himself against fraud, he proved a lack of political acumen and should lose. Few, except the loser, became upset over a stolen election.

In 1852, Henry Clay, the "Great Pacificator" and elder statesman from Kentucky, died. Although of opposite political parties, he and Breckinridge admired each other, and Breckinridge was selected to deliver a eulogy for Clay. While his speeches in Congress had gained him some national reputation, this speech pushed him toward the forefront of national politics.

Breckinridge was again elected to Congress in 1853 after a hard-fought campaign. He soon became involved in the presidential election and strongly supported and spoke for Franklin Pierce, thereafter forming a close alliance with the president.

What were perhaps the defining moments of Breckinridge's subsequent political career came during this second term as Congressman. In 1854, Breckinridge's friend Stephen A. Douglas of Illinois introduced a bill to organize the territories of Kansas and Nebraska on the basis of "popular sovereignty"—that is, letting the residents themselves decide the question of whether slavery would be allowed. The proposal would also in effect have repealed the Missouri Compromise, dating from the early 1820s, which had put the question of slavery in the territories in Congress's hands and ruled out slavery north of Missouri's border. Breckinridge played a key role in helping to broker the bill's final form and securing its passage in the House. Breckinridge's position in the debate (he nearly came to a duel with a representative from New York during consideration of the bill) caused him to be branded as a southern slavery sympathizer and destroyed any chance that he would be considered a moderate who might possibly be acceptable to both sections of a divided country.

Meanwhile, the Kentucky legislature had gerrymandered Breckinridge's district so as to expand the Whig vote. It appeared that he would be defeated if he ran again. He returned to Lexington, and though he decided not to seek office again—he turned down an appointment by President Pierce as minister to Spain—he did not leave politics. He launched a vigorous opposition to the antiforeign, anti-Catholic Know-Nothing (American) Party, which had scored a sweeping victory in Kentucky, electing a governor and many other officers.

Breckinridge was appalled not only at the Know-Nothings, but also at a party calling itself Republican that had developed in the Midwest and the North out of the Kansas–Nebraska Bill uproar. Breckinridge considered the new party to be purely sectional and a divisive threat to the Union.

As the Democratic Party approached its presidential nominating convention of 1856 in Cincinnati, it was clear that Breckinridge would be likely to play an important role. His prestige nationally had grown during his terms in Congress, despite his image among many as a pro-slavery southerner, and he had a major influence because Kentucky's votes were thought to be crucial to both the nominating process and the election to follow.

Breckinridge went to Cincinnati as a supporter of Franklin Pierce's renomination, but Pennsylvania Democrat James Buchanan and his strong organization seemed to have the upper hand. The sectional splits that threatened almost all aspects of the Union were at work also within the Democratic Party, so Buchanan could not swing a majority of the delegates immediately, and he calculated that he would need the support of Kentucky in order to win the White House in the Fall. Attention focused on the Kentucky delegation, from which two vice-presidential possibilities emerged: Breckinridge and Lynn Boyd. During the first fourteen ballots, Breckinridge at first supported Pierce but switched to Douglas when it became apparent that Pierce had no chance for renomination. At the end of the first day, Buchanan lead in the voting but without the majority needed. During that evening, Buchanan organizers came to Breckinridge and offered him the vice presidency in return for his support, but he declined.

On the following day, Douglas withdrew from contention after the sixteenth ballot, giving the presidential nomination to Buchanan. A delegate from Louisiana then nominated Breckinridge for the vice president's slot. The Kentuckian at first declined, but when he received the nomination by acclamation on the second vote, he graciously accepted his party's call to fill out the ticket.

The contest for the presidency reflected the growing fragmentation of American politics. Buchanan and Breckinridge represented the old Democratic Party, which would hold a majority if they could avoid too much splitting over the issues of slavery and sectionalism. The new Republican Party nominated John C. Frémont and William L. Dayton. The Know-Nothings recruited former President Millard Fillmore to head their anti-immigrant ticket. Breckinridge, along with other Democrats, feared that the Know-Nothings would again run strongly in Kentucky, which might siphon enough electoral votes from the Buchanan ticket to throw the election into Congress, where anything could happen.

Finally, Kentucky went Democratic and helped Buchanan and Breckinridge pile up a healthy win, polling nearly a half-million more votes than Frémont and a million more than the Know-Nothings. The Democrats coasted into office with a total of 174 electoral votes.

For Breckinridge, however, the move into the vice presidency proved to be a massive step downward. He hoped to influence Buchanan's cabinet appointments and secure places for Kentuckians among the diplomatic nominees, but the president pointedly ignored him. Worse yet, within a month of the inauguration, Buchanan not only denied a request from Breckinridge for a private audience but insultingly told the new vice president to call instead on the president's niece. Breckinridge was outraged at this treatment—resulting, apparently, from Buchanan's smoldering resentment that Breckinridge had originally supported Pierce and Douglas at the nominating convention—but could do nothing.

The vice presidency completely sidetracked Breckinridge. From that office he had little opportunity to exercise leadership and had no control or influence over the momentous events of the day. The *Dred Scott* decision came during Buchanan and Breckinridge's first year in office and poured new fuel on the national fires when the Supreme Court ruled that slaves had no rights and that Congress did not have the authority to restrict or interfere with slavery in the western territories. Breckinridge approved the decision. When Kansas burst into open warfare over the question of slavery and the Buchanan administration and Congress were faced with dire circumstances, Breckinridge could do or say virtually nothing. His only opportunities to cast deciding votes in the Senate during most of his term were on inconsequential issues such as a proposed tariff on codfishing.

As he neared the end of his vice-presidential term, Breckinridge moved to reestablish himself as a national leader. One of the senate seats from Kentucky was coming open, and Breckinridge wanted it. As a senator from an important swing state, he would likely wield considerable power and perhaps find a chance to play a key role in the divisive troubles that everyone knew lay ahead. In December 1859, while still vice president, Breckinridge was selected as Kentucky's new senator, but he was not scheduled to take office for more than a year—until after the new presidential election and inauguration.

Given the splintered condition of both the nation and the Democratic Party, when the time came for the 1860 Democratic national convention in Charleston, South Carolina, the heart of the southern opposition, there were candidates from all parts of the spectrum and much political maneuvering. Breckinridge was a serious contender for the Democratic nomination but carried the burden of a prosouthern label.

The Charleston convention was a disaster. The Deep South delegates demanded a pro-slavery plank in the platform and, failing to get it, walked out. The delegates remaining were divided, many preferring Stephen A. Douglas of Illinois over Breckinridge, but a final vote was not taken. On May 3, the convention voted to recess and to reconvene in Baltimore on June 18.

Between those dates, the Republicans nominated Abraham Lincoln.

At Baltimore, the Douglas faction brought in new delegates from Alabama and Louisiana to replace those who had walked out at Charleston. That provoked a second secession, and the "bolters" reconvened at the Maryland Institute, where they adopted the slave plank and, without his consent, nominated Breckinridge for president. On the same day, the original convention nominated Stephen A. Douglas.

Movements were made to get each man to withdraw in favor of the other. Douglas, from Illinois, was entirely correct in refusing, on the grounds that his northern supporters would shift to vote for Lincoln.

Breckinridge, knowing that his candidacy was a "forlorn hope" and calling it that, considered declining the nomination, which would in effect throw his support to Douglas. His reasons for deciding not to do so are hazy. William C. Davis, one of Breckinridge's biographers, credits the persuasiveness of Senator Robert Toombs of Georgia, who played on Breckinridge's ambition and insisted that Douglas would find so little support in the South that he would withdraw on his own accord within forty days. This did not occur. John W. Forney may have touched on the truth in his remark about Breckinridge's conduct during this period: "Having taken one wrong step, he was too proud to retract."

Election results were predictable, given the complete disintegration of the Democratic Party and the potential strength of the Republicans' alliance. Lincoln won the popular vote easily with a 400,000-vote plurality over Douglas. Breckinridge finished third, nearly a million votes behind Lincoln. Lincoln had 180 electoral votes, even though he won only 40 percent of the popular vote. Because of the peculiarities of the electoral system, Breckinridge received seventy-two electoral college votes to Douglas's twelve, even though the "Little Giant" from Illinois had greatly outpolled the Kentuckian. John Bell of Tennessee had been the candidate of the "Constitutional Union" Party, largely made up of old Whigs, Know-Nothings, and what might today be called Independents. They appeared to be living in—or wanting to return to—a dream world where the sectional issue of slavery would just go away. Bell received thirty-nine electoral votes. Breckinridge, a man who never lost an election, must have been galled that Kentucky, including his native Fayette County, voted for Bell.

Though Lincoln's election caused panic in the South, it was reasonably pointed out that the Senate and the Supreme Court were Democrat in the majority and that Lincoln could not hope to carry out any radical programs. However, on December 20, South Carolina seceded from the Union.

Congress struggled with proposals to preserve the Union, including the famous Crittenden Compromise, which was rejected by the Republicans. Breckinridge looked on it as the last hope. He accused the Republicans of "rejecting everything, proposing nothing," while the Southern states seceded one by one.

In March, no longer vice president but now a senator, Breckinridge was able to take an active part in the Senate's proceedings. He urged that federal armed forces be withdrawn from seceded states "where their presence can accomplish no good, but will certainly produce incalculable mischief."

Breckinridge and the Senate struggled for compromise of the slavery problem as one Southern state after another seceded. In one speech he warned of "what I think Kentucky will do," which was to secede if all else failed. Immediately, the Republicans classified him as a potential rebel, and so did the Southerners. Both sides exaggerated his remarks to suit their own views.

After Fort Sumter was fired on, Kentucky was swept by the impractical idea of declaring itself neutral. This idea arose from the grassroots, and politicians of all parties had to reckon with it for a time. Breckinridge, too, was driven to support this position. However, events were now driving him; he no longer had control.

He returned to Washington and the Senate, where every Democrat was now suspected of treasonous inclinations.

As a war measure, Lincoln suspended the writ of *habeas corpus.* Many persons who simply disagreed with Lincoln's policies were jailed without recourse. Stories of such abuses are innumerable. Breckinridge called this "despotism" in a speech to the Senate, and he was more than correct, but the administration would not allow a wire service to telegraph the speech.

After the battle of Bull Run (also called First Manassas) in July 1861, Breckinridge was still in the Senate, a lonely figure, futilely denouncing the policies of Lincoln at a time when to express such views was considered treason. It was plain that he no longer represented the official views of Kentucky. Many of her legislators, public officials, and influential citizens had "gone South," leaving the pro-Lincoln faction to take charge. Breckinridge spent his time attacking Lincoln while ignoring the Confederacy. He was still for Kentucky neutrality, but now he had no following, and he knew it. In the Senate he said:

> We are making our record here; I, my humble one, amid the snares and aversions of nearly all who surround me, giving my votes, and uttering my utterances according to my convictions, but with few approving voices, and surrounded by scowls.

Then, Breckinridge's sixteen-year-old son Cabell ran off to Tennessee and joined the Second Kentucky Infantry, a part of the Confederate Army.

Breckinridge returned to Kentucky and made a round of speeches, but the legislature, now pro-Union, abandoned the state's official neutral stance on September 8 in favor of adherence to the Union. Arrests began immediately, including that of former Governor Morehead. The prosouthern *Louisville Courier* was suppressed. The heads of both houses of the legislature requested that Union General George Thomas arrest Breckinridge, and Thomas issued the orders. Hearing of this, Breckinridge fled to the Confederacy. Ulysses S. Grant was to say of him: "He was among the last to go over to the south, and was rather dragged into that position."

Jefferson Davis and others thought Breckinridge could help bring Kentucky into the Confederacy. Accordingly, Breckinridge was made a brigadier general and commander of the First Kentucky Brigade. As in most wars, there was a dearth both North and South of professional officers, and many political generals were appointed on both side. Some of them turned out to be natural soldiers and displayed great competence; others did not. Surprisingly, Breckinridge demonstrated undoubted ability as a general. He commanded the reserve at Shiloh and was heavily engaged; subsequently, he was promoted to major general. His attempt to capture Baton Rouge was a failure because of insufficient numbers, and from there his command was moved east and participated in the bloody battle at Murfreesboro (Stones River). Had Braxton Bragg taken Breckinridge's advice, the Confederate Army might have avoided what became a costly near-disaster. Breckinridge's brigade suffered terrible casualties at Stones River, and forever after bore the name he gave it then, the Orphan Brigade. Both his sons, Cabell and Clifton, fought in this battle.

Next, in 1863, his command contributed greatly to the Confederate victory at Chickamauga and participated in the defeat at Chattanooga, a battle during which Cabell was captured (he was later exchanged).

On February 15, 1864, Breckinridge was called to the Confederate capital and given command of the Western Department of Virginia. For a nonprofessional officer to receive command of the area that had been defended by the already immortal Stonewall Jackson was a compliment to Breckinridge's now proven military ability. In

May 1864, Breckinridge's forces started north up the Shenandoah Valley, collided with Franz Siegel's much larger Union army at New Market, and, with the help of the Virginia Military Institute Corps of Cadets, routed the Union forces completely. The necessity of putting the cadets into line greatly grieved the general.

Because Grant's army was in motion toward Richmond, Breckinridge was ordered to join the opposing forces of General Robert E. Lee. In the battle of Cold Harbor, Breckinridge's horse was killed and fell on him, causing an injury that temporarily disabled him and that would plague him for years and eventually lead to his premature death. Breckinridge and his troops were ordered back to western Virginia and were later joined by General Jubal Early, to whom Breckinridge became second in command. Their combined forces moved north and without serious opposition proceeded into Maryland and within sight of the Capitol in Washington.

There followed defeats in the Shenandoah at the hands of overwhelming Union forces, with Breckinridge constantly in the thick of battle. Chided by Early for taking risks, he replied: "Well, general, there is little left for me if our cause is to fall."

Few Confederate generals fought over so great an area, from Baton Rouge in the west to the gates of Washington in the east.

On February 6, 1865, Jefferson Davis nominated Breckinridge for secretary of war. Within a month of taking office, Breckinridge found the South to be without resources to continue the war and urged "surrender as a government," opposing proposals for continuing the war as a guerilla operation. He said: "This has been a magnificent epic; in God's name let it not terminate in a farce."

On April 2, Richmond was evacuated, and the Confederate government fled south. Breckinridge made his way to Greensboro, North Carolina. Lee surrendered his army on April 9. On April 18, Breckinridge and Confederate General Joseph E. Johnston met with Union General William T. Sherman and arranged the surrender of the remaining Confederate army. Breckinridge was a wanted man and fled south through the

Florida swamps. He then embarked for Cuba in a small boat.

Breckinridge remained in exile in England and Canada for four years, with side trips to Europe, the Near East, and the Holy Land. Two of his five children were sent home to school at Washington College, then presided over by General Lee and now called Washington and Lee College.

At Christmas 1868, President Andrew Johnson issued an amnesty proclamation, and the following February, Breckinridge returned home to Lexington and a warm welcome. In August, he resumed the practice of law and was besieged by offers of corporate office, thus lending his name to the enterprises. His main interest was in railroads, and he became the equivalent of executive vice president of the Elizabeth, Lexington, and Big Sandy Railroad, personally supervising its construction east from Lexington to Mt. Sterling, where progress came to an eight-year halt due to the Panic of 1873. While he was inspecting a proposed right-of-way east of Mt. Sterling, Breckinridge became ill. His health declined over the following months, and although he rallied often, his lungs filled with fluid. Surgery to relieve the pressure revealed a badly damaged liver, probably the result of his wounding at Cold Harbor. He died on May 17, 1875.

What had raised Breckinridge to high positions in life? Foremost was a charisma projected by his physical appearance. He had blue eyes and black hair, with deeply sunk eye sockets. Basil W. Duke said of Breckinridge: "Often a glance over a crowd, while he remained seated and silent, would elicit wild cheers and a tumult. . . ." Champ Clark called him "the handsomest man, the most majestic human being I ever clapped eyes on." Percy Walker, a Washington friend, agreed: "There was a wonderful magnetism about him. You felt instinctively drawn to him. Meet him where you might . . . , there was the same rare power of attraction."

His wife Mary's remark reveals a lot: "I never saw him come without being glad, or leave without being sorry."

REFERENCES

William C. Davis, *Breckinridge: Statesman, Soldier, Symbol* (Baton Rouge: Louisiana State University Press, 1974); James C. Klotter, *The Breckinridges of Kentucky, 1760–1981* (Lexington: University Press of Kentucky, 1986); Frank H. Heck, *Proud Kentuckian: John C. Breckinridge, 1821–1875* (Lexington: University Press of Kentucky, 1976); Lucille Stillwell, *John Cabell Breckinridge* (Caldwell, Idaho: Caxton Printers, Ltd., 1936); A.J. Hanna, *Flight into Oblivion* (Bloomington: Indiana University Press, 1938, reprinted 1959); Alexander Brown, *The Cabells and Their Kin* (Orig. published 1895; reprint Harrisonburg, Va.: C.J. Carrier Company, 1978).

JOHN MARSHALL PREWITT is a retired attorney who lives in Mt. Sterling, Kentucky. He graduated from the U.S. Naval Academy in 1944 and the University of Kentucky College of Law in 1955. He is married to Katherine Carson Breckinridge, John C. Breckinridge's great-granddaughter.

HANNIBAL HAMLIN (1809–1891)

Vice President, 1861–1865

(President Abraham Lincoln)

HANNIBAL HAMLIN
(Library of Congress)

By H. Draper Hunt

The U.S. minister to Spain noted wryly that the Russian minister and several other guests at an 1882 Madrid diplomatic dinner stood in awe of the fact that he had once been vice president of the United States. Little did they know Hannibal Hamlin's low opinion of the "second office of the land," a post devoid of power and patronage. Yet, such is the fleeting nature of political fame that the only thing for which Hamlin is remembered even in his native state of Maine (he is virtually unknown elsewhere) is the fact that he was Abraham Lincoln's first vice president. And this was a statesman who served as a U.S. senator for twenty-five years!

Hannibal Hamlin was born on August 27, 1809, in an imposing white house overlooking the White Mountains in Paris Hill, Province of Maine. His roots lay buried deep in New England soil. His grandfather Eleazer Hamlin, sire of seventeen children by two doubtlessly weary wives, lived in Barnstable, Massachusetts. Geographical and ancient-world interests mingled to produce sons named Asia, Africa, Europe, and America, and twin sons Cyrus and Hannibal. Cyrus Hamlin, a physician, and his wife Anna Livermore settled in Paris Mill, where the doctor did some

138

farming and served as sheriff of Oxford County. Hannibal, named after his paternal uncle, nearly died during his first winter. Tradition has an Indian princess and healer named Mollyockett traveling through driving snow to save the baby with ointments, healing herbs, and a diet of cow's milk—and Dr. Hamlin was a pediatrician!

Young Han grew up surrounded by forests, streams, and mountains and came to know them well. He grew up tall and muscular, with black hair and eyes and an extremely swarthy complexion. Educated locally, Han spent a happy year at Hebron Academy (1826–27) studying the classics, math, and history, his favorite. His formal education ended when elder brother Cyrus became ill and Hannibal returned to run the family farm. He subsequently enjoyed a brief stint clerking in a Boston fruit store and flirted with the idea of a theatrical career, but his father summoned him home; this ended his stage aspirations.

Dr. Hamlin's financial situation worsened, and his youngest son had to earn money for college. Training briefly as a surveyor in an 1827 expedition deep in the Maine woods, he then combined surveying with schoolteaching in Paris Hill. His students ran the gamut in size and deportment, some of the bigger boys threatening to toss their eighteen-year-old teacher out the window, but the brawny Hamlin sternly announced, "You will find I will be the master." He proved an effective teacher during his brief career.

College plans went glimmering when Dr. Hamlin died unexpectedly in 1829. As a precaution in case higher education proved impossible, Hannibal had begun to read law even before his father's demise. Now he pressed on with his legal studies as he ran the family farm and cared for his mother and sisters.

He also plunged into politics. Influenced by Portland's Democratic *Eastern Argus*, which he had devoured in his late teens, Hamlin became an enthusiastic Jacksonian Democrat, delivering stump speeches during the 1829 state campaign. In 1830, he scraped together enough money to purchase the *Oxford Jeffersonian*, the Jacksonian weekly of Paris Hill. Its circulation proved disappointing, and Hamlin pulled out after less than a year, intensifying his legal studies. He combined potato-hoeing with law-book reading, a colorful but impractical method. But opportunity came knocking in 1832, and Hamlin journeyed to Portland to read law with the celebrated firm of Fessenden and Deblois. A serious fellow law student was William Pitt Fessenden, General Samuel Fessenden's son and future colleague of Hamlin's in the U.S. Senate.

Sam Fessenden, Maine's premiere abolitionist, discussed slavery at length with Hamlin, but the young man rejected the abolitionist solution. He loathed human bondage but felt that this radical approach simply made matters worse. Scotching the spread of slavery because of its inhumanity and his belief that free white labor could not flourish in slave territory became Hannibal Hamlin's approach as the slavery issue encroached increasingly on his future political career.

Fortified by a year's splendid legal training, Hamlin returned to Paris Hill. Easily admitted to the Maine bar, he won his first case on the same day against famed attorney Judge Stephen Emery. On December 10, 1833, he married Sarah Jane Emery, the judge's daughter, whom he had courted for some time.

A brief sojourn in Lincoln was followed by a move to Hampden, south of Bangor, where Hamlin hung out his lawyer's shingle and served as town attorney. Four Hamlin children were born in Hampden: George, Charles, Cyrus, and Sarah Jane.

As his law practice grew gratifyingly, Hamlin's long-time interest in politics bore its first fruits. Symbolically speaking, Captain Hamlin marched into the Maine legislature in 1836 at the head of his militia company, the green-clad Hampden Rifles, because his men unofficially "nominated" him for the house of representatives. He soon crossed swords with cranky, red-faced old John Holmes of Alfred, earlier Maine's first U.S. senator, who sneered at Representative Hamlin's dark skin. The captain neatly skewered his irascible antagonist: "If the gentleman chooses to find fault with me on account of my complexion, what has he to say about himself? I take my complexion from nature; he gets his from the brandy bottle. Which is more honorable?" From then on, Hamlin was treated with respect and emerged as the leader of younger legislators. He won the house speakership in 1837 and served as speaker twice more, with skill and authority. His aplomb only deserted him once. Governor John Fairfield, the recipient of a 400-pound cheese from an admirer, gave the bulk of it to the legislature, which added cider and brown bread for a collation. Some joker spiked the cider with brandy, and Hamlin, unable to adjourn his drunken colleagues, deserted the podium in confusion.

A true Jacksonian, Hamlin favored sound currency, coin over paper. He fought unsuccessfully to abolish capital punishment in Maine "on general humane principles, and also because it does not serve as a deterrent, finally, because it is not in accordance with the great and fundamental truths of the Sacred Book." Fifty years on, the death penalty would be rescinded, with Hamlin's enthusiastic support.

Hamlin's antislavery views were thoroughly aired as a member of the house committee charged with receiving abolitionist petitions. He loathed slavery, he said, and longed for its ultimate extinction. The peculiar institution "blights all it touches. . . . It is a curse, a moral wrong." He felt it should be bottled up, prevented from spreading, but abolitionists, although wrongheaded, had every right to be heard.

In 1840, amid the hoopla of the "Tippecanoe and Tyler, Too" campaign, Hamlin ran for Congress, losing by a tiny margin to Whig Elisha Allen. A reapportionment of the Penobscot congressional district delayed the next election until 1843, when Hamlin buried Allen in an avalanche of Democratic votes. And so, by a wearying combination of stagecoach, boat, and train, Mr. Hamlin went to Washington. For some thirty-three years, Hannibal Hamlin would make Washington his second home, dwelling in boardinghouses and hotels during congressional sessions.

Hamlin's four years in the federal House proved eventful, even turbulent. He supported rescinding the "gag rule" that effectively consigned antislavery petitions to legislative oblivion, arguing that the people had a right to have petitions of every kind heard and acted upon. "Old Man Eloquent" John Quincy Adams welcomed a fresh ally in his long and lonely fight, and both New Englanders rejoiced at the final destruction of the gag rule in 1844.

Hamlin took firm Jacksonian ground on banking, denouncing "that monster institution" the Second Bank of the United States and applauding Martin Van Buren's subtreasury plan; further, he opposed protective tariffs on principle. But the Maine congressman tempered ideology with pragmatism, pushing hefty duties for such Maine products as cordwood and potatoes.

In an expansionist decade, with the cry "Manifest Destiny" ringing across the land, Hamlin urged the immediate termination of joint British–U.S. occupation of Oregon and the acquisition of as much of that rich territory as the United States could legitimately claim. He favored the annexation of Texas, too, but balked at the slavery-expansion implications of admitting a single massive slave territory. He had hoped to "secure at least half of the territory as free" and voted against the Texas annexation joint resolution because it failed to provide this.

In 1846, Hamlin made his first run for the U.S. Senate. He had political friends all over Maine but powerful and resourceful enemies, too. The latter, so-called pro-slavery Democrats, in many cases enjoyed important shipping and other economic ties to the South and loathed men like the antislavery Penobscot congressman, whom they deemed troublemakers. They defeated Hamlin by the narrowest of margins in the Maine senate.

When the Mexican War came in 1846, Hamlin supported the war effort and voted military supplies, but he bitterly resented what he deemed a southern power play to expand slavery into fresh territory. Consequently, he vowed to rob the slave states of the "fruits of victory." An original "father" of the Wilmot Proviso barring slavery from any territory ceded by Mexico, Congressman Hamlin even introduced the proviso once when David Wilmot arrived in the House late. The proviso never became a law, but Hamlin enhanced his antislavery reputation.

Hamlin retired from Congress in 1847 but won election to the Maine house for service that same year. He offered powerful antislavery resolutions the thrust of which was that Maine stood adamantly opposed to slavery expansion because "the influence of slavery upon productive energy is like the blight of mildew; that it is a moral and social evil; that it does violence to the rights of man as a thinking, reasoning, and responsible being." All passed almost unanimously.

The following year, after the sudden, shocking death of U.S. senator John Fairfield at the hands of a medical quack, Hamlin moved with lightning speed and incredible energy to line up legislative votes for the succession. This time, he won, beginning what would be twenty-five years as a U.S. senator.

Picture a big, dark-skinned man, wreathed in smoke from his favorite cigar, sitting at his hotel-room desk surrounded by huge bags of public documents for franking to send to constituents. See him in trademark tailcoat and neck stock, without an overcoat even in frigid weather, hurrying through the streets of Washington, visiting government departments in his relentless pursuit of patronage for Mainers. Thus stood Hannibal Hamlin in the 1850s, a self-styled "working" rather than "talking" senator.

Much of his work stemmed from his prestigious chairmanship of the Committee on Commerce, involving shipping, customs and revenue, marine services, river and harbor improvements, lifesaving, and coastal survey. As a senator from a great maritime state, Hamlin was an obvious choice for this powerful, patronage-rich position.

The 1850s posed enormous challenges for Hamlin, with 1850 being a particularly trying year. Filling an interim term, he faced reelection for a full term in spring 1850. His enemies, those opposing the Wilmot Proviso and referred to variously as "Wildcats" (one of their leaders hailed from remote Aroostook County), "Mormons," and "Hunkers," had marked Maine's leading opponent of slavery expansion for political death. These "pro-slavery" legislators boycotted the Democratic legislative caucuses where Hamlin was the heavy favorite and refused to support him when the full legislature balloted. Deadlock ensued, only broken at last by timely aid from enough Free-Soil legislators to give

the incumbent U.S. senator the narrowest possible victory. (One doughty Hamlinite, ill with typhoid fever, had his bed carried into the House chamber to help put his hero over the top.)

On the national scene, stormy debate over what became the Compromise of 1850 transfixed Congress. Senator Hamlin wrote to a Maine supporter:

I shall be as glad as you or any one can be to see all vexed questions fairly settled, and that can and should be done in such a way as to preclude the extension of slavery. We have had some excitement here [i.e., Washington] but far less I apprehend than is supposed. We have disunion men here certainly, but they are few & harmless. I set them down with our abolitionists. And the disunionists of the South will destroy our Govt just about as soon as the abolitionists of the North. It is and has been all stuff, gasconade & bluster.

Hamlin bitterly opposed any comprehensive compromise package, holding out for admission of California as a free state, period. He dubbed Henry Clay's "Omnibus Bill" "a vicious log rolling scheme, which compelled one to vote for what was obnoxious to get at what he wanted." The senator from Maine voted against applying popular sovereignty (that is, allowing the people in each federal territory to decide to allow or bar slavery) to the territories of New Mexico and Utah because he believed that only the Wilmot Proviso approach would surely keep the peculiar institution from spreading.

In 1854, the Kansas-Nebraska Bill controversy convulsed the country and struck the American party system like an earthquake. Under powerful southern pressure, Senator Stephen A. Douglas of Illinois, chairman of the Senate Committee on Territories, reported a bill that, in its final form, specifically repealed the 1820 Missouri Compromise interdicting slavery in Louisiana Purchase territory north of the line 36°30′. It created two separate territories—Kansas and Nebraska—the former due west of the slave state of Missouri and presumably vulnerable to slavery expansion.

Hamlin asked:

What say the good people of Maine? Shall we repeal the Missouri Compromise line of 1820 to let it [Kansas] be made a slave country? Where will this spirit end? Shall we repeal freedom and make slavery? It comes to that.

The Maine Legislature seconded Hamlin's views by strongly condemning the Nebraska bill. The senator defied party discipline, including direct pressure from Democratic President Franklin Pierce, and voted against the bill, which passed notwithstanding.

Antislavery Whigs and Democrats deserted their parties in droves to form anti-Nebraska coalitions, which joined together to create a new free-soil organization called the Republican Party. In 1855, Maine's first Republican governor, Anson P. Morrill, pleaded with Hamlin to desert the foundering Democrats and join the Republicans, but Hamlin bided his time, hoping the party that he had served loyally since his youth would come to its senses. It did not: At its 1856 national convention in Cincinnati, the Democratic Party endorsed the Kansas-Nebraska Act and popular sovereignty.

On June 12, 1856, Hamlin took the Senate floor to resign the commerce committee chairmanship, symbolically severing his ties with his old party. Pressure mounted in Maine for him to become the Republican gubernatorial candidate, thus ensuring a huge state victory and helping elect Republican presidential nominee John C. Frémont in November. The governorship, a part-time job with a minuscule salary and a single-year term, held no charms for Hamlin, but his duty here was clear. To "sweeten the pot," a private understanding was reached that if he made the governor's race, he would be returned to the Senate in 1857.

Hamlin made ninety-nine speeches from "Kittery to Quoddy Head" and won an enormous September victory, becoming an instantaneous Republican celebrity nationwide. That same month, he married Ellen Vesta Emery, half-sister of his first wife, Sarah Jane, who had died in 1855. Young enough to be his daughter, Ellen would make him an ideal wife and the doting father of two sons, Hannibal Emery and Frank.

After less than two months in office, Governor Hamlin resigned to begin a full term as U.S. senator. During the next three years, he blistered his old party for its pro-slavery stance, especially its Kansas policy. As the presidential election of 1860 approached, Hamlin looked over the field of potential Republican nominees and ultimately rejected front-runner Senator William H. Seward of New York as unelectable. Abraham Lincoln of Illinois seemed a better choice, and so the senator told Chicago-bound Maine convention delegates, but he expected Seward to prevail.

Lincoln's surprise nomination stunned the Sewardites, who were offered the vice presidential spot as a consolation prize. They demurred but raised no objections to the nomination of Hannibal Hamlin when eager Maine delegates, sensing a golden opportunity, put his name forward. Hamlin's chief opponent, Cassius M. Clay of Kentucky, a legendary political abolitionist and formidable bowie-knife fighter, was deemed too radical by a majority of delegates. Hamlin won easily on the second ballot.

To say that Hamlin was horrified to learn of his nomination by euphoric Republicans, who stormed his Washington House room saluting him as "Mr. Vice President," would be a gross understatement. The powerless "second office of the land" seemed a one-way ticket to political oblivion to a powerful political leader like Hamlin. Farewell to influence and patronage! Later he declared that had he been at the convention, he would have declined the honor, but it was too late: He would have to run. The Republicans of his hometown of Bangor rejoiced at the Lincoln-Hamlin ticket. Some well-liquored celebrants began to fire cannon salutes, one man sacrificing his trousers for cannon-wadding until only the waistband remained. "You can fire *me* out of the cannon," he emoted, "if only it will kill the Democratic Party!"

The nomination of a prominent former Democrat from New England to balance former Whig Lincoln from Illinois made excellent sense politically, but Lincoln played no role whatever in the choice of his running mate. The two men had never even met. They corresponded during the campaign but, true to the tradition of the day, made no joint speeches or public statements. Hamlin's dark complexion became a minor issue when Southern ultras accused the perfidious "Black Republicans" of putting a mulatto on the ticket with Lincoln.

After their November victory, the president-elect summoned Hamlin to Chicago to discuss Cabinet appointments. The vice president-elect vowed to himself to do everything possible to get along well with his chief. Lincoln impressed him favorably, especially when he left the choice of the New England cabinet member to Hamlin. Working from a list the president-elect gave him, he finally designated former Democrat Gideon Welles of Connecticut, who became secretary of the navy. Hamlin also played a key role in the intricate negotiations by which Seward assumed the secretary-of-state position, but he failed to keep Simon Cameron out of the cabinet, despite his frank advice that the appointment of the allegedly corrupt Pennsylvanian would be damaging to the Republican Party.

Hamlin's February journey to Washington for the inauguration proved eventful. In New Haven, excited Republicans literally pulled him off the back of the train, and he had to run down the track to board again. He and Mrs. Hamlin rendezvoused with the Lincolns in New York. In Baltimore, an angry mob roiled outside the train, and liquored-up rowdies, searching for Lincoln, peered into Hamlin's compartment but failed to recognize the vice president-elect.

The new vice president fulfilled his sole constitutional function of presiding over the Senate for two-and-a-half weeks before leaving for Maine "in conformity with established usage, and with a view of affording the Senate an opportunity of choosing a President *pro tempore*. . . ." Back home, he learned of the firing on Fort Sumter and ten days later left for New York City, apparently to be available in case something untoward happened to President Lincoln. He itched for service. The national emergency and his own hardworking nature compelled him to action. But the vice presidency is not, by its nature, an activist office. Only the president could vest him with even a modicum of authority, and Lincoln's only request was that Vice President Hamlin inform him of troop movements in and out of New York. The vice president had returned to Maine before this message arrived. His reply foreshadows four years of frustration:

> I went to New York in the hope that I might be of some little service to you or the Gov't. I felt it my duty to contribute even a mite, if I could, for I thought I could feel something of the responsibilities you had to meet. I remained in N.Y. two weeks, and not hearing from you in any way, I came to the conclusion there was nothing for me to do. I even began to fear my motives might be misunderstood. . . . Had I read your note before I left, I would promptly and gladly have performed that service, or any other.

Hamlin concluded by vowing loyally to "*at once* repair to N.Y. or to any place you may desire and perform as well as I can that or any other service you may require." He journeyed to New York and Washington, but it is not known what, if anything, he did for the president in either place.

The impotent vice presidency chafed and galled its Civil War incumbent. President Lincoln seemed well disposed toward Vice President Hamlin personally but, despite his legendary sensitivity and kindness, seems not to have sensed Hamlin's unhappiness and gave him no significant role to play during the war.

When Jessie Benton Frémont urged the vice president to help her husband, General John C. Frémont, gain a new command in summer 1862, Hamlin replied with brutal frankness:

> What can I do? The slow and unsatisfactory movements of the Government do not meet with my approbation, and that is known, and of course I am not consulted at all, nor do I think there is much disposition in any quarter to regard any counsel I may give much if at all.

Hamlin grumbled that he was the most insignificant man in Washington, neglected by president, cabinet, and Congress. When Congressman William A. Wheeler of New York came to take Hamlin to lunch, he found the vice president asleep in his chair, worn out by an interminable Senate debate. "Wheeler, I will take lunch with you on condition that you promise me you will never be vice president. I am only a fifth wheel of a coach and can do little for my friends." Ironically, Wheeler became Rutherford B. Hayes's vice president in 1877.

One suspects that most vice presidents have found their one Senate duty boring, but Hamlin could have done without the excitement of tangling with drunken Senator Willard Saulsbury of Delaware, whose bitter denunciations of Lincoln and inebriated antics on January 27, 1863, forced the vice president to place him in the custody of the sergeant-at-arms.

Patronage, the lifeblood of Hamlin the politician, was conspicuously lacking during the war years. Having no power, the vice president's pleas for jobs and other government favors could be, and often were, safely ignored. Navy Secretary Welles considered Hamlin "rapacious as a wolf" for patronage, and the former's coldness and unhelpfulness angered the man largely responsible for Welles being in the cabinet.

Vice President Hamlin wanted to make the destruction of slavery an early Union war aim. He applauded President Lincoln's Emancipation Proclamation and his decision to use black troops, but he played only a peripheral role in these landmark policy decisions and others concerning the conduct of the war. Only the removal of the president by death or Confederate capture could have brought Hamlin to power. When President Lincoln took to his bed with a mild strain of smallpox immediately after returning from Gettysburg (he joked that now he had something he could give everybody), anxious discussion of the possible succession of the vice president ensued. But Lincoln recovered quickly, and Hamlin once again became anonymous. As to assassination, Lincoln rarely worried about it. Do you think, he quipped, alluding to the vice president's radicalism on the slavery issue, that "the Richmond people would like to have Hannibal Hamlin here any better than myself? In that one alternative, I have an insurance on my life worth half the prairie land in Illinois."

The seizure of Washington by the Confederates seemed a real possibility after the Southern victory at Second Manassas in August 1862. "Should the emergency . . . arise," Hamlin wrote from Bangor in September, "[be] assured I will be ready to act at once with all the energy and efficiency I possess." Washington remained safely in Union hands.

But Hamlin would have become the seventeenth president of the United States had he won renomination at the National Union Party Convention in June 1864. (The Republicans had temporarily adopted a new label to stress their premier war aim and to woo Democratic votes). Despite the second office's many frustrations, the vice president clearly anticipated a second term to validate his wartime fidelity to Union and party and to provide a secure post for the next four years. The substitution of Andrew Johnson of Tennessee for the doughty Mainer had momentous consequences and has been a source of considerable historical controversy. Lincoln's role has been the center of contention. Did he, as he indicated to some, intend not to interfere with the vice presidential nomination? Certainly he wrote exactly that to his private secretary, John G. Nicolay: "Wish not to interfere about V.P."

But other Lincoln intimates swore he favored Johnson and asked them to work for the Tennessean behind the scenes at Baltimore. Two political realities argue powerfully for this view. First, President Lincoln feared for his own reelection in June 1864, and strengthening the ticket by replacing Hamlin with a Southern war Democrat like Johnson made excellent sense. Second, as a Lincoln supporter and delegate from New Jersey pointed out " . . . so perfect was Abraham Lincoln's control of the Baltimore Convention . . . , that he need only have pointed his index finger toward the State of Maine to have had Hannibal Hamlin on that ticket." The president's secret efforts for Johnson doubtless proved decisive.

Hamlin put on a brave front in defeat but four years later voiced his anger and pain. When urged to run for the 1868 Republican vice presidential nomination, Hamlin wrote to a friend in a letter marked "For your eye only":

One thing I can say very distinctly. My name must not be draged [sic] into the canvass to be defeated. I am sure you will concur in that. I was draged out of the Senate, against my wishes—tried to do my *whole* duty, and was then unceremoniously "whistled down the wind." While I have *never* complained to any one, I did not fail to *feel* and *know* how I was treated. I do not want my name used to such an end again.

During the war, Vice President Hamlin had frequently absented himself from Washington, engaged in such activities as, stripped to his shirt-sleeves, harvesting hay and doing other chores on his Maine farm. During the summer of 1864, he served as color corporal in the Maine Coast Guards, a militia unit stationed at Fort McClary in Kittery. Corporal Hamlin stood guard for the first three nights until relieved and appointed company cook. In his biography of Hannibal Hamlin, this writer sums up his military service as follows:

> There is considerable charm and picturesqueness in Hamlin's brief tour of duty. Nothing, however, illustrates more graphically the insignificance of the Civil War vice presidency than the spectacle of its incumbent toting a musket, cooking up fish chowders, and generally playing at being a soldier for two months during one of the most critical periods of the war.

Inauguration Day, March 4, 1865, featured the most notorious vice presidential swearing-in in U.S. history. Vice President Hamlin had banished liquor from the Capitol's Senate wing, but he procured a bottle for his shaky successor, who was slowly recovering from a bout of typhoid fever and was hungover from a party the previous evening. Excitement, an overheated Senate chamber, and two stiff drinks converted the usually dignified Johnson into an inebriate with red face and waving arms, delivering a Tennessee-style stump speech to the stunned dignitaries before him. The *Bangor Jeffersonian* harrumphed:

> His whole manner and speech were the inspiration of a brain crazed by intoxicating liquors. There was not a respectable man in that whole assemblage . . . from the President to the humblest page, who did not hang his head for shame at such conduct and on such an occasion. Every decent man in the nation feels disgraced.

A few days after the inauguration, Hamlin said goodbye to President Lincoln and headed for Maine. The *New York Herald*'s March 10, 1865, issue carried a story headed "Going Home Disgusted" in which it described the former vice president as "thoroughly disgusted with every thing and almost everyone in public life, excepting the President." Among his gripes was William Pitt Fessenden's refusal to remain in the cabinet as treasury secretary "and leave Hamlin a clean track for his place in the Senate" (Fessenden was returned to the U.S. Senate in January 1865).

Hamlin last saw Lincoln in his coffin in the crepe-hung White House East Room. President Johnson completed a process begun by his predecessor by appointing the former vice president collector of the Port of Boston. The income of the office proved somewhat disappointing, but when Hamlin resigned in 1866, he did so on a matter of principle. He deplored Andrew Johnson's Reconstruction policy, which he believed turned the former Confederate states over to unrepentant rebels and completely abandoned the freed blacks to their fate. When the House impeached, and the Senate tried, President Johnson for high crimes and misdemeanors in 1868, Hamlin made clear that had he held the Senate seat, he, unlike Fessenden, would have voted to convict.

In 1869, Hamlin defeated incumbent Senator Lot M. Morrill by a whisker. He served until 1881, eventually rising to the chairmanship of the Senate Foreign Relations Committee. Senator Hamlin got along famously with President Ulysses S. Grant but clashed with President Rutherford B. Hayes over patronage and the ending of Reconstruction. Hamlin and James G. Blaine dominated the Maine Republican Party in the 1870s, and the senator labored for Blaine's nomination as president in both the 1876 and 1880 Republican National Conventions. In 1881, Blaine became secretary of state and engineered his political cohort's appointment as minister to

Spain. Hamlin found Europe fascinating, touring cathedrals and art galleries, meeting dignitaries, and comparing the Old World with the New:

> While absent, I was in, and saw much of the different nationalities, which enabled me to form opinions of the Governments and people of Europe. And while I tried to judge fairly of all that I saw, I must say that I love our Govt and its plain republican character all the better for what I saw.

During his nine retirement years, Hamlin farmed, fished, attended Grand Army of the Republic encampments, read biographies, novels and poetry, and enjoyed the comforts of his Bangor home. On July 4, 1891, he suffered a fatal heart attack while playing cards at Bangor's Tarratine Club, the month before his eighty-second birthday.

Hannibal Hamlin could scarcely be described as a great vice president. The office itself has no greatness in it. But during the Civil War he served his nation, his president, and his party with all the dedication and activism his painfully circumscribed role allowed. One should also not forget his significant role as a premier antiexpansionist in the 1840s and 1850s and his status as a mover and shaper of the Republican Party.

REFERENCES

H. Draper Hunt, *Hannibal Hamlin of Maine: Lincoln's First Vice-President* (Syracuse, N.Y.: Syracuse University Press, 1969); Charles Eugene Hamlin, *The Life and Times of Hannibal Hamlin* (Cambridge, Mass.: Riverside Press, Published by Subscriptlon, 1899); Lewis Clinton Hatch, ed.-in-chief, *Maine: A History*, 3 vols. Centennial Edition (New York: The American Historical Society, 1919); Lewis C. Hatch, *A History of the Vice Presidency of the United States*, revised and edited by Earl L. Shoup (New York: The American Historical Society, Inc., 1934).

H. DRAPER HUNT recently retired as professor of history at the University of Southern Maine, where he taught since 1965. He holds an A.B. degree from Harvard College and M.A. and Ph.D. degrees from Columbia University. From 1962 until 1965, he taught at Hunter College of the City University of New York. In addition to his biography of Hannibal Hamlin (above), Professor Hunt's publications include *The Blaine House: Home of Maine's Governors* (1974; rev. ed. 1994) and *Dearest Father: The Civil War Letters of Lt. Frank Dickerson, a Son of Belfast, Maine* (Unity, Maine: North Country Press, 1992).

ANDREW JOHNSON (1808–1875)

Vice President, March 4–April 15, 1865

(President Abraham Lincoln)

ANDREW JOHNSON
(Library of Congress)

By Richard Zuczek

ndrew Johnson, one of the most enigmatic figures in American nineteenth-century politics, had only a brief tenure as vice president, yet his experience dramatically illustrates two important roles of the office. In 1864, the Union Republican Party and Abraham Lincoln selected Johnson for the political advantage he could bring in the election, demonstrating the vital, if supporting, role vice presidents play in campaigns. Only months later Johnson, following the assassination of Lincoln, was thrust into the ex-

ecutive chair, providing an object lesson in the vice president's ultimate function. For Johnson, those few months also marked a rupture in his political career; his subsequent intransigence and short-sightedness as president eclipsed his earlier achievements and destroyed the reputation he had struggled his entire life to build.

That reputation may never be resuscitated, although historical opinion concerning Johnson—and in particular his presidency—has not remained constant. Many historians of the late nineteenth and early twentieth centuries saw a man valiantly protecting the Constitution from the radical designs of northern capitalists and ignorant blacks. Later, revisionists came along and beheld only a racist southerner, nearly traitorous in his support for former confederates and their outmoded values. The latest view lies somewhere in between, depicting an intense man of limited vision who never understood that in a society undergoing revolution, his zealous dedication to conservative principles was not only unproductive, but self-destructive.

Both the principles and the stubborn attachment to them were rooted deep in Johnson's past. Born in 1808 in Raleigh, North Carolina, Johnson knew hard times. His father, a porter, had died in 1811, forcing Johnson's mother to support the family by weaving. Johnson never attended school but at age fourteen was apprenticed to a tailor from whom he learned the rudiments of reading and writing. Perhaps believing Raleigh too constricting and hoping to improve his standing—once before he had run off to South Carolina with his brother—Johnson sought his future in East Tennessee. He finally settled in Greeneville in 1827, where he met and married Eliza McCardle (1810–1876) and became well regarded as a skilled tailor. He prospered both personally and professionally: He had five children (Martha, Charles, Mary, Robert, and Andrew) and continued his education under the tutelage of his better-educated wife. His commanding physical presence, frank opinions, and appealing oratorical style soon made him popular in the local debating society.

Johnson was a magnet for the town's younger artisans, a man who seemed to embody the Jacksonian Democracy of the 1820s and 1830s. (That Johnson's middle name was Jackson is a myth; he had no middle name.) Before long he started to look toward local politics. His humble roots, honest egalitarianism, strict constitutionalism, and distrust of government and the wealthy gained him enough admirers to win election as alderman in 1829 and mayor of Greeneville in 1831, but these principles also alienated many townspeople. His stoic adherence to principle caused Johnson political damage throughout his career; for instance, he was elected as a Democrat to the state legislature in 1835, 1839, and 1841 but was defeated in 1837 because he opposed—on constitutional grounds—the state aid to railroads that his constituents demanded. Among the Tennesseans who opposed his rise was William "Parsons" Brownlow, who attacked Johnson as much for his policies as for his admittedly "unaffiliated" religious stance.

Intelligent and ambitious, Johnson hoped to reproduce his local success at the national level. He won election to Congress in 1842 and served five consecutive terms until gerrymandered out of office by the Whig-controlled Tennessee legislature in 1852. In Congress, as in Tennessee, his devotion to his own narrowly defined principles won him both respect and derision. While Johnson opposed most Whig programs, including the tariff and government funding of internal improvements, he was also at odds with Democratic President James K. Polk. Johnson criticized patronage, military academies, the electoral college, and even the Smithsonian Institution. Johnson, who won praise as the defender of the "common man," saw such entities as elitist, costly, and dangerous to democracy.

Johnson's ouster from Washington in 1852 only redirected his energies. He spoiled Tennessee Whig celebrations by being elected governor in both 1853 and 1855. In 1857, when the Democrats retook control of the legislature, he returned to Washington, this time as senator.

Although the growing sectional crisis clouded the background of Johnson's rise to national prominence, it provided opportunities as well. The Tennessean seemed destined to be a major player in the national drama, for he embodied the contradictions and qualities of not only his idol Andrew Jackson but of the nation itself. A southern Democrat and slaveholder, Johnson was also a devout Unionist. A former critic of the Whigs who now saw Republicans as dangerous agitators, Senator Johnson nevertheless advocated the Homestead Bill, which would grant 160 acres of land to those willing to work it; this met with caustic opposition from southern Democrats but hearty support from Free Soilers and Republicans. Yet, while despising southerners' aristocratic pretensions and secessionist rhetoric, he was a longtime defender of states' rights and openly attacked Republicans in the wake of John Brown's raid on Harper's Ferry in 1859.

As the sectional crisis came to a head, Johnson found his values coinciding more with northern interests than southern ones. Above all else, Johnson believed in the sanctity of the Union and the Constitution. Hoping that his peculiar blend of values would merge with his ambition and Unionism, he saw himself as a compromise candidate for the Democrats in the 1860 presidential campaign—he, a man who had built a career on an unwillingness (or inability) to compromise. Realizing he lacked any real support, Johnson then backed Stephen A. Douglas, which further alienated southern Democrats; not even his last-minute support of John C. Breckinridge could repair the damage. The final break came in the winter of 1860–61, following the election of Republican Abraham Lincoln. Johnson adamantly opposed secession, worked furiously (but unsuccessfully) to keep Tennessee in the Union, and found himself allied with former enemies—Whigs like William Brownlow—against former friends. Johnson's support for Abraham Lincoln and his refusal to leave the Senate when Tennessee seceded (he was the only Southern senator who did not go out with his state) made him a hero among Republicans and Northern war Democrats.

A Tennessee Unionist, Johnson was the obvious choice for military governor when federal forces moved into central Tennessee in early 1862, but the attempt to rekindle latent Unionism and reinstate a civil government met with numerous obstacles, including Confederate forces, squabbles over authority with military commanders, and divisions within the pro-Union population. Although civil government was not restored until spring 1865, Republicans had liked what they had seen of Johnson. He had dealt severely with Confederates and sympathizers, and his no-nonsense approach to secessionists and advocacy of emancipation won wide acclaim. But many in the North overlooked other issues that would return after the war: Johnson's belief in *individual* disloyalty, rather than state disloyalty, and his overriding conviction in civil supremacy over the military.

Johnson's defiant stance toward secession and what he termed the "so-called Confederacy"—defiance would always be a character trait—made him an overwhelming choice as Lincoln's running mate in 1864. Carrying the new "Union Party" designation, Republicans hoped to attract as many war Democrats as possible, and the selection of Johnson for vice president increased their chances for bipartisan support. As the Tennessean campaigned during the election (it was rare for vice-presidential candidates to campaign, but Johnson was ever the political maverick) he became even more radical, driving home his stubborn save-the-Union-at-all-costs philosophy. He consistently pushed for emancipation in Tennessee and even admitted blacks to military service in a September militia call. Yet, other messages bothered some Republicans, especially those led by House power Thaddeus Stevens. According to Johnson, his status as a candidate from Tennessee proved his claim that secession was impossible and the states had not left the Union, an approach that would cause considerable conflict during Reconstruction.

The Union ticket of Lincoln and Johnson rode roughshod over the candidates of conservative Unionism, George B. McClellan and George Pendleton, but the November victory and Johnson's contribution to it were tainted by an embarrassing performance at the March inauguration. Exhausted from a rigorous campaign and a celebration the previous night, Johnson sought to steady himself with some whiskey; a packed Senate chamber listened in shock as the veteran stump speaker and new vice president babbled on incoherently, delivering a tirade of self-serving remarks and alienating nearly the entire cabinet. It was not the first time Johnson had acted without careful thought to consequences, nor would it be the last.

Unfortunately for Johnson and the nation, the Tennessean would not have the opportunity to learn the intricacies and nuances of functioning at the executive level. Abraham Lincoln was assassinated a month after his second inauguration, and on April 15, 1865, Johnson took the oath of office as the seventeenth President of the United States. At first many Republicans believed that Johnson might be more to their liking than Lincoln; a brilliant war leader and politician, Lincoln nonetheless opposed many of the more radical policies favored by some in Congress. Judging by Johnson's hard-line approach during the war, Radicals hoped they had found an ally ready to punish the South and levy a severe penance. In a way, the Radicals were correct, for Johnson was not Lincoln. Impatient, tactless, and egotistical, Johnson lacked his predecessor's ability to observe, assess, and then act, ever mindful of when to conform to the political climate and when to manipulate it. But neither did Johnson understand the men who would oppose him; the choice of the Republican Party and, by implication, of the northern population, he failed to realize the debts he owed. Moreover, he held widely differing views on the Constitution, the role of government, and the status of blacks in American society.

Johnson's first weeks in office gave little indication of the storm to come. Doing his best to ease the sudden transition, the new president retained Lincoln's cabinet and permitted Mary Todd Lincoln to stay in the Executive Mansion for several weeks. He backed Secretary of War Edwin Stanton's hunt for the assassins, even posting a $100,000 reward for the capture of Jefferson Davis. Johnson then coolly sentenced the conspirators—excluding Davis but including Mary Surratt, whose complicity was questionable at best—to their deaths. Radical mirth was short-lived, however, for Johnson's policies were even more war-oriented than Lincoln's: with the war over and the assassination conspiracy exposed, the new president was eager to get on with business as usual.

But business as usual was unlikely until the South was brought back into proper alignment with the rest of the nation. Johnson understood that the southern states needed to make certain concessions before their representatives would be readmitted to Congress. With Congress in recess, Johnson was free to act on his belief that Recon-

struction was an *executive* function, and he readily offered his own plan of restoration, rooted in his values as a limited-government southerner. The president appointed provisional governors to oversee the abolition of slavery, the writing of new state constitutions, the repudiation of secession and Confederate debts, and the election of new members of Congress and governors. Beyond this, Johnson required former Confederates to concede little, holding to the concept that *individuals*, and not states, commit treason. He did not require black suffrage or any economic assistance for the freed people and readily offered pardons to former Confederates who applied. In fact, few states even complied with his meager requirements; most refused to repudiate the Confederate debt, and some found clever wordings to avoid nullifying the principle of secession.

By fall 1865, with the passage of restrictive "black codes," the rise of antiblack and anti-Republican violence, and the election of former Confederates to local and national offices, Republicans in Congress decided Johnson was not the man they expected. The South did not appear penitent or remorseful, yet the president seemed unconcerned and even pleased. Battle lines were drawn in December 1865, when Congress, invoking its prerogative, refused to seat the newly elected members of Congress from the former Confederate states. This rejection and the subsequent formation of the Joint Committee on Reconstruction underscored the fundamental difference between the executive and the legislature. Johnson believed that the states held direction over their citizens and that it was the president's responsibility to protect states in their rights. Congress, on the other hand, was wallowing in the extension of federal power that grew out of the Civil War and fully intended that it determine the nature of a state's society.

Because Johnson was unwilling to push for real change in the South, Congress in 1866 attempted to provide the protection for former slaves that the South and the president would not. Through the Freedmen's Bureau Act, the Civil Rights Act, and the Fourteenth Amendment, Republicans hoped to protect blacks in their civil rights, limit southern power in Congress, and bolster the new southern Republican party. To Johnson these measures were unconstitutional infringements on states' rights and the fundamental precepts of American federalism, especially considering that Congress was making laws for states that were not represented! The president vetoed each bill—Congress overrode each veto—and actively campaigned against the ratification of the Fourteenth Amendment. His antagonistic veto messages and belligerent attitude toward Congress drove moderates into the radical camp, further fueling Johnson's own persecution complex.

As had happened before, Johnson's rigid adherence to principle would cost him dearly. His support for emancipation was a war measure, and he had no intention of granting black suffrage or, worse yet, allowing the federal government to impose it. But Johnson's conservative constitutionalism placed him firmly in the South's camp, which alienated him from his base of support in the North. Politically obtuse at times, Johnson could not see that he was binding his future to that of an impoverished, politically bankrupt region that was clutching at the last vestiges of a dying lifestyle. His callousness in the face of southern violence—in particular the New Orleans Riot in July 1866—and his formation of a new party for the fall congressional elections only increased the distance between himself and northern voters. Adding insult to injury was the debacle of his "Swing around the Circle," a speaking tour from New York to the Midwest that demonstrated just how out of touch he had become. The elections hammered the point home, as Republicans took control of two-thirds of each house, assuring them of a free hand in administering their own Reconstruction program. Despite the warning signals, Johnson not only stayed his course but took the offensive; he tinkered with the idea of replacing radical Secretary of War Stanton with General William T. Sherman, and delivered an annual message critical of Congress and its unconstitutional measures.

Congress responded by embarking on its own plan of Reconstruction. Bolstered by Republican successes at the polls, Congress in the spring of 1867 passed two military reconstruction acts that provided the blueprint for new governments in the South. Under the watchful eye of the army, new elections would be held, but without a white monopoly; blacks and whites would elect new governments, select new national officials, and write new state constitutions. Congress also planted the seed of Johnson's demise with the Tenure of Office Act (designed to prevent the president from removing Republican officeholders) and curtailed his authority by requiring that all orders to the army pass through General of the Army Ulysses S. Grant.

Johnson's reaction was immediate and hostile. Although Congress easily overrode his vetoes, the president found other ways to hamper what he believed were unconstitutional measures that illegally punished some people while dangerously elevating others. He encouraged opposition to the laws in communications to southerners, nurtured opposition in the North, and removed military commanders who he felt had transgressed against civil supremacy. His recall of commanders Philip Sheridan, Daniel Sickles, and later John Pope angered Radicals and worried Grant, who had been supporting them in their liberal approach to Congress's rulings. Congress matched the president move for move, and in summer 1868 the House Judiciary Committee held impeachment hearings but was unable to produce evidence of any criminal wrongdoing.

The final break with Congress came over the suspension of Secretary of War Stanton. For two years the president and the secretary had been at odds, yet Johnson had vacillated and procrastinated about Stanton's future despite his duplicitous actions and obvious complicity with Radical generals and congressmen. In late summer, during the congressional recess, Johnson suspended Stanton and appointed Grant Secretary of War *ad interim*, but Johnson's few victories—the purchase of Alaska from Russia and the Democratic resurgence in northern states in the fall elections, for instance—could not shield him from Republican wrath. Had Johnson moved more decisively earlier, he might have been spared impeachment, but now Republicans were armed with the Tenure of Office Act. The

House Judiciary Committee decided in favor of impeachment in late November, and while the House as a whole rejected impeachment in December, the Senate in January 1868 voted not to concur with the president's suspension of Stanton. Continuing to side with Congress over the president, Grant vacated the position, happy to avoid being crushed between the two warring branches of government.

Johnson, not without Congress's help, had worked himself into a corner with the Senate, General Grant, and Stanton allied against him. When Stanton resumed his old post (and barricaded himself in his office), Johnson formally removed him and appointed General Lorenzo Thomas interim secretary. Johnson's first choice, William T. Sherman, had succeeded in refusing his commander in chief; like Grant, another powerful potential ally had slipped through Johnson's fingers. Johnson's removal of Stanton only exacerbated the situation. Thomas was unable to take possession of the secretary's office, and Stanton's removal (as opposed to a suspension) convinced the House to vote in favor of impeachment on February 24. The same day, Johnson nominated Hugh Ewing, Sr., to take over the War Department (instead of the inept Thomas), but new affairs took precedence.

On March 30, the galleries were packed as the Senate, with Chief Justice Salmon P. Chase presiding, convened to decide whether the president was indeed guilty of "high crimes and misdemeanors." Benjamin Butler, Thaddeus Stevens, and the other five prosecutors attempted to prove that Johnson had violated both the Tenure of Office Act and the Army Appropriations Act of 1867 and had failed to execute the laws of Congress. The five defense counsels had their hands full, not only refuting Republican charges but keeping Johnson as inactive as possible (he did not even appear at the trial), trying to avert some other blunder that might antagonize Republican fence-sitters. While Johnson was convinced that the trial would vindicate his policy, his chief counsels, Attorney General Henry Stanbery (who resigned to defend Johnson) and noted attorney William Evarts, created a defense based on the legal details of the charges, deliberately avoiding the controversial larger issues of Reconstruction.

Arguments closed nearly a month and a half later, and on May 16, senators began to vote on the individual articles of impeachment. They began with Article 11, the refusal to faithfully execute the laws and found Johnson guilty by a vote of 35 to 19, one vote shy of the two-thirds required for conviction. Ten days later two more articles followed the same pattern. Sensing it was over, Republicans conceded, and the Senate adjourned without voting on the other charges.

Although Johnson attributed his acquittal to the righteousness of his course, other factors were at work. His counsels ably dismantled the prosecution's central charges, those involving the Tenure of Office Act, by showing that it covered officials only during the term of the president under which they were originally appointed. Thus, it was irrelevant here because while Stanton had been appointed under Lincoln, Johnson was now president. Timing also helped Johnson's cause; with his term nearly over and most southern states already readmitted, there was little left to win. Facing such meager rewards at best, many Republicans would rather stick with Johnson than turn the executive chair over to Benjamin Wade, president of the Senate. Since there was no vice president, Wade would succeed if Johnson were convicted, and his rabidly Radical politics were too controversial for many Republicans, who also feared he might complicate matters for the chosen successor, Ulysses S. Grant.

Historians like to believe there was also an element of "constitutional caution" at work, some last-minute fail-safe that stopped the wheels of party politics and forced senators to consider the significance of their actions. Never before or since has American government come so close to disintegration, so near to setting a disturbing, irrevocable precedent. Just as secession struck at the heart of democratic politics in general, impeachment struck at the heart of democratic government. The trial of Andrew Johnson demonstrated some admirable qualities of American politics: determination, loyalty, perseverance, adherence to principle. Unfortunately both sides lost sight of principles in the face of personalities and paranoia, nearly doing irreparable damage to the structure each intended to protect.

Although the final ten months of Johnson's presidency were relatively uneventful, Johnson still behaved with characteristic intransigence. He trusted to the end that he would receive the Democratic nomination for president (he did not) and in his last annual message reiterated his opposition to the Reconstruction Acts. Always a proponent of his own lost cause, Johnson even sought political office after he returned to East Tennessee in 1869, but as had happened in the past, Johnson fell between party stools: he remained a Republican enemy, while Democrats clearly remembered his defection during the Civil War. Not until 1874 did his political horizons brighten, when he was elected to the U.S. Senate—the only former president to earn this distinction. The years had not mellowed the man or his temperament, and in a special March 1875 session he attacked President Grant for his support of Reconstruction governments in Louisiana. His return to the national arena was short-lived: On a visit to Greeneville he suffered a stroke and died two days later on July 31, 1875.

Historians will continue to debate Johnson's policies and his legacy. Rather than condemning or justifying him, scholars should be content to try to understand him, a man trapped within his principles, unable to see beyond the past and into the future. Johnson had risen to prominence by challenging conservative views during the Jacksonian period, yet could not see how during the Union crisis, new times again required new thinking. His racism, constitutional conservatism, and shortsightedness were common among whites of the time, but many came to realize that the Civil War had forever altered the country: Revolution-ary times required revolutionary thinking. To Johnson, liberty could only be protected if people served the Constitution, rather than vice versa. That the Constitution was a "living" document, capable of growing and changing with the nation, escaped him. To be sure, his administration exacerbated the trauma of the period and damaged the presidency as both an institution and a symbol. Ironically, however, his obstinacy also unified the North and the Republican Party and forced his opponents to tear down the Constitution he so revered and erect a greater one in its place.

REFERENCES

Michael Les Benedict, *The Impeachment and Trial of Andrew Johnson* (New York: W.W. Norton and Co., 1973); *The Papers of Andrew Johnson*, Paul H. Bergeron, LeRoy P. Graf, and Ralph Haskins, eds., 11 vols. to date (Knoxville: University of Tennessee Press, 1967–); Albert Castel, *The Presidency of Andrew Johnson* (Lawrence, Kans.: Regents Press of Kansas, 1979); Richard B. McCaslin, *Andrew Johnson: A Bibliography* (Westport, Conn.: Greenwood Press, 1992); Eric McKitrick, *Andrew Johnson and Reconstruction* (Chicago, Ill.: University of Chicago Press, 1960); Hans Trefousse, *Andrew Johnson: A Biography* (New York: W.W. Norton and Co., 1989).

RICHARD ZUCZEK received his doctorate from Ohio State University in 1993 and is currently assistant editor for the Papers of Andrew Johnson Project at the University of Tennessee, where he also teaches American and European history. He has presented numerous papers on Reconstruction and has two articles on the subject due to appear in *Civil War History* and *The South Carolina Historical Magazine*. His book, *State of Rebellion: South Carolina During Reconstruction*, was published by the University of South Carolina Press in 1996.

SCHUYLER COLFAX (1823–1885)

Vice President, 1869–1873

(President Ulysses S. Grant)

SCHUYLER COLFAX
(Library of Congress)

By Patrick J. Furlong and Ann Leonard

Schuyler Colfax, though always associated with Indiana, was born in New York City on March 23, 1823. He was named for his father, who had died of tuberculosis six months earlier. Hannah Stryker Colfax, a widow at seventeen, struggled to support and educate her son. Schuyler Colfax was born into very modest circumstances, but earlier members of the family had distinguished themselves: His paternal grandfather was General William Colfax, who had served as commander of George Washington's Life Guard during the Revolutionary War, and his maternal grandmother, Hester Schuyler, was a cousin of General Philip Schuyler, whose name passed into the Colfax family.

Hannah Colfax lived with her mother and provided for her fatherless son until he reached the age of ten, when her resources were exhausted. Schuyler then went to work clerking in a store to help support his mother. On November 6, 1834, Hannah Colfax married George Matthews of Baltimore. Matthews was only fourteen years older than his stepson, and the two developed a lifelong attachment. Two years later, the family moved to the newly settled village of New Carlisle, Indiana, where Schuyler clerked in his stepfather's general store. In 1841, Matthews was elected auditor of St. Joseph County on the Whig ticket and the family moved to the county seat, South Bend. Matthews appointed his stepson deputy auditor, although Colfax was not yet of legal age when he began his public career. He remained deputy auditor until 1849, but the position was not time consuming.

From 1842 to 1844, Colfax served as assistant enrolling clerk of the Indiana senate. During this period he also studied law intermittently but never qualified as a lawyer. Colfax idolized Henry Clay, and he campaigned for him in the presidential election of 1844, addressing crowds in New York City as well as Indiana. On October 10, 1844, he married his childhood sweetheart, Evelyn Clark of Argyle, New York. From all accounts they had a happy marriage, though Evelyn Colfax suffered from ill health and was a semiinvalid for years until her death on July 10, 1863.

Religion was an important influence on Colfax from his earliest years, and his humanitarian principles of equality for all and his passion for justice grew out of Christian precepts and early training. He began and ended his life as a member of the Dutch Reformed Church, and though sincere, he was not doctrinaire. For a short time, he was a Presbyterian until expelled from that church for driving his horses on Sunday to an Episcopalian wedding. He spoke frequently on the evil of strong drink and encouraged establishment of a total abstinence society in South Bend.

Colfax began to contribute articles to local newspapers when he was only sixteen, and within a few years became a frequent contributor to Horace Greeley's *New York Tribune*, one of the nation's leading Whig newspapers. While working for the state senate he serve also as legislative correspondent for the *Indiana State Journal*, the state's leading Whig newspaper. In 1845, at the age of twenty-two, he was able to secure enough money to purchase a half-interest in a struggling South Bend weekly, which he soon renamed the *St. Joseph Valley Register*. Its circulation was only 250 copies, and it required several years of hard work for Colfax to increase its average weekly sale to 1,000 and to repay the money he had borrowed to buy the newspaper.

The *Register* was a good example of a small-town midwestern newspaper. It offered the usual selection of European and national news, heavily political of course, with a variety of fiction and human interest stories. Local news, except for politics, received little attention, for word-of-mouth was much faster than a weekly newspaper. Colfax energetically supported development of the St. Joseph Valley, praising the fertility of its soil, the healthy nature of its climate, and the industrial advantages of its streams. He was a vigorous advocate of railroad construction and frequently published long descriptions of his eastern travels by steamboat and railroad. Colfax continued as editor of the *Register* until 1864, with a deputy in South Bend while he attended congressional sessions. From Washington he sent regular reports of the debates in Congress and the social life of the nation's capital.

Politics continued to absorb Colfax's interests outside of journalism. In 1848, he was chosen as a delegate to the national Whig convention. He favored General Winfield Scott, but when General Zachary Taylor won the nomination Colfax worked energetically for his election. He voted with the majority to endorse the Wilmot Proviso, which prohibited the extension of slavery into the western lands acquired after the Mexican War.

Colfax often took time from his editorial duties to attend political gatherings. He was a leading Whig delegate to the Indiana Constitutional Convention in 1850. The Whig minority won few motions, but Colfax argued eloquently against the article that prohibited further black immigration into the state. He favored exempting debtors' homes from seizure for payment of debts and supported the majority in limiting the legislature's power to borrow. Much of the credit for an improved banking system in Indiana goes to Colfax and his ability to encourage compromise among the members of the convention.

Though liberal in his views regarding blacks, Colfax showed himself rigidly opposed to measures intended to protect the property of married women, widows, and orphans. This stand with respect to women is somewhat curious when Colfax is credited with being the leading spirit in the establishment of the Degree of Rebekah, the ladies' auxiliary to the Independent Order of Odd Fellows. In 1850, he was appointed chairman of a committee to consider accepting women, and he wrote the minority report favoring the proposition. When the proposal was accepted by the membership a year later, Colfax drafted the articles of incorporation for the Rebekah.

Slavery was never far from the public and private conscience of Colfax. Colfax disliked slavery on moral principle and opposed its expansion, without moving as far as favoring outright abolition. Henry Clay was his political idol, but he regarded the fugitive slave provisions of the Compromise of 1850 as "unnecessarily harsh and summary." On the other hand, Colfax did not believe that Congress possessed the power to abolish slavery in the District of Columbia without the consent of its residents.

Colfax's political views were firmly Whig, in favor of high protective tariffs and internal improvements. In 1847, he served as secretary of the Rivers and Harbors Convention in Chicago. This was the beginning of his association with a young Whig from Illinois, Abraham Lincoln, who made a stirring impromptu speech at the convention.

Colfax ran unsuccessfully for Congress on the Whig ticket in 1851. The next year at the party's national convention he helped to secure General Winfield Scott's nomination. Colfax declined the Whig nomination for Congress in 1852, but when the party broke apart on the slavery question two years later, he played a significant role in the organization of the new Republican Party in Indiana. He was nominated for Congress in 1854 and elected in a vigorous campaign across a sprawling district in northern Indiana. In 1855, Colfax attended a national convention of the Know-Nothing Party, a serious mistake on his part. When accused afterward of being a Know-Nothing himself, he pretended that he had attended only as a newspaper reporter.

As a member of Congress, Colfax was soon embroiled in the Kansas-Nebraska controversy. He denounced Stephen A. Douglas's scheme to allow settlers in the newly organized Kansas Territory to vote on the admission of slavery to an area long closed to slavery by the Missouri Compromise of 1820. Colfax's stirring denunciation of the oppressive Kansas slave code, delivered in the House on June 21, 1856, greatly advanced his reputation as an orator. More than a million copies of his speech were circulated in pamphlet form by the Republican Party.

In 1858, Colfax was appointed chairman of the Post Office Committee, and he performed his most significant work in Congress in this capacity. He reorganized the postal service and reformed gross abuses, while consolidating routes and extending daily overland mail service to California. He shepherded bills through Congress that greatly improved mail service to the Western mining regions and provided for both the return of undelivered mail and the delivery of articles in addition to letters. During the Civil War, Colfax was responsible for the establishment of the system that made recipients of mail from soldiers and sailors liable for postage.

During the Illinois senatorial election of 1858, Colfax gave Lincoln lukewarm support and met with Douglas on more than one occasion to discuss the latter's break with President James Buchanan over the troubles in Kansas. Colfax did not take an active role in the Republican convention of 1860, aside from his efforts to encourage the candidacy of the conservative former Whig Edward Bates of Missouri. Once Lincoln received the Republican nomination, Colfax campaigned enthusiastically for him, speaking in Illinois, Iowa, Missouri, and Michigan.

With Lincoln's victory and his own reelection, Colfax and his friends besieged the new president for a cabinet position, preferably postmaster general. Lincoln's political managers had promised the job to someone else, and the popular Colfax was passed over. Colfax faithfully supported Lincoln's war policies, except when Lincoln removed General John C. Frémont from command in Missouri because of his imprudent proclamation freeing the slaves. He said that Freémont "was like a man asked to make bricks without straw." Colfax urged the president to issue an early emancipation proclamation and even detailed the most effective methods of releasing the news to the Northern press.

Colfax and Lincoln attended many social events together, especially theater outings. Years later Colfax recalled that he and Lincoln "often went to Ford's opera house" to relieve the strains of the war. They found pleasure and relaxation watching "those southern girls with their well rounded forms, lustrous hair and sparkling voices," dancing and singing. One night in January 1863, soon after the release of the Emancipation Proclamation, a very dangerous situation developed outside Grover's Theater when an angry crowd surrounded the carriage carrying Colfax and the Lincolns as their coachman lay drunk on the sidewalk. The guards had left the president unattended, and the theater owner grabbed the reins and rescued them. It was Colfax who persuaded the president to attend the Baltimore Sanitary Fair on April 18, 1864, and he acted as host when Lincoln delivered his moving address on liberty.

In later years Colfax noted that two of the most important days of his life were concerned with Abraham Lincoln. He regarded February 1, 1865, the day he signed the House resolution for the Thirteenth Amendment outlawing slavery, as the happiest day of his life. As fate would have it, Colfax was the last public figure to shake Lincoln's hand the night he was assassinated. The two men met that morning to discuss the collapse of the rebellion and Lincoln's plans for Reconstruction. Colfax intended to leave early the next morning for the Pacific coast, and Lincoln gave him a personal message to deliver to the western miners. Colfax declined the president's invitation for the theater that evening but returned to the White House for a promised half-hour visit. He walked the president to the door when it was time for the Lincolns to leave for Ford's Theatre and said his farewell there. Colfax was summoned to Lincoln's deathbed and traveled to Springfield on the solemn funeral train.

The Republican majority chose Colfax as Speaker of the House on December 5, 1863, and reelected him in 1865 and 1867. As Speaker, Colfax was very popular, and though strongly partisan, he was not personally harsh to the Democratic minority. He preferred to use courtesy, tact, and his considerable parliamentary knowledge to guide his rulings. Thaddeus Stevens of Pennsylvania was the dominating figure in the House, and Colfax collaborated with him regularly, both because of Steven's power and because they shared many of the same ideas.

Colfax was severely criticized, however, when he left the chair on April 8, 1864, and introduced a resolution to expel Representative Alexander Long of Ohio on the charge that "he had given aid, countenance and encouragement to the enemy." Colfax had to accept a modification of his resolution, and Long was censured rather than expelled.

Originally favorable to President Andrew Johnson, Colfax lost confidence in him when the president appeared to favor former Confederate officers. Johnson took charge of the process of Reconstruction himself, rather than calling a special session of Congress to deal with the defeated South. Soon after Congress convened in November 1865, Colfax made an important speech on Reconstruction policy in which he asserted the constitutional right of the Congress to judge its members' qualifications. He also insisted that Congress would add its own requirements to those of President Johnson for restoration of the southern states. His speech received wide publicity and gave notice to the southerners that their newly elected representatives would not be seated.

Colfax also contended that a clear majority of the people of a state must give evidence of their loyalty before that state could be fully restored to the Union, that blacks as well as whites needed to be protected in their persons and property, and that the Declaration of Independence must be recognized as the law of the land. "Let us make haste slowly," was the dominant theme of this speech which ended with the hope that the executive and legislative departments would "cordially cooperate."

Colfax was again elected Speaker in December 1865, and the newly elected members from the seceded states were indeed refused their seats. When Thaddeus Stevens carried his motion to create a Joint Committee on Reconstruction, the speaker named nine Radicals to represent the House, including Stevens. Colfax also appointed Stevens as chairman of the newly created Committee on Appropriations, and another Radical, Justin S. Morrill of Vermont, as chairman of the important Ways and Means Committee.

For the next few months, Colfax tried to avoid a public split with President Johnson. Reports of southern whites working defiantly against the rights of newly freed slaves inflamed Colfax's prejudice against southerners and hardened his resolve to solidify the Union victory that had cost the lives of so many. The president's belligerence and lack of tact made powerful enemies in Congress. Colfax helped overturn Johnson's veto of the Freedman's Bureau Bill, and the break between the legislative and executive branches became complete by April 1866. Later in the session, the Joint Committee on Reconstruction reported proposals that eventually became the Fourteenth Amendment.

As a candidate for reelection in the fall of 1866, Colfax vigorously defended both Radical Reconstruction and the Fourteenth Amendment, while his Democratic rival appealed to the tradition of white supremacy. Back in Washington, Colfax again set the tone for the new session with a speech on December 31, 1866. He paved the way for more Radical legislation, including bills to enfranchise the blacks in the District of Columbia and to extend black suffrage to the territories. Naturally Colfax supported the drastic Reconstruction Act passed over a presidential veto in March 1867. That same day Congress passed the Tenure of Office Act over another presidential veto.

Two days later the Thirty-ninth Congress adjourned with a resolution of thanks to the Speaker and then immediately convened as the Fortieth Congress, the only time Congress, rather than the president, called a session. Elected Speaker for a third term, Colfax within the same hour gave both a valedictory and an inaugural address. President Johnson played into the hands of the radicals when he asked for Secretary of War Edwin M. Stanton's resignation on August 5, 1867, and then suspended him a week later because he refused to resign. There was already talk of removing the president, and in November the judiciary committee unsuccessfully recommended impeachment. Colfax urged Stanton to defy the president and continue in office.

When Thad Stevens moved for impeachment in February 1868, Colfax directed the clerk to call his name so that he too could vote for impeachment, although as Speaker he did not usually vote except in cases of a tie. Colfax allowed himself to be drawn into the hectic confrontation and privately urged the president's conviction and removal. The law of presidential succession then in force provided that when the vice presidency was vacant, the Senate president pro temp ranked before the Speaker of the House. Thus Senator Benjamin F. Wade would have become president had Johnson been removed, not Colfax, although the Speaker was more widely respected and trusted. Colfax was rather surprised when the Senate failed to convict the president.

The 1868 presidential campaign began before the impeachment trial ended, but it was already clear that General U.S. Grant would lead the Republican ticket. There was no clear favorite for the vice presidential nomination. When Colfax's name was placed in nomination, he knew that his strongest competitor would be Senator Wade. The Republican convention in Chicago required six ballots to decide that Colfax would be the party's choice for vice president. Republican newspapers portrayed him as reliable and experienced, and he was well known for his many speeches in support of Republican candidates. Democrats remonstrated with Colfax for his earlier connection with the antiforeign and anti-Catholic Know-Nothings, and he in turn waved the bloody shirt and reminded voters that disloyal Democrats were the ones responsible for the deaths of thousands of Union soldiers. Colfax spoke often during the campaign throughout the Midwest, while Grant remained quietly in Washington.

Senator Carl Schurz described with painful accuracy the general Republican view of Grant's running mate:

> Colfax is a very popular man and on that account a strong candidate. His abilities are not distinguished but are just sufficient to make him acceptable to the masses. They are fond of a happy mediocrity.

The genial "Smiler" Colfax, as he was known in Washington, had few illusions and knew well that his active political career was ending as he became vice president on March 4, 1869. An Indianapolis newspaper quoted an unnamed friend who spoke of "the dignified impotence of his present office," an apt description of the vice presidency during the Gilded Age. With his long experience as Speaker of the House, Colfax presided over the Senate effectively and with great dignity, but he was never part of the Republican leadership in Congress, and as vice president he was not invited to the party caucus. Colfax did remain active as a party orator, appearing often to speak in favor of Republican candidates, lecturing for Odd Fellow lodges and church groups and still turning down hundreds of speaking invitations each year of his vice presidency.

Impossible to satisfy were the hundreds of deserving Republicans who sought his help in securing government jobs. The vice president had no positions to fill on his own and little influence at the White House. So far as possible, Colfax recommend deserving Hoosiers for federal appointments.

Always of cheerful disposition, Colfax had long enjoyed Washington society, and his receptions as Speaker and vice president were always crowded, although he never served wine or liquor. Shortly after the 1868 election, the widowed Colfax married Ellen Wade, a niece of his convention rival, Ben Wade. His first marriage had been childless, but with the birth of Schuyler Colfax, Jr., two years later, the vice president became a doting father.

As editor and then as a member of Congress, Colfax supported internal improvements, particularly railroads. His western tour in 1865, which he often described in his lectures, enhanced his interest in railroad projects. Two years later he traveled to California on the newly completed Pacific railroad, delivered several speeches, and toured Yosemite and other scenic locations. In 1871, he was invited by Jay Cooke, the leading banker of Philadelphia, to participate in the Northern Pacific Railroad—Colfax replied that he was indeed interested in finding some such position when his term expired. To his surprise, Cooke immediately offered him employment as the railroad's chief lobbyist in Washington, if such

a position would not conflict with the vice presidency. Cooke assured Colfax that the Northern Pacific did not seek federal funds or favor. The vice president wisely declined the offer, although he was indeed in financial need because the cost of housing and official entertaining in Washington exceeded his salary.

No vice president had been elected to a second term since 1828, and Colfax spoke often of retiring to private life when his term ended in 1873. He never enjoyed comfortable relations with President Grant, although he vigorously defended the administration against the growing talk of scandal. Their differences were clearly personal rather than political, and although their relationship became strained, both Grant and Colfax avoided public disagreement. "I *do* love the party and its unity, far, far more than any selfish advancement . . . ," Colfax assured a friend. In 1871, Grant asked Colfax to consider resigning from the vice presidency and accepting appointment as secretary of state, but he declined and later joined with Republican senators to persuade Hamilton Fish to remain at the State Department.

For reasons never explained even in his private correspondence, Colfax changed his mind early in 1872 and sought renomination for a second term. Senator Henry Wilson had already won wide support among the Republican convention delegates, and Colfax struggled to make up for lost time. He lost to Wilson on the first ballot by a margin of 364½ to 321½, defeated but certainly not disgraced.

In the 1872 campaign Colfax loyally supported the Republican ticket of Grant and Wilson, although he did not speak as widely as usual, but instead of a graceful descent into retirement, the lame-duck session brought bitter controversy and accusations of corruption. Colfax, Wilson, and other prominent Republicans were accused of accepting bribes from the Crédit Mobilier, a construction company secretly owned by the directors of the Union Pacific Railroad. Oakes Ames, a Republican representative from Massachusetts and director of the Union Pacific, revealed that he had paid generous bribes to win political favors for the railroad.

Vice President Colfax first denied that he had received anything from Ames but was soon forced to concede that in 1868 he had briefly accepted shares in the Crédit Mobilier. As soon as he realized that the Crédit Mobilier might become controversial, Colfax said, he had returned the stock and forfeited his $500 down payment. Investigating committees discovered a deposit in Colfax's bank account that matched the amount of a payment Ames claimed to have made, and there was also a mysterious check payable to "S. C." that Colfax swore he had never seen. He desperately explained that the money he deposited came from an anonymous campaign contribution and the sale of the family piano, but nothing he could say ever cleared his reputation of the shadows of corruption.

When the Poland Committee in the House heard Ames's confusing account of bribes offered and received, Vice President Colfax voluntarily appeared to defend himself against every particular. He denied each of the accusations and then personally cross-examined his accuser. In his own sworn testimony, Colfax insisted: "I never did receive a dollar . . . no one ever gave, or offered to give me, any shares of stock in the Crédit Mobilier, or the Union Pacific Railroad." Still, Colfax had to admit that Ames had proffered Crédit Mobilier shares and that he had initially accepted the offer. Neither court nor congressional committee ever passed judgment on Colfax, and his fate was left to public opinion.

At the end of his term in March 1873, Colfax returned home to South Bend, where he was greeted by a cheering crowd. He was then only fifty years of age, despite his long service in Congress, and for the rest of his life he made his living as a public lecturer, earning far more than his vice presidential salary. He generally avoided politics, speaking most often about his western travels or his memories of Abraham Lincoln. Colfax died of a heart attack on January 13, 1885, at the railroad depot in Mankato, Minnesota, waiting for the train to take him to his next speaking engagement.

Although he presided over House and Senate for ten years during a tumultuous period in American politics, Schuyler Colfax was never among the leaders of the Republican Party. A faithful supporter of radical Reconstruction, Colfax played no role in shaping his party's policy. Easygoing, eloquent, and generous, "Smiler" Colfax fully satisfied his party's expectations: he was a competent presiding officer who upheld Republican principles as defined by the party leaders, as well as a stirring orator willing to travel great distances to speak in support of Republican candidates. Except for the Crédit Mobilier scandal during the final months of his political career, Colfax was always regarded as unusually honest for a political figure of his era. It was the great misfortune in the life of a former newspaper editor that his one political lapse, whether of memory or judgment, appeared prominently in every newspaper in the country. Colfax never blamed anyone but the lying Oakes Ames for his misfortune. He denied participation in the Crédit Mobilier affair as long as he lived, but he could never escape the suspicion of guilt. The public remembered nothing else of his term as vice president.

REFERENCES

Willard H. Smith, *Schuyler Colfax: The Changing Fortunes of a Political Idol* (Indianapolis: Indiana Historical Bureau, 1952); O.J. Hollister, *Life of Schuyler Colfax* (New York: Funk & Wagnalls, 1886); W. Allan Wilbur, "The Crédit Mobilier Scandal, 1873," in *Congress Investigates: A Documented History, 1792–1974*, ed. by Arthur M. Schlesinger, Jr., and Roger Bruns (New York: Chelsea House, 1975).

PATRICK J. FURLONG is professor of history at Indiana University–South Bend. He has long studied the American Congress as well as Indiana history and politics. He is the author of *Indiana: An Illustrated History* (Windsor Publications, 1985), as well as articles in historical journals such as *The William and Mary Quarterly*.

ANN LEONARD is an independent scholar and freelance writer who lives in Granger, Indiana.

She is a graduate of St. Mary's College, Notre Dame, Indiana. She has written on Sister Mary Francis de Sales Monholland for *The Encyclopedia of Chicago Women* (forthcoming from Indiana University Press) and is the author of "Red Rover, the Civil War, and the Nuns" in *The Lincoln Herald*. Her article on "Smiler Colfax and President Lincoln" appeared in the Spring 1995 number of the same publication.

HENRY WILSON (1812–1875)

HENRY WILSON
(Library of Congress)

By Richard H. Abbott

Henry Wilson, the son of Winthrop Colbath, Jr., and Abigail Witham Colbath, was born on February 16, 1812, near Farmington, New Hampshire, and christened Jeremiah Jones Colbath. His mother quickly bore four more sons, and her husband, an unskilled laborer who was indolent and often drunk, proved unable to provide an adequate living for his growing family. Jeremiah later recalled that "want" sat by his cradle. When he reached the age of ten, his father apprenticed him to a local farmer, for whom the young man worked for the next eleven years. On his twenty-first birthday young Colbath, apparently hoping to escape both

a dismal future and a humiliating past, changed his name to Henry Wilson and left New Hampshire in search of a better life.

Wilson's subsequent career, which carried him from the rocky soil of New Hampshire to the halls of the United States Senate and eventually to the vice presidency, provides a case study of the rise of the common man in early nineteenth-century America.

Although Wilson would overcome the handicaps posed by his origins, his early experiences shaped his life. Resolved never to be like his father, he would work hard, avoid alcohol, and strive relentlessly to improve himself. He would identify with other working men and devote his career to helping remove the handicaps that threatened their paths to success. Eventually this course would lead him to champion the abolition of slavery and the achievement of equal rights for African Americans, causes that would earn him his place in history.

When Wilson left Farmington in 1833, he headed for Massachusetts, eventually settling in Natick to learn the shoemaking trade; it remained his home for the rest of his life. In New Hampshire he had had little time for school; in Natick he managed to squeeze out a month here and there to attend local academies, giving him probably not more than a year of formal education in total. In 1840, he married Harriet Malvina Howe, who bore their only child, a son, six years later. Wilson had little time, however, to devote to his family, for his shoe business claimed most of his attention. He was quite successful at it, and by 1847 employed more than 100 workers.

Wilson was not satisfied simply to be a successful shoemaker. Manufacturing brogans provided him with an income but not with an outlet for his powerful ambition. In 1840, he was elected to the lower house of the Massachusetts legislature, and from that time on he sacrificed all else in order to build a successful political career. Between 1840 and 1852, he served for eight years in either the upper or lower house of the state legislature. Political activity seemed to suit Wilson's personality. He enjoyed courting voters and reveled in building coalitions and controlling elections, but he also was drawn to politics because it offered him a chance to use government to achieve the social and moral reforms that he championed. A self-made man himself, he wanted to help others to achieve similar successes in their own lives, so he worked to abolish imprisonment for debt, reduce the poll tax, institute a secret ballot, enact a mechanic's lien law, secure legislation to limit the consumption of alcohol, and promote free public schools.

It was the cause of the slave, however, that claimed most of Wilson's attention. Wilson had first seen slavery on a visit to Washington, D.C., in 1836, and the experience left him firmly resolved to do whatever he could to eradicate the institution. When he returned home he became an abolitionist, and later in his career one of his proudest moments came when, as a U.S. Senator, he sponsored legislation emancipating the slaves in the nation's capital. Probably Wilson's early experiences as a hardworking apprentice in New Hampshire had given him a sympathy for the oppressed blacks, a sympathy increased by the social ostracism that he experienced because of his own lowly origins. Of all laborers, he said, the slave was the most helpless and the most degraded. He recognized in slavery the absolute antithesis of the free-labor system that had enabled him to rise, and he warned that the same prejudices of class and race that subjugated blacks could also oppress white workers. Although slavery did not exist in Massachusetts, Wilson recognized that racism persisted there, and he sought to abolish segregated schools in the state, to repeal laws banning blacks from the militia and prohibiting interracial marriage, and to enact a state civil rights law.

Of all the northern states, the abolitionist movement was strongest in Massachusetts, where its chief spokesman was William Lloyd Garrison. Wilson shared Garrison's moral objections to slavery but disagreed with his insistence that abolitionists abstain from political action against the institution. Wilson believed that the political power southern slaveholders wielded in Washington helped to perpetuate slavery, and he was determined to break their hold on the national government. Wilson deeply resented the political influence of the southern planters, whom he decisively termed the Slave Power, and warned that this influence was undermining the foundations of republican government. From the time he entered politics, Wilson sought to organize an antislavery party strong enough to gain control of the U.S. government, terminate the baneful influence of the Slave Power, and ultimately abolish slavery itself.

Initially Wilson joined the Whig Party. He was not impressed with the party's economic views, which he believed favored banks and corporations, and frequently he voted with the Democrats on measures before the state legislature. The Whigs, however, controlled the state, and he thought their party was much more likely than the Democrats to take a stand against slavery. To ensure that it did, Wilson became a leader of the "Conscience Whigs," a group of antislavery advocates that encouraged the party to oppose the further expansion of slavery in the western territories of the United States. In 1848, when it had become clear that the Whig Party had not measured up to his expectations, Wilson left it to help found the Free Soil Party, which was dedicated to keeping slavery out of lands taken from Mexico after a war with that country, and for three years (1848–51) he edited the Boston *Republican*, a Free Soil newspaper. In 1851, while a member of the state legislature, Wilson was instrumental in organizing a coalition of Free Soilers and Democrats that sent an outspoken critic of slavery, Charles Sumner, to the United States Senate.

By 1854, the Free Soilers had collapsed, and Wilson then joined the newly organized American or Know-Nothing party, which had seized control of the Massachusetts government by exploiting nativist and anti-Catholic sentiment in the state. Wilson quickly became a power in the party, and in 1855 the Know-Nothing legislature sent him to Washington to join Charles Sumner in the U.S. Senate, a position he would hold until he became vice president in 1873. Although Wilson soon disavowed the American Party's nativist doctrines, his decision to join the Know Nothings, followed so quickly by his elevation to the Senate, left him open to charges of crass opportunism and helped create an image of him as a political manipulator that he never was able to shake. He remained firm in his antislavery convictions, however, and tried to turn the American Party into a vehicle for unseating the Slave Power in Washington. Instead, the Know-Nothings, who had support in both the North and the South, split over the slavery issue and soon dissolved.

Fortunately for Wilson, another party had appeared in the North by 1855 that would signal an end to his fifteen-year search for an antislavery political organization that he could support. The new party, which took the name Republican, was firmly opposed to slavery expansion, and Wilson willingly left the Know-Nothings to join it. He helped to organize the new party in Massachusetts and remained a loyal Republican for the rest of his life. Because of his strongly antislavery views, Wilson became a member of the newly organized party's radical wing. From 1855 to 1858 he spent much of his time in the Senate trying to keep slavery out of the Kansas Territory, a struggle that convinced him anew of the political power the South held in Washington. In 1856, in the middle of heated debates over Kansas, irate Representative Preston Brooks of South Carolina beat Wilson's colleague Charles Sumner senseless with a cane, furnishing Wilson with even more evidence of the arrogance of the Slave Power.

Two years later, Wilson received much applause in the North for his vigorous denunciation of a speech by South Carolina's James Hammond, who suggested that white workers functioned as slaves in northern society. Proudly Wilson identified himself as a manual laborer, and insisted that while the northern free-labor economy allowed men like himself to rise, in the South slavery kept poor whites in a servile condition. But while Wilson voiced the sentiments of northern workers, he realized that the Republican Party needed the support of farmers and businessmen if it was to gain control of the government, so he courted the support of such Massachusetts industrialists as Amos A. Lawrence and in the Senate cast votes for railroad land grants, tariffs, bounties for New England fishermen, and homesteads for western farmers. He also spent a great deal of time campaigning for the party: in 1860, he gave more than 100 speeches for Republican presidential candidate Abraham Lincoln.

Lincoln's election immediately precipitated a crisis, when eleven Southern states seceded from the Union to form the Confederate States of America. Both Massachusetts senators, along with other radical Republicans, refused to support compromise proposals that some hoped would resolve the crisis. In April 1861, Confederates fired on U.S. Fort Sumter in the harbor in Charleston, South Carolina, plunging the nation into a civil war. In July, a large Union army moved into Virginia to engage the Confederates, and in the ensuing battle near Bull Run Creek, the Union force was defeated and retreated hastily back to the capital. As people in Washington searched for answers for this disaster, some suggested that a Confederate spy, Rose Greenhow, had gained information about the Union advance from Senator Wilson. Although the senator was certainly embarrassed by these rumors, no one produced conclusive evidence of their veracity, and the charges were most certainly false.

Later that summer Wilson, who was eager to prosecute the war against the Confederacy, returned to Massachusetts, accepted a colonel's commission, and proceeded to recruit 2,300 men for the Twenty-second Massachusetts Volunteers. He might have been tempted to stay with the regiment, for he was fond of the military. During his political career in the Bay State, Wilson had taken an active role in the volunteer militia and, by 1846, had become a brigadier general. From that time on he relished being called "General Wilson." He decided to resign his colonel's commission, however, to resume his place in the Senate, for he had important responsibilities there as chairman of the Senate Military Affairs Committee. This post gave him the opportunity to play a major role in organizing the Union war effort. His solicitous attitude toward Union Army officers may account for the fact that when Republicans in Congress established the Committee on the Conduct of the War in December, 1861, which was intended to investigate the operations of the Union Army, Wilson was not named to it.

Drawing on all of his considerable political and legislative skills, Wilson guided a number of manpower procurement laws through the Senate during the war, including the 1863 Enrollment Act. In securing this legislation, which instituted the first federal conscription in the United States, Wilson had to protect both the interests of state governors, who were jealous of their prerogatives, and northern businessmen who feared that either they or their labor force would be drafted into the Union Army. One of the most controversial provisions of the enrollment measure allowed men to pay a $300 commutation fee to escape the draft, which Wilson ardently defended until it was repealed in 1864. He also introduced legislation authorizing the federal government to stimulate volunteering by paying bounties to recruits. These measures, while not producing an efficient national draft, nonetheless deflected criticism of the law, which helped raise and organize the armies that brought victory to the North.

When representatives of the seceding Southern states left the Congress, depriving the South of its political influence in Washington, Wilson realized that the long-sought opportunity to end slavery had arrived. The fact that the Southern states had taken up arms against the Union had given Washington a reason to abolish slavery, and Wilson and his fellow Radical Republicans were quick to urge this upon President Lincoln. He often visited the president to discuss the issue and sought to organize public opinion to pressure Lincoln as well. Not content with waiting for presidential action, Wilson sought congressional legislation to achieve the same end. In 1862, he proudly sponsored legislation abolishing slavery in the District of Columbia, and in the same year he drew up a militia draft bill that authorized the federal government to enlist African Americans, both free and slave, in the Union armed forces. In January 1863, Wilson rejoiced when Lincoln issued his Emancipation Proclamation, but noted that the president had exempted the border slave states from its effects. He urged Congress to compensate border state slave owners if they would emancipate their slaves, and when this effort failed, he secured legislation drafting border slaves into the army and granting them and their families freedom. An ardent advocate of the use of black soldiers, Wilson also secured legislation granting them the same bounty and pay as whites.

In 1865, as the war came to an end, Wilson saw the final realization of a dream when Congress passed the Thirteenth Amendment abolishing slavery everywhere in the nation and sent it to the states for ratification. He and his radical Republican colleagues in Washington, however, realized that the overthrow of slavery did not settle the question of the ultimate status of the almost four million freedmen. Before the war ended, he and Charles Sumner had obtained legislation granting equal civil rights for blacks in the District of Columbia. In 1864, Wilson had also played an important role in creating the Freedmen's Bureau, a federal agency charged with protecting the rights of blacks during the difficult transition from slavery to freedom. The war had only been over a few months before some southern states began to pass Black Codes severely restricting the rights of the former slaves; a horrified Wilson warned Congress that these laws demonstrated that the dark spirits of slavery still lived. In 1866, he and other Radical Republicans pushed through a Civil Rights Act that nullified the Black Codes, and they also obtained new legislation strengthening the Freedmen's Bureau.

Wilson drew back, however, at supporting the recommendations of some Radicals, including his colleague Sumner, that southern plantations be confiscated and their lands divided and given to the freedmen. Nor did he relish the idea of keeping Union troops in the South and governing the southern states by military authority. Instead he, like most of his Republican colleagues, believed granting the freedmen the franchise would be the best way to protect their newly won freedom. They could then vote for public schools, obtain state civil rights laws, and elect sympathetic public officials who would recognize their rights. Enfranchisement would be the capstone that would finish the process of giving laboring African Americans the same rights and opportunities as their white counterparts. It would then be possible, Wilson reasoned, for blacks to rise through the ranks of society as he himself had risen.

Securing suffrage for blacks in the face of resistance from whites not only in the South but in the North presented a difficult challenge to Wilson and his Radical associates. At first, Wilson said he would limit suffrage to blacks who could meet property or literacy tests. When the Republicans won increased control in Congress after the 1866 elections, however, he championed universal manhood suffrage and opposed any restrictions on the ballot. Wilson helped draft reconstruction legislation in 1867 under whose terms the southern states were to be returned to the Union, and he was overjoyed when the first

of these laws required these states to enfranchise adult black males. He and most of his Republican colleagues were bitter at the president, Andrew Johnson, who had resisted them every step of the way. They had been forced repeatedly to overcome his vetoes and were upset because he was removing generals in the South who were most active in implementing the Reconstruction acts. In 1868, Wilson became an ardent supporter of the impeachment of Johnson and was bitterly disappointed when the Senate voted not to remove him.

Despite the failure of impeachment, Wilson believed that the work of Reconstruction was nearing a successful conclusion. In 1868, the Republicans nominated northern Civil War hero General Ulysses S. Grant to run for president, and he was elected that fall. The following year Congress passed a Fifteenth Amendment enfranchising black men in the whole country, a step that Wilson and others hoped would forever settle the issue of their rights and freedom. He did try—and fail—to alter the amendment in order to guarantee African Americans the right to hold elective office as well as to vote. Three years after that, he gave firm support to his friend Charles Sumner's civil rights bill, which was designed to prohibit segregation in schools and in public accommodations throughout the United States.

It was Wilson's hope that once equal rights for blacks were spelled out in congressional legislation and in Constitutional amendments, whites would eventually acknowledge the legitimacy of these rights. He believed that former Confederates would be more likely to acquiesce in this new dispensation if they were treated with consideration. Wilson held no vindictive views toward the ex-Confederates, and shortly after the war's end, he endeavored to gain the release of incarcerated Confederate leaders. He opposed inserting provisions in the Reconstruction acts disfranchising them, arguing that coupling universal suffrage with universal amnesty would facilitate national and racial reconciliation. When, despite his opposition, the Fourteenth Amendment did bar some southern leaders from holding office, Wilson voted whenever he could to remove those disabilities.

In 1867, Wilson took a tour of the South, one of the few national Republican leaders to do so. The purpose of his visit was to encourage southern whites to accept the Reconstruction acts, and he promised them that if they did, there would be nothing more asked of them. He encouraged his white listeners to join those freed in supporting the Republican Party, which he believed would work to advance the interests of both races in the South. Constant outbreaks of white violence against blacks in the South, while disappointing to Wilson, did not destroy his hope for a biracial party there, and he continued to work for it the rest of his life. He was outraged by the activities of the Ku Klux Klan and supported legislation designed to destroy the white vigilante group, but he believed there was a limit to what federal coercion of whites could achieve. Rather than force, he preferred to rely on moral suasion and public education to bring racial harmony to the South.

Buoyed by the fervor of a religious conversion he had experienced in fall 1866, Wilson urged Christian churches to combat the spirit of caste and prejudice that still remained. He also wanted the federal government to help finance the expansion of public education in the South. Denied an opportunity for much schooling himself, Wilson had long struggled to guarantee it to others, both black and white. In every Congress after he entered the Senate, Wilson had introduced legislation to finance education for both races in the District of Columbia, and in 1867 he had assisted in the incorporation of Howard University there. In 1871 and again in 1873, he introduced bills in Congress to distribute revenues from public land sales to the southern states to finance public schools, contending that education would be an effective way to overcome the adverse effects of slavery on both races.

None of these efforts for federal aid to education came to fruition, but they did reveal the depths of Wilson's commitment to a society that afforded all of its citizens equal rights and opportunities. In the early 1870s, sensing that the Republican party was losing sight of its purpose and warning that it was in danger of falling into the hands of a new class of wealthy men, which

he now characterized not as the Slave Power but as the Money Power, Wilson called on his colleagues to awaken the party's dormant reform zeal and to take on new challenges. For example, he supported an eight-hour day for government workers and called for the creation of a government commission to investigate laboring conditions in the country. In addition, he championed civil service reform, temperance legislation, and the enfranchisement of women.

Wilson had little success in convincing his Republican colleagues to take up these new issues. His influence in the party, which had been strong throughout the 1860s, was waning by that decade's end. Younger men, more interested in tariffs and banking legislation than in humanitarian reform, began replacing the older generation of antislavery leaders. Wilson became increasingly dissatisfied with the Grant administration: Evidence of corruption among some of Grant's appointees had led Wilson to champion civil service reform. He was also unhappy with the president for pushing a scheme to annex Santo Domingo, a proposal that led to a breach between Grant and Wilson's colleague and friend Charles Sumner, Senate Foreign Affairs Committee chairman.

By 1872, a number of discontented Republicans, including Sumner, formed a "Liberal Republican" Party to nominate and elect someone other than Grant. Wilson, however, refused to join the new movement; instead he tried to mitigate some of the discontent by praising the administration, and he urged Grant's reelection. Wilson's course was probably influenced not only by a strong sense of party loyalty but also by his own ambition because in 1872 many Republicans were talking of nominating him for vice president. The incumbent in that post, Schuyler Colfax, had declared that he would not run again, allowing Wilson to express interest in replacing him. When Colfax then changed his mind, Wilson chose not to withdraw his own name. As a result, the Republican convention, while easily renominating Grant, had a contest for second spot on the ticket, which Wilson won on the first ballot. During the ensuing campaign, Wilson had to defend himself against charges of bigotry arising from his earlier association with the Know-Nothings.

He also faced even more damaging charges when a newspaper revealed that in 1868 he was among several congressmen who had received stock from the Crédit Mobilier, a construction firm that was receiving federal aid to build a transcontinental railroad. As it turned out, Wilson had indeed obtained some of the stock for his wife but a few months later had canceled the deal. Because his long public career provided ample evidence of his incorruptibility, the charges had little effect, and the Republicans easily won the election. Early the following year, as Wilson relinquished his Senate seat to assume his new office, he was without a dollar in his pocket; he had to borrow money from Sumner for a suit of clothes for his inauguration.

Wilson's nomination and eventual election to the post of vice president brought his career to its culmination. The honor awarded him by the Republicans, however, was made more in appreciation for past services than in anticipation of future contributions. To his frustration, he found he had little influence either with the president or with the Republican Congress. His relentless ambition allowed him little rest, for he harbored dreams of succeeding Grant in 1876. Wilson was critical of the president's Reconstruction policy and still hoped to build the Republican Party in the South on the votes of both races. In 1875, he took another trip through the South and came back convinced that hundreds of thousands of southern ex-Whigs could be made into Republicans if the president would offer them representation in his cabinet and if Congress would provide assistance in building southern railroads. Wilson's suggestion anticipated the southern policy that would be implemented not by Grant but by his successor, Rutherford B. Hayes, in 1877.

Wilson would not live to see that happen. Having lost his political influence, he spent his remaining years in Washington, working on a multivolume history of the rise and fall of the Slave Power. By the time he had become vice president, both his wife and son had died, followed soon by colleagues and friends like Sumner who had shared his struggle against the Slave Power. Feeling lonely and forgotten, Wilson was determined to write a history that would record his own role in the great events of his era. By 1868, he had already produced several legislative histories chronicling the passage of the various military, antislavery, and reconstruction measures that he had either authored or supported. He then began to collect material for a three-volume history, portions of which he began to publish in newspapers in 1870. In spring 1872, the year he was elected vice president, Wilson published the first volume. Desperate to finish the work and hopeful of additional income from its sale, Wilson devoted up to sixteen hours a day to his writing, even though his physical condition was failing. On May 19, 1873, Wilson suffered a stroke that partially disabled him. Invoking a friend's aid to help him with his writing, he plunged ahead, and in 1874, the second volume appeared, and the third neared completion. In October 1875, he suffered a second, more-serious paralytic attack, and in November, yet another. He died later that month, lying on a bed in the plain surroundings of the vice president's room in the Capitol.

The nation grieved Wilson's passing. During his career, Wilson had probably campaigned more than any other prominent politician. He had traveled hundreds of thousands of miles, had crisscrossed the North, and had visited the South on two occasions. By the time he died, he was one of the most well-known politicians of his day. Many eulogists took note of his rise from lowly origins, and while they quarreled about the quality of his statesmanship and recalled his penchant for political manipulation, most agreed that his legislative achievements and his devotion to the cause of freedom and equality were unparalleled. A year after his death, the third and final volume of his history appeared to stand as a monument to Wilson's life and achievements. Although his election as vice president brought him to the second-highest office in the land, he is best remembered for his leading role in the political antislavery movement, for his work to organize the Union effort during the Civil War, and for his struggle to secure for African Americans the rights and opportunities accorded to whites.

REFERENCES

Richard H. Abbott, *Cobbler in Congress: The Life of Henry Wilson, 1812–1875* (Lexington, Ky.: The University Press of Kentucky, 1972); Ernest McKay, *Henry Wilson, Practical Radical: Portrait of a Reformer* (Port Washington, N.Y.: Kennikat Press, 1971); John L. Myers, "The Writing of the *Rise and Fall of the Slave Power in America*," *Civil War History*, 31 (June 1985), 144–162.

RICHARD H. ABBOTT teaches American history at Eastern Michigan University. In addition to *Cobbler in Congress,* his 1972 biography of Henry Wilson, Abbott is author of a number of other books and articles on the Civil War period, including *The Republican Party and the South, 1855–1877* and *Cotton and Capital: Boston Businessmen and Antislavery Reform.*

WILLIAM A. WHEELER (1819–1887)

WILLIAM A. WHEELER
(Library of Congress)

By Frank P. Vazzano

William A. Wheeler was born on June 30, 1819, in Malone, the seat of Franklin County in upstate New York, an area dominated geographically by Lake Saranac, some 60 miles from the Canadian border. Wheeler's Puritan ancestors had settled first in Concord, Massachusetts, then in Fairfield, Connecticut, and finally in Vermont. Both of his grandfathers fought in the Revolutionary War. Wheeler's father, Almon, a lawyer, died in 1827, too young to have left his family an estate or any other means of support, and his widow Eliza sustained herself and her three children by boarding students enrolled in Franklin Academy in Malone.

At best, Wheeler was an average student, although sharp in mathematics. From the common school in Malone, he moved on to highly regarded Franklin Academy, from which he graduated in 1838. Wheeler then attended the University of Vermont but dropped out after two years. He returned to Malone to study law with Franklin County District Attorney Asa Hascall. After a five-year apprenticeship, Wheeler was admitted to the New York bar. In that same year, 1845, he married Mary King.

While honest and sure, he was not a spectacular lawyer, but he was politically ambitious and won election to various town and school clerkships. When Hascall's failing health forced him to relinquish the district attorneyship in October 1846, Franklin County officials appointed Wheeler to the post. Subsequently, county voters elected him to the job, which he held for three years.

Wheeler used the district attorneyship as a political springboard. Running as a Whig, he was elected to the New York Assembly in 1849. He seemed a born parliamentarian and was also quick to grasp public issues. He so impressed some of his fellow legislators that they suggested he seek the speakership in 1850, although he had already agreed to support another for the post. Wheeler resisted the enticement. The next year, during his second term in Albany, he was named chairman of the Ways and Means Committee, a singular distinction for so junior an assemblyman.

Despite his success, Wheeler spurned a third term and returned to Malone. He became cashier of the newly organized State Bank of Malone, a position that he kept for fifteen years. Solid and honest as cashier, Wheeler attracted the attention of officers of the Ogdensburg and Rouse Point Railway, part of the Northern New York Railroad Company that passed through Malone. Eventually, he became a trustee and then president of the line. He was so astute a financial manager that he retained the latter office for eleven years.

While Wheeler enjoyed much personal success in the 1850s, the nation was rent, North and South, over the issue of slavery. Passions kindled by the "peculiar institution" helped spawn the Republican Party in 1854. Antislavery forces of all stripes, particularly old Whigs, found its philosophy attractive. Wheeler was among those drawn to the party. He helped organize the Franklin County Republicans

in 1855 and supported the soldier-explorer John C. Frémont for president in 1856.

Frémont's defeat at the hands of James Buchanan did not sour Wheeler on Republican politics. In 1857, urged on by friends who persuaded him to run for the good of the fledgling party, Wheeler campaigned as a Republican and won a seat in the New York Senate from the Seventeenth District, representing Franklin and St. Lawrence counties. Recalling Wheeler's reputation for honesty and efficiency as an assemblyman, his fellow partisans elected him president pro tempore in both 1858 and 1859.

By 1860, Wheeler was ready and eager for a larger political stage. While the Union was disintegrating, he campaigned for and won election to the United States House of Representatives from New York's Sixteenth District. This Thirty-seventh Congress began the formal prosecution of the Civil War. It supported President Abraham Lincoln's recognition that a state of war existed and approved his requisition of militias and volunteers from the loyal states. The same Congress abolished slavery in the District of Columbia and passed a measure calling for the death penalty or fine and imprisonment for those convicted of treason against the United States. In all this, Wheeler voted a strict Republican line.

The frenzy of the Thirty-seventh Congress convinced Wheeler that one term was enough. In 1863, he retired to private life and spent the next four years quietly in Malone with his wife. Only his banking and railroad interests intruded upon the tranquility of the lake and mountain life.

Politics, however, remained in Wheeler's blood. In 1867, when New York State prepared to draft a new constitution, the still-popular Wheeler won election as a delegate to the convention. His fellow Republicans, predominant at the convention, nominated him for presiding officer, and he won. His new honor enabled him to appear as more the statesman than the partisan because he was now removed from debate but yet could still direct his colleagues on the convention floor. Even his friends expressed surprise at how easily and effectively he assumed the executive's role.

Heartened by his successful reentry into politics at the constitutional convention, Wheeler in 1868 once more ran for Congress. He won easily and did so again in 1870, 1872, and 1874. His continuous service spanned from March 3, 1869 to March 3, 1877. House Speaker James G. Blaine, acknowledging Wheeler's railroad experience, named him chairman of the Pacific Railroad Committee, a post he filled until 1873. Later, Wheeler served on the Appropriations Committee.

George Frisbie Hoar of Massachusetts, who befriended Wheeler when both entered the House in 1869, said of the New Yorker that he had "little respect for the devious and self-seeking. . . ." Hoar recalled how Wheeler's unwavering honesty provoked a storied confrontation with Roscoe Conkling, the consummate spoilsman and unquestioned martinet of the United States Senate. Conkling, attempting to entice Wheeler to his side in state politics, propositioned his fellow New Yorker: "Wheeler, if you will act with us, there is nothing in the gift of the state of New York to which you may not reasonably aspire." An indignant Wheeler snapped: "Mr. Conkling, there is nothing in the gift of the state of New York which will compensate me for the forfeiture of my self-respect."

That kind of bravery in the face of pressure from one of the most powerful and vindictive politicos of the day not only established Wheeler's independence but also spoke eloquently to his character. Fortifying his reputation as an honest man, Wheeler spurned the infamous "Salary Grab" of 1873. While many of his congressional colleagues embraced the proposal that increased their salaries from $5,000 to $7,500 a year and gave them an additional two years of the raise as back pay, Wheeler, who had opposed the measure from the beginning, returned the money to the United States Treasury.

It was Louisiana politics that gave Wheeler the national reputation needed to enter the lists for the vice presidency. Difficult though Reconstruction was in any of the seceded states, nothing could match the fraud, intimidation, and violence that dominated Louisiana electioneering in the 1870s. In trying to regain control of their state's political machinery, the so-called Redeemers had virtually declared open season on their opponents, whom they considered to be carpetbaggers and scalawags. In 1874, after Democrats concluded that the Republicans had cheated them out of the recently contested governorship, gunfire broke out in the streets of New Orleans. Fifty-six people died before the military, acting upon direct orders from President Ulysses S. Grant, restored order.

Grant's intervention, however, only temporarily eased tensions. Later in the year, Congress sent Wheeler as part of a committee to Louisiana to arbitrate the angrily contested gubernatorial election. Under Wheeler's lead, the contending forces worked out a compromise in 1875, allowing Republican Governor William Pitt Kellogg to keep his office. In return, Democrats received most of the nineteen disputed seats in the lower house of the state legislature. The Wheeler Compromise restored as much peace to Louisiana politics as was possible in that fractious state and, by enhancing Wheeler's reputation, opened the way to his vice-presidential nomination in 1876.

Republican politics in America's centennial year were muddled. The scandal-scarred but still popular Grant dared not risk the nation's traditional aversion to a third-term and stepped aside. Among the possible successors, James G. Blaine of Maine seemed the favorite, although several other aspirants, including Benjamin Bristow of Kentucky, Oliver P. Morton of Indiana, Roscoe Conkling of New York, and Rutherford B. Hayes of Ohio, all hoped to win Grant's presidential mantle. The Republicans at the Cincinnati nominating convention chose Hayes on the seventh ballot.

The din of Hayes's nomination had scarcely subsided when the convention's presiding officer, Edward McPherson of Pennsylvania, called the vote for a vice-presidential nominee. Wheeler, nominated by Luke P. Poland of Vermont, surged immediately to the front and remained there when the roll call reached New York. The Conkling-supported candidate, Stewart L. Woodford, recognizing that his chance for nomination was slim, stepped aside for Wheeler. New York's delegates then promptly cast their seventy votes for the man from Malone. Shortly thereafter, the convention bowed to the inevitable and moved for the unanimous nomination of William A. Wheeler for vice president of the United States.

At the moment of his triumph, Wheeler was two weeks short of his fifty-seventh birthday. He stood taller than most of his nineteenth-century contemporaries and, despite his fifty-seven years, was ramrod straight and strong of limb, although he frequently complained of ill health. Clean shaven and crisply turned out, in sharp contrast to the bushy-bearded and typically rumpled Hayes, Wheeler looked more "presidential" than the chief nominee himself. Moreover, his life could bear any scrutiny, *The New York Times* declared in its postnomination assessment. His geography was right too: A New Yorker on the ticket with an Ohioan assured widespread support in both the Northeast and the Midwest. Both sections of the country were essential to victory in November.

Within days of his nomination, Wheeler began to offer Hayes advice. The Democratic presidential nominee, Samuel Jones Tilden, the millionaire governor of New York who had fashioned a reform reputation for himself by smashing the notorious Tweed Ring, Wheeler warned, was a "wonderful organizer and manipulator" and would gladly put his considerable wealth to "unscrupulous use." "But his foes are many and bitter . . . ," Wheeler continued, and if "Ohio and Indiana swing out right in October, we shall not despair of New York."

Wheeler also had sound thoughts about the organization of the Republican National Committee. Do not let Conkling control the committee by engineering the election of his lieutenant Alonzo B. Cornell as chairman, he cautioned, and sage advice this was, because Cornell's allegiance to Conkling would have boded ill for Hayes. The senator from New York, unable to forget his failure and Hayes's success at Cincinnati, bore a perpetual grudge against the Ohioan and constantly tried to undermine his presidency.

Wheeler proffered other advice as well. Knowing that civil service reform and sound money were Hayes priorities, he suggested that "capacity and character" ought to be prerequisites for government appointment and that there was no need of enlarging on Hayes's well-known fiscal conservatism. Regarding treatment of the South, Wheeler was sufficiently radical to appeal to those Republicans who were still mentally fighting the Civil War.

As the campaign of 1876 began to crystallize, Wheeler disappeared from the public eye. He begged off active campaigning, informing Hayes that poor health, perhaps accentuated by his wife's death earlier in the year, prevented him from taking to the stump. He was quick to add, however, that he did "not intend by any means to be an idle spectator. New York is to be fought inch by inch, and there is work to be done here far more effective in results than speech making." What Wheeler had in mind was working with New York State Republicans to nominate a gubernatorial candidate who would strengthen the national ticket in November.

Interestingly, pressures to campaign, although not coming from Hayes, soured Wheeler on his vice-presidential nomination. In August, when James G. Blaine asked Wheeler to stump Maine, the nominee once again pleaded ill health. Typhoid fever in 1872 had weakened him, and he suffered constantly from insomnia as well. Of the latter affliction, he complained: "No resident of the grave or a lunatic asylum has suffered more from this cause than I have. Speaking, and the presence of crowds, excite me and intensify my wakefulness. I regret that I was nominated."

By September his enthusiasm seemed to return. From his home in Malone, he wrote Hayes that he was optimistic about New York in the coming election. Republicans there had a few weeks earlier nominated Edwin D. Morgan for governor, not the Conkling-run Alonzo B. Cornell, and close Democratic friends had confided to Wheeler that they held little hope of carrying New York in the presidential canvass.

Three weeks before the election, Wheeler noted that the Democrats were desperate in New York, even trying to convince the Catholic French of the northern part of the state that the Democratic party "was a friend of their church." "The contest in this state," he observed, "is the combination of every evil agency within it, in intense action, marshaled by the cunning, adroitness and energy of the devil himself, against its intelligence, conscience and decency."

Wheeler was more prescient than he knew. The presidential election of 1876 did indeed combine "evil agencies" and "intense action" as Republican and Democratic managers sank to new depths of chicanery and deceit.

The heated campaign in New York—and everywhere else for that matter—served as a prelude to one of the most notorious presidential elections in U.S. history. Three southern states, Florida, Louisiana, and South Carolina, submitted dual sets of votes, one for each candidate. Conflicting returns were problem enough, but the absence of a constitutional or traditional procedure to determine which ballots were valid complicated the situation. Tilden had already beaten Hayes by more than 250,000 popular votes and led in the electoral count, 184 to 165. But the three southern states, and Oregon where a Republican postmaster—in violation of the Constitution—served as an elector represented twenty disputed votes. If Hayes captured them, he would win.

In January 1877, Congress compromised its way to a solution. Both houses agreed to the creation of an Electoral Commission of five members each from the House, the Senate, and the Supreme Court; those fifteen commissioners would determine the validity of the disputed returns. The Democratic House named three Democrats and two Republicans; the Republican Senate selected three Republicans and two Democrats. With a congressional representation of five men from each party, it was hoped that a fair judgment could be assured with the appointment of two Republican and two Democratic justices and the neutral David Davis. However, the partisan balance tipped toward the Republicans when the Illinois legislature elected Davis to the United States Senate. He stepped aside and was replaced by Joseph P. Bradley, a Republican. During the deliberations over the Electoral Commission, Wheeler, like Hayes, deliberately faded from view.

The Electoral Commission began its work on February 1, 1877. For a month the committee examined the returns and heard arguments from lawyers representing both sides. First Florida, then Louisiana and Oregon, and finally South Carolina were declared for Hayes. In each instance the partisan vote was 8–7.

Congressional Democrats saw the handwriting on the wall after Hayes received the votes from Florida and Louisiana. They threatened to stop his installation by filibustering to prevent the election returns from being officially counted. The resultant interregnum could prove disastrous, especially because rumors of outright revolution already ran rampant in the capital. With Hayes's tacit sanction, some of his supporters, notably James A. Garfield, John Sherman, and Stanley Matthews, met with moderate southern leaders, including John Young Brown of Kentucky and John B. Gordon of Georgia, to effect a compromise. The bargainers were bold and explicit; Hayes's men asked what concessions they would have to make to ensure his inauguration. The reply was equally explicit—withdrawal of all federal troops from the South, the appointment of a southerner to Hayes's cabinet, and government subsidies for internal improvements in a South still reeling from the Civil War. None of the conditions was distasteful to Hayes. Although much was made of the bargain afterward, he was already committed to a conciliatory southern policy. By February 28, 1877, barring revolution, Rutherford B. Hayes and William A. Wheeler were secure in their positions as the next president and vice president of the United States.

Grant's term ended on March 4, a Sunday. Custom dictated that an inauguration could not take place on the Sabbath, so, to avoid a potentially dangerous interregnum, Hayes privately swore the presidential oath on March 3 after slipping off to the Red Room during a White House dinner party hosted by the outgoing president.

Wheeler's inauguration took place during the formal ceremonies on Monday, March 5. Although the country's newspapers tracked Hayes's every movement for the next several days, they reported nothing about the new vice president. Already Wheeler headed into the obscurity that seemed inevitably to stamp the second highest office in the land.

Wheeler, however, stayed close to Hayes. The two discussed the formation of the new cabinet, with the vice president pressing his views. The cabinet, he told Hayes, would set the tone for the new administration and must contain the best possible men. The president should not retain anyone from the previous cabinet because Hayes's administration should stand in marked contrast with Grant's scandal-plagued regime.

Wheeler successfully recommended Charles Devens of the Massachusetts Supreme Court for attorney general. Wheeler ultimately disapproved, though, of William M. Evarts, Hayes's choice for secretary of state because Evarts equivocated too much on patronage appointments, refusing, for instance, to tell aspirants that they stood no chance of gaining a place in the government. Although he appointed Evarts, Hayes agreed with the vice president that candor in patronage was safest and fairest to all.

Where Wheeler could have been most helpful to Hayes, he begged off. The president, in accordance with promises hinted if not sworn in the hectic months while his election was still in dispute, wished to inquire into Louisiana politics with the intention of withdrawing the last federal troops from the state. To that end, in early 1877 he sent a five-man commission to Louisiana. Wheeler, because of his experience in the state, seemed an obvious choice for the commission. By late March, however, the vice president had already left Washington for Malone and was too weary to assume any official responsibilities. Furthermore, Wheeler explained, he had to tend to his invalid sister until she improved. In any case, he told Hayes's secretary, William K. Rogers: "I should be utterly at [a] loss what to advise as to the Louisiana problem."

He was less reluctant to comment about the South in general, though, even when his opinion differed from the president's. In 1878, when Hayes still held hope of reconciling the South, Wheeler warned the president that southerners were not to be trusted. "*I* never had a particle of faith in their beguiling professions," he wrote, "and long before you leave the Executive Mansion any lingering confidence *you* may have in them will be fully dispelled." The next year, when Hayes became embroiled in a bitter appropriations struggle with congressional Democrats,

most of whom were southerners, he accepted his vice president's views more readily.

Wheeler's support heartened the president in that contest with his Democratic Congress. In seven vetoes that followed rapidly one upon another, Hayes refused to allow the Democrats to repeal laws calling for federal troops to protect the polls during national elections and requiring a loyalty oath for southern jurors. Hayes's vetoes broke the Democrats' resolve and united a Republican Party badly divided over the president's conciliatory policy toward the South.

Wheeler congratulated Hayes for his determination. He described one of the president's vetoes as "a document impregnable in form and substance and which, alone, would secure [the president] a place in the history of the country." Two weeks later, in response to still another Hayes veto, he wrote: "It is rarely given to a man to defend the constitution of his country by both sword & pen. . . . [I] rejoice in your marked success."

Wheeler's fidelity continued as Hayes moved into the second half of his term, but his official duties were few, and he was consequently free to chair the Republican state convention at Saratoga, New York, in September 1879. Hayes's and Wheeler's old nemesis, Roscoe Conkling, dominating that convention, got his man Cornell nominated for governor. Hayes's earlier purge of Conkling's patronage plum, the New York Custom House, was so complete, however, that he could afford to be generous to the New York senator, even to the point of allowing Secretary of the Treasury John Sherman, Secretary of State Evarts, and a reluctant Wheeler to stump the state for Cornell.

With few formal responsibilities, much of Wheeler's relationship with Hayes was personal. Not only were the president and the vice president warm friends, but their cordiality spread to the entire Hayes family. Wheeler was a regular visitor at the White House, particularly on Sunday evenings when the First Family gathered in the library or Red Room for an evening of song. Typically, the vice president provided copies of *The Presbyterian Hymn and Tune Book* for all. Hayes's Secretary of the Interior Carl Schurz or some other guest accompanied on the piano. The songfests provided a welcome respite from Washington politics and at least a semblance of family life for the widowed and childless vice president.

Lucy Webb Hayes's visit to Malone in the spring of 1878 attested more than anything else to the closeness between Wheeler and the Hayes family. Without her husband but accompanied by her daughter Fanny, Mrs. Hayes spent three weeks as Wheeler's guest traveling in the Adirondacks and fishing Saranac Lake. Not only did she find the vacation itself invigorating, but Lucy also enjoyed testing her angling skills. She virtually gushed at the prospect of landing some of the huge trout for which Saranac was so renowned.

The trip also gave her a chance to see the home of the man who so frequently visited hers. Wheeler's house reminded her of their own in Fremont, Ohio, perhaps even nicer in some respects, she informed her husband. Wheeler, too, enjoyed Mrs. Hayes's visit:

> Scarcely an hour of the day passes that some Adirondack experience is not marshalled up in memory. Would that some friendly, artistic hand could have sketched for our own eyes the postprandial on Flood-wood Pond. The splendor of a White House reception would pale in the contrast,

Lucy's presence in his Malone home, brief though it was, allowed Wheeler to forget momentarily the lingering sadness occasioned by his wife's death. Months later he still reminisced about the excursion.

Hayes not only entrusted his wife to Wheeler for the Adirondack holiday, but he also thought the entire country could be entrusted to his vice president. As a publicly avowed single-term advocate, Hayes refused to run for another term, but in late 1879, during a conversation with several journalists and members of the Republican National Committee in the White House library, the President seemed to favor Wheeler as his successor in 1880. Such a man could likely carry the important state of New York, Hayes thought. Too, Wheeler's nomination would validate Hayes's presidency, and considering the longtime

hostility between the vice president and Roscoe Conkling, it might also weaken the New York senator's control of politics in the Empire State. John Sherman was Hayes's final favorite, but the prospect of a Wheeler candidacy was appealing.

Neither Wheeler nor Sherman, however, was the Republican Party's choice in 1880. The honor fell to James A. Garfield, the House minority leader and Hayes's chief congressional liaison. With Garfield's narrow victory in the November election, Hayes and Wheeler's term drew to a close. Neither man appeared disappointed at the prospect; indeed, both seemed relieved, as if their service had been more burden than pleasure.

Wheeler's final Washington appearance was at Garfield's inaugural ball on March 4, 1881. He then escaped, with great relief, to a holiday in Tennessee, intending to avoid the late winter snows of upstate New York. Returning finally to his home in Malone, he was greeted by a brass band and hundreds of well-wishers. In April, he wrote a happily retired Lucy Hayes that after his trip to Tennessee he stopped for a day in Washington to gather some personal effects. He lamented:

> Oh how changed everything seemed. I encountered new faces at every hand. I did not go near the White House. When I parted with you on the eve of the 3d. of March, I felt that I should never again enter its portals, nor have I a desire to.

Even during retirement, Wheeler and Hayes stayed close. Through a mutual friend, Hayes learned in 1885 that Wheeler, now sixty-six, looked well but suffered from vertigo. Later, Hayes let their correspondence lapse, but Wheeler remained in contact with various members of the former president's family. In 1886, the former vice president still felt sufficiently familiar with Hayes to complain about his bladder and bowel problems. Although he claimed to be an invalid, Wheeler confessed that most of the time he was up and dressed and able to walk short distances.

Serious illness struck in early 1887. On March 8, Wheeler caught a chill, became feverish, and grew so weak that his doctors thought he was dying. He never fully recovered. On May 30, after weeks of irrationality, he lost consciousness and, save for a few moments here and there, never regained it. Finally, surrounded by friends, members of his deceased wife's family, his physician, and his pastor, Wheeler died. In Malone, and later in the nation's capital, flags fluttered at half-mast. At home in Fremont, a saddened Hayes reflected on Wheeler's perseverance and integrity. He was a "'rare man,' sound and true. In character he was sterling gold," the retired president confided to his diary as he made plans to attend the funeral.

The immediate assessments of Wheeler's life and career were neither untrue nor exaggerated. The New York *Tribune* described him as "not a man of brilliant, showy parts" but of "natural sagacity, and sturdy common-sense with unswerving moral rectitude." The *New York Times* judged him similarly: "He had the confidence of those who knew him. He was not an orator or great leader. . . . But he was above all things trustworthy." His old friend George Frisbie Hoar recalled how adroitly Wheeler had run the Senate, a body not known for its self-restraint or altruism during Hayes's stormy term. Wheeler, Hoar claimed, kept testy senators in check with "as little show of force as if [he] were presiding over a company of guests at [his] own table."

In retrospect, Wheeler's professional relationship with Hayes, unlike his personal one, seemed distant. Certainly in the nineteenth century, by tradition and function, the first and second officers of the land shared few official duties. On one occasion, Wheeler actually had to write the president to learn if the latter intended to call the Senate into special session during the appropriations crisis of 1879. Hayes, too, at times had to resort to correspondence with his vice president for information about Senate proceedings. Once the president waited four months for records of the Senate's executive sessions before asking Wheeler: "Can you make the waters move?"

Wheeler never considered the vice presidency as a stepping stone to the White House, nor did he use the position for personal gain. Early in his term, he succinctly described his vice presidential role to Hayes: "no advice to proffer,

no positions to seek, but always at your command, with my best energies to do anything within my power in furtherance of your great purpose." Such a promise, ardently expressed and genuinely fulfilled, was refreshing in a day when the likes of Blaine and Conkling, who felt political and personal gain were natural prerequisites of office, dominated politics.

Wheeler's penchant for hearth and home bespoke a sensitivity almost antithetical to the rough and tumble of late nineteenth-century political life. In his leisure he read Shakespeare and, too often for his own good, brooded over personal tragedies, particularly the passing of his wife Mary in 1876 and his sister Delia in 1879. With their deaths, Wheeler seemed to lose much of his zest for politics and life itself.

Given Wheeler's temperament, the vice presidency was probably best suited for him in 1876. He had long been a political animal and likely was unprepared to abandon the public calling to which he had already devoted most of his life. The vice presidency was visible enough to provide him comfortable ingress to retirement and welcome repose in his beloved lake and mountain country.

REFERENCES

Frank P. Vazzano, "Who Was William A. Wheeler?" *Hayes Historical Journal: A Journal of the Gilded Age*, IX, 4 (Summer 1990), 5–23; James T. Otten, "Grand Old Partyman: William A. Wheeler and the Republican Party, 1850–1880" (Ph.D. diss., University of South Carolina, 1976); James T . Otten, "The Wheeler Adjustment in Louisiana: National Republicans Begin to Reappraise Their Reconstruction Policy," *Louisiana History*, XIII (Fall 1972), 349–367; Frederick J. Seaver, *Historical Sketches of Franklin County* (Albany, N.Y.: J.B. Lyon Company, 1918).

FRANK P. VAZZANO is professor of history at Walsh University in North Canton, Ohio. His research interests are in the Hayes presidency, the Great Depression, and immigration and ethnicity. His articles have appeared in *Louisiana History, Ohio History, The Hayes Historical Journal, Congress & the Presidency*, and in various publications of the American Italian Historical Association.

CHESTER ALAN ARTHUR (1829–1886)

Vice President, March 4–September 19, 1881

(President James A. Garfield)

CHESTER ALAN ARTHUR
(Library of Congress)

By Justus D. Doenecke

When the Republican Party convention, meeting in Chicago in early June 1880, chose Chester Alan Arthur as its vice-presidential candidate, the move was widely perceived as a cynical political bargain.

Arthur had been a prominent lieutenant of New York Senator Roscoe Conkling, head of the Grand Old Party's Stalwart faction and the epitome of spoils politics. The party's presidential candidate, James A. Garfield, had been backed by the rival Half-Breed group, led by

Maine senator James G. Blaine. Hence Republicans deemed it necessary, indeed urgent, to unite the party by giving the vice-presidential slot to the defeated wing.

When Arthur was first notified that he was in the running for the nomination, Conkling commented: "Well, you should drop it as you would a red hot shoe from the forge." Garfield, predicted the New York State boss, was bound to be defeated at the polls. Arthur, however, accepted the bid, saying: "The office of the Vice-President is a greater honor than I have ever dreamed of attaining." Perhaps he saw the nomination as vindication of his conduct as collector of the Port of New York, a post from which he had been removed by President Rutherford B. Hayes on the grounds that he tolerated illegal conduct. Perhaps he sought to enhance his own political standing within New York State party ranks.

The reformist weekly *The Nation*, in commenting on the ticket, expressed a kind of ironic relief, finding

> no place in which [Arthur's] powers of mischief will be so small as in the Vice-Presidency. . . . It is true General Garfield, if elected, may die during his term of office, but this is too unlikely a contingency to be worth making extraordinary provisions for.

As a political candidate, Arthur played a crucial role in the campaign, coordinating scores of rallies and securing contributions from scores of public servants. As vice-president elect, however, he undercut his own running mate Garfield on a crucial matter as he vehemently backed Conkling's efforts to push Stalwarts into the major government positions. Even after Garfield and Arthur were inaugurated respectively as president and vice president of the United States, Arthur fought his own president on a crucial matter, the collectorship of the Port of New York, a major patronage plum.

In a shocking turn of events, Garfield was shot early in July 1881 and died on September 19. The general reaction was later recalled by Cornell University President Andrew Dickson White: "It was a common saying at the time among those who knew him best, 'Chet' Arthur president of the United States. Good God.' That Arthur ended up a competent president was one of the nation's great political surprises.

Chester Alan Arthur was born on October 5, 1829, in a small log cabin in Fairfield, Vermont. Arthur's father, William, an Ulsterman born in Dreen, Ireland, was an itinerant Baptist minister who served parishes in Vermont and New York State. His mother, Melvina Stone Arthur, was of English descent; her father had fought in the Revolution.

In 1845, Arthur entered Union College, where he chose the traditional classical curriculum and coedited the school newspaper. By now a tall, strikingly good-looking youth, Arthur was elected to Phi Beta Kappa. Upon graduating in 1848, he taught in rural schools and in 1851 became principal of a small academy located in his father's church basement in North Pownal, Vermont. A year later he became a principal in Cohoes, a village near Troy, New York.

But Arthur's real interest lay in law, and in 1854—after private study—he was admitted to the New York City bar and made a partner in the firm of Culver, Parker, and Arthur. As an attorney, he participated in the famous Lemmon Slave Case of 1858, centering on the rescue of eight slaves passing through the city, and also in a test case that led to the racial integration of the New York streetcar system. In 1859, Arthur married Ellen ("Nell") Lewis Herndon, a Virginian who could trace her ancestry to colonial times and whose late father, Captain William Lewis Herndon, had been a prominent explorer.

Originally a Whig, Arthur became active in the newly organized Republican Party. He was a protégé of the wealthy New York merchant Edwin D. Morgan, who was elected governor in 1858. Three years later, Morgan appointed Arthur state engineer-in-chief. When the Civil War broke out, Arthur was made brigadier general, being given the task of representing the quartermaster general's office in New York City. His task: the feeding, housing, and equipping of thousands of troops. Sometimes working on no more than three hours sleep per night, Arthur proved to be an effective administrator.

In February 1862, Arthur was appointed inspector general and in July quartermaster general, in which capacity he established thirty-two recruitment camps in the state. He was an efficient and respected leader, known for his firmness and integrity. In some ways, these two years were the high point of his life.

Yet, a new governor assumed office on January 1, 1863, an event that caused Morgan and his staff, including Arthur, to lose their commissions. Arthur did not reenlist but left the service the day Lincoln issued the Emancipation Proclamation.

Speculation remains as to his motives: the possible influence of his wife, whose close relatives were fighting for the Confederacy; the possible fear that the war might turn into an antislavery crusade; the possible desire for additional income.

All this time, Arthur was keeping his political fences mended, and he was closely affiliated with the conservative wing of the Republican Party, headed by Thurlow Weed and William Henry Seward. A dutiful functionary of the Weed-Seward machine in the 1864 election, Arthur collected assessments (that is, compulsory contributions) from postmasters and tapped donations from army contractors. By 1868, he chaired the executive committee of the Republican State Central Committee. In addition, he served as chairman of the Central Grant Club and again raised funds for the party. A year later, Arthur—whose law practice was now slipping—became counsel to the New York City Tax Commission, a plush job that came through the influence of Democratic boss William Marcy Tweed.

By now Arthur was becoming Roscoe Conkling's chief political lieutenant. Tall, vain, and dressed like a dandy, Conkling was a ruthless boss who suspected all men's motives but his own. He once summarized his political statement in a single sentence: "I do not know how to belong to a party a little."

In 1871, President Ulysses S. Grant appointed Arthur collector of the New York Customhouse. The Customhouse was the largest single federal office in the nation, collecting about 75 percent of the nation's customs receipts, and was also the greatest source of patronage as well. The collector directed appointments and removals, guided the assessment of hundreds of employees, and in the process held the highest-paying job in the federal government. Arthur tolerated, at times encouraged, the illegal conduct that made the office a national scandal. He had a better command of office tasks than several predecessors but still devoted most of his time to machine politics. Although popular with businessmen, subordinates, and politicos, he discreetly bypassed civil service rules and gave party supporters the lucrative positions. For Arthur, politics had remained a struggle for spoils.

By now Arthur was a corpulent figure, though always dressing in subdued elegance. He ate, drank, and smoked cigars with Republican cohorts until 3:00 A.M. As Arthur biographer Thomas C. Reeves notes, the world of Arthur was

the world of expensive Havana cigars, Tiffany silver, fine carriages, and grand balls; the "real" world where men manipulated, plotted, and stole for power and prestige and the riches that bought both.

In 1876, Arthur was a delegate to the Republican national convention, in which capacity he pushed Conkling for president. Once Governor Rutherford B. Hayes of Ohio was nominated, however, Arthur threw himself into the presidential race, engaging in his usual drive for assessments and possibly assisting Republican leaders in influencing the outcome of the disputed election.

Yet if Arthur hoped for continued support from the White House, he was soon disappointed, for within a year Hayes ordered an investigation of customs corruption. By the middle of 1878, in a move that became a *cause célèbre*, the president suspended Arthur. True, Secretary of the Treasury John Sherman, in specifying the reasons for Arthur's removal, stressed matters of efficiency and fiscal responsibility, but partisan use of the office was obviously at stake. When in February 1879, Arthur's replacement was confirmed by the Senate, the humiliation was complete. Again a mere lawyer, not a civil servant, Arthur collected assessments for his party in the 1879 New York gubernatorial campaign, an effort that cemented Conkling's control of the governor's office, the state legislature, and the state Republican Party.

Despite the glitter, however, Arthur's life was becoming marred by tragedy. When Arthur was thirty-four, a son died; when he was fifty, his wife passed away. The latter event in particular caused him grief, for he realized how often he had neglected her for the late hours devoted to machine politics. The marriage, in fact, was on the verge of dissolution when in 1880 she succumbed to pneumonia.

Arthur again found national visibility at the Republican convention of 1880, meeting in Chicago. Part of the New York delegation, Arthur worked with fellow Stalwarts to try to gain a third-term nomination for Grant, who had been out of office for four years. Members of the Stalwart faction of the party, led by Roscoe Conkling and Senators J. Donald Cameron and John A. Logan, were united by their hostility to the South and their "stalwart" allegiance to Grant. Opposing the Stalwarts within the Republican Party were the Half-Breeds (a pejorative label affixed by their Stalwart enemies), led by James G. Blaine and Whitlaw Reid. While each side claimed to have significant differences from the other, in truth the split was more on matters of personality and control of the party than on policy or doctrine. Both sides were vehemently opposed to civil service reform, for example.

The party rejected Grant however, and Senator James A. Garfield of Ohio, a dark horse with Half-Breed leanings, was chosen as standard bearer, with Arthur put forward as running mate to appease the Stalwarts. Garfield had not authorized the overture to Arthur and indeed turned pale when he heard of the bid. Yet, he realized that any successful candidacy needed the cooperation of the Stalwarts and therefore acquiesced.

Arthur was soon chosen, receiving the blessing of the New York caucus in a session chaired by Conkling (who had strong misgivings) and of the convention as well. On the only ballot conducted, he won 468 of the 611 votes cast. The nomination, however, was declared unanimous.

In his letter of acceptance, Arthur supported suffrage for black Americans. He praised Hayes's vetoes of army bills, as they contained riders that would have prevented federal troops from keeping peace at the polls. In addressing himself to the spoils system, a major political controversy of the post–Civil War era, Arthur opposed civil service examinations: "They have seemed to exalt more educational and abstract tests above general business ability, and even special fitness for the particular work in hand." Yet, he continued, "positions of responsibility should, so far as practicable, be filled by the promotion of worthy and efficient officers."

Indeed "the punishment of all official misconduct should be prompt and thorough."

If, during the campaign, Arthur's tasks as running mate were minimal, he ably served the Republican machine. He coordinated many mass meetings and took charge of tours made by Conkling and Grant throughout the Middle West. Indeed, he might have been the first "advance man" in American political history. More important, as chairman of the New York State Republican Committee, he collected assessments from city, state, and federal employees, with the normal request being 3 percent of an annual salary. Arthur played a particularly crucial role in collecting a secret fund aimed at securing a Republican victory in Indiana, an important state that had gone Democratic two and four years before.

When on November 2, 1880, Arthur was elected vice president, he refused to stand aloof from the party's still warring factions. Rather he strengthened his ties to the Conkling machine. Indeed, so anxious was he to bolster Stalwart power that he journeyed to Albany to fight over a Senate slot. On February 11, 1881, at a meeting of the Union League Club at Delmonico's famous restaurant in New York, Vice President-elect Arthur boasted of his role in paying for Indiana voters and thereby securing that crucial swing state for the Republicans. Obviously somewhat inebriated, he said: "If it were not for the reporters present I would tell you the truth, because I know you are intimate friends and devoted adherents to the Republican Party."

Upon hearing the day before the inauguration that Garfield had not slated a Conkling protégé as postmaster general, which was a powerful major patronage position, Arthur, Conkling, and New York Senator Thomas Platt stormed to the president-elect's Washington hotel room. There Conkling castigated the president-elect for more than an hour, claiming that Garfield deceived his friends and betrayed his party. Arthur sat on the edge of Garfield's bed, listening in silent approval. To Arthur, tacit or overt support of a man about to be president meant far less than continued loyalty to a party faction. Far from thinking that he was acting treacherously, he saw himself as obedient to the political code upon which he had been raised.

After his inauguration on March 4, 1881, Arthur as vice president presided over the Senate. Party strength in the upper chamber was practically even; both Democrats and Republicans had thirty-seven members. One independent, David Davis of Illinois, sided with the Democrats. Virginia's William Mahone, a former Democrat who won his seat as a "readjuster" of his state's debt, agreed to support the Republicans in return for control over state patronage and GOP pledges to keep the party ticket off future state elections. Within this deadlocked Senate, Arthur cast deciding votes, though at one point he was so nervous his hands shook and he called a tally incorrectly.

By this time, Garfield sought a showdown with the Stalwarts, who were continually demanding more lucrative patronage positions. On March 23, he appointed William H. Robertson, a Half-Breed who was president pro tem of the New York senate, to the collectorship of the New York Customhouse. Garfield sought to make the issue one of presidential prerogative, writing a friend: "This brings on the contest at once and will settle the question whether the President is registering clerk of the Senate or the Executive of the United States." Because Half-Breed leader Blaine, now secretary of state, was really behind the move, nothing could have insulted the Stalwarts more.

As the controversy developed, Arthur made little secret of his loyalty to Conkling. In a petition to the president dated March 28, Arthur joined with Postmaster General Thomas James, Conkling, and Platt in accusing Garfield of violating senatorial courtesy. Visiting the White House on April 14, the vice president implored Garfield to withdraw Robertson's name, arguing that the move could only lead to the Republican's national defeat. Along with Conkling, Arthur pushed a petition among New York importers: It criticized Robertson's record in the state legislature and called for the retention of the current reformist collector, General Edwin A. Merritt. Arthur's New York home was the center of several anti-Robertson strategy meetings.

On May 16, Conkling and Platt resigned their senate seats. Were they to be sent back by the New York legislature, the Stalwart cause—they believed—would be vindicated. Conversely, were the legislature to turn them down, their political machine would be weakened beyond repair. Arthur personally opposed the move, no doubt doing so in the realization that the New York legislature had earlier endorsed Robertson. Once, however, Platt and Conkling made their move, he backed them to the hilt.

The U.S. Senate had long been tied up over a Democratic filibuster, one not centering on the Robertson imbroglio but over a different controversy: whether to offer favors to renegade Virginia Senator Mahone. Once, however, the Republicans abandoned the effort to back Mahone, the Senate could vote on Robertson. On May 18 he was easily confirmed. Arthur continued his support of the two recalcitrant New York senators, journeying with Conkling to Albany on May 24 to rally the Stalwart forces. His efforts did little good, for on May 31 the legislature turned down both Conkling and Platt.

Not surprisingly, Arthur's moves were tarnishing his image even further. Democrats, Half-Breeds, and independents alike portrayed him as a man of sheer expediency. Arthur might well have resented such attacks, but he would not let them interfere with his opposition. Arthur told the Stalwart editor of the *New York Herald* that Garfield, "spurred by Blaine, by whom he is easily led, has broke every pledge made by us; not only that, but he seems to have wished to do it in the most offensive way."

Biographer Thomas Reeves ably captures Arthur's thinking:

> He had been a Stalwart too long to surrender an inch—much less the war—to Blaine and those he controlled. If he could not be popular, at least he could be true to his friends; and if Conkling regained his political power there would soon be admirers enough.

On the morning of July 2, Arthur and Conkling had barely stepped off the steamer from Albany to New York when they heard that the president had been shot. Charles Guiteau, a lunatic who felt slighted in his quixotic quest for major office, had shot Garfield at Washington's Baltimore and Potomac Station. Upon arrest, Guiteau said: "All right, I did it and will go to jail for it. I am a Stalwart, and Arthur will be president." Arthur took the midnight train to New York. Conkling carried his bags to the depot.

Over the ensuing weeks, Garfield steadily grew weaker. A bullet had lodged near his spinal column, and his physicians deemed him too weak for a probe. In genuine agony, Arthur was overwhelmed by the prospect of becoming chief executive, stunned by the situation that had brought him to Washington, and crushed by savage press attacks. Old friends had not found him so moved since the death of his wife.

Secretary Blaine was obviously no friend of the Stalwarts but feared that Garfield might linger incapacitated for months, perhaps years. On August 27, the cabinet sounded out Arthur on his willingness to serve as acting president. Despite Blaine's support, Arthur refused, finding the proposal improper. Having returned to New York City in mid-July, he refused to go back to Washington.

There was also the matter of the U.S. Senate, where there was again fear of Democratic control. The resignation of Conkling and Platt had given the Democrats a majority, and the party undoubtedly desired to elect Maryland's Thomas Bayard its president pro tem. Arthur prevented the move by refusing to vacate his chair, so the Senate adjourned without a constitutional successor to the presidency if the vice president was incapacitated. Bayard in particular was far from pleased with such crude partisanship, and he wrote to reformer Carl Schurz: "May heaven avert the contingency of Arthur's promotion."

Bayard was not alone. To many, Arthur represented, a bit unfairly, the worst of the spoils system, and Guiteau was seen more as a disappointed office seeker than a certified madman. The press did give Arthur credit for conducting himself with propriety during the assassination crisis, but his unsavory reputation remained. E.L. Godkin, editor of the *Nation*, wrote: "It is out of this mess of filth that Mr. Arthur will go to the Presidential chair in case of the President's death." Ex-president Hayes wrote in his diary: "Arthur for President! Conkling the power behind the throne, superior to the throne!"

On September 19, Garfield died at Elberon, a village on the Jersey shore. At 2:15 A.M. the following day, a judge administered the oath of office to Arthur. Three days later, he again took the presidential oath, this time before Chief Justice Morrison R. Waite. He gave a brief inaugural speech, referring to his predecessor's "example and achievements" and the "pathos of his death." He called attention to the nation's prosperity and, as a hard-money man, praised its "well-grounded" fiscal policy. There was, he said, "no demand for speedy legislation," and as president he would never find any.

Few then realized that a man of such limitations would take the presidency seriously. Ohio Governor Charles Foster was almost alone in claiming that "the people and the politicians will find that Vice-President Arthur and President Arthur are different men."

Once he became chief executive, Arthur made some strong appointments, even if most were Stalwarts: Former U.S. senator Frederick T. Frelinghuysen became secretary of state; Charles J. Folger, chief justice of the New York State Supreme Court, was made secretary of the treasury; Pennsylvania's former Attorney General Benjamin Harris Brewster served as attorney general. Arthur sought prosecution of a postal scandal—the star route affair—though he knew full well that former cronies were among the guilty. Indeed, he was extremely embarrassed when the courts found the defendants not guilty.

The Stalwart faction received so few favors that one member complained of Arthur: "He has done less for us than Garfield, or even Hayes." Arthur did ask Conkling, who was an able attorney, to serve on the U.S. Supreme Court, but "Lord Roscoe" had his eye on the State Department and refused. Eventually Conkling found the Hayes administration by comparison "reputable, if not heroic." As former old Arthur cronies of customhouse days mourned: "He isn't 'Chet' Arthur any more; he's the president."

Arthur could not entirely escape his shady past. Both William E. Chandler, his secretary of the navy, and Timothy O. Howe, his postmaster general, were perceived as typical spoilsmen. The removal of reformer Silas Burt, naval officer to the New York Customhouse, was a spiteful act against an able administrator, and certain other appointments—such as Arthur's first choice for chief examiner to the Civil Service Commission—aroused the ire of reformers.

In his first annual message, Arthur endorsed civil service reform. Only, however, after the congressional elections of 1882 was the cause taken seriously. The Democrats had won the House and almost captured the Senate. It was better, realized the lame-duck Republican Congress, to back the civil service bill advanced by Ohio's Democratic senator George Hunt Pendleton than to take the blame for delaying the inevitable; indeed, by moving quickly, the GOP could protect the tenure of their own incumbent officeholders before any ax fell.

With his second annual message, Arthur became a vocal reformer par excellence, and on January 18, 1883, he signed the Pendleton Act. On the plus side, the bill provided for a five-member Civil Service Examination Board, with authority to hold competitive examinations for positions on a classified list. On the minus side, it exempted the vast majority of federal employees and all municipal and state ones. Indeed one Democratic senator caustically called the measure "a bill to perpetuate in office the Republicans who now control the patronage of the Government."

Like other Gilded Age presidents, Arthur used his veto power generously. In 1882, he successfully vetoed a Chinese exclusion bill that would have excluded Chinese laborers from entry into the United States for twenty years and denied U.S. citizenship to Chinese residents. While conceding that unrestricted Chinese labor might threaten American livelihoods, he claimed in his veto message that twenty years—"nearly a generation"—was unreasonable. Moreover, the bill violated a treaty made with China in 1880, disdainfully ignored those Chinese laborers who had contributed to the U.S. economy, and risked a lucrative Far Eastern trade. Arthur also vetoed a steamboat safety bill, claiming that the wording contained several technical errors, and a rivers and harbors bill that was heavily weighted in favor of one section—the South.

Arthur promoted naval development to such a degree that he could be called one of the fathers of the modern navy. In his annual message of 1881, he referred to the protection of "the highways of commerce, the varied interests of our foreign trade." Furthermore, he said: "We must be prepared to enforce any policy we think wise to adopt." His secretary of the navy, William E. Chandler, was a ruthless party organizer who had been judge advocate under Lincoln and was the only pronounced Half-Breed (though a strong Arthur partisan) in the cabinet. With Arthur's full approval, Chandler instituted a surprising number of reforms: a much-needed Naval War College at Newport, Rhode Island; the closing of superfluous navy yards at Pensacola, Florida, and New London, Connecticut; and a new naval advisory board that recommended the construction of armor-plated cruisers. In March 1883, Arthur signed a bill that gave the nation its first three steel-plated cruisers and a new dispatch boat.

In some areas, Arthur was quite limited. As with most Gilded Age presidents, he so believed in laissez-faire that he was unable to cope with a declining economy. In 1883, the Supreme Court found unconstitutional the Civil Rights Act of 1875, a law that provided that all persons, irrespective of race, were entitled to equal access to "inns, public conveyances on land or water, theaters, and other places of public amusement." In response to the decision, the president said he would unhesitatingly support any "right, privilege, and immunity of citizenship" that Congress might pass. Yet, when congressional Republicans introduced five different bills to replaced the defunct 1875 Civil Rights Act, Arthur offered little support. His annual messages spoke only of educational needs.

Arthur also had some major setbacks. Congress, for example, overrode his veto of a rivers and harbors bill. When examining his foreign policy, it is hard to find a single success. His administration was unable to mediate the war between Peru and Chile, to alter the Clayton-Bulwer Treaty of 1850 that recognized British rights over any canal built through Central America, or to secure a treaty with Nicaragua that would give the United States co-ownership of any canal strip there. The Germans and French blocked the entry of American pork. Congress tabled the Berlin agreement of 1885, a treaty that formally recognized the Congo Free State; it also refused to act on reciprocity efforts concerning Mexico, Cuba, Puerto Rico, and Santo Domingo.

Within a year after assuming office, Arthur became extremely lethargic. Much of his apparent listlessness was caused by Bright's disease, a fatal kidney ailment that led to spasmodic nausea, mental depression, and inertness. His deteriorating condition, however, was probably the best-kept secret of his administration. A courageous man, he refused to court public sympathy, and in fact found it undignified to burden others with his plight. All the time he was failing, he carried on his official duties, refusing to go into seclusion. He realized that the performance of official tasks was hastening his end, but he did not want to be remembered as a caretaker executive.

In 1884, he made a nominal bid for election to a term in his own right, but he was simply going through the motions. Reluctance would merely raise suspicions about his health, competency, and courage. After leaving the White House, Arthur moved back to New York City where he assumed the position of counsel to his old law firm. Within a year, he was an invalid. On November 17, 1886, Chester Alan Arthur died in New London, Connecticut.

REFERENCES

Justus D. Doenecke, *The Presidency of James A. Garfield and Chester A. Arthur* (Lawrence, Kans.: Regents Press of Kansas, 1981); George Frederick Howe, *Chester A. Arthur: A Quarter-Century of Machine Politics* (New York: Dodd, Mead, 1935); David M. Pletcher, *The Awkward Years: American Foreign Relations under Garfield and Arthur* (Columbia, Mo.: University of Missouri Press, 1962); Thomas C. Reeves, *Gentleman Boss: The Life of Chester Alan Arthur* (New York: Knopf, 1975).

JUSTUS D. DOENECKE is the author of *The Presidencies of James A. Garfield and Chester A. Arthur* (1981) and has written numerous other books and articles. In 1991, he received the Arthur S. Link Prize for Documentary Editing from the Society for Historians of American Foreign Relations. He received his Ph.D. from Princeton. He is professor of history at the New College of the University of South Florida, where he has taught since 1969.

THOMAS ANDREWS HENDRICKS (1819–1885)

Vice President, March 4–November 25, 1885

(President Grover Cleveland)

THOMAS A. HENDRICKS
(Library of Congress)

By Thomas Burnell Colbert

It was probably the largest funeral ever in Indianapolis, Indiana. On December 1, 1885, a mass of mourners came to lay to rest Thomas A. Hendricks, the twenty-first vice president of the United States. For more than three decades, Hendricks had been one of the state's most prominent political leaders. Four times he had been a candidate for the Democratic Party's presidential nomination, and twice he had been the party's candidate for vice president. Indeed, Hendricks had played a conspicuous role in state and national politics during a tumultuous period in American history.

As with any notable politician, any attempt to assess his career, achievements, and qualities confronts conflicting viewpoints. To his many admirers, Hendricks was an admirable person. This understanding of Hendricks was summed up well by historian Louis Clinton Hatch, who wrote: "Personally, Hendricks was thoroughly honest, a man of culture but without hauteur, fond of mixing with his fellows, agreeable and conciliating." Furthermore, present-day Indiana historian Ralph D. Gray has concluded that Hendricks "had talent, firm convictions, a simple but powerful style of oratory, and the common touch. He was indeed a most eloquent spokesman for the Indiana Democracy, and for Democrats everywhere, during a critical two decades." To his critics—in both national parties—Hendricks lacked commitment to defining political policies. To them, he was more of a political operator, an office seeker rather than a statesman. Consequently, Whitelaw Reid, the editor of the Republican *New York Tribune*, called Hendricks "the Professional Candidate," and Oliver P. Morton, Indiana's powerful Republican leader, caustically said that Hendricks's "thirty years of nonachievement in office set some sort of record." A brief review of his life shows how all these views have basis.

Thomas Andrews Hendricks was born on September 7, 1819, in Zanesville, Ohio, to John Hendricks and his wife, Jane Thomson Hendricks. In 1822, John Hendricks moved his family to Shelby County, Indiana. Thomas grew up in Shelbyville, first in a log cabin and then in a brick house his increasingly successful father built. John Hendricks, a staunch Presbyterian who helped found the First Presbyterian Church in Indianapolis, sent Thomas to Hanover College, a Presbyterian school, in Hanover, Indiana, in 1836. After spending one year in the preparatory courses, Thomas began college work, graduating in 1841. He decided to study law, first with Judge Stephen Major in Shelbyville and then with his uncle, Judge Alexander Thomson, who conducted a law school in Chambersburg, Pennsylvania. In 1843, Hendricks was admitted to the Indiana bar.

For the next few years, Hendricks worked to develop a practice. On September 26, 1845, he married Eliza Morgan. In 1848, their only child, Morgan, was born; sadly, the boy died in 1851. Eliza gave much attention to helping Thomas advance his career, becoming not only a social hostess but also a trusted advisor.

In 1848, Hendricks entered politics and was elected as a Democrat to the Indiana assembly's lower house. His family had a history of political life:

His grandfather, Abraham Hendricks, had been elected to four terms in the Pennsylvania assembly, but more important, his uncle, William Hendricks, was a bulwark of the Democratic Party in Indiana, having served as Indiana's first member of the U.S. House of Representatives, as the second governor of the state, and then as a two-term U.S. senator. Ironically, though, Thomas did not distinguish himself in the legislature. Apparently, his interest was not piqued, and he refused renomination.

What did propel Hendricks into a leadership role was the state constitutional convention. Indianans in 1850 prepared to revamp their state constitution, and Shelby Countians sent Hendricks to the convention. As a Jacksonian Democrat, Hendricks attracted notice for his critical views on paper money and banks. Additionally, he was also outspoken in his opposition to allowing blacks to enter Indiana. While he claimed to be no friend to slavery, he called for separation of the races—an attitude held by many Indianans who approved the new constitution and its exclusion article.

In 1851, buttressed by his new-found popularity, Hendricks was elected to the U.S. House of Representatives from the Indianapolis district. In Congress, Hendricks fulfilled the expectations of his supporters, and in 1852, having to run so soon because of the new constitution's election-date changes, Hendricks was easily reelected. During this term, Hendricks more closely aligned himself with Senator Stephen A. Douglas of Illinois. In particular, as a Western Democrat, Hendricks supported the Homestead Bill to open free land to settlers and Douglas's controversial Kansas-Nebraska Act to nullify the Missouri Compromise on the extension of slavery through popular sovereignty. Consequently, in 1854, Know-Nothings, old Whigs, prohibitionists, and other non-Democrats fused to defeat Hendricks for reelection.

Much to Hendricks's surprise, newly elected President Franklin Pierce asked him to become commissioner of the General Land Office. Initially, Hendricks wanted to refuse the offer, for he suspected that Pierce wanted to gain approval of Indiana Democrats more than having any particular desire for Hendricks in the administration. However, John Hendricks convinced his son to accept the post, and Pierce informed Thomas that he did indeed desire him for the office because of his strong support for the Homestead Bill.

As commissioner, Hendricks proved an able and efficient administrator. Many land claims were processed under his leadership, and when James Buchanan became president in 1857, he asked Hendricks to continue in the job. Unfortunately, Buchanan and Hendricks did not get along. Hendricks resisted the president's efforts to use clerkships in the Public Land Office for patronage payoffs. Furthermore, not only did Buchanan not endorse the Homestead Bill, but he was also at odds with Douglas, his rival in the Democratic Party. Therefore, in 1859, Hendricks resigned.

After returning to Indiana, Hendricks was nominated for governor by his fellow Democrats in 1860. The growing Republican Party, however, won many contests in Indiana that year, and Hendricks lost by 25,000 votes. Following his defeat, Hendricks moved from Shelbyville to Indianapolis to practice law.

By 1862, the political situation had changed somewhat. Abraham Lincoln's winning of the presidency had led to Southern secession, the creation of the Confederacy, and finally the Civil War. While some Northerners with Southern ties and sympathies in Indiana opposed the war, most Indianans were unionists; however, many were not emancipationists, including Hendricks. Moreover, the war effort at first went poorly for Union forces, especially in the East. All of this fostered a frustration played out at the state Democratic convention in 1862. Hendricks was chosen as president of the convention, and he and others spoke out against the possible emancipation of slaves and the recruitment of black soldiers. (Several years later, in 1880, he conceded that he was wrong in opposing the abolition of slavery during the war.) Hendricks opined that it would hurt the morale of white Indianans to be joined by blacks, for he maintained that blacks were inferior to whites and that the races should be kept unequal and separated. Later that year, a mass state convention was held, and Hendricks was elected its president by acclamation. Once more, he voiced his views and concerns, and certainly, he had become one of the Indiana Democratic Party's major leaders. The efforts of Hendricks and other wheelhorses paid off when Democrats gained control of the state legislature. In turn, on January 14, 1863, they elected Hendricks to the U.S. Senate.

Throughout the Civil War, although accused by Republican enemies of being a Copperhead (one of a group of Republicans who worked actively to end the war and whom many regarded as traitors), Hendricks remained a staunch Unionist. In fact, contrary to the carping of his opponents, he strove to curb Copperhead activities. Although he opposed conscription (he favored enlistment and the payment of bounties), emancipation, high taxes, and the issuance of greenback currency, he always admonished Indianans to obey the laws—he denounced civil disobedience and treason. At the same time, he supported legislation in the Senate for prosecuting the war. Most notable, perhaps, was his opposition to the Thirteenth Amendment to the Constitution. Again arguing that blacks were inferior to whites, he said that while he did not like slavery, the issue should be calmly and judiciously resolved by all the states, not just those in the North. He argued that the states in rebellion had not left the Union; they were merely not at the time capable of considering the amendment, which should be withheld from consideration until after the war. In all, Hendricks became a leading Democratic spokesman in the Congress at a time when his party was in the minority. At the same time, he professed to enjoy a friendly cordiality with President Lincoln despite their disagreements.

When Andrew Johnson became president following the assassination of Lincoln, Hendricks took a lead in supporting Johnson's Reconstruction actions. He opposed the Radical Republicans' Freedmen's Bureau Act, the Civil Rights Bill, reapportionment legislation with the destruction of the three-fifths clause, the Fourteenth Amendment, and the Fifteenth Amendment. He continued to argue that the southern states had never left the Union and should have a say in any future constitutional amendments. As for civil rights, he offered that the term was vague, and with his well-known views on race relations, he expressed his fear of black suffrage and potential interracial marriages. Additionally, while he had nothing against opening federal lands to black homesteaders, he did oppose confiscating land to be given to former slaves.

On issues not directly connected to Reconstruction policies, Hendricks was more pragmatic. Indeed, his detractors said he was a "trimmer," an opportunistic and unprincipled politician. Thus, for example, he could cooperate with like-minded Western Republicans in opposition to high tariffs or could modify his position on greenbacks ("soft money") when farmers in the West desired inflation after the war.

Hendricks's strength as a Democratic leader was evinced in January 1868, when he was nominated for governor of Indiana. At the state convention, he again assailed black suffrage but then implied that he could accept gradual and restricted enfranchisement for qualified freedmen. He had supported such a policy with his votes in the Senate.

More important, at that year's national Democratic convention Hendricks sought the presidential nomination. The leading contender from the West before the convention was George H. Pendleton of Ohio, who had gained prominence as a result of his opposition to reducing the amount of greenbacks in circulation. With the war's end, the economy had soured. In Indiana and in the West, farmers faced low prices on their produce, coupled with heavy debt from high-interest loans that had been made in depreciated greenbacks. Nonetheless, the administration's fiscal conservatives wanted to make the economy more monetarily sound by reducing the amount of paper money, which would deflate prices even more and make repayments even harder. Many westerners, both Republicans and Democrats, opposed "contraction" (as it was called) of the money supply. Consequently, Pendleton proposed not only the curtailment of contraction but also that the principal of government bonds be redeemed in greenbacks in order to place more paper money in circulation. On the basis of this so-called Ohio Idea, Pendleton cast his eyes toward the presidential nomination. Eastern Democrats, however, who did not care for Pendleton, looked to Hendricks as an alternative, even though the Indiana delegation came to the convention committed to Pendleton and Hendricks had accepted the Democratic gubernatorial nomination in Indiana.

Hendricks's position on soft money was ambiguous. Before and during the war, he had opposed the issuance of greenbacks. In 1866, when the Contraction Bill came before the Senate, he did not vote. But in 1868, when Indianans of both parties voiced opposition to contraction, he voted to repeal the act. Thus to some he was at heart a hard-money man; to others he was an advocate of soft money. Consequently, Hendricks's name was placed in nomination, and he seemed to have a chance at victory as Pendleton's support peaked. On the twenty-first ballot, Hendricks had the most votes. At that point, Pendleton's Ohio delegation moved to defeat Hendricks by nominating Horatio Seymour, the hard-money governor of New York. The convention was being held in New York and Seymour was chairman. On the fourth ballot, his name had been offered, and he had it removed. Seymour did not, however, stop the stampede for his candidacy on the twenty-second ballot.

After Hendricks failed in his surprise bid for the presidential nomination in 1868, he also lost in the Indiana governor's race. His apparent early lead dissipated, and he lost by 961 votes. On the other hand, his personal popularity was equally evidenced by the fact that Republican presidential candidate U.S. Grant carried the state by more than 20,000 votes.

Although Hendricks retired to private life and his partnership in a very successful law firm in 1869, he remained active in politics. In 1872, after the national Democratic convention merged with the new anti-Grant Liberal Republican Party and endorsed its presidential candidate, Horace Greeley, some "straight-out" Democrats who were opposed to Greeley looked to Hendricks as a possible presidential candidate. Hendricks, however, announced at the Indiana Democratic state convention that he would be willing to support Greeley. Following the lead of Hendricks and his ilk of Democrats, the party both wrote a state platform that adopted much of the Liberal Republican positions and ran Hendricks for governor. At the same time, the rumor spread that if the Democrats gained control of the state legislature, Hendricks would be sent to the U.S. Senate, which he desired more than the governorship. The Republicans, however, carried the state except for the offices of governor and superintendent of public instruction. Hendricks thus in 1872 became governor in his third attempt. His victory had been determined by the support of temperance advocates, for he said that he would sign a local option liquor law if the legislature passed one, even though he personally preferred a license law.

His gubernatorial victory again made Hendricks important in national Democratic politics. He had become one of the first Democrats to lead a northern state after the Civil War. In fact, the degree of his new importance was symbolized when the Electoral College met in 1869. Greeley died not long after the presidential election, and of his eighty-one electoral votes, the electors gave forty-two of them to Hendricks.

In 1873, the nation headed into an economic depression, and once more the agitation for greenbacks and inflation began. The so-called Inflation Bill to put more greenbacks in circulation was passed by both houses of Congress in 1874, but President Grant vetoed it. This action raised the ire of western Democrats, and at the Indiana Democratic convention Hendricks half-heartedly accepted soft-money planks for the state platform. However, when the Democrats gained control of the legislature, Hendricks supported the senatorial candidacy of hard-money Democrat Joseph E. McDonald. McDonald's main competitor for the office was Congressman Daniel Voorhees, an outspoken advocate of soft money. Supposedly, Hendricks had rejected Voorhees for McDonald on the condition that McDonald and other conservative Indiana Democrats endorse Hendricks for president in 1876.

By 1875, the money controversy took a new turn when the Republican-controlled Congress passed the Resumption Bill, which called for the resumption of specie payments by the government

in 1879. President Grant signed the measure, and opposition to the Resumption Act made a strong issue for soft-money Democrats. As for Hendricks, he said that gold and silver were true money and that resumption was necessary. However, he also said that because it should not be accomplished so quickly as to hurt businesses and farms, the Resumption Act should be repealed at this point. Hendricks proposed instead that bonds be sold for the government to build a stock of gold over a longer period of time than four years. Furthermore, he offered that an increase in production and rebuilding the South would do much more to enhance the national economy than the premature resumption of specie payments.

To the astute, it seemed clear that Hendricks was hedging on the money issue, sounding paradoxically like both a hard-money and a soft-money advocate. Hendricks, however, was trying to position himself for the Democratic presidential nomination in 1876.

Hendricks did not attend the Democratic national convention that year; rather, the Indiana delegation, led by Senator McDonald, was pledged to Hendricks's presidential candidacy. Furthermore, he let it be known that he would accept nothing less than the head of the ticket. At the convention, however, Samuel J. Tilden, the reform-minded governor of New York, received the nomination, and despite his wishes, Hendricks was unanimously nominated for vice president. His selection was based on geography. Democratic strategists hoped that Hendricks could at least carry the important state of Indiana and perhaps some others in the West with his financial views, and that Tilden could carry New York, and then with victories in the "redeemed" Democratic states in the South, Tilden would win. Regardless of the political logic behind his selection, Hendricks only reluctantly acquiesced to accepting the nomination, and then only after the strenuous urging of political allies.

Tilden and Hendricks, unfortunately, were not overly agreeable with each other. Tilden termed the call for repeal of the Resumption Act a "barren promise," while Hendricks campaigned for repeal, although conservative Eastern Democrats working for Tilden promoted Hendricks as a proponent of hard money. Moreover, Hendricks openly felt snubbed by not receiving the presidential nomination. The final controversy came with the results of the election. Twenty electoral votes were in dispute and claimed by both parties. Tilden and Hendricks needed only one of the votes to claim the election, in which they had outpolled the Republican ticket by more than 200,000 votes. The impasse was resolved when a special electoral commission was established. It consisted of eight Republicans and seven Democrats who voted on partisan lines on every questioned electoral ballot. Republican Rutherford B. Hayes thereby became president. Tilden begrudgingly accepted the decision of the commission. Hendricks, however, chided Tilden for his passivity in the controversy. He believed that Tilden should have demanded that he be declared president and then asked the Supreme Court to act on the electoral count question.

In 1877, Hendricks again returned to private life while still thirsting for a presidential candidacy. In 1880, the Indiana delegation to the national Democratic convention was instructed to support Hendricks for president. However, Senator McDonald, who also harbored presidential aspirations, likewise had a following in the delegation. Nonetheless, Daniel Voorhees nominated Hendricks, and the Indiana delegation stayed solidly behind him, though he garnered few other votes. General Winfield Scott Hancock won the nomination, and to placate some Indianans and to carry the state, W.H. English, a conservative banker from Indianapolis, was chosen as his running mate. Hendricks took no pleasure in English's selection. As congressmen in the 1850s, the two had split between supporting Douglas and Buchanan, and they had not gotten along well since then. Indeed, it was even said that English was nominated for the vice presidency, in part, just to upset Hendricks.

In another close election, the Republican ticket won again. More personal to Hendricks, though, was a blow to his health. He suffered a stroke, which left him with some paralysis in his right arm. Two years later, he endured a second stroke. This one left him lame.

Regardless of his deteriorating health, Hendricks did not forsake politics, especially as he experienced popularity on the Democratic speakers' circuit. Again in 1884 he and Tilden were mentioned for another national ticket. Hendricks, however, now could not abide Tilden, and they no longer even spoke to each other. Tilden said he was too old and sick to consider another run. As for Hendricks, that spring he publicly professed his distaste for civil service reform and his support for tariff reductions, as well as reminding everyone that he and Tilden had been cheated out of office in 1876.

The Democratic national convention of 1884 was the largest such political gathering held in the United States up to that time. Hendricks was a delegate-at-large from Indiana, and he had agreed to place Senator McDonald's name in nomination for the presidency, although McDonald and his supporters more realistically viewed the senator as a contender for the vice-presidential slot. The strongest contender for the presidential nomination, however, was Grover Cleveland, the governor of New York. Cleveland had a reputation as an efficient administrator and an advocate of civil service reform. As such, however, he did not enjoy the backing of the patronage-based Tammany Hall New York City Democratic machine. John Kelly, "the Grand Sachem of Tammany," was not only opposed to Cleveland but also a friend of Hendricks. He and his cohorts tried to turn the convention toward Hendricks when, on the second ballot, a delegate from Illinois cast his vote for Hendricks just as he appeared dramatically in the doorway. The hoopla that followed did not change the outcome: Cleveland was nominated easily. However, the memory of the "old ticket" of 1876 helped lead to Hendricks being nominated for vice president. The reasons for Hendricks's selection were much the same as before: he could carry an important state; he was a soft-money man while Cleveland was for hard money; he had the support of machine politicians who opposed Cleveland on civil service reform. Moreover, he carried the martyr's baggage of having been defrauded of the vice presidency.

Hendricks was reluctant to accept the nomination. His health was poor, and he had earlier declared his support for McDonald. Nor was Cleveland enthusiastic about Hendricks. Nonetheless, Hendricks agreed to run; campaigned well in New York, Ohio, Illinois, and Indiana; and even joined in the mudslinging for which the contest became infamous by charging the Republican Navy Department with corruption. However, as with Tilden, not only were there political differences between Hendricks and Cleveland but also personal ones. In particular, when it was discovered that Cleveland was supporting an illegitimate son, some thought he should surrender the nomination. (Reportedly, Hendricks was one who uttered such a view.) However, in a public letter, Hendricks stated that it was too far into the race for Cleveland to bow out. Besides, Hendricks offered, this "moral" issue was not so great as to disqualify Cleveland for the presidency.

Cleveland and Hendricks won a majority of electoral votes although they outdistanced the Republican ticket by only 20,000 popular votes. When asked about the contest, Hendricks remarked: "It's very unpleasant. . . . This is the fourth time that an election in which I was a candidate has been so close that both sides claimed it, until the official count was declared." Furthermore, the relationship between Cleveland and Hendricks, who met for the first time after the election, did not improve. Cleveland cared little for the patronage concerns of Hendricks and his wing of the Democratic Party, but probably more distancing was Cleveland's resentment of Hendricks's propensity for compromise and especially his equivocating monetary views. The situation was further exacerbated when it was reported that inasmuch as Cleveland was a bachelor, Mrs. Hendricks intended to oversee social functions at the White House. Hendricks was compelled to show the press his telegram to Cleveland saying there was "no truth in the assertion."

Regardless of any strained relations, both men took their oaths of office on March 4, 1885, and Hendricks turned to presiding over the Senate. The task lasted for only a month while the senators considered cabinet appointees. Hendricks attended every Senate meeting and did not allow the Republican majority to select a president pro tem to preside in his absence. He probably not only wanted to perform his one official duty faithfully, but he also chose to deny the Republicans the opportunity to advance one of their own.

Soon, however, Hendricks and Cleveland became embroiled in a dispute over patronage. Cleveland both wanted to fulfill his promise of civil service reform in government appointments and didn't care to spend his time dealing with office seekers. On the other hand, Hendricks wished to put his supporters into patronage jobs. This difference spilled into a public controversy over who would become the postmaster for Indianapolis. Hendricks backed Aquila Jones for the position, but Indiana congressman William D. Bynum wanted someone else. Hendricks won out, but not before a congressional committee investigated the matter. At the same time, Hendricks faced the hostility of Senator McDonald, who claimed that Hendricks had kept him from receiving the Democratic presidential nomination in 1880 and now had Cleveland deny him either a cabinet post or a foreign mission. (He did not mention Hendricks gaining the vice presidential nomination in 1884!) For his part, Hendricks complained: "The Democratic party isn't in power. Grover Cleveland is making a party of his own." When asked by a reporter if he and Cleveland did not get along, he replied: "Our relations when we meet are decidedly cordial. I have not seen the President in four months, but I have no doubt when I meet him it will be on terms of the most cordial Democratic fellowship."

While waiting for the Senate to reconvene in December, Hendricks not only rested but also accepted speaking engagements at Yale and Harvard, following which the *New York Times* reported that he looked "worn." Nonetheless, despite his age and health, Hendricks was again mentioned as a possible presidential candidate in 1888 by some who disliked Cleveland. Hendricks, however, confided to a close friend that all the talk about my being a candidate in 1888 is the veriest twaddle. I shall never be a candidate for that or any office again. I was not a candidate for Vice President last year, but having been elected, I am satisfied, more than satisfied. A happier man than I am today you never saw.

Hendricks died suddenly a week later on November 25, 1885, in Indianapolis, after attending a major reception in his honor.

Thomas Andrews Hendricks served as vice president of the United States for only nine months. He did little to distinguish himself in that office. On the other hand, he had been a major player in the Democratic Party for three decades. Perhaps he merited some of the invective heaped upon him by his political enemies. Hendricks certainly found no solace in observations such as Oliver P. Morton's that Hendricks had "fearlessly refused to commit himself upon any question until after his party has taken a position on it." Yet, that was a characteristic that many party brokers sought in candidates. Hendricks could, when advantageous, comfortably compromise on party concerns. He spoke well, he made many friends, and he worked the spoils system. In all, he functioned creditably at politicking and electioneering. Therefore, while Hendricks's time as vice president was brief, his role in national politics had been established for many years, and the vice presidency was only the capstone to his place in history.

REFERENCES

John W. Holcombe and Hubert M. Skinner, *Life and Public Services of Thomas A. Hendricks with Selected Speeches and Writings* (Indianapolis, Ind.: Carlon and Hollenbeck, 1886); *American Biographical History of Eminent and Self-Made Men in the State of Indiana, District 7* (Cincinnati, Ohio: Walden & Stowe, 1880); Ralph D. Hayes, ed., *Gentlemen from Indiana: National Party Candidates 1836–1940* (Indianapolis: Indiana Historical Bureau, 1977); Emma Lou Thornbrough, *Indiana in the Civil War Era 1850–1880* (Indianapolis: Indiana Historical Bureau and Indiana Historical Society, 1965); G.R. Tredway, *Democratic Opposition to the Lincoln Administration in Indiana* (Indianapolis: Indiana Historical Bureau, 1973); William G. Carleton, "The Money Question in Indiana Politics 1865–1890," *Indiana Magazine of History*, 42 (June 1926), 107–150; Edward L. Gambill, *Conservative Ordeal: Northern Democrats and Reconstruction 1865–1869* (Ames: Iowa State University Press, 1981); James Rawley, *The Politics of Union: Northern Politics During the Civil War* (Lincoln: University of Nebraska Press, 1974). While obviously biased, a sense of Hendricks and the politics of the times can be found in the several presidential campaign biographies in which he was featured.

THOMAS BURNELL COLBERT is professor of history and chair of the Social Sciences Division at Marshalltown Community College in Iowa. He holds a B.A. and an M.A. in history from the University of Iowa and a Ph.D. in History from Oklahoma State University. One of his main areas of research and publication is nineteenth-century political history of the West and Midwest.

LEVI PARSONS MORTON
(Library of Congress)

By Robert S. La Forte

$\mathcal{T}$iming is everything in politics. With it, Levi Parsons Morton could have been president of the United States. James A. Garfield wanted him as his running mate in 1880, but Morton refused because Roscoe Conkling, his faction's party boss in New York State, asked him to. Eight years later Benjamin Harrison gave Morton a second chance to be vice president, and he accepted, but unlike the ill-fated Garfield, Harrison served a full four years. If Morton had

wished, he could have been on the Republican ticket with William McKinley in 1896, but having been beaten for the top spot, he eschewed second place. Had he been nominated and later renominated, he, not Theodore Roosevelt, would have become president in 1901.

The presidency was not the only office to elude Morton's grasp. He wanted to be United States senator from New York but failed to win enough support on at least four occasions when his party controlled the state legislature. But while his fondest political goals eluded him, he was, nevertheless, an important Republican leader in the late nineteenth century. In addition to his vice presidency, he was twice elected to Congress, served four years as United State minister to France, and was a one-term governor of New York.

Morton was the person censured by the famed Populist orator, Mary Elizabeth Lease, who allegedly advised Kansas farmers to "raise less corn and more hell!" In her best-known speech at Kansas City in March 1891, she denounced American government as "a government of Wall street, for Wall street, and by Wall street," noting that "Money rules and our vice president is a London banker." By then, Morton was a senior partner in the English banking firm of Morton, Rose and Company.

But what makes Morton truly significant is that he personifies the successful businessmen who cast aside class aversions to politics to dominate the Republican Party during its early years as a national political organization. These are the men discussed by Robert Marcus in his admirable study, *Grand Old Party: Political Structure in the Gilded Age, 1880–1896* (1971). Although Morton was not the supreme leader at any national convention, he used his wealth to be close to those who were. In 1880, he headed the Republican Party's national finance committee, and on other occasions, notably in 1888, he raised impressive amounts for the party, donating freely of his own riches.

Morton was allied with the Stalwart Republican faction in New York headed by Conkling until 1881 and by Thomas C. Platt in the 1890s. He united with these men to make certain that the party continued "to foster and to protect" America's "business interests and industries." A nationalist and tariff protectionist, Morton believed that business and industrial prosperity meant a higher standard of living for the majority of Americans and a strong and peaceful nation. He said so when he accepted the vice-presidential nomination in 1888.

Born in Shoreham, Vermont, on May 16, 1824, Morton was descended on both his mother's and his father's sides from Puritan families that arrived in the Massachusetts Bay Colony during the 1620s and 1650s. His father, the Reverend Daniel O. Morton, was a Congregational preacher, and his mother, Lucretia Parsons, a housewife. Even after assuming a new ministry in Springfield, Vermont, in 1833, Daniel Morton's salary never exceeded $600 a year, and, as a result, he could provide his son with only a common school and academy education. Thus, the youth left school at fourteen to take a job at a country store in Enfield, New Hampshire, for $50 a year.

In 1841, the younger Morton taught briefly in the Boscawen common school but left the next year for a clerkship at a general store owned by a Mr. Esterbrook in Hanover. A Boston merchant, James M. Beebe, took control after Esterbrook's business failed and allowed Morton to run the store until eventually selling it to him. During these years Morton learned the fundamentals of commerce and prospered, but not as much as he wished. With a fortune of $13,000 he left New Hampshire in 1849 to join the wholesale dry-goods firm of James M. Beebe and Company in Boston. Two years later, it became J.M. Beebe, Morgan and Company, with Junius Spencer Morgan added as a partner. Here, Morton made the acquaintance of J. Pierpont Morgan, who had been brought into the business by his father.

During the next several years, Morton became knowledgeable in more than the textile trade, as Beebe, Morgan and Company added railroads, private banking, and insurance to their interests. Despite an improved business position, in 1855 Morton moved to New York and, with F.B. and W.F. Grinnell, nephews of a business associate, began the wholesale dry-goods commission house of Morton, Grinnell and Company. Until the Civil War, the firm profited, doing considerable business in the South, but after 1861, unable to collect debts owed it by Southern merchants, it failed. Reorganized following bankruptcy, Morton and Grinnell initially paid its creditors fifty cents on the dollar, but within two years Morton was reportedly able to host a banquet at which he placed under each creditor's plate a check for payment-in-full with interest.

Having put his affairs in order, in 1863 Morton formed the banking concern of L.P. Morton and Company. Among his partners was J.S. Morgan's son-in-law, Walter H. Burns, who opened a London branch of the firm, Morton, Burns and Company. Six years later Morton and Company increased its capital and membership, adding George Bliss and John Rose as partners. As reconstituted, the firm became Morton, Bliss and Company in the United States and Morton, Rose and Company in London. Rose, who had been Canada's finance minister, returned to England to head the London branch of the business.

From its beginning, Morton's financial house did both private and public business, helping to finance the closing years of the Civil War. Morton, who had married Lucy Young Kimball in 1856, began a friendship with General Ulysses S. Grant, and at Grant's behest he began to dabble a bit in politics. His earliest political associations had been as a Whig, but with the party's demise he supported John C. Frémont in 1856. He remained a Republican for the rest of his life and began to help finance some of the party's campaigns. His wife, who wanted him to enter electoral politics, died in July 1871, delaying, perhaps, his actively seeking office.

By then Morton was immersed in affairs surrounding the settlement of the *Alabama* Claims, which were preferred against Great Britain for depredations caused by Confederate commerce raiders built in England during the Civil War. His partner, Sir John Rose, was instrumental through unofficial talks with Secretary of State Hamilton Fish in setting the stage for creation of the Joint Anglo-American High Commission of Ten, which negotiated the Treaty of Washington of 1871. Rose's role in helping settle outstanding difficulties between the United States and England and Morton's friendship with President Grant undoubtedly contributed to Morton, Rose and Company being appointed as an agent in the arbitrational award payment to the United States of $15.5 million for the *Alabama* Claims

and $5.5 million to Great Britain for the subsequent Halifax award to continue American fishing liberties in Canadian waters.

At about this time, Morton, Rose and Company could have replaced the Baring Brothers as managers of the London account of the U.S. State Department. Not wanting to offend Barings, they eschewed the offer, but at the failure of Jay Cooke's banking house, which had taken the account, Grant gave it to Morton and Rose. When Secretary of the Treasury John Sherman began to resume specie payments in 1879, under the law of 1875, Morton's bank in conjunction with several others formed a syndicate to take 4 percent government bonds so that resumption might be possible. By this time, Morton had become a man whose financial advice was sought by government and Wall Street; indeed, J.P. Morgan and he were considered the nation's premier financiers.

Two years after his first wife died, Morton married Anna Livingston Read Street in 1873. She too was interested in politics and may have contributed to his decision to run for Congress from Manhattan's "silk-stocking" Eleventh District in 1876. He was supported by both of the party's important factions. Conkling's pro-Grant Stalwarts and Whitelaw Reid's anti-Grant Half-Breeds.* Unskilled in oratory, his few campaign speeches dealt with the money question then being agitated by Greenbackers and silver money advocates. A banker, Morton supported a sound currency, that is, gold, and favored the resumption of specie payments under the 1875 law. He was attacked by his opponent, Benjamin A. Willis, the incumbent Democrat, as a "plutocrat" who was merely "a tool of Wall Street." Although defeated, Morton ran well ahead of the Republican presidential candidate in the district. He also trimmed Willis's margin of victory from 2,500 votes in 1874 to only 500 in 1876.

Smitten by politics, Morton began to prepare for the 1878 congressional election. He helped to finance the ailing Republican New York *Evening Mail* and became a charter member of the New York Civil Service Reform Association. He also gained recognition when President Ruther-

---

*Editor's note: See CHESTER A. ARTHUR for further explantion of the Stalwarts and the Half-Breeds.

ford B. Hayes appointed him honorary commissioner to the Paris Exhibition of 1878. Morton had helped raise money to hire the lawyers who argued the Republican case in the contested election of 1876. But internal difficulties in the Democratic Party helped Morton most of all, and he defeated Willis by 7,018 votes. In 1880, he was reelected over James W. Gerard, Jr., by an even larger margin. Irving Katz, in a brief biography of Morton, quotes Morton's daughter as saying that "in New York society the prejudice against politicians was very great, so that when my father first entered public life, his friends behaved as if my father had almost committed a crime and as if he were abandoning respectability."

As a member of the Forty-sixth Congress, Morton was appointed to the Committee on Foreign Affairs, addressing those issues that rose naturally from this position: immigration, the tariff, and the building of an isthmian canal in Nicaragua. He spoke in support of immigration but wanted laws excluding paupers, destitutes, criminals, and lunatics enforced; he was a tariff protectionist, who later helped organize the Protective Tariff League, a group of 1,000 "defenders" of American industry who each contributed $100 annually to advance their cause; the New Yorker also wanted a canal constructed in Central America that would be controlled by the United States. To this end, several American politicians, naval officers, and financiers, including Morton, organized the Provisional Inter-Ocean Canal Society to obtain concessions from Nicaragua. This group was ultimately restructured as the Maritime Canal Company of Nicaragua.

Morton joined the debate on the use of silver as money, endorsing the gold standard as the only fair means of coinage. He opposed a silver dollar that contained only "84 cents worth of silver" at open market prices and was against a move to make the trade-dollar, which was silver, legal tender. As created, trade-dollars, authorized in February 1873 and put into use in 1876, were not to circulate in the United States but were to be used only for export.

Although Morton was not an orator, he spoke on a variety of topics during his time in Congress, supporting an effort to convince the Czar of Russia to allow U.S. citizens of Jewish ancestry to own property in Russia. He advocated the repeal of taxes on bank checks and bank deposits, and favored official United States support for the Argentine Republic.

Morton's most active moment in Republican politics came during the election of 1880. His friendship for General Grant caused him to accept the leadership of Roscoe Conkling, who favored Grant's nomination while opposing a second term for Hayes. Despite considerable work by the Stalwarts at the Chicago convention, Grant failed to win sufficient backing, and James A. Garfield, a candidate of conciliation, was nominated by the Republicans. Knowing that New York would have to be placated if the Republicans were to win, Garfield and his Ohio backers offered the vice presidency to Morton. The banker-congressman accepted before checking with his friends.

The vice presidency was not what Conkling wanted for New York's support. The "boss" wished to control all patronage in the state and hoped to name the secretary of the treasury, who along with the postmaster general and secretary of state supervised most national patronage. Apparently, Conkling informed Morton that he hoped "no sincere friend of mine" would accept the vice presidency, and cleverly recommended that Morton seek advice from George S. Boutwell, former governor and then senator from Massachusetts. As expected, Boutwell advised Morton to reject the offer. Some historians think that Conkling also hinted that he thought the Wall Street tycoon should be appointed secretary of the treasury. After Morton withdrew, Garfield's supporters offered the vice presidency to Chester A. Arthur, another New York Stalwart of the Conkling faction. Before Conkling knew what had transpired, Arthur accepted and would not later forswear the opportunity when told to do so by the New York boss.

That Morton was interested in becoming secretary of the treasury became apparent in the few months after the national convention. With Garfield's campaign lagging and his position in New York appearing weak, the Republican nominee agreed to meet with leaders of the Empire State's Stalwart faction to enlist their aid, specifically, to ask Morton to raise money. Morton later claimed that at a meeting in the Fifth Avenue Hotel he was promised the treasury position if he would take charge of the campaign's finances—a task he performed to almost everyone's satisfaction, the president-elect later telling him that he had been of "great and effective service." Additionally, other New York Stalwarts, including Conkling and Thomas C. Platt, believed that Garfield had promised to allow them to name all federal appointees in New York State.

With Morton's help, Garfield carried the pivotal states of New York and Ohio, in part through the use of a "special fund" that Morton raised. Garfield's plurality was only 9,000 votes, but he defeated Democratic candidate Winfield Scott Hancock 214 to 155 in the electoral college. What happened next is subject to different interpretations by historians. As the president-elect dillydallied in naming his cabinet, Morton grew apprehensive, finally confronting Garfield directly about the treasury appointment. To his dismay, the future president said: "I will not tolerate nor act upon any understanding that anything has been pledged to any party, state, or person." Among the several reasons given for the decision not to appoint Morton, the most important seems to be that Garfield did not think it politic to name a major Wall Street banker as the secretary of the treasury. Moreover, the Stalwart's chief enemy, James G. Blaine, had been made secretary of state and was apparently exercising considerable influence in selecting the cabinet. Morton's judgment of what happened, which he later passed on to a friend, was "that an Ohio man cannot be relied on to stand by his pledges."

The new president's unwillingness to allow Stalwarts a determining role in New York appointments and his selection of a Half-Breed as collector of the Port of New York eventually led to a bizarre turn of events when Conkling and the recently elected Platt foolishly decided to resign in protest from the Senate, assuming that they would be reelected. When they were not reelected, Morton may have made his second unsuccessful bid for the United States Senate. He had tried a few months earlier, in January 1881, when Platt replaced Senator Francis Kernan. Just before Conkling and Platt resigned, Morton accepted the position of secretary of the Navy, but when Conkling denounced him for betraying the Stalwarts, the congressman reversed himself and asked Garfield to release him from the commitment.

While the president may have misled Morton regarding the treasury, he was grateful to him and apparently fond of the New Yorker. After his 1892 defeat, the only time Garfield appeared publicly for a candidate was at the Carnegie Music Hall during Morton's 1894 gubernatorial campaign. More immediately, at Blaine's suggestion, Morton was made minister to France, an assignment he gratefully and graciously accepted. He resigned from the House of Representatives, put his private affairs in order, and presented his credentials to the French on August 5, 1881. He served until May 14, 1885, when President Grover Cleveland replaced him with Robert M. McLane.

Morton enjoyed his duties in Paris, although when he first arrived the embassy was located over a laundry and a butcher shop on the Rue de Chaillot, a dingy area that the new minister found distasteful. He moved it to a mansion in the Place de la Bitche, which the French renamed the Place des États-Unis. As was the case in New York and Washington, Morton had the wealth to entertain lavishly, and he did, both at the embassy and at his palatial summer residence, the Château Champ Fleuri, near the forest of St.-Germain. His tour of duty became memorable as a social success for the United States.

On July 4, 1884, Morton drove the first rivet into Frédéric-Auguste Bartholdi's Statue of Liberty ("Liberty Enlightening the World"), which he accepted on behalf of the American people from the Franco-American Union. He subsequently helped arrange for its shipment to Bedloe's (now Liberty) Island in New York Harbor. He also represented the United States at Le Pui, the birthplace of the Marquis de Lafayette, when a statue of that patriot was unveiled.

Politically, Morton convinced the French government to modify its commercial regulations so that U.S. businesses could place agencies in

France; saw them recognize as U.S. citizens the sons of Frenchmen born in the United States; and, although nothing of importance happened, played a role in trying to convince the French to accept America's good offices to settle their difference with China. He was modestly involved in trying to mitigate French colonialism in the Congo and Madagascar. Fearing French imperialistic moves in areas of American interest, he discussed with them potential commercial violations in Hawaii and infringements against the Monroe Doctrine in Venezuela.

The most controversial development during Morton's stay in France dealt with exclusion of American pork from French markets. The ban was part of difficulties American packers faced throughout Europe, as nation after nation asserted that U.S. pork was diseased and blocked access to their markets during the 1880s. Scientific and medical studies disproved the allegations, but American officials realized that Europeans feared cheap bacon and lard, not the trichina worm, as they claimed.

Morton abandoned the tactics used by his predecessor, Edward F. Noyes, who, on the advice of Secretary Blaine, had hinted at retaliation against French wine, which was frequently adulterated when sold in the United States. Morton set out to ingratiate himself with French leadership, trusting in his ability to reason with them. He did succeed in getting France's president, François P.J. Grévy, to withdraw the decrees momentarily, only to have the Chamber of Deputies reverse the president's action. Even though Morton failed, he laid some of the groundwork that allowed Whitelaw Reid, another New Yorker who subsequently represented the United States in Paris, to get the ban lifted later.

Although Morton's ministry lasted officially until May 14, 1885, he returned to New York in October 1884 to take part in that year's presidential election. Despite promising Secretary of State Frederick T. Frelinghuysen that he would not be involved in the race, he raised funds for Blaine, who lost the election when he failed to carry New York. After the Republican defeat, Morton reentered banking and spent time developing his country estate, "Ellerslie," near Rhinecliff, a village on the Hudson River, about seventeen miles north of Poughkeepsie.

Politics still occupied much of his time, and he made his two most serious efforts at becoming U.S. senator after his return from France. In March 1885, when the term of Elbridge C. Lapham ended, Morton seemed to be the favorite to replace him; however, New York reformers opposed Morton because of Platt's role in the campaign. At the last minute they were able to push forward former Secretary of State William M. Evarts, a man not aligned with any wing of New York's Republican party. The final tally when taken was not even close: Evarts 61, Morton 28, and Chauncey M. Depew, a noncandidate, 3.

Morton seemed to be Platt's candidate for governor at the New York State Republican convention in 1886, although this was a ploy: It was the U.S. Senate that he coveted. In 1887, three men emerged as important senatorial candidates in the January elections: Morton, Warner Miller, the incumbent, and Congressman Frank Hiscock. As balloting commenced, Hiscock, who ran third, held the balance of power, the vote running about 35 for Morton, 44 for Miller, and 12 for Hiscock. Senator Miller was the candidate who had defeated Platt when he ran after resigning his seat in 1881. Sometime before the sixteenth ballot, Platt became convinced that Morton could not win. Not wanting the much despised Miller to be reelected, he had the banker's supporters switch their votes to Hiscock, who was nominated, 50 to Miller's 43.

Having lost what he most desired, Morton became something of an object of pity, and many party members momentarily put aside their differences to advance him as a favorite son for president in 1888. He was not terribly interested in the matter until talk, coaxed by Platt, developed in favor of a Harrison–Morton ticket. Such a combination had tremendous advantages. It assured the campaign of adequate funding and united candidates from the key states of Indiana and New York, both of which were needed for an electoral college victory.

After Harrison was nominated on the eighth ballot in the Chicago Republican convention, the New York delegation advanced their favorite son for second place. Despite opinions such as those of Wisconsin Senator John Coit Spooner that Morton "would be denominated all over the country as a boodle candidate," he was selected on the first ballot; the vote was Morton 592, William W. Phelps of New Jersey 119, William O. Bradley of Kentucky 103, and 11 votes scattered. Harrison wired him: "Let me assure you that the association of your name with mine upon the ticket gives me great satisfaction."

Morton played what for him was an active role in the campaign. Harrison, an accomplished orator, did most of the public speaking, but Morton was important in articulating the party's commitment to the protective tariff, the main issue in 1888. Republicans, also, raised a multimillion-dollar war chest, and Morton's presence on the ticket was one of the reasons they were so successful. Knowing that he would be attacked for his wealth and business connections, he resigned from Morton, Bliss and Company, from his directorship of the Canadian Pacific Railroad, and from the Pacific Postal Telegraph Cable Company. Despite his efforts, he was attacked by *The New York Times* and *Nation* for his alleged involvement in what was billed the "Peruvian guano scandal." They claimed he used his governmental and political connections to secure a lucrative contract to sell guano at a high commission for the Société Générale de Crédit Industriel et Commercial. The Crédit Industriel was a European financial group that held large amounts of Peruvian government bonds and was forcing the sale of the country's immense guano deposits to secure repayment.

Despite losing the popular vote—Grover Cleveland and Allen G. Thurman 5,540,050; Harrison and Morton 5,444,337; with 399,830 for third-party candidates—the Republicans won the electoral vote: Harrison 233 and Cleveland 168. In his inaugural statement to the Senate on March 4, 1889, Morton acknowledged that he lacked experience as a presiding officer and asked for the body's "indulgent consideration." He added that he hoped to "administer the rules of procedure with entire fairness, and to treat each senator with courtesy and consideration." "I hope," he concluded, "that our relations officially and personally will prove mutually agreeable."

Morton is best remembered for his social role as vice president. He and his wife entertained lavishly at their Scott Circle home in northwest Washington, D.C. One of his daughters recalled a typical Wednesday during his tenure: "In those days hordes of people went from one official house to another . . . [Mother] used to have as many as two thousand people pass through her rooms on an afternoon." He did have trouble with prohibitionist groups because of his less than abstinence, particularly when the Women's Christian Temperance Union discovered that liquor was served in the Shoreham Hotel, a property he purchased in Washington.

Morton was considered a gentlemanly, evenhanded, competent presiding officer, and several important pieces of legislation passed during his years as Senate president, including the Dependent Pension Act, McKinley Tariff, Sherman Antitrust Act, and Sherman Silver Purchase Act. North Dakota, South Dakota, Montana, Washington, Idaho, and Wyoming were also admitted to the Union in 1889 and 1890. In fact, Congress passed 1,100 bills, a record for its time; however, Morton's legislative participation in these actions was inconsequential, his only crucial role was during consideration of the Federal Elections, or Force, Bill.

The Force Bill began in the House under the sponsorship of Congressman Henry Cabot Lodge of Massachusetts. It provided that bipartisan election supervisors, appointed by U.S. district judges, inspect registration books and attend to elections in all congressional districts. In towns of 20,000, the supervisors were to make house-to-house canvasses, informing registrants of the mechanics, place, and time of elections. A three-member board of canvassers was to certify the results of elections, checking the voter turnout of each district every November 15. Designed primarily to protect African American voters in the South, the so-called Lodge Bill passed the house during the first session of the Fifty-first Congress, 155 to 149; all affirmative votes were

Republican and only two members of the G.O.P voted in the negative.

In the Senate, opposition from Democrats, "mugwumps," silver interests, and commercial groups stalled the legislation. Nevertheless, its proponents were able to secure a promise that the bill would be given priority in the second session, which convened in December 1890. When debate began on the measure, Democratic senators used a variety of parliamentary tactics to delay a vote, including a thinly disguised filibuster. At this juncture, western Republicans who were dissatisfied with existing legislation and wanted greater expansion of the currency joined Democrats to set aside the Federal Elections Bill to consider a new silver-coinage measure, which passed but as predicted was buried in the recently elected Democratic House.

In January 1891, a motion was introduced to make the Force Bill an order of business. It passed when Vice President Morton cast the tie-breaking vote. Once again Democrats filibustered, but this time Republican leaders decided to force a vote on an ad hoc cloture rule that Senator Nelson Aldrich had cleverly devised to allow a majority to stop debate. To achieve their ends, Republicans needed Morton's support, expecting it because President Harrison made passage of the legislation one of his main considerations. To their dismay, the vice president refused to force a vote on the Aldrich rule: He maintained that his duty required him to be nonpartisan, impartially enforcing all existing rules, and that until the new cloture was adopted he could not stop debate. Republicans tried to get him to step down temporarily from the chair, suggesting on one occasion that he take a vacation to Florida. Morton refused, even abandoning his custom of going out for lunch. One New York newspaper declared that Republican leaders might "wail," or "tear their hair, in impotent rage, but Morton will not surrender." Inevitably, by a vote of 35 to 34, the Senate moved to other legislation; there would be no Force Act in 1891.

Morton's action was critical in defeating the Federal Elections Bill, which may have changed the course of American history and, if administered as planned, would have effected a major change in southern elections. The episode illustrated how much the Civil War Republican Party had changed and was perhaps the last gasp of what some call "bloody shirt" Republicanism. Born in part as an economic reform group, the party was now almost wholly engrossed in matters of the marketplace.

Perhaps it is understandable that Morton was not chastised for his inaction, albeit one historian suggests that he was dropped from the ticket in 1892 because of it. Actually, his failure to be renominated seems to have had little to do with the Force Bill. He failed to state clearly a desire to be renominated by Republicans at a time when continuation of vice presidents was not the tradition it is today. Moreover, his New York opponents wanted the publisher of the *New York Tribune*, Whitelaw Reid, to replace him. Further, Platt was disenchanted with Harrison because of the latter's patronage practices. He felt Morton would help the president's reelection. Senator Spooner, a Republican supporter of the Force Bill, wrote that if the nomination "had been left to the Convention without the influence of the New York delegation your support would have been in my judgment overwhelming." His main biographer says that Morton received the news of Reid's nomination at Minneapolis, Minnesota, "without the least appearance of resentment," but another described him as being "chagrined, but dignified."

In February 1893, the Senate honored Morton with an unprecedented banquet at the Arlington Hotel in Washington, D.C. At the gathering, Charles F. Manderson, Nebraska Republican and president pro tempore of the Senate, said: "Our tribute to the genial gentleman who has for four years presided over the Senate is not an empty compliment. It is given to him out of the fullness of our affection for him." A few days later, the Senate passed a resolution thanking him "for the dignified, impartial, and courteous manner" in which he presided over its deliberations. Congratulations arrived from many quarters, including the nation's press. After Harrison's failed reelection *The Washington Post* suggested that the Republicans lost because Morton was not on the ticket; in fact, his absence had little to do with the defeat.

When Morton returned to New York he expected his time in public life would be over—he was sixty-eight years old—but Tom Platt had other ideas and convinced him to run for governor in 1894, telling him the job was not very demanding. By attacking Democratic corruption, Morton defeated David B. Hill, 673,818 votes to 517,710, with 84,173 scattered. For the next two years, Morton proved to be what Theodore Roosevelt maintained was "far and away the best Governor we have had for many a long day."

Morton's relationship with Platt was interesting. While he often followed the boss's advice on patronage, he also championed the state's recently adopted merit system of civil service appointments, nor did he slavishly accept Platt's recommendations on policy. When the mayors of New York and Brooklyn objected to creation of a Greater New York City by the legislature, his response was dilatory maneuvering, which incensed Platt. Supporting Morton's presidential ambitions in 1896 and realizing that the banker depended on him, Platt wrote that if Morton continued stalling: "I will not feel like taking off my coat and doing the work I contemplated in the presidential matter. I might as well be frank with you now." Greater New York City was ultimately created, and within a few years it satisfied almost everyone. On the whole, Platt considered the former vice president, "the safest governor New York ever had."

Other important changes that Morton championed and secured for New York included adoption of the Australian ballot, regulation of horse racing, creation of a four-man bi-partisan New York City police board, and the Raines Liquor Law. The Raines Act established state regulation and taxation of traffic in alcoholic beverages and eventually removed liquor as an issue from New York politics. He also improved the existing civil service system.

Morton could have been renominated for governor in 1896 but chose not to be. His defeat as a presidential contender that year convinced him to leave public life. In truth, he never had the slightest chance of beating McKinley, who overwhelmed his opposition at the St. Louis Convention.

Morton remained interested in politics and the Republican Party for most of the rest of his life. He was opposed to war with Spain in early 1898, but as a good nationalist supported the country's effort once war was declared. His feelings toward Theodore Roosevelt are illustrated by his opinion that a conservative Democrat could beat the president in New York in 1904 because of the "the direction in which . . . Roosevelt's economic policies were aimed."

In 1897, Morton, Bliss and Company became the Morton Trust Company. Thirteen years later, the former vice president reached what might be considered the pinnacle and end of his financial career when Morton Trust merged with J.P. Morgan's Fifth Avenue Trust to form Guaranty Trust. Although Morgan arranged the merger, Morton became chairman of the board of the new organization. The position was more honorary than functional, but Morton was now recognized as the "Grand Old Man" of Wall Street. Morton almost died in 1913, but recovered to live seven more years, passing away on his ninety-sixth birthday, May 16, 1920.

REFERENCES

Robert McElroy, *Levi Parsons Morton: Banker, Diplomat and Statesman* (New York: G.P. Putnam's Sons, 1930); Irving Katz, "Investment Bankers in American Government and Politics: The Political Activities of William W. Corcoran, August Belmont, Sr., Levi P. Morton, and Henry Lee," (Ph.D. diss., New York University, 1964); *Testimonial to Vice-President Levi P. Morton Upon His Retirement from Office March 4, 1893; Proceedings at the Banquet, Given to the Vice-President by the United States Senate . . .* (Concord, N.H.: Monitor Press, 1893); Justus D. Doenecke, *The Presidencies of James A. Garfield and Chester A. Arthur* (Lawrence: Regents Press of Kansas, 1981); Brigham Duncan, *Whitelaw Reid: Journalist, Politician, Diplomat* (Athens: University of Georgia Press, 1975); Harold F. Gosnell, *Boss Platt and His New York Machine, A Study of the Political Leadership of Thomas C. Platt, Theodore Roosevelt and Others* (Chicago, Ill.: University of Chicago Press, 1924); Stanley P. Hirshson, *Farewell to the Bloody Shirt: Northern Republicans and the Southern Negro, 1877–1893* (Bloomington: Indiana University Press, 1962); David M. Jordan, *Roscoe Conkling of New York: Voice in the Senate* (Ithaca, N.Y.: Cornell University Press, 1971); John D. Long, ed., *The Republican Party: Its History, Principles,* and Policies (New York: M.W. Hazen Co., 1888); Robert D. Marcus, *Grand Old Party: Political Structure in the Gilded Age, 1880–1896* (New York: Oxford University Press, 1971); Richard L. McCormick, *From Realignment to Reform: Political Change in New York State, 1893–1910* (Ithaca, N.Y.: Cornell University Press, 1979); David M. Pletcher, *The Awkward Years: American Foreign Relations Under Garfield and Arthur* (Columbia: University of Missouri Press, 1962); Thomas C. Reeves, *Gentleman Boss: The Life of Chester Alan Arthur* (New York: Alfred A. Knopf, 1975); Thomas Clarke Smith, *The Life and Letters of James Abram Garfield* (New Haven, Conn.: Yale University Press, 1925); Homer E. Socolofsky and Allan B. Spetter, *The Presidency of Benjamin Harrison* (Lawrence: University Press of Kansas, 1987); William O. Stoddard, *Men of Business* (New York: Charles Scribner's Sons, 1904); Richard E. Welch, Jr., *George Frisbie Hoar and the Half-Breed Republicans* (Cambridge, Mass.: Harvard University Press, 1971); Beckles Willson, *America's Ambassadors to France (1777–1927): A Narrative of Franco-American Relations* (New York: Frederick A. Stokes Company, 1928). Congressional Record, 1st, 2nd, and 3rd sess., 46 Cong.; 1st and 2nd sess., 51st Cong.; *The New York Times*, 1888–1920.

ROBERT S. LA FORTE, former department chair and professor of history at the University of North Texas, is the author and editor of *Leaders of Reform: Progressive Republicans in Kansas, 1900–1920* (1974), *Down the Corridor of Years* (1989), *Remembering Pearl Harbor* (1991), *Building the Death Railway* (1993), *With Only the Will to Live* (1994), and *Our Nation's Heritage* (1995). He is currently researching Kansas Republicans' response to Populism.

ADLAI EWING STEVENSON (1835–1914)

Vice President, 1893–1897

(President Grover Cleveland)

ADLAI EWING STEVENSON
(Library of Congress)

By Leonard C. Schlup

Adlai E. Stevenson, patriarch of a political family, experienced a rewarding but sometimes frustrating career in politics that spanned nearly half a century. While he has usually been relegated to a footnote in history, in his day he achieved recognition as a shrewd politician. A highly sociable person and master raconteur who respected his opponents, Stevenson, the quintessential gentlemen who avoided making personal enemies of political adversaries, was a political insider who forged alliances with disparate groups while deflecting insensitive comments with humor and skillfully turning political setbacks to his advantage. He sought harmony in an era of transformation and intense partisanship, offered soothing words to heal intraparty dissension, and refused to indulge in personal vendettas. The vice president was a coalition Democrat who preached the politics of accommodation. Emerging on the right side at the right time, Stevenson, a consummate survivor, was an American Talleyrand and a political rarity. His political genius lay in a careful mix of principle and pragmatism.

Born in Christian County, Kentucky, the son of John Turner Stevenson, a farmer, and Eliza Ann Ewing Stevenson, the young Adlai Stevenson moved to Bloomington, Illinois, with his parents in 1852. There he worked at his father's sawmill and taught school to earn money to attend Illinois Wesleyan University and later Centre College in Danville, Kentucky. Upon the death of his father in 1857, Stevenson returned to Bloomington, studied law under Robert E. Williams, and was admitted to the bar in 1858, the year in which the Lincoln–Douglas debates stimulated his interest in politics. He began his practice in Metamora, where on occasion he rode circuit with Abraham Lincoln. In 1860, Stevenson and Robert G. Ingersoll, a lawyer, traveled the state in support of Steven A. Douglas for president. During the Civil War, Stevenson served as a master in chancery of Woodford County's circuit court, helped to organize the 108th Regiment Illinois Volunteer Infantry, and was a presidential elector in 1864 for the Democratic ticket of McClellan and Pendleton. After the war, from 1865 to 1869, he was prosecuting attorney for the Twenty-third Judicial District. In 1866, at Chenoa, Stevenson married Letitia Barbour Green, the daughter of Lewis Warner Green, a former Presbyterian clergyman and college president.

In 1869, Stevenson and his wife returned to Bloomington, where they raised their four children in a Victorian home on Franklin Square. Stevenson and his double cousin, James Stevenson Ewing, formed a law partnership that prospered over a period of twenty-five years. Stevenson was the politician and office lawyer, while Ewing was the trial lawyer who promoted his colleague's political career. In one sensational case, they won a $50,000 damage verdict for an attractive young woman who claimed that a Bloomington physician had contributed to her downfall through the use of drugs. Stevenson also served as president of the McLean County Coal Company, a family operation, which was the city's largest industry, with nearly 300 employees. A successful businessman and lawyer, Stevenson gained the respect of his neighbors and friends, including David Davis, associate justice of the United States Supreme Court, who urged him to pursue a political career.

Stevenson entered national politics in 1874 when the Democrats of his congressional district nominated him for a seat in the U.S. House of Representatives. Endorsed also by the Greenback Party, Stevenson defeated the Republican incumbent. Two years later, he lost his bid for reelection, but he regained the House position in 1878, only to lose again in 1880 and 1882. Serving in Congress for two nonconsecutive terms and representing a rural Republican constituency, Stevenson in large measure managed to win a House seat due to his persuasive skills, political instincts, and ability to make politics out of the issue of nonpartisanship. Assiduous salesmanship on his part sustained his image of evenhandedness among his constituents. Yet, he won only in off-year contests that coincided with national Democratic victories and majority control of the lower chamber, and he narrowly lost reelection bids in presidential years when he suffered the effects of high voter turnout, intense partisanship, and Republican presidential coattails. These defeats tempered Stevenson as a politician and bred a cautious outlook, making him cognizant of his political vulnerability and the patterns of ticket splitting in subpresidential voting.

A member of the Forty-fourth and Forty-sixth Congresses, Stevenson earned a reputation for honesty, commitment to service, and exceptional talent for making friends. He advocated laissez-faire policies, tariff reduction, low taxes, balanced budgets, railroad regulation, agricultural growth, antitrust legislation, electoral college reform, and immigration restriction. Stevenson differed from party conservatives and spokesmen for business in that he favored silver coinage to reduce indebtedness and to provide for a more elastic currency. In the process of balancing interacting forces, he applied on the national level the lessons he learned from prairie Republicans to camouflage differences among Democrats. These years constituted a preparatory period on which he built his reputation as a flexible accommodationist.

A turning point in Stevenson's career occurred in 1884 when, as a delegate to the

Democratic national convention in Chicago, he endorsed the presidential nomination of Governor Grover Cleveland of New York. He also formed a crucial political association with William F. Vilas, a Wisconsin lawyer whom Cleveland appointed to head the Post Office Department. Shortly after assuming the presidency in 1885, Cleveland selected Stevenson for the position of first assistant postmaster general. While functioning in this role, Stevenson removed nearly 40,000 Republican postal employees across the nation, replacing them with Democrats. He relished this assignment, for he typified the spoilsman of the 1880s who earned the wrath of civil service reformers such as Carl Schurz. For a short time, Stevenson was acting chief of the Post Office Department in the absence of Vilas and attended cabinet meetings during this interlude. While performing his patronage duties as first assistant postmaster general for four years, Stevenson collected valuable IOUs from Democrats across the nation and in one case established a local post office in order to fill the vacancy. His duties and responsibilities gave him a new sense of purpose and whetted his appetite for higher office. He had become infatuated with Washington life. After Cleveland's defeat for reelection in 1888, he selected Stevenson for an associate justiceship on the Supreme Court for the District of Columbia, but Republicans, who controlled the Senate, blocked the nomination.

Stevenson returned to his law practice in Bloomington in 1889 but remained an astute observer of political events. A clever political practitioner and political chameleon who could take on the characteristics of diverse constituencies, Stevenson preached the politics of pacification while campaigning for Democratic congressional candidates in 1890. He communicated with Cleveland and traveled the country in spring 1892 to enlist support for the former chief executive's presidential bid that year. Tying his own political aspirations to Cleveland, Stevenson carefully laid the foundation for his vice-presidential nomination. His failure to obtain second place on the ticket with Cleveland in 1888 only enhanced his fierce sense of ambition and determination to succeed in 1892.

Stevenson played an important role at the 1892 Democratic national convention in Chicago. At the Hotel Richelieu on June 17, he chaired a session of pro-Cleveland delegates. Chairman of the Illinois delegation, Stevenson persuaded his colleagues to cast all their votes for Cleveland, which contributed to his first-ballot victory. Stevenson also delineated clear directives regarding the vice presidency, mentioned his availability and encouraged a small coterie of friends to work in his behalf. He easily won the coveted prize on the revised first ballot, securing support from all regions of the nation. Although Cleveland considered several possibilities for his running mate, he did not contribute in any direct way to Stevenson's victory but wholeheartedly approved the outcome.

Stevenson's vice-presidential nomination, a political development based on the demands of practical politics, stemmed from several factors: Foremost among these was the meticulous planning by Stevenson and his cohorts both before and during the convention; a second reason concerned his ability to unite discordant elements within the party. A political moderate of unquestioned personal integrity, Stevenson did not antagonize diverse internal groups and found himself in the advantageous position of being a compromise choice. Lacking ideological rigidity, Stevenson fashioned a career of centrist positions, espousing the politics of consensus. He emerged in 1892 as the Great Conciliator.

Stevenson provided both philosophical and geographical balance to the Democratic ticket. Cleveland forged a political alliance in 1892 in order to strengthen his chance of carrying Illinois and to placate southern farmers, upset with his sound-money policies, who were flirting with the Populist Party and its stand on transportation, land, and currency. Because Cleveland and Stevenson held divergent views on the volatile currency question, Stevenson wisely sidestepped the matter, preferring to concentrate on tariff reform. Even though, on Cleveland's insistence, he pledged his approval of the hard-money plank in the Democratic platform, Stevenson continued to cherish his associations with soft-money advocates who favored the free and unlimited coinage of silver at a ratio of 16 to 1 with gold. The vice-presidential nominee pursued a policy of reticence that would neither offend nor threaten Cleveland while preserving his own independence. In his acceptance speech at Madison Square Garden in July, Stevenson appealed to the sober judgment of the people. He later wrote his acceptance letter in Charleston, West Virginia, with the assistance of George F. Parker, a journalist and close Cleveland confidant.

To counteract the Populist threat to Democratic success in the South, which was a solid part of the Democratic presidential coalition, Stevenson met with Cleveland in a postconvention strategy session at the former president's summer home in Buzzard's Bay, Massachusetts. There they devised a carefully crafted plan for a conservative counterattack. This compromise of 1892 consisted of five parts: First, southern Democrats who refrained from voting for the Populist Party would be rewarded by victorious Democratic opposition to Republican efforts in Congress to enact a federal elections law to protect African American suffrage; second, the Democratic administration would continue to direct economic benefits to the South; third, the Democrats would demonstrate their appreciation for southern support through patronage; fourth, the new administration would resume its past endeavors to reinstate the South to a proper place in the Union by harmonizing relations between sections; and fifth, the Democrats would lower the tariffs and practice frugality in government. Together these proposals constituted a significant challenge to the Populist danger, and with this program the Democrats bargained to hold a wavering South.

Stevenson functioned as the main proponent of this strategy in the presidential campaign of 1892. The Democratic plan for economic and political revitalization, he argued, would compensate for the more radical programs of the Populists. To consolidate Democratic strength and thwart the third-party movement, Stevenson visited several midwestern, border, and deep southern states, including Indiana, Kentucky, Tennessee, Alabama, North Carolina, Maryland, West Virginia, and Virginia. In these appearances,

Stevenson sought to generate support for the Democratic platform and convince discontented Democrats that too many votes for the Populists would only concede the presidential election to Benjamin Harrison, the Republican standard bearer. While touring these states, he assured Cleveland by letter that nothing was being left undone and that he was putting into operation, in private talks with party leaders and public speeches, the principles outlined in the compromise that year between the national party and the southern electorate.

Opposed to federal interference in elections, Stevenson contended that a Republican Congress and White House would attempt to implement a new federal elections law. Its passage, he theorized, would lead to economic calamities, heavy taxes, and the election of Republican congressmen from the South. He easily translated this personal belief into public rhetoric to squash the Populists and Republicans by recalling the bleak era of Reconstruction. Raising his hands in a gesture for emphasis, he scolded his audience in the manner of a stern father. Working closely with local conservative southern leaders, Stevenson, concerned that a new West–South agrarian alliance might replace the old East–South Bourbon alignment, provided them with the oratorical justification for the compromise package of 1892, which enabled these groups to exploit their opposition and repair their tenuous position in countless speeches throughout the region. Although warning southerners of the direct threat that awaited their interests should Harrison recapture the White House, Stevenson prudently avoided mentioning the race question in his prepared statements. Nor did he comment about black rights and opportunities. In common with Democratic politicians of his era, he made no effort to protect African Americans, who voted overwhelmingly Republican.

Stevenson did his part to help the Democrats win the presidential election of 1892. The chairman of the Democratic National Committee, William F. Harrity, thought that Stevenson's work had contributed largely to the result. A dedicated and competent public servant, Stevenson attained stature in the Democratic Party in

1892 and brought a broader trend toward personal campaigning in American politics. His most fundamental political skill revolved around an ability to charm audiences and attract support, regardless of geographic area. Stevenson championed party loyalty and regularity, intertwining Democratic fortunes with his own destiny and endeavoring through compromise to ease the transition from the politics of the antebellum era to that of the Gilded Age. Having fought for years to define the center, Stevenson in 1892 created a political posture in the middle of the spectrum that enabled him to avoid crossfires between Democratic factions. It was perhaps the defining event of Stevenson's political life.

Stevenson received the news of his victory in Bloomington, where he had begun and ended the campaign. He immediately wired a congratulatory telegram to Cleveland. Neighbors and friends welcomed the vice president-elect at a public reception. There Stevenson accepted the cheers while putting partisanship aside for the moment. He reminded the crowd that the glory attached to the American name and flag belong exclusively to no party or section but was instead the common heritage of all the people. Shortly thereafter, Stevenson contacted Vice President Levi P. Morton to make arrangements for a smooth transition. In late February 1893, the Stevenson family left Bloomington by train for Washington and the inaugural ceremonies.

In a brief ceremony conducted in the Senate chamber on March 3, 1893, Stevenson took the oath of office as vice president. The next day, in a special session of the Senate, he delivered a short inaugural address in which he pledged to discharge the important duties as president of the Senate with impartiality, courtesy, and fidelity. After witnessing Cleveland's inauguration on March 4 and attending an inaugural ball at the Pension Office, Stevenson and his family went to their temporary living quarters, a large suite on the second floor of the Normandie Hotel. Later, they moved to the Ebbitt House. At an even later date, they occupied a large suite on the second floor of the Normandie Hotel.

Stevenson entertained frequently and earned a prominent place in Washington's social circle.

He presided over several banquets, including dinners for Secretary of the Treasury John G. Carlisle and Secretary of War Daniel S. Lamont. Two of Stevenson's children married during his vice-presidential tenure. Stevenson's wife, president of the Daughters of the American Revolution and member of other organizations, was also active socially in Washington as the nation's second lady. On more than one occasion she assisted Frances Folsom Cleveland with receptions at the White House.

In addition to social responsibilities, Stevenson maintained his interest in politics. He regarded the vice presidency as an important office and accepted his position despite its constitutional shortcomings. Although he did not attend the cabinet meetings and voted only twice on minor bills to break a Senate tie, Stevenson never wavered in his belief that he was a representative of all the people. He opened his office door to reporters, allowing them easy access for interviews and questions, so that they could inform the citizenry of his activities. The vice president usually went to his office in the Capitol in the morning to work on his mail before presiding over the Senate, a parliamentary procedure with which he was familiar and liked immensely. His son, Lewis Green Stevenson, served as his clerk for a time.

Nearly four months after taking office, President Cleveland underwent surgery to remove a malignant growth on the roof of his mouth. His precautions for secrecy were so elaborate that only his wife, doctors, a close friend, and Secretary of War Lamont had any knowledge of the president's serious condition. The clandestine operation occurred aboard a slowly cruising yacht on Long Island Sound, while doctors worried about the effects of an anesthetic upon the corpulent chief executive and the possibility of a stroke of apoplexy occurring without a properly equipped hospital. Cleveland neglected to inform Stevenson of this event; in fact, Stevenson was a "near president" without ever learning the events that could have catapulted him into power. Cleveland's enigmatic reticence may have prevented a sudden fluctuation in the economy, but he was guilty of concealing a presidential illness from both his colleagues and the people. By denying Stevenson, who was then in Illinois, the right to important information and not providing him with the necessary briefings to assure a continuation of governmental activity in case of temporary incapacitation, Cleveland adopted principles that were inconsistent with the national interest and displayed a limited view of presidential prerogatives.

Stevenson was vice president during a severe economic depression. Rising unemployment and distressed conditions spawned political protest and social unrest, including a march on Washington in support of a public works relief program by an "army" led by Jacob Stevenson Coxey. To restore public confidence and strengthen the economy, Cleveland asked Congress to repeal the Sherman Silver Purchase Act of 1890. Sentiment in the Senate ran strongly in favor of compromise, but Cleveland refused to consider alternative legislation. Some western and southern senators thereupon engaged in a filibuster to resist the revocation. Displaying no feelings of disloyalty toward Cleveland or secret sympathies with the silverites, Stevenson, who regarded the Sherman law as an ill-advised enactment, did nothing to break the filibuster. Although supporting repeal, he permitted the verbal marathon to continue because of his deep regard for the established tradition of unlimited debate in the Senate. He contended that his oath bound him to obey the traditions of the upper chamber. Personally believing that wise legislation and good government resulted from debate, Stevenson worried that hasty legislation without reasonable discussion could imperil the public welfare. In the end, the bill repealing the Sherman measure passed Congress in 1893.

Stevenson's political endurance was greatly tested in 1894. He was caught in the middle that year in a dispute between Cleveland and Governor John Peter Altgeld of Illinois. Cleveland dispatched federal troops to Chicago to safeguard the mail, protect interstate commerce, and restore order during the Pullman Strike, an action called by the American Railway Union under Eugene V. Debs that immobilized railroads in the Midwest. The president's decision to quell the

disturbance by force met with opposition from Altgeld, who angrily condemned Cleveland. Wishing to antagonize neither Cleveland nor Altgeld, the governor of his home state, Stevenson remained silent on the issue, though his secret sympathies probably were with Cleveland.

Other issues confronted Stevenson in 1894. Democrats had pledged in 1892 to reform the tariff, and the House of Representatives in 1894 passed a measure to reduce taxation. Projectionist senators, on the other hand, added numerous amendments to safeguard certain items, which emasculated the original purpose of the legislation. The Wilson–Gorman Tariff of 1894 became law without Cleveland's signature, for he disliked the final version and denounced those Democrats who had contributed to protectionism. A disappointed Stevenson chose not to condemn fellow Democrats; instead, he blamed selfish interest for the defeat of reform. He also rationalized that the Democratic tariff was a step in the direction of lowering duties and that it was better than the Republican McKinley Tariff of 1890. As the depression deepened and farmers grew more restless, Cleveland's popularity plummeted, and he remained virtually secluded in the White House, shunned by segments of his own party.

During the congressional elections of 1894, Stevenson campaigned for Democratic candidates. The outcome reaffirmed his apprehensions: The Democratic Party sustained a stinging rebuke in one of the most profound off-year electoral routs in American history. A voter rebellion swept Republicans into power in Congress, which reconfigured political leadership. The stunning Republican revolution transformed the nation's political landscape, producing a political realignment outside the South. The nation's long electoral and ideological leaning toward the Republican Party since 1860 reached its watershed in 1894 when Democrats lost 113 seats in the House and 5 in the Senate. This enormous redistribution was such that Democrats failed to elect a single member of Congress in twenty-four states. Without much of the Democratic infrastructure left standing, demoralized Democrats recognized that there existed a widening sectional division between

East and West and a shrinking base of Democratic political power.

During his four years as vice president, Stevenson traveled extensively across the nation. He and Cleveland attended the opening of the Chicago's World Fair in 1895. In 1893, Stevenson and his wife, accompanied by the chief justice of the Illinois Supreme Court and other guests, boarded a private car of the Great Northern Railroad to tour several western areas. After seeing the Dakotas and Rocky Mountains, the entourage passed through the territories of New Mexico and Arizona, stopped at Los Angeles, and then arrived in San Francisco. A flotilla in the bay greeted the vice president, along with a nineteen-gun salute and a formal reception. There he met with Governor Henry M. Markham of California. After departing San Francisco, the group went home by way of Oregon, Montana, and Minnesota.

Stevenson also did a great deal of traveling in 1895. He and Altgeld were present at the dedication of the Chickamauga National Park, where Stevenson addressed the issue of healing sectional wounds and emphasized the indivisible union of indestructible states. Certainly the vice president's most notable trip that year was his train ride across the nation to Washington and his excursion by ship to Alaska, where he spent several days sightseeing and conferring with local officials. When he visited the state of Washington, people there wanted to know if he thought their majestic mountain should be called Mount Rainier or Mount Tacoma. Not wishing to antagonize anyone on this important but divisive local matter, Stevenson adroitly resolved the dilemma his own way: In a speech from the rear platform of the train, he devoted his peroration to discussing the beauty of the mountain, pledging not to rest until the mountain had a name. Then the vice president pulled a secret cord to notify the engineer. As a result, his last words, at the very point when he was supposed to mention his choice regarding this northwestern nomenclature, were drowned out by the noise of whistles and steam as the train pulled away from the station, leaving Stevenson, white of mane and dressed in a Prince Albert coat, bowing graciously to a cheering crowd, with his position still unknown.

Although Cleveland and Stevenson shared a mutual friendship and high regard for each other, the two never became close confidants. The president did not allow the vice president to share in decision making, but on one occasion Cleveland did ask Stevenson to review a Thanksgiving proclamation. Despite being on the outside, Stevenson loyally defended his chief's decision in both domestic and foreign affairs. This was apparent in speeches and writings in which he supported Cleveland's stand with regard to the Venezuelan boundary controversy with Great Britain, the maintenance of the Monroe Doctrine, and opposition to the annexation of Hawaii. Yet, it was the division within the Democratic Party in 1895 and 1896 over the money issue that tested Stevenson's ability as a versatile politician.

Neglecting to comprehend the political situation in 1895, Stevenson failed to seize the advantage he enjoyed that year over potential presidential rivals. He had reached his zenith and needed to create a national feeling for his presidential candidacy, as well as to generate a groundswell of support among Democrats that would make opposition to his presidential ambitions unpalatable. With Altgeld's blessing and with endorsements from the South, where he counted numerous political allies, Stevenson would have been in good shape to try for the nomination without directly attacking Cleveland's policies. Instead, he found himself in a quandary in 1896 and in the position of bearing ultimate responsibility for his own actions.

The most trying time politically for Stevenson occurred in 1896 when the contentious currency question strained his relationship with sound-money and free-silver friends. There existed a conflict inside the vice president—a contest between the gentlemen and the politician. The problem was how far Stevenson, dexterous accommodator, could go without antagonizing the Cleveland conservatives to perpetuate his political viability. Stevenson's instinct told him to keep his two jobs—vice president and practicing politician—distinct, but this was a self-defeating policy that crippled his chance for the presidency. An aura of invulnerability clouded his judgment and prevented him, until it was too late, from seeing the danger that he faced from opponents. Eager to please, Stevenson not only misjudged the political situation early in 1896, but everything he did prior to the Democratic convention seemed desperate and insincere. In short, Stevenson's style of leadership was both his strength and his undoing.

In spring 1896, a handful of free-silver senators, including James K. Jones of Arkansas, George G. Vest of Missouri, and Isham G. Harris of Tennessee, planned to promote Stevenson's presidential candidacy and urged the vice president to postpone announcing his intentions until an appropriate moment. While these senators were working to line up support for Stevenson's nomination on a free-silver platform, the vice president quietly met with sound money Democrats to gauge their sentiment concerning his possible presidential bid. In April 1896, Stevenson attended a dinner-table conference in New York at Wolfert's Roost, the home of Senator David B. Hill of New York. Present on this occasion were Senator Calvin Brice of Ohio, Senator Arthur P. Gorman of Maryland, Judge Alton B. Parker of New York, and John R. McLean, owner of the *Cincinnati Enquirer* and *The Washington Post*. While conferring with this group, Stevenson considered the possibility of stopping the free-silver movement from overtaking the badly divided party.

Stevenson was looking in two opposite directions in his quest to gain the nomination and heal intraparty wounds. He desired the endorsement of conservative and free-silver-coinage Democrats, talking unostentatiously with each side in an endeavor to gauge his strength, mollify differing factions, and endanger nothing. The vice president sought to emerge as the compromise choice of both Democratic factions and to compete for the presidency on a moderate platform. Ever eager to please, Stevenson showed a preference for compromise that by 1896 displeased all sides. His reputation as a dexterous accommodator always concerned with preserving his political viability raised questions that year about his leadership. Stevenson's strong point was empathy, but many wondered if it was adequate for the times.

The growing strength of the free-silver crusade and the Republican nomination of William McKinley on a sound-money platform weakened Stevenson's chance of obtaining the Democratic nomination on any kind of platform. By the end of June, when it had become obvious that prosilver forces would control the Democratic National Convention, Stevenson's free-silver allies in the Senate abruptly withdrew their support of his candidacy, and their cabal collapsed before the onslaught of free-silver ideologues determined to choose a more acceptable candidate.

An incensed Stevenson purportedly took umbrage over the unexpected turn of events and notified his cohorts that he would make his own fight for the nomination. Resenting the manner in which he had been used and then discarded when radical silverites gained control of the convention, Stevenson, instead of backpedaling to the safety of his vice-presidential suite, accused the senators of political cowardice and complained of the contemptible manner by which he had been deserted by his friends. Stevenson thereupon used the press as a vehicle to enhance his prospects and dispel the fear that he was not loyal to silver, conveniently forgetting his 1892 declaration in favor of sound money. Newspapers quickly capitalized on the beleaguered vice president's activity. The plan failed to generate enthusiasm, leaving Stevenson in a political quagmire. Radical silver ideologues, such as Altgeld, viewed Stevenson as an unlikely patron of change, accusing him of straddling the currency issue and being incapable of rebuilding a winning coalition. At the Democratic national convention in Chicago, Stevenson received no votes from either Kentucky or Illinois, and only a small handful from other states. Secluded in his Bloomington home, the vice president experienced a rapid fall from grace.

Stevenson's innate political cautiousness, a successful trait in the past, proved calamitous in the tumultuous arena of Democratic politics in 1896. It was the ultimate irony for a lawyer who had achieved success in the political world with his talent for fashioning compromises. Disliking divisive politics, Stevenson preferred to merge groups into the middle ground of happy consensus. Regrettably, the explosive political situation in 1896 put the vice president in a position that did not play to his natural strengths. He ultimately had to displease one group or the other by stating what kind of monetary system he envisioned for the nation. Unable to escape the cloud of discontent hanging over the Cleveland administration, the vice president, practicing the politics of preservation to immunize himself from extremism, endeavored to play politics for the silver vote but lost while trying to deflect criticism that he had not done enough for free silverism. Caught between the vacuum that was Cleveland and the resentment that was William Jennings Bryan, Stevenson faced his worst political identity crisis.

Struggling to reconcile a divided party by using his outmoded conciliatory style, Stevenson tried to appease all factions with concessions but went down to a humiliating defeat. His presidential ascendancy in 1896 would have been the result of deep intraparty wrangling, fueled by a policy clash over the money issue, a deadlocked convention, and an ultimate Stevenson coronation as a compromise choice. It did not happen. Vice President Stevenson lacked the personal dynamism to energize Democrats with frenzied enthusiasm; he was not the heroic figure that the occasion demanded. Instead, Bryan steamrollered his opposition, crushing Stevenson in the process. An older group of party stewards exited while the torch was passed to a new generation of Democrats. Stevenson quickly joined the group and wholeheartedly endorsed Bryan as the Democratic presidential nominee.

Although he failed to obtain the Democratic presidential nomination in 1896, Stevenson worked for party unification in a way that Bryan refused to do in the postconvention period. Unlike Bryan, whose victory infuriated conservatives, Stevenson did not make the Chicago platform a litmus test of faith, and he rejected all unyielding positions on party purification and attempts to purge those Democrats who refused to pledge their loyalty. Unalterably opposed to the principle of excommunication from the party, Stevenson minimized differences, preached assimilation, and warned that Democratic divisions would result in Republican control of Congress and the White House. The vice president was the highest official in the Cleveland administration supporting Bryan, who, along with the new chairman of the Democratic National Committee, miscalculated badly by neglecting to use the soothingly sensible Stevenson in the national campaign to ease the clash among party factions. Stevenson's careful blend of pragmatism and partisanship constituted an important counterpart to the more ideologically charged agenda of Bryan. Nevertheless, Stevenson campaigned for Bryan, introduced him to the crowd when the nominee visited Bloomington, and decided against discussing his stand with Cleveland, who supported the independent presidential candidacy of Senator John M. Palmer, an Illinois sound-money politician chosen in Indianapolis by bolting Democrats. Although Palmer, Cleveland, and Stevenson remained friends, the vice president did not endorse Palmer on a separate third-party ticket, nor did he question the sincerity of his conservative colleagues who favored Palmer over Bryan.

At the end of September 1896, before participating in the quadrennial convention of the National Association of Democratic Clubs in St. Louis, Missouri, Stevenson went to Burlington, Iowa, to represent the administration in the semicentennial celebrations of that state's admission to the Union. In the midst of this festival, the reviewing stand on Main Street, hastily erected against the wishes of some local businessmen, suddenly collapsed from the crowd's weight, sending dignitaries and guests falling to the rain-soaked ground. Stevenson, seated near the center of the stand, was thrown into a wildly struggling mass of people. His left leg was badly bruised, and his knee was slightly sprained. He appeared dazed for a moment by the force of the fall, and concern grew when he was unable for a time to leave the scene of the accident. Eventually, the vice president entered his carriage for the ride to the hotel, where he recovered after a short rest. Stevenson took the incident good naturedly and only seemed concerned about the injuries of those who fell about him.

After leaving Iowa and Missouri, Stevenson returned to Illinois to await the results of the presidential election. William McKinley, the Republican presidential standard bearer and former governor of Ohio, easily won the presidency on a conservative platform. Stevenson immediately dispatched a congratulatory telegram to Vice President–elect Garret A. Hobart of New Jersey. He then made preparations for his final months in office. Members of the U.S. Senate individually and collectively expressed their appreciation to Stevenson for his fairness and efficiency in presiding over the upper chamber. They unanimously passed a resolution of thanks and presented the vice president with a handsome silver service and a signed testimonial.

On March 3, 1897, Stevenson administered the oath of office to his successor, Vice President Hobart. He then delivered his farewell address, in which he thanked the senators for their courtesy and urged that they extend the same spirit of cooperation to Hobart. Stevenson stated that it had been a great honor and a rewarding experience to preside over the Senate, and that he carried with him no feelings of unkindness toward any senator. Adding that he had endeavored to interpret and execute faithfully the rules of the Senate, Stevenson reiterated his support of its rules and traditions.

After attending McKinley's inaugural ceremonies at the Capitol on March 4, 1897, Stevenson returned to his home in Bloomington. He resumed his legal career and duties as president of the McLean County Coal Company. The former vice president also served for a time as president of the Interstate Building and Loan Association of Bloomington and as director of the People's Bank of Bloomington. He looked forward to a relaxed life with his family and neighbors.

In April 1897, one month after he left office, Stevenson was back in Washington to accept the invitation of President McKinley to serve as one of three members of the Bimetallic Monetary Commission, headed by Senator Edward O. Wolcott of Colorado. McKinley chose Stevenson to represent the Democratic Party, but the two men had long been good friends. The three commissioners immediately sailed to Europe to discuss with world leaders the monetary question and to explore the possibility of bimetallism, which would establish the proper mint ratio between gold and silver. Stevenson secretly believed the Democrats would not be able to convert the nation to free coinage and that the only hope for silver rested with an international agreement. With this goal in mind, he discussed international bimetallism with British and French spokesmen.

While waiting for final negotiations and a decision from India, Stevenson and his wife visited Norway, Sweden, Denmark, Italy, and Switzerland. Upon returning to London, where he was presented to Queen Victoria, Stevenson learned that European leaders had declined the American offer.

The following year Stevenson and McKinley renewed their relationship when they shared a platform at a Peace Jubilee Banquet in Chicago. On that occasion Stevenson warmly praised McKinley's successful conduct of the Spanish–American War, referring to the brief conflict in 1898 as the marvel of the closing century.

Stevenson surfaced again politically in 1900, when events took a surprising turn at the Democratic National Convention in Kansas City. There, delegates extricated Stevenson from political retirement by choosing him as a vice-presidential candidate to run with Bryan. Mayor Carter H. Harrison II of Chicago assumed the initiative by presenting Stevenson's name to the Illinois delegation. Altgeld's gubernatorial defeat in 1896 had created a Democratic void in Illinois, and Stevenson's friends again controlled the political machinery. Easily eliminating other contenders, Stevenson triumphed on the first ballot. He received the vice presidential nomination in 1900 because he was the most available man in the Democratic Party to provide the stability and harmony that the party needed that year. Nominated in 1892 as a liberal to balance a slate led by a conservative, the rehabilitated Stevenson, a spokesman for traditional Democratic nostrums, obtained a second nomination in 1900 as an elder conservative statesman to stabilize a ticket headed by a progressive who championed reinvented government.

The Democrats changed presidential leaders and philosophical direction in eight years but kept

Stevenson, who also received the vice-presidential nominations of the Silver Republican and Populist parties, which had fused with Bryan. The belated attempt of the Bryanites to assuage differences with Democratic conservatives by selecting Stevenson would have been more useful and effective had they chosen Stevenson as Bryan's running mate in 1896. In any event, Bryan, who had preferred another candidate, did nothing to prevent Stevenson's nomination in 1900, praising him as a person of splendid character and, in an unprecedented move, announced his determination to increase the importance of the vice presidency by having the incumbent attend cabinet meetings.

In 1900, Stevenson regarded the vice presidency as a suitable conclusion to his long career of public service. His nomination, which marked the first time that a vice president had recaptured his party's nomination after having left office, propelled him once again into the political spotlight, and the prospect of serving his party and country prompted him to campaign widely. Again conferring with Bryan in Lincoln, Nebraska, on campaign strategy and following his acceptance speech in Indianapolis, Stevenson visited several states, including Maryland, Delaware, New York, New Jersey, and West Virginia. He denounced monopolistic growth and the trusts but avoided mentioning the currency issue, which he did not regard as paramount in the campaign of 1900.

Stevenson took special interest in foreign affairs in 1900. He was particularly opposed to the provision in the Paris peace treaty of 1899 for acquiring the Philippine Islands. An implacable opponent of overseas expansionism, Stevenson predicted that the acquisition and retention of the Philippines would compromise America's original altruistic purpose. He presented a number of constitutional, political, economic, diplomatic, historical, and radical reasons to substantiate his opposition to imperialism. A product of the isolationism that flourished in the midwestern heartland, Stevenson repeated the warnings of George Washington and Thomas Jefferson regarding alliances and internal involvement. Although Stevenson espoused continental con-

tainment, he lacked the xenophobic paranoia and pessimism characteristic of some rabid antiimperialists. In essence, he was a traditionalist who tried to steer the country away from permanent entanglements and belligerent interventionism. To Stevenson, isolationism meant maintaining maximum freedom of action and not total withdrawal from world affairs. He advocated a coherent foreign policy for the future while fully recognizing America's aversion to interventionary politics. Stevenson also hoped for the establishment of a tribunal of all nations, including the United States, that would resolve issues and preserve peace. Ironically, his grandson and namesake, Adlai E. Stevenson II, Democratic presidential nominee in 1952 and 1956, served as United States ambassador to the United Nations from 1961 to 1965.

After the defeat of the Bryan-Stevenson ticket in 1900 at the hands of McKinley and Roosevelt, Stevenson returned to Bloomington. There he lived a quiet but active life as a respected elder party spokesman. He addressed various groups, delivered lectures, and favored New York Democrat Alton B. Parker for the presidency in 1904. In 1908, after handily winning the Democratic primary, Stevenson narrowly lost the Illinois gubernatorial election, but he ran ahead of Bryan, who unsuccessfully sought his third try at the White House. Vote frauds in Chicago wards controlled by Republican Mayor Fred A. Busse may have cost Stevenson, who commanded the backing of Republican Congressman William Lorimer, the governor's office. Four years later, in a letter to President-elect Woodrow Wilson, Bryan suggested Stevenson as a possibility to fill a position in the new Democratic administration. The offer never materialized, and Stevenson died shortly thereafter in a Chicago hospital.

Stevenson must be analyzed in connection with the complicated political context in which he lived and the ambiguities of his beliefs and policies, for he embodied the contradictions of an age that was simultaneously resisting and welcoming ongoing changes in society. Like most Gilded Age politicians, Stevenson suffered from an inability to recognize that the major problem of his generation reverberated around the adjustment of American politics to the enormous economic and social transformations imposed on the United States by industrialization and urbanization, which brought the nation to a new stage of self-awareness. Stevenson, whose politics combined a generally conservative social and political agenda with a strong dose of moralism, was a Gilded Age Jeffersonian who lived in the agrarian Midwest. His fidelity was to the Democratic Party, whose faithful servant he tried to be throughout his career. Partly progressive and partly conservative, both a reformer and a conformer, he sought the society of Old Guard security but often registered dissenting opinions. Admittedly, he was a complex political figure who zigzagged across stereotypes, both naturally and by calculation.

Although not in the first rank of great men of his generation, Stevenson was a good vice president and an honest politician in an era when the public neither expected nor sought great political leaders. He also served as a transitional figure in bridging the passing of the Democrats from the conservatism of Cleveland to the progressivism of Bryan and Wilson. Like many nineteenth-century vice presidents, however, Stevenson failed in his quest for lasting fame. His glory, like that of many who preceded him, rested in achieving, rather than holding, high political office. On the other hand, as the founder of a political dynasty whose grandson ran for president in 1952 and 1956, he thrust his family onto the political stage where they remained for the next three generations. Stevenson's contribution to the American political tradition was a legacy for his family and the nation.

REFERENCES

Leonard C. Schlup, "The Political Career of the First Adlai E. Stevenson" (Ph.D. diss., University of Illinois at Urbana-Champaign, 1973); Leonard C. Schlup, "The American Chameleon: Adlai E. Stevenson and the Quest for the Vice Presidency in Gilded Age Politics," *Presidential Studies Quarterly*, 21 (Summer 1991), 511–529; Adlai E. Stevenson, *Something of Men I Have Known: With Some Papers of a General Nature, Political, Historical, and Retrospective* (Chicago, Ill.: A.C. McClurg and Company, 1909).

See the entry for Garret Hobart for a biographical note on Leonard C. Schlup.

GARRET AUGUSTUS HOBART (1844–1899)

Vice President, 1897–1899

(President William McKinley)

GARRET AUGUSTUS HOBART
(Library of Congress)

By Leonard C. Schlup

Garret A. Hobart was one of the nation's first modern vice presidents. Although he entered office with a modest résumé, he demonstrated that conventional credentials are not always the main indicators of political success. Hobart gave a new distinction to the vice-presidential office, increased its stature, served as a loyal personal friend and political companion to President William McKinley, skillfully presided over the United States Senate, and performed duties assigned to him by McKinley. Because of his important role and responsibilities, combined with his close relationship with McKinley, Hobart was often referred to as the "assistant president." In the public mind, he was clearly identified with the administration. Hobart was more than the titular president of the Senate with a reversionary right to the presidency; he was for more than two years a factor in the political and social life of the nation.

Born in Long Branch, New Jersey, the son of Addison Willard Hobart, a teacher and farmer, and Sophia Vanderveer Hobart, Garret Hobart attended elementary and preparatory schools before graduating third highest in his class with honors in mathematics and English from Rutgers College in 1863. He taught school for a short time before relocating to Paterson, New Jersey, where he studied law in the office of Socrates Tuttle, whose daughter, Jennie, he married in 1869, the year of his admission to the bar. Hobart became a counselor at law in 1871 and a master in chancery the following year. He advanced quickly in the fields of law, business, and politics. In 1871, he was chosen city counsel of Paterson, and in both 1872 and 1873, Hobart won a seat in the lower chamber of the New Jersey state legislature, becoming speaker of the house in 1874. Elected state senator in 1876 and 1879 by large majorities, he served as president of the senate in the sessions of 1881 and 1882, thereby becoming the only person in New Jersey history ever to be both speaker of the state assembly and president of the senate.

Early in his career, Hobart developed interests in national politics. Chairman of the New Jersey State Republican Committee from 1880 to 1891, he was a delegate-at-large to five successive Republican national conventions, where he made many friends. In 1884, he joined the Republican National Committee. Unsuccessful as the Republican candidate for the U.S. Senate in 1883 in an age when state legislators selected senators and Democrats then controlled the New Jersey legislature, Hobart, declining to run for a seat in the U.S. House of Representatives, refused to allow his defeat to terminate his political interests. In 1888, he dispatched letters to Republican presidential nominee Benjamin Harrison to outline the political situation in New Jersey and offer his advice.

A constructive moderate from an important eastern state, Hobart supported sound-money principles, a protective tariff to safeguard American industry, expanded markets, development of transportation systems, and federal spending for projects of regional and national importance. He accepted the industrial United States and the ethic of the day. Eager to see the country grow, Hobart was a nationalist who possessed the emotional attitude for increased governmental action. The dogmas of localism, retrenchment, and antifederalism were foreign to him as he embraced his party's growing nationalism and the rapid social and economic changes in the nation. In New Jersey he represented an industrial constituency of business, agriculture, labor, and the professional middle class.

Hobart's political and business interests were intertwined; he regarded himself as a businessman who engaged in politics for recreation. In 1885, he assumed the presidency of the Passaic Water Company. A director of several banks and a receiver for the New Jersey Midland Railroad and the First National Bank of Newark, Hobart earned a reputation for business sagacity, eventually having connections with sixty corporations. In the process, he accumulated a fortune and surfaced as a leading Republican of northern New Jersey. The practicing businessman/politician in 1895 secured the Republican gubernatorial nomination for his friend, John W. Griggs, and managed the campaign. Griggs's election ended a long reign of Democratic control and heralded a new era of Republican rule in the state.

The beginning of a long Republican reign in the Garden State began when the GOP took control of the state legislature in 1894 and the governor's mansion the next year. Several factors were responsible for this emerging Republicanism, among them the severe depression that engulfed the nation, the decrease in the number of farms, the increase of the conservative commuter vote, the support for tariff protection, and the disapproval of the free-silver movement. Republican domination of New Jersey opened the door to Hobart's vice-presidential nomination.

The depression that gripped the nation following the Panic of 1893 weakened the Democratic Party. Legions of unemployed workers and scores of failed businesses contributed to a bleak picture of the American economy. This economic distress spawned political protest and social unrest. President Grover Cleveland's popularity plummeted, and he was shunned by segments of his own party. His handling of the currency issue, among other actions, divided Democrats, with southern and western free-silver advocates aligned against the East in a battle of the monetary standards. As a result of overwhelming Republican victories across the nation in the off-year congressional elections of 1894, Republicans felt confident of success in 1896.

Hobart also sensed a Republican victory in 1896. His duties as a Republican National Committee member and as a delegate-at-large from New Jersey occupied his time in the immediate weeks prior to the party's state and national conventions. Endorsed by the New Jersey convention as a vice-presidential favorite son, Hobart left Paterson on June 8 to entertain the New Jersey delegation at the Lawyer's Club in New York City and make arrangements for the national convention. He also conferred with Senator Matthew S. Quay of Pennsylvania, who endorsed Hobart for the vice presidency. On his way to the national convention in St. Louis, Hobart stopped at McKinley's home in Canton, Ohio, to discuss politics with the former congressman and governor who was the front-runner for the presidential nomination. Meanwhile, the stage was being set for his vice-presidential nomination. Confident of Hobart's nomination, Senator John M. Thurston of Nebraska, Republican national convention chairman, arrived in St. Louis wearing a McKinley-Hobart button. Senator Redfield Proctor of Vermont also sported a similar ornament. Illinois lawyer, banker, and businessman Charles G. Dawes, who later served as vice president, lined up the Illinois delegation for Hobart.

At first dismayed and overwhelmed at the thought of his possible nomination, Hobart expressed his innermost feelings and trepidations in letters and conversations with his wife and close friends. His concerns centered mainly on the work, the worry, and the loss of home life connected with political office. He was also cognizant of the impenetrable vacuum that characterized the vice president, a person usually viewed as the trailer to the ticket, a fifth wheel in the national bandwagon who rolled painlessly into oblivion. Knowing that McKinley needed a running mate from an eastern-seaboard state, Hobart hoped that Thomas B. Reed, Speaker of the House of Representatives, would consent to accept second place, but Reed adamantly refused to consider this possibility. Although he approached the convention with misgivings, Hobart ultimately decided that he would neither seek nor avoid the vice-presidential nomination; he would allow events to take their own natural course.

Republican delegates convened in St. Louis on June 16, 1896, for their quadrennial national convention. McKinley easily triumphed on the first ballot to become the party's presidential standard bearer. The platform, which called for a protective tariff and sound money, contained ideas and words offered by Hobart; in fact, his unwavering endorsement of the gold standard helped to influence the party's position on that vexatious issue.

When delegates began to consider vice-presidential possibilities, Thomas C. Platt, the recognized leader in New York Republican politics, attempted to force upon the convention the name of Governor Levi P. Morton of New York, who had served as vice president from 1889 to 1893, during the administration of Benjamin Harrison. Because there was no one candidate from New York upon whom the Republicans could agree, the delegates needed to look elsewhere. Mark Hanna, a wealthy Ohio industrialist who shrewdly managed McKinley's campaign, preferred Hobart, and he used his powerful influence to further the ambitions of the New Jersey contender. United States Senator William J. Sewell, the boss of New Jersey Republicanism, also favored Hobart for the vice presidency, contending his presence on the ticket would guarantee Republican success in the Garden State. The New Jersey delegation thereupon presented Hobart as the state's candidate for the vice presidency. Hobart was nominated by Judge John Franklin Fort, later to serve as governor of New Jersey, who emphasized that his politically regenerated state merited the recognition. J. Otis Humphrey, an Illinois attorney who later served as a federal district judge, seconded Hobart's nomination. Hobart scored an easy victory on the first ballot over his nearest competitor, Henry Clay Evans of Tennessee.

McKinley and Hanna joined forces with Hobart in 1896 for a variety of reasons. First, Hobart was politically acceptable to and ideologically compatible with McKinley. Hobart and McKinley belonged to the same wing of their party; neither political doctrine nor a separate allegiance divided the two men. Second, Hobart entertained no presidential ambitions and carried no burdensome baggage. Although he had not been governor or senator and was without a national reputation, Hobart was a moderate and noncontroversial politician who possessed personal integrity and wealth although he lacked political enemies. In short, he did little to strengthen the ticket, but he did nothing to weaken it either. Third, Hobart lived in a region that provided geographical balance to the ticket in an era when both parties, by prevailing practice, selected their presidential and vice-presidential nominees from the Midwest and East. As a native of New Jersey, Hobart was expected to help carry that pivotal state for the Republican slate and add vigor to the ticket in the East. For these reasons, Hobart, a conservative pragmatist, emerged as a national political leader in the Republican coalition of 1896.

After receiving the vice-presidential nomination, Hobart thanked his New Jersey colleagues and the Republican delegates for their expression of confidence in his ability to discharge the duties of the vice presidency. He pledged to employ his best efforts to further McKinley's election. Hobart thereupon returned to New Jersey, where on July 17 the committee appointed by the convention to notify Hobart of his nomination arrived at his Paterson home. Charles W. Fairbanks of Indiana, chairman of this committee, who would later serve as senator and vice president, remarked that the vice presidency had been graced by eminent statesmen who had contributed to the upbuilding of the strength and glory of the nation.

In his reply, Hobart accepted the nomination. He promised to help the party achieve electoral success and reaffirmed his support for the gold standard and protective tariffs as sound principles on which to restore the nation's prosperity. The nominee pointed out that monetary uncertainty or instability could lead to serious consequences and that the gravity of the financial question could not be overestimated. Because gold was the one standard of value among all enlightened commercial nations, Hobart declared that the issue could not be compromised.

The presidential election of 1896 was a crucial contest in U.S. history, constituting a fundamental turning point in American electoral politics and demonstrating the periodicity of political realignment. By 1896 the economic depression had led to an erosion of living standards for many, including farmers who watched their incomes plummet and their debt skyrocket throughout the course of the national malaise. A crisis of confidence gripped Cleveland's presidency at the time of the campaign. Years of violence, sectional antagonisms, class conflicts, social unrest, political protest, and economic disillusionment, combined with the problems of growing urbanization and industrialization, fostered frustration and triggered national anxiety. These forces climaxed in the campaign of 1896, the most significant election in the Gilded Age, a term coined by Mark Twain to describe a post-Civil War generation characterized by excess.

Hobart assumed an active role in the 1896 presidential campaign. He delivered speeches, corresponded with McKinley, visited the most important cities of New Jersey, helped to manage the campaign from an office in New York City, and received delegations of visitors on the front lawn of his home in New Jersey. Like McKinley, who conducted a front-porch campaign from his home in Canton, Hobart abstained from the national barnstorming method identified with the Democratic and Populist presidential nominee, William Jennings Bryan, who ran on a free-coinage platform. Maintaining that the Republican Party was right in its principles and that issues were more important than personalities, Hobart emphasized that he was not fighting the old Democratic Party but rather a new group that had seized power and overturned traditional party nostrums. The new group's proposal of such fiscal alterations and heresies, Hobart warned, would lead to a financial revolution, inflation, and the collapse of sound money; in a speech at Newark, he predicted that the election's outcome would teach the greatest lesson in political morality that had ever been taught in America.

Twice during the campaign, Hobart journeyed to McKinley's home to confer with the head of the ticket. On the second visit, he brought his letter of acceptance with him. Hobart met McKinley and Herman H. Kohlsaat, editor and publisher of the *Chicago Times-Herald*. The New Jersey Republican read his letter of acceptance while McKinley, who had supervised its preparation, smoked a cigar and offered suggestions. McKinley was exceedingly cautious about the exact wording, but Hobart gladly accepted the revisions.

Hobart's formal letter of acceptance, dated September 7, was addressed to Fairbanks and other members of the notification committee. The letter, devoted chiefly to the monetary issue, contained several graphic illustrations of the horrendous consequences of free silver, referring to this question as the supremely important subject in the campaign. Hobart claimed that the money standard of a great nation should be as fixed and permanent as the nation itself and that the free coinage of silver at the ratio of 16 to 1 was a policy that no country had ever before proposed. Noting that the foundation of a house is not always in sight but that the house would not stand without its foundation, Hobart warned that any depreciation in the value of the dollar would defraud those who had accumulated savings and would hurt the pensions of Civil War veterans, a situation that would be tantamount to war upon the people. He believed that no person should be made homeless because a political party wanted to experiment with the money standard for its own selfish purposes. Contending that the country could not afford to give its sanction to wholesale spoilation, Hobart wrote that it was neither wise nor patriotic to make a political platform the medium of assault upon property, the peace of society, and civilization itself. He equated the Democratic platform with revolutionary propaganda embodying a menace of national disintegration and destruction, and he urged all men regardless of political affiliation to unite in defense of individual and institutional rights and of the nation's endangered interests.

Although he emphasized the currency issue, Hobart did not neglect the tariff question. Reminding Americans that their paralyzed industrial system had resulted from a mistaken economic system deliberately enacted by Democrats, he stressed that the duty of government was to protect and encourage in all practical ways the development of domestic industries, the elevation of home labor, and the enlargement of prosperity. Hobart remained convinced that the voters would understand the issues during the campaign and would choose safe and sure remedies rather than trust the Democratic Party, which under Bryan had dishonored its pledges and repudiated its past principles and policies.

McKinley and Hobart made the election of 1896 a contest between the forces of law and decency versus those of radicalism and violence. Their supporters distributed American flags, thereby making the nation's banner a symbol of conservative politics. Mounting a great publicity and mass-marketing effort, Hanna raised millions of dollars on behalf of the McKinley-Hobart team, whose campaign was the first to be professionally run. A new era had dawned in American politics.

McKinley triumphed nationally to win the presidency in 1896, while Republicans retained control of both houses of Congress, further cementing the political realignment that had begun two years earlier. Republican nationalism scored an impressive victory in that McKinley, a safe midwesterner, represented the conscience of the country and symbolized the ideals of nationality in an age of industrial growth and uncertainty. A political collision of two ideologies occurred in 1896. The fuel that fired the political revolution that seminal year was a blend of anger and fear that adverse economic and social forces were slipping out of control. The outcome demonstrated that business and industrial groups had conquered agrarian forces, and the result, plus the passage of the Gold Standard Act of 1900, helped to destroy free silver as a powerful political issue.

The immediate result marked a victory for conservatism and the politics of census, the very cornerstone of McKinleyism. From this election, Republicans built a presidential coalition that, with the exception of eight years of Woodrow Wilson, dominate American politics until the Great Depression.

A few days after the election, in which the Republican ticket swept New Jersey with 60 percent of the popular vote, Hobart acknowledged his victory in a spirit of nonpartisanship. He said that he did not consider the election a personal victory; rather, it was a triumph of American patriotism that belonged to no party. The vice president-elect observed that many voters had abjured their past political affiliations and had voted as their consciences dictated for the supremacy of law and to maintain the national honor. Seeking to assuage campaign wounds, Hobart magnified principles and patriotism instead of personalities.

During the postelection period, Hobart prepared himself for his new position. He studied the history of the vice presidency, mastered and memorized the rules of the Senate, and learned the names of all the senators. He arrived in Washington on March 2, 1897, establishing his headquarters and temporary living quarters at the Arlington Hotel. Vice President Adlai E. Stevenson paid a courtesy call on his successor. Hobart returned the nicety by visiting with Stevenson at the Ebbitt House the next day.

On March 4, 1897, Stevenson administered the oath of office to Hobart as the nation's twenty-fourth vice president. The ceremony occurred in the Senate chamber with members of Congress, President Cleveland, President-elect McKinley, governors, cabinet officers, and other dignitaries present for the occasion. After taking the oath, Hobart delivered a brief inaugural address in which he promised to abide by a conservative, equitable, and conscientious construction and enforcement of the upper chamber's rules while at the same time conserving the precedents and established traditions that had contributed to making that tribunal the most distinguished of the world's legislative bodies. He pledged to assist the senators to move expeditiously in the interests of good government and positive legislation, maintaining that any attempt to obstruct the regular course of wise and prudent legislative action after the fullest and freest discussion was neither consistent with true senatorial courtesy nor conducive to the welfare of the people. Hoping to form genuine friendships with members of the Senate, the vice president announced his intention to discharge his duties in such a manner as to lighten their labor and promote the pleasant and efficient transaction of the public business in such a way that their work would redound to the peace and honor of the country and the prosperity and happiness of all the people. Upon the conclusion of Hobart's speech, Cleveland leaned over to McKinley and whispered that it was the sweetest oration he had heard in a long time.

Although abhorring unnecessary procrastination and prolonged debates, Hobart entertained no plans to usurp the prerogatives of the Senate, to change its rules and customs, or to claim unconstitutional powers; instead, he frankly expressed his views, promising to set an example of facilitation in his endeavor to conduct sessions in a businesslike fashion. A business-politician oriented toward goals and achievements, Hobart wanted to see concrete results in ways similar to those he had witnessed in his private business transactions over the years. Moreover, he propounded the idea that the results of the presidential election demonstrated that the people demanded action from their elected representatives.

Skillfully presiding over the Senate, using a gavel made from his father's apple tree, Hobart took his duties seriously and prepared assiduously for the legislative agenda. Regularly attending Senate sessions, the vice president became known as a chronic audience. He enjoyed sitting in the presiding officer's chair, listening to the debates, strolling the corridors, visiting committee sessions, lunching with senators, attending afternoon smokers, holding dinner parties, and smoothing things over for McKinley in the upper house. He was somewhere between the powerful Speaker of the House Thomas B. Reed on the one hand and passive insignificance on the other.

With his quick perception and keen memory for legislative details, Hobart speeded proceedings by providing rapid answers to parliamentary questions. In the process, he surfaced as a popular president of the Senate who avoided making political enemies. A kindly gentleman with modest dignity and a good conversationalist who was known for his charm and his willingness to compromise, he gave new meaning to the vice presidential office, gained the respect of the Senate and the president, influenced the Senate to promote the administration's policies, and sought harmonious feelings between the executive and legislative branches. McKinley had an invaluable ally in Hobart.

The Hobarts leased the Cameron Mansion at 21 Lafayette Square, which stood diagonally across from the White House. Often called the Cream White House, the home was owned by Senator James D. Cameron of Pennsylvania, who at first wanted a $10,000 rental agreement, which Hobart, whose salary was only $8,000, refused outright. Fortunately, the two Republicans came to an agreement. The proximity of the Cameron Home to the White House facilitated frequent social meetings between the McKinleys and the Hobarts. Jennie T. Hobart often served as the White House hostess for Ida S. McKinley, an invalid who experienced seizures of unconsciousness. Unable to fulfill all her social duties, Mrs. McKinley often turned to Mrs. Hobart for assistance. The vice president's charming wife, who popularized the title "second lady," thoroughly enjoyed her role as a Washington hostess with a busy social calendar. From these frequent contacts, a close personal relationship developed between the two families. On more than one occasion, they vacationed together at Bluff Point on Lake Champlain and shared certain holidays, including Thanksgiving Day 1898 in the White House. Hobart even served as an investment counselor to the president and manager of McKinley's income.

Hobart loyally supported McKinley's programs. In 1897, he endorsed the Dingley Tariff, a high protectionist measure. Later that year, upon the resignation of Attorney General Joseph

McKenna, Hobart persuaded McKinley to appoint Governor Griggs of New Jersey to the vacant cabinet spot. Although McKinley did nearly everything possible to promote Hobart as a vital part of the administration, such as soliciting his views on issues and consulting with him on affairs of state, he neglected to invite the vice president to attend cabinet meetings, a surprising oversight. Socially, Hobart was the first vice president to assert predominance over Sir Julian Paunceforte, dean of the diplomatic corps in Washington, who previously had claimed a position next to the president in receiving lines. Recognizing Hobart as the second-highest official, McKinley, asserting unmistakably that second place at diplomatic receptions belonged to the vice president, ordered Hobart to stand next to him instead of the British ambassador.

As presiding officer, Hobart had the opportunity to address the Senate on various occasions in which he related his personal impressions of the character and scope of the upper chamber. At the close of the session in which the Dingley Tariff had been approved in 1897, he conceded that his inaugural remark about Senate promptness had been made in innocence and that he had since learned that his definition of reasonable expedition differed considerably from the Senate's conception of the meaning of that phrase. He praised Senate Democrats for refraining from abusing the rules of the Senate and congratulated Republicans for their endeavors to promote the public welfare by passing legislation designed to restore healthy industrial and economic conditions, adding that senators represented well the desires of their constituents. Defining the Senate as a remarkable body and the sine qua non of legislation, Hobart asserted that the smallest state was just as powerful as the largest one in the upper house. He opined that the cloud of depression and distrust was evaporating and then bluntly lectured U.S. socialists on the work ethic, telling them that no industrial rewards existed for the idle.

In 1898, Hobart turned his attention to foreign affairs. The desire of the Cubans for independence from Spain received his warm blessing. After the sinking of the U.S. battleship *Maine*, Hobart joined the president, the secretary of state, and Catholic archbishop John Ireland in a meeting on March 10 at the White House, where they reviewed the Cuban situation. Hobart used that occasion to notify McKinley of the growing pressure for war that was prevalent in Congress and to express his belief that the nation had no alternative except to declare war on Spain. Congress approved the war declaration on April 25. The swift military triumphs in the popular Spanish-American War of 1898 heightened Hobart's patriotic and nationalistic sentiments. He boasted of the brilliant military victories; yet he opposed annexing a free Cuba to the United States. Like McKinley, Hobart was not an imperialist by inclination but a reticent expansionist eager to gain new markets for American business and industry. He favored the annexation of Hawaii in 1898, scoffing at the impassioned rhetoric and warnings of antiimperialists over American acquisition of distant lands.

The single casting vote of Hobart as president of the Senate took place on February 14, 1899, eight days after the Senate had ratified the Treaty of Paris, the formal document concluding the war with Spain. Democratic Senator Augustus O. Bacon of Georgia proposed a resolution to limit American control over the Philippine Islands, which the United States had acquired from Spain, urging that the United States disclaim any intention to exercise permanent jurisdiction over the islands and affirming that the United States would withdraw once a stable independent government had been formed by the people. McKinley disapproved this restriction, suggesting that it would place restraints on his conduct of foreign policy in the region. Because some Republicans were absent when the resolution came up for a vote in the Senate, the outcome resulted in a tie of 29 votes for each side. Empowered by the Constitution to break a tie vote, Hobart cast his vote against the resolution, thereby relieving McKinley of an embarrassing situation. When Hobart administered the coup de grâce by voting to defeat the resolution, he opened a new political struggle in the United States between imperialists and antiimperialists.

On March 4, 1899, before declaring the Senate adjourned, Hobart addressed the members. Recalling the Spanish–American War as a conflict undertaken in the interest of humanity and conspicuous for the brilliant deeds of the army and navy, he bragged that an imperial domain had been added to American possessions. The vice president expressed confidence that future Congresses would also meet grave questions with wisdom and patriotism and would resolve them properly. Hobart also confessed that he cherished a profound faith in the spirit of the American people and that his confidence in the strength of American political institutions had been increased during his tenure in office.

No doubt the most difficult personal assignment Hobart completed for McKinley occurred in the summer of 1899. Public outcry over unpreparedness, mismanagement, and incompetence in the army during the Spanish-American War led to an investigatory commission and public requests for the resignation of Secretary of War Russell A. Alger, a former governor of Michigan whom McKinley had appointed to his cabinet in 1897. Blamed for wartime mistakes and sins of omission, Alger, who tried to shuffle the blame, became the scapegoat and an embarrassment to the McKinley administration. Several daily newspapers severely censured his conduct. At first the president showed no inclination to dismiss Alger, but everyone except the secretary knew that the end was near. McKinley's baffling silence, which led Alger to believed he had been vindicated, only compounded the tense situation and lengthened the tortured affair.

In June, Alger offered to resign, effective January 2, 1900, when he planned to run for the U.S. Senate from Michigan, but the president demurred. Demonstrating surprisingly squeamish behavior, McKinley refused to demand his secretary's immediate resignation under fire to placate public feeling or to unburden the administration from a ticklish dilemma or a potentially dangerous political problem. Rather than meet Alger face to face, McKinley devised a surreptitious scheme to remove the secretary of war: He asked Secretary of State John Hay to notify Alger that he must resign his position. Hay tactfully declined to perform this disagreeable duty, and

McKinley then gave to Hobart, Alger's close friend, the delicate task of requesting the secretary's resignation from the cabinet. Attorney General Griggs journeyed to New Jersey as the president's messenger to inform an ailing Hobart of McKinley's decision. The vice president accepted the unpleasant burden out of duty and friendship for his chief. He immediately summoned Alger to visit him at his summer home at Norwood Park, where, assisted by his wife, he told the secretary that the president wanted him to resign at once. Alger received the news with surprise and pain, leaving the house deeply chagrined. After reflecting on the episode, Alger returned to Hobart's home the next morning. Seeing the sick vice president sitting on the piazza, Alger ran toward his friend and threw his arms about him.

Hobart found his task doubly painful in that he was desperately ill at the time and had long been friends with Alger. Still, he performed the job with such understanding and finesse that the New York *Sun* called the vice president a man of crystal insight and velvet tact. Happily, neither the Hobarts nor the Algers allowed this pathetic incident to mar their friendship. In an attempt to console Alger, Hobart dispatched a telegram, assuring the deposed secretary that he would appreciate his freedom more and more each day.

When Alger returned to Washington, he confronted McKinley. He remonstrated against the president's failure to see him directly and deplored the roundabout method of forcing his resignation, which he submitted to the president, effective August 1, 1899. Alger had a valid point: On this issue McKinley showed weakness, indecisiveness, and an absence of common sense, which were totally out of character with his administration. He should have handled the matter forthrightly from the beginning rather than delegating an unpleasant presidential duty to his terminally ill vice president. McKinley's action was inexcusable. Grateful in the end for Hobart's services, McKinley wired his thanks to the vice president. The drama officially ended when Elihu Root of New York entered the cabinet as secretary of war.

The battle in the Senate over the ratification of the controversial peace treaty with Spain and the Alger affair took their toll on the vice president. Long hours of hard work and a weak heart exhausted him, resulting in a physical collapse in spring 1899 from which he never recovered. He went to Long Branch, New Jersey, to recuperate and stayed at Norwood Park, his seaside home on the coast. Failing to improve, he returned to his Paterson home, where McKinley visited him. The two corresponded that autumn: Hobart wrote of his sleepless nights, nervous indigestion, the diagnoses, and the remedies the doctors has prescribed to give him relief. He grew weaker and weaker in October, knowing that he would not live much longer.

Hobart died in Paterson on November 21, 1899, from complications resulting from a heart attack. He was the sixth vice president to die in office. A grieving McKinley attended the funeral. Hobart was buried at Cedar Lawn Cemetery in Paterson. Following his death, John Hay became next in line of succession to the presidency, while Republican senator William P. Frye of Maine, president pro tempore of the Senate, presided over that chamber. Senators eulogized Hobart in speeches from the floor. In 1903, the citizens of Paterson erected a bronze statue of the vice president next to that of Alexander Hamilton on the City Hall plaza.

Although not an outstanding national leader or orator in the first rank of his generation, Hobart was a competent and cautious government official. He shared with Vice President Charles W. Fairbanks many of the same personal and political qualities. Hobart's short term as vice president was soon overshadowed by the presidential election of 1900, the assassination of McKinley, and the presidency of Theodore Roosevelt. Yet, during his nearly three years in office, Hobart laid the foundation for twentieth-century vice presidents from Theodore Roosevelt to Albert Gore. A model presiding officer of a deliberative assembly and adviser to the president, Hobart made the vice-presidential office what the framers of the Constitution properly intended it to be and lifted the office to the dignity and importance it deserved in the Gilded Age. Massachusetts Republican senator Henry Cabot Lodge argued that Hobart restored the vice presidency to its proper position. By honoring the office Hobart honored himself. A successful businessman with a vision and an individual possessed of a tremendous capacity for hard work, Hobart was a man of conscience who brought a business-oriented pragmatism to the vice presidency. He also mirrored McKinley's attitudes and proved loyal to his chief. His personal integrity exerted a healthy influence in late nineteenth-century American politics. Hobart's death in 1899 paved the way for Theodore Roosevelt.

REFERENCES

Jennie Tuttle Hobart, *Memories* (Paterson, N.J.: privately printed, 1930); David Magie, *Life of Garret Augustus Hobart, Twenty-Fourth Vice-President of the United States* (New York: G.P. Putnam's Sons, 1910); Leonard Schlup, "Republican Nationalist in the McKinley Era: Garret A. Hobart of New Jersey and His Political Career and Letters," *The North Jersey Highlander*, 32 (1996).

LEONARD SCHLUP, an independent scholar and writer, lives in Akron, Ohio. He earned a B.A. degree from the University of Akron, an M.A. from Kent State University, an M.L.S. from Indiana University, and a Ph.D. from the University of Illinois at Urbana-Champaign. The author of more than 200 articles in professional history and political science journals, he has written fifty biographical essays for the forthcoming *American National Biography*. He has also written entries for the *Encyclopedia of the United States Congress* and the *Tennessee Encyclopedia of History and Culture*. He is preparing other articles, as well as a biography of Vice President Adlai E. Stevenson. Dr. Schlup has also participated in numerous professional conferences and meetings connected with the men's movement.

THEODORE ROOSEVELT (1858–1919)

Vice President, March 4–September 14, 1901

(President William McKinley)

THEODORE ROOSEVELT
(Library of Congress)

By John Allen Gable

Vice President Theodore Roosevelt became the twenty-sixth president of the United States on September 14, 1901, taking the oath at the home of his friend Ansley Wilcox in Buffalo, New York, after the death of President William McKinley, who had been shot by an anarchist while attending the Pan American Exposition in Buffalo. Theodore Roosevelt won the presidential election of 1904 and was the first vice president to become president because of the death of his predecessor who then went on to be elected president in his own right. TR was the fifth vice president elevated to the presidency by the death of his predecessor; the eighth man to serve as vice president to become president; and the third vice president to become president due to assassination.

Theodore Roosevelt was born on October 27, 1858, in a fashionable brownstone at 28 East 20th Street, Manhattan, and is the only president of the United States born in New York City. His ancestors were an immigrant couple, Claes Martenszen van Rosenvelt and his wife, Jannetje, who came from the Netherlands to what was then

New Amsterdam in the 1640s, and their descendants became wealthy importers, merchants, bankers, and holders of real estate. Many members of the family held public office over the years. Theodore Roosevelt's father, also named Theodore Roosevelt, was an importer, merchant, and philanthropist. The future president's mother, Martha Bulloch, was from Roswell, Georgia, the daughter of a noted family of the old South.

The Civil War was a personal crisis for young Theodore's household. Martha's brothers were officers in the Confederate Navy, but Theodore, Senior, was an ardent supporter of Abraham Lincoln, the Republican Party, and the Union. Out of deference to his wife's feelings, Theodore, Senior, did not join the army, but he was active in war work. Theodore, Junior, watched Lincoln's funeral procession in 1865 and Lincoln became TR's hero and Lincoln's democratic nationalism became TR's creed. Because of his family heritage and his years as a cattle rancher in the Dakota Territory, TR claimed to be a son of both the North and the South, a westerner as well as an easterner. These claims were useful politically, but they also reflected the importance and centrality of nationalism to Roosevelt's philosophy and politics.

Theodore Roosevelt was a politician most of his adult life, but he found time and had the talents to be the kind of American admired by a wide spectrum. "Roosevelt was a many-sided man and every side was like an electric battery," said his friend, the nature-writer John Burroughs. "Such versatility, such vitality, such thoroughness, such copiousness, have rarely been united in one man." Brander Matthews, literary critic and professor at Columbia, once wrote: "The more closely we scrutinize Theodore Roosevelt's life and the more carefully we consider his many ventures in many totally different fields of human activity, the less likely we are to challenge the assertion that his was the most interesting career ever vouchsafed to any American. . . ." In 1915, the writer Julian Street published a portrait of Theodore Roosevelt and entitled his little book, simply, *The Most Interesting American*.

For Julian Street, as for Brander Matthews, it was TR's many-sidedness that made him supremely interesting. Only Benjamin Franklin and Thomas Jefferson among his countrymen seem obvious rivals to the multiplicity of TR's roles and accomplishments. His entertainment value has never been in doubt. The question of his greatness, however, is another matter—one that has been endlessly debated.

Theodore Roosevelt was a naturalist, hunter, conservationist, historian, explorer, soldier, winner of the Nobel Peace Prize, rancher in the "Wild West," intellectual, deputy sheriff in cowboy country and head of the New York City Police Department, author of more than thirty books on a wide variety of subjects, politician, magazine editor and newspaper columnist, and founder of his own political party. He was Phi Beta Kappa at Harvard, one of the original members of the National Institute of Arts and Letters, and one of the first fifteen elected to the American Academy of Arts and Letters. He was a founder of the Boone and Crockett Club, the National Municipal League, the Bird Club of Long Island, and the National Collegiate Athletic Association. He was president of the American Historical Association. He spoke French and German fluently. He put a river on the map in Brazil. He climbed the Matterhorn and led troops into battle. He wrote essays and reviews on a dazzling variety of topics, ranging from primeval man to polar exploration and from poetry to politics. A.A. Norton in a recent study of Roosevelt as a writer has said that TR was "perhaps the outstanding generalist in his era."

As a child, TR suffered from asthma and other ailments and was seldom able to attend school or lead a normal life. At the urging of his father, young Theodore took up body building and then sports. TR's youthful struggle for health eventually became part of the Roosevelt saga that served as inspiration to generations of American boys. "He was frail; he made himself a tower of strength. He was timid; he made himself a lion of courage," asserted the memorial resolution passed by the Boy Scouts of America when TR died in 1919.

TR's devotion to physical fitness, outdoor adventure, sports, and strife on behalf of noble causes became a philosophy of living that TR called the "strenuous life." TR said in 1899:

I wish to preach, not the doctrine of ignoble ease, but the doctrine of the strenuous life, the life of toil and effort of labor and strife; to preach the highest form of success which comes, not to the man who desires mere easy peace, but to the man who does not shrink from danger, from hardship, or from bitter toil, and who out of these wins the splendid ultimate triumph.

For TR the "ultimate triumph" was that he became a hero to millions of his countrymen in his time and since.

From early boyhood, TR was deeply interested in natural history. He learned taxidermy as a boy, and eventually the bird specimens he collected in his childhood and teenage years enriched the collections of museums all over the world. He published papers on ornithology while in college and in his twenties became an authority on North American big game. His books on hunting and his adventures in wild places won a wide audience, were reprinted again and again, and earned the respect of the scientific community. During his lifetime, TR hunted, collected, and wrote about wildlife in North America, the Near East, Africa, and South America. His many outdoor books include *Outdoor Pastimes of an American Hunter* (1905), *African Game Trails* (1910), *Through the Brazilian Wilderness* (1914), and *A Book-Lover's Holidays in the Open* (1916). In the 1890s, TR was George Bird Grinnell's coeditor and contributed to three volumes published by the Boone and Crockett Club: *American Big-Game* (1893), *Hunting in Many Lands* (1895), and *Trail and Campfire* (1897). In 1914, TR was co-author with Edmund Heller of *Life-Histories of African Game Animals*, published in two volumes. TR's love and knowledge of nature found further expression through his leadership in the conservation movement.

Roosevelt wrote history before he made it. While a senior at Harvard, he began work on what would become his first book on any subject, *The Naval War of 1812*. The 500-page scholarly work was published in 1882 when TR was in his early twenties. Roosevelt went on to write biographies of Thomas Hart Benton (1887), Gouverneur Morris (1888), and Oliver Cromwell (1900); a history of New York City (1891); and an epic study of the westward movement, *The Winning of the West*, published in four volumes, 1889–1896.

Both *The Naval War of 1812* and *The Winning of the West* were in print in the 1990s and still consulted by scholars. TR's biographies of Senator Benton and Gouverneur Morris were volumes in the prestigious "American Statesmen" series, edited by John T. Morse, Jr. Other contributors to the series included Henry Adams, William Graham Sumner, and Moses Coit Tyler. TR's biographies of Benton and Morris have been attacked by later critics as superficial and opinionated, but at the time they were favorably reviewed, and both volumes were widely used and cited by historians for many years. TR's concise history of New York City was part of the noted and classic "Historic Towns" series, edited by E.A. Freeman. Roosevelt's work on the naval aspects of the War of 1812 was so respected that he was asked to contribute the section on the War of 1812 for the English history of the Royal Navy edited by William Laird Clowes, but nobody on either side of the Atlantic ever has had much to say in praise of TR's biography of Oliver Cromwell.

TR's work on naval history predated Alfred Taylor Mahan's books, and the first volumes of *The Winning of the West* came out before the publication of Frederick Jackson Turner's frontier thesis. TR influenced Mahan and Turner. He knew both historians, conducted a continuing dialogue with them, and was influenced in turn by their thinking.

Roosevelt's views on the writing of history were eloquently expressed in his famous inaugural address as president of the American Historical Association in 1912, "History As Literature," which is a defense of history as a didactic epic, or story with a moral, and an attack on the German school of "scientific" history. "History As Literature" is still widely cited in works on historiography. Although TR did make his mark as an historian, he is of course remembered more as a maker rather than a writer of history.

Theodore Roosevelt graduated from Harvard in 1880, and that year married Alice

Hathaway Lee of Chesnut Hill, Massachusetts. He studied law at Columbia for a time but soon became a lawmaker rather than a lawyer. TR was elected a Republican member of the New York State Assembly from Manhattan's Twenty-first District in 1881, shortly after his twenty-third birthday. There were annual elections at that time, and TR was reelected in 1882 and 1883. He was the Republican minority leader in one session during his tenure and the youngest member of the state assembly. He won a reputation as a reformer and was a nationally known figure in the Republican Party by 1884.

TR and historian Henry Cabot Lodge, his friend and fellow Harvard graduate, gained much attention at the Republican national convention of 1884 for their opposition to James G. Blaine, whom they considered corrupt. However, when Blaine won the nomination, both TR and Lodge backed the Republican ticket, refusing to bolt the G.O.P. in company with reform-minded independents known as the "Mugwumps" who went over to Grover Cleveland and the Democrats. Roosevelt's refusal to bolt confirmed his status as a professional politician.

On February 14, 1884, devastating personal tragedy struck TR when his wife and mother died on the same day in the same house. TR's mother died of typhoid, and Alice Lee Roosevelt succumbed to Bright's Disease after giving birth, on February 12, to a girl, named Alice. TR turned from politics for a time and became a cattle rancher, near Medora, in the Badlands of western Dakota Territory. Roosevelt's trilogy on his western experiences, *Hunting Trips of a Ranchman* (1885), *Ranch Life and the Hunting Trail* (1888), and *The Wilderness Hunter* (1893), became classics, promoted the careers of such artist-illustrators as Frederic Remington, and helped formulate the images of cowboy life and the "Wild West" that have come down to us.

In 1886, Roosevelt returned east to run for Mayor of New York City against labor leader Henry George and the winning Democrat, Abram S. Hewitt. TR came in a poor third. Shortly after the election, TR married a childhood friend, Edith Kermit Carrow (1861–1948), in London on December 2, 1886. After an extended European wedding trip, the Roosevelts returned to live at Sagamore Hill, the house TR had built in 1885 at Cove Neck in Oyster Bay, New York, on the North Shore of Long Island, where the couple were to raise a lively brood of six children, Alice (born to TR's first wife), Theodore, Kermit, Ethel, Archibald Bulloch, and Quentin.

Having campaigned loyally for the Republican Party over the years, TR was rewarded in 1889 when he was appointed to the U.S. Civil Service Commission by President Benjamin Harrison. He continued in the post during part of Democrat Grover Cleveland's second term and served from 1889 to 1895.

On the Civil Service Commission, Roosevelt did much to replace the traditional spoils system of partisan appointment to government jobs with the merit system that had been authorized by the Pendleton Act in 1883. While enforcing the law, TR fought with spoilsmen from both political parties. He put the cause of civil service on the front page of the newspapers and reestablished his credentials as a reformer. During TR's tenure on the commission, the number of jobs covered by the civil service more than doubled. The historian William H. Harbaugh writes:

> His imaginative and energetic enforcement of the laws had virtually institutionalized the civil service system; and had he never performed another service for the American nation, that alone would have assured perpetuation of his memory as a secondary figure of substantial accomplishment.

Theodore Roosevelt was appointed to the four-member board of police commissioners of New York City in 1895 and was chosen president of the board. In two years as president, he revolutionized the New York Police Department and made his mark in the history of American law enforcement. He attacked corruption in the NYPD; hired women and Jews; enforced the law rigidly, regardless of political consequences; and transformed police work through civil service reforms and the use of modern techniques and technologies. TR set minimum professional standards for recruits (height, weight, age, ability to do basic arithmetic, and so on); published a manual of rules and regulations; adapted the use of the Bertillion system for identification; started a much-publicized bicycle squad; and established a school for training in the use of firearms. The New York School of Pistol Practice, founded in 1895, was at the time one of the two schools for police training that existed in the United States. There was a dramatic increase in arrests and a systematic attack on graft under Roosevelt.

As usual, TR was front-page news on virtually a daily basis. Probably most Americans knew the name of the police commissioner of New York City and what he was doing, but Roosevelt was attacked by the leaders of both political parties, and his enforcement of the Sunday closing law for saloons and other unpopular laws alienated much of the public. Frustrated by growing opposition to his police policies, TR sought a new job when the Republicans again won the White House in 1896.

President William McKinley appointed TR to the post of assistant secretary of the Navy in 1897. Roosevelt was in the Navy Department for a year, and during his tenure, Roosevelt sought to prepare American naval forces for the war he saw coming with Spain over the independence of Cuba, the last remnant of the Spanish empire in the New World. Biographers have given TR much credit—probably too much—for the subsequent spectacular American naval triumphs in the Spanish–American War, and TR's influence in bringing about the war has been exaggerated by both his admirers and his severest critics. Yet, that assistant secretary is remembered while his superior, Secretary of the Navy John Davis Long, is forgotten, and TR went on to become one of the most famous heroes of the Spanish–American War.

After protracted quarreling over the future status of Cuba between the United States and Spain, on April 24, 1898, Spain declared war on the United States. The next day, Theodore Roosevelt was appointed lieutenant colonel, and his good friend Leonard Wood, an officer in the regular army, was named colonel of the First United States Volunteer Cavalry Regiment, soon popularly known as the Rough Riders. The Rough Riders, who assembled at San Antonio, Texas, in May, were composed in large part of cowboys and Indians from the West, and Ivy League athletes and eastern aristocrats. These men represented Roosevelt's Knickerbocker–Harvard background and his days as a cattle rancher in the West. What did these groups have in common? They could ride and shoot, were fit, and needed relatively little training to be ready for battle.

The Rough Riders were shipped out from Tampa, Florida—without their horses, thus turning them into infantry—and landed at Daiquiri, in Cuba, on June 22. They defeated the Spanish at the Battle of Las Guasimas on June 24. On June 30, the day before the major advance on Santiago, Leonard Wood was promoted in the field to brigadier general, and TR was made colonel of the Rough Riders. On July 1, 1898, TR and the Rough Riders charged uphill into immortality at the Battle of San Juan Hill. He led the assaults on first Kettle Hill and then San Juan Hill on the ridges overlooking the city of Santiago. The U.S. forces won the day, and soon Santiago fell. The Rough Riders had the highest casualty rate of any regiment in the war.

After the fall of Santiago, the Rough Riders, many suffering from yellow fever and other ailments, were shipped to Montauk Point, at the eastern end of Long Island, to rest and recuperate. There at Montauk, Colonel Roosevelt was approached about becoming the Republican candidate for governor of New York State, and there the Rough Riders mustered out, on September 16, 1898, after 137 days in the army.

Senator Thomas Collier Pratt, the boss of the Republican Party in New York State, mistrusted Roosevelt because the Rough Rider's reputation as a reformer and an independent. But there was a big scandal with the Erie Canal in 1898, and the Republicans dared not run their incumbent governor for reelection. It was thought that only Roosevelt the war hero could win. Accordingly, TR was nominated for governor of the Empire State on September 27, and after a spirited campaign, in which Colonel Roosevelt emphasized national issues and the glories won by his regiment, he was elected on November 8, receiving a vote of 661,715 to his opponent Democrat Augustus Van Wyck's 643,921 votes.

The year 1898 had indeed been busy for Theodore Roosevelt: In January, he was in the Navy Department in Washington, working to prepare for war with Spain; in July, he was leading the Rough Riders at the Battle of San Juan Hill; and in November, he was elected governor of New York. He had seized and made the most of every opportunity. Fortune seemed to smile on TR in his youth; events seemed to break in his direction. In his last years, the reverse appeared to be the case, but to a considerable extent Theodore Roosevelt made his own luck.

By 1898, TR had been a political celebrity for more than fifteen years, but the governorship of New York was really the first top-level job Roosevelt had. He had been head of the police in New York City but was defeated for mayor. He had been a civil service commissioner and an assistant secretary but never a member of the cabinet. He made it to colonel but not general in the Spanish-American War. Yet, he was famous, quoted, and admired, and he influenced events and shaped public policy from the time when he was in his midtwenties. TR's career up to the governorship seemed to follow one of Roosevelt's favorite adages, "Do what you can, with what you've got, where you are."

In his inaugural address as governor, on January 2, 1899, TR declared:

It is only through the party system that free governments are now successfully carried on, and yet we must keep ever vividly before us that the usefulness of a party is strictly limited by its usefulness to the State, and that in the long run, he serves his party best who most helps to make it instantly responsive to every need of the people, and to the highest demands of that spirit which tends to drive us onward and upward.

In other words, TR was a professional partisan politician, but he was also a reformer. To fellow partisans he preached the need for honesty and a positive program. To reformers he spoke of the necessity of working "through practical methods and with a readiness to face life as it is, and not as we think it out to be."

As governor of New York, Roosevelt brought about the passage of legislation taxing corporate franchises, strengthening the state's civil service system, setting up a tenement commission, increasing the power of factory inspectors, raising teachers' salaries in New York City, limiting working hours for drug clerks and state employees, and other reform measures. He did much for conservation, working to preserve the Palisades and reforming the forest, fish, and game service. He saw to it that factories in the state were not allowed "to make bird-skins or bird feathers into articles of ornament or wearing-apparel."

TR regularly consulted with Senator Platt and avoided any open breach with the Republican machine, but Platt was displeased when the governor refused to accept the senator's orders on job appointments, nor was he happy with most of the governor's reform measures. Platt therefore decided to rid himself of Roosevelt by making him the next vice president of the United States. Vice President Garret A. Hobart, elected with McKinley in 1896, died on November 21, 1899, and thus Republicans needed to find a new running mate for President McKinley in 1900.

TR wanted to be reelected governor in 1900, and as for the vice presidency: "The more I have thought it over the more I have felt that I would a great deal rather be anything, say a professor of history, than vice-president," he said. At the time, the vice presidency was seen as a dead end for politicians, a high honor, no doubt, but also the end of the line. Yet, TR's close friend Henry Cabot Lodge urged TR to take the job and was certain that the vice presidency would be Roosevelt's stepping stone to the White House.

Senator Mark Hanna of Ohio, Republican national chairman and President McKinley's closest friend and advisor, was strongly opposed to Roosevelt for vice president, as was McKinley. But McKinley refused to repudiate Roosevelt openly or make known any choice for the vice presidency. Republicans from the West wanted the Rough Rider on the ticket to counter the appeal of westerner William Jennings Bryan, Democratic presidential candidate in 1896 and again in 1900, and many party leaders saw TR as a match against Bryan's dynamic campaigning.

Both Hanna and McKinley considered TR unstable and dangerously independent of party discipline. Hanna warned G.O.P. delegates to avoid Roosevelt. He asked them to consider that with TR as vice president there would be "only one life between that madman and the White House." But Senator Platt found an ally in Senator Matthew Quay, the powerful boss of Pennsylvania, who disliked Mark Hanna. Platt and Quay deftly outmaneuvered both Hanna and their candidate at the G.O.P. convention in Philadelphia, the western delegates had their way, and the Rough Rider was nominated.

The campaign of 1900 was largely a running debate between William Jennings Bryan and Theodore Roosevelt, who both strenuously stumped the country. In 1896, McKinley, in contrast to Bryan's whistle-stop campaign, had spoken to visiting delegations from his front porch in Canton, Ohio, and in 1900, the president wanted to maintain the same style. It was TR who was sent out to whistle-stop for the G.O.P. TR ignored his opponent for vice president, sixty-five-year-old Adlai E. Stevenson of Illinois, who had been vice president in Cleveland's second term.

Bryan attacked the Republicans on imperialism, the high tariff, and the trusts, and, as in 1896, he advocated free-silver inflation. TR pointed with pride to prosperity and to "full dinner pail," the results of the protective tariff and a stable gold-standard dollar. TR embraced the responsibilities of world leadership and overseas commitments brought about by victory over the Spanish empire. He denounced the evils of the trusts, surrendering no ground to Bryan and the Democrats on that issue, and attacked free silver and the Democrats' irresponsibility on foreign and domestic policy. According to observers then and since, the outcome of the election was never in doubt because the incumbent administration presided over good times and had just won a war. The ticket of McKinley and Roosevelt defeated Bryan and Stevenson in a landslide, 292 electoral votes to 155.

Theodore Roosevelt was inaugurated as vice president of the United States on March 4, 1901.

He presided for four days over a special session of the Senate, and that, as it turned out, ended the only official duties he was to have as vice president. Senator Platt happily remarked on his way to the inauguration that he was going "to see Teddy take the veil."

As vice president, TR felt that he had little influence in the administration. He explained to office seekers that he now had less power over federal appointments than when he was the governor of a large state. To Leonard Wood, Vice President Roosevelt wrote on April 17, 1901: "You know that the Vice-Presidency is an utterly anomalous office (one which I think ought to be abolished). The man who occupies it may at any moment be everything; but meanwhile he is practically nothing."

To occupy his time, and with an eye to future employment, TR made plans to study law and seek admission to the bar. TR also worked on an innovative program to educate college students about politics and draw them into public life. He held a seminar for selected undergraduates and recent graduates from Harvard and Yale at Sagamore Hill on June 29, 1901. An unexpected dividend of the seminar was that one of the Harvard men, Richard Derby, later married TR's daughter Ethel Roosevelt. In 1901, as his correspondence clearly reveals, Roosevelt also began to work to line up support for himself for the 1904 Republican presidential nomination.

On May 20, 1901, Vice President Roosevelt opened the Pan American Exposition at Buffalo, New York, delivering a speech entitled "The Two Americas." President McKinley visited the exposition on September 6 and at a public reception was shot twice by an anarchist, Leon Czolgosz. TR was attending an outing of the Fish and Game League at Isle la Motte, Vermont, when he was notified of the shooting. The vice president hurried to Buffalo, where he stayed at the home of his friend, the attorney and reformer Ansley Wilcox. McKinley seemed certain to recover, said the doctors, and TR left Buffalo on September 10, soon taking his family for a vacation at the Tahawus Club in the Adirondacks. On September 13, the vice president climbed Mount Marcy, and while returning, late in the afternoon, he saw a man coming toward him on the trail. TR later recalled: "When I saw the runner I instinctively knew he had bad news, the worst news in the world."

The news was that McKinley appeared to be dying. TR headed for North Creek, New York, to board a special train. He traveled all night on country roads, and when he reached North Creek at dawn he was informed that President McKinley had died at 2:15 A.M. After TR's train reached Buffalo, he went to offer his condolences to Mrs. McKinley and then took the oath of office at the Wilcox Mansion, on Delaware Avenue, from U.S. District Judge John R. Hazel at about 3:30 P.M. on September 14. He was forty-two years old, the youngest president in history, before or since. In 1904, TR was elected in his own right. TR served as president from September 14, 1901, to March 4, 1909.

Theodore Roosevelt was a prolific phrase-maker and wordsmith, enriching the public discourse with such terms as *muckrakers*, *nature fakers*, *weasel words*, *Ananias Club* (whose members were liars), *malefactors of great wealth*, *race suicide* (birth control), *clean as a hound's tooth*, *mollycoddlers*, and *hyphenated Americans*. TR felt as fit as a "bull moose" as he led the "strenuous life" and preached to Americans from the "bully pulpit" of the White House about a "square deal" in domestic policies, while advocating in foreign affairs a policy of "speak softly and carry a big stick."

TR's square-deal policies emphasized the conservation of natural resources and the regulation of big business. He sought to reverse the traditional policy of laissez-faire and to bring order, social justice, and fair play into the workplace and the marketplace. When he entered the White House, virtually his only instrument for dealing with big business was the Sherman Antitrust Act of 1890, which had been made a dead letter by the rulings of conservative courts.

Shortly after becoming president, TR brought the Sherman Act back to life with a suit against the Northern Securities Company, a holding company owned by J.P. Morgan, E.H. Harriman, and James J. Hill. After a lengthy fight in the courts, the Supreme Court by a five to four decision dissolved the Northern Securities trust, thereby reversing earlier court rulings that weakened corporations and monopolies. The Roosevelt administration launched antitrust suits against American Tobacco, Du Pont, Swift and Company, Standard Oil, and other giants, forty-five antitrust suits in all, most won by the government.

TR said that government by lawsuit left much to be desired. What was needed, TR insisted in every annual message, was continuous regulation of all important aspects of economic life by commissions, but a Congress dominated by "standpat" Republican conservatives and Bourbon Democrats rejected most of the president's recommendations for comprehensive legislation to regulate big business. TR was able, however, to get through Congress an impressive list of laws, including the Elkins Antitrust Act (1903) and the Hepburn Act (1906) to regulate railroads; the Pure Food and Drug Act and the Meat Inspection Act, both signed on June 30, 1906; and the Federal Employers Liability Act (1908). The Pure Food and Drug Act and the Meat Inspection Act were the beginning of consumer protection by the federal government.

TR's conservation policies were broad and multifaceted. He worked for the preservation of wildlife, natural beauty, and wilderness areas and also promoted the planned use, development, and control of natural resources. Under the Newlands Act of 1902, TR started the first twenty-one federal irrigation projects, including what became Theodore Roosevelt Dam in Arizona. Under the Antiquities Act of 1906, the president preserved eighteen national monuments, the first being Devil's Tower in Wyoming, set aside on September 24, 1906. TR's other national monuments include the Grand Canyon, Muir Woods, Mount Olympus, and Arizona's Petrified Forest. He also expanded the forest reserves from about 43 million acres to 194 million acres, doubled the number of national parks, and set up the first federal wildlife preserves, including the National Bison Range in Montana and some fifty-one reservations. TR's work for conservation also included the first inventory of natural resources, the appointment of commissions, and the calling of conferences to promote conservation. If he had done nothing else, surely TR could be called a great president on the basis of his conservation legacy.

His record on conservation has won universal praise from posterity, but the Rough Rider's conduct of foreign affairs has always been controversial. Historians have been highly critical of Roosevelt's dealings with Colombia and Panama in building the Panama Canal and of the Roosevelt Corollary to the Monroe Doctrine, which defined the role of the United States as a police officer for Latin America. Yet, the record shows that TR worked hard on behalf of peace.

TR was the first world leader to submit a case to the Court of Arbitration at The Hague and to call for holding the Second Hague Peace Conference, which met in 1907. Successfully mediating an end to the Russo-Japanese War in 1905 led to his being awarded the Nobel Peace Prize in 1906. He prevented a war from starting between France and Germany in 1906 by resolving the Moroccan Crisis through the Algeciras Conference. Roosevelt firmly upheld the Monroe Doctrine, preventing European occupation of first Venezuela and then the Dominican Republic over debts. At the Second Hague Peace Conference, the Roosevelt administration secured the adoption of the Drago Doctrine, which outlawed the use of force in the collection of foreign debts. The Roosevelt administration also was responsible for setting up the Central American Court of Justice.

In foreign affairs, TR's "big stick" was the Navy. Under him, the U.S. Navy was expanded greatly, and by 1909 the United States was second only to Great Britain as a naval power. The voyage of the U.S. "Great White Fleet" around the world in 1907–1909 showed that American national interests and military capabilities were now global.

The Democrats nominated William Jennings Bryan, the "Great Commoner," in 1896, 1900, and 1908, but in 1904 the party turned from progressivism and nominated for president a conservative, "safe and sane" eastern Democrat, Alton B. Parker, the chief justice of the Court of Appeals of New York State. For vice president, the Democrats chose an elderly millionaire, Henry G. Davis of West Virginia.

TR drafted as his running mate in 1904 Senator Charles W. Fairbanks of Indiana. The choice was a case of traditional ticket balancing. Fairbanks was a conservative from a midwestern state running with a progressive reformer from the East. In an article published in 1896, commenting on the vice-presidential candidates of that year, Roosevelt wrote: "It is an unhealthy thing to have the Vice-President and the President represented by principles so far apart that the succession of one to the place of the other means a change as radical as any possible party overturn." So it had been in 1901 when TR followed McKinley, and yet in 1904 Roosevelt was guilty of doing the "unhealthy thing" by choosing a running mate at odds with the president's philosophy. In his 1896 article, TR had also suggested that the vice president be included in cabinet meetings, but he did not give Fairbanks, as Arthur M. Schlesinger, Jr., puts it, "a seat in the cabinet or anywhere else."

In 1904, the Roosevelt-Fairbanks ticket received 7,628,834 popular and 336 electoral votes to the Parker–Davis totals of 5,084,491 popular and 140 electoral votes. TR had won by the greatest popular-vote majority to that time, and Parker had carried no states outside the South.

In his seven-and-a-half years in the White House, TR had transformed the presidency to the center of a powerful federal government and made the president a world leader. The man for whom the Teddy bear was named had entertained and inspired the public as few presidents before or since. TR's view was that the president "was a steward of the people bound actively and affirmatively to do all he could for the people." He was an activist on behalf of the public, recognizing no bounds except the specific prohibitions of the Constitution and the statutes. "Is there any law that will prevent me from declaring Pelican Island a Federal Bird Reservation?" TR asked his attorney general in 1903. No legal barrier could be found. "Very well, then I so declare it," said TR, thus creating the first federal bird refuge. He would establish fifty more by 1909.

TR is generally seen as the first "modern president," and historians and political scientists rate him among the greatest of the presidents. When the experts are polled, TR always makes the top ten presidents, and recently he has been found in the top five. His importance is as obvious as his visage on Mount Rushmore.

There was nothing of the anticlimatic in Theodore Roosevelt's last years, but there was frustration, defeat, and tragedy.

Returning to the United States in 1910, after a postpresidential expedition to Africa and tour of Europe, TR found the Republican Party seriously divided between conservative and progressive factions. TR's own handpicked successor, the former secretary of war, President William Howard Taft, sided with the conservatives, abandoning his promise to follow the Roosevelt policies. Progressive Republicans looked to TR for leadership. TR responded with his "New Nationalism" speech in 1910, which the historian George E. Mowry says is "probably the most radical speech ever given by an ex-president."

In 1912, with the progressive movement at high tide, Roosevelt opposed President Taft for the nomination. TR swept the newly instituted popular primaries, but the Taft forces prevailed at the Republican national convention. TR's followers then bolted the Republican Party and founded the Progressive Party, which nominated him for president and Governor Hiram W. Johnson of California for vice president. The new party was popularly known as the Bull Moose Party, after its robust presidential nominee. Roosevelt ran on a detailed and advanced reform platform that advocated most of the major reforms adopted since 1912, including old-age pensions, unemployment and health insurance, the graduated income tax, wages and hours laws, and women's suffrage. In the midst of the campaign, Roosevelt was shot by an anti–third-term fanatic. The Bull Moose insisted on making his speech before going to the hospital and was back on the campaign trail in a few weeks.

In the November election, Democrat Woodrow Wilson was elected due to the split in the normal Republican vote. TR came in second, and for the first and only time in history the Republican candidate came in third. During the next four years, the Wilson administration co-opted much of the 1912 Bull Moose platform. In defeat Roosevelt had firmly established the presidential primary system—the voters had strongly rebuked the G.O.P. leadership—and he had provided his opponent and nemesis Woodrow Wilson with a program for the next four years.

World War I began in 1914, and soon Roosevelt was the leading advocate in the United States for military preparedness and a hard-line policy toward Germany. Wilson preached neutrality and at first did little to strengthen the army and navy. Seeing Wilson's defeat as the prime national need, the old Rough Rider turned down a second Bull Moose nomination in 1916 and backed the Republican candidate, Charles Evans Hughes. Wilson was narrowly reelected and asked for a declaration of war a few weeks after his second inauguration. TR volunteered for military service; Wilson turned him down.

TR's last years were a time of frustration for the old Rough Rider: He was unable to regain office and tasted defeat again and again. Yet, in those final years, with both major parties against him most of the time, without office, Roosevelt still set the agenda, still decided what issues were to be faced by the politicians and the people, and usually his view prevailed in the end.

On July 14, 1918, TR's youngest son, Quentin Roosevelt, an army pilot, was shot down and killed behind German lines in France. After Quentin's death, the boy in TR died, as his friend Hermann Hagedorn observed. The man soon followed. Theodore Roosevelt died in his sleep in the early morning hours of January 6, 1919, at the age of sixty.

REFERENCES

William H. Harbaugh, *Power and Responsibility: The Life and Times of Theodore Roosevelt* (New York: Farrar, Straus, and Cudahy, 1961); David McCullough, *Mornings on Horseback* (New York: Simon and Schuster, 1981); Edmund Morris, *The Rise of Theodore Roosevelt* (New York: Coward, McCann and Geoghegan, 1979); Frederick W. Marks, III, *Velvet on Iron: The Diplomacy of Theodore Roosevelt* (Lincoln: University of Nebraska Press, 1979); John Allen Gable, *The Bull Moose Years: Theodore Roosevelt and the Progressive Party* (Port Washington, N.Y.: Kennikat Press, 1978); Lewis L. Gould,

The Presidency of Theodore Roosevelt (Lawrence: University of Kansas Press, 1991); John Allen Gable, "Theodore Roosevelt: A Selected and Annotated Bibliography," in *Theodore Roosevelt: Many-Sided American,* edited by Natalie A. Naylor, Douglas Brinkley, and John Allen Gable (Interlaken, N.Y.: Heart of the Lakes Publishing, 1992) 645–654; Joseph Bucklin Bishop, *Theodore Roosevelt and His Time, Shown in His Letters,* 2 vols. (New York: Charles Scribner's Sons, 1920); Elting Morison, John M. Blum et al., ed., *The Letters of Theodore Roosevelt*, 8 vols. (Cambridge, Mass.: 1951–1954); Hermann Hagedorn, ed., *The Works of Theodore Roosevelt: Memorial Edition*, 24 vols. (New York: Charles Scribner's Sons, 1923–1926).

JOHN ALLEN GABLE graduated from Kenyon College and received a Ph.D. in history from Brown University. He has been the executive director of the Theodore Roosevelt Association, an historical society and public service organization, since 1974 and an adjunct professor of history at Hofstra University since 1989. He is the editor of the quarterly *Theodore Roosevelt Association Journal* and is the author and editor of numerous books and articles on the twenty-sixth president.

CHARLES WARREN FAIRBANKS (1852–1918)

Vice President, 1905–1909

(President Theodore Roosevelt)

CHARLES WARREN FAIRBANKS
(Library of Congress)

By Ray E. Boomhower

A conservative former railroad attorney and senator from Indiana, Charles Fairbanks was selected by the Republican convention in 1904 to balance the ticket with the more progressive Theodore Roosevelt. In 1916, Fairbanks made a second try for the vice presidency by running with G.O.P. presidential candidate Charles Evans Hughes but lost to fellow Hoosier Thomas Marshall and his presidential candidate, Woodrow Wilson.

Fairbanks was a native of Union County, Ohio, born on May 11, 1852. One of the few politicians who could truthfully say that he had been born in a log cabin, the house was owned by his farmer father, Loriston Monroe Fairbanks. According to the younger Fairbanks, he absorbed his abiding interest in politics and political discussion from his father, a waggonmaker and an abolitionist who often built "liberty wagons" for political rallies and parades held at the county seat.

During his youth Fairbanks displayed the same quiet, steady character that marked his subsequent career in law and politics—a demeanor that won for him the unflattering nicknames the "Indiana Icicle" and "Senator Icebanks." In a 1904 campaign biography for the GOP vice-presidential candidate, Fairbanks's uncle, William Henry Smith, said that although biographers often delight in relating exciting stories about their subjects' young lives, there were, unfortunately, "few incidents connected with the boyhood life of Mr. Fairbanks that would interest the reader. He was not bad, as boys go, nor was he especially good." In a sketch prepared on his life for the Indiana State Library in Indianapolis, Fairbanks said of his early days that he was an "active young farmer, with a predominating love of books."

At the age of fifteen, Fairbanks entered Ohio Wesleyan University, a small Methodist institution located in Delaware, Ohio. Although he worked his way through school, the Ohio farm boy still found time to serve as one of three editors for the campus newspaper, the *Western Collegian*. Reminiscing about his college days with a newspaper reporter, Fairbanks noted that he and his roommate subsisted on a diet of "mush and milk and boiled potatoes with an occasional dish of stewed dried apples."

Graduating with honors in 1872 (he ranked eighth in a class of forty-four students) his uncle, William Henry Smith, Western AP general manager, offered Fairbanks a job as a reporter for the Associated Press in Pittsburgh. After a year in Pittsburgh, the young reporter received a transfer to the news service's Cleveland office. While in that city, Fairbanks attended law school for six months, receiving a degree from the Cleveland Law College on July 10, 1874.

In fall 1874, Fairbanks took two important steps in his life: On October 6, he married Cornelia Cole, a fellow editor on his college newspaper and daughter of Judge P.B. Cole of Marysville, Ohio, and he accepted an offer from another uncle, Charles Warren Smith, Chesapeake and Ohio Railroad System general manager, to become claims attorney for the Indianapolis, Bloomington, and Western Railroad. The young couple moved to Indianapolis, and Fairbanks set out his shingle for a law career that saw him try only one criminal case. Instead, he turned his legal talent to working with railroads, becoming a general solicitor for the Ohio Southern and the Dayton and Ironton railroads; president and principal stockholder of the Terre Haute and Peoria Railroad; and director, general solicitor, and principal stockholder of the Cincinnati, Hamilton and Dayton Railroad.

During his days with these various railroad enterprises Fairbanks amassed a considerable personal fortune, which he made with assistance from relatives who provided him with investment tips. His railroad ties not only made him rich but also made Fairbanks popular with politicians and other public officials—especially because he regularly granted free passes on railroads in which he had a stake to these influential people. In 1888, Fairbanks, at age thirty-six, entered the hurly-burly world of Hoosier politics as manager of his friend Judge Walter Q. Gresham's attempt to capture the Republican presidential nomination. Gresham's effort failed, and the nomination went to rival Indiana candidate Benjamin Harrison. Despite losing out to the former Civil War general, Fairbanks remained true to the GOP, campaigning energetically on Harrison's behalf during the general election, which Harrison won.

Fairbanks's entrance onto the Hoosier political scene came at a time when Indiana played an important role in national politics. With both parties having almost equal strength in the state, the national organizations vied furiously to capture Indiana's fifteen electoral votes in presidential elections. In an attempt to woo Indiana voters to their side, each party often placed Hoosiers on their tickets, earning for the state the designation as the "mother of vice presidents."

With the Harrison faction's loss of control of the Indiana GOP following the president's 1892 reelection defeat, Fairbanks became a powerful force in Hoosier Republican Party circles. "I intended to be a lawyer," Fairbanks told an *Indianapolis News* reporter in 1918, "but out here in the states west of the Alleghenies, politics and the law, you know, somehow run together." Fairbanks began to build an impressive political machine. In 1892, as the Indiana Republican Convention's permanent chairman, he worked to place men loyal to him on the Republican state committee. To help solidify his political power in the Hoosier state, Fairbanks, in 1893, became a silent partner with his uncle William Henry Smith in purchasing the *Indianapolis News.*

It was during Harrison's failed 1892 campaign that Fairbanks first met a man who would do much to advance his political career in the coming years—Ohio politician and future president William McKinley, who told the railroad lawyer that he belonged in the United States Senate. Four years later, with Indiana solidly behind McKinley thanks to Fairbanks's efforts, the Hoosier G.O.P. leader delivered the keynote speech at the Republican national convention in St. Louis. In 1897, with the support of now President McKinley, Fairbanks was elected by the Indiana general assembly to a seat in the U.S. Senate.

Fairbanks's career in the U.S. Senate was less than inspiring. In his biography of the Hoosier politician, *Charles Warren Fairbanks: Conservative Hoosier,* Herbert J. Rissler noted that Fairbanks "spent more time opposing what he considered to be unwise proposals than in formulating new proposals of his own." Fairbanks did serve as a U.S. representative on the United States and British Joint High Commission that was formed in 1898 to settle between the two countries the Alaskan boundary dispute. When the commission failed to come to a final agreement, Fairbanks spoke out against the suggestion of submitting the issue to a foreign arbitrator. His role on the commission won for him the admiration of Alaskan citizens, who named the community of Fairbanks after the vice president.

Although his political mentor McKinley was assassinated in 1901, Fairbanks remained a potent force in state and national G.O.P. affairs. He harbored hopes that the party would look to him as its presidential candidate in 1904. The increasing national popularity enjoyed by McKinley's successor, Theodore Roosevelt, however, offered a major roadblock to Fairbanks's presidential ambitions. Although conservative Republican leaders were concerned about Roosevelt's crusading tendencies, it seemed likely that the former Rough Rider would be the party's choice for president.

With Roosevelt's nomination all but assured, political insiders began to wonder who might be selected as his running mate. Despite making no public statements about his choice, Roosevelt did admit to his son, Theodore, Jr., that

> strictly between ourselves, I very earnestly hope that Mr. [Congressman Robert R. of Illinois] Hitt will be nominated for Vice-President with me. He would be an excellent candidate and if I should be elected he would be of all men the pleasantest to work with.

There were, however, a number of factors working in favor of Indiana's favorite son, Fairbanks. To party insiders, a Roosevelt/Fairbanks ticket made perfect sense as it matched an easterner with a midwesterner and a progressive with a conservative. Even Roosevelt could see the handwriting on the wall. On May 27, 1904, Henry Cabot Lodge wrote Roosevelt to tell him about a visit from Fairbanks that morning in which the Indiana senator indicated

> that he was at your service in any way you might indicate. He would not say that he wanted the V. Presidency; held off as before but yet made it perfectly evident to me that he did want it and is after it,—and means to get it. If he pushes for it he will get it.

Fairbanks got it; in June Republican delegates at the GOP national convention in Chicago selected the Hoosier politician as the party's vice presidential candidate.

In congratulating Fairbanks on his selection, Roosevelt offered scant personal enthusiasm for his new running mate: "I do not see how you could refuse [the nomination] in view of the unanimous feeling of the representatives of the Republican party that you were the man above all others needed for the place," Roosevelt wrote Fairbanks, leaving unsaid whether the Indiana politician was his personal choice for the post. Although the two men were never close friends—Roosevelt even once proclaimed that Fairbanks was nothing but a "reactionary machine politician"—their coolness toward each other had no effect on the 1904 election's outcome. As he had in other elections, Fairbanks traveled throughout the country touting the glories of the Republican Party, ending with a whirlwind tour through Indiana. His efforts did not go unrewarded; the G.O.P. national ticket swamped Democratic candidate Alton B. Parker by more than 2.5 million votes (336 to 140 electoral college votes). Hearing about the overwhelmingly Republican election returns, an excited and pleased Roosevelt exclaimed, "How they are voting for me! How they are voting for me!"

After the excitement of a landslide election triumph, Fairbanks settled down into the drudgery of being vice president. Although Roosevelt had once advocated increasing the office's power and responsibilities, he made no such changes. During his four years in office, Fairbanks played little or no role in the Roosevelt administration. In fact, the vice president worked with conservative House Speaker Joseph "Uncle Joe" Cannon to halt Roosevelt's Square Deal program, vowing to delay "all progressive measures in committee so that they [will] never come to vote."

One anecdote highlights the conservative Hoosier's isolation from the more progressive president. Irritated one day by the continued tinkling sound made by a White House chandelier, Roosevelt is reported to have turned to his butler and said: "Take it to the vice president. He needs something to keep him awake." The president often received reminders from others on Fairbanks's ambition to succeed him in office. When Roosevelt planned to inspect a new, and dangerous, device—a submarine—humorist Finley Peter Dunne warned him not to go on the trip unless he took Fairbanks with him. It came as no surprise that Roosevelt turned to Secretary of War William Howard Taft to succeed him as president instead of Fairbanks.

Contributing to the tension between Roosevelt and Fairbanks was an incident in the vice president's home state. Roosevelt had in 1907 agreed to travel to Indiana on Memorial Day to help dedicate a statue honoring Henry W. Lawton, a Spanish-American War general later killed fighting forces opposed to America's control of the Philippines. Problems soon arose,

however, when Civil War and Spanish-American War veterans squabbled over their rightful places in the proceedings. A Spanish-American War veteran himself, Roosevelt nevertheless wrote Fairbanks that "both because of their age and because of the infinitely greater nature of the war, our claims must not be put forward against the claims of the Civil War veterans."

A greater controversy resulted from ceremonies before Roosevelt's speech dedicating the statue at the Marion County Courthouse. Arriving in Indianapolis's Union Station a little before 11 A.M. on Memorial Day, the president journeyed to the Fairbanks home at 1522 N. Meridian Street to be guest of honor at what he called "a big political lunch."

The forty guests for lunch were divided into two parties, one hosted by Fairbanks in the dining room, and the second headed by U.S. Senator from Indiana James Hemenway in the library. One item on the menu received nationwide attention—Manhattan cocktails.

A teetotaling Methodist, Fairbanks may not have drunk any liquor himself at the luncheon, but he bore the brunt of nationwide newspaper attacks on his character when they learned of the cocktail incident. Already nicknamed "Buttermilk Charlie" for his advocacy of buttermilk instead of hard liquor, Fairbanks had a brand new moniker after the affair—"Cocktail Charlie." A leading Methodist official proclaimed that the vice president had been "crucified by a cocktail."

At first, Fairbanks took full responsibility for the entire matter, writing a Methodist bishop in Buffalo, New York: "I followed the usual custom in such entertainments. For what was done, I was entirely responsible. I have never had any apologies to make for it." But with the frigid relations between the president and vice president, Fairbanks had some nagging doubts about Roosevelt's role in the affair.

These doubts came to light at a Washington, D.C., Gridiron Club dinner honoring Roosevelt as he prepared to leave office. In his speech, Fairbanks said that although he had often been assailed and misunderstood during his career, he himself had "never thrown a line to trip an adversary." Roosevelt, the next and last speaker, responded in kind to Fairbanks's remarks, telling the audience: "The Vice President says he never threw a line to trip an adversary. In that he and I differ. I have thrown a line to trip an adversary, and—I would do it again."

Despite the president's angry words at the Gridiron Club function, earlier he had expressed sincere bewilderment about the uproar caused by the incident. In his memoirs, Indiana Congressman James E. Watson told about a visit he made to see Roosevelt during the controversy. The president told Watson that the treatment afforded Fairbanks had been uncalled for and termed the situation "ludicrous and preposterous." Ironically, Roosevelt confided to Watson: "I don't like cocktails anyhow. I like champagne, and that made the incident at Fairbanks's home all the more gruesome to me."

Of course, the negative publicity Fairbanks received on the "cocktail affair" did not in itself cost the vice president the 1908 Republican presidential nomination. Even with that incident hanging over his head, Fairbanks proved to be a potent force at the convention. He could not, however, prevent Taft—Roosevelt's handpicked successor—from winning the G.O.P. presidential nomination.

After leaving office, Fairbanks and his wife embarked on an around-the-world trip. Even though he was out of politics, he made headlines again when the Pope denied Fairbanks an audience after the former vice president tried to address students at the Methodist schools at the American Church in Rome. On his return to Indiana, Fairbanks kept active in Republican Party affairs but failed to exercise the control he once enjoyed. He kept busy by serving as a trustee for his alma mater, Ohio Wesleyan University, and for DePauw University and American University. In 1912, Congress made Fairbanks a regent of the Smithsonian Institution.

The last political hurrah for Fairbanks came in 1916 when he was once again the G.O.P.'s choice as vice president. Although Fairbanks helped his running mate Charles Evans Hughes to carry Indiana, the duo lost in a close race to incumbent President Woodrow Wilson and his Hoosier running mate, Thomas Marshall. The defeat ended Fairbanks's political life.

Fairbanks died on June 4, 1918. Today, when Fairbanks is remembered, it more often is not for his political stature but rather for his physical stature. Naming Fairbanks one of Indiana's two greatest senators in 1957 for a selection committee choosing the United States Senate's five most distinguished senators of all time, former President Harry S. Truman could only give this rationale: "It is said that the mirror in the Vice President's office, which once belonged to Dolly Madison, is placed at its present height so that Vice President Fairbanks could see to comb his hair."

REFERENCES

Herbert J. Rissler, "Charles Warren Fairbanks: Conservative Hoosier" (Ph.D. diss., Indiana University, 1961); James H. Madison, "Charles Warren Fairbanks and Indiana Republicanism," in *Gentleman from Indiana: National Party Candidates, 1836–1940* (Indianapolis: Indiana Historical Bureau, 1977); William Henry Smith, *The Life and Speeches of Hon. Charles Warren Fairbanks: Republican Candidate for Vice-President* (Indianapolis, Ind.: Wm. B. Burford, 1904); *The Letters of Theodore Roosevelt*, Elting E. Morison, ed. (Cambridge, Mass.: Harvard University Press, 1951); James E. Watson, *As I Knew Them: Memoirs of James E. Watson* (Indianapolis, Ind.: The Bobbs-Merrill Co., 1936).

RAY BOOMHOWER is public relations coordinator for the Indiana Historical Society. He also serves as a contributing editor for the Society's popular history magazine, *Traces of Indiana History and Midwestern History*. Boomhower's work has also appeared in *History News*, *Indiana Magazine of History*, and *Outdoor Indiana*.

JAMES SCHOOLCRAFT SHERMAN (1855–1912)

Vice President, 1909–1912

(President William Howard Taft)

JAMES SCHOOLCRAFT SHERMAN
(Library of Congress)

By William H. Cumberland

The nation's twenty-seventh vice president during the administration of William Howard Taft (1909–13) was James Schoolcraft Sherman, a conservative, business-oriented New Yorker. Veteran of nearly two decades in the House of Representatives, Sherman was known more for his parliamentary than his legislative skills. He remained firmly attached to the stand-pat wing of the Republican Party where he played an influential though not dominant role during the Progressive Era. His genial demeanor and civility earned him the name "Sunny Jim." In 1912, Sherman became the first Republican vice president to be renominated since the party's founding in 1856. However, he died a few days before the election was held.

James Schoolcraft Sherman was born in New Hartford village, New York, then a suburb of Utica, on October 24, 1855. His parents were Richard Updike Sherman and Mary Frances Schoolcraft Sherman. The family name was originally spelled *Shearman*, and the first ancestor on his father's side to arrive in America in the seventeenth century was Henry Shearman, son of Sir Henry Sherman of Dedham, Essex County, England. James Schoolcraft Sherman was of the ninth generation of descendants from Henry Sherman, a line also connected to Roger Sherman, signer of the Declaration of Independence, and William Tecumseh Sherman, the Union general during the Civil War.

The family moved from Connecticut to Massachusetts and finally to Oneida County, New York, where James's father, Richard Updike Sherman, was born. Richard's father, Willet Sherman, was a successful glass manufacturer and captain of the steamboat *Burlington*, which was featured in Charles Dickens's *American Notes.*

Richard Updike Sherman was a Democrat and quite prominent in political and civic affairs, serving as a state constitutional convention member in 1867. He was tally clerk of the U.S. House of Representatives for ten years, and in 1853 wrote a legislative manual that remained in use into the twentieth century. He also served for fifteen years as president of the New York State Forest and Game Commission and had worked as a journalist in Rochester, New York.

James S. Sherman was educated in the Utica public schools and at Whitestown Seminary. His advanced education came at Hamilton College in Utica, where he received the B.A. in 1878 and the L.L.B. in 1879. Sherman distinguished himself as a debater and, although not a brilliant student, was popular with both professors and peers. After gaining admission to the bar in 1880, he entered the Utica law firm of Cookinham, Gibson and Sherman. Henry J. Cookinham, a former New York assemblyman, was married to Sherman's sister, Mary Louise.

Sherman's role in the partnership appears to have been that of a business adviser, and he remained with the firm until 1907. Meanwhile, his father's career stimulated in James an interest in politics, but his decision to enter the political arena as a Republican was contrary to the senior Sherman's advice. An early effort to obtain the Republican nomination to the state senate failed by one vote.

Sherman's first political triumph was his election as mayor of Utica in 1884 at the age of twenty-nine, making him the youngest mayor in the city's history. One of his brothers had been elected mayor of Utica earlier on the Democratic ticket. James Sherman served only one term, declining renomination, as he prepared to move into national politics. Sherman was a supporter of the Half-Breed faction in Republican Party politics and associated with the machine known as the "gang" which for years made its power felt on the Oneida County political scene.

Actually, Oneida County and Utica had been the spawning ground of a number of outstanding political careers—among them Francis Kernan, a prominent Democrat and United States senator, Horatio Seymour, Democratic presidential nominee in 1868, and Senator Roscoe Conkling, powerful Republican leader during the Gilded Age. The area was also the home base for Elihu Root, distinguished lawyer and secretary of state during the administration of Theodore Roosevelt. Root's father and brother taught mathematics at Hamilton College during the nineteenth century, where they were known as Square and Cube. Elihu Root and James Schoolcraft Sherman became warm personal friends. Both men had close ties to Hamilton College and had belonged to the same fraternity.

Although there appears to have been no outstanding municipal achievement during Sherman's one term as mayor, he managed to work his way into position for the Republican nomination for Congress in 1886. He defeated his democratic opponent, Thomas J. Spriggs, who had held the office for two terms. Sherman's congressional election victory started him on a long and successful career in national politics that would culminate only with his death in 1912. However, a strong anti-Sherman faction soon developed over his support of the McKinley Tariff bill and his alleged unwise use of patronage. This led to his only election defeat and caused the often critical *New York Times* to describe Sherman as "a rosy cheeked genial young lawyer whose political pull is based upon a native cunning rather than any reputation for ability." Except for that single election loss by a close margin in 1890, Sherman served in the House, representing the Twenty-seventh (earlier known as the Twenty-third) District, until selected as Taft's running mate in the 1908 election. His career spanned the last phase of the laissez-faire Gilded Age and most of the reform-minded Populist and Progressive Era that followed and during which he never wavered from the principles of the Republican Party's Old Guard wing.

Meanwhile, Sherman's personal life and career were steadily progressing. He had married Carrie Babcock of East Orange, New Jersey, on January 26, 1881. Carrie Babcock Sherman's father, Lewis Babcock, was a prominent lawyer, and her grandfather, Colonel Eliakim Sherrill, had been killed on the third day of fighting at Gettysburg. Carrie and her future husband had attended school together in Utica and had known each other since childhood. They had three sons, Sherrill, Richard U., and Thomas M., all of whom were destined for successful business careers. Carrie Babcock Sherman has been described as a "regal Victorian lady," whose gentle manners made her much respected and loved. She was short of stature, prematurely gray, with attractive, round facial features. She was always solicitous of the well-being and proper accommodations of the Sherman household's servants. When her husband was elected vice president in 1909, Carrie Sherman became the first second lady to accompany her spouse in the inaugural parade. During her husband's tenure as vice president, she founded the Congressional Club for senators' and representatives' wives. When in Utica, the Shermans attended the Dutch Reformed Church, where the congressman was president of the trustees and church treasurer.

Upon his father's death in 1895, Sherman assumed the presidency of the New Hartford Canning Company and was also instrumental in the Utica Trust and Deposit Company's formation in 1899. Sherman served as president of this corporation, one of the most important financial institutions in Central New York.

He was a popular "stump" speaker throughout his career, although during his years in Congress he rarely addressed the galleries. As an emerging politician and successful businessman,

Sherman furthered his contacts as a trustee of Hamilton College as well as serving as president of that institution's Washington Alumni Association, as president of the Oneida County Historical Society, and as a member of several golf clubs, the Washington Metropolitan Club, Union League, Chevy Chase, and the Order of Elks. He received honorary L.L.D. degrees from Wesleyan University and the University of Pittsburgh. While vice president, he was on the board of the Smithsonian Institution.

One of Sherman's favorite hobbies was cultivating flowers, and he always wore a boutonniere. It was Sherman's custom to be finished with breakfast before 8:00 A.M. and then take a brief outing either by buggy or in one of the three autos his sons possessed. He enjoyed playing golf and frequently attended baseball games. Sherman's desire to play baseball was only tempered by his stocky, 190-pound frame, which limited his mobility. His amiable disposition soon led to the nickname "Sunny Jim," which was attached early and remained with him throughout his life. It was said that "he was a man of cheerful yesterdays and confident tomorrows."

Sherman's national career began with his election to Congress during the first Cleveland administration in 1886. He was not known as a legislative leader or innovator, and there are few bills that bear his imprint. His main contribution appears to have been as parliamentarian. Here, Sherman developed a reputation for being fair and for his detailed knowledge of parliamentary procedure. He was chairman of the Committee of the Whole during important debates, and there were few men in either party whose parliamentary knowledge was more highly respected.

He often presided over the House during the fierce debate over the Dingley Tariff in 1897. Sherman was entrusted with this position by Speaker Thomas "Czar" B. Reed, a major influence in the congressman's career. Sherman was also a member of the Committee on Interstate and Foreign Commerce and despite the fact that he was not from a western state was appointed Committee on Indian Affairs chairman, a post he held for twelve years. Other committees on which he served were the judiciary, civil service, and census. His leadership was, according to his colleagues, one of firm dignity as he demonstrated both fairness and executive ability.

Sherman gradually worked his way into the Republican Party's upper echelons and was a trusted colleague of House Speakers Thomas Reed, David B. Henderson, and Joseph G. Cannon. When his close friend Thomas Reed died, Sherman eulogized him as "a lofty patriot, the great and representative citizen of the American Republic who has gone into history." Sherman himself was eventually regarded as one of the House of Representatives "big five," which included Speaker Joseph G. Cannon (Illinois), Sereno E. Payne (New York), John Dalzell (Pennsylvania), and James A. Tawney (Minnesota). Champ Clark remarked that Sherman was "the slickest of the bunch."

A successful career in Congress led Sherman to aspire to further political ambitions. In 1899, he was nominated and confirmed for the post of general appraiser for New York. At first Sherman accepted the position, but then he declined because he claimed his constituents wished him to remain in Congress. Shortly thereafter, when Speaker Reed retired, Sherman entered the contest for Speaker of the House. The position went instead to David Henderson of Iowa. At this point in his career, Sherman may have entertained the prospect of running for the Senate. "Uncle" Joe Cannon, another close colleague of Sherman's, followed Henderson as Speaker in 1903. All three Speakers held enormous power over legislation, which ultimately led to a revolt against Cannon by House insurgents during the Taft administration. Sherman further enhanced his reputation by chairing the New York Republican convention in 1895, 1900, and 1908, was Republican national convention delegate in 1892, and in 1906 chaired the Republican Party's National Congressional Committee.

During the 1906 midterm election, Sherman was instrumental in devising a scheme by which every Republican would contribute a dollar to the campaign. For a time thereafter, "Sunny Jim" was given a new sobriquet, "Dollar Jim." He also endeavored to solicit a political contribution for a good deal more than a dollar from railroad magnate E.H. Harriman, only to be curtly refused. Harriman, not pleased by Roosevelt's reform policies, indicated that he was indifferent to the GOP's electoral success. Republican Congressional Campaign Committee chairman Sherman reported the incident to the president. The dispute that surfaced between President Roosevelt and Harriman had been festering since 1904, when the railroad executive had raised (supposedly at Roosevelt's request) $250,000 to assist the campaign in New York, where GOP success was in doubt. This included Harriman's personal contribution of $50,000. Subsequently, Harriman thought Roosevelt had failed to keep commitments, including a promise to appoint Old Guard Senator Chauncey Depew as ambassador to France. The episode became public in April 1907, when a discharged employee of Harriman's sold to the *New York World* a letter Harriman had written to Sydney Webster, revealing the details of the 1904 arrangement with Roosevelt. Roosevelt denied that he had requested the contribution and produced a letter to Sherman dated October 8, 1906, to validate his position. "Sunny Jim," returning from a cruise on the Spanish Main with House Speaker Joe Cannon, received a wireless telegram from an unidentified source "J.O.," ordering him to avoid all political interviews. Sherman found himself in the uncomfortable position of maintaining silence concerning his knowledge of whether or not Roosevelt had made a personal appeal for campaign funds.

Sherman's congressional career came to an end in 1908 when he was selected, somewhat to the chagrin of the party's Roosevelt wing, as Taft's running mate. While there are few who questioned Sherman's party loyalty or his organizational skills, some wondered whether or not he was suitable for the responsibilities of the office. Three assassinations of presidents in forty-three years, one as recently as 1901, might well have prompted caution concerning the qualifications of the second man on the ticket. Furthermore, because of Sherman's close affiliation with the standpatters, the progressive wing of the Republican Party would have preferred Jonathan Dolliver of Iowa, or at least Dolliver's Iowa colleague, Albert B. Cummins. Albert J. Beveridge of Indiana and Charles Evans Hughes of New York (who himself harbored presidential aspirations) were other possibilities. None of these men was interested, and Roosevelt and Taft, although not enthusiastic, acquiesced in the selection of "Sunny Jim."

The New York delegation strongly supported Sherman throughout the Chicago Republican convention. Sherman's main qualifications were his parliamentary skills. Also, he was well liked in the Senate, had been an effective Congressional Campaign Committee chairman, came from a doubtful state, and of course was acceptable to the party's conservative wing. His candidacy also received a boost when House Speaker Joe Cannon made an unprecedented appearance before the convention and gave a rousing speech in support of Sherman's nomination.

Some Progressives like W.R. Nelson, editor of the *Kansas City Star*, protested that the second post on the ticket should go to someone who could strengthen the cause against Bryan, "not to please reactionaries." One concern of progressives was Sherman's general hostility to labor, exemplified by his support of injunctions in labor disputes, which progressives wished to see modified. Samuel Gompers, president of the American Federation of Labor, referred to Sherman's place on the Republican ticket as a "slap in the face." However, the Taft-Sherman Republican ticket swept easily to victory, defeating William Jennings Bryan, the perennial Democrat standard bearer, by more than a million votes.

Sherman, who wanted a job that was seemingly scorned by more-renowned men, was at least a competent vice president during a period that saw growing divisions within Republican Party ranks. Sherman, it was generally conceded, presided over the Senate with "skill and affability." In 1909, he became the first vice president to be included on the inaugural medal, an honor repeated only by Richard Nixon in 1957 and Spiro Agnew in 1973. Despite declining health and reports that he might retire from politics, Sherman was renominated in 1912—becoming only the seventh vice president in U.S. history to achieve this distinction. No Republican vice president had been renominated since the party's beginning in 1856. The *New York Times* in an editorial on December 23, 1911, stated that in spite of rumors, Sherman's retirement was unlikely; "his alert mind and persuasive speech will be actively employed for the good of his party, the country and Mr. Sherman."

Ideologically, Sherman remained a conservative throughout his life, a fact that his selection as Taft's running mate on a relatively progressive platform in 1908 could not change. He was a man of limited horizons and belonged, as an November 9, 1912, editorial in *Outlook* put it, to the type of men "who conserve the material interests rather than advance the spiritual interests of the nation." However, his executive ability, geniality, parliamentary skill, and devotion to the country's business interests contributed to his consistent reelection and gradual emergence as a party stalwart. During the heyday of Progressivism, he would be included among the ranks of the standpatters who resisted reform championed by the progressives. "Sunny Jim," insisted author William Manners, "during a long twenty years in the House had not backed a single thing of value." Henry Pringle in his biography of President Taft referred to him as a "conservative political hack."

Certainly, this assessment is true if one examines Sherman's views on the tariff, railroad reform, conservation, and antitrust legislation, all important issues to the Progressives. The battle over the Payne-Aldrich tariff bill perhaps best illustrates Sherman's standpattism. It appeared in 1908 that Taft (with Sherman as his running mate) adhered to the Progressive demand for lower rates. Taft, however, vacillated and accepted the Payne-Aldrich bill, which failed to meet the Progressives' demands and threatened by 1910 to split party ranks. Sherman, who had always favored protection, found the legislation to his liking. He even advised Taft to warn Republicans that "any person who tries to defeat the party wishes must necessarily be considered hostile."

The controversial Payne-Aldrich tariff bill, he felt, signified that the party had "fulfilled every campaign pledge." He not only supported the bill, to the chagrin of Progressives like Dolliver of Iowa and even Theodore Roosevelt, but dared venture into the Middle West, where antagonism toward the legislation was strongest. This effort was sharply resented by those midwestern Republican insurgent congressmen who valiantly fought to ward off Old Guard party dominance. Sherman even dared ascribe the return of prosperity and the increase in wages to the tariff—arguing that its provisions did not go far enough. Some insurgents went so far as to advocate reading Sherman out of the party.

Nor does Sherman seem to have shared the Progressive desire to protect the nation's natural resources. As vice president during the Ballinger-Pinchot controversy, Sherman sided with the Old Guard. Ballinger was the secretary of the interior who aroused the suspicions of Louis Glavis, government agent, and Gifford Pinchot, head of the Forest Service, by transferring rich Alaska coal deposits to the Guggenheim-Morgan interests. The charges of corruption against Ballinger led to demands by the Progressives that a special investigative committee be appointed. This meant that Sherman, as vice president, appointed the committee, which Progressives like Dolliver of Iowa correctly predicted would consist mostly of standpatters.

However, Sherman was somewhat more flexible in other matters. He supported labor's demands for an eight-hour day and a child-labor law for the District of Columbia. As a congressman, he favored safety legislation for railroad employees and a limited measure of federal control over industrial and transportation corporations. Sherman was a member of the House committee that worked out a compromise with the Senate in the passage of the Hepburn Act in 1906, a bill that mildly strengthened the regulatory powers of the Interstate Commerce Commission. He was among those who sponsored legislation along the lines of the Pure Food and Drug Act, contributing as early as 1902 a measure that prevented the false branding of food and dairy products from the state or territory in which they were made. However, in congressional hearings on Pure Food and Drug legislation itself in 1906, Sherman remarked that the legislation was designed to "protect not the pocketbook so much as it is the stomachs of the American people," and he opposed compulsory labels that stipulated the weight of cans and bottles. Dr. Harvey W. Wiley, Department of Agriculture chief chemist and a crusader for reform, referred to Sherman as "short weight Jim" and reminded everyone that the New York congressman was a canner.

Sherman was particularly interested in the nation's Indian policy and headed the Committee on Indian Affairs for twelve years prior to his vice-presidential nomination in 1908. He was quite proud of the fact that he was a descendent of early nineteenth-century historian of Indians Henry Schoolcraft. The Riverside, California, Indian school was named in Sherman's honor, and he received the Indian name of Wau-be-ka-chuck (Four Eyes). He also collected numerous Indian artifacts. While Sherman's work as chairman of the Committee on Indian Affairs appears to have won high praise from Congress and may have played a role in his obtaining the vice-presidential nomination in 1908 when the "Indian States" supported him, it does not stand up under close scrutiny. Sherman's goal, as Committee on Indian Affairs chairman and as vice president, was to advance the policy of severalty stemming from the Dawes Act of 1887—that is, to break up the traditional tribal arrangement and encourage the Indians to become individual farmers—a misguided policy that was eventually deemed disastrous to the well-being of the tribes, who were separated from much of their land.

The vice president's lack of sensitivity was revealed in a speech before 400 prominent men and women at a conference held in 1911 at Lake Mohonk, New York, where he stated that the government had fulfilled all of its treaty obligations with the Indians. Chief Choctaw Victor Locke, finding this assertion ridiculous wrote: "If the Commission of which he was chairman took that view we have the explanation of many evils of the past fifteen years." Between 1883 and 1912, Lake Mohonk was an annual conference instituted by a member of the Indian Commission, Alfred Smiley and supported by such well-known humanitarians as Henry Dawes

(Dawes Act author and Senate Committee on Indian Affairs chairman) and the Indian Rights Association. Sherman shared their goal of lifting the Indian to a "higher plane of civilization" and believed the day would come when the Native American would be self-supporting. He often attended Lake Mohonk Conferences, and feeling that great progress was being made in solving the Indian problem through education, he supported federal appropriations for education for Native American children. Furthermore, his colleagues in Congress credited him with endeavoring to reduce fraud in the government management of Indian Affairs.

Sherman, during the U.S. acquisition of a global empire in the 1890s, advocated government support in the completion of an interoceanic Nicaraguan Canal as early as 1896. Furthermore, he fathered the first bill advocating laying a cable to the Philippine Islands, and he also advocated strengthening both the army and the navy in order to give it a two-ocean capability. Sherman also stressed the importance of an improved revenue-cutter service and was among those congressmen who launched an investigation of hazing at the Military and Naval academies. Sherman considered hazing nonsense and brutal and believed that the American people were opposed to it.

There were a few hints of political scandal during Sherman's twenty-six years in national politics. One ugly tale surfaced in the presidential election of 1908, when it was rumored that he had diverted congressional campaign funds in order to secure reelection to Congress and that he had invented dummy corporations to exploit tribal oil lands in Oklahoma. Supposedly, Sherman had secured for a relative a position paying ten dollars a day for inspecting clothing for Indians. He ignored the charges, which were not pressed by the Democrats, as he triumphed in his last campaign. The charges were of little consequence and did not impede Sherman's nomination as Taft's running mate in 1908. However, Sherman's culpability in Indian policy cropped up again in 1910 while he was vice president. Oklahoma lawyer and lobbyist J.F. McMurray was seeking congressional approval

for contracts he had solicited pertaining to the sale of Choctaw and Chickasaw land rights in coal and tar. McMurray and his accomplices, who represented the tribal nations, were to receive exorbitant fees of up to $3 million for their efforts. Senator Thomas P. Gore of Oklahoma, who attacked the contracts, was offered a bribe of between $25,000 and $50,000 for dropping his opposition, but he instead reported the incident, thereby setting forth an investigation during which, along with several other senators, a "higher up" was alleged to be involved. The "higher up" turned out to be Vice President Sherman, who stoutly denied the accusations, and even Gore acknowledged that there was no evidence to implicate him. However, Sherman's critics pointed out that as a congressman he had been Committee on Indian Affairs chairman, making it likely that he had knowledge of the McMurray contracts.

One of Sherman's main interests throughout his life was the law. His familiarity with the legislative process was enhanced by his considerable parliamentary skills—Sherman's peers regarded him as one of the best presiding officers in American history. While chairing a session at the fourteenth annual meeting of the American Academy of Political and Social Sciences in Philadelphia in 1910, Sherman delivered an address explaining the mechanism of legislation by which a bill made its way through Congress. He also equated American greatness with the Founding Fathers' constitutional wisdom and their national respect for the law. The vice president, in a not unusual surge of early twentieth-century patriotism, argued that the progress of the United States was "tied with respect for law." He expanded his address by pointing out that the United States occupied only 5 percent of the world's area, with just 7 percent of the population, while "commercially and financially we about equal one-half of all the rest of mankind."

As the Taft-Roosevelt conflict intensified, Sherman sided with President Taft and would be in position for the unique distinction of receiving the vice-presidential nomination on the Republican ticket for the second time. President Taft, elected as a Progressive in 1908, soon found himself in difficulty with the more liberal wing of the party. The president's support of conservation and tariff reform seemed weak and angered Progressive forces who sought to maintain control of the party organization. Taft's once cordial relationship with Roosevelt cooled. This conflict escalated prior to the 1910 midterm elections. Vice President Sherman traveled from Washington, D.C., to Milwaukee and criticized the Progressives for "arraying class against class and interest against interest."

Several weeks later, the struggle between Sherman and Roosevelt forces in New York intensified when the predominantly Old Guard Republican Committee, without consulting Roosevelt, nominated Sherman for temporary chair of the state convention. However, during the Republican convention at Saratoga, the Old Guard forces were thwarted and Roosevelt was elected. Roosevelt was alarmed over the decline of liberal Republicanism in the state and hoped to rally support for progressive candidate Henry L. Stimson as governor. President Taft played an ambiguous role during the contest (at first appearing to support Sherman and then denying it). This served to further the divisions within the Republican Party prior to the campaign of 1912, which would pit two Republican candidates (Roosevelt on the Progressive ticket and Taft) against an articulate and progressive Democrat, Woodrow Wilson. Sherman, never a strong Roosevelt supporter, said that Roosevelt's defeat in the election was essential "both for the life of our party and the continuation of all government."

Sherman, reluctant to accept renomination because of his declining health, would not live to see the outcome of the election, in which all Republican forces went down to defeat as Woodrow Wilson became the first Democrat to win the White House since Grover Cleveland. The vice president had actually been in ill health for nearly four years, suffering from Bright's Disease. His health worsened while on vacation in August 1912, and he was rushed back to Utica, where he slowly improved. While Sherman had the best medical advice available, he did not always follow that advice. His health was dealt a final, fatal blow

when, contrary to his physician's insistence that he speak only five minutes to a visiting delegation that was to notify officially him of his renomination, he insisted upon speaking for thirty minutes. "You may know all about medicine," he told his physician, "but you don't know about politics." The effort was too much and the vice president never recovered, dying on October 30, 1912. Throughout late summer there had been rumors of his impending resignation from the ticket, but there was no pressure from the Taft forces to bring this about.

Overall, Sherman's vice-presidential years were uneventful. He was an efficient spokesman for the GOPs conservative wing, he was generally supportive of the president in the struggles over conservation (Ballinger-Pinchot) and the tariff (Payne-Aldrich) and in trying in 1912 to thwart Theodore Roosevelt's renewed presidential aspirations. But he was not at the center of decision making. Furthermore, no one in the party considered Sherman as a possible future aspirant for the presidency, nor does he appear to have harbored such ambitions. Although Sherman had been in ill health for some time, his death at age fifty-seven shocked both the nation and the Republican Party.

The vice president's untimely death did not help Taft forces in the 1912 election because he could not be replaced at that late date. While Sherman's premature demise did not cause Taft's defeat, the lack of a second candidate on the ticket did create some confusion as Taft came in third in the popular balloting. Sherman was the seventh vice president to die in office and the first candidate in either major party to die between nomination and the date set for election. Although James Schoolcraft Sherman hardly qualified for a place among the nation's great men, and although his congressional and vice-presidential achievements were no more than average, he was well liked and respected by both major political parties.

The vice president's body lay in state in the rotunda of the Utica Courthouse, where as many as 5,000 mourners filed by the casket, with 25,000 others outside in the streets. Even the Army–Holy Cross football game at West Point was canceled due to the vice president's death. The funeral was held on November 4 in the First Presbyterian Church of Hamilton College. The vice president was buried in Forest Hill Cemetery in Utica. President William Howard Taft summed up the nation's feelings when he said: "Those who knew him loved him; those who knew the services he rendered to his country respected him."

REFERENCES

There is no full biography of Sherman, but short articles appear in some standard biographical compilations, such as *The Dictionary of American Biography*. Material on his life and career comes from publications such as *The Congressional Record* and *The New York Times*. Specific articles: "Career in Congress," *Independent*, May 28, 1908, 1188–1189; "James S. Sherman," *Independent*, June 24, 1908, 1424–1426; "Republican Candidates," *Outlook*, June 27, 1908, 410–412; "Sunny Jim Sherman," *Current Literature*, 45 (August 1908), 151–155; William E. Weed, "James S. Sherman, Republican Candidate for Vice-President," *Review of Reviews*, 38 (August 1908), 167–171; "Vice President Sherman and the Tariff," *Independent*, May 5, 1910, 993–994; "Portrait," *Literary Digest*, November 9, 1912, 827; "The Death of Vice-President Sherman," *Outlook*, November 9, 1912.

WILLIAM H. CUMBERLAND received his B.A. from the University of Dubuque and his M.A. and Ph.D. from the University of Iowa. He is the author of *The History of Buena Vista College*, (1966, 1991), and *Wallace M. Short, Iowa Rebel* (1983), as well as articles in the *Palimpsest*, *Annals of Iowa*, *Books at Iowa*, and *Midwest Review*. He is professor of history, emeritus, at Buena Vista College and currently resides in Cedar Rapids, Iowa.

THOMAS RILEY MARSHALL (1854–1925)

Vice President, 1913–1921

(President Woodrow Wilson)

THOMAS RILEY MARSHALL
(Library of Congress)

By Peter T. Harstad

Lawyer, politician, governor of Indiana from 1909 to 1913, one of six two-term vice presidents, popular speaker and raconteur, Thomas Marshall is best known for a quip that became part of American political culture: "What this country needs is a really good five-cent cigar."

A smoker whose personality contrasted sharply with that of President Wilson's, Marshall very likely uttered these words while presiding over the U.S. Senate during the Sixty-third Congress. However, the statement cannot be found in the *Congressional Record* or any other authoritative source close to the event. Marshall's principal biographer, Charles M. Thomas, concluded that the remark was an aside heard by a Senate clerk and others during a long speech by Senator Joseph L. Bristow of Kansas about the country's needs. In his 1970 doctoral dissertation, John E. Brown presented this and other explanations of Marshall's famous utterance.

Marshall deserves to be remembered for more than his humor, which is amply documented in his *Recollections* and elsewhere. Before he arrived on the national scene, Marshall was an effective lawyer and progressive governor of Indiana who sought to adjust the machinery of state government to the twentieth century. The 1912 election that brought Wilson and Marshall to Washington proved to be the national high-water mark for progressivism. Marshall played a role in the progressive agenda of Wilson's first term; then, when war engulfed Europe, he presided over debates in the Senate about American entry into World War I and, subsequently, over bitter debates about the country's participation in the League of Nations.

President Wilson's stroke tested Marshall, who had ambitions beyond the vice presidency. A lesser man might have thrown the country into constitutional turmoil. Instead, Marshall used the vice presidency to stabilize the executive branch and to calm the nation. Operating without precedent during a president's incapacitation, Marshall conducted affairs of state with dignity. A wise and kindly man, he deserves the designation *statesman.*

Born in North Manchester, Indiana (thirty miles west of Fort Wayne), on March 14, 1854, Marshall was a third-generation Hoosier whose paternal grandfather, Riley Marshall, came from Virginia in 1817. Whether the latter "belonged to the first families, the second families, was just well spoken of, or was downright white trash," the vice president could not determine. He thought he might be the only Marshall "who does not trace his origin . . . to the great chief justice." The family had owned slaves in the Old Dominion and had manumitted them, but a great-uncle managed to take some of the blacks to Missouri before they knew they were free. On the eve of the Civil War, that relative owned a plantation and 300 slaves. At this point in his recollections Marshall inserted: "God does not pay at the end of every week, but He pays."

Hard-working people, the Indiana Marshalls made the most of their opportunities. Daniel, Thomas's father, became a country doctor. The vice president's maternal ancestors, Pennsylvanians who came to Indiana via Ohio, were Presbyterians. "That does not necessarily make a good man," he quipped, "but it makes a religious one." In the Indiana setting, it also tended to make a political man.

Thomas and an older sister who did not survive infancy were the only children born to Daniel and Martha Patterson Marshall. Because of vast swamps, malaria was the bane of northeast Indiana in the 1850s. Marshall spun a yarn in which heredity, environment, and malaria explained why he became a Democrat: A man of "domineering character and predatory wealth" lived in town. When summer came and malaria seized the townspeople, that man took sick with third-day ague. "He was an aristocrat. The rest of us shook every other day. We were democrats."

In the Marshall household, each day began with a Presbyterian prayer "that began in Indiana and ended in China." Thereafter "we had a teaspoonful of quinine and then we had breakfast." Thomas admired and respected his parents, both of whom valued learning. One chapter of his *Recollections* is a tribute to the country doctor, "adviser, counselor, friend" personified by his father, a staunch Democrat and minor officeholder. The loving son asserted: "I could be elected to any office" if I could rehabilitate the old family physician.

Thomas believed that he received his sunny disposition from his mother, with whom he lived, except when attending college, until he was forty. During Thomas's early years, Martha Marshall was sickly. Coupled with Dr. Marshall's understanding of medical geography, this explains several family moves. When Thomas was two, the family went west by covered wagon to the prairies near Urbana, Illinois, to try the open-air treatment for Martha's tuberculosis. In the fall of 1858, Dr. Marshall, a Stephen A. Douglas Democrat, took his son to a political debate at Freeport. A suggestive memory led Thomas to believe that he "sat on Lincoln's lap while Douglas was talking, and on Douglas' lap while Lincoln was talking." Although the youthful Marshall liked "the tall man," it pleased the aged raconteur to think that "something of the love of Lincoln and of Douglas for the Union, the Constitution and the rights of the common man flowed into my childish veins."

Again for health reasons, the Marshalls moved to Kansas but stayed only long enough to conclude that it was a dark and bloody ground. Next, the family went to LaGrange, Missouri, across the Mississippi from Quincy, Illinois, where Martha's health was restored. Late in October 1860, Dr. Marshall, a unionist, got into a street altercation with a pro-slavery guerrilla leader. Relatives convinced the doctor that his life was in danger unless he left Missouri immediately. Thomas and his parents saw the sun go down from the stern of the evening boat for Quincy.

Back in Indiana by November, the month Abraham Lincoln was elected president of the United States, the family took up residence at Pierceton, between Warsaw and North Manchester. Here Thomas went to public school for six years. He attended seventh and eighth grades in Warsaw, where an uncle, Woodson Marshall, practiced law, and spent the 1868–69 academic year in high school at Fort Wayne. A fellow student remembered Thomas as "very bright." Sectionalism, Civil War, and the legacy that followed colored Thomas's world. Even as vice president he saw his role as soother and pacificator but not always as compromiser.

After but one year of high school, Thomas went to Wabash College, operated by the Presbyterian church in Crawfordsville, Indiana. The Marshalls were active in that denomination, and Martha hoped that her son would become a Presbyterian minister. Thomas thrived at Wabash College and his personality developed, but not in the direction of the ministry. He studied classical Greek and Latin, modern French and German, mathematics, a cluster of critical thinking courses, science, religion, military drill, and the Constitution of the United States. On a nine-point scale, his lowest college grade was 8.5; in fourteen of his thirty-seven classes he received the highest possible grade.

Fraternities, literary societies, political activities, and the *Geyser*, a student newspaper, offered diversion from the curriculum of the all-male college. A Phi Gamma Delta fraternity member, Marshall actively participated in campus life. Fellow students had confidence in him, particularly when trouble threatened, as it did during Marshall's senior year. Thomas wrote an article that defamed the character of a female lecturer and visitor to Crawfordsville and published it in the *Geyser*. She hired Lew Wallace, Civil War general and Crawfordsville novelist, as her attorney and filed a $20,000 libel suit against Marshall and the *Geyser* staff. Marshall went to Indianapolis and engaged the services of another Civil War general, Benjamin Harrison, destined also to become president of the United States. Harrison extricated the boys from their predicament, charged nothing, and then gave them a stern lecture on ethics. "It was a great lesson to me," Marshall recorded fifty-two years later, "and I have never again been sued for either slander or libel." Through this episode and by visiting courthouses and witnessing trials, the bright young student met leading members of the Indiana bar.

At Wabash College, Marshall learned to reason quickly and keenly and to speak and write well—valuable skills that he would soon put to use. Thomas's Greek professor tried to persuade him to take up that occupation, but by his senior year he had made up his mind to become a lawyer. Elected to Phi Beta Kappa, he graduated with honors in June 1873.

Rather than attend law school (which the family could not afford), Thomas, on the advice of members of the bar, decided to work and study law in the Warsaw law office of his uncle, Woodson Marshall. Why he soon left is not clear, but the chronology of his departure coincided with his parents' move to Columbia City, midway between Warsaw and Fort Wayne.

Before 1873 was out, Marshall was preparing himself for the bar in the offices of Hooper and Olds in Columbia City. Walter Olds took to the bench, opened offices in Fort Wayne, and eventually became a judge of the Indiana Supreme Court. Therefore, accounts asserting that Marshall studied for the bar under a Fort Wayne judge do not conflict with the facts. Marshall was admitted to practice before the Whitley County Circuit Court at age twenty-one.

The Wabash and Erie Canal and several railroads had opened north central Indiana to development well before Marshall came to Columbia City. In his day, the wetlands were being ditched, tiled, and drained. A girl of the nearby Limberlost swamp, writer Gene Stratton-Porter, viewed draining from a nature lover's perspective; farmers regarded it as physical labor. Marshall came to see the "gum-boot era" of Whitley County development from a lawyer's perspective. Draining projects required legal arrangements, hydraulic engineering, capital, and loans. The aftermath of the Panic of 1873 brought mortgage foreclosures, collection cases, and litigation involving farmers, bankers, and merchants. Life was becoming complicated even in the countryside. Frustrated men attempted to solve their problems with their fists. It was a dull Saturday if Marshall did not get a half-dozen assault-and-battery cases. As a young lawyer, he eked out an existence trying them before the justice of the peace.

In time, Marshall's practice diversified and became profitable, but he never specialized in any particular aspect of the law. He liked the county-seat town of 3,000 inhabitants. According to his biographer, "ditch diggers, local bankers, town sots, ministers of the gospel, small town lawyers, and later, diplomats and kings" accepted him as a friend. Here was a man who understood them and their problems. Marshall's matchless humor relieved tense situations and made him good company. By the close of the 1870s, he and his partner, William F. McNagny, were involved with nearly half the cases before the local circuit court. During the 1880s, the influence of Marshall & McNagny spread throughout the Twelfth Congressional District of northeast Indiana. Although Marshall also had other partners for shorter durations, his affiliation with McNagny lasted from 1877 until 1909.

In his *Recollections*, Marshall discussed some of his cases as well as insights he received into the twistings and turnings of human nature while practicing law in Indiana. With tongue in cheek, he claimed that he could tell whether a witness was telling the truth by watching his Adam's apple.

In a 1913 speech to George Washington Law School students in Washington, D.C., Marshall offered his "legal ten commandments," which a reporter paraphrased as follows:

Don't put a fee before a just cause.
Don't worship money to the extent of being willing to write a dishonest contract in order to get a large fee.
Be a peacemaker; that is the lawyer's business.
Don't chase ambulances.
Honor your profession as your own sacred honor; therefore, do not seek or confound litigation.
Don't accept contingent fees.
Use your influence against the system of allowing attorneys' fees in advance of divorce cases. . . ; when that has been abolished half the divorce cases will be stopped.
Use your influence to compel a person charged with crime to testify in the cause; the innocent man cannot be harmed thereby.
Take the part of the known criminal, but only to see that justice is tempered with mercy.
Don't inquire as to your client's pocketbook before fixing your fee.

Knowledge of the law and of men could be valuable in politics. Marshall and McNagny, both Democrats, worked for the well-being of their party. As their legal reputations spread, so too did their influence in Democratic circles. In a day when political activity doubled as entertainment, Marshall was in demand as a quick-witted speaker and Democratic torchbearer. In 1892, McNagny ran to represent the Twelfth District in the Fifty-third Congress (1893–95); he won, but failed in his reelection attempt. William Jennings Bryan and "free silver" were not popular in Indiana in 1896, but Marshall hewed to the party line—one of the few Democratic state central committee members to do so.

As Marshall approached forty, he appeared to be successful. He had a good law practice and held the respect of many Hoosiers. On Sundays he attended both morning and evening services at the Presbyterian church. He had taught Sunday school, served on the school board, organized the county fair two years in succession, and gave generously to charities. A Masonic Lodge member, he climbed the grades of the Scottish Rite through the thirty-third degree by 1898. His oratory, at its best in banquet halls and temple dedications, brought resounding applause and more speaking engagements.

But Marshall's genial exterior and gregarious personality masked heartaches; moreover, he drank too much.

During his early years in Columbia City, Marshall had asked Catherine Hooper, daughter of a partner in the the law firm of Hooper and Olds, to marry him. She consented but died soon after buying her trousseau. For the next two decades, Marshall kept the company of several women but did not fall in love with any of them. He lived with his mother. Friends reached the conclusion that he was a confirmed bachelor. While trying a case in Angola few months after his mother's death, Marshall met Lois I. Kimsey, a vivacious twenty-three-year-old deputy county clerk, and married her on October 2, 1895. Marshall adored her and dedicated his *Recollections* to two women "uninjured in the fall of Eden"—his mother and his wife.

Lois Kimsey Marshall helped her husband gain the upper hand over his alcoholism. This did not come easily. By his own account, he never cared for a "drink" of whiskey; he "wanted a barrel." By 1897, according to his biographer, Marshall began to appear in morning court sessions "with after effects of intoxication which made it impossible for him to conduct his business." Marshall's drinking threatened his marriage until in 1898 he took the cure. He continued to struggle with alcoholism but, thereafter, no one saw him drink alcohol in public. "I do not drink," he replied when tempted at political gatherings. When Marshall was governor and then vice president, he and his wife did not serve liquor in their home.

It is unlikely that Marshall would have been successful in Indiana and national politics without a loving wife's encouragement and without Thomas Taggart's influence. As mayor of Indianapolis (1895–1901) and a wheel horse in the Democratic Party on the state and national levels, Taggart had a eye for political talent. Marshall had served with Taggart on the Democratic state central committee beginning in 1896. When the party faithful talked with Marshall about doing his duty and running for Congress in 1906, he declined on grounds that he "might be elected" and then hinted that the only elective office that interested him was the governorship. Republicans had held that office for a decade, but a friend, Louis Ludlow, began to tout Marshall as the Democratic candidate for governor a full year before the 1908 gubernatorial election.

The liquor issue then divided Indiana Republicans and Democrats alike. At the Democratic state convention in March 1908, Taggart's candidate, Samuel M. Ralston, could not muster enough votes in four ballots to carry the convention. To prevent the nomination from going to a temperance candidate, Taggart maneuvered enough votes to Marshall so that he won the nomination on the fifth ballot. Several factions then rallied to Marshall's call for party unity.

Marshall's Wabash College and Masonic connections raised interest beyond the Democratic Party. So too did his speaking style and adept handling of the liquor issue when he began to campaign. To assure his independence, Marshall paid his own campaign expenses. Neither a "dry" nor controlled by the brewers, he favored local option. He also supported such progressive planks in his party's platform as direct election of U.S. senators, primary election laws, tariff reform, and control of trusts. Republican opponent Congressman James E. Watson bogged down when the incumbent governor called a special session of the legislature in September to consider the liquor issue. The Republican majority passed a county option law, whereupon Marshall pilloried the opposition for taking the decision away from the people in the fall election.

Marshall campaigned hard in 1908, using his homespun approach to good effect. Neither formidable in appearance nor particularly handsome, he was friendly and approachable. Well trimmed gray locks covered his large head and a bushy mustache obscured his mouth, into which he frequently stuffed a cigar. Observant reporters noted that he was well groomed, that he wore a Phi Beta Kappa key, and that a dash of whimsy flavored his otherwise dignified appearance. Marshall delivered his points deliberately, "as if addressing a jury," reported the *Indianapolis*

News of June 3, 1908; "the whole people seemed to be in a jury box before him."

People liked the man, his progressive message, and the way he delivered it. In the November election, Marshall won a four-year term as governor with a plurality of nearly 15,000 votes. More Hoosiers voted for him in 1908 than for Bryan, the perennial Democratic candidate for president. Marshall also came within 150 votes of outpolling the Republican candidate for president, William Howard Taft. Gubernatorial victories then being rare for Democrats, Marshall's success commanded national attention. Two years later, another progressive Democrat, Woodrow Wilson, would be elected governor of New Jersey.

In office, Marshall distanced himself from the machinery of his party and refused to take orders from party boss Thomas Taggart. As his four-year term unfolded, Marshall proved to be a sound administrator who wielded the powers of his office decisively, including the veto and the use of the militia during labor disputes. He understood the citizens he governed as evidenced by his words and deeds.

The 1910 election, midway in Marshall's term, brought strong Democratic majorities to both houses of the legislature. This enabled the governor and his party to replace the Republicans' county option law governing the sale of intoxicants with their own township option law in 1911. The time had also arrived for action on a progressive agenda related to child labor, correctional institutions, drugs, education, elections, hygiene, railroad safety, trusts, voter registration, and workman's compensation. Governor Marshall signed reform legislation into law in these and other categories. Upon analyzing the details, later generations may conclude that their accomplishments were minimal; for the times, they were significant.

Marshall recognized the limits of what society should attempt through legislation. His theory was that reform should not work downward upon the citizenry but outward from the individual and, when appropriate, be capped off by legislation. The legislature "cannot baptize the state," he insisted.

Because of his interest in penal reform Marshall became known as the Pardoning Governor. One day, he was jostled in a crowd and a man said, "Pardon me," whereupon Marshall replied, "Certainly, what crime have you committed?"

During his tenure as governor, Marshall reached the conclusion that to meet the needs of the twentieth century, Indiana government needed to be overhauled. Amending the 1851 state constitution was exceedingly difficult; therefore, in 1911 Marshall proposed a new and more easily amendable one. Although its principal author was actually Jacob Piatt Dunn, Jr., an Indianapolis lawyer and historian, the document came to be known as the Tom Marshall Constitution. Sections embodying much of the reform thought of the day about state government (including the initiative, referendum, and recall) passed both houses with ease. Curiously, liberalized voting rights were not part of the package.

The question arose: Did the legislature have the power to draft a new constitution and to submit it to the people? Negative answers came back from the circuit court of Marion County and also, by a margin of one vote, from the Indiana supreme court. This rankled Marshall, a stickler on the doctrine of the separation of powers, who thought that the court had overstepped its authority. The U.S. Supreme Court eventually ruled that it had no jurisdiction; therefore the decision of the Indiana supreme court held.

Master politician that he was, Marshall could not steer around the impasse. He closed out his statehouse career as a "liberal with the brakes on."

While he was yet governor, and even before the fate of the Tom Marshall Constitution was sealed, another chapter of Marshall's life was beginning to unfold: He sought the Democratic nomination for president in 1912. Months before the convention, he drummed up speaking engagements for himself in various parts of the country. He had no illusions about his reputation on the national scene but reasoned that he might have a chance at the nomination if the major candidates deadlocked. That prospect was not farfetched because the Democratic nominee then needed the votes of two-thirds of the delegates. Thomas Taggart allegedly led the Indiana delegation to Baltimore in June 1912 with the goal of securing the vice-presidential nomination for Indiana and its popular governor, although Marshall and Taggart were not political cronies (nor were Woodrow Wilson and "Boss" James Smith, Jr., of New Jersey).

The fifth man to be nominated at Baltimore, Marshall received only one vote from beyond Indiana in the initial balloting. On the tenth ballot, Champ Clark of Missouri received a majority of the delegates' votes but could not muster enough to clinch the nomination. The convention deadlocked. On the twenty-eighth ballot, Indiana switched all but one of its votes to Wilson. Marshall's biographer offered the explanation that Taggart used the occasion to gain favor for a vice-presidential slot for Marshall, and further, that Taggart also used his influence with delegations from Illinois and other states to push Wilson over the top and to shore up support for a Wilson-Marshall ticket. On the forty-sixth ballot, Wilson received the necessary two-thirds majority. The vice-presidential nomination for Marshall then came easily. It made political sense to counterbalance a liberal easterner of southern birth with a popular midwestern liberal "with the brakes on." Marshall was not a confidant of Wilson, but Wilson acquiesced in the selection of his running mate.

During a vigorous campaign, Wilson and Marshall traveled the country separately, focusing on the tariff and the trusts. As he had done in his 1908 gubernatorial campaign, Marshall paid his own expenses. He began his campaign in the Northeast in late August, worked his way to the West Coast, and then came back to Indiana. Marshall reserved his strongest rhetoric for lambasting Theodore Roosevelt, the Progressive candidate. In the thick of the campaign, he attended a Scottish Rite banquet along with William Howard Taft, the Republican candidate for president. The Democratic ticket won overwhelmingly in the electoral college.

While the Marshalls were preparing to leave Indiana for Washington, D.C., the Phi Gamma Delta fraternity held a national meeting in Indianapolis. It was on this occasion that Marshall, now a superb after-dinner speaker, told the story of the man who had two sons, one of whom went to sea and drowned and the other of whom entered politics and became vice president. "The poor father died of a broken heart—he never heard of either one afterward."

Marshall began his vice presidency auspiciously on March 4, 1913. A special honor guard consisting of the Black Horse Troop of cadets from his home state's Culver Military Academy escorted Marshall to the inauguration ceremony (and did so again four years later). In his inaugural speech, termed "novel and naive" by *The New York Times*, Marshall referred to the "forced silence" he was about to enter as the presiding officer of the Senate. The realities of the vice presidency began to dawn on Marshall when he found his office, a single room near the Senate chamber. He described it as "a monkey cage, except that the visitors do not offer me any peanuts."

Washington society received the Marshalls graciously. Thomas attributed this to his nimble tongue, which could pay a compliment and "tell a story out of the book of my life, which had not been read by the people of that city." He might have added that his wife added gaiety to private parties and dignity to functions of state. The Marshalls did not have sufficient wealth to entertain lavishly and needed the income from the vice president's speaking engagements to afford even their modest lifestyle. In demand throughout the country, Marshall entertained his audiences and also stumped for the president's program. He spoke of Wilson as a man of ideas who had the courage to express them, the desire to get things done, and "the nerve to insist on their being done."

While Marshall was learning the rules of the tradition-bound Senate, progressivism flowered. With the passage of the Underwood Tariff Act in October 1913, Wilson and Marshall fulfilled their tariff-reform campaign promises. In Marshall's opinion, banking issues generated "the most illuminating and exhaustive discussion of a public question ever held in the Senate." The Federal Reserve Act, also passed in 1913, gave flexibility to the money supply and overhauled the nation's banking system. The Clayton Antitrust Act of 1914 delivered on more campaign promises.

Marshall presided over the Senate while that body debated and passed landmark measures. His friendliness and evenhandedness won him the respect of senators of all political persuasions. As one who had been present at the Lincoln-Douglas debates and whose family had witnessed intense sectionalism, it gave Marshall great satisfaction one day to observe Senator John Hollis Bankhead of Alabama, a former Confederate soldier, locked arm in arm with Senator Knute Nelson of Minnesota, a former Yankee soldier.

The vice president enjoyed his front-row seat on the great American drama. However, he soon ascertained that he was "of no importance to the administration beyond the duty of being loyal to it and ready, at any time, to act as a sort of pinch hitter; that is, when everybody else on the team had failed, I was to be given a chance." He therefore decided to accept the situation,

> to take it in a good-natured way; to be friendly and well disposed to political friend and . . . foe alike; to be loyal to my chief and at the same time not to be offensive to my associates; and to . . . deal justly with those over whom I was merely nominally presiding.

During the eight years that Marshall spent presiding over the Senate, he did not cast a tie-breaking vote on any legislation of paramount importance.

Every two years, Marshall traveled the country on behalf of Democratic candidates for the House and Senate. As was the case in his Indiana days, he proved to be a loyal and useful party member. In 1916, the Democrats renominated Wilson and Marshall. The Republicans nominated Charles Evans Hughes for president and Charles W. Fairbanks as his running mate. This was awkward for the two vice-presidential candidates because they were fellow Hoosiers, fraternity brothers, and friends. The Democrats ran on their reform record, but by election day the war in Europe overshadowed domestic issues.

Both Marshall and Wilson failed to carry their home states. When it was clear that they had won by a narrow margin nationally, Marshall, quoting Shakespeare, telegraphed Wilson:

'TIS NOT SO DEEP AS A WELL
NOR SO WIDE AS A CHURCHDOOR;
BUT 'TIS ENOUGH 'TWILL SERVE.

The two men exchanged pleasantries, but no deep relationship developed that could be counted upon to sustain them through a serious crisis. The 1916 victory made Marshall the first vice president since John C. Calhoun to be reelected.

Marshall's *Recollections* provides commentary on events leading to the American declaration of war on April 6, 1917, the war itself, and its aftermath. Nothing what transpired caused Marshall to revise the conclusions he had reached earlier about the vice presidency.

Himself no early or rabid enthusiast for American entry into the war, Marshall refused to be swept along by wartime hysteria. An incident involving Wisconsin Senator Robert M. La Follette motivated the vice president to revise a senate procedure. As did other midwestern progressives, La Follette drew fire for opposing U.S. entry. When a Senate committee temporized about how it should respond to petitions from citizens calling for La Follette's expulsion from the Senate, Marshall halted the Senate's tradition of acting upon petitions from individual citizens and held to this policy for the rest of his term.

The war changed Marshall's duties: In addition to presiding over the Senate and making political speeches, he also traveled the country in support of the Liberty Loan campaigns. According to his biographer, the war transformed "the merry companionable 'Tom' Marshall" into "a serious, serviceable and earnest Vice-President."

When Wilson went to Paris after the armistice, Marshall presided over cabinet meetings—the first vice president to do so. But in accordance with his scruples over the separation of powers, he informed cabinet members that he was "acting in an unofficial and informal way . . . out of deference to your desires and those of the President." He explained that it would be embarrassing "to be in a confidential relationship to both the legislative and the executive branches."

Wilson returned to the United States in February 1919 to discuss both early drafts of the peace treaty and the League of Nations with the senators. With Marshall presiding, an acrimonious debate broke out in the Senate during the waning days of the third session of the Sixty-fifth Congress. The senators filibustered all night. Nerves became frayed and some said things in anger. When Marshall banged down the gavel on March 4, 1919, to close the session, he declared the Senate adjourned "Sine Deo" (without God).

Characteristically, Marshall's humor belittled no one; this time it did have a bite.

The major challenge of Marshall's vice presidency struck in late September 1919, intensified a week later, and continued until the end of his term. On September 25, President Wilson took sick on his return to Washington, D.C., from a national speaking tour presenting his case for the League of Nations to the people. His physician, Dr. Cary T. Grayson, informed the press that the president had "suffered a complete nervous breakdown" (in fact, it was a stroke) and would rest in the White House. Marshall began to fill in for the president on ceremonial occasions, but for several days he knew no more than the public about the situation's seriousness. On October 2, for example, he welcomed the king and queen of the Belgians and their son to the United States on the president's behalf.

That day the president suffered a second stroke, a cerebral thrombosis that left him a physical and mental invalid. Marshall received a briefing on the gravity of the situation a few days later in a bizarre manner. J. Fred Essary, the *Baltimore Sun*'s respected Washington correspondent, made his way quietly to the vice president's office and explained that the massive stroke of October 2 left the president deathly ill. The stunned vice president did not speak or even look up. The reporter waited for a response from Marshall but received none and left. Years later when Essary and Marshall met in Indiana, Marshall apologized for the incident: "I did not even

have the courtesy to thank you for coming over and telling me. It was the first great shock of my life."

Wilson's advisers had method in their manner of informing Marshall. They did so unofficially through a nongovernmental source so that the vice president would have no grounds for invoking Article II of the Constitution and assuming the presidency due to the president's "Inability to discharge the Powers and Duties of the said Office."

In his 1992 book *Ill Advised: Presidential Health and Public Trust*, historian Robert H. Ferrell stated flatly: "The president should have resigned immediately." Instead, Wilson, his physician, his wife, and his secretary, Joseph P. Tumulty, disguised his illness. The vice president repeatedly tried to visit the stricken president but was not allowed to see him until his last day in office, March 4, 1921.

Volumes have been written about Mrs. Wilson's "petticoat government," as Senator Albert Fall called it. Edith Bolling Wilson termed it "her stewardship," which probably went so far as to guide the president's hand as he signed necessary papers to sustain him in the presidency. Even in full health, Wilson had not regarded Marshall highly (although he had headed off a move to drop Marshall from the ballot in 1916). Wilson's advisers had less regard for Marshall than did their chief. Colonel Edward M. House, for example, told a reporter that an "unfriendly fairy godmother" had presented Marshall with a keen sense of humor. "Nothing is more fatal in politics." He acknowledged that Marshall made friends, "but they looked upon him as a jester."

Tumulty and Secretary of State Robert Lansing both left accounts describing a conference they had with Dr. Grayson on October 3, 1919. The threesome discussed the possibility of having Marshall "assume the executive authority temporarily in the absence of precedents as to what constituted disability under the Constitution." Heated discussion followed, with the upshot that Tumulty and Grayson concurred that neither man would certify the president's disability. Tumulty then notified Lansing that "if anybody outside of the White House circle attempted to certify to the President's disability, that Grayson and I would stand together and repudiate it."

Not privy to such discussions and barred from seeing the president, Marshall realized that his inquiries into the president's health might be interpreted as self-serving or worse. In the deluge of advice that came to him, people of many political persuasions urged Marshall to seize the presidency; he consistently declined to do so. Marshall's secretary, Mark Thistlethwaite, asked him if he would assume the presidency if Congress decided that Wilson was unable to serve. "No," Marshall replied. "It would not be legal until the President signed it, or until it had a two-thirds vote. . . ." The only conditions under which Marshall would have taken over, according to his biographer, would have been for Congress to have passed such a resolution and for Mrs. Wilson and Dr. Grayson to have approved it in writing. "I am not going to seize the place and then have Wilson—recovered—come around and say 'get off, you usurper.'"

There the issue rested for the remainder of Marshall's term. "These were not pleasant months for me," Marshall recorded in his *Recollections*. He remained reluctant to ask about the president's health "for fear some censorious soul would accuse me of a longing for his place. I never have wanted his [Wilson's] shoes," he wrote. No evidence contradicts the genuineness of this assertion.

An ambitious man could have made much of the situation; an unscrupulous one could have thrown the nation into turmoil. Aware of this, Marshall on one occasion confided to his wife: "I could throw this country into civil war, but I won't." Historian John D. Hicks concluded that had Marshall countenanced the idea, "it is probable that he might have been declared president." Marshall rose above personal ambition. His idols were two Democrats, Stephen A. Douglas and Samuel J. Tilden (who showed restraint in the disputed presidential election of 1876). He wrote:

> They are the two men in all American history who when the peace and good order of their country were at stake cast aside every hope of personal preferment for the sake of the Republic.

As vice president, Marshall did what he could from September 1919 to March 4, 1921, to keep the executive branch of the government functioning. (Ratified in 1967, Amendment Twenty-five of the U.S. Constitution addresses the issue of the incapacitation of the president and the transfer of powers to the vice president.) Marshall hosted foreign dignitaries with republican dignity. While presiding over the Senate, he remained loyal to the president's objective of supporting the League of Nations. Had he been president, it is likely that he would have been more flexible in dealing with the Senate. His considered opinion was that more than executive flexibility would have been required to get two-thirds of the senators to approve Article Ten of the League covenant, which provided for collective action against aggressors.

Marshall was not proud of his nation's rejection of the League of Nations. He wrote in his *Recollections* that it reminded him

> of a man going to the relief of his neighbor who was being assaulted by a burglar. After he had assisted in throwing the burglar out of the house, although his neighbor was wounded and in sore stress, he picks up his hat, says good night and goes home.

Following the Republican national convention of June 1920, Marshall greeted his possible successor, Calvin Coolidge, with a message of commiseration. His telegram read: "Please accept my sincere sympathy." Only for fleeting moments following the vice presidency did Marshall entertain thoughts of continuing his political career. He moved back to Indianapolis and used his time to travel, speak, and write. In 1925, he offered to the public *Recollections of Thomas R. Marshall, Vice-President and Hoosier Philosopher—A Hoosier Salad* "in the hope," as he explained in the front matter, "that the Tired Business Man, the Unsuccessful Golfer and the Lonely Husband whose wife is out reforming the world may find therein a half hour's surcease from sorrow." He also served as a trustee of his alma mater, Wabash College. In 1922, President Harding appointed Marshall to the U.S. Coal Commission.

Marshall died on June 1, 1925, of a heart attack while on a visit to Washington, D.C. The body was returned to Indianapolis and is buried in Crown Hill Cemetery. The Marshalls had no children.

John D. Hicks's decades-old assertion that Marshall "was perhaps the most popular vice president the country ever had" still holds.

REFERENCES

Thomas R. Marshall, *Recollections of Thomas R. Marshall, Vice-President and Hoosier Philosopher—A Hoosier Salad* (Indianapolis, Ind.: The Bobbs-Merrill Co., 1925); Charles M. Thomas, *Thomas Riley Marshall: Hoosier Statesman* (Oxford, Ohio: The Mississippi Valley Press, 1939); John Eugene Brown, "Woodrow Wilson's Vice President: Thomas R. Marshall and the Wilson Administration" (Ph.D. dissertation, Ball State University, 1970).

PETER T. HARSTAD received his Ph.D. in history from the University of Wisconsin, Madison in 1963. He has spent most of his career in three "I" states: as professor of history at Idaho State University, 1963–72; as director of the State Historical Society of Iowa, 1972–81; and as executive director of the Indiana Historical Society, 1984 to the present. He has published on a variety of subjects, most of them related to the history of the Midwest.

CALVIN COOLIDGE
(Library of Congress)

By Paul L. Silver

Calvin Coolidge has provoked a range of views. He is often stereotyped as "Silent Cal" and a thoroughly unaggressive administrator, but has also been described as sound and wise, particularly in his handling of the Boston police strike, and as thoughtful and well informed. Both biographer Claude Fuess and Thomas Silver (in a more recent study of the treatment of Coolidge by historians) have argued that their subject was unfairly maligned by politicians and academicians. Indeed Fuess, in his 1940

biography, *Calvin Coolidge: The Man from Vermont,* concludes his introduction with the statement that its subject "was not only a useful public servant but a great and good man."

Coolidge, one of two Vermont-born presidents, both of whom reached that high office through the vice presidency, was born, appropriately, on July 4, 1872, in Plymouth, Vermont. Most of the technological marvels with which we are familiar—the telephone, radio, movies, television, computers, and such—were long in the future, and Coolidge's native state was more remote from the centers of culture and power than it is a century and more later. Interstate highways and E-mail tie Vermont to the rest of New England and the country today; in the 1870s Vermont was more detached, and Plymouth was a small community that was rather remote from population centers even within the state. Though he spent most of his adult life outside the state of his birth, Coolidge never lost his devotion to and admiration for it, and he declared his feelings on several occasions, notably September 21, 1928, at Bennington, where he said frankly: "Vermont is a state I love."

In the crossroads town of Plymouth, Calvin's father, John Coolidge, storekeeper and landowner, was also active in local politics and a sometime member of the state legislature. Calvin's education, both at the local ungraded school at Black River Academy and, briefly, at St. Johnsbury Academy, covered a variety of subjects including English grammar, Latin, Greek, French, mathematics, history, and rhetoric. He performed capably with an interest in history and biography, though Fuess in his 1940 biography characterized young Coolidge as "an ordinary boy, who seemed likely to end his days on the farm or in the village store."

Coolidge's life had its share of tragedy as well as chores, education, and entertainment. His mother, Victoria, died when Calvin was twelve years old, and his sister Abigail, of whom he was very fond and who was three years younger than he, died of appendicitis in 1890 leaving a lonely brother and father. The void in the father's life was filled after six years as a widower by Carrie Brown with whom Calvin was close for the remainder of her life.

In fall 1891, the young Vermonter did what no member of the family and few in southern Vermont had done: he went off to college. Amherst College was in the 1890s a small liberal arts institution that introduced young Coolidge to the wider world both of learning and of people beyond Vermont. His shyness and reserve made his absorption into the community slower than for others, though he made friends, participated in fraternity activities, and achieved some promi-

nence as a speaker, delivering an oration as part of his commencement exercises. Coolidge biographer Donald McCoy summarized this part of his subject's life and looked ahead when he wrote that the graduates

> marched out into life and among them marched Calvin Coolidge, who though not last among them in college was far from being first. As so often happens, some of the top members of the class were to disappear into the jungles of life and a number of the obscure were to become worthies in their communities, businesses, and professions. Calvin Coolidge, marching to his own tune, was to surpass them all.

The young graduate's next stop was Northampton, Massachusetts, in which he spent a good part of the rest of his life, both before and after his presidency. He had already decided to study law, but during the summer after graduation, in 1895, he discarded the idea of attending law school because of the cost and opted instead for reading law with an established lawyer, clerking in that lawyer's firm and being admitted to the bar by examination. (This is still an option in Vermont, though not in many other states.) At the end of two years of clerking and reading law, he was presented by one of the lawyers in the firm in which he worked, examined by a committee of lawyers and judges, and admitted to the bar forthwith, opening his law office in Northampton in February 1898.

At virtually the same time, Coolidge began his rise up the political ladder. Unlike Herbert Hoover, who ran for only one political office—president of the United States—winning once and losing once, the young lawyer started at the bottom as a campaign worker in the effort of Henry Field, a partner in the firm in which Coolidge had clerked, to become mayor of Northampton. He was also chosen to be on the Republican city committee and a delegate to a local convention and in December 1898 was elected to the Northampton city council, the first of many elective offices he held. He used this relatively insignificant position to learn the mechanics and people of the political process. He then won election by the city council to the city solicitor's post, served two terms, and was defeated for a third. This was one of his few defeats; another was for a position on his chosen city's school committee.

Prior to his next political move, Coolidge met Grace Goodhue, also a Vermonter, who after graduating in 1902 from the University of Vermont, had accepted a teaching position in Northampton. Though they seemed almost opposite in personality as well as in diversity of interests, Grace and Calvin found each other congenial and in the summer of 1905 decided to be married; the ceremony took place in Burlington in October.

Following a short honeymoon, the couple returned to Northampton where he resumed his law practice and political career. The latter next moved to the state level, Coolidge having won a seat in the Massachusetts house of representatives. Though he is often seen as a staunch conservative, the young legislator's record was reasonably progressive. In his two terms as representative, he supported direct election of U.S. senators, women's suffrage, a six-day workweek, and fewer hours of work for women and children.

After two terms as a representative, the young attorney had a brief period out of office but in 1909 was the Republican candidate for mayor of Northampton, an office he also held for two terms, "beginning," as Donald McCoy notes, "his continuous service in public office until he left the White House twenty years later." As mayor he worked to better the fire and police departments, increase teachers' pay, and improve the city streets, and he did it all efficiently and honestly.

A state senate seat from Hampshire County was Coolidge's next political office. The young politician's return to Boston coincided with the turmoil in the Republican Party marked at the national level by the split between President William Howard Taft and former President Theodore Roosevelt and in Massachusetts by the textile strike in Lowell. At a critical point in this latter contentious dispute, a legislative committee was appointed with Coolidge at its head. Because

of his previous record, he was acceptable to both labor and management, and while the settlement reached did not entirely please the strikers, in general Coolidge was perceived as having acted in a fair manner. He served a total of three terms—three years—as state senator; in the final year he was chosen as president of the senate. In the latter position he had considerable power, including the naming of committees and the assignment of bills to those committees. Once again, both as senator and senate president, Coolidge had retained the support of conservatives and moderates and favored measures of interest to the progressives. He backed both women's suffrage and a minimum wage for women as well as a state income tax and primary elections, and he renewed his support for direct election of U.S. senators. Further, as senate president Coolidge was perceived as fair, honest, and efficient with a concern for stability and economy.

Coolidge's upward climb continued with his election in 1915 as lieutenant governor; here, too, he served three one-year terms. In this position, though he did not preside over the senate, he was chair of the governor's council, which had the job of advising the governor on matters as wide ranging as finances, appointments, and pardons. At Governor Samuel McCall's behest, Coolidge was assigned the task of speaking frequently across the state, thus improving his chances for higher office by making him and his ideas and his aura of soundness and stability widely known.

Among those whose attention Coolidge attracted was Frank Stearns, a wealthy Boston merchant who was ultimately to be a major backer of the future president. With Stearns's financial and promotional help, Coolidge became the Republican gubernatorial candidate and entered a campaign made more difficult by a split in the Republican organization between then Governor McCall and U.S. senator John Weeks. Indeed Coolidge at one point thought he might lose the election, and though he won, he did so by the relatively small margin of 16,000 votes.

The new governor began the first of his two one-year terms with an inaugural address characterized by Claude Fuess as "one of his most liberal pronouncements." In it the governor urged the legislature to work diligently and under the law for all citizens:

> Let there be a purpose in all your legislation to recognize the right of man to be well born, well nurtured, well educated, well employed, and well paid. This is no gospel of ease and selfishness, or class distinction, but a gospel of effort and service, of universal application.

In his tenure as governor, Coolidge dealt with the problems and dislocations of the months immediately following World War I. Professor McCoy's assessment of the governor's performance—"an effective, responsible, and conscientious executive"—seems fair. His actions and statements during perhaps the single most difficult event of his governorship, the Boston police strike, more than any other action thrust him into national prominence. Historians disagree about the specific events and most particularly Coolidge's role in them. Some such as McCoy accuse him of being hesitant and uncertain, while others such as Fuess and Silver praise his firmness, determination, and consistency, particularly in his support of Police Commissioner Edward Curtis.

The Boston police strike occurred in the late summer of 1919, a year in which various disputes had occurred as labor went after gains it had refrained from seeking during World War I. The most notable dispute was the threatened Seattle general strike early in the year, though Massachusetts had had its share of strikes, including a work stoppage by telephone workers and a street railway workers' strike in Boston. Coolidge entered that dispute, helping to achieve an agreement under which the workers went back to work while matters in dispute were arbitrated; eventually the workers achieved significant improvement in their wages.

Two primary issues dominated the police strike—the wages, hours, and working conditions of the police, and the effort to form a union and affiliate with the American Federation of Labor. The governor was fully aware of the long hours, the low wages, and the dirty police stations, and said so. However, he consistently backed Police Commissioner Curtis, who refused to allow the Boston police officers to join a union and found guilty those who disobeyed his orders and received a charter from the A.F. of L. Curtis delayed implementing punishment in hopes that these leaders would cease their association with the A.F. of L. Further, just prior to the strike, these men were suspended instead of being dismissed. Silver and McCoy disagree on how vigorous, forthright, and involved the governor was in all of this, but it seems reasonably clear that Coolidge consistently supported Police Commissioner Curtis and, while sympathizing with the policemen, would not condone the strike.

When policemen walked off the job and disorder and violence resulted, Mayor Andrew Peters removed Commissioner Curtis, who was shortly reinstated by Coolidge. Peters had called out the State Guard within Boston; Coolidge called out most of the rest, and order was restored. A.F. of L. Head Samuel Gompers sent telegrams to the governor in which Gompers asserted that the police commissioner had denied the right of policemen to affiliate. The governor replied in his own telegram that became the single most-famous statement in the whole controversy. In it he declared: "The right of the police of Boston to affiliate has always been questioned, never granted, is now prohibited." He added that it was wrong to leave the city unprotected, declaring: "There is no right to strike against the public safety by anybody, anywhere, any time." Coolidge's actions heartened the people of Boston. His telegram, and particularly the above sentence, were quoted across the country, and together his actions and statements helped to propel the governor onto the national scene and into the vice presidency.

In 1920, Governor Coolidge entertained ambitions to be the Republican Party's nominee for president. He had support within Massachusetts and some outside of it, but many Massachusetts delegation members to the Republican national convention were pledged to Leonard Wood, and its most prominent member, Senator Henry Cabot Lodge, would not support Coolidge, in part because of the governor's association with the Murray Crane faction in

Massachusetts politics and because, in the opinion of Claude Fuess, of differences in style and background as well as the senator's determination to retain what Fuess calls Lodge's "supremacy in Massachusetts politics." The convention, deadlocked between Wood and Governor Frank G. Lowden of Illinois, was firmly in the control of what Coolidge in his autobiography referred to as "a coterie of United States Senators." These leaders succeeded in nominating for president Senator Warren G. Harding of Ohio, but they were blocked in their efforts to have Wisconsin Senator Irvine L. Lenroot chosen by the delegates as the vice-presidential nominee. Oregon delegation member Wallace McCamant placed the Massachusetts governor's name in nomination, and it was seconded by North Dakota, and though several others were also named, the convention running away from the senatorial group's control quickly chose Coolidge, the nomination being made unanimous.

In the meantime, back in Boston, the governor, perhaps disappointed at not making a better showing in the effort to gain the top place on the ticket, left his Boston residence for a walk and returned from it for a long talk with his wife Grace. When the results from the convention were telephoned to Coolidge, he told his wife: "Nominated for Vice President!" She at first thought he might be kidding, but when it was clear that he was not, she said: "You are not going to accept it, are you?" to which he replied: "I suppose shall have to." Coolidge then prepared a short statement in which he declared the nomination "unsought" and accepted "as an honor and a duty." He added:

> It will be especially pleasing to be associated with my old friend Senator Warren G. Harding, our candidate for President. The Republican Party has adopted a sound platform, chosen a wise leader and is united. It deserves the confidence of the American people. That confidence I shall endeavor to secure.

Coolidge's role in the campaign was not large and usually not outside of New England. He made a speech in Philadelphia in October and in the same month, on orders from the Republican national committee, made an eight-day swing through the South with other party leaders. Coolidge protested the assignment as keeping him too long away from his responsibilities in Massachusetts and added that "my abilities do not lie in that direction," but he carried out the assignment. Following a speech and parade in New York City, he returned to his home state and concluded his campaign with speeches in Boston.

The new vice president's role in the Harding administration promised, at least at the beginning of the campaign, to be significant, certainly larger than was usually the case. On June 30, 1920, Harding and Coolidge had breakfast at the presidential candidate's Washington, D.C., residence. At the press conference that followed, Harding said:

> I think the vice president should be more than a mere substitute in waiting. In reestablishing coordination between the Executive Office and the Senate, the vice president can and ought to play a big part, and I have been telling Governor Coolidge how much I wish him to be not only a participant in the campaign, but how much I wish him to be a helpful part of a Republican administration. The country needs the counsel and the becoming participation in government of such men as Governor Coolidge.

The Harding-Coolidge ticket easily defeated the Democrats, headed by James M. Cox. The Republicans campaigned on a "return to normalcy" theme that had great national appeal after the war. Harding and Coolidge took 61 percent of the popular vote.

After being sworn in in 1921, Coolidge took over his prescribed duty of presiding over the Senate and attended cabinet meetings though according to both Claude Fuess and Donald McCoy, rarely involved himself in the discussions that took place. Coolidge presided over the Senate in a competent and, after one or two troublesome situations, cautious manner. In his autobiography, he declared that "presiding over the Senate was fascinating to me" but in the next paragraph said, wryly, that "the Senate had but one fixed rule, subject to exception of course, which was to the effect that the Senate would do anything it wanted to do whenever it wanted to do it." He thereafter relied on the secretary to the Senate for information on questions of parliamentary procedure.

The vice president also participated in various ceremonial events, and made numerous speeches, either as representative of the Harding administration or to boost his personal income. He later laconically summarized this aspect of his vice-presidential career: "During these two years I spoke some and lectured some. This took me about the country in travels that reached from Maine to California, from the Twin Cities to Charleston. I was getting acquainted." This was not an insignificant benefit to him because, as he himself noted, he had no experience at the federal level and needed to learn the ways of Washington.

He participated in the capital's social side, often accepting invitations to luncheons and dinner—surprisingly perhaps, given his shyness and well-known aversion to idle chatter. Once, when asked about this, he replied "Got to eat somewhere!" This and other stories merely strengthened his reputation for taciturnity punctuated by an occasional dry jest.

During his vice-presidential years Coolidge, though not a major force in either the Washington political arena or social scene, remained a power in Massachusetts politics. Donald McCoy attributes this in part to what came to be called "Coolidge luck," by which he, though not always the strongest candidate, had moved up the ladder from one elective office to another in Massachusetts and then on to the vice presidency. In fact, many expected that this same good fortune would move him into the presidency. People in Northampton reportedly said: "I wouldn't give two cents for Warren Harding's life."

Coolidge's strength in his home state was also based on his political faction's need for a well-known figure to head the group after the death of its longtime leader, Murray Crane, as well as on the strength of that faction, holding as it did in addition to the vice presidency the speakership of the U.S. House of Representatives and the Massachusetts governorship. In addition, the vice president was perceived as a primary reason why Massachusetts Republicans had done well in the elections of 1920.

However, in Washington Coolidge, though supportive of the president, was not close to him or his cronies, having little in common with people like Charles Forbes and Harry Daugherty, of whose activities and character he must have become aware. Fuess noted that: "It could not have been agreeable for Calvin Coolidge, with his innate Puritanical virtue, to watch the deterioration of the Harding administration." While the president was cordial to his vice president, in private he referred to him as "that little fellow from Massachusetts." Claude Fuess asserted, nonetheless, that "Harding had great confidence in Coolidge, consulted him frequently, and was influenced by him to a marked degree." Donald McCoy disagrees, saying rather gently that he found no direct evidence to back up Fuess's assertion, and believes that "The relationship between the Chief Executive and the Vice President, though friendly, was not close." Robert K. Murray, in *The Politics of Normalcy,* is more blunt: Fuess, he says, in arguing that Harding had a high opinion of Coolidge and often sought his views "was wrong on both counts." Mrs. Harding was much less friendly to the vice president than was her husband. In response to an offer of an impressive house as the vice president's residence, Mrs. Harding purportedly said: "Not a bit of it, not a bit of it. I am going to have that bill defeated. Do you think I am going to have those Coolidges living in a house like that? An hotel apartment is plenty good enough for them." A bill to have Congress accept the offered house and appropriate money to maintain it was not passed, though it is unclear whether Mrs. Harding was actually involved.

Perhaps more significant, Coolidge had few close friends and was not aided in making more by those, like Lodge, whom he had known before his arrival in Washington. Indeed, Senator Henry F. Ashurst of Arizona noted in his diary in early 1923 that Senate Republicans were seeking another vice-presidential nominee for the coming election.

In any case, President Harding was increasingly distressed by what he learned of the indiscretions and illegalities of his subordinates. When he left Washington for a trip to Alaska and the West Coast, he was not well. Coolidge had seen Harding at the end of the congressional session in March 1923, then spent much of the time between then and midsummer in Northampton, and in early July drove to Vermont to spend several weeks in Plymouth. It was here that the news of President Harding's death reached him early on the morning of August 3, 1923. Thus ended Coolidge's service as vice president, years which he later termed "a period of most important preparation."

The notification of the vice president and his swearing in as president, the oath being administered by his father, a notary, make a charming and well-known story. The absence of a telephone at the Coolidge home, the rural setting, his father's role in the proceedings all captured the public's attention and that of historians since. It is interesting to note that while this was the first instance of a father swearing in his son as president, there was some question as to whether John Coolidge, a state official and not a federal one, had the authority to do this. To cover this possibility, the oath was administered a second time by a judge of the Supreme Court of the District of Columbia.

Later on the day of his initial swearing-in, the new president traveled to Washington to begin to establish himself as the head of his own administration. He first issued a proclamation of a period of mourning for Harding, then met with various government leaders, urged all cabinet members to retain their posts, and chose a personal secretary. His choice was C. Bascom Slemp, a Virginia congressman and highly knowledgeable individual whose appointment was taken to mean Coolidge's intention to seek nomination and election in 1924.

The new president's concern for Mrs. Harding was striking: He took care of some details personally, told her that she could stay in the White House as long as she wished, and delayed his own family's move into the executive mansion almost four days beyond her departure. "It was," said Professor McCoy, "a magnificent performance for the taciturn Yankee, and for a man who knew how little Mrs. Harding had thought of him."

Coolidge might have found his life as vice president a bit boring, leaving him with time on his hands. As president, he now had more than enough to keep him fully occupied. An increasingly pressing matter—a series of matters, really—involved Harding administration scandals that were becoming public. The president was under significant pressure both to keep and to dismiss Attorney General Harry M. Daugherty. Coolidge eventually did ask for Daugherty's resignation in March 1924, after the attorney general refused to open Justice Department files to a Senate investigation. Professor McCoy asserts that the president "had kept his head and his self respect: he had not acted until he had unquestionable reason to do so." He had indicated earlier, said McCoy,

> that he was not going to condemn a man on the basis of adverse public opinion or loose-knit circumstantial evidence, a virtue perhaps better understood after the McCarthyite scares of the 1950s than it was in the 1920s.

Though occasionally a target of the Teapot Dome investigations, Coolidge was not seriously linked to this scandal, and his cautious and judicious actions combined with several praiseworthy appointments, notably of Harlan Fiske Stone as attorney general, helped to bring the president through this crisis in as good shape as was likely.

Coolidge's relations with Congress in 1923 and 1924 were rather contentious, involving the Immigration Act, which the president signed though he criticized the provisions excluding Japan from any immigration quota, and a veterans' bonus bill on which he was opposed by major Republican leaders in Congress and which he nevertheless vetoed. The veto was being overridden. Also in this period the McNary-Haugen bill, an effort to raise farm prices by buying up surplus production of several major commodities at prewar prices and selling abroad for whatever could be gained, failed to pass the Congress; it would subsequently be passed and be vetoed by Coolidge. On most major issues, the president had been defeated and abused by the Congress, though the public still had great confidence in him.

The campaign of 1924 began, in the opinion of Robert K. Murray, with the congressional election of 1922. For Coolidge it began with his accession to the presidency. In his autobiography, the former president wrote, somewhat disingenuously, about his role:

> Many people at once began to speak about nominating me to lead my party in the next campaign. I did not take any position in relation to their efforts. Unless the nomination came to me in a natural way rather than as the result of any artificial campaign, I did not feel it would be of any value.

While the campaign was not personally directed by the president and while, as he noted in his autobiography, he made no "purely political speeches" during the campaign, he did make remarks at ceremonial occasions and did not in any way discourage efforts to gain for him the Republican nomination at the party's 1924 convention. He certainly indicated what he liked or disliked about the plans others made for his nomination. National Committeeman (subsequently chair of that committee) William M. Butler took charge, ensuring a united Massachusetts delegation, and then controlled equally firmly the following campaign.

The Republicans were aided in 1924 by the deep divisions within the Democratic Party, the inept campaign conducted by Democratic nominee John W. Davis, and the lack of public interest in anything the Progressives and Robert M. La Follette had to offer. The scandals, particularly the Teapot Dome oil scandal, touched the Democrats as well as the Republicans and certainly did not damage Coolidge in any significant way. To the degree that the Democrats attacked the Republicans about the scandals, some have argued, the Republicans believed it necessary to support the president more firmly. John W. Davis's summary, in a later oral history interview, is on the mark: "I went about the country telling people I was going to be elected, and I knew I hadn't any

more chance than a snowball in hell. . . . Not only was the Democratic party ripped apart, but it was impossible to hang the responsibility for the Harding era ills on Coolidge." Coolidge had run on this Harding record and program, and the public supported that program and the stability that the president offered.

In his full term as president, Coolidge continued his support for Andrew Mellon's tax policies and the secretary of the treasury's program for debt reduction; remained consistent in his opposition to the McNary-Haugen bill; continued his effective combination of action and inaction in regard to the scandals of the Harding administration; and dealt with numerous other matters, including U.S. relations with Latin American countries. The tax policies have long been criticized as evidence of Secretary Mellon's effort to shift the tax burden from the rich to the middle class and the poor and in general to reduce government revenues and improve the condition of business. It is clear that Calvin Coolidge favored the business community and admired many of its leaders, but Thomas B. Silver, in his work *Coolidge and the Historians,* comes down strongly in support of Coolidge administration tax policies and excoriates John D. Hicks and Arthur M. Schlesinger, Jr., for distortion, inaccuracy, bias, and overlooking sources and documents that would not support their case.

Though the president had favored American participation in the World Court, he did not push the Congress on this matter, nor did he achieve American membership. He also did not back efforts to have the United States join the League of Nations. Among the legacies of World War I were the war debts owned the United States by various nations. It is not clear that Coolidge ever said "they hired the money, didn't they," but he opposed the cancellation of those obligations, though he did agree to a reduction in the interest rates on these debts.

In summer 1927, Coolidge vacationed in South Dakota and there handed to news reporters a brief announcement that said: "I do not choose to run for President in nineteen twenty-eight." Historians and others have debated ever since exactly why Coolidge made the announcement and what he really meant by it. Claude Fuess declared that this statement was the result of "a deliberate and carefully planned decision." Coolidge, Fuess added, "never allowed his emotions to dominate his reason, and he knew precisely what he was doing when he prepared the statement which precipitated so much controversy." McCoy, after noting that contemporaries of the president, including Herbert Hoover, his successor, reached differing conclusions, asserts that "there was and still is no absolute proof of what Coolidge had in mind." In his autobiography, the former president wrote that "I had never wished to run in 1928 and had determined to make a public announcement at a sufficiently early date so that the party would have ample time to choose someone else. An appropriate occasion for that announcement seemed to be the fourth anniversary of my taking office." Certainly the president believed he had been clear and, as usual, concise. He offered no comment when he personally handed the announcement to the reporters.

The effect of the announcement was to encourage others to be more active in their campaigns. The eventual Republican nominee in 1928, Herbert Hoover, spoke to Coolidge on two occasions in that year in an effort to elicit further comment. Interested in entering the Ohio primary, Hoover asked the president if he, Coolidge, would be in that primary and was told that he would not. To Hoover's question about his own entry, the president answered, "Why not?" Two months later Hoover believed he had the backing of approximately 400 delegates of the 1,000 who would attend the convention. In another meeting with Coolidge, the candidate said that he would be happy to try to swing these delegates to the president, who replied: "If you have four hundred delegates, you better keep them." Hoover was apparently convinced that the president did not want to be renominated and pursued his own ultimately successful effort to become his party's candidate.

Whether or not Coolidge was pleased with Hoover's actions has been a subject of some comment. On the one hand, he is reported to have said: "That man [Hoover] has offered me unsolicited advice for six years, all of it bad!" and referred to Hoover as the "wonder boy." On the other hand, as McCoy notes, Hoover had remained in Coolidge's cabinet and was supported by the president in the 1928 election campaign.

On March 4, 1929, Coolidge's public career of more than twenty years ended, and he returned to Northampton, where he remained interested in politics. He wrote articles for popular magazines, published his autobiography in 1929, and in 1930 contracted with McClure Syndicate for a daily column to be headed "Thinking Things Over with Calvin Coolidge." Increasingly, in 1932, the former president said he felt "worn out." On January 5, 1933, after working at his office with his secretary on some correspondence, he went home and was shortly thereafter found dead of coronary thrombosis.

Many have attempted to evaluate the life and career of Calvin Coolidge. An examination of some of the literature on this public servant casts up some of the following attributes. Coolidge was decent, honest, and politically ambitious in the best sense of the word, with a circumscribed view of the world. He revered stability and largely accepted society and government as he found them. Even Claude Fuess, a staunch defender of the former president, declared that "Coolidge during his career displayed very little constructive imagination" and in his speeches no "evidence of broad vision stretching into the shadowy future." Coolidge had a successful public career in part because he was honest, decent, and hardworking, and in part because he appealed to a public that did not want politicians to demonstrate broad vision and imagination.

REFERENCES

Calvin Coolidge, *The Autobiography of Calvin Coolidge* (New York: Cosmopolitan Book Corporation, 1929); Claude M. Fuess, *Calvin Coolidge: The Man from Vermont* (Boston: Little, Brown, 1940); Claude M. Fuess, *Calvin Coolidge: Twenty Years After* (Worcester, Mass.: American Antiquarian Society, 1954); Donald R. McCoy, *Calvin Coolidge: The Quiet President* (New York: The Macmillan Company, 1967); Robert K. Murray, *The Politics of Normalcy: Governmental Theory and Practice in the Harding-Coolidge Era* (New York: W.W. Norton and Company, Inc., 1973); Robert K. Murray, *The Harding Era: Warren G. Harding and His Administra-*

tion (Minneapolis: The University of Minnesota Press, 1969); Thomas B. Silver, *Coolidge and the Historians* (Durham, N.C.: Carolina Academic Press for the Claremont Institute, 1982); William Allen White, *A Puritan in Babylon: The Story of Calvin Coolidge* (New York: The Macmillan Company, 1938); manuscript collections at the Library of Congress, Forbes Library in Northampton, Massachusetts, Amherst College, and Holy Cross College.

PAUL S. SILVER is professor of history at Johnson State College, Johnson, Vermont. He received his B.A. from Oberlin College and his M.A. and Ph.D. from the University of Pennsylvania. He has been at Johnson State College since 1971; previously he taught at Pennsylvania Military College (now Widener University) and the University of Akron. He has particular interests in the Progressive Movement and the New Deal. Also a clarinetist, Professor Silver is a member of the Vermont Philharmonic Orchestra and of Cadenza, a woodwind quintet. He has been a member of numerous pit orchestras accompanying musical theater productions.

CHARLES GATES DAWES (1865–1951)

Vice President, 1925–1929

(President Calvin Coolidge)

CHARLES GATES DAWES
(Library of Congress)

By Robert A. Waller

The inauguration of the vice president immediately preceding that of the president is usually a ritualistic, routine affair worth only a passing note in newspaper accounts describing the beginning of a new administration. Not so the festivities surrounding the inauguration of the thirtieth vice president, Charles Gates ("Hell and Maria") Dawes, on March 4, 1925. As a successful Chicago businessman, former comptroller of the currency, and former purchasing agent for the American Expeditionary Forces during World War I, Dawes used the occasion for a lengthy diatribe against the Senate's antiquated rules, especially the filibuster, which interfered with effective and efficient dispatch of the people's business. The Dawes proposals for the reform of the Senate captured national headlines that overshadowed the inaugural address of President

Calvin Coolidge as he began his second term in the White House. This incident foretold the political chasm between Capitol Hill and 1600 Pennsylvania Avenue in the mid-1920s. What circumstances and experiences caused this set of conditions to prevail during the next four years?

Charles Gates Dawes was born on August 27, 1865, in Marietta, Washington County, Ohio, the oldest son of Rufus Republic Dawes (a lumber merchant, Civil War general, and Republican member of Congress, 1881–83) and Mary Berman (Gates) Dawes. After receiving his basic education at Marietta Academy, he attended Marietta College and earned a Bachelor of Arts degree in civil engineering in 1884 with auxiliary interests in music, especially flute and piano. At the age of nineteen, he studied law at the Cincinnati Law School, earning the LL.B. in 1886. Following admission to the Ohio bar that same year, Dawes continued to work for the Marietta, Columbus and Northern Ohio Railway Company as a civil engineer. Eventually he became chief engineer for construction.

On the invitation of James W. Dawes (his father's cousin and former governor of Nebraska), Dawes moved to Lincoln in April 1887. Admitted to the bar there, he began his legal practice with the firm of Dawes, Coffroth and Cunningham. His law office was two floors above that of William Jennings Bryan. The two exchanged political barbs occasionally but became lifelong friends with ideas firmly planted in opposing party platforms. Bryan's brother Charles (later Nebraska governor and 1924 Democratic vice-presidential candidate) was also a member of this frontier community. Another of Dawes's Lincoln acquaintances was a young second lieutenant instructor in military affairs at the University of Nebraska named John J. Pershing. In addition to the legal practice, Dawes became vice president of the Lincoln Packing Company and a director of the American Exchange National Bank, forerunners of his commercial interests.

On January 24, 1889, Dawes married Caro D. Blymyer (1865–1957), a Cincinnati girl whom he had met while a law school student.

They had two children, Rufus Fearing and Carolyn, and adopted two, Dena McCutcheon and Virginia. Rufus, a Princeton student, drowned in a Lake Geneva boating accident on September 5, 1912. Among the many philanthropies associated with the future vice president was the Rufus Fearing Dawes Hotel for Destitute Men, with facilities in Chicago and in Boston. In memory of his mother, Dawes also established the Mary Dawes Hotel for Women in Chicago, which provided bed, bath, and breakfast in clean, inexpensive quarters for the impoverished. Another Dawes philanthropy was the Chicago Grand Opera Company.

While his Lincoln law practice proved lucrative, Dawes's successes in the administrative reorganization of faltering companies led him to move to the Chicago area in January 1895. Though he lived in Evanston, Chicago became his operations base, and subsequent careers would take him to Washington (four times), France, and Great Britain. Dawes's early business interests included real estate ventures and the accumulation of a public utilities empire centered on the North Shore Gas Company in 1900. Ultimately, Metropolitan Gas and Electric Company became a holding company that owned seven companies with twenty-eight plants in ten states.

In a state known for its factionalism within the two major political parties, Dawes's Republicanism brought a fresh perspective. Through his congressman father, Charles Dawes had met Mark Hanna and William McKinley. Although only twenty-nine and an Illinois resident for only two years, Dawes volunteered to rally Illinois Republican support on behalf of McKinley's presidential nomination in 1896. He delivered the four delegates-at-large to McKinley.

President McKinley rewarded Dawes with appointment as comptroller of the currency, a position in which he served from 1898 to 1901. Dawes had published an eighty-three-page tract on *The Banking System of the United States* in 1894 in which he supported the gold standard and argued for better public comprehension of the need for "proper understanding of the monetary problems of the day." From this perspective

Dawes proposed banking structure reforms that would obviate the conditions that had caused the depression of the 1890s. He also collected $25 million due to the federal government from various national banks that had failed.

In October 1901, Dawes resigned from the comptroller's position to campaign for election to the U.S. Senate from Illinois. State legislatures selected upper house members to Congress until 1913. Dawes believed that he could be nominated and then elected with the McKinley administration's help, with assistance from federal officeholders, and with the personal friendship of Hanna and McKinley, but the assassination of McKinley changed the political equation. Theodore Roosevelt was not friendly with Hanna; Dawes's hopes for a senatorial role faded.

Rebuffed by the party kingmakers, Dawes withdrew from the race and poured his considerable energies and talents into business and banking affairs. From 1902 until 1921 he served as president of the Central Trust Company of Illinois (the Dawes Bank). Then he served as chairman of the board until he went to Washington as vice president in 1925.

In 1915, Dawes published *Essays and Speeches*, a 400-page collection of his observations on the nation's economy, trust policy, the Federal Reserve System, political reform, and public philanthropy. His conservative views were kept in the public eye and his business ventures prospered.

Then World War I intervened. Despite his age (fifty-two), he volunteered for the army artillery. Ultimately his enlistment was accepted, and he was commissioned a major in the Seventeenth Engineer Corps (Railway) on June 11. Promoted to lieutenant colonel on July 16, Dawes was in one of the advance units of the American Expeditionary Forces sent directly to France. Commanding General John J. Pershing plucked Dawes from the ranks on September 27, 1917, to coordinate all purchases for the U.S. Army overseas. Commissioned a colonel on January 16, 1918, and a brigadier general on October 15, 1918, Dawes carefully regulated purchases to avoid inflated prices and duplicate buying. Following the war he published a two-volume *Journal of the Great War* (1921) which logged his wartime experiences as chief of supply procurement for the A.E.F. under Pershing.

When the Allied and Associated Nations' forces were unified under Marshal Ferdinand Foch, Dawes became the U.S. member of the Military Board of Allied Supply, continuing to work his business magic in this inter-nation environment. For these services he received the Distinguished Service Medal awarded by his own government and several military recognitions as well from the Belgian, British, French, and Italian governments. At the war's end, Dawes became a member of the Allied Liquidation Commission. While most doughboys headed home, he remained behind in an administrative capacity to dispose of the accumulated war materials and supplies. The task completed to his satisfaction, Dawes resigned from the Army on August 31, 1919. He held a brigadier general position in the Officer's Reserve Corps from 1921 to 1926.

Dawes returned to the United States to resume direct responsibility for his far-flung business interests. Politically he was a supporter of Woodrow Wilson's campaign to ratify the Versailles Treaty and to participate in the League of Nations. Understandably, Dawes was drawn into the inevitable postwar investigation of military spending. By taking a closer look at how the Democrats had conducted the war, Republican congressmen hoped to expose graft and corruption. Dawes went before the committee, not as a guilty-looking Democrat or profiteer but as a justifiably outraged, hand-waving, shouting ex-general who happened also to be a Republican. His seven hours of testimony in 1921 did much to take the wind out of the investigation.

His congressional inquisitors asked him many questions concerning the price the United States had paid for mules from Spain. Dawes roared this response, as stated in the *New York Times* of February 3 and 4, 1921:

> Sure we paid. We didn't dicker. Why, man alive, we had to win the war. We would have paid horse prices for sheep if sheep could have pulled artillery to the front. Oh, it's all right now to say we bought too much vinegar and too many

cold chisels, but we saved the civilization of the world. Damn it all, the business of an army is to win the war, not to quibble around with a lot of cheap buying. Hell and Maria, we weren't trying to keep a set of books, we were trying to win the war!

Long after this committee is dead and gone and forgotten the achievements of the American army will stand as an everlasting blaze of glory. You have tried to make a mountain out of a molehill. The people are tired of war talk and fault finding. The army was American, neither Republican [n]or Democratic.

From that day forward, he was known as "Hell and Maria" Dawes. In point of fact, he had said "Helen Maria" (an expletive he was fond of using in polite company), but he spoke so rapidly that the stenographers did not catch the distinction.

After this episode, Dawes's prominence catapulted him into consideration for the Republican presidential nomination in 1920. The men in the famous smoke-filled room turned instead to Ohio's Senator Warren G. Harding. Dawes declined an offer to become Harding's secretary of the treasury but instead accepted appointment for one year as first director of the Bureau of the Budget, with promises of unfaltering presidential support. Harding finally achieved in the Budget and Accounting Act of 1921 what Theodore Roosevelt, William Howard Taft, and Woodrow Wilson had sought in their efforts to rationalize the fiscal operations of the federal government. As Dawes recorded in his published notes, *The First Year of the Budget of the United States* (1923), the purpose of the Bureau was " . . . to inaugurate a system of coordinating business control over the various departments and independent establishments of government which, for one hundred and thirty-two years, have been almost completely decentralized." From the start it was clear that the bureau would deal with no question of policy "except that of economy and efficiency." It was to be "impersonal, impartial and non-political." With characteristic energy and zeal from Room 372½ in the Treasury building, Dawes threw himself into the task of organizing a new unit of presidential administration. Drawing upon his Washington acquaintances from the turn of the century and his

military compatriots, he quickly assembled the staff and established the principles under which the bureau would operate. At this time, he acquired the habit of smoking the underslung pipe that became his trademark thereafter.

True to his word, Dawes resigned in July 1922 after launching an agency that was to continue virtually unchanged until the Reorganization Act of 1939. Although he hoped to return to his Chicago business pursuits full-time, he instead at Coolidge's request became chairman of a League committee of experts that was addressing the unsettled question of war reparations. What came to be known as the Dawes Plan (announced on April 9, 1924) suggested methods of balancing the German budget and stabilizing that nation's currency. Undoubtedly this is the work for which Dawes is most noted. It gained him the Nobel Prize for Peace in 1925.

This international prominence enhanced Dawes's credentials for the Republican vice-presidential nomination in 1924. As with most incumbent presidents, the Coolidge nomination was virtually assured. "Silent Cal" left the choice of a running mate to the Republican convention. The initial choice was Illinois former Governor Frank O. Lowden (whom Dawes supported), an ardent spokesperson for the plight of the midwestern farmer. Since the party platform on this issue was unsatisfactory to the Prairie State's ex-governor, he declined by telegraph.

The party chieftains consulted about an alternative candidate while the convention recessed. Among the remaining contenders were Senator Charles Curtis of Kansas (the floor whip); Secretary of Commerce Herbert C. Hoover; and Dawes, whose chairmanship of the Reparations Commission made him newsworthy and noteworthy. Dawes, selected on the third ballot (682½ votes to Hoover's 334½), recorded in *Notes as Vice President* (1935) that he gained the honor ". . . notwithstanding the efforts of the Chairman of the Republican National Committee who . . . endeavored to unite his followers for Hoover." It is significant that Dawes was not blessed by President Coolidge. Distant, if not actually hostile, relations between the Republican standard-bearers could be forecast.

In spite of possible tensions, the Republican nominees conferred in Washington on July 1 with Party Chairman William M. Butler. A campaign strategy was agreed upon with the president, partially due to inclination and partly due to Calvin, Jr.'s tragic death, staying close to the White House or to Vermont. Dawes assumed the bulk of the speech making and traveling. The content of the vice president's acceptance speech was established, and the law-and-order theme became the campaign's leitmotiv. Dawes reported traveling 15,000 miles and making 108 speeches on behalf of the Grand Old Party.

Interestingly, Dawes virtually ignored Democratic candidates John W. Davis and Charles W. Bryan, his acquaintance from Lincoln days. His focus instead was on the third-party candidacies of Robert M. La Follette and Burton K. Wheeler. Especially repugnant to Dawes was a Progressive Party platform plank urging an Constitutional amendment to give Congress the power to override judicial review of legislation. Dawes prophesied to his audiences: "The bill of inalienable rights, the general recognition of which is the foundation of civilization, would be, under the La Follette proposition, at the mercy of Congress." While reporters covering his campaign tired of the repetitious theme, Dawes retorted: "There is one issue in this campaign, and only one. That is whether you stand on the rock of common sense with Calvin Coolidge, or in the sinking sands of Socialism."

Another of the themes in Dawes's campaign swings was opposition to the Ku Klux Klan, a topic that Chairman Butler encouraged him to avoid. He spoke out vigorously, sometimes to the discomfort of local dignitaries seated behind him on the platform, who would have preferred to ignore the subject. Typical are these remarks made at Augusta, Maine, on August 24, 1924:

Appeals to racial, religious, or class prejudice by minority organizations are opposed to the welfare of all peaceful and civilized communities. Our Constitution stands for religious tolerance and freedom.

I have told you why I am opposed to the Klan.

Take what I say into your hearts and consciences and think it over calmly. However it may be with the mind, there is no acrimony in conscience.

Such a stand was not popular in some circles at that time, but it indicated Dawes's independence and spirit of fairness.

"Keeping Cool with Coolidge" was the order of the day. Neither the Democrats nor the Progressives were able to lay the Harding scandals at the doors of Coolidge or Dawes. The voters affirmed their support for prosperity on November 5, 1924, by providing a Republican landslide: a popular plurality of 7 million votes and an electoral college majority of 382 votes to 136 for Davis-Bryan. La Follette and Wheeler garnered 4.5 million popular votes, but only 13 electoral votes from La Follette's home state of Wisconsin.

Normally the period between election and inauguration is one of speculation as the press and the public contemplate the new administration's direction. In those days the vice president's role did not loom large in the considerations, but Vice President-elect Dawes made his wishes known. President Harding had established the practice of asking Vice President Coolidge to attend cabinet meetings. President-by-accident Coolidge had admitted that such exposure was helpful when he was unexpectedly thrust into the Oval Office. The Constitution itself makes no provision for a cabinet, let alone a role for the vice president in attending.

When faced with the prospect of being invited to attend cabinet meetings, Dawes rebelled in a very public and embarrassing manner. In his *Diary* Dawes wrote: "After my election, not knowing how Coolidge felt about it, I wrote him stating my views on the subject." He further explained:

Long before my election and before I had any thought that I would ever have an individual interest in the question, I said the plan . . . was unwise. The Cabinet and those who sit with it always should do so at the discretion and inclination of the President. Our Constitution so intended it. The relationship is confidential, and the selection of a confidant belongs to him who would be injured by the abuse of confidence, however unintentional. No precedent should be established which creates a different and arbitrary method of selection.

Should I sit . . . the precedent might prove injurious to the country. With it fixed, some future President might face the embarrassing alternative of inviting one whom he regarded as unsuitable into his private conferences or affronting him in the public eye by denying him what had been generally considered his right.

My friendship and high respect for President Coolidge are such that it would be personally a pleasure to sit . . . but I will not do so because, in my judgment, it involves a wrong principle.

Unexplainedly, Dawes did not write personally and privately to his superior to forestall an expected but nonexistent invitation. Rather, he made his views known through a press interview on February 5, 1925, as reported in the *New York Times* even before the letter reached the president. The editorial pandemonium that resulted reflected no credit on the vice president but increased the strain between the chief executive and his supposed right hand. Coolidge followed his custom of silence, so the controversy was one-sided, though prolonged.

Beyond Dawes's public expression of constitutional qualms about the role of the vice president vis-à-vis the cabinet, his publications offer no insight about the further rationale behind his position. Reporters speculated about the hidden agenda. Among the best of these is the analysis presented by Arthur Sears Herring in the *Chicago Tribune* (November 27, 1924), which listed these considerations: (1) as a potential presidential candidate in 1928 Dawes did not wish to be too closely associated with Coolidge's policies should there be a need to criticize them in the future; (2) given Dawes's reputation for pungent and spontaneous expressions of views, Coolidge had no desire to upset the tranquility of his meetings with an irascible competitor; (3) philosophical differences of opinion on such issues as agricultural subsidies and veterans' bonuses made Dawes unpopular in the Coolidge inner circle; and (4) practical experience had suggested to Coolidge that friction

would be reduced if executive and legislative spheres remained separate. Whatever the real reason in the matter, the gratuitous manner in which the issue had been aired served to strain relations between Dawes and Coolidge. Rarely has such an unwarranted slight been made to a president by a vice president.

President Coolidge's comments in his *Autobiography* (1929) suggest that Dawes was not invited to sit with the cabinet because he was perceived to be both indiscreet and insubordinate. In spite of Dawes's strict constructionist approach and Coolidge's personality assessment, the practice of the vice president sitting with the cabinet was resumed by the Herbert Hoover–Charles Curtis team and by every succeeding presidential administration. This tactic to enhance the role of the vice president was only interrupted, not derailed, by Dawes's very indiscreet argument for the status quo.

The next clash between the federal government's two principals occurred on inauguration day, March 4, 1925. Coolidge anticipated the day as the culmination of a thirty-year career in public life and savored the opportunity to create an agenda and atmosphere for his own administration. Dawes, on the other hand, saw the occasion of the "other" inauguration as an opportunity to bring his businesslike approach to conducting the affairs of the U.S. Senate over which he was to preside. Unfortunately, a blustery inaugural address from the new vice president overshadowed Coolidge's day in the sun.

Never having held elective office or presided over a deliberative legislative body, the new Senate presiding officer endeavored to establish his leadership style. As reported in the March 4, 1925, *Congressional Record* he noted:

> What I say upon entering this office should relate to its administration and the conditions under which it is administered. Unlike the vast majority of deliberative and legislative bodies, the Senate does not elect its presiding officer. He is designated for his duties by the Constitution of the United States.

So far, so good.

Dawes continued that he was elected by the people of the United States. Thus he viewed his trust to be opposed on behalf of the people to the implementation of Senate Rule XXII, the one concerning a filibuster. He continued:

> That rule which, at times enables Senators to consume in oratory those last precious minutes of a session needed for momentous decisions, places in the hands of one or a minority of Senators a greater power than the veto power exercised under the Constitution by the President of the United States.

For nearly twenty minutes, he vigorously and pungently attacked the rules conducive to filibustering. He concluded with the declaration that: "Reform in the present rules is demanded, not only by American public opinion, but, I venture to say, in the individual consciences of a majority of the members of the Senate itself." As presiding officer, Dawes considered it his duty to call attention to defective methods in the conduct of Senate business.

Reporters noted an "icy silence" in the Senate chamber when Dawes finished his tirade. If the senators did not appreciate the tongue-lashing about their archaic rules, the nation's reporters applauded the good copy "Hell and Maria" Dawes had provided them. Dawes proceeded to add insult to injury. The customary practice following the remarks had been for the vice president to call the thirty-two newly elected senators in groups of four to the Senate well for an individual inauguration ceremony to facilitate public relations opportunities and to sign the roll as duly sworn members of the new Congress. Tiring of this tedious practice after the second group of four, the vice president called all the remaining senators to the well for administration of the oath en masse. In his haste to conclude the proceedings, Dawes neglected to have the roll inscribed. He endeavored to inject some much needed efficiency into the operations of the government, but he succeeded in offending Senate sensibilities.

During the ensuing four years, Dawes returned frequently to this efficiency theme in speeches and articles. While he viewed his attack on the cloture system with a sense of achievement, neither the Senate nor the public moved to make or demand changes. His valedictory comments on March 4, 1929, gave him one last opportunity to chide his colleagues when he administered the oath of office to his successor, Charles Curtis. Dawes again urged the easing of the cloture rules. His brief remarks ended with a cryptic, good-natured phrase, "I take nothing back." Scarcely two minutes later, the new vice president assured his former colleagues that he was "not one of the makers of the law nor is he consulted about the rules governing your actions." The Dawes tilt at the windmill of Senate procedures had come to naught, for the rule remains virtually unchanged.

However, the Dawes remarks had other consequences. Senators and Capitol reporters could think and talk of nothing else but Dawes's campaign to streamline the operations of the nation's oldest deliberative body. President Coolidge's own inauguration ceremony and his carefully crafted address were quickly overlooked and easily forgotten. The focus this inauguration day in news headlines and coverage was this version of the "Dawes Plan" for revamping the U.S. Senate. Another source of irritation between the president and the vice president was identified. Although Coolidge professed in his *Autobiography* never to have been perplexed by the Senate rules, at the time the president clearly thought the timing of the issue was inauspicious.

Excitement over the Dawes's declaration of war on the Senate rules continued as the president sent over a batch of administrative appointments for approval. When Coolidge named Attorney General Harlan Fiske Stone to the Supreme Court, he nominated Charles B. Warren of Michigan as his successor. Democrats and insurgent Republicans united to oppose the confirmation on the ground that Warren was too closely tied to the Sugar Trust, which would make him an unsuitable candidate to enforce the nation's laws against combinations in restraint of trade. The debate was long and fierce, occupying the first several days on the calendar of the new Congress.

As presiding officer of the Senate, the vice president breaks tie votes. On the average a vice president exercises this privilege twice in a term. On March 10, the debate on the Warren appointment continued. Dawes was notified that at least six more senators wished to be heard on the issue that day. After checking with both floor leaders, Curtis and Joseph T. Robinson, who assured him that no vote would be taken later that day, Dawes went to the new Willard Hotel, then the home of vice presidents, and took an after-lunch nap.

In the Senate, however, the action quickened. Curtis, now believing that the savage assaults on Warren were having an impact, decided to press for an immediate vote. As the roll call progressed, it became apparent that the result would be close. E. Ross Bartley, the vice president's secretary, telephoned to request that Dawes return to the Senate in case there should be a tie. When the result was a 40 to 40 deadlock, the Republicans tried several parliamentary maneuvers to delay, but their efforts proved unavailing. The death blow was given when Lee S. Overman of North Carolina, the lone Democrat who had voted for confirmation, announced a change in his vote. By the time Dawes arrived in the chamber, there was no tie to break. The vote now stood at 39 for confirmation and 41 against. For the first time since Andrew Johnson's presidency, the Senate had rejected a cabinet appointment.

Privately, Coolidge held Dawes accountable, but publicly he said nothing. In a rare show of temper and tenacity, Coolidge resubmitted the nomination six days later. This time Warren was rejected, 39 for and 46 against. Dawes never had the opportunity to make amends for his absence; indeed, it may have been less than coincidence that Dawes was asleep at the switch. At the 1924 Republican convention, the one vote in the Michigan delegation against Dawes and for Hoover was cast by delegate Charles B. Warren. It is probably a curious happenstance but reporters wondered if there were substance in the speculation.

As can be imagined, Dawes suffered considerable ridicule and embarrassment over his failure to be present to support the administration's nominee. Having been lectured on decorum, duties, and responsibilities, the senators now reciprocated. Most clever of all was the needling presented by Senator George W. Norris of Nebraska in the March 12, 1925, *Congressional Record*. Recalling that Dawes was the great-great grandson of William Dawes, the forgotten patriot who rode with Paul Revere on that famous night in '75, Norris offered this parody based on "Sheridan's Ride":

> Hurrah, hurrah for Dawes!
> Hurrah, hurrah for this highminded man!
> And when his statue is placed on high,
> Under the dome of the Capitol sky,
> The great Senatorial temple of fame,
> There with the glorious general's name,
> Be it said, in letters both bold and bright:
> 'O, Hell and Maria, he has lost us the fight!'

The *New Republic* on March 25, 1925, was far more severe in its criticism. After describing the wild taxi ride up Pennsylvania Avenue, the editor concluded that: "It is extremely doubtful whether he will again be able to get himself taken seriously in political circles." Some wag added the indignity of hanging a sign on the Willard: "Dawes slept here!" Within five months the vice president had thrice placed himself beyond the pale when cooperation with the new administration was expected. It is little wonder that Dawes's four years as vice president are devoid of significant legislative or policy impact. Unlike his success as an administrator of great affairs, Dawes seemed ill suited to the legislative halls.

Where the Dawes name figures prominently in the years 1925–29, it frequently appears in opposition to administration stands. For example, Dawes favored the soldiers' bonus legislation, which Coolidge found it necessary to veto as an unprincipled raid on the federal treasury. The greatest source of irritation over policy arose over the plight of American farmers and the role of the federal government in providing relief. The Republican Party platform of 1924 had recognized that a farm problem existed and promised to study the issue to achieve a solution. Coolidge elected to ignore Dawes's recommendations for select committee membership to explore the issue.

The farm bloc, meanwhile, rallied around the McNary-Haugen legislation as offering the best hope for relief from depressed prices due to surpluses. Without publicly proclaiming his assent to this particular legislation, Dawes gained a reputation for providing an office headquarters for proponents of parity prices and surplus disposal abroad. In February 1927 Dawes's parliamentary intervention enabled the McNary-Haugen bill to come to a vote; it passed the Senate and met the inevitable veto from the White House. Coolidge did not appreciate the fact that he was forced to take a negative action on this political hot potato. He faulted the senators and Dawes for having passed the buck when the proffered legislation could have remained dormant in Congress. Dawes's usual conservatism on policy matters with budgetary implications was dampened when it came to matters affecting farmers and veterans. Expressing support for these two groups could prove beneficial if he had aspirations in 1928 to retain the vice presidency or to run for the presidency.

The presidential political picture for 1928 became both clearer and clouded when Coolidge announced on the fourth anniversary of his succession to the presidency that he did not "choose" to run in 1928. Political pundits were unclear whether he meant it or wished to be drafted for another term. In an interview long after the fact, Dawes told Chicago historian William T. Hutchinson that "a man close to Coolidge" had reported that the president "ardently desired" the nomination and was "sore as a pup" when the Republican convention bypassed him. Acting on this assumption, Dawes made little effort to seek the presidency himself, although he doubtless would have been willing to serve if nominated.

In the 1928 Republican convention, Dawes received four votes (one from Illinois, one from Ohio, and two from Missouri) for president. He figured more prominently in the vice-presidential selection because he was the incumbent. The inner circle at the convention agreed that Dawes should have a chance to "qualify" for the renomination. The principal sticking point was his attitude toward the resolution of the farm problem. With Hooverites dominating the convention, the GOP platform refused to endorse McNary-Haugenism. Instead, there was a general palliative that appropriate but alternative relief measures would be sought. When questioned by the kingmakers on the issue, Dawes agreed that Coolidge's vetoes had probably shelved the opportunity to pass the McNary-Haugen principles for the next four years. When asked to make a public declaration to that effect, Dawes's hackles rose and he refused to abandon this farm relief measure. Thus, his name was eliminated from the eligibles. The convention then turned to Hoover's rival, Charles Curtis, who had been most active in the stop-Hoover movement.

After a term as presiding officer of the Senate, Dawes came to respect the institution in spite of its perceived flaws. As a valedictory summary of the role he had played, he wrote the following:

> The office is what the man in it makes it—which applies to all public offices. The fact that the Vice President in the Senate Chamber cannot enter into debate is considered a disadvantage, yet for that reason he is removed from the temptation to indulge in the pitiable quest of that double objective so characteristic of many Senate speeches—the placating of general public opinion and of an opposing local constituency at the same time. For his prestige as a presiding officer, it is to his advantage that he neither votes nor speaks in the Senate Chamber. Outside . . . his position as Vice President gives him a hearing by the general public as wide as that accorded any Senator, other things being equal. If he lacks initiative, courage, or ideas, he of course will be submerged; but that is true also of a Senator or any other parliamentary member.
>
> Whatever may be said to the contrary, as anyone discovers who occupies the office, the

people hold it in great respect. While I shall serve eight months more . . . and make future mistakes, I see the prospect of closing my public career at least without discredit. The occupancy of a public office, unless decorated with public respect, is a curse to anyone.

There were no future "mistakes," so the self assessment showed a credible record.

Charles Gates Dawes's public service was not yet ended. Toward the close of his vice presidential term, he had accepted an invitation from President Horacio Vásquez of the Dominican Republic to serve as chairman of an economic commission that would study and revise that new republic's finances. This he did within a month with the aid of a team of U.S. experts. Even before this task was concluded, President Hoover appointed Dawes as ambassador to Great Britain in April 1929. In the Court of St. James, he became involved in the preliminary discussions leading to the London Conference on Naval Limitation in 1930. After resigning this diplomatic post in 1932, Dawes became deeply involved in assuring the financial success of the Chicago World's Fair, known as the Century of Progress.

The Hoover administration was not yet through with his services. As an anti-Depression measure, the Congress had established the Reconstruction Finance Corporation in February 1932. The RFC aimed to provide loans to the states for relief and to provide direct governmental loans to collapsing businesses. Hoover convinced Dawes to accept the presidency of this precursor of the New Deal. He resigned on June 6, 1932, to return to Chicago to protect his banking interests, now known as Central Republic Bank and Trust Company, from a series of consolidations, including getting a controversial $90 million RFC loan for his endangered bank, a loan repaid in full by 1944.

During the 1930s and 1940s, Dawes busied himself with several publications recounting his experiences, including *Notes as Vice President* (1935), *A Journal of Reparations* (1939), *A Journal as Ambassador to Great Britain* (1939), and *A Journal of the McKinley Years* (1951). He served as Chairman of the Board for Chicago's City National Bank and Trust Company from 1932 until his death in Evanston on April 23, 1951, at the age of eighty-five. He was buried in Chicago's Rosehill Cemetery. With a certain irony, the year 1951 experienced a revival of his 1911 musical composition "Melody in A Major"; Now with lyrics and a new title, "It's All in the Game," the song became one of the most popular of that year.

Among historians and political scientists, the ranking and rating of presidents is a professional avocation, but similar attention has not been accorded vice presidents unless elevated to the Oval Office. The typical rating system ranges from great, near great, above average, and below average, to failure. Based on the evidence, a rating of "above average" seems appropriate when restricting the judgment to the vice-presidential years when Dawes exhibited a forceful, independent, and efficient spirit as the Senate's presiding officer. If his total career as author, banker, servant of four presidents, winner of a Nobel Peace Prize, and administrator par excellence were included, then the evaluation becomes "near great." In the pantheon of vice presidents since 1789, Charles Gates Dawes stands among the luminaries.

REFERENCES

Carl William Ackerman, *Dawes—the Doer!* (New York: ERA Publications, 1924); Paul Roscoe Leach, *That Man Dawes* (Chicago: The Reilly and Lee Co., 1930); John Erwin Pixton, "The Early Career of Charles G. Dawes [to 1905]" (Ph.D. diss, University of Chicago, 1952); Richard Garrett Sherman, "Charles G. Dawes: An Entrepreneurial Biography, 1865–1951" (Ph.D. diss, State University of Iowa, 1960); and Bascom N. Timmons, *Portrait of an American: Charles G. Dawes* (New York: Henry Holt and Co., 1953).

Books by Dawes: *The Banking System of the United States and Its Relation to the Money and Business of the Country* (Chicago: Rand, McNally and Co., 1894); *The First Year of the Budget of the United States* (New York: Harper and Bros., 1923); *Essays and Speeches* (Boston: Houghton Mifflin Co., 1915); *A Journal as Ambassador to Great Britain* (New York: Macmillan Co., 1939); *A Journal of the Great War*, 2 vols.

(Boston: Houghton Mifflin Co., 1921); *A Journal of the McKinley Years* (Chicago: Lakeside Press, 1950); *A Journal of Reparations* (London: Macmillan, 1939); *How Long Prosperity?* (Chicago: A.N. Marquis, 1937); *Notes as Vice President, 1928–1929* (Boston: Little, Brown and Co., 1935); Charles G. Dawes Papers at Northwestern University Library include 20,000 letters by Dawes, 10,000 letters to him, and journals from 1887 to 1907.

ROBERT A. WALLER recently retired as professor of history and dean of the College of Liberal Arts at Clemson University in South Carolina where he had been since 1981. Before that, he taught history and was associate dean of Liberal Arts and Sciences at the University of Illinois at Champaign-Urbana.

CHARLES CURTIS (1860–1936)

Vice President, 1929–1933

(President Herbert Hoover)

CHARLES CURTIS
(Library of Congress)

By William E. Unrau

Charles Curtis was born in North Topeka, Kansas, on January 25, 1860, the son of Orren Arms Curtis, a Union soldier, and Ellen Gonville Pappan, a quarter-blood member of the Kansa (now Kaw) Indian tribe. As the only person of Indian blood and legal membership in an Indian tribe to be elevated to the second-highest office in the land, Curtis has been the focus of considerable interest as well as disagreement re-

garding the precise character of his genealogy. On occasion the popular press in the twentieth-century described him as one-quarter Kaw or as one-eighth Kaw and one-eighth Osage. The official Kaw tribal census taken in 1929, the year he assumed the vice presidency, listed Curtis as one-eighth Kaw, but in 1940 another tribal census changed it to one-quarter Kaw. In the interim, and over objections Curtis himself voiced soon after he relinquished the vice presidency, one scholar expressed certainty that Curtis was a half blood.

The available documents confirm that on the maternal side Curtis was a blood descendant of Kansa Chief White Plume, who married a daughter of the distinguished Osage Chief Pawhuska sometime prior to 1825. Unlike the majority of his tribe, White Plume came under the influence of Catholic missionaries from St. Louis and insisted that the marriage of one of his nieces to Louis Gonville, a French fur trader from Canada, be conducted by a Catholic priest in what White Plume considered a legitimate manner. The Kansa half-blood daughter of this union, Julie, was raised a Catholic and eventually married Louis Pappan, another French trader from the St. Louis area. Pappan entered the ferry business near the Kansa reservation and the future site of North Topeka, where his wife gave birth to Ellen (sometimes Helen), who was educated in a Catholic convent in St. Louis. In 1859, Ellen married Orren Arms Curtis, native of Indiana, and on January 25, 1860, the future vice president was born to them on Kaw Allotment Four, a tract of land in North Topeka granted to Ellen's mother by the Kansa Treaty of 1825. Charles Curtis was thus an eighth-blood Kaw with, perhaps, a modest Osage heritage, and by Indian Office standards of the day, a legal member of the Kaw tribe.

Ellen Pappan Curtis saw to it that her infant son received a Catholic baptism in the St. Mary's Immaculate Conception Church on the Potawatomi reservation nearby. She also taught young Charles the French language and apparently was determined to raise him apart from the Kaw tribe, then located on a reservation some sixty miles west of North Topeka. Her untimely death in 1863 altered the situation dramatically. A few months after Ellen's death Orren Curtis married but soon divorced Rachel Hatch. Perhaps deeming it necessary to remove himself from the setting of his recent bereavement and domestic difficulties, he secured an officer's appointment in the Fifteenth Kansas Cavalry for service against the Confederacy in Missouri and Arkansas. Thus at age three Charles and his older sister Permelia were placed in their maternal grandmother, Permelia Hubbard Curtis's care; with her husband William and their family, who had followed Orren from Indiana to Kansas Territory in 1860. While her husband engaged in Indian land speculation in the North Topeka vicinity, Permelia ruled her family (including her young Indian grandson) with stern dedication. As Charles Curtis's sister recalled years later, membership in the Republican Party and the Methodist Church were seen by the grandmother as prerequisites to the good life on earth as well as to eternal salvation. In 1866, however, young Charles was abruptly placed in the care of Julie Gonville Pappan, his maternal grandmother, on the Kaw reservation at Council Grove.

Why Charles was sent to live with his Indian grandmother is difficult to determine. The Civil War was over and the Council Grove reservation was dominated by full-bloods alien to their mixed-blood relatives in eastern Kansas. Certainly there were few Republicans and even fewer Methodists among the Kaw traditionalists. The most plausible explanation is that in 1866 there were rumors of an impending Kaw removal treaty, one that once and for all might settle their tribal land affairs in Kansas. With the possibility of a generous financial settlement, it was desirable for Charles and his sister to be reservation residents, thus guaranteeing their legal tribal membership and qualifying them for annuity disbursements. Or it simply may have been a case of the two grandmothers wishing to share in the expense and responsibilities of raising the young mixed bloods. Whatever the case, Charles Curtis lived with his Indian grandmother until the Southern Cheyenne raid on the Kaw reservation in spring 1868.

On June 3, 1868, some 100 mounted Southern Cheyenne from the High Plains to the west appeared at Council Grove and heaped insults on the Kaws with whom they had been bickering for several years. A few shots were fired and shouts and insults from both sides continued for about four hours, but no one was injured. In fact there was no serious military danger because federal troops from nearby Fort Riley were prepared to intervene in case threats on either side turned to violence. The Cheyennes did steal some food and livestock from nearby non-Indian farms, but they later agreed to pay for the modest amount of plunder taken. Young Curtis was unaware of these details but in later years never wearied of challenging those who suggested that he had fled the reservation for fear of personal injury. To the contrary, he claimed that tribal leaders gave him the responsibility of traveling alone and on foot to North Topeka to alert Kansas authorities and the mixed bloods of the Cheyenne attack. The records indicate that Kansas Governor Samuel Crawford was informed of the attack by Joseph James, Kaw half-blood interpreter, under orders of Kaw Agent E.S. Stover. James, a distant relative of Curtis, apparently took the young mixed-blood with him on his mission to Topeka and to the less perilous home of William and Permelia Curtis. Certainly these events contributed to Curtis's developing aversion for traditionalist reservation life—an aversion that intensified in the face of his father's enlistment in the Nineteenth Kansas Cavalry later that year for military action against the tribe that had "attacked" his Kaw relatives at Council Grove.

Excluding some hesitation before he decided, in 1874, to stay in Topeka rather than join his tribe on a new reservation in future Oklahoma, Curtis's interest and involvement with his tribe or with Indian affairs in general were minimal until he entered national politics two decades later. Yet, his name remained on the Kaw annuity roll until 1878, when it was officially deleted by the Indian Office for his having failed to reside with his people in Indian Territory. Even so, he continued to retain the status of a legal Kaw for the reason that his maternal grandmother was so designated by the Kansa Treaty of 1825.

Curtis attended common school in North Topeka and worked on weekends as a hack driver and fruit salesman in the railyards near his grandfather's hotel. During the summer months, he also rode as a jockey at county fairs in Kansas and at racetracks in Indian Territory and Texas. In 1876, he entered Topeka High School and in 1879 began to read law under Topeka attorney Aderial H. Case. Soon he was handling some of Case's minor court appearances and in 1881, at age twenty-one, the future vice president was certified by the Kansas bar. Criminal law became his specialty and the Republican Party his political preference, as it was of most Topekans of that time. On November 27, 1884, Curtis married Anna E. Baird of Topeka, to which union were born two daughters and one son: Permelia, Harry, and Leona, in that order.

Following his election as Shawnee County Attorney in 1884, Curtis's rigid enforcement of the recently passed (1880) Kansas prohibition amendment brought the young politician to Republican leaders' attention in the Jayhawk state. Illicit saloon keepers in Topeka had supported Curtis's election in 1884 on the belief that as an Indian he surely was also against prohibition and thus would go easy on them; in fact, he virtually ended the illegal flow of alcohol in Topeka and in 1886 was easily reelected to the Shawnee County prosecutor's office. In the meantime he had organized a home-talent theatrical company to stage several well-attended renditions of the famous antidrinking play *Ten Nights in a Barroom*, which spoke well of his political savvy and ambition in a state where the Republican Party was reaping great dividends on the volatile prohibition issue. Years later, he recalled how important his Grandmother Curtis's counsel was at this point in his political career.

In the 1892 election that saw Kansas cast its vote for the Populist James B. Weaver and elect a Populist legislature and governor, Curtis made headline news by being elected to Congress on the Republican ticket, representing Kansas's old Fourth District. It was a dramatic victory for the conservative Curtis and a testimony to his remarkable talent for working what William Allen White termed the human side of politics. White, who knew Curtis well, recalled that issues never interested or bothered the Indian. Indeed, said White, in all his life he had never encountered a politician who could better soothe a hostile audience with a smile, a handshake, piercing dark eyes, and seemingly endless small talk at strictly the human level of communication. Curtis always carried a book containing the names of his constituents, which he carefully memorized prior to a political appearance so that he could address audience members by first name and know something about their jobs, marriages, children, relatives, local gossip, and the like. According to one report from the nation's capital after he became a congressman, Curtis received 1,400 letters from folks back in Kansas in one 24-hour period and that with the help of a battalion of secretaries answered every one within the day, often including some personal note taken from his constituent book. One national reporter was persuaded that the famous Curtis handshake and smile could convince a stone image of sincere intent and that few politicians could match his palavering and small talk on the campaign stump or his ability to deflect serious questions regarding the pressing political issues of the day.

There was another side to the Curtis popularity, what some observers attributed to a kind of natural wisdom consequent to an indiscriminate fusion of Indian blood and white, at a time when the government's policy of forced assimilation and tribal dissolution was beginning to prompt public concerns regarding the decline—indeed, the demise—of the continent's first North Americans. In Congress, the hardworking mixed blood from Kansas exploited the "Vanishing American" belief with dramatic fineness. As a member of committees dealing with tribal annuities, Indian Territory legislation, development and exploitation of public lands vis-à-vis tribal claims dating back to the beginning of the republic, and, after 1903, as chairman of the powerful House Committee on Indian Affairs, Curtis assumed a dominant role in the present and future status of the American Indians.

He vigorously supported the distribution and allotment of tribal lands on grounds that individual land ownership would promote assimilation and provide Indian families with the means to engage in the competition that in his mind was the very cornerstone of the democratic process. He sponsored the Curtis Act of 1898, which abolished tribal courts and established the legal machinery for dissolution of the once-powerful Five Civilized Tribes in Indian Territory, and more than any other person in Congress, Curtis laid the foundation for Oklahoma statehood. He championed the legal rights of full-bloods and

mixed bloods alike and especially orphaned Indian children, while at the same time earning lucrative fees as an attorney representing energy companies that were swindling tribal governments of their natural resources in oil, timber, gas, and coal. He also assumed a leadership role in the legal destruction of his own tribe while gaining valuable allotments for himself and his children in the Kaw Allotment Bill of 1902.

With his shabby hat, ruffled trousers, and generally unkempt look, "Charley" (as both his supporters and critics often called him) preferred to work behind the scenes. For him, formal debate on the House floor was a waste of time and, more important, confusing to the public who neither knew nor could understand the inner workings of politics. Getting things done with a slap on the back and the sealing of a deal "without a fuss" in committee were the more efficient (and productive) tactics of democracy in action. As a fixer, concluded one Washington reporter shortly after the Kaw allotment business had been completed and Oklahoma statehood was a sure thing, Curtis clearly was one of the best in the business.

The fact is that Curtis was a conservative Republican regular who during the Populist and Progressive Eras was able by sheer power of personalized politics to ignore important economic and social issues. He furthered his political career by appearing to be a concerned protector of high tariffs and hard money against the threat of foreign competition, and he evoked the enduring nature of the capitalistic dream. He stood as living proof that an Indian could succeed at the highest levels of government, and when all else failed, he was not above waving the "bloody shirt" to remind his constituents that Lincoln, the Republican Party, and Jayhawk soldiers like his father had saved the Union from Democratic slave mongers in his beloved home state of Kansas.

Curtis remained in the U.S. House until 1907, when he was selected to fill the unexpired term of Kansas Senator Joseph R. Burton. He was returned to the Senate in 1914, where he served continuously until he became vice president in 1929. With his abiding interest in party organization and parliamentary detail, it surprised no one that he was selected to head the Senate Rules Committee or that he eagerly accepted the onerous responsibilities of party whip. At least at the onset of "normalcy" following World War I, keen political observers were not surprised that Curtis—vocal opponent of the League of Nations and avid supporter of high tariffs, restrictive immigration, and reduced federal spending—joined Henry Cabot Lodge, Frank Brandegee, and George Harvey in the smoke-filled room at the Republican convention in Chicago in 1920 to cast his lot for the darkhorse nomination of Warren G. Harding. With Senator Lodge's death one week after Coolidge's election in 1924, Curtis reached the apex of his political career by being selected Senate majority leader.

President Coolidge soon realized that congressional determination to act independently of the executive branch was a fact of political life and that Curtis's legislative support was indispensable to the executive strategy. So it was, again and again, that the so-called "silent" president relied on Curtis's support of the conservative agenda, which at bottom line was economy in government, disengagement at the international level, and support of private enterprise unobstructed by government interference—regardless of the economic implications for industrial workers or, for that matter, Curtis's own agrarian constituents, who were beginning to suffer severe economic depression several years prior to the stock crash of 1929.

No better example may be cited than Curtis's legislative support of the McNary-Haugen Farm Bill of 1927, a federal assistance program for the agrarian sector, and then his hearty upholding of Coolidge's veto of that same legislation soon thereafter. Thus when Coolidge announced in October 1927 that he would not seek another term, it came as no surprise that the mixed-blood Indian from Kansas had set his sights on the White House. He was confident that the Republicans owed him a presidential nomination for his hard work and party regularity, and that an anticipated deadlock between front-runners Herbert C. Hoover of California and Frank Lowden of Illinois might result in a draw in the 1928 Republican Convention in Kansas City—ironically, only a few miles from where Curtis's Indian grandmother more than half a century earlier had advised him to take the white man's way.

The convention's selection of Hoover was a severe blow to Curtis's personal ego and political ambition. Even though he stated publicly that to nominate Hoover would place a heavy burden upon the Republican Party, Curtis agreed to second place on the ticket after Hoover was selected on the first ballot. Curtis won easily on the vice-presidential ballot with 1,025 votes—215 more than Hoover had received for the presidency—thus indicating firm recognition of his tireless and dedicated service to his party. Subsequently, on the campaign stump, however, Curtis was no great asset to the Republican ticket. As in the past, he relied on platitudinous and repetitious speeches and handshaking rather than on addressing the complex economic and social issues of the times. Some dismissed him as an anachronistic Harding crony. Others made derogatory remarks regarding his heritage, and on one important whistlestop appearance in the Midwest (where his support was strongest), Curtis clumsily played into the hands of an angry farm heckler by angrily charging him with being too dumb to understand the nation's mounting economic crisis.

Even so, his close political supporters in Washington viewed him as a statesman of great accomplishment. Just prior to his taking the oath of office, Curtis was showered with praise by his good friend and colleague, Senator Reed Smoot of Utah. Smoot dwelt at length on Curtis's long and dedicated career in both houses of Congress, applauded Curtis for his industry and self-reliance, and emphasized how the Indian from Kansas had reached his zenith without benefit of money or powerful influences. Continued Smoot, as reported in the *Congressional Record*:

> Senator, now Vice President Curtis, began life amid primitive and humble surroundings. In his veins runs the blood of a Puritan Englishman, a French-Canadian, and an Indian maiden. That remarkable fusion brought forth the real American, whose career demonstrates the boundless possibilities in the land we love. . . . We will feel

more tolerant, more considerate, and more wise, as we look into his kindly eyes. We will profit by the example you have set for us.

As vice president, Curtis busied himself wielding the gavel over the Senate. He moved from a modest residential section in Washington to a ten-room suite in the Mayflower Hotel and hosted hundreds of official dinner parties. President Hoover invited him to attend cabinet meetings, but Curtis's advice was seldom sought—perhaps, as one observer noted, because he had little to offer. He sought to influence farm policy but with little success. He supported prohibition and protective tariffs, criticized the Federal Reserve System on grounds that its actions were too speculative and that it drained too much money from the country to the city, supported Hoover's dispersal of the Bonus Marchers, and in general called on the entire nation to support courts, the country, and the Constitution. The Depression, insisted Curtis repeatedly, was simply a natural occurrence that inevitably would run it course and give way to even greater prosperity.

During the presidential campaign of 1932, Curtis continued to deliver dull and plodding speeches that insisted that the Depression was nearly over and that prosperity was just around the corner if only the Hoover–Curtis team were retained in office. In fact, Curtis's campaign efforts had a negative effect on voters and played havoc with Hoover's attempt to win a second term.

When early election returns indicated a Democratic victory in 1932, Curtis stubbornly predicted that the Republicans would prevail in the end, and according to most accounts, he was genuinely shocked with the Hoover-Curtis de-feat. Even his home state of Kansas cast its support for Franklin D. Roosevelt, which may explain Curtis's decision to remain in Washington after the election to resume his law practice while maintaining a nominal association with his old law firm in Topeka. On February 8, 1936, the former vice president died of a heart attack in the Washington home of his half-sister, Dolly Gann (his wife Anna had preceded him in death in 1924). Final interment was in a Topeka cemetery, not far from where he was born three-quarters of a century earlier.

REFERENCES

William E. Unrau, "Charles Curtis: Politics of Allotment," in *Indian Lives: Essays on Nineteenth and Twentieth Century Native American Leaders*, L.G. Moses and Raymond Wilson, eds. (Albuquerque: University of New Mexico Press, 1985); William E. Unrau, *Mixed Bloods and Tribal Dissolution: Charles Curtis and the Quest for Indian Identity* (Lawrence: University Press of Kansas, 1989); William E. Unrau, "The Mixed-Blood Connection: Charles Curtis and Kaw Detribalization," in *Kansas and the West: Bicentennial Essays in Honor of Nyle H. Miller*, Forrest R. Blackburn, ed. (Topeka: Kansas State Historical Society, 1976); Don C. Seitz, *From Kaw Tepee to Capitol: The Life Story of Charles Curtis, Indian, Who Has Risen to High Estate* (New York: Frederick A. Stokes, 1928); Marvin Ewy, "Charles Curtis of Kansas: Vice President of the United States, 1929–1933," *Emporia State Research Studies*, 10 (December 1961) 1–58; Dolly Gann, *Dolly Gann's Book* (Garden City, N.Y.: Doubleday, Doran, 1933).

WILLIAM E. UNRAU is Endowment Association Distinguished Research Professor at Wichita State University, where he specializes in the history of Indian/White relations and the American West. His latest book is *White Man's Wicked Water: The Alcohol Trade and Prohibition in Indian County, 1802–1892* (University Press of Kansas, 1996).

JOHN NANCE GARNER (1868–1967)

Vice President, 1933–1941

(President Franklin D. Roosevelt)

JOHN NANCE GARNER
(Library of Congress)

By J. Kent Calder

Best remembered for his acerbic quips about the worthlessness of the office, John Nance Garner of Texas was one of this country's most powerful vice presidents. He served fifteen terms in the House of Representatives before his inauguration on March 4, 1933, and during his last term in the House he was elected Speaker. No vice president has ever brought to the office as much legislative experience and influence, and only one other man, Schyler Colfax, has ever served as both vice presi-

dent and Speaker of the House of Representatives. As President Franklin D. Roosevelt's liaison with Congress, Garner played a major role in pushing through the legislation that initiated the New Deal. Early in his second term, however, Garner split with the president, and their resulting feud led to Garner's unprecedented presidential challenge in 1940 and one of the great stories of American political history.

Born in a log cabin in Red River County in East Texas on November 22, 1868, two weeks

289

after the election of President Ulysses S. Grant and Vice President Colfax, Garner was the fourth in line with his name. His father, John Nance Garner III, had come to Texas from Tennessee at the age of six with his widowed mother, Rebecca Walpole Garner, a descendant of Sir Robert Walpole of England. The Walpoles of Tennessee were affluent and cultured, as were the Garner and Nance families, into which Rebecca married. After the Walpoles lost their fortune in the panic of 1837, they followed the trail to Texas that fellow Tennesseans such as Sam Houston and Davy Crockett had blazed. Rebecca's good management and hard work, along with that of her two sons and three daughters, enabled the family to survive, but the children did not receive the education that had been customary for their ancestors.

Nevertheless, John Nance Garner III inherited qualities that helped to make him a successful cotton grower, even in Reconstruction Texas. He was honest, companionable, thrifty, and determined to succeed. By the time Texas came back into the Union in 1870, he had begun to build the impressive and comfortable colonial home that his son, the future vice president, grew up in. It was the place where neighbors gathered to discuss politics and agriculture, share a drink from the ever-present whiskey barrel, and play poker. These occasions shaped the attitudes and interests of the future politician.

Garner long remembered the resentment in Texas, and especially in his own house, that surrounded the prospect of Grant seeking a third term in 1876. Texas Democrats who hailed from Tennessee were well aware of the efforts of their revered Andrew Jackson to push a constitutional amendment through Congress that would have limited a president to one term of four or six years. Garner also retained vivid memories of the premature celebration of Samuel J. Tilden's election to the presidency, as well as the disappointment with which those around him greeted the electoral commission's designation of Rutherford B. Hayes as president. The most significant event of the campaign year for Garner, however, occurred when he attended with his father a political rally at Coon Soup Hollow and heard the declama-tions of two candidates for constable. The youngster came away from this event with a desire to become an orator.

Garner attended local schools and did well as a student, though one teacher described him as "not physically capable of prolonged application." At a boarding school in nearby Bogata, he acquired a love of literature from a stern teacher with an excellent library. When he was fifteen, he decided to further his education by going to school in adjoining Lamar County, where a relative, J.R. Walpole, was a teacher. According to biographer Bascom N. Timmons, Garner told his mother: "I don't wish to ask father for assistance. I don't believe I will have to." He supported himself by playing shortstop on semiprofessional baseball teams and by working at odd jobs. His ideas on fiscal responsibility were fully formed at an early age. Even as a student he continually added to his bank account. "My father told me that if I had a dime and owed no one I was solvent," he later recounted.

At the age of eighteen, Garner enrolled at Vanderbilt University in Nashville, Tennessee. Although he considered attending the newly established University of Texas, he succumbed to the ancestral pull of Tennessee. He stayed only one semester. While he might have overcome his educational inadequacies with hard work, physical ailments brought his college career to an abrupt halt. Developing problems with his eyes and lungs, Garner consulted a doctor. "He told me I wouldn't live many years," the vice president remembered; "I decided under these circumstances the money I'd saved was worth more than an education, so I took it and went home."

Returning to Texas, Garner studied law in Clarksville and continued to supplement his income by playing baseball. He was admitted to the bar in 1890 at the age of twenty-one and set up his own practice, which did not prosper. In 1892, he ran unsuccessfully for city attorney and soon afterward was diagnosed with tuberculosis. Seeking a drier climate, he found an opening with the law firm of Clark and Fuller in the south-central Texas town of Uvalde. Years later Garner recalled that his father advised him upon leaving to "Tell the truth and be a gentleman."

The young lawyer's first impressions of Uvalde were not positive. "Hell's bells," Timmons records Garner as saying to himself when he arrived, "I'd rather be dead in Clarksville than alive here." Nevertheless, he immediately opened a bank account with the $150 he had brought with him and finalized arrangements to join the law firm henceforth known as Clark, Fuller & Garner. Appointed to fill a vacancy as county judge, the junior partner rode the circuit in the nine surrounding counties, bringing in substantial revenue for the firm, regaining his health, and developing useful contacts that would later serve his political ambitions. When Garner ran for the regular term, the opponent he defeated was Mariette (Ettie) Rheiner, whom he married on November 25, 1895. The couple's only child, Tully, named after Garner's law partner, was born on September 26, 1896, breaking the line of John Nance Garners.

Defeated for reelection in 1896, the aspiring politician set his sights on a seat in the Texas house of representatives, which he acquired in 1898. He served on the Appropriations Committee, where he opposed pork-barrel legislation and established a reputation for championing economy in government and mediating disputes. Although he sought regulation of large corporations, including insurance companies and railroads, he also understood the need for economic development. Reelected in 1900, Garner chaired the redistricting committee that created a new federal congressional district, the Fifteenth, which contained twenty-two counties, including his own. He had been frank with his colleagues about his intentions to be elected to the new seat, and in 1903 his straightforwardness paid off when he became the Fifteenth's Democratic representative in the Fifty-eighth Congress.

Thirty-four years old at the time of his election, Garner entered the House on a sound financial footing and with well-developed political ideas. His law practice, ranch, and bank holdings provided assets of nearly $50,000, and his political focus from the beginning was on fiscal issues. He considered an income tax the most equitable means of raising revenue, and he was a strong supporter of good economic management in government. "It is just as necessary to watch the expenditure of the people's money after it is collected as it is to devise means for taxing people to produce revenue," he proclaimed during his first campaign; "I, therefore, oppose centralization of government at Washington." As a southerner, a westerner, and a Democrat, Garner also strongly opposed a protective tariff: "We must buy from other countries if we are to sell to them. Therefore, the tariff should be competitive."

Though he was a talented debater, the young legislator maintained a low profile in the Republican House, which Speaker Joseph G. Cannon had just begun to dominate. Instead of making speeches, Garner became an ardent student of legislation and people. "For the first few years," he said, "I just answered roll calls, looked after chores for my constituents, studied, played poker and got acquainted." When Cannon assigned the freshman congressman to the Committee on Railways and Canals, however, Garner immediately introduced legislation calling for a survey for a coastal canal to connect his district along the Gulf of Mexico to the Mississippi and Ohio rivers, much to the astonishment of the committee's chairman. According to the *Galveston News*, one purpose of Garner's bill was "just to find out if such a committee really existed." "Mr. Garner is always admirable in the beginning of a game to find out exactly how it is played." The Garner bill eventually became a law, and many years later the 1,100-mile-long Gulf Intracoastal Waterway became a reality.

Just as honesty, industry, and amiability enabled his father to prosper under the trying conditions of post–Civil War Texas, Congressman Garner became extremely popular as a minority member of the House of Representatives by exercising similar traits. Known as Cactus Jack to constituents and colleagues, he made friends with both Democrats and Republicans. Shortly after Garner entered the House, the *Houston Post* reported that he "had not been in the Capital two weeks before he was acquainted with more members of the House and the Senate and with public men generally than many members who have been here for years."

He met Joe Cannon during a poker game at the exclusive Boar's Head poker club. Biographer Timmons's account of the meeting has Garner ending the contest and winning a large pot by beating the Speaker's three aces with four fours. "Will that be enough, Mr. Speaker?" queried the freshman. "Sir," Cannon answered, "any man who can do that honestly—honestly mind you—has my profound admiration." By all accounts, the meeting was expensive for Cannon, but the two were thereafter fast friends. Garner, nevertheless, remained a committed Democrat and in 1910 played a leading role in the successful revolt against the Speaker's authoritarian leadership. As a result, the Texan established himself as an expert in parliamentary maneuvering and one of the party's most promising leaders.

In 1905, Cannon moved Garner to the Foreign Affairs Committee, where he served for the next eight years. After his first state dinner, the second-term congressman pulled no punches in providing his impressions: "As near as I have been able to figure out the chief functions of the Committee on Foreign Affairs is [*sic*] to attend as many dinners and banquets and do as little work as possible." Despite such opinions, or perhaps because of them, Garner eventually became the committee's ranking Democrat. While on the committee, he met junior Republican member Nicholas Longworth of Cincinnati, Ohio, establishing the foundation for what would become an extraordinary friendship.

Talented and ambitious, Garner advanced steadily in the House. He became party whip in 1909 and, after Woodrow Wilson's election to the presidency and the brief return of Democratic dominance to the legislature, a member of the Ways and Means Committee in 1913. Although Garner was not as influential in the new administration's first term as he had been with the two previous Republican presidents, he played an important role in financial legislation. He also made it clear that he would continue to advocate economy for Democrats just as he had for Republicans. He fought for a graduated income tax against those who favored a flat-rate tax and succeeded when his plan was enacted as a part of the Underwood Tariff Act of 1913. He supported as well currency and banking reform

efforts that led to the institution of the Federal Reserve System.

Cactus Jack's status within the Wilson administration rose during World War I, however, as the president's relations with Speaker Champ Clark and Ways and Means Chairman Claude Kitchen soured. Having lost the Democratic majority in the House in the 1916 election, Wilson made Garner his liaison in that body. If the country was going to war, it would have to raise revenue, and Garner became the president's point man and the acknowledged expert on tax and tariff issues. Yet, even as he endeavored to raise the necessary sums to support the war, he never lost sight of his fundamental belief in fiscal responsibility. Garner told Wilson:

> This war is going to cost us from $10,000,000,000 to $20,000,000,000 a year. Congress has never had any experience in raising such sums. The problem now is to get it to thinking in such astronomical terms. After the war the problem will be to get it out of the habit of thinking in such terms.

The Republican landslide of 1920 left only 132 Democrats in the House. Having no relish to serve again in the minority, Garner made retirement plans. The Ku Klux Klan, however, changed his mind. When Garner discovered that Texas congressmen had joined the organization, he publicly condemned it. The Klan, then, burned a cross near Garner's home and announced plans to facilitate his retirement. As usual Garner did not campaign, but he did win the election.

During the ensuing years of Republican ascendancy, Garner pursued his established policy of making friends rather than speeches. Only a handful of Democrats with more seniority had survived the 1920 election in the House, clearing the Texan's way for accelerated advancement within the party. In 1923, he became the ranking minority member of the Ways and Means Committee and chairman of the House Democratic Committee on Committees. Six years later he attained the post of minority leader, and at the same time his friend and political adversary Nicholas Longworth became Speaker.

These years marked the beginning of a Washington institution presided over by Garner and Longworth in which the two party leaders dispensed political wisdom and influenced legislation in a nonpartisan atmosphere made cordial by whiskey. Not yet liberated from Prohibition by the Twenty-first Amendment, the two legislators resorted to euphemism when describing the practice of sharing a drink with colleagues. They were "striking a blow for liberty," and meetings became known as the "Board of Education."

During one of the first meetings of the board, Garner informed his counterpart that passage of the Smoot–Hawley tariff bill, then being considered, would allow the Democrats to regain a majority in the House and lead to Longworth's defeat as Speaker. "Put a ring around that date, December 7, 1931," he warned, "if you have a calendar that far ahead." Smoot–Hawley was enacted on June 17, 1930, and Garner's prophecy was fulfilled. He became the thirty-ninth Speaker of the House of Representatives on the very date he had foretold. He did not succeed Longworth, though, for his friend and rival had died the previous April.

As Speaker, Garner presided over a slim Democratic majority of three. Keeping that majority intact and available for votes on a daily basis was a task that demanded the full measure of the new Speaker's legislative experience and skill. In the midst of a deteriorating economic crisis, Garner decided that he could best serve the country by supporting the relief program of President Herbert Hoover's Republican administration rather than by thwarting it. "I'll be criticized for following Hoover and not offering a program of our own and I'll be accused of sabotaging Hoover," he told Timmons; "I'm not going to let it bother me. I've got skin as thick as cowhide."

The speed with which proposed legislation, such as the creation of the Reconstruction Finance Corporation, a moratorium on European debts, and strengthening of the Federal Reserve system, passed through the House of Representatives in the early part of the session astonished the White House. By February 1932, however, when the president praised Democrats for their nonpartisanship, a number of prominent party members had begun to revolt. Representative Fiorello H. La Guardia of New York, who controlled as many as fifteen votes and generally supported the Speaker, was quoted as saying: "This isn't a session of Congress. This is a kissing bee."

When Garner pushed for a federal sales tax in order to counter the rapidly growing budget deficit, he was defeated. In one of his rare speeches before the House on March 29, a few days before the vote, he outlined his fundamental beliefs regarding the importance of maintaining the financial integrity of the country. "The paramount duty of the House of Representatives," he stated, "is to levy sufficient taxes of some kind, of some nature, that will sustain the credit of this country in the eyes of the world, as well as our own people." Although the Speaker regained lost political ground with this "camp meeting" speech, his mishandling of sales tax legislation, according to some commentators, weakened his candidacy as his party's presidential nominee and boosted that of Franklin D. Roosevelt.

Backed by publisher William Randolph Hearst, Garner was a serious presidential contender in the spring of 1932. Although the Speaker did not campaign actively, he controlled the crucial votes of California and Texas by the time the Democrats convened in Chicago. When it became apparent by the convention's third ballot that Cactus Jack had no chance for the nomination, he released his delegates to Roosevelt. Indebted to Garner and to the state of Texas, Roosevelt offered the Speaker the vice-presidential nomination, which Garner reluctantly accepted. "Hell, I'll do anything to see the Democrats win one more national election," he told his friend and colleague Sam Rayburn. On November 8, 1932, as the regionally and ideologically balanced Roosevelt-Garner ticket carried 42 of the 48 states, the new vice president also regained his seat in the House. Though in theory he had a choice in the matter of which office to accept, in actuality he had none. He resigned from Congress on March 4, 1933, and began his eight-year tenure as vice president.

Upon assuming the office, he described for the press the nature of its power, or its lack thereof: "The Vice-President has no . . . offices to bestow or favors to extend. He can only make power for himself sometimes by his personality and ability. Only if by his association with men they come to have friendship for him and faith in and respect for his judgment can he be influential." Understanding well the limitations of the office, perhaps no holder was ever in such a good position to maximize its potential. Though the role was new, it was still familiar, and few could equal the capacity of John Nance Garner for making friends or for commanding the respect of his peers. The Board of Education moved to the Senate side of the Congress along with Garner, and 20 percent of the body he now presided over contained men who had served with him in the House.

Astutely, Roosevelt assigned Garner to serve as his liaison with Congress and requested that as such the vice president also attend cabinet meetings. Concerned about potential resentment in the Senate, Garner accepted the offer under the conditions that he would not make public statements or recommendations for public office or national policy unless asked to do so. Not only did the vice president utilize his vast legislative knowledge to push administration measures through the Senate, but he exercised as well considerable clout in the House. He maintained excellent relations with both Senate Majority Leader Joseph T. Robinson and House Speaker William B. Bankhead. Moreover, his numerous friends in the House included the powerful Texas delegation, which supplied no fewer than eight regular committee chairmanships at any time during the New Deal years. As historian Lionel V. Patenaude explains: "Little New Deal legislation could go through Congress without passing through one of these committees."

Garner served the president especially well during the One Hundred Days, a special legislative session from March 9 to June 16, 1932, that inaugurated the New Deal and extended executive power beyond that of any previous peacetime president. He believed the emergency measures were necessary to combat the deepening economic crisis and that they had saved the country. By early 1934, however, along with many conservative businessmen and politicians, he thought that the crisis was over and that government spending should be curtailed. In October, Garner asked the president to "cut down as far as possible, the cost of government," and Roosevelt indicated that he would do so.

Feeling pressure from both ends of the political spectrum, Roosevelt hesitated for a few months before deciding to follow the advice of other key advisers in co-opting the initiatives of the Left by introducing new programs of reform. Though the vice president disagreed with the liberal measures of the Second Hundred Days, referring to a number of them such as the Wagner National Labor Relations Act, the Social Security Act, and the Revenue Act as "plain damn foolishness," he nevertheless worked diligently and effectively during 1935 to secure their passage. At this point his party loyalty overcame his distaste for what he believed the New Deal had become. Yet, he found it increasingly difficult to tolerate the new capitalized phrase, especially as administration officials began referring to themselves as "New Dealers" rather than Democrats.

Despite his misgivings, the landslide Democratic victory of 1936 was immensely satisfying to the vice president. Remembering the overwhelming Republican victories of the 1920s, when some thought that the Democratic Party had outlived its usefulness, Garner took great pleasure in the vast majorities his party now realized in both the Senate and the House and also in the number of governorships and state legislatures that Democrats controlled. The new federal government's duty as he saw it was to "amend, amend, amend." "We have passed a lot of experimental legislation," he stated, "and any experimental legislation has to be amended in the light of the experience with it. . . . We are not putting out a fire now." The lopsided victory only served to fuel the president's arrogance, however, and as the administration moved further to the Left, the differences between the president and the vice president grew. Their inevitable split came not long after the historic 1936 election.

The first significant fissure appeared because of disagreements between Roosevelt and Garner on how to handle the sit-down strikes that closed the automotive industry at the end of 1936. New Deal initiatives that protected the right of workers to organize and bargain collectively had provided new impetus to a moribund labor movement, and by 1936 the Committee for Industrial Organization, led by John L. Lewis, had begun major organization drives in the automobile and steel industries. Late in the year, automobile workers in Detroit adopted the sit-down strike, in which they refused to leave the shop until they were granted collective bargaining. Though Roosevelt disagreed with the method, he refused to denounce the strikers, whose right to unionize the Wagner Act protected. Garner, on the other hand, saw sit-down strikes as illegal: "They permitted men to take over other people's property," he recalled protesting in a cabinet meeting. "In Texas we would call that stealing," he said. In January 1937, the president and the vice president exchanged heated words over the sit-down strikes, and thereafter Garner worked behind the scenes to oppose his boss.

The ever widening rift became irreparable during the fight over the president's Court Reform Plan. Thwarted by a Supreme Court that had by 1936 ruled against New Deal laws in seven of nine major cases, Roosevelt sought to rectify the problem by naming as many as fifty new federal judges, including six Supreme Court justices, and by limiting the power of judges who had served ten or more years or reached the age of seventy. Though Congress had the power to determine the size of the Court, the president had not consulted that body before introducing the bill, which its elder statesmen, as well as the vice president, considered an affront. Garner eventually worked out a compromise that added no new judges, but his vacation to Uvalde in the midst of the struggle publicized the split not only between Garner and Roosevelt but also between the liberals and the conservatives within the party.

Roosevelt's unsuccessful efforts in 1938 to purge from Congress the senators and representatives who had opposed him by campaigning against them in their district primaries exacer-bated the divisions within the administration. By 1938, Garner was the second most powerful man in Washington and the leader of conservative opposition to the New Deal, that voted against nearly all of the president's congressional initiatives. In that year the Texas state Democratic convention endorsed Garner as a candidate for president in 1940, as did the Texas legislature in March 1939. Opinion polls showed him to be the leading candidate if Roosevelt did not run, and in June a Garner-for-President campaign committee formed.

The concept of a third term for any president was anathema to Garner: "I would be against a third term on principal even if I approved every act of Roosevelt's two terms," he told Bascom Timmons; "I would oppose my own brother for a third term." If Roosevelt was ever undecided about whether or not to run, his path became clearer as Garner gained momentum. He was certainly not going to allow a successor to undo all that he had accomplished. Believing that Roosevelt's third-term campaign was inevitable, Garner declared his candidacy for the presidency in December 1939, three months after Great Britain and France declared war on Germany. It was the first time since the development of the party system that a sitting president and a vice president competed for their party's nomination.

Crushed in the primaries by the presidential machine, Cactus Jack Garner ended his campaign at the Chicago convention in July 1940 when Roosevelt received the Democratic nomination with Henry A. Wallace as his running mate. Roosevelt defeated Republican nominee Wendell L. Willkie in the fall election by a comfortable margin as Garner retired from public life to his home in Uvalde. He lived there quietly until his death on November 7, 1967, a couple of weeks before his ninety-ninth birthday. In 1965, when asked by a Washington journalist for suggestions on running the government, he admonished: "Stop the spending!"

Garner's vice-presidential legacy is mixed. While he played a major role in implementing Roosevelt's programs during the first term, he might also be held accountable for preventing completion of the New Deal. His entire career, however, serves as a testament to the importance of legislative power. As vice president, he resisted the transfer of power from the legislative to the executive branch that occurred during his tenure. A colorful character who always provided good copy for the journalists, Garner is perhaps most often recalled for his widely misquoted statement that the office of vice president was not "worth a pitcher of warm spit." (He actually said "piss.") After his first term, he said: "The job is delightful. I like it. But it is almost entirely unimportant." Although he had little regard for the office, some historians, such as Lionel V. Patenaude, have called him "the most powerful Vice President in the history of the United States."

REFERENCES

Bascom N. Timmons, *Garner of Texas: A Personal History* (New York: Harper and Brothers Publishers, 1948); Lionel V. Patenaude, *Texas, Politics and the New Deal* (New York: Garland Publishing, Inc., 1983); Michael J. Romano, "The Emergence of John Nance Garner as a Figure in American National Politics, 1924–1941" (Ph.D. diss., St. John's University, 1974); Robert A. Caro, *The Years of Lyndon Johnson: The Path to Power* (New York: Random House, 1982).

J. KENT CALDER a native Texan, now writes and edits in Indiana. He is a graduate of the University of Texas at Arlington and Butler University in Indianapolis. Since 1989, as managing editor for the Indiana Historical Society, he has edited its illustrated magazine, *Traces of Indiana and Midwestern History.*

HENRY AGARD WALLACE (1888–1965)

Vice President, 1941–1945

(President Franklin Delano Roosevelt)

HENRY AGARD WALLACE
(Library of Congress)

By Mark L. Kleinman

Henry Wallace is usually remembered for the events that followed his tenure as vice president, particularly for his resounding defeat as a third-party candidate for the presidency on the Communist-tainted Progressive Party ticket in 1948. Yet during the three decades prior to his political demise in 1948, Wallace had a highly successful public career of which his term as vice president during U.S. participation in World War II was something of a culmination. As vice president, he set modern historical precedent by playing a real administrative role in government. He also gained worldwide notoriety during his vice presidential years as a champion of international political and economic democracy, calling for what he termed the "Century of the Common Man." Through the 1910s, 1920s, and early 1930s, the decades before he became vice president, Wallace was a highly successful agricultural scientist as well as an influential farm editor and Midwestern agrarian spokesman. He was also a central participant in Franklin D. Roosevelt's

New Deal as secretary of agriculture, overseeing what are considered some of the most successful programs of the New Deal years.

Despite Wallace's very real successes, from the time he began his political career in 1933 he was often attacked as an impractical, starry-eyed idealist. These attacks were augmented during the 1948 presidential campaign by widespread assertions that Wallace was a dupe of the Communist Party and later by the general cultural climate of the early cold war years and the McCarthy era. Such characterizations also gained impetus from persistent rumors of Wallace's actual interests in different forms of spiritualism. Wallace's reputation, both contemporary and historical, was probably damaged as well by an awkward, somewhat distant personality. Indeed, by nature he was not a politician at all; he was rather a reformer and, to a great degree, a visionary.

Wallace was born on a farm outside the village of Orient, Iowa, south of Des Moines, the third in an agrarian leadership "dynasty" of three Henry Wallaces. His grandfather, "Uncle Henry," from whom Henry A. gained much of his spiritualistic bent, went to Iowa from Pennsylvania in the 1860s as a progressive minister in the United Presbyterian Church, but he later left the ministry for reasons of health and took up farming and farm journalism. With his sons, Uncle Henry took over a small farm journal in 1895 and transformed it, as *Wallace's Farmer*, into one of the leading farm newspapers in the nation. In 1921, his eldest son, Henry C. Wallace, took up the portfolio of secretary of agriculture in the Harding administration, and Henry C.'s son Henry A. Wallace—trained in the agricultural sciences at Iowa State College and already an international pioneer in corn hybridization—took over the editorship of *Wallace's Farmer*. In 1914, Henry A. had married Ilo Browne of Indianola, Iowa. They had three children and were married for more than fifty years.

It was in his editorials in *Wallace's Farmer* that Wallace worked out the framework and much of the detail of the extensive critique of modern American culture that lay behind his social, political, and international affairs commentary of the 1930s and 1940s. In thousands of editorial columns and articles written between 1921 and 1933, Wallace presented social criticism analogous in many ways to that of various commentators of the era, liberal and conservative. The centerpiece of Wallace's perspective, framed by his spiritualism and his science, was a quintessential American communal philosophy. He developed a commentary grounded in midwestern American agrarian values. Above all, he invoked the ethic of "cooperation," a touchstone of nineteenth-century agrarian politics in the United States. Around the notion of cooperation, Wallace fashioned an analog to the European constructions of socialism and communism, a vision of a different and, in his view, better American civilization based on ideals that he saw embodied in an increasingly threatened rural culture.

Wallace's profound curiosity about the spiritual world led him, during the 1920s, to explore Hinduism, Bahaism, astrology, and Native American religion. He focused the most, however, on the "wisdom religion" of Theosophy, a belief system eminently suited to his philosophical intertwining of science and spiritualism. Wallace's attraction to the movement led to his involvement in something of a network of spiritualists by the early 1930s.

The best-known and most controversial of Wallace's spiritual associations was that with Russian emigré artist, poet, essayist and Theosophist Nicholas Roerich. In the 1920s and 1930s, Roerich promoted an international treaty providing for the protection of the art treasures of all nations during wartime. The so-called Roerich Pact became a reality in 1935 with Wallace, a champion of the pact and a member of Franklin Roosevelt's cabinet, as the signatory for the United States. At about the same time, Wallace, as secretary of agriculture, commissioned Roerich to lead a Department of Agriculture expedition to Asia in search of drought-resistant grasses that might be of some benefit to the drought-ravaged American Midwest. The expedition ultimately collapsed in an embarrassing international relations controversy that arose out of some dubious political activities that Roerich undertook while in China.

Wallace contributed to the controversy by first defending Roerich unquestioningly against various accusations of misconduct and then completely disengaging from him when it became apparent that the accusations were accurate.

Wallace first entered government as Franklin Roosevelt's secretary of agriculture at the commencement of the New Deal in 1933. He moved quickly to address the desperate circumstances into which American farmers had slipped during the previous twelve years. Shortly after taking office, he called a national agricultural conference to determine what sort of emergency legislation to create. Wallace backed what was known as the Voluntary Domestic Allotment Plan (VDAP), a strategy he had advocated in various forms since the late 1920s. The VDAP called for controlling agricultural production by limiting the acreage of certain crops under cultivation in a given year. The aim of the legislation that contained the VDAP, the Agricultural Adjustment Act (AAA) of 1933, was to restore "reasonable parity" between the prices of farm products and manufactured goods. Farmers would voluntarily agree to produce less of various commodities and would receive in return compensatory payments funded by a special tax on companies that processed agricultural commodities. This would not only raise farm income in the short term but, by decreasing the overall supply of the specific commodities, raise agricultural prices over the long term as well. Wallace and his advisers intended to establish an agricultural system that would guarantee farmers a fair enough return on their production so as to enable them to function for the foreseeable future as consumers in the larger U.S. economy.

The program was wide ranging and controversial, and certain aspects of its controversy redounded negatively upon Wallace himself. This was particularly true regarding aspects of the AAA that in 1933–34 required large portions of the American cotton crop to be plowed under and thousands of baby pigs to be slaughtered in order to drive up cotton and pork prices. The destruction of the piglets was particularly controversial at a time when some 25 percent of American workers were without work and millions more

were unable to provide themselves and their families with basic necessities. Although the administration made real attempts to distribute the surplus piglets and crops when appropriate, perceptions of the policy proved easily manipulable by Roosevelt's and Wallace's political opponents. Indeed, exaggerated allusions to the episode were used against Wallace from time to time for the rest of his public career.

In fact, the policy of crop destruction was utilized only during the first year of the AAA and in the case of wheat was not necessary at all. The wheat allotment program worked from the start, greatly helped along by a drought that radically decreased the size of the American wheat crop, augmenting the effects of the AAA's policy. The results in wheat foreshadowed the overall relative success that the entire act attained. By 1936, farm income in the United States increased by some 50 percent, while farm debt plummeted by several billion dollars. In this sense, agricultural policies under Wallace's supervision arguably can be characterized as the New Deal's most effective.

Also controversial was the AAA's impact on tenant farmers, particularly in the cotton agriculture of the South. Because the program decreased the need for farm labor, many tenant farmers were pushed off their land by owners who opted to put the tenants' acreage out of production. The AAA tried to moderate the effects, but at the local level affairs were generally dominated by landlords. The situation led to a battle within the AAA between liberal reformers and more-traditional agrarians. In the end Wallace was put in an untenable position, one over which he was deeply torn: he sympathized with the reformers but acceded to the political practicality of the agrarians (including the need to maintain Democratic support for the administration in the South). His ultimate and infamous "purge" of the liberals from the AAA in 1935 was the only way Wallace believed he could preserve support for the overall reform program.

Despite being declared unconstitutional by the Supreme Court in 1936—a fate shared with many other components of the early New Deal—the AAA survived the New Deal era essentially intact. This was in great part due to the fact that Wallace and his advisers were prepared for just this eventuality, having watched New Deal industrial policy succumb altogether to a negative Supreme Court decision the year before. Within months, virtually all of the AAA's components were re-created in constitutionally acceptable forms and in some cases have remained in place to the present day.

Wallace's ascension to the vice presidency was also characterized by controversy. Roosevelt, running for an unprecedented third term, chose Wallace to run with him in 1940 both for the latter's demonstrated administrative abilities and as a counterbalance to the concessions Roosevelt had made to conservatives in the Democratic Party during his first two terms. At the Democratic convention that summer, Roosevelt was insistent, explicitly threatening to decline the presidential nomination if the Democrats rejected Wallace as his running mate. In this context, the convention experience was humiliating for Wallace. Delegates who resented Roosevelt's dictatorial behavior, as well as those who were specifically opposed to Wallace, focused their anger on Wallace who was shocked by the crowd's vehemence. Ilo Wallace was driven to tears by the antagonism aimed at her husband. Wallace eventually won the nomination in a close vote over House Speaker William Bankhead of Alabama, but was unable to deliver his acceptance speech to the convention due to the delegates' hostility. He gave it the following month instead at a campaign kickoff in Des Moines, Iowa.

Wallace took on something like an enforcer's role in the campaign of 1940, frequently attacking the Republicans in the realm of foreign affairs. Most pointedly, he tried to taint them with the stain of Nazism, arguing that FDR's efforts in global affairs were impeded internationally by Hitler and domestically by partisan opponents. He developed an image of a protofascism nascent in the United States arising out of isolationism and monopolistic corporate capitalism, both of which he associated with the Republican Party. Wallace's quite vicious attacks drew a great deal of criticism not only from the Republicans but also from less partisan sources, including the moderate press. His rhetorical strategy was attacked for being unjust and even irresponsible in its exaggeration. Indeed, it is clear that Wallace did go too far in some of the aspersions he cast on the Republicans in 1940, but he did so out of his real belief that the United States had to move quickly to prepare for an inevitable war and that any group that hindered that preparation was, in effect, "appeasing" the fascists. In the wake of the Munich crisis of 1938 and the advent of the ideologically powerful "Munich analog," Wallace's view was not in any sense an extraordinary one for a liberal in the United States to hold by 1940.

Wallace undertook his first vice-presidential task prior to actually taking office. A few weeks after the election Roosevelt appointed the vice president-elect to head a U.S. delegation to the December 1 inauguration of Manuel Ávila Camacho as president of Mexico. It was an assignment that gave Wallace an opportunity to work to bring about the realization of his long-time hope for hemispheric cooperation, a goal he had advocated since entering government. Wallace was an excellent choice for the mission. As his interest in Latin America had blossomed over the years, he had become an ardent student of Latin American culture as well as of the Spanish language. By the time he left for Mexico, he was fully conversational in Spanish, which greatly impressed the Mexicans. His penchant for visiting with the common people as well as his ability to communicate in their native tongue drew enthusiastic responses wherever he traveled.

While in Mexico, Wallace conducted an extensive correspondence with Washington in which he advocated an amicable settlement of several issues of contention between the United States and Mexico, most connected to the reformist policies of the outgoing president, Lázaro Cárdenas. It was Cárdenas's administration that had expropriated foreign—including U.S.—oil companies' holdings in Mexico in 1938, causing an international dispute that had seriously threatened the viability of Roosevelt's Good Neighbor Policy throughout Latin America. Wallace contended that the new Mexican regime was likely to be amenable to reaching some sort of final settlement of the oil issue. Doing so would in turn open the door to further Mexican–U.S. cooperation, and Wallace hoped that such cooperation would take a course close to his own heart. He believed that the United States could greatly help the Mexicans by, among other things, setting up an agricultural experiment station in Mexico. As a farm leader and now former secretary of agriculture, he knew how helpful such stations had been to U.S. farmers over the years. Wallace felt that if the United States established such an agency in Mexico, it might have a similarly beneficial impact on Mexican agriculture and so ultimately improve the lives of thousands of impoverished Mexicans.

After the inauguration, Wallace had little difficulty taking up the formal tasks of the vice president. He proved himself fully capable of presiding over the Senate, both in terms of mastering procedure and acquainting himself with its members. By nature Wallace had little interest in the convoluted political machinations of the senators. He did, however, attempt to raise their health consciousness by getting rid of his predecessor's infamous liquor cabinet (Wallace was for the most part a teetotaler) and presenting himself as a physical fitness role model through his constant participation in sports ranging from boxing to tennis. He also maintained the wide range of intellectual interests that he had pursued since his youth. His office was known for its extensive and varied collection of reading material. In addition, as vice president, Wallace continued to nurture U.S. cooperation with Latin America by keeping up his Spanish language studies, supporting a national radio program that popularized Latin American culture in the United States, and advocating various educational and cultural exchange programs between the United States and the other nations of the Western Hemisphere.

In July 1941, Wallace was given a task that established a new administrative aspect for the office of vice president. Roosevelt appointed him to head the Economic Defense Board (EDB), made up of eight members of the cabinet. The agency was renamed the Board of Economic Warfare (BEW) after Pearl Harbor, and Wallace remained as its wartime director.

The BEW's primary responsibility was locating and obtaining items of strategic importance to the United States from all over the globe. In supervising these operations, Wallace came into direct and highly visible bureaucratic conflict with Secretary of Commerce Jesse Jones, a conservative Texas Democrat who was also director of the Reconstruction Finance Corporation (RFC) as well as, ultimately, federal loan disbursement in general. The main circumstance behind the controversy was that the RFC was the BEW's "banker," which meant that disagreements over procurement, whether philosophical or in regard to specific goals, were likely to lead to classic bureaucratic battles. For Wallace, there were two interconnected concerns that together formed the crux of the conflict: efficient matériel procurement and the assumption that procurement policies had to be socially just, not only for humanitarian reasons but also to attain optimum efficiency. The problem was that Wallace and his subordinates at the BEW believed that the simple fact of being at war meant that peacetime assumptions regarding the flow of goods were to be disregarded. The exigencies of war demanded innovation and particularly might mean foregoing what would normally be considered sober business practices. For Wallace's BEW the profit motive was not a driving strategic principle, but for millionaire businessman Jones and his like-minded team, following sound business practices was of paramount importance.

The intertwining of Wallace's concern for procurement efficiency with his liberal humanitarianism was evident in his regard for the well-being of the workers in other nations who were producing the supplies the BEW sought to procure, especially in Wallace's much-beloved Latin America. To Wallace the working conditions and health of those he had come to term collectively the common man were bound to the question of efficiency. Healthy workers would produce more and do so more efficiently, benefiting the United States both during and after the war. What was humane actually made the best business sense.

By spring 1943, the conflict between Wallace and Jones ranged over various procurement issues. It had also become acrimonious and public, the latter quality being one that Roosevelt ultimately would not tolerate. Jones had used a Senate Banking and Currency Committee hearing the year before to attack the BEW's rubber procurement policy. Wallace and his assistant, Milo Perkins, given an opportunity to respond, implied that Jones and the RFC through their obstructionism had failed to protect the nation's strategic interests in numerous instances. The whole exchange appeared in newspapers across the country. In June 1943, the BEW was attacked in an inflammatory manner on the Senate floor by Jones's allies. This, along with similar, concurrent attacks in the House, led Wallace and Perkins to issue a lengthy press release detailing the impediments created by Jones and the RFC in the creation of adequate stockpiles of a whole list of strategic materials. The statement included the assertion that by obstructing BEW efforts at obtaining supplies of quinine for U.S. troops in the Pacific theater, the RFC had actually caused the deaths of U.S. servicemen. Jones responded with public outrage, insisting that Wallace in effect had called him a traitor.

Roosevelt intervened at first indirectly, having Wallace and Jones meet under mediation to attempt a reconciliation. They agreed to a public statement, but Jones decided after the fact to issue a statement of his own that once more attacked in vehement language Wallace's criticism of the RFC. Then on July 5 he issued his own press release in response to Wallace's and Perkin's of the previous month. The obvious failure of reconciliation over the next week impelled Roosevelt to direct action. On July 15 he abolished the BEW altogether by executive order, thus ending the conflict. While the RFC did lose some of its authority over foreign contracts, the president's action clearly was a defeat for Wallace, and the episode contributed to the mounting desire of conservative Democrats to force him from the vice presidency the following year. At the time, however, Wallace accepted his defeat with equanimity.

Wallace's poise in the face of public defeat may have derived in part from the fact that by the time of the BEW's liquidation in summer 1943 he had firmly established himself not only as the United States's leading progressive liberal, but also as the nation's great champion of cooperative internationalism. He had done so in May 1942 when he gave what was the best-known and perhaps most important speech of his career. Formally titled "The Price of Free World Victory," the speech, widely published and republished over subsequent weeks and months, became known by its most poignant phrase, the "Century of the Common Man." It was an address that not only articulated Wallace's liberal internationalism as it had evolved through the 1920s and 1930s, but also laid out his vision for postwar global affairs as well. He attacked U.S. tariff policy as he had in the 1920s for the manner in which it had contributed to international economic upheaval, and he spoke to the historical and moral contexts of the war, characterizing it dramatically as a "fight to the death between the free world and the slave world." Wallace once more attacked fascism abroad and industrial monopoly at home as the great threats to both international and domestic democracy. He declared that modern technological knowledge could overcome inequities in the world and create the "shared abundance" he had long championed. At the same time, he was demanding, as director of the BEW, foreign procurement contracts that protected the health and well-being of the workers of other nations, Wallace asserted in "Century of the Common Man" that modern technological know-how made such a demand wholly reasonable. Wallace insisted that by 1942 modern technology was capable of ensuring "that everybody in the world has the privilege of drinking a quart of milk a day." The statement was not an offer to use national wealth without restraint to support the world's poor, as it was often and sometimes deliberately misconstrued. Rather, Wallace was arguing that the knowledge existed to enable the citizens of all nations to attain the means to supply themselves with the necessities of life. His use of the dietary metaphor arose from his belief that children who ate well would learn well—well enough to master the technology that would industrialize their nations, enabling those nations to participate in the cooperative postwar global prosperity that Wallace envisioned. With such hopes in mind, Wallace declared that this war against fascism could be viewed as one more, perhaps culminating step in a "Great Revolution of the people" that began with the American Revolution and continued with the French, Latin American, German, and Russian revolutions.

By 1944, Wallace was an extremely popular political figure in the United States. A July Gallup poll showed that 65 percent of Democratic voters favored his renomination as vice president. He was viewed by many Americans as the torchbearer of progressive liberal domestic reform and the great champion of cooperation in international affairs. Because of such perceptions, as well as the battles he fought with Jesse Jones while at the helm of the BEW, conservative Democrats were determined by summer 1944 to force him from the vice presidency, particularly in view of widespread doubt that Roosevelt's health would allow the president to complete a fourth term. Roosevelt's own feelings on retaining Wallace as vice president remained ambiguous throughout the spring and early summer, but by the time of the Democratic convention in mid-July, his actions worked against Wallace's renomination.

Earlier in the year, Wallace had proposed to Roosevelt that he make a vice-presidential tour of Soviet Asia and China. Wallace expected both to become areas of important social, economic, and political development in the postwar era. Roosevelt readily agreed, perhaps seeing the trip as a way to remove the vice president from the domestic political scene. Thus from late May through early July, Wallace traveled in Asia while preconvention political machinations in the United States heated up. He visited mines, farms, and factories in Russia and made speeches that he hoped would establish the foundation for what he termed "world security on the basis of broader understanding." In Siberia, Wallace was received warmly and with great respect, in part because of his clearly exceptional agricultural knowledge. But he was also welcomed enthusiastically because he had taken the time, characteristically, during the months preceding the trip to study enough of the Russian language to enable himself to deliver a speech in his hosts' native tongue. Upon his return to the United States, Wallace recounted the great respect he felt for Soviet accomplishments in Siberia, in notable comparison to the serious doubts and even disdain he felt for the corruption he witnessed under Chiang Kai-shek's regime in China. He was only vaguely aware that much of what he was shown by the Russians—model factories and mining towns peopled by enthusiastic workers—was a false front put up by the Soviets to guarantee his positive report to the U.S. president and people.

By the time Wallace returned home, his hold on the vice presidency was quite tenuous. Despite the strong support he had among rank-and-file Democrats, southern democratic leaders and party bosses wanted him out. In conversation, the president himself was vaguely contradictory, telling Wallace that if he, Roosevelt, were a delegate to the convention, "he would vote for Henry Wallace" but that there were many in the party who felt otherwise. By the time of the convention, Roosevelt's perhaps false ambivalence led him to desert Wallace effectively by indicating that he would be willing to share the ticket with either Supreme Court Justice William O. Douglas or Senator Harry S. Truman of Missouri, both of whom were viewed by party conservatives as acceptably moderate alternatives.

Roosevelt was formally renominated on the evening of July 20, and Wallace made a dramatic speech from the platform seconding the president's nomination. In bold terms, he asserted a powerfully progressive position, including a call for racial equality in education, economics, and politics. He spoke with a candor that probably cost him whatever chance remained for the renomination. The speech was followed by a huge demonstration on Wallace's behalf. Some historians have argued that had the party bosses not succeeded in having the convention adjourned at that moment, Wallace might have been nominated the same evening. In fact, much of the demonstration was made by Wallace supporters in the galleries who were not actual delegates. In any case, the convention was adjourned and the next day Wallace was beaten in the balloting by Truman.

After his reelection that November, Roosevelt nominated Wallace for secretary of commerce, and Wallace's confirmation by the Senate became yet another acrimonious battle over his liberalism. He finally won confirmation, but not before his Senate opponents stripped the position of its traditional control of important federal lending agencies. Nevertheless, Wallace was heading the Department of Commerce when Roosevelt died in April 1945 and Harry S. Truman became president.

Truman kept Wallace in the cabinet, at first believing that he needed Wallace to retain the support of the left wing of the Democratic Party, which continued to view Truman with great skepticism. But by summer 1946, Wallace was increasingly in disagreement with Truman over the course of U.S. foreign policy, particularly over U.S. relations with the Soviet Union, the nation's World War II ally. In a letter he wrote to the president in July, Wallace predicted not only the arms race to come but the sort of international paranoia and tension that would result from such a race. He laid the blame for tensions at the feet of both nations but suggested that the United States could ease them by slowing down the tremendous expansion of its military establishment that was taking place especially in atomic weapons and delivery systems.

In September, Wallace reiterated many of the same points in a speech he gave at a progressive political rally at Madison Square Garden in New York. The speech engendered great controversy, both within the administration and the national press. The positions that Wallace advocated seemed to oppose strongly those being established by Secretary of State James Byrnes, who was in Paris at the time, attending a meeting of foreign ministers. It was ultimately at Byrnes's irate insistence that Truman demanded Wallace's resignation from the cabinet.

After leaving public office Wallace became the editor of the *New Republic* magazine. Through his editorials, he continued to oppose the Truman administration's hard line toward the Russians as well as what he viewed as the increasingly conservative course of U.S. politics. By late December 1947, motivated by such issues, he decided to run for the presidency against Truman on the ticket of the resurrected Progressive Party. For Wallace, the campaign of 1948 was a culmination of the various controversies that had followed him throughout his public career. To those of his critics who viewed him as too far to the Left, his association with communists in the Progressive Party seemed to prove their greatest fears, and his path-breaking insistence on integrated rallies while campaigning in the South enraged conservative Southern Democrats even while it foreshadowed aspects of the Civil Rights movement of the 1950s and 1960s.

Wallace's relationship with Nicholas Roerich, particularly its spiritual aspects, became an issue during the campaign of 1948 as well. Their association was brought to light by conservative columnist Westbrook Pegler, who smeared Wallace by publishing and critically interpreting several letters Wallace had written during the 1930s to Roerich and Roerich's secretary on both political and spiritual issues. Pegler harped on aspects of the correspondence in such a way as to make it seem that Wallace had been under the mystical sway of Roerich, with Roerich pejoratively characterized as Wallace's guru. Wallace's failure to squarely address the Roerich connection as well as the larger issue of his spiritualistic inclinations contributed to the further degradation of his reputation in the midst of the disastrous campaign.

Throughout the campaign, Wallace was portrayed in the mainstream press as a foolish dupe of the Communists. Truman and the anticommunist liberals who eventually came to support him went so far at times as to imply Wallace's disloyalty. The election itself was anticlimactic: The Progressives were crushed in the presidential election, with Wallace receiving only 1.1 million votes, less than 2.5 percent of all those cast.

The debacle of the 1948 election was the effective end of Wallace's public career. Although he did speak out on various issues occasionally over the next decade and a half, he in fact retired to a farm he had purchased in upstate New York, returning to his earliest passion, experimental agricultural genetics. He spent his later years developing various strains of garden flowers, hybrid corn, chickens, and strawberries. In 1964, he was diagnosed with amyotrophic lateral sclerosis (Lou Gehrig's disease) and after a year battling the illness he succumbed to it, dying on November 18, 1965, at the age of 77.

REFERENCES

Norman D. Markowitz, *The Rise and Fall of the People's Century: Henry A. Wallace and American Liberalism, 1941–1948* (New York: The Free Press, 1973); Edward L. and Frederick H. Schapsmeier, *Henry A. Wallace of Iowa: The Agrarian Years, 1910–1940* (Ames: The Iowa State University Press, 1968) and *Prophet in Politics: Henry A. Wallace and the War Years, 1940–1965* (Ames: The Iowa State University Press, 1970); *The Price of Vision: The Diary of Henry A. Wallace, 1942–1946*, John M. Blum, ed. (Boston: Houghton Mifflin, 1973); Torbjorn Sirevag, *The Eclipse of the New Deal and the Fall of Vice-President Wallace, 1944* (New York: Garland Publishing, 1985); Graham White and John Maze, *Henry A. Wallace: His Search for a New World Order* (Chapel Hill: The University of North Carolina Press, 1995).

MARK L. KLEINMAN is assistant professor of U.S. history at the University of Wisconsin, Oshkosh. He received his Ph.D. in history in 1991 from the University of California, Los Angeles. He specializes in modern U.S. intellectual history and political culture and history of U.S. foreign relations.

$\mathcal{H}$ARRY S. TRUMAN (1884–1972)

Vice President, January 20–April 12, 1945

(President Franklin D. Roosevelt)

HARRY S. TRUMAN
(Library of Congress)

By Robert H. Ferrell

$\mathcal{H}$arry S. Truman was appallingly ill-prepared for the grand questions of military strategy and foreign policy that would take most of his time as president, and for that lack of preparedness the blame has to rest on his predecessor, Franklin Delano Roosevelt, who told him virtually nothing before or after his inauguration as vice president. As Lieutenant Commander William M. Rigdon of the White House Map Room, the president's secret operations center in the White House, put it: "I was custodian of the President's secret war files, but not once had I been instructed to show any document to the Vice President. He simply had not been worked into the Roosevelt administration." The vice president saw the president only a few times, mostly with other people; he met privately with the president twice.

Beyond question, Truman was well informed on domestic politics and on those issues might be considered one of the best-informed vice presidents in all of American history. He had been in the Senate for ten years and knew the membership of the upper house and many members of the lower house. He knew the principal officers of the administration, for beginning in 1941 he had been chairman of a special Senate committee to investigate the war effort. The committee was very active, making reports that involved conversation with, and reception of documents from, the highest government officials as well as the principal officers of corporations with war orders. He sometimes excoriated administration officials in his reports, which the committee always issued unanimously.

But when it came to military strategy and foreign policy, he knew no more than what the average intelligent reader of the nation's newspapers would have learned. That, alas, was not much, for censorship kept many details, and most serious disagreements among the Allies, out of the newspapers.

Truman was sixty years old when he became vice president—older than the usual holder of the nation's second-highest elective office. He had not gotten into politics early in his life. After graduation from high school in 1901 he spent three years working in Kansas City banks, 1903–06, and for the next eleven years, until 1917, he was a farmer on a big 600 acre farm near Grandview, Missouri, a few miles south of Kansas City. After two years in the U.S. Army in World War I, he and a regimental friend, Edward Jacobson, conducted a Kansas City haberdashery for three years until it failed in the economic recession after the war.

Beginning in 1923, the banker-farmer-soldier-haberdasher took a two-year term as "county judge," county commissioner, of Jackson County, the county of Kansas City in 1923–24, and then after losing an election because of a division among the local Democrats, Truman came back as "presiding judge" for two four-year terms (1927–34) presiding over a three-man court. In this task, Truman's political instincts developed markedly because much of his duties consisted of ensuring that the county possessed good roads. At this time, automobiles were rapidly increasing and road construction was one of the large county tasks throughout the United States. By the time Truman ended his two terms as his county's principal executive officer, Jackson County had one of the best road systems in the nation, comparable with Wayne County (Detroit) and Westchester County, next to New York City. He accomplished this in an honest way, without graft, despite the presence in Kansas City of Boss Thomas J. Pendergast, whose fiefdom was included in Judge Truman's bailiwick. Truman managed good relations with Boss Tom by not challenging—as indeed he could not have even if he had wanted—Pendergast within the city and simultaneously keeping the county honest.

In the senatorial election of 1934, Truman was backed by Pendergast, as was necessary for anyone running for office from western Missouri, against the rival faction of the Democratic Party in St. Louis, and Truman won the primary in a three-way race. His first term in the Senate was difficult, as he was a newcomer, but gradually it became apparent to the Senate's leadership that he was a work horse, not a show horse, and after shepherding through the upper house the Civil Aeronautics Act of 1938, he became coauthor with Senator Burton K. Wheeler of Montana of the Truman-Wheeler Transportation Act of 1940, a combination of rules governing water and rail transport in the country, a major administrative achievement.

Truman's tightest race, moreso than the presidential election of 1948, was his bid for senate reelection in 1940, against the destroyers of the Pendergast machine, Federal Attorney Maurice Milligan and Governor Lloyd C. Stark (a nurseryman of "Stark Delicious" apples fame). Stark had Roosevelt's secret support, and Truman squeaked through the primary because of 8,000 machine votes in St. Louis, votes from what were described as delivery wards, which came to him because of a trade of Kansas City and other votes in an intraparty contest for the governorship. Truman's plurality in the state was less than 8,000.

In his second Senate term, he quickly turned to the special committee, which consumed his time until he was nominated for the vice presidency.

The nomination in summer 1944 was a piece of derring-do by the Democratic Party bosses. It was not so much an effort to choose Truman as to remove the sitting vice president, Henry A. Wallace, whom the party leaders distrusted and—the word is not too strong—despised. Wallace was an amateur in politics, and had never run for office until 1940, when Roosevelt put him on the national ticket. He did not enjoy politics and politicians, and said openly that he was interested in issues, not people—a prime error for any would-be successful candidate. Roosevelt began to tire of Wallace when the vice president tangled with Secretary of Commerce Jesse H. Jones in 1943, even though Jones was no favorite of the president, who privately described the crusty Texan as Jesus H. Jones. The contention between the vice president and secretary became public, and to the surprise of observers, for it was not the president's usual way with squabbling subordinates, he pronounced a plague on both their houses. Roosevelt continued to say publicly and privately that he admired Wallace and that he was the obvious vice-presidential candidate. A cabal consisting of party treasurer Edwin W. Pauley, party secretary George E. Allen, the president's appointments secretary Major General Edwin M. Watson, together with national chairman Robert E. Hannegan and preceding chairman and then Postmaster General Frank C. Walker, thereupon determined to destroy Wallace. General Watson kept Wallace admirers out of the president's office and brought in Wallace antagonists. Gradually, the group brought the president around to their point of view.

The party leaders had made their calculation carefully, and it was uncomplicated in the extreme. The reason for ridding the ticket of Wallace was in part distrust and dislike, but also a belief that Roosevelt could not survive a fourth term and whoever was vice president would become president. After Roosevelt's return from the Teheran Conference late in 1943, his health had visibly worsened. He seemed to suffer from bronchitis. The party leaders did not know what ailed him, though there was talk of cancer, but it was obvious, they believed, that the president needed a healthy vice president and a trustworthy party man, such as Truman.

Roosevelt indeed was wearing out. On March 27, 1944, well before Truman's nomination at the Democratic national convention in Chicago on July 21, the president underwent a physical examination at Bethesda Naval Hospital and was seen by the staff cardiologist, Howard G. Bruenn, who was appalled by the president's condition. Bruenn knew the minute he helped lift the president out of the wheelchair onto the hospital table for the examination that Roosevelt was in trouble, for the president was short of breath. From that moment on, the diagnosis was of the worst: Bruenn found him in heart failure. The results of the examination were not made public, nor told to the president—who never asked Bruenn about his condition nor inquired whether Bruenn, who thereafter saw him almost daily and virtually became his personal physician, was a cardiologist (although the president did know that, as he indirectly mentioned to Secretary of the Treasury Henry Morgenthau, Jr., the night before he died).

One might ask why the leaders allowed Roosevelt to run. The truth was that the president wanted to run, and he was so powerful a figure within the party that no one dared try to convince him otherwise. Moreover, the party needed him. That year the Republicans nominated an attractive candidate, Governor Thomas E. Dewey of New York, and only "the champ," the party's strongest vote getter since Andrew Jackson, could win against Dewey.

At the convention Truman was duly nominated but not without a fight by Wallace, who defied the president. Through intermediaries Roosevelt had advised him not to run. There was a strong bid by a White House insider, the ambitious James F. Byrnes, who scented not the vice presidency but the presidency, as did Wallace. Byrnes was a former member of the House and the Senate, associate justice of the Supreme Court, and Roosevelt's "assistant president," to use the president's phrase, beginning in 1942. The president told both Wallace and Byrnes in advance of the convention that he was backing them, but after maneuvering them out he passed the nomination to Truman. The nominee had claimed that he did not want the nomination, which is the usual claim in American politics, but it is difficult to believe that Truman, who was ambitious, did not want the nomination that he knew meant the presidency. Moreover, to have been forward in seeking the post would not have endeared him to Roosevelt, who disliked Byrnes for that reason. The nominee also had labored under a singular awkwardness, namely, that his wife, Bess, for reasoning that defies imagination, did not want to live in the White House as she knew the nomination would mean, in view of Roosevelt's ill health.

Truman had not seen Roosevelt since March and met with him on August 18 for luncheon outside the White House on the south lawn, where the two Democratic candidates posed for photographers, and then after Roosevelt sent them, away the president told Truman about the atomic bomb, albeit in general terms, for the president's daughter, Anna Boettiger, soon joined them. The vice-presidential nominee was alarmed by Roosevelt's physical condition. Afterward he spoke with his senatorial assistant, Harry H. Vaughan, and said: "I had no idea he was in such a feeble condition. In pouring cream in his tea, he got more cream in the saucer than he did in the cup." He told Vaughan that the trouble did not seem mental, but that physically the president was going to pieces.

On September 7, the vice-presidential nominee and a World War I friend, Edward D. (Eddie) McKim, attended a White House reception, where McKim studied the president for an hour and a half. Afterward when he and Truman left the mansion, he stopped Truman and said: "Hey bud, turn around and take a look. You're going to be living in that house before long." Truman's response was: "Eddie, I'm afraid I am."

The resultant campaign did not focus on the vice-presidential candidate but upon Roosevelt, even though the president did not campaign much, if only because he was physically unable. Truman's speeches received little attention. The candidate afterward told a reporter friend that he drew crowds of two or three dozen, all over the country.

At a huge rally in Madison Square Garden, Truman had an unnerving experience, but it was about the only one—other than an accusation that he once had been a member of the Ku Klux Klan (which was not the case). He and Vice President Wallace were scheduled to enter the auditorium together. Truman had to wait until the very last moment before Wallace arrived because Wallace had decided to walk to the rally and it took more time than he anticipated. Truman was not certain about this explanation and was inclined to believe that this former rival for the nomination was stalling so he could make a separate entrance and receive applause from the pro-Wallace crowds. Nevertheless, they walked in together, arm in arm. After the two men entered that important evening, there were no more problems. A Truman confederate was in charge of broadcasting the meeting over the radio, and when each man was introduced separately, he saw to it that the "gain" was up for Truman and down for Wallace so that the radio audience, much more important than the Garden audience, would receive the proper impression.

After taking the oath from Vice President Wallace in an abbreviated ceremony held behind the White House because of wartime conditions and the need for ceremonial modesty, Truman remained the same unassuming individual he had been before. He continued in the same Connecticut Avenue apartment he had been living in since 1941, a five-story Moorish-style brick building dating to the 1920s. There, Trumans lived with their daughter Margaret (a junior and history major at George Washington University), and Mrs. Truman's mother, in two bedrooms with a single bath, a living room, a dining room, and a kitchen. The vice president received secret service protection, albeit with a single agent on duty.

The family enjoyed much the same life as before, except that the hectic duties of the investigating committee, together with heavy mail from Missouri constituents and the need to attend votes if not debates on the Senate floor, now were matters of the past.

The vice presidency appears to have been a time of relaxation for Truman. Bess Truman certainly enjoyed herself, and it was perhaps memory of that last, unfettered time that caused her toward the end of her husband's presidency to show some willingness to continue living in Washington where, after Truman's retirement from the White House, he might possibly remain as junior senator from Missouri in the way that John Quincy Adams a century and more before had gone to the House of Representatives. There was a pleasant round of parties in which the vice president and his lady substituted for the busy (or so said the newspaper accounts) chief executive.

Otherwise the family members did what pleased them. In a letter to her husband's cousin, Ethel Noland, Bess conveyed a charming scene of domestic contentment. "Marg," she wrote, "has gone to a picture show and Harry to a poker party. Mother is practically asleep in her chair—so it's very peaceful." The date of this idyllic scene was the day before President Roosevelt left Washington for Warm Springs, for a much-needed rest.

During this period, the vice president liked to show Missouri visitors and friends what he described as his "gold-plated" office ("pretty good for a country boy"), the special suite in the Capitol that went with his recent elevation. He kept his old Senate office, which made him feel more at home, especially the back room, with its wall covered with photographs and cartoons of his Senate years—the room he referred to as "the doghouse," in which he used to confer with important visitors.

He was sensitive to his new duties, and to a reporter for the *New York Times* he gave an interview that in its frankness showed what lay in store for reporters who for years had endured Roosevelt's general evasions of awkward questions. "What are you going to do with your spare time?" the reporter asked. "Study history," was the response. But then Truman got down to something more interesting. He said he would not follow the vice-presidential example of Charles G. Dawes during President Coolidge's second term. (Dawes had spent his time telling the Senate not to waste time, had gone to sleep at a crucial moment during a confirmation, and spent the rest of the time telling everyone how to shape up.) Nor would he follow that of his predecessor. He warmed to the latter example. He said,

Well, while Garner was Vice President there was hardly a day when at least half the members of the Senate did not see him in his office or talk to him somewhere around the Capitol. In the past four years I doubt if there are half a dozen Senators all told who have been in the Vice President's office. You can draw your own conclusions.

One of the first tasks Truman undertook as vice president was to fly out to Kansas City when Boss Tom Pendergast died on January 26, 1945. Pendergast was an ex-convict, having gone to Leavenworth in 1939, where he spent a year and a day for income tax evasion (he had forgotten to tell the internal revenue bureau about a huge bribe he had taken from fourteen fire insurance companies in exchange for obtaining for them a favorable settlement of $11 million in impounded premiums). Without hesitation Truman attended the funeral, going out in an army bomber; he could have found something to keep him away but refused. "He was always my friend," he told reporters unabashedly, "and I have always been his."

Vice President Truman saw Roosevelt only a few times—Roosevelt either was abroad at the Yalta Conference or at Warm Springs. On such occasions Truman was inconspicuous. One of Roosevelt's secretaries, Roberta Barrows, remarked years later when Truman had become famous, that: "Three or four times, he claims he came, but I can't remember the visits at all." He went to the White House for the president's meetings with the Big Four, the leaders in the House and Senate, but there were only a few meetings. The cabinet meetings did not count for anything. Truman told his biographer, Jonathan Daniels, that "Roosevelt never discussed anything important at his Cabinet meetings. Cabinet members, if they had anything to discuss, tried to see him privately after the meetings." He saw the president by appointment privately only on March 8 and March 19.

During the vice presidency, Truman had to perform one difficult task, which was to ensure the confirmation of former Vice President Wallace as secretary of commerce. This was no simple assignment, and Truman later told Daniels that when Roosevelt told him he was going to give Wallace the commerce department, his initial response was "Jesus Christ!"

The Wallace confirmation was nothing if not complicated. Wallace's preference for commerce was understandable. The president had felt sorry for his former running mate and faithful vice president for four years, and told Wallace, with more generosity than perhaps he should have displayed, that he, Wallace, could have any cabinet department save the department of state and the military departments. Without hesitation, Wallace asked for commerce, the department then presided over by his mortal enemy, Byron Jones.

FDR may not have felt too badly about the choice, for he was angry with Jones, who in the arrangements for the recent national convention in Chicago had seemed to be behind a division in the Texas delegation between pro-Roosevelt and anti-Roosevelt forces—Jones's nephew was a member of the anti-Roosevelt faction. The president proposed that Jones become an ambassador, an assignment Jones first indignantly rejected. He then left the cabinet in a huff.

However, for the president and thereby for Truman, who had to preside over the arrangement, the confirmation of Wallace at once turned into a bitter fight. Jones's partisans, who were many, especially in the South and among conservatives generally, raised up the possibility that Wallace would be unable to handle the Reconstruction Finance Corporation, the lending agency that was a part of Jones's bailiwick. Soon senators were whispering that with Wallace running the RFC, federal money would go out for every fad and scheme in creation, perhaps for giving each Hottentot a quart of milk. The latter accusation had been invented by the president of the National Association of Manufacturers, but it hurt Wallace's reputation. President Roosevelt, during discussions with the then vice president over renomination, had mentioned the canard.

The Wallace confirmation hearings and debate on the Senate floor turned into a great argument, which in its purposes probably was twofold. One was genuine concern that Wallace could not handle federal money. The other was, one strongly suspects, an indirect revolt against the president. During the war, Roosevelt represented the government to his fellow citizens and also to the nations of the world, and now that the war was coming to an end, the time had come to embarrass the president, to cut him down to size. Wallace's confirmation could be the occasion.

In the event, Truman was forced to break a tie—contrived or real must be a question—in favor of Wallace.

It is interesting that during Truman's short vice presidency he cast another deciding vote, two days before Roosevelt's death, that broke a Senate deadlock over whether recipients of lend–lease could use such funds for postwar reconstruction. Without Truman's intervention, all nonmilitary lend–lease shipments would have ceased upon the end of the war. One of Truman's early embarrassments in the presidency would be cessation of lend–lease to the Soviet Union, announced shortly after the end of the war in Europe, an order that he signed without reading it or thinking about it and which he was forced to change after furious protests from Moscow. Earlier he had broken the Senate tie on this issue, in favor of nonmilitary shipments.

During the vice presidency, Truman sought as best he could not to think of what lay ahead, although he knew full well. In a television series years later, entitled *Decision: The Conflicts of Harry S. Truman,* he said that: "It would have been very foolish not to realize that President Roosevelt was a very sick man. It became perfectly obvious to me that due to [his] health I would eventually inherit the presidency." When he saw FDR on March 19, "His eyes were sunken, his magnificent smile was missing from his careworn face. He seemed a spent man."

But as the weeks passed, the future seemed to extend itself and spring was in the air in the capital. One of Truman's ardent supporters (in part because of belief that Truman had to replace Wallace because of the president's ill health), the New Orleans builder of flat-bottomed landing craft, Andrew J. Higgins, had sent Truman his congratulations in November 1944 and ended on the note of "keep your good health." On April 4, 1945, Truman wrote Higgins: "I am just a figurehead now and don't have any hand in what takes place." Two days later he went from Washington to Buffalo and was accompanied by a single secret service agent.

What he did not know was that after the president came home from the Yalta Conference and made the speech to Congress sitting down in the well of the House chamber—the speech that seemed distressingly anecdotal, in which he mentioned his infirmity because of poliomyelitis—the president's immediate assistants were so concerned for Roosevelt's health that there was talk of a veritable regency. Anna Roosevelt took Jonathan Daniels aside—the later Truman biographer was then a White House aide—and expressed her fears, not of the president's death but of his increasing incapacity. She hinted at a regency in which she and her husband John would hold what would be dynastic positions.

As he remembered, "I was to be a sort of front." Daniels was shocked. He did not think it would work. Important people such as Congress of Industrial Organizations leader Philip Murray would not be willing to come to the White House to speak with a regent; they would insist on seeing the president. Daniels was so taken aback by the very idea that when he made an oral history for the Harry S. Truman Library, he enjoined his interlocutor not to release this portion of his history until he, himself, was ready to release it—even though by that time eighteen years had elapsed since President Roosevelt had died.

An interesting aspect of Anna Roosevelt's tentative proposal of a regency was that it did not even consider a role for the vice president. It was an evidence of how low in esteem Truman was held in the Roosevelt White House.

The afternoon of April 12, 1945, seemed at first like every other afternoon in the Senate, for discussion concerned water power and irrigation. Senator William Langer of North Dakota was holding forth on that subject, with the vice president in the chair. Leverett Saltonstall of Massachusetts was almost the only other senator on the floor, and a page approached him with a pink slip in Truman's handwriting: "Governor, will you take this seat for a while? I want to see a soldier boy from home in my office." Saltonstall

nodded and went down to sit on the dais. Truman said he would be gone no more than half an hour. Someone had placed an apple on his desk, and Saltonstall asked what he would do if he, the senator, ate the apple. The vice president said he would have to fine the senator. About an hour and a half later he returned, recessed the Senate, and walked over to the other side of the capitol for a drink with the Speaker of the House, Sam Rayburn, and some friends.

Then lightning struck in the form of a telephone message from Stephen T. Early from the White House. In a tight voice, he asked the vice president to come to the front entrance of the White House and go directly up to the family quarters on the second floor. There Mrs. Roosevelt rose to meet Truman, put her arm around his shoulder, and said gently: "The President is dead."

He asked Mrs. Roosevelt if there was anything he could do for her.

She asked the new president if there was anything they could do for him.

Truman's subsequent presidency of almost eight years, until January 20, 1953, was marked by partisanship, some of it caused by the fact that Truman himself was a partisan, accustomed to fight rather than negotiate. The times also were out of joint, as too many things were happening too quickly, and public opinion—and for that matter congressional opinion—could not always keep up.

The initial problem was to end the wars in Europe and Asia. The European war petered out after the suicide of Adolf Hitler, but ending the Japanese war seemed to require what Secretary of War Henry L. Stimson described as a shock. This was effected by nuclear bombs dropped on Hiroshima and Nagasaki.

Thereafter came reconversion, accompanied by labor strife and inflation. In 1945 and again in 1949, President Truman asked for expansion of the New Deal measures of his predecessor and with only a few exceptions, such as amendment of the Social Security Act, discovered that the country had turned conservative in domestic measures, unwilling to support further change until the 1960s and the presidential administration of Lyndon B. Johnson. Perhaps Truman's most notable domestic action was to stand up for the rights of black Americans in a way that his predecessor had not done and that looked forward to the Supreme Court decision of *Brown v. Board of Education of Topeka* (1954). During Truman's administration the armed forces were desegregated.

Perhaps his most notable domestic failure was to institute an internal security check on federal employees that not merely turned up almost no Communists but gave an excuse for extremists to abuse Americans' civil liberties under claim that they, the extremists, were protecting internal security.

In foreign policy, the Missouri president made a large contribution and in the Truman Doctrine (1947), Marshall Plan (1948), and North Atlantic Treaty (1949) turned the country away from the policy of isolation. Isolation had been championed by Presidents George Washington and Thomas Jefferson, embodied in the Monroe Doctrine, and confirmed in U.S. withdrawal from the political affairs of Europe after World War I. President Roosevelt told Premier Joseph Stalin at Yalta that U.S. troops would not remain in Europe. It was Truman who turned policy to what for the next half century would be a marked participation in the affairs of Europe and the world. This change was evident in his swift intervention in the Korean War in 1950.

After the presidency, Truman went back to the rambling Victorian house in Independence, from which he could see the skyscrapers of Kansas City ten miles to the west, and was active in writing his memoirs and raising money to build the Harry S. Truman Library on a knoll in a park a few blocks from his house. In his spare time, he made speeches around the country in support of Democratic candidates and causes. In 1964, his physical energy flagged. He was confined ever more to his house, where he died in 1972.

Underestimated during his presidency (in 1951 a Gallup popularity poll gave him a rating of 23 out of 100, one point below the rating of President Richard M. Nixon on the eve of his resignation), Truman's striking qualities came again to public attention in the early 1970s, at the time of the nation's defeat in the Vietnam War and President Nixon's increasing troubles and resignation. "Trumania" made its appearance; Truman's memory took on evidences of a cult, and popular enthusiasm for the Man of Independence has continued to the present day. Scholarly appreciations have been less enthusiastic, although it is of interest that three biographies in 1992–95, one of which received the Pulitzer Prize and was a massive best-seller, all announced his greatness.

REFERENCES

Robert H. Ferrell, *Choosing Truman: The Democratic Convention of 1944* (Columbia: University of Missouri Press, 1994); R.H. Ferrell, *Harry S. Truman: A Life* (Columbia: University of Missouri Press, 1994); Alonzo Hamby, *Man of the People: The Life of Harry Truman* (New York: Oxford University Press, 1995); David McCullough, *Truman* (New York: Simon and Schuster, 1992); Roberta Barrows, Jonathan Daniels, Edward D. McKim, and Harry H. Vaughan oral histories, Harry S. Truman Library, Independence, Mo.

ROBERT H. FERRELL is professor emeritus of history at Indiana University in Bloomington. He is the author of books on U.S. foreign policy and author or editor of ten books on President Truman.

ALBEN W. BARKLEY
(Library of Congress)

By *James K. Libbey*

arkley was a progressive politician and a partisan Democrat who became one of the "working" vice presidents in American history. It was during his term that the Heraldic Branch of the United States Army designed a special seal and flag for the Office of the Vice President.

Willie Alben Barkley was born near the village of Lowes, Kentucky, on November 24, 1877. His parents, John Wilson and Electra Eliza Barkley, immersed the child in the sanctity of family designations by christening him not only with the name of John's father, Alben, but also for good measure with "Willie" to honor uncles on both sides of the family. The first name, however, was favored by neither father nor mother who grew into the habit of calling their firstborn by his middle name, especially after Grandfather Alben died in 1880. Moreover, their son came to dislike his christened name and later changed it to Alben William Barkley.

Whether Willie or Alben, the son's name was not as important to the child as the nearly primitive environment and subsistence existence that surrounded his early years. Barkley was born in a log cabin. Sometimes half-jokingly and yet half-seriously, he would ponder the rustic birthright that had been a stepping stone into the White House for several of America's illustrious presidents. Such rustic circumstances, though, were not due to the family's existence on the wild frontier. John Barkley was an impoverished tenant farmer who specialized in raising dark tobacco, the sugary leaf used for chewing instead of smoking.

Without benefit of modern impediments to nature's course, the harsh but loving life shared by John and his wife produced like clockwork a succession of seven siblings for Alben. While children and their labor can be a blessing for a farm owner, the biennial appearance of a new mouth to feed spelled financial disaster for the tenant farmer. Almost frenetically, the Barkleys moved from one rented farm to another at least six times between 1877 and 1891 in John's efforts to provide for his family. Thus Alben was raised in an impecunious household whose members bordered daily on achieving the indistinction of being described as indigent.

Alben probably did not realize that he was poor until a family shopping trip to Mayfield when he was twelve revealed that store clerks wore Sunday suits during the week. He had, though, little time to contemplate his humble surroundings. From an early age he had to accept his share of work. As the Barkley family grew larger and Alben grew older, he began to assist his father on the farm, to help his mother with household chores, and to watch over his younger brothers and sisters. The interludes between sessions in country schools were filled with chopping wood, splitting rails, digging out stumps, setting tobacco, plowing fields, and dozens of other backbreaking tasks. All this work at an early age helped build a strong young man with a physical constitution that gave Alben enough durability to enjoy a long life in robust health.

At least twice in their early years together, the Barkleys had to draw deep from the wellspring of neighbors' good graces when their home was destroyed or damaged, first by fire and then by tornado. Spontaneously, friends gathered clothes and furniture and lent their labor to help the beleaguered family rebuild their home. As a result, the Barkleys never locked their smokehouse door; and if neighbors wanted to borrow tools, utensils, or food, they always received a welcome greeting. Certainly, this general lesson in reciprocity, so fundamental to the covenant of humanity in rural America and so basic to human relations, was driven home to the oldest Barkley child.

A primeval equality emerged from this hard rural life, reinforced in part by the old English custom of calling out each year all males regardless of race and fortune to improve county roads. These positive values were strengthened in Alben Barkley by a happy but strict upbringing by religious parents. His father held the position of elder in the Presbyterian church of Lowes, and his mother refused to light the stove on Sundays unless the pastor joined them for dinner. Liquor and playing cards never entered the home, and without radio, television, CD players, and other electronic gadgets that often promiscuously fill the modern mind, conversation absorbed the Barkleys' evening hours, and Alben Barkley became an apt student of the art.

In 1891, John Barkley made a decision of great importance to Alben's future. With the help of friends and neighbors, the family packed three wagons, tied their Jersey cow to one, and moved twenty-five miles southwest from Lowes to Clinton, the Hickman County seat. The nearby Mississippi River and the town's two colleges combined to provide Alben with a cultural atmosphere far in excess of anything he had experienced in Lowes. The move little helped the family fortunes, for John, expert in tobacco, found meager success in raising corn. Despite John's failure to improve the family's status through farming, Alben was able to fulfill his youthful desire for a college education. Shortly after the family had settled into the new home, Alben enrolled in Marvin College.

Alben never graduated from high school, but then, to describe Marvin as a "college" in modern terms would be as impossible as equating Alben's country education with the rigid K–12 grades so familiar to us today. Marvin, a Methodist school no longer in existence, accepted adolescents and trained them for adulthood. A single building housed most of its activities, and years later Alben could remember the names and count the numbers of his class of 1897 on a single hand. In this personal atmosphere, Alben's fine mind, which had been stimulated mainly by the raw frontier-like life of Lowes, grew with the knowledge and civilizing influences of tradition and the humanities. He would also become a lifelong Methodist.

He could attend Marvin only because of the kind patronage of President J.C. Speight, who provided the youth with a job as janitor. Five years later Barkley graduated, earning a Bachelor of Arts degree and a medal for oratory. Because Marvin functioned as a preparatory institute, his BA represented something between a high school diploma and a college degree. Regardless, his study of classical rhetoric and debates over current issues sharpened his interest in law and politics, an interest heightened by the success of his mentor, Speight, in winning a seat to the Kentucky State Senate in 1896.

Understandably, then, Barkley wanted to continue his education. He borrowed money, moved to Atlanta, Georgia, and enrolled as a sophomore in Emory College (now a university), a Methodist school closely connected with Marvin. Barkley spent the 1897–98 academic year in Georgia studying the classics and making speeches as a member of Emory's Few Debating Society. His poverty, though, forced him to return to Clinton and to accept a teaching position in the intermediate department of Marvin College. It was an unwise decision: the college struggled to pay its faculty and Barkley floundered as a teacher. In the midst of a disastrous term, his father abandoned the hazards of a farm for the security of a paycheck by moving his family to Paducah and accepting employment at a cordage mill. Forced to rent a room and buy his meals and uncertain about his college pay and teaching abilities, Barkley resigned from Marvin in December 1898 and joined his parents in Paducah, the city that later became synonymous with his name.

Barkley abandoned his dream of earning a law degree. Instead, he took the self-study route available at the time. He prevailed upon Charles K. Wheeler, Democratic representative for Kentucky's First Congressional District, to give him access to the attorney's library. In the summer of 1899, barristers William S. Bishop and John K. Hendrick hired Barkley as their law clerk. After two years of reading and working in the law, he passed the bar exam and opened his own office in 1901. Moreover, he received an appointment from Hendrick's friend, Judge L.D. Husbands, to serve as court reporter for the circuit court. The steady income subsidized Barkley's law practice and enabled him to pay off his college debts. Sensitive to his shortcomings in formal education, Barkley also saved money to attend, in 1902, a two-month law course at the University of Virginia. He listened to fifty lectures by leading experts and gained confidence in the law. As important, he used his leisure time to tour the campus and read about its architect, Thomas Jefferson. These readings left an indelible mark on his character. Then and thereafter he tended to measure people and politics against the Jeffersonian ideal of the common man.

Meanwhile, Barkley entered Paducah's social milieu with an enthusiasm that bordered on frenzy. One explanation for his behavior is that he had to overcome his outsider status by building those contacts that other lawyers, native to Paducah, acquired as their birthright. He joined the Broadway Methodist Episcopal Church, attended dances and socials, and sought membership in every local organization in sight. Each club not only acquired an energetic member but also a talented speaker. His rich baritone voice could be heard mellifluously preaching a lay sermon on Sunday from behind a Methodist pulpit or gleefully telling an anecdote on Monday before a sportsmen's group. Besides making a name for himself, Barkley's activities brought another benefit. He met and courted Dorothy Brower of Paducah and Tiptonville, Tennessee. Married on

June 23, 1903, in Tiptonville, their shared lives produced three children: David Murrell (1906), Marian Frances (1909), and Laura Louise (1911).

A year after his marriage, Barkley chose to enter the Democratic primary for county attorney. Simple ambition accounts for his decision; nevertheless, the campaign he waged is interesting because he demonstrated a style and pattern that served him well in most elections between then and 1954. First, he announced his candidacy in December 1904, well in advance of the March primary. Similar to most later contests, the primary rather than the general election was the key to gaining office in the heavily Democratic region. Second, Barkley's campaign hinged on his performance and often on his resources. Generally, the organization and leadership of his campaigns emerged solely at the time and place of his physical presence. Third, and for the humble post of county attorney, he overwhelmed the voters with personal appearances. Indeed, the energy and drive he displayed became his hallmark. Fourth, Barkley's gregarious nature fused with another quality he long possessed: a supreme ability to make speeches and engage opponents in debates. Finally, he won the 1905 election because of his rural background and his kinship with farmers, who showered him with their votes.

Barkley prosecuted approximately 300 individuals who transgressed the law and saved taxpayers thousands of dollars by challenging padded contracts and inflated claims against the county government. His diligent work and speaking abilities earned him a statewide reputation. In 1907, the Democratic State Central Committee invited him to serve on the Speakers' Bureau, and the State Association of County Attorneys elected him to the post of president. Barkley's rising star contrasted sharply with the sour image of the scandal-ridden Democratic courthouse clique. Not surprisingly, the local Democratic Club looked to Barkley to save the party by tapping him as the Democratic nominee for county judge. The 1909 election turned out to be the most vicious campaign in Barkley's career. His victory, in an unusual year when Republicans captured a majority of seats on the fiscal court, marked Barkley as a formidable political force.

Judge Barkley repaid his most loyal constituents—farmers—by nearly bankrupting McCracken County in order to widen and gravel each county road. Road building, in fact, became the prime feature of his administration. But he also inaugurated a number of progressive measures, such as appointing a purchasing agent and auditing county books, that served as benchmarks of integrity for later officeholders. In the midst of a vigorous term, Barkley told the press late in 1911 that he planned to be a candidate for First District representative to the U.S. Congress. The abrupt move can only be understood by the fact that Barkley had decided early in public life to make Congress a milestone if not a capstone to his political career. Ollie James precipitated the judge's plans when the incumbent congressman revealed his intention to seek a seat in the U.S. Senate. Once again, the Democratic primary proved crucial, as Barkley faced three strong contenders, including his former employer, Hendrick.

Barkley quickly plucked for himself two issues most dear to the hearts of farmers: lowering the tariff and lowering the boom on railroads through stricter regulation by the Interstate Commerce Commission. Moreover, he advocated federal support for highway construction. His opponents chided the judge for his liberal views and maligned him with the socialist tag. Midway through the 1912 campaign, however, Democrats at the Baltimore national convention selected Woodrow Wilson as the party's presidential nominee and adopted a progressive platform that bolstered Barkley's position. Adroitly, he converted the socialist label into party regularity. With the support of First District farmers, Barkley garnered nearly half the votes in the four-way primary and easily won the general election. He would be reelected six times to the U.S. House of Representatives and serve on the important Interstate and Foreign Commerce Committee.

Barkley's early years in Congress further shaped the political views he would hold in his maturity. He admired President Wilson and found that they shared a number of similarities, including a regional heritage and a strong belief in party. By the same token, Wilson went out of his way to cultivate the favor of Barkley and other lawmakers elected for the first time under the Wilson ticket. It was easy, then, for Barkley to enlist in Wilson's New Freedom program, which tried to restore economic competition by sweeping away special privileges. He strongly supported, among many others, the Clayton Antitrust Act of 1914, but once Barkley accepted the idea that federal power should be used to break up monopoly, he pragmatically moved beyond the New Freedom to seek governmental solutions to a variety of social problems. Thus by 1916 he spoke in favor of legislation restricting the use of child labor in interstate commerce and coauthored a bill to ban the sale of liquor in the District of Columbia.

The Shepard-Barkley Act laid the foundation for future prohibition measures. While the experiment in abstinence eventually turned sour and had to be abandoned, the issue put Barkley in the national limelight and in the forefront of the Progressive movement. Colleagues in Congress, from Maine to Missouri, asked him to spark their campaigns with his wit. Because his own reelection was generally assured after the primary, he could afford to spend most electoral seasons from 1916 to 1922 giving hundreds of talks for fellow Democrats and gaining credit as a party stalwart. Coupled with his solid base of support in western Kentucky, Barkley's brush with national prominence subtly colored his own ambition. On November 11, 1922, he declared his candidacy for the 1923 gubernatorial race in Kentucky.

The single four-year term provided in the state constitution tends to make the governorship either a launching pad for higher office or a rewarding honor to a lengthy political career. Because Barkley had no thought of retiring, most commentators argue that the 1923 canvass merely set the stage for his quest of a seat in the U.S. Senate. Regardless, he conducted a spirited campaign and exhibited such stamina that journalists labeled him the Iron Man. Understandably, Iron Man Barkley advocated the immediate completion of Kentucky's highway network as well as substantial improvements for public education,

but he also attacked coal-mining and horse-racing interests by suggesting higher taxes on coal and a ban on parimutuel betting. While he narrowly lost the primary, his behavior during and after the campaign gained the plaudits of most Commonwealth Democrats and strengthened his hand for the future. When Barkley announced for the Senate in 1926, no Democrat opposed him in the primary, and even the coal and racing lobbies quietly supported his bid, if only to prevent the reformer from running for governor in 1927.

Barkley unseated Republican incumbent Richard P. Ernst in the general election and, after fourteen years in the House, moved to the Senate in 1927. Assigned to the Library, Finance, and Banking and Currency committees and later to the Interstate Commerce Committee, he possessed a status far beyond his official position as a newly elected junior senator. As early as 1928, Democrats seriously considered Barkley for the second spot on the presidential ticket, and by 1932 he was selected temporary chairman and keynote speaker for the Democratic national convention. The intervening years witnessed the onslaught of the Great Depression. Barkley's background, experience, and progressive lineage enabled him to assume a major role as a national spokesman and political leader during the dramatic and eventful years of the several administrations of President Franklin D. Roosevelt.

The Wilsonian liberal became an apostle of the New Deal, a term more synonymous with Barkley than with any other figure of the 1930s except Roosevelt himself. Barkley assisted Senate Majority Leader Joseph T. Robinson in debating measures, effecting compromises, and securing votes for a host of New Deal bills. So identified did Barkley become with FDR's program that he often served as its defender on national radio. Moreover, Roosevelt picked this loyal lieutenant for the unique role of delivering the second consecutive keynote address before the party's convention of 1936, and, when Robinson died in July 1937, FDR urged Democratic senators to elect Barkley as Robinson's successor. The new Senate majority leader faced an early and major defeat in managing FDR's court-packing plan. Nevertheless, his accomplishments far outweighed his failures, and Barkley impressed his contemporaries by his mastery of legislative detail and his skill in the art of persuasion.

These skills received their greatest test during World War II. FDR's focus on foreign affairs left to Barkley extraordinary powers over domestic issues. The senator generally cooperated with the president, but he also felt compelled to preserve those internal interests of the nation's people that Roosevelt neglected because of external events. Barkley, then, slipped uneasily between roles as the administration's cheerleader and watchdog. He attacked, for example, the War Production Board for its habit of assigning military contracts to large rather than small businesses, and in February 1944 when FDR turned down as too little a tax bill, Barkley engineered a stinging rebuke to presidential power by successfully leading the fight to override FDR's veto. Barkley resigned his majority leader post, but his Democratic colleagues immediately reelected him. The whole affair established a precedent for autonomy not found among earlier congressional leaders.

The episode may have also profoundly affected contemporary events, for it kept Barkley from becoming president when FDR died on April 12, 1945. In 1944, Roosevelt changed vice presidents, picking Harry S. Truman to be his running mate. Political analysts admit that the February incident cost Barkley the chance of having his name, rather than Truman's, in the second spot on the Democratic ticket. Regardless, the seemingly indestructible Barkley endured after FDR's death as the statesman of American politics and as "Mr. Democrat" for his party. Although Barkley suffered the loss of his wife Dorothy to heart disease in 1947, he achieved new heights of popularity in the postwar years. He received awards for distinguished congressional service, ranked ahead of President Truman as the most requested of the Democratic Speakers' Bureau, and vied with war hero General Dwight D. Eisenhower as the most "fascinating American," according to *Look* magazine.

Small wonder that in 1948, when Democrats seemed to be on the ropes and awaiting the knockout punch, Truman asked the popular Kentuckian to serve again as keynote speaker for the party's convention. Barkley's rousing defense of New Deal liberalism so stirred the delegates that Truman felt compelled to name the senator as his running mate. It was a decision the president would not regret. In fact, the pair proved to be a dynamic team. While Truman mercilessly assaulted the nation by train, Barkley audaciously captured the attention of the electorate by his novel use of the airplane. He flew 150,000 miles and delivered 250 speeches, providing an awesome display of vocal and physical powers. When the November tally was complete, Truman and Barkley had fashioned a major upset.

On January 20, 1949, Barkley stopped being a senator when fellow Kentuckian and Supreme Court Associate Justice Stanley F. Reed administered the oath of office that converted Barkley into the nation's thirty-fifth vice president. He was proud of the honor bestowed on him by his party's nomination and the people's votes, though he never made a fuss over the additional distinction that he was also the oldest man to enter into these duties. However, coping with obscurity, not age, had been the prerequisite of office before Barkley walked onto the stage. In fact, one of Barkley's more famous but unoriginal anecdotes—removed from his repertoire after he became vice president—told to a friend shortly before the 1948 convention stated: "There once was a farmer who had two sons. Both boys showed great promise early in life. But the elder son went to sea and the younger son was elected Vice President and neither has been heard from since."

Barkley and many of his contemporaries had good reason to stop joking about the vice presidency after he took the oath of office. Not only did the Kentuckian bring stature to the position, but the course of the president's life reminded the voters that Truman was the third vice president to move up to the White House in the first forty-five years of the twentieth century. Over the years, the vice president had become more than just the Senate's presiding officer and tie-breaker and the president's replacement in time of tragedy. The office permitted its occupant to appoint a few Senate committees, sign congressional resolutions, select five candidates each for the Naval Academy and West Point, and represent the government on the Smithsonian Institution's Board of Regents.

Truman wanted Barkley's legislative experience made available to the entire executive branch of government and so insisted on Barkley's presence for each cabinet-level meeting. Also, when a congressional bill created the National Security Council, that important policy-making body included the vice president. Finally, Barkley's national fame and speaking abilities prompted the administration to use the vice president as its principal spokesman. One reporter calculated that in the first eight months of 1949, Barkley traveled across the country to deliver forty major addresses in support of the president's positions. This constant visibility in the national limelight turned Barkley's joke about the vice presidency on its ear.

Recognizing that Barkley brought extraordinary qualities to his post, President Truman ordered the Heraldic Branch of the U.S. Army to design a special seal and flag for the Office of the Vice President. These prestigious symbols, however, were not nearly so endearing as the title Barkley and his family gave to the office. One evening in the spring of 1949 he spent a quiet time with daughter Marian and grandson Stephen Truitt. The conversation turned to the awkward address, *Mr. Vice President*, that people used when they met Barkley. Ten-year-old Stephen thought *Gramps* should insert two *e*'s between the initials *V.P.* to form *Veep*. At his next news conference the proud grandfather told this story and the reporters picked up and began to employ the title *Veep* when they wrote articles about the vice president. Unlike the symbols of office created by the Heraldic Branch, Barkley did not pass this label on to his successors. The Veep became a special sign for Barkley alone and one that would be used with affection then and thereafter.

As if Barkley had not broken enough new ground to alter permanently the importance and style of the vice presidency, he added another first. On July 8, 1949, he attended a party given by the Clark Cliffords on board the White House

yacht *Margy*. One of the guests, Jane Rucker Hadley, caught the attentions and later the affections of the Veep. Mrs. Hadley—vivacious, attractive, and charming—was the middle-aged widow of a St. Louis attorney and secretary for the Wabash Railroad. She had come to Washington for a brief vacation with her close friends, the Cliffords. The moonlit night and the strains of "Some Enchanted Evening" struck a romantic chord in the hearts of Jane and the Veep. Although Jane returned to St. Louis, Barkley's affinity for planes allowed him to woo her in a cross-country romance that every American faithfully followed in the daily press. This whirlwind courtship ended on November 18, 1949, when Alben and Jane shared marriage vows in a simple ceremony before close friends and relatives. Thus Barkley was the first vice president to wed while he held that office.

Not all the accomplishments and activities Barkley undertook as vice president acquired the sympathetic interest of the nation. In his traditional and constitutional function as the Senate's presiding officer, the Veep more than once engaged in controversies that mirrored beliefs and principles he had long held and also shared with the administration. The most publicly disputed act Barkley performed occurred in March 1949. He ruled on a motion to end a ten-day filibuster conducted by southern senators who opposed a civil rights bill then being considered. Technically the motion, not the legislation, caused a bitter debate, and both sides had quoted Barkley extensively to buttress their views. The Veep's decision on the motion placed him squarely on the side of those legislators who strove to implement civil rights, but before he presented his emotion-packed ruling he led off with an anecdote. "The Chair," Barkley said, "feels somewhat like the man who was being ridden out of town on a rail. Someone asked him how he liked it. He said if it weren't for the honor of the thing, he would just as soon walk."

Barkley's peers marked his ruling as scurrilous or statesmanlike depending on their position, but few senators could sustain any genuine hatred for a man who so deftly encapsulated a potentially distasteful ruling in a syrup of digestible humor. Fortunately for the Veep's emotional stability, most of his chores in the Senate could be quietly performed or tactfully and wittily fulfilled without arousing the rancor that occurred over the civil rights motion. Congress responded to Barkley's masterful charm by awarding him a special gold medallion for his service, and on March 1, 1951, the thirty-eighth anniversary of his first year in Congress, President Truman made a surprise visit to the Senate chamber to honor the Veep. Truman carried a special gavel for the Senate's president, a gavel fashioned from the ancient timbers of the renovated White House.

Despite his unique role, executive knowledge, and high visibility, Barkley's age (seventy-four) prevented his dark-horse candidacy for president from reaching the finish line during the 1952 convention. January 1953 found Barkley unemployed and without political office for the first time in nearly a half-century. After a brief stint with his own national television show "Meet the Veep," Barkley and his bride retired to their Angles estate in Paducah, where he wrote his memoirs with the assistance of journalist Sidney Shalett. Retirement, however, did not suit Barkley, and, perhaps to redress the "too old" label that had ended his 1952 candidacy for president, he entered the 1954 Senate race, defeating Republican incumbent John Sherman Cooper by 80,000 votes. Barkley relished his return to Congress as a freshman legislator, though his colleagues honored him with an appointment to the prestigious Senate Foreign Relations Committee. He also remained a popular, much sought after speaker. Thus on April 30, 1956, he traveled to Lexington, Virginia, to give a keynote speech before a mock convention conducted by students at Washington and Lee University. At the conclusion of his address, he suffered a fatal heart attack, dying as he had lived, in the public arena. He was buried in Paducah.

REFERENCES

James K. Libbey, *Dear Alben: Mr. Barkley of Kentucky* (Lexington: University Press of Kentucky, 1979); Alben W. Barkley Papers, King Library, University of Kentucky, Lexington; Alben W. Barkley, *That Reminds Me* (Garden City, N.Y.: Doubleday, 1954); Jane R. Barkley, *I Married the Veep* (New York: Vanguard, 1958); Polly Ann Davis, "Alben W. Barkley: Senate Majority Leader and Vice President" (Ph.D. diss., University of Kentucky, 1963); Gerald S. Grinde, "The Early Political Career of Alben W. Barkley, 1877–1937" (Ph.D. diss., University of Illinois, 1976); Charles A. Leistner, "The Political Campaign Speaking of Alben W. Barkley" (Ph.D. diss., University of Missouri, 1958); William Ray Mofield, "The Speaking Role of Alben Barkley in the Campaign of 1948" (Ph.D. diss., Southern Illinois University, 1964); William O. Reichert, "The Political and Social Thought of Alben W. Barkley" (M.A. thesis, University of Kentucky, 1950); Jack R. Yakey, "Prelude to Defeat: Alben Barkley's Quest for the 1952 Democratic Presidential Nomination" (M.A. thesis, Central Missouri State University, 1973).

JAMES K. LIBBEY is a former administrator at Eastern Kentucky University in Richmond, Kentucky, and is an associate professor of social sciences at Embry-Riddle Aeronautical University. He is the author of more than a hundred historical publications, including a book and six articles on Alben W. Barkley.

RICHARD MILHOUS NIXON (1913–1994)

Vice President, 1953–1961

(President Dwight Eisenhower)

RICHARD M. NIXON
*(By permission of the Richard Nixon Library
& Birthplace)*

By Joan Hoff

Richard Milhous Nixon, born in Yorba Linda, California, on January 9, 1913, became the thirty-seventh president of the United States in 1969. On August 9, 1974, as a result of the Watergate affair, he resigned during his second term, becoming the only president in the country's history to leave office in this manner. Before this unprecedented event, however, he had served eight relatively uneventful years as vice president under Dwight D. Eisenhower.

The Irish ancestors of both his mother and his father dated back to the colonial period, and each grew up in the Midwest before migrating to California. Although Frank Nixon became a Quaker upon marrying Hannah Milhous in 1908, Nixon commented in his *Memoirs* (1978) that the type of Quakerism his family practiced—first in Yorba Linda and then in Whittier—resembled the Protestant churches in the area rather than the stricter version the Milhous family had known in Butlerville, Indiana. Nixon's novelist cousin Jessamyn West was more explicit in a 1976 interview with Fawn Brodie, saying: "[There was] no difference between preachers in the Yorba Linda Quaker church and hard shell Baptists. . . . [They were] very evangelical. . . . and rambunctious, singing, crying, going up [to the] front [of the church]." West hastened to add, however, that the Nixons did not personally participate in this unorthodox Quaker display of emotions, although she herself had once become a "born-again."

Because his father was neither a particularly good nor a lucky businessman, Nixon grew up as many boys of his generation did, poor but by no means impoverished. Although he was imbued with a 1920s ethos that combined hard work with the dream of unlimited opportunity, his father was only a marginally successful grocer. As a result, Nixon grew up realizing how difficult it was to make a living and acutely sensitive about preserving his own good name financially. (This is one of the reasons he defended himself in his 1952 "Checkers" speech so emotionally against charges of setting up a slush fund and why he went to great lengths at the height of Watergate to point out repeatedly that he and his aides had not profited financially from the affair.) "The problems you have during the time you are growing up as a member of a working family," Nixon later told an early biographer, "are the ones that stay with you all of your life."

A good student because he applied himself, Nixon excelled scholastically at both Whittier High School and College. His special talent turned out not to be football but debating, although he doggedly tried to make "first string" on his high school and college football teams. Interestingly, these interests helped him develop skills he later used as a politician: perseverance and rhetorical attack. They also reinforced his combative, aggressive personality and came to be both respected and resented in the course of his long political career.

After earning a scholarship to Duke Law School in 1934, Nixon worked even harder in law school, graduating third in his class. However, he did not obtain the hoped-for offer from a prestigious law firm upon graduation, so he returned to Whittier, where he practiced law from 1937 until 1942. Perhaps his meeting, courtship, and marriage to Thelma Catherine (Pat) Ryan between 1938 and 1940 constituted the most memorable episodes in Nixon's life prior to his entering politics in 1946.

World War II found the newlyweds in Washington, D.C., where Nixon worked in the tire-rationing section of the Office of Price Administration (OPA). Quickly disillusioned with the red tape of government bureaucracy, Nixon obtained a commission and served in the South Pacific between 1942 and 1946, rising to the rank of lieutenant commander. There was nothing particularly distinguished about either his civilian or military career during these years, and those who knew him best did not perceive any overt political ambition.

Like most American politicians since 1945, Nixon's views on government and domestic, as well as foreign, policies appear more influenced by his adult experiences beginning first with the Great Depression and then with World War II than with any unresolved childhood psychological crises or ideological influences that he may have experienced as a young man while going to school or establishing himself as a lawyer.

In contrast to his rather nondescript background, Nixon's political career prior to assuming the presidency proved as controversial as it was meteoric. Elected to the Eightieth Congress in 1946 at the age of thirty-three, he served two terms and then ran successfully in 1950 for the California seat in the U.S. Senate. By 1952, he was elected vice president of the United States at thirty-nine and only narrowly missed being elected president in 1960 when forty-seven. Eight years later, Nixon won the presidency in an almost equally close contest.

Nixon's twenty-three years as a politician before becoming president were peppered with controversy beginning in 1946 when he defeated the five-term liberal Democratic Congressman

Jerry Voorhis, and later in 1950 when he defeated the equally liberal Democrat Helen Gahagan Douglas for a Senate seat. In both campaigns, Nixon charged his opponents with having left-wing political views. In retrospect, however, the latest biographies of Nixon either strongly imply or actually conclude that because of the increasing postwar conservatism, he probably would have defeated Voorhis and Douglas without any Red-baiting.

Before becoming a Senator in 1950, as a freshman House of Representatives member of the House Committee on Un-American Activities (HUAC), Nixon initiated the successful attempt to end the diplomatic and governmental career of Alger Hiss by exposing his connections with the Communist Party in the 1930s. Nixon achieved national prominence during the course of this investigation of the relationship between self-confessed member of a communist spy ring Whittaker Chambers and Hiss who was convicted of perjury on January 21, 1950, after Nixon had been elected to the Senate.

Later studies of the Hiss case concluded that he was guilty of perjury as charged, and documents released from Russian archives in the 1990s indicated that Hiss, indeed, had passed documents to the USSR. At the time, liberals never forgave Nixon for stumbling onto the "pumpkin papers" (five rolls of microfilm that contained photographs of secret State Department documents hidden in Chambers's pumpkin patch) and then using them to promote his own career in the early years of the cold war.

Advisers to Dwight Eisenhower recommended that Nixon become the general's running mate in 1952, in part because of his well-publicized anticommunist activities. But, as Herbert Brownell later said, Nixon was also chosen because "he was young, geographically right [being from California], had experience both in the House and the Senate with a good voting record, and was an excellent speaker." Moreover, he was a team player, had expert knowledge of domestic politics, and among Republicans had become a popular critic of Truman and Democrats. Nixon viewed his own role on the ticket as that of peacemaker between the Eisenhower and

Robert Taft factions in the Republican Party that had developed before the convention when the two men vied with each other for the presidential nomination.

Within two months after accepting the nomination, however, Nixon faced a charge published on September 18 that he had created a private slush fund of slightly more than $18,000 from rich southern Californians. Nixon acknowledged the existence of such a fund, saying that he was actually saving the taxpayers money by using private donations to pay for political expenses in excess of the amounts allowable by law to a senator. After the *Washington Post* and New York *Herald Tribune* called for his resignation from the ticket and when a few of Eisenhower's advisers began to wonder if he should, Nixon decided to go on nationwide television on September 23, 1952, to defend himself.

In this broadcast, he presented embarrassingly detailed information about his family's finances, including the fact that his wife Pat did not own a fur coat like so many Democratic politicians' wives but only "a respectable Republican cloth coat." This speech is probably best remembered, however, because of his maudlin declaration that his children would keep a dog named Checkers, even though the cocker spaniel had been a political gift.

The mere hint at financial wrongdoing threatened Nixon's sense of working-class integrity, and so he felt impelled to defend the fund with an emotional and very personal financial narrative. His performance in this broadcast also demonstrated his by then famous ability to attack opponents by innuendo. In this instance, he drew upon statements he had already made on the West Coast about his wife's cloth coat compared to the mink ones worn by wealthy Democrats, the fact that Democratic vice presidential candidate John Sparkman had placed his wife on the federal payroll, and that Adali Stevenson also had such a fund. For good measure and in typically overkill fashion, he also implied that he was being unfairly charged because of his role in the Hiss case and reiterated the Republican campaign slogan of corruption, communism, and Korea.

This speech has been so satirized and condemned by Nixon haters from 1952 down to the present that it is often forgotten that it marked Nixon's debut as a successful television personality. Denounced for its emotionalism, its illogical assertions, and its implicit attacks on Democrats, much of what Nixon said he had already previewed during the campaign on live audiences with good results. Its success among Republicans at large sealed its fate among his opponents as the worst political speech in history. Some have even maintained that the memory of it contributed to his defeat in 1960 and that dislike for Nixon among left-of-center intellectuals stemmed as much from the "Checkers" talk as from his early campaigns against Voorhis and Douglas, and his role in the Hiss case.

One thing is sure: when seen today in its uncut version, it still makes for powerful television and shows Nixon at his debating best—looking directly into the camera and delivering an effective, engaging, and emotional speech. Not until John Kennedy made similar use of television in 1960 did Democratic liberals think such performances could be respectable. Today personal testimonials by politicians about their private lives have become so commonplace that few question their authenticity or effectiveness. Nixon successfully defended himself in this famous Checkers speech, forcing Eisenhower to keep him on the Republican ticket as vice president.

Except for the anticommunist hysteria known as McCarthyism, the 1950s were relatively quiet domestic years for the country, as well as for Nixon politically, despite the fact that he later placed five of his *Six Crises* (1962) in that decade. Of these, probably only one was—the 1952 charge about a slush fund. Following the guilty verdict in the Hiss case, Nixon did not take much advantage of McCarthyism (a term meaning charging people indiscriminately and without substantiation of being communists) in the first half of the 1950s.

Despite his early Red-baiting campaigns in California and the Hiss affair, it became clear that Nixon simply did not make the single-minded pursuit of domestic communists *the*

major goal of his public life. He was too much of a political pragmatist and centrist to place all his eggs in one basket.

Although he found Joseph McCarthy "personally likable," he recognized that his extremism was "leading him and others to destruction." Instead, he "kept some distance between himself and McCarthy" as McCarthyism emerged in the early 1950s and Eisenhower used Nixon "to put . . . out brushfires started by McCarthy" because as vice president he had credibility on both sides of the issue. Despite numerous private meetings with McCarthy at the president's request, in which he attempted to modify or redirect the subcommittee's activities, by 1954 Nixon could not tolerate the direct attacks on the administration of the Senate's Permanent Investigations Subcommittee (known as the McCarthy Committee) hearings of alleged spying at the army base at Fort Monmouth, Wisconsin. As president of the Senate, Nixon appointed the select committee that ultimately voted to censure McCarthy on December 2, 1954.

During his first term as vice president, Nixon concentrated on becoming an expert on international affairs, making many trips abroad and becoming acquainted with leading heads of state. The first, in 1953, lasted sixty-nine days, during which Nixon visited nations in Asia and the Middle East. He later said in his memoirs that the trip had been highly educational and convinced him that "foreign policy was a field in which [he] had great interest and at least some ability."

While Nixon was vice president, the Eisenhower administration faced several serious foreign policy crises. The first occurred in spring 1954 when the French were defeated and overrun at their military outpost in Vietnam called Dien Bien Phu. Despite the fact that the United States had heavily financed the French occupation of Vietnam since World War II, Eisenhower decided—against the advice of Nixon, Secretary of State John Foster Dulles, and Admiral Arthur Radford of the Joint Chiefs of Staff—not to bomb or commit U.S. troops there once the French withdrew. Thus, Nixon's first attempt to influence foreign policy as vice president failed. Although the United States did not sign the 1954

Geneva Accords dividing Vietnam into North and South, it promised not to oppose the settlement by force. Nonetheless, in the same year the United States took the lead in setting up the Southeast Asia Treaty Organization (SEATO), pledged to the defense of South Vietnam. In 1956, the Eisenhower administration refused to honor nationwide elections in Vietnam because it was clear that the South under Ngo Dinh Diem would lose. In July, Nixon made a thirteen-day trip to the Far East, visiting South Vietnam on the second anniversary of Diem as president, thus giving him the approval of the administration.

In October, during the 1956 presidential campaign, two foreign policy crises occurred almost simultaneously: the popular rebellions in Poland and the Hungary and the Israeli invasion of Egypt over control of the Suez Canal. Nixon quickly made headlines by calling Nikita Khrushchev the Butcher of Budapest. The United States did nothing to aid the uprisings after rhetorically encouraging such actions in Eastern Europe. In his memoirs, Nixon said that he thought Eisenhower and Dulles were wrong in pressuring Britain, France, and Israel (with the concurrence of the USSR) into withdrawing their forces from the Suez because it meant that "from this time forward the United States should by necessity be forced to 'go it alone' in the foreign policy leadership of the free world." Thus, as vice president, he once again failed to affect foreign policy under the Eisenhower administration.

Part of the problem was, as Nixon himself said in a July 1958 interview in *Saturday Evening Post*, as vice president under Eisenhower he was more willing to take risks than the president: "I am not necessarily a respecter of the *status quo* in foreign affairs. I am a *chance taker* in foreign affairs. I would take chances for peace." However, he approved of allowing the CIA to help overthrow the nationalist government of Iran in 1953, of sending marines into Lebanon in 1958, and of organizing indigenous military units to invade both Guatemala and Cuba.

The election year of 1956 proved difficult for Nixon not only because of foreign policy crises not resolved to his satisfaction, but also because his place on the ticket as vice president was once

again challenged. This time it was by Harold Stassen, who in the summer of 1956 was at the height of his prominence as Eisenhower's "Secretary of Peace" and cabinet-level adviser because of his conduct of Geneva "Open Skies" disarmament talks with the Soviets. In July, Stassen apparently told the president that a private poll showed that Nixon would lose the Republicans more votes (4 to 6 percent of the electorate) than other possible running mates, such as Governor Christian Herter of Massachusetts.

At the beginning of the year Eisenhower had announced he would run again but refused to announce his choice for vice president. In fact he offered Nixon a cabinet post, excepting State and Justice, saying that he needed administrative experience if he wanted to run for president in 1960. When Nixon responded that he would be happy to serve again, Eisenhower did not respond negatively. Stassen announced in July that he would support Herter for vice president. Nixon immediately obtained the endorsement of 180 of 203 Republican members of the House, and Eisenhower responded by offering Herter a State Department job if he did not vie for the vice presidential nomination. Herter then offered to renominate Nixon at the forthcoming Republican convention. Not until the convention in August did Stassen finally capitulate and agree to second Nixon's renomination.

It is still not clear who prompted Stassen to initiate a "dump Nixon" campaign. Columnist Drew Pearson said that it was Milton Eisenhower, the president's brother, but he specifically denied this charge in a private letter to Nixon. There is circumstantial evidence indicating that Dulles may have encouraged Stassen to discredit himself and therefore remove him from his cabinet position because Stassen had more direct access to the president than had the secretary of state. In 1957, Stassen was transferred to the State Department and immediately resigned to run unsuccessfully for governor of Pennsylvania.

In addition to the 1952 Checkers speech, two other media events at the end of the decade enhanced Nixon's political fortunes and popularity with the general public: the stoning of his car in Caracas in 1958 and his 1959 "kitchen" encounter with Soviet leader Nikita Khrushchev in Moscow, during which the two men jabbed their fingers at one another and argued the merits of their two very different systems of government and economics. In a word, Nixon was a television success in the 1950s before he became a television failure in the 1960s following two major political defeats. None of these three events, however, added up to a common pattern of constant controversy or crises, as much as they represented sporadic and potentially negative incidents that Nixon turned into politically profitable media opportunities during the valuable, but often discouraging, learning process he underwent during his two terms as vice president.

His major publicity faux pas occurred in 1958 when the State Department leaked to *The New York Times* information about 5,000 letters, 80 percent of which opposed the administration's policy of defending Quemoy and Matsu, two small offshore islands held by the Chinese Nationalists that the Chinese Communists shelled periodically. Nixon overreacted, threatening government employees who "sabotaged" foreign policy through leaks. Accused of "fascist tendencies" by the press, the vice president sent out a defensive form letter and later said that he was only defending Dulles's Far East policies against a small group in the State Department. At the same time, he launched a full-scale attack on the previous foreign policy of Harry Truman and Dean Acheson as having promoted appeasement and war rather than peace. Eisenhower forced Nixon to say that he did not "question the sincerity or patriotism of those who criticize our policies."

Always outside President Eisenhower's private group of advisers, especially those on the National Security Council who advised the president on foreign policy, and occasionally humiliated by Ike in public, Nixon bided his time and mended his own political fences by courting both moderate and conservative Republicans and creating a "centrist" image of himself among supporters within his own party. This ensured his presidential nomination in 1960. Eisenhower gave him few formal responsibilities during the 1950s; yet, in eight years Nixon permanently upgraded the office of vice president and gave it a much more meaningful and institutionalized role. In part he accomplished this through several well-publicized trips abroad on behalf of the president in the 1950s. (Nixon nostalgically repeated the 1953 trip to Asia and the Middle East as ex-president in 1985.)

The vice presidency also assumed greater importance because Eisenhower suffered a heart attack in 1955, a bout with ileitis in 1956, and a stroke in 1957. Throughout all these illnesses, Nixon handled himself with considerable tact and self-effacement while presiding over nineteen cabinet sessions and twenty-six meetings of the National Security Council. Following his stroke, President Eisenhower worked out a plan with Nixon, Secretary of State Dulles, and Attorney General William Rogers to create the office of acting president in the event he became incapacitated from illness. This formal agreement substituted under Presidents Eisenhower and Kennedy for a constitutional amendment (not ratified until 1967) that granted the vice president full authority to govern when the president could not discharge the powers and duties of his office.

Nixon was so well positioned to run for the presidency in 1960 that despite the trouncing the Republicans experienced in the 1958 midterm elections and potential challenges from the governors of New York and California—Nelson Rockefeller and Ronald Reagan—he won the Republican nomination for president. Once again, he received only lukewarm support from Eisenhower because their relationship had always been an ambiguous one. The president had always approved of Nixon's aggressiveness and partisanship but questioned his maturity. It did not help when Eisenhower was asked at a press conference in August about Nixon's role in the decision-making process and replied: "If you give me a week, I might think of one. I don't remember."

Instead of taking an active public role in Nixon's campaign, Eisenhower held back. Nixon later said in his memoirs that this was because Eisenhower did not want to "overshadow my own appearances," while the president remembered that Nixon did not want him in the campaign until the very end. (Moreover, he ignored Eisenhower's advice not to debate Kennedy, because Nixon was still bedazzled by his victory over Khrushchev in their "debate" the year before.) Whichever interpretation of Eisenhower's lack of participation in the campaign is true, it proved a costly mistake as Kennedy successfully zeroed in on a mythical missile gap and other failures of the Republican administration to be tough enough on communism.

Nixon's unsuccessful campaign against John F. Kennedy for the presidency was fraught with ironies and political lessons he never forgot—not the least of which was that he had to answer the charge that he was soft on communism in Castro's Cuba without being able to reveal that the administration had a plan to invade the island. He also was left holding the bag after Eisenhower lied about the mission of a U-2 spy plane shot down by the Russians. Once again Nixon had to defend an administration that looked inept in dealing with communism abroad when he had not been privy to many of the foreign policy decisions he defended.

To make matters worse, the press repeatedly described Kennedy as a "youthful front-runner" representing a new generation, when in fact both men came from approximately the same age cohort, Nixon being only four years older than his forty-three-year-old Democratic opponent. In the course of the campaign, Kennedy was successfully packaged to appear what, in fact, he turned out not to be: a devoted father and family man in good health, an intellectual, a bona fide war hero, and a liberal Democrat. The fact that Nixon's congressional and vice-presidential records on social issues, especially civil rights and foreign policy, were more liberal than Kennedy's were lost in this media blitz, as were JFK's womanizing, chronic back ailments and Addison's disease, mediocre cultural and intellectual interests, his cold warriorism, his conservative fiscal views, and his cautious, at best, attitudes about social reform. Nixon also learned the hard way that television would play a most significant role in the 1960 election—the closest one in U.S. history since Grover Cleveland defeated James G. Blaine in

1884. Nixon's successful television tactics of the 1950s proved outmoded in one-on-one debates with Kennedy. Almost overnight, the man who had been touted as a "handsome" young returning veteran in 1946 became "ugly" after he "lost" four nationally televised debates with Kennedy in September and October—losses based not on substantive points made but on style and image. Nothing new was said or revealed in any of the debates, and those who listened to them thought Nixon carried the day, but those who watched them on television rallied to Kennedy.

Nixon's speaking style had long been described as "effective" but not "eloquent." It stemmed from his high school and college days, when he had employed standard debating techniques such as thorough preparation, immediate feedback to improve the next time around, and the use of surprise attacks whenever possible rather than defensive tactics. These debating techniques stood him in good stead until the rules of political debate changed dramatically with television, as Nixon found out so painfully in the 1960 debates with John Kennedy. Forced then to adapt to a situation where scoring points did not matter as much as image, Nixon adapted his debating skills after 1960 to the age of television more successfully than is usually thought.

Even more frustrating to Nixon during the 1960s presidential campaign was his inability to capitalize on his civil rights record among African American voters. As vice president, Nixon had been a stronger supporter of civil rights in the 1950s than either Eisenhower, Kennedy, or Johnson. When he presided over the Senate, his rulings consistently favored those who opposed the use of filibusters to block civil rights legislation, and he chaired the Committee on Government Contracts that oversaw enforcement of nondiscrimination provisions of government contracts, recommending in his final report the establishment of "a positive policy of nondiscrimination" by employers that he later supported as president. In the fall of 1957, during the integration crisis at Little Rock Central High, Nixon strongly defended the administration's use of troops against attacks from southern newspaper editors and congressmen, even though he was never able to persuade Eisenhower to meet directly with African American leaders. He later said that he supported civil rights for blacks and equal rights for women not because it would "help" members of either group but because "it was fair" and good for the nation because it prevented "wasted talent."

Nixon always denied that he was a conservative on civil rights at any time during his career, citing his support as vice president for the 1957 Civil Rights Act and Equal Right Amendment every time it was introduced in Congress. Although he adopted a white-oriented southern strategy for the Republican Party in the late 1960s, earlier in the 1960 presidential campaign Nixon had expected to be able to increase black support for the Republican Party beyond Eisenhower's 39 percent in 1956 because of his previous civil rights record and Martin Luther King, Jr.'s, personal promise to register African Americans for the Republican Party in the South. He also had the support in 1960 of such prominent African American athletes as Jackie Robinson.

After the Democrats nominated Kennedy, whose Catholicism brought an unexpected number of white southern Protestants over to the Republican Party, Nixon appealed more carefully to both blacks and whites in the South than he had originally intended. As it turned out, Kennedy's highly publicized intervention when Martin Luther King, Jr., was arrested in October won over a crucial number of black voters, including Robinson. Before this incident King (and Robinson) had openly praised Nixon above all other presidential candidates for caring about the race issue. Despite Kennedy's "grandstanding" on King's arrest and subsequent jailing, Nixon still captured 32 percent of the black vote in 1960, but in such a close election that was not enough. Later, as a very public private citizen in the 1960s, Nixon, unlike George Bush, supported the Civil Rights Acts of 1964 and 1966—not southern segregationist planks in Republican state platforms. Nixon also consistently opposed the poll tax and supported antilynching legislation. Far from being a bland supporter of civil rights, Nixon's record was better than any of the political opponents he ran against for the Senate, vice president, and president (with the exception of Hubert Humphrey).

To his credit, Nixon did not challenge the election he lost to John F. Kennedy by only 113,000 popular votes (less than one-half vote per precinct nationwide), although there was every indication that the Democrats did not legally win in either Illinois or Texas, whose combined electoral college tally tipped the election in their favor, 303 to 219. Moreover, there were confused returns from Alabama and such close votes in Missouri, New Mexico, Nevada, and Hawaii that a shift of less than 12,000 votes would have given Nixon a majority in the electoral college. Such luminaries of the Republican Party as Bryce Harlow, Herbert Klein, Len Hall, Thruston Morton, and even Eisenhower all urged Nixon to challenge the results because of the many reported cases of fraud, but he steadfastly refused. "Our country can't afford the agony of a constitutional crisis," Nixon remarked in an unconsciously prescient moment to a reporter who had unearthed a number of voting irregularities in Illinois and Texas, "and I damn well will not be a party to creating one just to become President or anything else." Nonetheless, after 1960, Nixon resolved never again to take any preelection lead for granted—not in 1968 or even in 1972. All future campaigns became "no holds barred" contests.

During his years as Eisenhower's vice president, Nixon campaigned widely for Republican candidates and in the process obtained the unenviable reputation of being the party hatchet man, especially because of his attacks on Adlai Stevenson, twice the Democratic presidential candidate in the 1950s. As a result, elements within the press, many academics, and liberals in general found it easier to criticize the conservatism of the Eisenhower administrations by concentrating on the personality and campaign tactics of his vice president rather than by attacking a popular president. What they overlooked in his performance then (and later after he became president) was his consistent support for liberal educational reform, civil rights, and for moderate, as well as conservative, Republican candidates on the campaign trail, thereby building up a broad base of support among Republicans that belied the one dimensional view his critics projected of him.

Richard Nixon's apprenticeship under Eisenhower left him with strong negative impressions about cabinet government in general, and the National Security Council in particular—impressions he would act on later when he became president in 1969. He is considered one of the most successful vice presidents, if for no other reason than his institutionalization of that office, so that future occupants could play a more significant role in policy formulation that he had been able to in the 1950s.

By 1968, Richard Milhous Nixon was once again positioned to win his party's nomination for the United States presidency. This time, unlike in 1960, he faced a Democratic Party hopelessly divided over the Indochinese war and haplessly led by Hubert Humphrey in the wake of LBJ's unexpected refusal to run again, Robert Kennedy's assassination, and a strong third-party bid by George C. Wallace. During the 1968 campaign, Nixon's more-liberal opponent Hubert Humphrey appeared to be defending past U.S. efforts to win the Vietnam War more than was Nixon, his Republican opponent whom many considered to be an original Cold Warrior. Had President Johnson halted the bombing of North Vietnam and renewed the Paris peace talks before the end of October, Humphrey might have been able to squeeze by Nixon, for the election results proved to be almost as close as they had been in 1960, with Nixon winning by 500,000 popular votes and receiving 301 electoral votes compared to 191 for Humphrey and 46 for Wallace. In 1972, Nixon won by a landslide with 520 electoral votes to 17 for George McGovern and a margin of almost 18 million popular votes.

Had Nixon left office after his first term, his administration would have been remembered as one of the most successful since the World War II, largely because of his often overlooked domestic achievements and his highly publicized, but rather ephemeral, foreign policy. Unfortunately, he precipitated the constitutional crisis known as Watergate and was forced, in August 1974, to resign from office or face a Senate impeachment trial.

In the areas of civil rights, it was Nixon, not Eisenhower, Kennedy, or Johnson, who actually desegregated southern schools rather than simply talk about it. His administration also enforced such affirmative actions programs as the Philadelphia "set-asides," one in the construction industry, and increased funding that so the Equal Economic Opportunity Commission could effectively implement the 1964 Civil Rights Act, making his civil rights record with respect to women and Native Americans one of the best. With respect to the environment, Nixon both led and accepted from Congress the first concrete federal legislation on this issue. His administration was also impressive in retrospect for its reorganization of the executive branch of government that most of his successors in office simply emulated or tinkered with but did not basically change, including his restructuring of the National Security Council. Nixon failed to achieve welfare and health care reform, but his bold attempts in both areas (opposed by liberals and conservatives alike at the time) remain the most comprehensive suggestions made by any president after FDR and before Bill Clinton and the One Hundred Fourth Congress.

Of all his innovative foreign policy endeavors, only one—the opening of China—survived. Détente with the Soviet Union became a dirty word in the Ford administration and was not pursued by Presidents Ford, Carter, or Reagan until Gorbachev appeared on the scene. Nixon formulated no coherent Middle East foreign policy before the 1973 October war and then it consisted largely of Kissinger's shuttling around telling both the Arabs and Isaelis what they wanted to hear. This proved more show than substance. Nor did Nixon develop a third-world policy except to use certain countries as pawns in the geopolitical battle with the USSR. In fact, his policy toward Africa favored the white minority regimes in that part of the world.

But it was the Watergate scandal that will forever cast a shadow on Nixon's presidency because it involved the highest officials of government. The cover-up by the president and his top aides of the original break-in and bugging at Democratic national committee headquarters located in Washington, D.C.'s Watergate complex on June 17, 1972, and related corrupt or criminal political activities ultimately resulted in the indictment, conviction, and sentencing of twenty men. These included the top White House aides to Nixon (John Ehrlichman and H.R. Haldeman), the president's counsel (John W. Dean III), the president's special assistant (Charles Colson), one former cabinet member (Attorney General John Mitchell, Jr.), and others who worked for the Committee for the Reelection of the President (CRP, but usually derogatorily referred to as CREEP) and/or the White House Special Investigative Unit known more commonly as the Plumbers, whose members engaged in break-ins before Watergate occurred.

Most of these men functioned as Republican election officials or presidential advisers in whom public trust had been placed. A few Plumbers such as E. Howard Hunt, James McCord, and G. Gordon Liddy—all former CIA or FBI agents—were specifically employed by the White House with private funds to carry out political espionage; they in turn hired the four Cubans arrested in the Watergate complex. All served time for their participation in the original crime burglary and bugging of the Democratic Party national offices. Despite multiple investigations and books, many factual questions remain unanswered about both the Watergate incident itself and its still-disputed historical significance.

Yet, most scholars and journalists, and quite a few prolific ex-felons continue to skew Nixon's legacy as president by attributing too much of Nixon's foreign policy to Kissinger; by almost entirely ignoring his constructive domestic achievements; and by refusing to recognize the downhill course in American politics that Watergate exacerbated, but neither originated nor ended. The system worked during Watergate in that it held Nixon and his aides accountable, but it has not held any other major politician or policy maker constitutionally accountable since.

REFERENCES

Stephen E. Ambrose, *Nixon*, 3 vols. (New York: Simon and Schuster, 1987, 1989, 1991); Fawn M. Brodie, *Richard Nixon: The Shaping of His Character* (New York: W.W. Norton, 1981); Belinda Kornitzer, *The Real Nixon: An Intimate Biography* (New York: Rand McNally, 1960); Earl Mazo and Stephen Hess, *Nixon: A Political Portrait* (New York: Harper & Row, 1968); Joan Hoff, *Nixon Reconsidered* (New York: Basic Books, 1994); Roger Morris, *Richard Milhous Nixon: The Rise of an American Politician* (New York: Holt, 1990); Richard M. Nixon: *Memoirs*, 3 vols. (New York: Grosset & Dunlap, 1978); Richard M. Nixon, *Six Crises* (New York: Doubleday, 1962); Herbert S. Parmet, *Richard Nixon and His America* (Boston: Little, Brown, 1990); Tom Wicker, *One of Us: Richard Nixon and the American Dream* (New York: Random House, 1991); Garry Wills, *Nixon Agonistes: The Crisis of the Self-Made Man* (Boston: Houghton Mifflin, 1970).

JOAN HOFF is a professor at the Contemporary History Institute at Ohio University. Previously, she was president and CEO of the Center for the Study of the Presidency and a professor of history at Indiana University, Bloomington. A specialist in U.S. foreign policy and politics, and women's legal history, she is author of *American Business and Foreign Policy, 1920–1933; Ideology and Economics: United States Relations with the Soviet Union, 1918–1933; Herbert Hoover: Forgotten Progressive*; and *Nixon Reconsidered*. Her books on women include *Law, Gender, and Injustice: A Legal History of U.S. Women* and *The Rights of Passage: The Past, Present and Future of the ERA*.

LYNDON BAINES JOHNSON (1908–1973)

Vice President, 1961–1963

(President John F. Kennedy)

LYNDON BAINES JOHNSON
(Library of Congress)

By G.L. Seligmann

For some—Adams, Jefferson, Van Buren, Nixon, and Bush—the vice presidency was but one rung in ascending the political ladder. For others—Tyler, Fillmore, Andrew Johnson, Arthur, Teddy Roosevelt, Coolidge, Truman, and Ford—it was the route to an office they probably would not have otherwise held. For many—Aaron Burr, George Clinton, Levi P. Morton, and Alben Barkley, among others—it marked the peak of their political careers. For a few—John Nance Garner comes to mind—it was

a decline in their political power. But for none did the office of vice president represent such a low point of their political career, sandwiched between the considerable power of a Senate majority leader and the awesome power of the presidency, as it did for Lyndon Baines Johnson.

Johnson was born in 1908 in the hill country of Texas, the eldest of Sam and Rebekah Johnson's four children. Sam was a teacher, farmer, and sometime member of the Texas state legislature, but he went broke early in the agricultural depression of the 1920s and moved his family to Johnson City, named after Lyndon's grandfather. Johnson graduated from high school in 1924 and spent a year as a laborer in California, followed by a return to Johnson City and a series of menial jobs. At age eighteen, Johnson borrowed a small stake and enrolled in Southwest Texas State Teachers College in San Marco. He struggled to pay his way through school and dropped out for a year to teach Hispanic children in the small town of Cotulla—an experience that had great influence on his later views of what society owed the poor and the disadvantaged.

After teaching in Houston briefly following graduation from college, Johnson embarked on his first job in politics, moving to Washington as secretary to Texas millionaire Representative Richard Kleberg. The young aide became an ardent New Dealer, absorbing and championing the programs of FDR. While serving at his Washington post, Johnson met, wooed, and married a Texan, Claudia Alta Taylor (known to all as Lady Bird). The couple eventually had two daughters, Lynda Bird and Luci Baines.

In 1935, Johnson became Texas state director of the New Deal National Youth Administration, but he was elected U.S. Representative in 1937 and returned to Washington, where his good personal connections and immense legislative skills moved him rapidly ahead. He briefly served on active military duty during the first months of World War II but returned to Congress at the president's request.

LBJ's most important electoral race came in the Texas state Democratic primary for the U.S. Senate in 1948. Whoever won the Democratic nomination was assured of winning the Senate seat. LBJ ran a vigorous and energetic campaign, using a helicopter to jump from appearance to appearance, but the voting came down to a margin of a mere 87 votes out of more than 988,000 cast. Johnson's victory was almost certainly due to fraudulent vote counting and a stuffed ballot box in a key precinct. Despite challenges, the thin margin held, and LBJ went to the Senate, where his rise was meteoric. He became Senate minority leader and was reelected to his Senate seat by a

huge margin in 1954 as part of a national Democratic victory, following which he assumed the office of Senate majority leader. He rapidly became one of the more powerful Senate leaders in modern times, able to manipulate people and processes masterfully.

Why then, in 1960, did Johnson accept nomination as Kennedy's running mate, which was a major retreat from his very powerful position as Senate majority leader? What motivated this quintessential political power seeker to agree to serve, over the opposition of very powerful elements within the Democratic Party, in an office succinctly characterized by a former vice president and a fellow hill-country Texan as "not worth a bucket of warm spit"? Then, too, why did presidential nominee John F. Kennedy offer the number-two spot to LBJ over the opposition of influential groups, while simultaneously removing LBJ from his position of power—a position that could be very useful to a Democratic president? These are not simply rhetorical questions, although no definitive answer can be given to either. Moreover, it is in the probable answers to these questions that one can find the clues to explaining and understanding the LBJ vice presidency.

From JFK's perspective, the offer can be readily understood. A powerful Senate majority leader would be of little value to a defeated Democratic candidate. LBJ's presence on the ticket would be valuable in the region where a New England Catholic would be most vulnerable—the South. The powerful elements on the Democratic left that feared, disliked, and mistrusted LBJ did not fear, dislike, or mistrust JFK; indeed, he and his close circle had strong ties to these groups, and the nominee knew full well that when all was said and done these groups would support the Democratic candidate. There was, moreover, in addition to this calculated political analysis another reason for adding Johnson to the ticket. Senator Kennedy believed that in the case of his incapacity or death, Johnson was qualified by virtue of knowledge, temperament, and ability to fill the office of the president. To be sure, rumors circulated at the time and since, often by members of JFK's outer circles, that the offer was made in the expectation that it would be refused. No evidence, however, other than the rumors themselves exists to validate this contention.

Given the reasons for making the offer, the question then becomes: Why was it accepted? The answers to this question both complement and go beyond JFK's reasons for making the offer. Johnson agreed with the arguments that he would strengthen the Democratic ticket where it was the weakest—the South and the West. But LBJ's reasons were not altogether altruistic. In 1968 he would be sixty years old, and he wanted to be president of the United States. The office of the vice president, if used well, could aid in that goal. LBJ knew well the nature, strength, and depth of the liberal Democrats' opposition to him. He believed that he could use the eight years as vice president to demonstrate to these groups that he was not the enemy they thought him to be. As a senator from Texas, even with the prestige of being Senate majority leader, he could not be too far ahead of his Texas constituents. He knew well the first two rules of politics: (1) Represent your constituency, and (2) do not break (1) until you are strong enough at home to withstand the challenge. Having won the 1948 primary vote by eighty-seven illegal votes, LBJ was in no position to challenge the conservative tastes of the Texas electorate. His 3–1 victory in 1954 had made it possible to begin to move away from distinctive conservative voting patterns toward the center of the national Democratic Party. As vice president, he would no longer be tied to a purely Texas voting base.

In the late 1950s, essentially four groups made up the liberal wing of the Democratic Party—big city bosses, labor, intellectuals, and civil rights groups—and, to be sure, the groups overlapped on occasion. Of these four groups, only the bosses supported Johnson.

Labor leaders, refusing to recognize the political realities of an eighty-seven vote victory in an antilabor state, opposed him for voting for both the Taft-Hartley and Landrum-Griffin bills. In this they were encouraged by the almost impotent liberal wing of the Texas Democrats. This union opposition Johnson understood, and al-

though he considered it wrongheaded, he felt it could be finessed over the next eight years.

The gap between LBJ and the intellectual community was one of both substance and style. These professional nonpoliticians were never comfortable with what their idol, JFK, called "the nature and the necessity for compromise and balance." Johnson's J.C. Penney–polyester style clashed with their tweedy Brooks Brothers look. They talked about things and, in only talking, avoided the hard-and-fast realities of practical politics. He did things and thus was forced to confront realities headlong. But LBJ knew he needed them, so he wooed them, and for this reason, plus the fact that he was the choice of JFK, they accepted him in the short run.

The opposition of civil rights leaders was a more difficult thing. They did not trust LBJ, and although he had gotten the best civil rights bills possible through the Congress in 1957 and 1960, they doubted his conversion. In this lack of trust they, like their labor allies, failed to take Texas political realities into account. In addition, they did not consider LBJ's racially liberal political antecedents. His father, Sam Ealy Johnson, when in the Texas legislature, had voted for a resolution opposing the Ku Klan Klan and had, indeed, called the Klan "un-American." Furthermore, LBJ's early experience teaching Mexican American children in South Texas, an experience which later led him to note "somehow you never forget what poverty and hatred can do when you see its scars in the face of a child," had taught him much. To the civil rights community, LBJ had joined the successful southern filibuster in 1949 against the Fair Employment Practices Commission, and in this opposition they had chosen not to hear some of what the new senator was saying:

> Perhaps no prejudice is so contagious or so unreasoning as the unreasoning prejudice against men because of their birth, the color of their skin, or their ancestral background. Racial prejudice is dangerous because it is a disease of the majority endangering minority groups. . . . For those who would keep any group in our nation in bondage, I have no sympathy or tolerance. Some may feel moved to deny this group

or that the homes, the education, the employment which every American has the right to expect, but I am not one of those.

Perhaps it is natural that words so out of place in a filibuster against a civil rights measure might be missed.

In 1957, LBJ had maneuvered a civil rights bill through the Senate at the cost of eliminating a section concerning contempt trials from the final bill. The part of the original bill had provided for nonjury contempt trials for those who violated the bill's provisions. This title quickly became the focus of the southern and conservative opposition to the measure. In a successful effort to pass this early civil rights measure, New Mexico Democrat Clinton P. Anderson, a liberal senator of impeccable credentials, moved to remove the embattled title. In this maneuver Anderson was joined by such liberals as Hubert H. Humphrey, Jacob Javits, and JFK, but the fury of the civil rights leaders fell on Johnson. That the offending section was in violation of our legal traditions made no difference to these civil rights leaders. They believed the only way to secure civil rights convictions in the South was to bypass jury trials, and this weapon had been stripped from them. It would be difficult indeed to win this group's support, but to become president in 1968 LBJ had to have it, and the office of vice president would give him eight years to change their opinions.

These then were the reasons JFK wanted LBJ on the ballot and the reasons LBJ accepted second-place billing to a younger, less experienced man. He brought strength to the ticket and he wanted the position. When Robert F. Kennedy informed his brother and others that Johnson is "willing to fight for it," he did not mean, as Arthur M. Schlesinger, Jr. and others have argued, that LBJ would fight the nominee for the vice president slot, but rather that LBJ would join JFK to fight for the nomination. Indeed, such close friends of JFK as Joseph Alsop and Philip Graham had consistently predicted a JFK–LBJ ticket.

With the ticket completed, the campaign commenced. As expected, Johnson campaigned extensively but not exclusively in the South, and his campaigning was most effective. As was expected, Kennedy's Catholicism was a major issue in the South, often masking southern opposition to other issues. Afraid to confront the electorate in open support of their party's nominee, many Deep South politicians used the candidate's religion as their out. Against this hypocrisy, LBJ used an indirect but not very subtle approach:

> I know you boys know how strong your people feel about this Catholic thing. Both Senator Kennedy and I think you should vote your conscience on this matter. Course we do want to win pretty badly and I am going to feel real bad if we don't. Now I don't know how them Irish Catholics take losing but I would be real surprised if they like it. But that's just something him and me are gonna have to live with. Course now I'm still gonna be majority leader and Senator Kennedy is going to be much more of a leader then he is now and that'll help some. And of course both of us have good memories. But now on this religion thing you just go ahead and go with your conscience and your people.

Given this sort of treatment, many southern politicos were able to rise above their religious prejudices.

The election was a squeaker, but Texas, helped by JFK's defense of his religious beliefs before a group of Houston Baptist ministers and a backlash of sympathy caused by the hostile if not threatening treatment Senator and Mrs. Johnson received from a group of Republican conservatives in Dallas, as well as several other southern states helped put the Kennedy–Johnson ticket over the top. The JFK-LBJ gamble had paid off.

The administration began as have all recent administrations with the president and vice president in complete accord as to how to involve the vice president more completely and at a higher level than previous vice presidents. As Johnson put it: "If there is one the President can turn to, I want it to be me." But additionally Johnson thought he could continue his rigid control of the Democratic majority in the Senate. The method to be used was for LBJ instead of newly elected Majority Leader Mike Mansfield of Montana to preside over the meetings of the Democratic Caucus. When this idea was presented to the Democratic senators, it was accepted by a 46 to 17 vote after some complicated political and parliamentary maneuvers. Although the vote was almost 3–1 in Johnson's favor and the opposition almost all liberals, it was a large enough bloc to convince Johnson the idea was a mistake. He never again attended a Senate Democratic Caucus meeting.

True to his word, JFK assigned several meaningful tasks to his vice president. LBJ, in addition to his general political duties in the United States, was often sent abroad to represent the president and the country, a job for which he soon demonstrated considerable proficiency. Domestically he was placed in charge of the Space Council and the Presidential Committee on Equal Employment Opportunity, two positions of importance both to the new administration and to Johnson's political future.

To Kennedy, the race to control space was one the country had been publicly losing since *Sputnik* and central to his concept of how to deal with the Soviet Union. Consequently the Space Council, which set and coordinated our national space effort, was of great importance. Therefore, although the Space Council had been underutilized during the Eisenhower years, JFK and LBJ revitalized its activities. Johnson, who had long pushed U.S. efforts in this area, threw his full energies into the project. These efforts, while neither dramatic nor well studied, of course, resulted in placing a man on the moon during the Nixon administration. In addition to the Space Council's support of the moon landing program, it also played a leading role in developing COMSAT (Communication Satellite).

Perhaps the major reason this important activity has been so ignored lies in the fact that it was so noncontroversial. It was an area that found those oftimes opponents, Johnson and Robert Kennedy, in full agreement. It was also an area where the president appreciated the advice he was getting from the vice president. President Kennedy did not welcome the general and political advice that was LBJ's forte because of his ego and self-perceived personal strengths. However, the vice president's expertise in the area of space issues, dating back to LBJ's long-standing congressional interest, was such that he could give JFK the kind of technical advice the president wanted.

Yet another area where Johnson was given a number of assignments and achieved considerable success was that of representing the United States abroad. His first trip abroad, to Senegal, set the pattern. After performing his official duties celebrating Senegalese Independence Day, he and Lady Bird were off and running. Awakening at 4:30 A.M., the Johnsons traveled by car to the small fishing and peanut-growing village of Kayar, some miles distant from Dakar, the capital. There they met the people, shook hands, and kissed babies. When asked by the village chief why he was there, John replied:

> I came to Dakar for Independence Day festivities because of President Kennedy's deep interest in Africa, but I came to Kayar because I was a farm boy too in Texas. It's a long way from Texas to Kayar, but we both produce peanuts and both want the same thing: a higher standard of living for the people.

Later, during a visit to Lebanon, Johnson discussed dump trucks with a Beirut road crew. When he asked what the truck held and was told five yards, he noted that his first job was filling a one-yard capacity truck with a shovel. He then noted to a nearby Lebanese official: "You're going to realize great benefits from work like this. In my country, one of the most important developments was getting the farmers out of the mud. In my own state of Texas now, no farmer has to drive more than a mile to get to a paved road." To the Ivy League–educated State Department personnel and the intelligentsia who understood JFK and joked about Johnson, this was "Uncle Cornpone" at his worst. His hosts, however, loved it. In Teheran on a state visit, Johnson shook an estimated 300 hands in 5 minutes. It was as though, one reporter noted, "he was running for Shah."

It was this gregariousness that resulted in Johnson's invitation to the illiterate Pakistani cameleer, Basher Ahmed, to visit the United States. An offhand invitation, "You all come to Washington and see us some day" was given to Ahmed, who took it seriously. When news of this hit the anti-American elements of the Pakistani press, it was passed on to Washington. LBJ then arranged through the People-To-People program for the Pakistani to come to the United States. The vice president and the camel driver toured the United States, where Ahmed's natural dignity and the vice president's presence turned a casual remark into a major news story. When Basher Ahmed's return trip was routed through Mecca so that he could make his pilgrimage, the diplomatic triumph was complete.

However, Johnson's major overseas triumph was his trip to Berlin, undertaken as one U.S. response to the construction of the Berlin Wall. There were three purposes to the trip: to make clear U.S. neutrality in the political struggle between Konrad Adenauer and Willi Brandt; to inform the German people and their leaders of the U.S. position on Berlin; and to attempt to moderate the West German political leaders' near hysteria. The first goal was achieved by Johnson's meeting with Chancellor Adenauer in Bonn and later his appearance in Berlin with the city's mayor, Willi Brandt. U.S. support of a Western-controlled Berlin was highlighted by the return of retired General Lucius Clay, the commander of the city during the Berlin blockade, and by the dispatch overland of a token force of some 1,500 additional combat troops. Support for the city was further made clear in the vice president's speech to the Berliners. "I have come to Berlin by direction of President Kennedy. . . . To the survival and to the creative future of this city we Americans have pledged, in effect what our ancestors pledged in forming the United States . . . 'Our Lives, Our Fortunes, and Our Sacred Honor. . . .'" More formal perhaps, less dramatic possibly than JFK's "*Ich bin ein Berliner*" but no less effective under the circumstances.

The same could be said of his trip earlier in 1961 to Southeast Asia. Here also, the purpose of the trip was to signal U.S. support of an ally, South Vietnam's President Diem. As with all of his overseas trips, Johnson's scope of maneuver was carefully defined. In his reassurances and his commitments, he could not go beyond the president's guidelines. On this trip, in addition to bolstering the South Vietnamese government's resolve, he was to urge other U.S. allies in Southeast Asia to support one another and to hold firm. While believing that Diem was too aloof to be a truly successful leader, LBJ's report to the president noted that Diem was the best choice in that troubled country. The significance of this report in determining future U.S. policy and involvement in the affairs of South Vietnam is impossible to determine.

Although his overseas trips were extremely successful, they did not result in Johnson's being seen as an indispensable part of the leadership team. Indeed the repetitious, clichélike quality of the president's remarks—"strengthened the forces of freedom," "well represented," "an invaluable service"—tended to give the impression that these missions were pro-forma endeavors. Despite this, these trips did demonstrate Johnson's ability to negotiate with foreign leaders and to communicate with the people.

Although helpful in his long-term quest for the presidency, these activities were at best peripheral. Johnson was widely viewed as a conservative on domestic and, particularly, racial matters and this was an impression he had to change. His best hope of reshaping his image lay in chairing the President's Committee on Equal Employment. Here he could demonstrate to the civil rights community, to the intellectuals, and to the liberal union leadership that his commitment to racial equality was heartfelt and real.

Prior to 1961, the government's involvement in the area of equal employment opportunities had been ineffective. To be sure, Nixon, a strong supporter of these goals, had tried but had lacked both a public mandate and the determined support of President Eisenhower, and he had consequently fallen short of his hoped-for goal. Perhaps Johnson could do better. Again there was no public mandate for this activity, but JFK had at least talked about it in his campaign and he had certainly gotten, and needed, the African American vote. In fact, not only had JFK endorsed the concept of equal employment, but he also had noted that the situation could be changed by a presidential "stroke of a pen." Given the possibilities and the potential, Johnson had good reason to view the situation with optimism.

This optimism was reinforced by the president's willingness to accept Johnson's suggestion that longtime friend and confidante Abe Fortas draw up a new executive order creating the President's Committee on Equal Employment. Under the terms of Fortas's directives, all government contractors would have to agree not to practice racial discrimination. The way the pledge was worded was designed to put the burden of proof on the contractors to prove that they didn't discriminate, not on an appellant to prove they did.

The first test of the new policy came when the Lockheed Corporation's Marietta, Georgia, plant received a billion-dollar government contract. Despite the fact that the company only employed blacks in menial jobs and that restrooms, eating facilities, water fountains, and so forth were segregated, the company submitted the necessary certificates of nonsegregation only to have them rejected by the committee. Despite intense political pressure brought by Johnson's former political mentor Richard Russell and others, the committee held firm and the company integrated its facilities. It was a major victory for the policies and demonstrated that local racial patterns would yield to economic pressure.

However, even before this victory, prominent committee members were complaining that LBJ's political style was playing havoc with the committee's proceedings. In addition to these complaints, there was also dissatisfaction with the president's choice of the committee's executive and associate executive director. For director, JFK had chosen one of his earliest southern supporters and a former college roommate of his dead brother Joseph, Robert Troutman, an Atlanta businessman. Troutman had seriously and courageously supported the goals of the committee, but he also advocated a "go slow" approach that several committee members opposed; the associate director, John Feild, was just the opposite—he supported compulsion where Troutman argued voluntary compliance. The result was con-

flict and confusion. Because both men were presidential appointees, the matter had to be resolved by Kennedy, but LBJ was caught in the middle. He agreed with Troutman's approach, but he didn't approve of Troutman. Johnson's suggestion was to reorganize the staff structure, creating a single head of staff who would work closely with the vice president. Eventually, JFK accepted this idea and Troutman and Feild were replaced by Hobart Taylor, Jr., an African American personally selected by LBJ. From then on things went better; still, by 1962 not much had been achieved.

Frustrated by this lack of progress, the president asked Robert Kennedy to look into the matter. The attorney general, who had long suspected Johnson's sincerity on ending segregation, compiled data on black employment by the federal government. The record was not encouraging. Appearing at one of the committee's meetings, Kennedy dropped this information into their laps with the very strong implication that the president expected results—and soon. The attack was unexpected and devastating. Although LBJ was not mentioned by name, it was clear that RFK was implying that the White House lacked faith in LBJ's ability and/or desire to improve the employment situation.

To make things worse, the charge was not a particularly valid one. Within the administration and in his public speeches, LBJ had done much to keep the issue of civil rights in the forefront. In an eloquent 1963 speech delivered at Gettysburg as a part of the Civil War centennial, Johnson had begun his remarks by noting that "One hundred years ago the slave was freed. One hundred years later the Negro remains in bondage to the color of his skin." He went on to note that the dead at Gettysburg were neither answered nor honored when our reply to the Negro is "patience." His conclusion noted that: "Until justice is blind to color, until all education is unaware of race, until opportunity is unconcerned with the color of men's skins, emancipation will be a proclamation, but emancipation will not be a fact."

Shortly after this speech Johnson, in a lengthy and recorded telephone conversation, gave Theodore Sorenson, JFK's principal speechwriter, a lecture on how the president should push his civil rights legislation. At one point in this remarkable conversation, LBJ advised Sorenson to have the president speak on the matter in the Deep South. LBJ went on to say that the president should ask his audience how they thought he could order a black soldier to risk death for his country when that soldier couldn't eat in a restaurant in the city where he was speaking. The audience might disagree with the president, the vice president noted, but they would respect him. Sadly, JFK never gave this speech.

By this time, it was clear that although LBJ had enemies in the administration he still had the president's support. Johnson had walked the narrow path between appearing to be unimportant and suggesting that he was more important than the President. Yet, the rumors and the attacks continued: Johnson had been out of the loop during the crisis over a potentially crippling strike in the steel industry; he had not been a major player in the Cuban missile crisis; he was "Uncle Cornpone" with the funny accent and the inferior education; he wore boots, not deck shoes; he was the square dancer at what was later to be called Camelot.

Despite Johnson's best efforts, he was still distrusted by liberals, and in Texas that distrust approached loathing. Being unable to defeat either LBJ or his lieutenant, John Connally, the best hope of Texas liberals was to work with Johnson's other enemies to remove him from the national ticket. That was easier said than done, but still they tried. They hoped to unite behind Senator Ralph Yarborough and seize control of the state party while sending a message to Washington that LBJ was more of a hindrance than a help in securing the state's twenty-five electoral votes. Johnson's response was to attempt the defeat of Yarborough. Both strategies cast a cloud over the chances of JFK carrying the state in the 1964 election.

Thus it was that the president and the vice president and their wives came to Texas in November 1963 to make peace within the Texas Democratic Party. Kennedy would support Con-

nally for governor and Ralph Yarborough for the Senate. The nature of Texas politics had made it impossible for LBJ to gain the Democratic nomination in his own right. The nature of Texas politics would thrust him into the presidency.

By midafternoon of November 22, Kennedy was dead, and LBJ had been sworn in as the thirty-sixth president of the United States. Johnson did a masterful job of rallying the country during his first months in office and used his great legislative skills to pass programs that had been stalled under Kennedy, notably a landmark civil rights act and a tax cut. In addition, LBJ pushed through Congress a series of programs aimed at attacking poverty in the United States.

By the 1964 presidential election, LBJ had solidified his position as national leader and was able to portray skillfully his conservative Republican opponent, Arizona Senator Barry Goldwater, as a dangerous right-wing warmonger. Johnson and his running mate, Hubert Humphrey, smashed the Republican ticket, winning 61 percent of the popular vote and taking 44 states in one of the greatest landslides in history.

LBJ used this mandate to push through Congress a monumental package of social legislation, which he referred to as the Great Society. Large-scale government programs in health, education, environmental protection, and minority rights that were put in place set the U.S. domestic agenda for the following thirty years. At LBJ's behest, Congress passed more than 200 bills that created more than 500 programs.

Unfortunately for Johnson, his domestic successes were not mirrored in the foreign policy area. He had inherited an intractable problem in Southeast Asia in the form of U.S. involvement in the ongoing war between South and North Vietnam. Often against his better judgment, Johnson slowly allowed the war to escalate until it included tens of thousands of U.S. troops on the ground and a massive bombing campaign against Communist North Vietnam. By 1966, the war was the consuming issue in the United States, with large-scale protests and political divisions becoming standard fare. LBJ strove mightily to solve the problem and to open negotiations with the communists but was essentially frustrated at every turn.

When domestic violence broke out in the form of riots in the black ghettos of several U.S. cities, Johnson's hold on the country slackened even more, and in March 1968 he stunned the nation by announcing that he would not run for a second full term as president. His lame-duck efforts to bring the war to a close failed, and he retired to his ranch near Johnson City.

Lyndon Baines Johnson died of heart failure in January 1973, only one day before his successor announced an end to the war.

References

Leonard Baker, *The Johnson Eclipse: A President's Vice-President* (New York: The Macmillan Company, 1966); Paul K. Conkin, *Big Daddy From the Pedernales: Lyndon Baines Johnson* (Boston: Twayne Publishers, 1986); Rowland Evans and Robert Novak, *Lyndon B. Johnson: The Exercise of Power* (New York: New American Library, 1966); Doris Kearns, *Lyndon Johnson and the American Dream* (New York: Signet Books, 1976); Merle Miller, *Lyndon: An Oral Biography* (New York: Putnam, 1988); Arthur M. Schlesinger Jr., *A Thousand Days: John F. Kennedy in the White House* (Boston: Houghton Mifflin and Co., 1965).

G.L. Seligmann received a B.A. and an M.A. in history from New Mexico A&M (now New Mexico State University) in 1957 and 1958 and a Ph.D. in history from the University of Arizona in 1967. His special research interest is New Mexico politics in the late nineteenth and early twentieth centuries. In 1964, he directed the Johnson-Humphrey campaign for the Third Congressional District of Louisiana, thus triggering an ongoing fascination with LBJ. He has given several papers on the general topic of LBJ and his biographers and published "LBJ versus His Biographers: A Review Essay" in *Social Science Quarterly*. He is currently coediting a book-length bibliography of New Mexico and beginning work on a study of nineteenth-century political campaign songs. He is on the faculty of the University of North Texas.

HUBERT H. HUMPHREY, JR. (1911–1978)

Vice President, 1965–1969

(President Lyndon Baines Johnson)

HUBERT H. HUMPHREY, JR.
(Library of Congress)

By Karen M. Hult

For observers of U.S. politics from the late 1940s into the 1970s, the name Hubert Humphrey likely triggers a torrent of memories. Among such images may be his 1948 speech pleading with the Democratic Party "to get out of the shadow of states' rights and walk forthrightly into the bright sunshine of human rights," the ebullient "Happy Warrior" on the presidential campaign trail, his incongruous reference to the "politics of joy" in the midst of televised coverage of violent demonstrations during the 1968 Democratic convention, or a haggard U.S. senator advising a president while himself dying of cancer.

Humphrey's vice presidency was scarcely the high point of a long and distinguished career of public service. As vice president, Humphrey struggled to balance loyalty to a domineering and often ungrateful Lyndon Johnson, his own sense of responsibility to the nation, and his searing ambition to be president himself. Despite sporadic involvement in foreign policy and more regular participation in domestic policy and politics, Humphrey's talents and energies were largely checked—and his weaknesses magnified—by a suspicious president and a polarizing polity. Little wonder then that Hubert Humphrey compared being vice president to " . . .

being naked in the middle of a blizzard with no one to even offer you a match to keep you warm."

Humphrey was a quintessentially public man. Not only did he spend most of his adult life in elective office, but he also was deeply committed to preserving and enhancing democratic governance. Throughout, too, Humphrey evidently craved recognition and affection and strove untiringly (if futilely) to become president.

Hubert Horatio Humphrey, Jr., though a second son, was named after his father; the junior Humphrey also had an elder and a younger sister. Humphrey was born in Wallace, South Dakota, but he spent most of his childhood in nearby Doland, where the family moved when he was four. In both Humphrey's telling and that of others, the roots of his love of politics and of many of his policy commitments can be traced to these early years. Humphrey's father, a pharmacist and small-drugstore owner, was an especially important influence. The young boy's rhetorical skills and political values were nurtured by a father who regularly read his children Woodrow Wilson's Fourteen Points and William Jennings Bryan's Cross of Gold speech and who conducted ongoing political debates at the drugstore soda fountain. Although the senior Humphrey was one of only a handful of Democrats in South Dakota, he was well respected, later serving as mayor and state legislator.

Like most members of his generation, Humphrey was deeply affected by the Great Depression. Economic troubles began early in South Dakota as its agricultural economy faltered and banks closed even before the devastating dust storms began. Humphrey's parents lost their house in 1927 and eventually moved to Huron, South Dakota, where his father opened another pharmacy in 1931. Hubert Humphrey, Jr., recalled being impressed by his parents' capacity to survive such setbacks without becoming bitter. Although he watched as his father extended credit and accepted barter for goods, he also became a staunch supporter of Franklin Delano Roosevelt and the New Deal.

The Depression also interfered with the young Humphrey's college plans. Initially, he and his older brother Ralph attended the University of Minnesota during alternate years. However, both returned home in March 1931 to help their father with the new drugstore. The following winter, Hubert completed a six-month course at Capitol College of Pharmacy in Denver, apparently resigned to life as a small-town pharmacist.

Humphrey married Muriel Buck in September 1936, but, he remembered, "[t]he depression, the dust storms, and the demands of family on a newlywed couple were finally too much." Using Muriel Buck Humphrey's savings, the two moved back to Minneapolis in September 1937, where Hubert resumed college; Muriel, who did not return to school, worked as a bookkeeper. In Minneapolis, the trademark Humphrey energy and speaking talents quickly surfaced. Humphrey completed his degree in political science in June 1939, graduating *magna cum laude*; he also was elected to Phi Beta Kappa and won a Big Ten debating championship.

Humphrey's next stop was Louisiana State University, which awarded him a graduate fellowship to study political science. At least by his own account, the year Humphrey spent at LSU taught him painful lessons about the discrimination blacks suffered in the United States and exposed him to southern politics (an experience he would draw on later in the Senate).

After finishing a master's degree (with a thesis on the political philosophy of the New Deal), Humphrey returned to the University of Minnesota to begin doctoral work. Needing more money than a teaching assistantship provided to support a growing family (his first child was born in 1939, with three others to follow), however, he started working in summer 1940 in a series of Works Progress Administration (WPA) positions. Humphrey trained adult-education teachers in Duluth, directed the Workers' Education Program for the Twin Cities, and served as state director of workers' services. By 1942, Humphrey was charged with liquidating WPA programs in the state, and in 1943 he was named assistant director of the Minnesota War Manpower Commission. Despite persistent efforts to join the armed services, though, Humphrey initially failed physicals and then received deferments as a "critical" domestic worker.

Humphrey's childhood fascination with politics persisted. Meanwhile, his university connections put him in contact with several political activists, and his WPA positions had introduced him to local labor leaders. It did not take much encouragement to convince Humphrey to challenge the incumbent mayor of Minneapolis in 1943. Although he ultimately lost to the sitting mayor, Humphrey was able to reach a runoff, drawing support from the local AFL and the Jewish and black communities.

Although Humphrey next accepted a teaching job at Macalester College in St. Paul, he later readily admitted: "[T]eaching . . . was a pale second choice. . . . I was permanently hooked on politics." Meanwhile, the future vice president plunged into numerous political activities. Working with local labor groups had catalyzed his opposition to the communist left that had infiltrated Minnesota unions. Humphrey worked with Philip Murray (the president of the national CIO) to rid the Minnesota chapter of communists. More important for later national political endeavors, Humphrey also became one of the founders of Americans for Democratic Action, which sought to articulate an ideology that was both strongly anticommunist and liberal. In addition, concerned about the inability of liberal candidates to win statewide elections, Humphrey enlisted the help of the national Democratic Party (itself worried about the narrow Roosevelt victory in Minnesota in 1940) to achieve the "fusion" of the Minnesota Democratic Party with the Farmer-Labor Party. With the merger accomplished, in 1944 Humphrey ran FDR's campaign in the state and attended his first national convention as a delegate.

Humphrey succeeded at moving into politics full time when he was elected mayor of Minneapolis in 1945. The new mayor moved quickly to "clean up" the city, notorious for its police corruption, gambling, and prostitution. He also worked to reduce racism and anti-Semitism among police officers and is credited with creating the nation's first municipal Fair Employment Practices Commission.

Although Humphrey was easily reelected in 1947, the sirens of national politics beckoned. As he later wrote: "The Cold War and international events seemed more compelling than veterans' housing and liquor licenses."

In 1948, the mayor exploded into national consciousness, igniting a firestorm of controversy. At the Democratic convention, he spoke advocating passage of a strong civil rights plank to the party's platform, an action that most in the party hierarchy opposed and a majority of the platform committee refused to take. To the surprise of many (including Humphrey himself), the plank was approved, triggering Strom Thurmond and thirty-five other southern delegates to walk out. Although mobilization by key big city bosses (led by Ed Flynn from the Bronx) mostly accounted for the plank's success, Humphrey's speech is likely the most remembered and most effective speech he ever delivered. (Surprising to critics of Humphrey's longwindedness may be that the speech was a mere ten minutes long.)

The year 1948 also marked Humphrey's first election to the U.S. Senate, where he would serve until 1964 and again from 1970 to 1978. He was the first Democrat to be elected to the Senate from Minnesota since it became a state in 1858.

At the outset, Humphrey faced considerable opposition and mistrust. He recounted: "My actions at the Democratic convention had elicited bitterness and antagonism far beyond what I expected. . . . [I was] treated like an evil force that had seeped into sanctified halls." The new senator made matters worse by violating hoary institutional norms. For example, he was silent for a mere six weeks; then, the urge to speak that would generate criticism throughout his career took over. "His cocky attitude caused [a Republican senator] to whisper to a colleague during a Humphrey speech that the brash Minnesotan reminded him of some tomatoes he once planted 'too early in the spring and the frost got them.'"

Humphrey's biggest mistake during this early period was giving a floor speech that criticized the Joint Committee on Reduction of Nonessential Federal Expenditures, chaired by the powerful Harry Byrd from Virginia. Worse yet, the novice senator attacked the committee when Byrd was away attending to his ill mother. Despite Humphrey's apology, the next day Byrd delivered a scathing lecture on the floor of the Senate on the institution's norms; more than twenty-five senators followed to deliver their own attacks.

As humiliating as this well-reported experience was to Humphrey, it showed his resilience and willingness to learn from his mistakes. Earning the respect of his colleagues took time and hard work, features that would mark the rest of Humphrey's tenure. In the Senate, Humphrey's breakthrough came when he and Paul Douglas from Illinois offered a series of amendments to 1950 tax legislation. Although virtually all of the proposed changes lost, the two senators were well prepared. The acknowledged experts on the Finance Committee congratulated the pair on the constructive and responsible nature of a week-long debate.

After this rocky start, Humphrey embarked on an extraordinarily productive Senate career. In his first two terms, the Minnesota senator sponsored 1,044 bills and joint resolutions. Moreover, among these proposals were several pathbreaking initiatives. Humphrey, for example, was one of the architects of P.L.–480 (which evolved into Food for Peace), authored the 1958 National Defense Education Act, and was instrumental in the creation of the Arms Control and Disarmament Agency and the ratification of the 1963 Limited Nuclear Test Ban Treaty.

Not all of Humphrey's proposals, of course, immediately became law. For example, the first bill Humphrey introduced in 1949 was to establish a program providing health care to the elderly through the Social Security system, a direct ancestor of Medicare, enacted in 1965. Meanwhile, throughout his Senate service, Humphrey took special interest in legislation in the areas of civil rights, public education, labor, and the Peace Corps. Long interested in foreign affairs (and acutely aware that presidential candidates are expected to have some foreign policy credentials), Humphrey pushed for the creation of a Senate subcommittee on nuclear disarmament in 1955 (which he chaired) and also served for a time as the Congressional Delegate to the United Nations.

Once Kennedy was elected president, Humphrey was chosen by the Senate Democrats as majority whip under Mike Mansfield, a position that made him the chief enforcer of party loyalty in the Senate. Far more energetic and adept at legislative maneuvering than the majority leader, Humphrey was an effective advocate for JFK's legislative program. After Kennedy's assassination, Humphrey joined Johnson in pushing hard to get the remaining Kennedy agenda through Congress. Most observers (including the new president) credit Humphrey with being instrumental in securing Senate passage of major legislation like the 1964 omnibus tax bill and the Civil Rights Act of 1964.

At the same time, Humphrey could not boast an unblemished record of accomplishment in the Senate. For example, perhaps reflecting Humphrey's own strong anticommunism, he did not distinguish himself by opposing Senator Joseph McCarthy, even though he was a member of McCarthy's Government Operations Committee. Indeed, some of Humphrey's language was written into the Communist Control Act of 1954, which sought to outlaw the Communist Party altogether.

More generally, at least one former legislative assistant has questioned the depth and quality of the Minnesota senator's deliberativeness:

[Humphrey was] a whirling dervish who absorb[ed] things fantastically quick, but the idea of Humphrey reading a book or sitting down long enough to seriously think about the implications of what he was doing is hard to imagine. He was so active that I don't think he had time to think about the big things.

The U.S. Senate, of course, also was where Humphrey and Lyndon Johnson developed the difficult and complex relationship that would so bedevil the former's vice presidency. Each man always claimed to have deep, genuine affection for the other; moreover, their relationship produced mutual benefits. For example, Humphrey credited LBJ (along with his LSU debate partner Russell Long) with establishing his credibility among southern senators. For his part, Johnson saw Humphrey as his link with the liberal-intellectual wing of the Democratic Party, which had long suspected the Texan. After JFK was assassinated, Humphrey worked to convince many Kennedy advisers to stay on in the White House and contributed the memorable phrase, "Let us continue" to LBJ's first speech as president.

One also can interpret LBJ's actions in a less benign light. According to historian Paul Conkin, Johnson "used and wooed" Humphrey when they were senators, making the latter "a bit of a protege. He befriended him and to some extent bought his loyalty." As minority leader, for instance, LBJ got Humphrey on the coveted Foreign Relations Committee in January 1953. Thus, "Lyndon recognized his worth, flattered his ego, and inhibited Humphrey from agitating domestic issues that divided Senate Democrats" because the Minnesota senator had to give up assignments on the Agriculture and the Labor and Public Welfare committees. More fundamentally, Conkin argues, LBJ had

. . . considerable disdain for men like Humphrey. Behind his exuberance and talkativeness . . . , Humphrey was an intellectual with a few scholarly credentials. This side of him, and his identification with the Senate's northern liberals, created elements of jealousy and resentment on Johnson's part.

Despite his clear love of the Senate, Humphrey, like many of his colleagues there, nursed presidential ambitions. For this, he offered few apologies: "I thought lack of ambition was sinful and that a politician without it was ready for retirement." In 1956, Humphrey became one of the first candidates ever to campaign openly for the Democratic vice-presidential nomination. He believed that Adlai Stevenson had promised to name him as his running mate, and Humphrey was stunned when Stevenson opened the nomination to convention vote. Utterly unprepared, Humphrey ran fifth on the first ballot and then shifted his support to Senate colleague Estes Kefauver, who won the nomination on the second ballot.

Again, Humphrey rebounded from a humiliating experience and shifted his attention to the presidency, becoming the first formal candidate in 1960. He entered only two primaries—Wisconsin and West Virginia—and was decisively defeated by John Kennedy in both. The Humphrey camp attributed Kennedy's Wisconsin victory to a heavy Catholic "crossover" vote, but the Minnesota senator's disastrous loss in West Virginia produced more lasting scars. In West Virginia, he was hamstrung by the issue of Kennedy's Catholicism, which had surfaced in Wisconsin: Humphrey could scarcely discuss it without appearing to be a religious bigot. At least as important, the Kennedy campaign had insurmountable funding and organizational advantages. Humphrey was most bitter, however, about Franklin Delano Roosevelt, Jr.'s, attack on his World War II service record, which Humphrey believed Robert Kennedy instigated (though whether this was the case is considerably less clear). Humphrey withdrew after garnering only 39.2 percent of the vote in West Virginia to JFK's 60.8 percent. The West Virginia contest produced lasting coolness between Humphrey and the Kennedys and apparently led the Minnesota senator to reject out of hand tentative offers from the Kennedy camp to become the vice-presidential nominee. Ever the good soldier, though, Humphrey did help quell a liberal revolt against LBJ at the 1960 Democratic convention.

Humphrey's ambition to attain higher office soon resurfaced, accelerated by events. Relatively soon after JFK's assassination, Humphrey began "an intensive effort to woo labor leaders I knew, journalists and commentators who wrote and rewrote the vice-presidential story, and leaders of the business community, an area where I was very weak." Despite strong support from party, civil rights, and labor leaders, he found himself competing for the nomination with his fellow senator from Minnesota, Eugene McCarthy. Characteristically, Johnson toyed with Humphrey, adding conditions for the nomination and refusing to make an iron-clad commitment until well after the convention had started. Humphrey remembered campaigning hard, delighting in the first plane solely under his campaign's command, the redoubtable "Happy Warrior."

Serving as vice president likely was the most agonizing period of Hubert Humphrey's public life. Still, Humphrey maintained his frenetic pace. He made twelve foreign trips as vice president, visiting thirty-one countries—a record unequaled until the vice presidency of Humphrey's Minnesota protégé, Walter Mondale. Like his immediate predecessors, Humphrey was a member of the cabinet and the National Security Council. He also for a time coordinated the federal government's civil rights programs as chair of the President's Council on Equal Opportunity. In addition, the vice president chaired, among others, advisory councils to the Office of Economic Opportunity and the Peace Corps, the President's Council on Youth Opportunity, the National Aeronautics and Space Council, and the President's Council on Recreation and Natural Beauty. Much like Johnson before him, Humphrey worked with Congress to help pass the administration's programs, including the flurry of Great Society initiatives in the mid-1960s. The vice president sought as well, with ever mounting difficulty, to be LBJ's link to liberals, blacks, and Democratic party leaders.

In early 1965, LBJ moved local government liaison from the White House (where it had been lodged since the Eisenhower years) to the vice-president's office. Mayors generally were pleased with the new arrangements, praising Humphrey's staffing, his personal interest in the nation's cities, and his office's ability to resolve snarls involving federal grants quickly. For his part, Humphrey's aides claimed that he spent more of his time on this than on any of his other assigned tasks.

Like many vice presidents, however, Humphrey soon faced challenges from senior White House staffers, who were concerned about protecting both the president's interests and their own political and policy turfs. Humphrey clashed most frequently with Johnson aide Joseph Califano, who directed an ever-expanding domestic policy operation within the White House Office. Rather quickly, the Equal Opportunity Council that Humphrey chaired was abolished and the vice president lost his civil rights responsibilities to Califano.

Even more galling perhaps were the ongoing indignities to which the president subjected Humphrey. Despite their apparent closeness as senators and his own unhappy experiences as vice president, LBJ sometimes treated his vice president—as he did many others—with cruelty and contempt. Conkin contends that LBJ, the master manipulator, "had a hook in [Humphrey]—Humphrey's presidential ambitions—and on occasions he twisted it." At a time when Humphrey was delivering as many as twenty-five prepared major speeches a month, he was forced to get direct presidential approval to use a White House plane or boat, and his speeches needed to be approved by senior White House aides. Humphrey's only visit to Camp David was at Jimmy Carter's invitation in 1977.

Vietnam, however, presented by far the worst problems for Humphrey. The new vice president's growing doubts about U.S. involvement in Vietnam almost immediately got him in trouble with LBJ. Despite his preconvention pledges to Johnson that he would never disagree with the president in a meeting with others present, at a National Security Council session in February 1965 Humphrey expressed concerns about both using retaliatory air strikes to bring North Vietnam to the negotiating table and expanding U.S. presence more generally. Humphrey followed up with a memo elaborating on his arguments, once more violating a rule of the leak-obsessed LBJ. As a result, the vice president was excluded for nearly a year from the inner circle of presidential foreign policy advisers and not invited to Johnson's informal Tuesday lunches, the chief forum for discussing Vietnam. Meanwhile, according to David Halberstam, " . . . every one of the other principals [including the other "dove," George Ball], wanting to keep their own effectiveness and credibility with this tempestuous President . . . became wary of being seen with Humphrey; he had become a cripple and everyone else knew it."

Humphrey's status within the administration rose marginally as he proved to be a capable roving presidential ambassador in early trips to India and France. Finally, in February 1966, the President sent Humphrey (on less than a day's notice) on a grueling two-week trip to nine Asian countries. To underscore his continuing lack of trust, though, LBJ also ordered White House aides to accompany him and report back daily on the vice president's activities. The ostensible purpose of the trip was to spread the "Honolulu Doctrine": the U.S. approach in Southeast Asia would increasingly focus on the pursuit of positive social and economic development goals. Instead, the U.S. party was treated to the kind of positive reporting by the South Vietnamese on the war's progress that George Romney would later call brainwashing. In Humphrey's case, the trip worked as intended, and he came home persuaded of the correctness of U.S. policy (though his doubts would return after a second trip in 1967).

For a time, the vice president became, in the words of his biographer, Johnson's "most articulate and indefatigable advocate of the war." Once again, Humphrey was invited to participate in high-level foreign policy discussions; yet, his hard-charging defense of administration policy also produced serious rifts with old liberal allies, and his general approval ratings in public opinion polls dropped.

As the Johnson years continued, controversy over Vietnam mounted—both within the administration and more generally in the country. This polarizing conflict, along with the vice president's own doubts, his painful separation from former friends and growing vilification on college campuses, and his sense of loyalty to, and ultimate dependence upon, Lyndon Johnson plagued Humphrey even after LBJ withdrew from the presidential race on March 31, 1968. Although Humphrey quickly threw his own hat into the ring, he feared that Johnson would reenter the race (especially after Robert Kennedy was killed in early June) until he actually received the formal Democratic nomination.

The 1968 Democratic convention was, from Humphrey's perspective, disastrous. Not only did Johnson forces retain control over virtually all of the logistics of the convention, but because there was an incumbent president likely to seek reelection, it had been scheduled late in the summer, reducing time for intraparty wounds to heal and

for an effective fall campaign plan to be crafted and put in place. Control of the platform committee by Johnson loyalists and the Soviet invasion of Czechoslovakia virtually on the eve of the convention conspired to make compromise on a Vietnam plank impossible. Meanwhile, a national television audience watched violent protests on Chicago streets as delegates inside the convention hall celebrated.

For much of the fall campaign, Humphrey was hampered by his unwillingness to express his own views on Vietnam. LBJ continued to demand absolute consistency with administration policy on Vietnam from his vice president. Humphrey reluctantly complied until the end of September, evidently driven both by the high value he placed on loyalty and by the concern that any apparent straying from the administration line could disrupt the Paris peace talks. In September, Humphrey trailed Republican nominee Richard Nixon by more than fifteen points and faced extraordinary difficulties raising funds and mobilizing traditional Democratic supporters. While Independent candidate George Wallace was siphoning away blue-collar and southern voters, many liberals deeply opposed Johnson's Vietnam policies. Of the three candidates, Humphrey endured by far the most interference from antiwar activists, who tried to keep him from delivering speeches and engaged in numerous verbal and physical confrontations with the candidate and his entourage.

Finally, Humphrey escaped LBJ's "fatal embrace" in a speech he delivered in Salt Lake City on September 30. Although the speech failed to outline any major departures from current policy, it did signal the vice president's increased willingness to halt U.S. bombing of North Vietnam and to pursue peace more vigorously. Opinion polls narrowed considerably, and many Democratic constituencies returned to spark the last weeks of the campaign. The renewed enthusiasm, however, was not enough. Humphrey lost to Nixon by less than 1 percent of the votes cast nationally.

In such a close election, a variety of factors could have tipped the scales. Not surprisingly, some Humphrey supporters blamed the lack of presidential support for his vice president. LBJ made only one campaign speech for Humphrey until their joint appearance in the Houston Astrodome in early November; nor was the machinery of the federal government used for partisan purposes during the campaign. Johnson aide Harry McPherson has observed that Johnson evidently had mixed feelings about the vice president's candidacy:

> On the one hand, an old and deep affection for Humphrey; his own lifelong fidelity to the Democratic party; and surely a desire that the Administration's record be vindicated by the election of its Vice President. On the other, apprehension that Humphrey was preparing to repudiate the war policies for which he had once been a zealous advocate; the desire to remain "above politics" in the search for peace; and, surely, resentment that another man now carried the banner that was his by right of achievement. . ."

Others point to characteristic weaknesses in all three of Humphrey's bids for the presidency. First, the candidate himself routinely talked too long, obscuring his message and plunging daily schedules into chaos. (Indeed, Conkin reports: "LBJ once remarked to Lady Bird: 'If only I could breed him to Calvin Coolidge.'") More important, Humphrey's campaign organizations tended to be weak, shot through with staff infighting and sometimes stunning gaps in expertise. His close friend and personal physician Edgar Berman has contended that Humphrey had a staff of "warm hearts and fuzzy heads." Meanwhile, Berman continued, Humphrey was a "terrible" fund-raiser, and his campaigns routinely faced financial problems.

Out of national elective office after the election for the first time in twenty years, Humphrey went home to Minnesota. He accepted offers to teach at both Macalester College and the University of Minnesota, became the chairman of the board of the Encyclopedia Britannica Education Foundation, and sat on several other boards of directors. Yet, the former vice president was wounded by the resistance of some students and faculty to his return to college campuses, and he clearly missed being out of the national spotlight.

Humphrey leaped at the chance to run again for elective office when Eugene McCarthy decided not to seek reelection to the U.S. Senate in 1970. Returning to the Senate created its own adjustment problems: not only was Humphrey again a lowly junior senator with no seniority, but the Senate itself had changed. Still, he set out to try to reestablish his credentials among liberals—voting, for example, to cut off financial support for the supersonic transport, which environmentalists opposed.

Humphrey made a final bid for the presidency in 1972. He ran second to Wallace in the Florida primary but trailed both Wallace and McGovern in Wisconsin. Despite familiar funding problems, Humphrey then swept the primaries in Pennsylvania, Ohio, Indiana, and West Virginia. Again, though, financial and organizational weaknesses haunted him. George McGovern won the California primary and became the Democratic nominee.

For reasons that may never be clear, Humphrey at the last minute decided not to run for his party's nomination in 1976, declaring that he did not want to be "humiliated again at this stage" of his life. He was diagnosed as having bladder cancer in August 1976, but his physician insists that he had a clean bill of health in the spring.

In spite of the cancer diagnosis, Humphrey was reelected to the Senate in 1976. He also advised President Carter and served as an advocate for his programs in the Senate. As his illness worsened, Humphrey talked with Nixon and specifically asked that the former president be invited to his Washington funeral service. Hubert Humphrey died in January 1978 and became only the twenty-second person to lie in state in the Capitol Rotunda. Nixon did attend Humphrey's funeral, his first visit to the capital since his resignation.

Hubert Humphrey's public life was marked by significant achievement and considerable disappointment, which reflected both the immense challenges of the times and his own characteristic strengths and weaknesses. His era was marked by periods dominated by oversimplification, dramatic overstatement, and extreme rhetoric. Yet, Humphrey viscerally disliked confrontation and seemed to genuinely believe that " . . . there is not a single problem in this country that is not subject to reason and negotiation and at least some form of conciliation. . . ." The urge to compromise produced clear successes in civil rights and in Senate leadership but less-impressive results in challenging McCarthyism or responding to polarization over Vietnam.

More generally, Humphrey's strengths and weaknesses seem inextricably linked. For example, his almost superhuman energy helped mobilize others to generate social change but on occasion likely drove out thoughtful reflection. The "lesson" that Humphrey drew from his first electoral defeat in 1943—that "loyalty, above all else, seems important"—served him well in building coalitions and attracting lifelong supporters. It also, however, heightened his vulnerability to LBJ's manipulation. The vice president's unwillingness to challenge U.S. policy in Vietnam consistently and openly was a consequence, one magnified and only belatedly overcome by Humphrey's presidential ambitions. Nonetheless, given the complexities and constraints of both the man and his times, Hubert Humphrey was a valuable contributor to the polity he so revered.

REFERENCES

Edgar Berman, M.D., *Hubert: The Triumph and Tragedy of the Humphrey I Knew* (New York: G.P. Putnam's Sons, 1979); Vaughn Davis Bornet, *The Presidency of Lyndon B. Johnson* (Lawrence: University Press of Kansas, 1983); Paul K. Conkin, *Big Daddy from the Pedernales: Lyndon Baines Johnson* (Boston: Twayne Publishers, 1986); Robert Dallek, *Lone Star Rising: Lyndon Johnson and His Times, 1908–1960* (New York: Oxford University Press, 1991); Albert Eisele, *Almost to the Presidency: A Biography of Two American Politicians* (Blue Earth, Minn.: The Piper Company, 1972); Dan B. Fleming, Jr., *Kennedy vs. Humphrey, West Virginia, 1960: The Pivotal Battle for the Democratic Presidential Nomination* (Jefferson, N.C.: McFarland and Company, 1992); Joel Goldstein, *The Modern Vice Presidency: The Transformation of a Political Institution* (Princeton, N.J.: Princeton University Press, 1982); David Halberstam, *The Best and the Brightest* (Greenwich, Conn.: Fawcett Publications, 1972); Hubert H. Humphrey, *The Education of a Public Man: My Life and Politics*, Norman Sherman, ed. (Minneapolis: University of Minnesota Press, 1991); Harry McPherson, *A Political Education: A Washington Memoir* (Boston: Houghton Mifflin, 1988); David M. Welborn and Jesse Burkhead, *Intergovernmental Relations in the American Administrative State: The Johnson Presidency* (Austin: University of Texas Press, 1989).

KAREN M. HULT is associate professor of political science at Virginia Polytechnic Institute and State University. Her publications include *Agency Merger and Bureaucratic Redesign, Governing Public Organizations: Politics, Structure, and Institutional Design* (with Charles Walcott), *Governing the White House: From Hoover through Johnson* (with Charles Walcott), and numerous journal articles. Her primary scholarly interests are the design and dynamics of government organizations; her current research focuses on the evolution of White House staffing in the Nixon and Ford administrations.

SPIRO T. AGNEW
(Library of Congress)

By John Robert Greene

On August 8, 1968, at about 1:00 P.M., Richard M. Nixon went down to the ballroom of his Miami Beach hotel to talk to the press for the first time since winning the Republican Party's nomination for the presidency. The room was buzzing with anticipation, as everyone expected that Nixon would use the occasion to announce the name of his running mate. Smart money was riding on either one of Nixon's two defeated rivals for the nomination—New York Governor Nelson Rockefeller and California Governor Ronald Reagan—or on longtime Nixon confidant Robert Finch. When Nixon announced his choice—Governor Spiro T. Agnew of Maryland—the press was stunned. As Nixon walked out of the room without taking any questions, several reporters cried out, "Spiro *Who?*"

The son of a Greek immigrant, Spiro Theodore Agnew attended Johns Hopkins University and Baltimore Law School before his education was interrupted by World War II. He married Elinn Judefind in 1942, during the war (the couple eventually had four children). He served in Europe as a captain in an armored division. He received his law degree from Baltimore in 1947 and began a law practice while seeking a career in politics. A Republican in a heavily Democratic state, it took until 1957 for Agnew to secure his first official post, an appointment to the Baltimore County Zoning Board of Appeals. Five years later, in a surprising upset, he was elected Baltimore County Executive. The Baltimore Democratic Party spent much of Agnew's tenure planning to unseat him in 1966. Recognizing that reelection was probably out of the question, Agnew began to sound out Maryland Republican leaders about a run for governor. He was not given much of a chance, but no other Republican wanted the nomination. Agnew once again won in an upset, thanks to the rabidly segregationist stand of his Democratic opponent and the correspondingly solid support of Agnew by the Baltimore black community.

Agnew's black support helped earn him a label as a moderate, sometimes left-of-center Republican. Part of this reputation was borne out by events, as Agnew put forth a progressive Fair Housing Act and appointed many blacks to statewide positions. However, Agnew's moderate tendencies were not deeply held, as was soon evidenced by his actions following the riots in Baltimore after the April 1968 assassination of Martin Luther King, Jr. Agnew called some 100 of the city's black leaders to his Annapolis office and, rather than offering them sympathy and help, berated them and laid the blame for the riots squarely at their door. Agnew called them "caterwauling, riot-inciting, burn-America-down type of leaders," and saw to it that his harangue was leaked to reporters in detail.

Agnew's response to the black leadership appealed to Pat Buchanan, then working as a speechwriter for Richard Nixon's campaign to win the 1968 presidential nomination. Buchanan reported Agnew's tirade to his boss, who arranged for a dinner with Agnew and Nixon law partner John Mitchell, then serving as Nixon's campaign manager. During the course of the dinner, Nixon asked Agnew if he would place his name in nomination before the convention. Ag-

new agreed, and Nixon came away from the dinner convinced that the governor would make a good running mate. This was a remarkable stroke of luck for Agnew, who not weeks before had been a supporter of Nelson Rockefeller's presidential candidacy, only to be left behind and embarrassed (literally standing in front of the Maryland press corps, about to make a speech of support) when Rockefeller announced that he wasn't sure that he wanted to run.

Despite Agnew's stroke of good fortune, he was far from Nixon's first choice. Nixon offered the vice-presidential nod first to Robert Finch, who, citing the appearance of cronyism, declined. Nixon then asked House Minority Leader Gerald Ford, who also declined in hopes of becoming the Speaker of the House after a Republican victory that fall. Nixon then turned to Agnew, arguing to those in the party who did not know the governor (it was reported that when Nixon told him of his final choice, Ford laughed out loud) that he was a good speaker who had shown courage during the Baltimore riots.

Yet the choice was a carefully considered one. Agnew—like Nixon in 1952—was largely chosen for his appeal to a constituency that distrusted the head of its ticket: the conservative wing of the Republican Party. It is clear that many early supporters of Alabama Governor George Wallace, not wanting to "waste their vote" on a third-party candidate, finally came home to the Republican Party because of Agnew. Nixon also had an important campaign role for Agnew, one that Nixon had been assigned by the head of *his* ticket in 1952. Dwight Eisenhower, who was anxious to run a campaign that showed him to be "presidential," instructed Nixon to go on the attack, while Ike took the smoother, high road. Sixteen years later, with an equal desire to be perceived as presidential timber but with Vietnam hovering as an issue that threatened to destroy any candidate who mishandled it, Nixon wanted to deflect as much attention from himself as possible. Thus, the low road was consigned to Agnew, and it was a road that he traveled well. During the campaign, Agnew called Maryland reporter, Eugene Oishi, a "fat Jap" (apologizing later, saying that they were old friends); he responded to the criticism that he was not campaigning in many inner cities by snapping that "when you've seen one slum, you've seen them all"; and he accused Democratic candidate Hubert Humphrey of being "squishy-soft on communism." Nixon's choice had proved to be a masterful one. Far from being embarrassed that Agnew was panned by the press, Nixon was pleased that Agnew's press contingent had doubled before October, thus deflecting attention from the issues of the day. More important, in an election that was this close (Nixon won with just 43.4 percent of the popular vote), postelection polls made it clear that, as Nixon had predicted, many conservatives voted for the Republican ticket *because* of Agnew's rhetoric.

However, despite Agnew's political value, Nixon was not about to allow him to have an active role in the formation of administration policy. From the start, Agnew was given low-level assignments, kept out of the limelight, and given only limited access to the president. Agnew himself made the situation worse by exhibiting a decided lack of political tact. As the first man since Calvin Coolidge to step directly to the vice presidency from a statehouse, it was logical that he be put in charge of relations with other state executives. The Office of Intergovernmental Relations was thus created as part of the Office of the Vice President in 1969. However, Agnew was far from diplomatic in his dealings with his former colleagues—Rockefeller simply refused to talk with him, sending his messages to Nixon through National Security Adviser Henry Kissinger. As chair of a Space Advisory Committee, Agnew's dogged support of a costly manned mission to Mars angered the White House. As a statutory member of the National Security Council, he advocated the immediate bombing of the Viet Cong sanctuaries in Cambodia and Laos. This belief mirrored Nixon's own, but Agnew was so strident about his support that Nixon, feeling that he had been overshadowed by an adviser, cut Agnew out of the foreign policy loop for the rest of the administration. The CIA even reported that while on an African trip, Agnew had told leaders that he opposed Nixon's overtures to the People's Republic of China. Agnew did make one

solid contribution to the administration's policy: Sharing Nixon's belief of Indian self-determination, Agnew's National Council on Indian Opportunity committee officially proposed the establishment of an Indian Revenue Sharing Program in October 1971, a plan that was supported by the Department of the Interior and eventually adopted. But this was not enough. By 1970, Nixon was openly speculating with his aides about getting rid of Agnew by naming him to the Supreme Court—then he could name John Connally, Nixon's choice as his heir apparent, vice president.

However, as much as he would have liked to have done so, Nixon was not able to rid himself of Agnew. By mid-1970, it was clear that Nixon was losing support of the conservative wing of the Republican Party, largely due to its opposition to détente with China and the Soviet Union. Despite Nixon's problems, Agnew found a home in the right wing, thanks to some of the most inflammatory rhetoric of the modern political period. Unneeded in Washington, Agnew hit the road, using speeches largely crafted by Buchanan. His first target was what he perceived to be a growing permissiveness on the part of the U.S. middle-class toward their children. At the University of Utah in May 1969, he railed against the dress of college students ("I didn't raise my son to be a daughter"). The next month at Ohio State, Agnew charged that any society that feared its young was "effete." Later that fall in New Orleans, he attacked the "effete corps of impudent snobs" who were teaching in the colleges and universities and poisoning the minds of the nation's young. These liberals soon were labeled with one of the most famous of the Agnewisms, "Radiclibs." But his most famous attack came in November 1969, when Agnew turned on the nation's broadcast media. In a speech at the Midwest Republican Conference held in Des Moines, Agnew savaged a media "whose minds were made up in advance" on Nixon's Vietnam policies. Agnew charged the networks with a conspiracy to slant the news through "a handful of commentators who admit their own set of biases," and encouraged like-minded people to call in and voice their support of his attack. All three networks were flooded with phone calls and telegrams; Agnew had become a celebrity.

By July 1970, several Republican congressional candidates, including Robert Taft of Ohio, publicly stated that they did not want Agnew campaigning for them in the off-year elections that fall, but Nixon wanted Agnew on the campaign trail. Using Agnew as the administration's chief campaign surrogate would allow Nixon to stay in Washington and avoid the political fray. It would also allow the administration to strike out at Republicans who had criticized the administration's policy on Vietnam without involving the president. With Buchanan at his side, the vice president plunged into the first substantive job given him by Nixon since their election. As he had been in 1968, Agnew was both coarse and effective. His attacks on antiwar New York Republican Senator Charles Goodell were so stinging (in a reference to the first person who had undergone a sex-change operation, Agnew called Goodell the "Christine Jorgensen of the Republican Party") that they brought private complaints from Republican Party leaders like Ford. Regardless of Ford's objections, Goodell lost his race, and the White House was ecstatic. Agnew played a large part for the administration in keeping its off-year losses to a minimum that fall.

Agnew's worth to the Nixon administration was clearly as a campaigner who galvanized the far right with his outlandish oratory. Despite his belief that his vice president was not up to the job, Nixon was quick to announce—during a January 2, 1972, televised interview with CBS's Dan Rather—that Agnew would stay on the ticket that fall. During the campaign, Agnew went after Democratic presidential candidate George McGovern, calling him "one of the greatest frauds ever to be considered as a presidential candidate by a major American party." Agnew also followed Democratic vice-presidential contender Sargent Shriver from city to city, answering the speeches of the former director of the Peace Corps with speeches that specialized in claiming that Shriver's position on the ticket was a result of his being an in-law of liberal senator Edward M. Kennedy.

Agnew's invective was less necessary in 1968 than in 1972 (the Republican ticket won with 60.7 percent of the popular vote). It also did not earn for him a place at Nixon's side during the second term. Quite the contrary; because the Constitution disqualified him from seeking a third term, Nixon no longer needed Agnew to rally the conservatives on the campaign trail. Immediately following the campaign, any access he may have had to Nixon virtually disappeared. Agnew was stripped of the Office of Intergovernmental Relations and virtually shut out of White House councils.

Yet, Agnew soon had much greater worries than a lack of access. In Baltimore, U.S. Attorney George Beall had found evidence that real estate developers in and around Baltimore County had been paying kickback money to Agnew since 1962. The payments began as a quid pro quo for lucrative building contracts, but one developer, Lester Matz, fell behind, and at least two installments were delivered to Agnew after he became vice president. Throughout the spring of 1973, Agnew had heard the rumors of an investigation, but the Watergate revelations had spurred the press to new heights of investigative reporting. Agnew dared not interfere with the investigation, lest an enterprising reporter pick up the scent.

Nixon had already heard. On April 14, 1973, during a meeting with Chief of Staff H.R. Haldeman and Domestic Policy Adviser John Ehrlichman, Nixon was first given details of the investigation. This news settled on a White House that had long been bunkering itself against Watergate; Nixon made it clear that there would be no attempt made to cover up Agnew's transgressions. Left without White House support, it was only a matter of time before the press picked up the story. On August 6, the *Wall Street Journal* called Agnew to tell him that it was running a story that reported that there was an investigation underway. That same day, Attorney General Elliot Richardson, who had been kept appraised of the investigation by Beall, met with Nixon and told him that Beall's case against Agnew was airtight.

The next day, August 7, Nixon met with Agnew. The vice president emerged to report that the president supported him in his fight against charges that Agnew labeled "damned lies." But Nixon's support never consisted of anything more than benign neglect. Watergate-implicated White House aides, including Haldeman and Ehrlichman, had been allowed to resign, as Nixon was faced with investigations by both the Congress and a Justice Department Special Prosecutor, both of whom wanted to hear recordings from an Oval Office taping system. As Nixon fought the battle of the tapes—which had every indication, even as early as the summer of 1973, of being a fight that would find its way to the Supreme Court—Nixon clearly wanted to rid himself of Agnew as soon as was politically possible. Before the end of August, he sent Alexander Haig, Haldeman's replacement as chief of staff, to ask the vice president to resign. Agnew refused, holding out until mid-September when both Haig and White House Counsel J. Fred Buzhardt told Agnew that he had no chance. Agnew's lawyer contacted Beall, and the plea bargaining began.

But when the *Washington Post* reported on September 22 that bargaining had begun, a seething Agnew tried one more offensive. Ordering the plea bargaining to come to a halt, he demanded to be afforded the formal impeachment process before the House of Representatives. This terrified the administration—once the impeachment process had been dusted off and tested, Agnew's case might well serve as a model for Nixon's own. Fortunately for Nixon, Speaker of the House Carl Albert refused to intervene. Agnew then tried one last gambit. Arguing that the Constitution prevented a sitting vice president from being indicted for a crime, his lawyers filed a suit against the Justice Department, enjoining them not to turn over any further evidence to the grand jury. On October 4, the court ruled that while a president was protected from indictment, a vice president was not.

Agnew had no further legal avenues, and his attempt to garner public opinion had failed miserably. The country was Watergate-weary; both the president and the people wanted Agnew gone, and the vice president finally accepted the inevitable. On October 10, Agnew appeared in a federal courtroom in Baltimore to plead nolo contendere (no contest) to a charge of income tax evasion. He received a $10,000 fine and a three-year jail sentence, which was suspended immediately. Later that afternoon, Agnew delivered his resignation to Secretary of State Kissinger. On October 12, Nixon announced that he would nominate Gerald Ford to replace Agnew under the terms of the Twenty-Fifth Amendment.

Five days after his resignation, on October 15, Agnew delivered a farewell address to the nation. It was vintage Agnew, as he continued to claim his innocence and to blame the media for his problems. In the national sigh of relief that followed the Ford nomination, Agnew's protests fell largely on deaf ears.

In the more than two decades after he left the vice presidency—a period that saw Agnew retreat into a retirement that did not include either an attempt to return to public office or to the public arena—Agnew continued to maintain his guiltlessness. In his memoirs, *Go Quietly . . . or Else* (1980), Agnew widened his indictment to include Attorney General Richardson and Nixon himself. In May 1995, the Republican-dominated Congress accorded Agnew an honor which, to that point, he had been the only vice president not to receive: His bust was included with the other vice presidents just outside Statuary Hall on the Senate side of the U.S. Capitol building—in a ceremony that received a great deal of media attention.

Spiro Agnew died on September 18, 1996, at age 77 in a hospital in Berlin, Maryland. He was admitted with a previously undiagnosed case of acute leukemia and died within three hours.

REFERENCES

Spiro Agnew, *Go Quietly . . . or Else* (New York: William Morrow and Co., 1980); Richard M. Cohen and Jules Witcover, *A Heartbeat Away: The Investigation and Resignation of Vice President Spiro T. Agnew* (New York: Viking Press, 1977); John Robert Greene, *The Limits of Power: The Nixon and Ford Administrations* (Bloomington: University of Indiana Press, 1992); Anthony J. Lukas, *Nightmare: The Underside of the Nixon Years* (New York: Viking Press, 1976);

Jules Witcover, *White Knight: The Rise of Spiro Agnew* (New York: Random House, 1972).

JOHN ROBERT GREENE is a professor of history and communication at Cazenovia College, Cazenovia, New York, where he has taught since 1969. In 1993, the faculty voted him the honor of Distinguished Faculty Member. Greene holds both a B.A. and an M.A. from St. Bonaventure University and a Ph.D. from Syracuse University. His books include *The Limits of Power: The Nixon and Ford Administrations* (1992) and *The Presidency of Gerald R. Ford* (1995). He is currently completing a history of Syracuse University during the years 1942–69 and has begun work on a history of the administration of George Bush, as well as a bibliography of the Bush and Nixon years.

GERALD RUDOLPH FORD (b. 1913)

Vice President, 1973–1974

(President Richard M. Nixon)

GERALD R. FORD
(Library of Congress)

By John Robert Greene

On October 10, 1973, pleading no contest to a charge of income tax evasion, Vice President Spiro Agnew resigned. Later that day, President Richard Nixon asked House Minority Leader Gerald R. Ford (a Republican from Michigan) to a private meeting at the White House. Aware that he would be the first president to utilize the Twenty-Fifth Amendment, ratified in 1967 to give the president the opportunity to fill a vice presidential vacancy by "nominat[ing] a vice president who shall take office upon confirmation by a majority vote of both houses of Congress," and equally aware that Watergate had squandered away much of his support on Capitol Hill, Nixon wanted Ford's advice on potential candidates who would be confirmable. After Ford left, Nixon spoke with advisers Bryce Harlow and Melvin Laird and Democratic Speaker of the House Carl Albert. All three men told the president that Gerald Ford was the only confirmable choice. Nixon instructed Laird to call Ford to sound him out about the nomination.

That evening, Laird called Ford at his home to inquire whether Ford would accept the vice-presidential nomination if offered the position by the president. Despite the protests of his wife, Betty, who said that she wanted him to run for one more term in the House and then retire, Ford agreed. The next day in the Oval Office, Nixon formally asked Ford if he wanted the job, and Ford accepted. Later that evening, Nixon publicly announced his choice of Ford to the nation, and those assembled in the room to hear the announcement went wild with cheering and whistling. Somewhat surprised, Nixon turned to Ford and whispered: "They like you."

Born in 1913 in Omaha, Nebraska, Leslie Lynch King was brought to Grand Rapids by a mother who had been the victim of spousal abuse. Once divorced, Dorothy King married Gerald R. Ford Sr., who gave his name to her only child. Young Jerry—called Junior by his neighborhood friends—was reasonably well insulated from the suffering of the Great Depression by the success of his stepfather's paint and varnish company. As a result, he had a relatively carefree childhood, one that centered around school, Boy Scouting, and football. As a football player, Ford had few peers. He was an All-City and All-State center for South High and won a full-year's tuition ($100) to the University of Michigan. In his senior year of college, Ford was regarded as one of the country's best centers, and in the balloting for the 1935 Collegiate All-Star Game played against the Chicago Bears at Soldier Field, Ford was the number four vote getter of fans around the nation. Had he not chosen to study law at Yale University that fall, Ford might have played for either the Detroit Lions or the Green Bay Packers, both of which offered him a professional football contract.

Ford earned his law degree from Yale University in 1941 and after a brief stint practicing law in Grand Rapids joined the Navy in 1942. After service in the South Pacific he returned to Grand Rapids, and in 1948 married Elizabeth Bloomer, a union that produced three sons and a daughter. In the same year, Ford was elected to the first of twelve consecutive terms in the House of Representatives. Throughout his years in Congress, Ford developed an expertise in the area of defense appropriations, as well as a reputation as a member whose political word could be trusted. It was this reputation for evenhandedness that was Ford's biggest asset as he rose up the leadership ladder.

In January 1963, he was elected head of the House Republican Conference, and in December of that year, President Lyndon Johnson tapped Ford to serve on the commission to investigate the assassination of John F. Kennedy. Thanks in part to the national recognition earned from his participation on the Warren Commission, Ford was chosen House minority leader in January 1965. He served in this position under both Lyndon Johnson and Richard Nixon until Nixon turned to him to replace Agnew in the fall of 1973.

In his memoirs, Nixon was crystal clear why he chose Gerald Ford for the vice presidency: "There was no question that he [Ford] would be the easiest to get confirmed." Yet, before the nomination could go to the floor of both houses of Congress, it had to clear both the Senate Rules Committee and the House Judiciary Committee. Anti-Nixon feeling ran deep on Capitol Hill, and Ford could expect to face many questions that were Watergate related. The overwhelming majority of the questions probed Ford's personality and his institutional views; his views on policy were virtually ignored. This comes as no great surprise—it was widely assumed, by Democrat and Republican alike, that in Ford, the Congress was confirming the next president.

For the most part, Ford said all the right things during his committee testimony. He argued that he saw himself as "a ready conciliator between the White House and Capitol Hill" (he would say in a later interview with Dom Bonafede of the *National Journal Reports* that while he felt that he *did* have an obligation to both president and Congress, "the obligation to Congress is one of my own choosing") and described himself as a "moderate on domestic affairs, conservative on fiscal affairs, but a very dyed-in-the-wool internationalist in foreign policy."

Ford testified that no official had the right to disobey a direct order of the Court. He also promised to be more accessible to, and honest with, both the public and the Congress. In response to a question on whether or not he would have the power to prevent or terminate any investigation or prosecution of his predecessor, Ford replied that "I do not think the public would stand for it. I think—and whether he has the technical authority or not, I cannot give you a categorical answer." On the few questions of policy, however, he indicated a solid agreement with the policies of the Nixon administration. He continued his long-standing loyalty to Nixon when he made it clear that he felt that Nixon was "completely innocent" of any wrongdoing in Watergate.

The hearings were far from a cakewalk, however. There were several serious accusations raised against Ford. He was questioned about contributions totaling some $11,500 in 1970 from several business groups and a union, the Marine Engineers Beneficial Association, which had a rather unsavory reputation. Ford stated "categorically" that no funds collected on his behalf in 1970 "were for my personal benefit," and testified that he had endorsed all the checks over to the Kent County Republican Committee. He was also grilled on his role as Nixon's chief defender on the floor of the Congress, his civil rights record, and claims that as minority leader he had used his influence to slow down the initial phases of the investigation into financial improprieties during the 1972 election, an investigation that later implicated the Nixon White House.

The oddest charges were made by an ex-lobbyist acquaintance of Ford's. Robert N. Winter-Berger, former public relations man and lobbyist, had claimed in a 1972 book, *The Washington Payoff*, that in 1966 he had paid a friend $1,000 and "a number of favors" to be introduced to Ford. Winter-Berger viewed this "a good investment," one that Ford "knew about . . . and it did not faze him." Winter-Berger's book went on to document the number of times that he had visited Ford's office and a vacation that he had arranged for the Minority Leader "at the home of some friends of mine in Kentucky." He

further charged that Ford had routinely granted favors for Winter-Berger associates in return for campaign contributions; one enumerated was that Winter-Berger had arranged for $125,000 to be contributed to the Republicans by Francis Kellogg, a State Department official, in return for consideration for his being named assistant to the secretary of state, a position that carried the rank of ambassador. In a second book, *The Gerald Ford Letters*, written after Ford had been confirmed as vice president, Winter-Berger claimed that he had rewritten speeches for Ford, consulted with Ford on the congressman's wardrobe, and had been instrumental in pushing Ford to get an extension on the visa of a New York psychiatrist who was facing deportation to his native Holland. Winter-Berger also claimed that he had "loaned" Gerald Ford about $15,000 and that he had introduced Ford to a New York psychiatrist who had treated Ford for nervous exhaustion.

Ford's memoirs reflect how he felt at the time:

> All these allegations, of course, were lies. . . . I had met Winter-Berger—I didn't dispute that—but it didn't take me long to determine that I didn't want anything to do with him. I had told my staff that and they made sure that he was kept out of my way.

Ford countered by offering to take a lie-detector test, but it was unnecessary; Winter-Berger's story immediately began to self-destruct. The *Ann Arbor News* reported that Winter-Berger's newest claims directly contradicted an April 17, 1972, interview with one of their reporters, during which Winter-Berger was quoted as contending that "Jerry Ford never personally received a cent from me." The House Rules Committee decided to call Winter-Berger in on November 7 to testify during a closed session. During that testimony, one committee member confronted Winter-Berger with a copy of his tax returns, which showed that he only had a gross income of about $28,306 over the three-year period of the loan. Reeling, Winter-Berger tried to change his story. After hearing his contradictory testimony, the committee did not try to hide its scorn.

The votes to confirm Ford's nomination were overwhelmingly positive. The Senate Rules Committee supported him, 9–0. Nine days later, the House Judiciary Committee voted 24–8. In the full House, the vote was 387–35; in the Senate, it was 92–3. All of the nay votes were cast by Democrats. Nixon wanted to have the swearing-in at the White House; however, a Nixon aide told Robert Hartmann, then Ford's Chief of Staff, that he was afraid that Nixon would be booed when he walked down the center aisle with Ford. Adamant, Ford insisted upon the Capitol, and Nixon finally agreed. Ford's December 6, 1973, swearing-in was a simple ceremony, followed by a short speech from the new vice president during which he cautioned the nation not to overinflate their expectations of his abilities, quipping that "I am a Ford, not a Lincoln."

As soon as he was confirmed, Ford solicited the advice of many of his Capitol Hill colleagues as he searched for a job description. Some of the most prescient advice, in a letter now deposited in the Gerald R. Ford Library, came from a former vice president, Minnesota Senator Hubert Humphrey, who characterized the office as "awkward . . . at best. The man who occupies it will have many responsibilities and no authority with the one exception [of the tie-breaking power in the Senate]." Humphrey recognized that the vice president was expected to serve as the "alter-ego of the president," but cautioned Ford that "it is important for a vice president to remember that he is not the president, and, therefore, can only speak for the government when he is authorized to do so." Nixon's staffers had the same idea. Bruce Kehrli, staff secretary to Alexander Haig and then Nixon's chief of staff, grandly announced in a meeting with Robert Hartmann that "what we want to do is to make the Vice President as much as possible a part of the White House staff." Hartmann remembered in his memoirs that "as I shook [Kehrli's] damp hand, it occurred to me that this was really intended to be a compliment."

Ford would later tell a reporter that "I feel that I am an active, participating vice-president."

That was certainly the case. Either by statute or by tradition, the vice president was a member of the cabinet, vice chairman of the Domestic Council, and a member of the National Security Council. Nixon also appointed Ford as the chairman of both the Committee on the Right of Privacy and of his Energy Action Group. However, Ford shed two assignments that had been routinely turned over to the vice president—that of White House liaison for Indian Affairs and the role of administration representative with the governors and mayors.

Yet, it was in his role as Nixon's lightning rod that Ford played his most public role as vice president. During his confirmation hearings, Senator Mark Hatfield asked Ford if he thought that Nixon could still save his presidency. Ford's reply: "I think so. It's going to take a lot of help from a lot of people. And I intend to devote myself to that." True to his word, Ford was constantly on the road, defending the president to any audience who would listen. During his eight months in office, more than 500 groups in forty states heard the vice president speak to them. He also gave more than fifty press conferences, and more than eighty interviews. Ford consistently gave an uncompromising defense of Nixon, and it was almost his undoing. On January 15, 1974, before the American Farm Bureau Federation in Atlantic City, Ford identified the president's antagonists as "a few extreme partisans," whose "aim is total victory for themselves and the total defeat not only of President Nixon but of the policies for which he stands." The next day, both Nixon and Ford's staff acknowledged that the speech had been drafted by the White House speechwriters. Sharp press criticism followed, and rather than be castigated any further as a Nixon shill, Ford hired two speechwriters of his own. The Farm Bureau speech was a turning point for Ford. From that point on, he was less effusive in his defense of Nixon. For example, when on May 1, 1974, the White House made public only a highly sanitized version of the Watergate tapes, Ford quipped that he was a "little disappointed."

The mutually exclusive requirements of political loyalty (he was, after all, vice president, and

Nixon had been one of his oldest friends in Congress) and good political common sense (Nixon was clearly doomed) played havoc with Ford. In his memoirs, Ford lamented:

> By the nature of the office I held, I was in an impossible situation. I couldn't abandon Nixon, because that would make it appear that I was trying to position myself to become president. Nor could I get too close to him, because if I did, I'd risk being sucked into the whirlpool myself.

The closest he came to admitting it in public was in a June 8, 1974, speech at Logan, Utah: "why do I uphold the president one day and the next day side with Congress, which is deliberating his impeachment? . . . [I will] remain my own man, fix my own course and speak my own conscience. . . ." Yet his time for political agony was almost over. Events sped through the consciousness of the United States in summer 1974 with a blinding speed. On July 22, the Supreme Court ordered that the White House release all the subpoenaed tapes.

Ford spent the first days of August preparing for the inevitable. On August 1, he met with Haig, who floated the idea of a deal—Nixon's resignation for the promise of a presidential pardon by Ford for any and all offenses that Nixon may have committed during Watergate—Ford turned Haig down in the presence of two aides. On Friday, August 2, Ford met with the Senate leadership to discuss plans for the now probable Senate trial of Nixon, and it was agreed that Ford should not even attend but should be waiting in the wings to take the oath of office when Nixon was convicted. On August 5, the day that the tapes were finally released, Ford announced that

> I have come to the conclusion that the public interest is no longer served by repetition of my previously expressed belief that on the basis of all the evidence known to me and to the American people, the president is not guilty of an impeachable offense.

In a cabinet meeting the next day—the final cabinet meeting of the Nixon administra-

tion—Ford told the president that "had I known and had it been disclosed to me what has been disclosed in reference to the Watergate affair in the last twenty-four hours, I would not have made a number of the statements that I have made, either as Minority Leader or as Vice President of the United States." In his memoirs, Ford was blunter: "No longer was there the slightest doubt in my mind as to the outcome of the struggle. Nixon was finished."

Equally convinced that the end was near, Haig asked for another meeting with Ford. On the morning of August 7, Ford remembered that Haig was formal: "Mr. Vice-President, I think it's time for you to prepare to assume the office of President." He was right. The next morning, Nixon summoned Ford to the White House. Nixon told his vice president that "I have made the decision to resign. It's in the best interest of the country." He paused, and then quietly said, "Jerry, I know you'll do a good job." Following Nixon's speech to the nation that evening, Ford came out onto the steps of his home in Alexandria, Virginia, and spoke to reporters, saying that "this is one of the most difficult and very saddest incidents I've ever witnessed." He praised Nixon for making "one of the greatest personal sacrifices for the country and one of the finest personal decisions on behalf of all of us as Americans by his decision to resign."

The next day, at about 12:00 P.M., the East Room of the White House was filled with staffers who, less than an hour before, had been teary eyed as they attended Nixon's farewell to them. Chief Justice Warren Burger, just off an Air Force jet that had whisked him back from a conference in the Netherlands, walked in alone, wearing a full black judicial robe. When Ford entered with his wife Betty at his side, he was met with an almost cathartic standing ovation. As the oath of office was administered, Ford's voice never wavered. His first speech as president was clearly his best speech as president. In words that would, for many, become both the symbol of the administration and the standard by which it would be judged, Ford attempted to bring an end to Watergate:

I believe that truth is the glue that holds government together, not only our government but civilization itself. That bond, though strained, is unbroken at home and abroad. . . . In all my private and public acts as your president, I expect to follow my instincts of openness and candor with full confidence that honesty is always the best policy in the end. . . . My fellow Americans, our long national nightmare is over. Our constitution works. Our great republic is a government of laws and not of men. Here, the people rule. . . .

As he closed, Ford came close to tears when he asked the country to pray for Richard Nixon and his family so that "our former President, who brought peace to millions, find it for himself. . . ."

Ford's presidency was a difficult one. Not having the luxury of a three-month transition period as president-elect, he had little time to plan, and he and his advisers faced many dilemmas: The economy, beset both by inflationary pressures and rapid unemployment, grew worse by the day. The nation growled at his pardon of Richard Nixon, a proclamation that came so early in his administration that, despite Ford's protests to the contrary, the majority of people believed he had made a deal with Nixon. Although he was not responsible for U.S. failure in Vietnam, it was on Ford's watch that the North Vietnamese began their final offensive against the South—the most vivid image held by many people of the Ford years was that of helicopters evacuating thousands from the U.S. embassy in Saigon. There were moments of national pride—most notably the rescuing of the crew of the *Mayaguez*, a tanker ship that had been detained by the Cambodian government, and the national celebration of the bicentennial anniversary of the signing of the Declaration of Independence on July 4, 1976.

However, as the nation headed toward the presidential election of 1976, Ford found himself faced with a challenge from within his own party: Conservatives, led by California governor Ronald Reagan, assailed Ford as a weaker clone of Nixon, and Reagan came breathlessly close to upsetting Ford for the Republican nomination. Weakened by the Reagan challenge, the Ford campaign did not withstand the fall challenge by Jimmy Carter, and the former governor of Georgia won the White House back for the Democrats for the first time since 1968. Ford retired to private life, dividing his time between homes in California and Colorado.

REFERENCES

John Robert Greene, *The Presidency of Gerald R. Ford* (Lawrence: The University Press of Kansas, 1995); James Cannon, *Time and Chance: Gerald Ford's Appointment with Destiny* (New York: HarperCollins, 1994); Gerald R. Ford, *A Time to Heal: The Autobiography of Gerald R. Ford* (New York: Harper and Row, 1979); Lester Sobel, ed. *Presidential Succession: Ford, Rockefeller, and the Amendment* (New York: Facts On File, 1975).

See the entry for Spiro Agnew for a biographical note on John Robert Greene

NELSON A. ROCKEFELLER (1908–1979)

Vice President, 1974–1977

(President Gerald Ford)

NELSON A. ROCKEFELLER
(Library of Congress)

By Leroy G. Dorsey

Nelson Aldrich Rockefeller represented a larger-than-life figure in American history who achieved nearly every prize he desired except the one he most sought: the presidency. As an heir to one of the largest family fortunes in America, Rockefeller funded many philanthropic projects. As a special counsel to six presidents, he helped to shape U.S. foreign and domestic policy. As four-time governor of New York State, he promoted major social and political reforms. During these decades of public philanthropy and political service, Rockefeller pursued the office of the presidency. Ironically, after three unsuccessful attempts to become president as well as his legendary disdain to be second in anything, Rockefeller accepted President Gerald Ford's offer to become the forty-first vice president of the United States.

362

Rockefeller's term as vice president held many trials and triumphs. Despite his political savvy and ability to manage people, Rockefeller faced numerous challenges. He encountered a highly controversial and lengthy confirmation process for the vice presidency. He experienced the emotionally draining conflicts fostered among competing interests in the Ford White House, and endured the overwhelming demands placed on him as both vice president and staff assistant to the president. Having survived these challenges, Rockefeller succeeded in making the vice presidency more substantively involved in the policy processes of the contemporary presidency. Given the fact that he neither sought nor wanted the vice presidency, he took an office that is often considered virtually useless and propelled it into a position that initiated and developed policy proposals that had far-reaching consequences for the country. Furthermore, he lent a sense of energy to a presidential administration that might well have languished in the aftermath of Watergate if not for him.

Born in Bar Harbor, Maine, in 1908, Rockefeller was a third-generation heir to the name and fortune of the Rockefellers. In fact, both sides of his family had attained prestige and wealth. Maternal grandfather Nelson Aldrich became a self-made millionaire and was a respected majority leader in the U.S. Senate for seventeen years. Paternal grandfather, John D. Rockefeller had formed the Standard Oil Corporation and by 1908 had seized control of nearly every aspect of oil production in the United States; as a result of this, John D. had become what President Theodore Roosevelt labeled a "malefactor of great wealth."

Rockefeller lived with his parents and five siblings in several of their family homes, including a town house in New York City and a country estate at Pocantico Hills, Westchester. Despite the magnificence of these homes—complete with art treasures, family infirmaries, and private playgrounds—Rockefeller's father instilled in him many of the traditional values that his father had taught him, frugality and altruism being primary among them. When Rockefeller received his allowance of thirty cents a week at age eight, his father allowed him to spend only ten cents on himself with the remainder to be split equally between savings and charity, and like his grandfather, Rockefeller became adept at making money. As a young boy he raised rabbits to be sold to the Rockefeller Institute, raised vegetables that he sold to the family kitchen, and performed household chores for money. Both his mother and his father wanted their son to respect the physical and financial benefits of hard work.

Rockefeller found his formal education, especially in the early years, to be difficult due to left-handedness and dyslexia. In the early 1900s, many people considered left-handedness an aberration. To counter this "abnormality" in his son, Rockefeller's father would inflict a mild pain by snapping an elastic band on his son's right hand when Nelson used his left hand. Although he became right handed in most activities, this conversion process probably intensified his learning disability: Rockefeller transposed numbers and juxtaposed letters in words. These problems nearly caused him to fail the ninth grade and placed him in his high school class's bottom third. While his grades prevented him from attending Princeton University like his older brother, he remained undaunted. Working tirelessly and with unflinching perseverance, and confident to the point of cockiness in his own abilities, Rockefeller improved his grades enough to allow him to enter Dartmouth College in 1926.

Rockefeller's college years helped to crystallize his beliefs and character. First, his experience with fraternities, which he considered snobbish, made him more aware of the need to promote democratic institutions and to consider the welfare of people not as privileged as himself. Second, college became an arena for Rockefeller to face tough competition and to experience both defeat and victory. In a foreshadowing of later events, he lost the class presidency and became instead the class vice president. His first political upset, however, did not prevent him from achieving success as a scholar. Rockefeller's senior thesis, a forty-five-page essay on Standard Oil, earned him an A and the respect of his teachers, fellow students, and family; in addition, it gave him greater insight into the power and the consequent responsibility of the Rockefellers. In 1930, he earned membership in Phi Beta Kappa and graduated *cum laude*.

Less than a month after graduation, Rockefeller married Mary Todhunter Clark whom he had courted during his school vacations. Nicknamed Tod, she also had come from a distinguished family: her family's estate in Philadelphia had been granted to them by their ancestor, King George III, and her maternal grandfather had served as president of the Pennsylvania Railroad. During their thirty-one-year marriage, Tod gave birth to five children. With a keen intelligence and wit, and the requisite social graces, she appeared to be the perfect mate (albeit temporarily).

After an around-the-world honeymoon lasting nine months, which included appointments with business associates and foreign leaders at every stop, Rockefeller and his wife returned to New York City in 1931. Despite the Depression, he had his choice of business opportunities. He quickly became bored with a minor post at Standard Oil and so went to work with his uncle at Chase Bank. During the morning, Rockefeller learned the banking business and in the afternoon devoted his energy to a company he started, Special Work, Inc; its mission involved finding tenants for the new Rockefeller Center, then the world's largest office complex. Rockefeller excelled at leasing space and at public relations for the Center. He frequently made the news with special ceremonies and speeches that paid tribute to the opulent structure. He proved so successful in the promotion of Rockefeller Center that his father named him its executive vice president in 1937 and its president in 1938. One year later Rockefeller became more involved with his second love: art. Having acquired a genuine appreciation for fine art from his mother, he eagerly accepted the position of president of the Museum of Modern Art.

It was, however, a small investment that Rockefeller made in the Creole Petroleum Company (CPC) in 1935, a Venezuelan subsidiary of Standard Oil, that altered the course of his life. After becoming a member of the CPC board of directors, he recruited a group of oil and eco-nomic experts to accompany him on a fact-finding mission to Latin America. He discovered that the U.S. executives of the Venezuelan CPC chose not to learn the native tongue, managed the company autocratically, and even separated themselves from the workers with barbed wire fences. Thanks to Rockefeller's report to the CPC board of directors on his return to the United States, the company instituted major reforms to serve better the interests of the host country. Rockefeller also took note of the growing anti-U.S. sentiment being created by companies like the CPC and the cultivation of that negative sentiment by German, Japanese, Italian, and Soviet agents. If these were left unchecked, he believed, Latin America would fall prey to the Axis powers and lead ultimately to the ruin of the Rockefeller interests and those of the United States.

Rockefeller's fervent interest in Latin America brought him to the attention of President Franklin Roosevelt. Roosevelt wanted him to head a program that would strengthen Latin American ties to the United States. After clearing it with his family, Rockefeller headed the Office of the Coordinator for Inter-American Affairs (CIAA) in 1940, earning a salary of one dollar a year. Working long hours every day as well as emerging relatively unscathed from bureaucratic in-fighting, Rockefeller made this small office one of the most popular agencies to work for during World War II, earning for himself a notoriety evidenced by his picture on the cover of *Life* magazine in 1942. Thanks to him, Latin American commodities were purchased at higher than market prices by the United States and other allied countries, which, in turn, caused critical shortages for the Axis powers; U.S. companies in Latin America were forced to terminate their anti-U.S. agents or be blacklisted by the State Department; and the CIAA's information campaign involving newspapers, radio, and movies met and turned back the tide of Nazi propaganda in Latin America. Roosevelt, impressed and pleased with Rockefeller's accomplishments, appointed him assistant secretary of state for American republic affairs in 1944. As assistant secretary he lobbied successfully to have the fascist-ruled Argentina admitted to the United Nations and reinforced the Monroe Doctrine by maneuvering the United Nations into agreeing that aggression against one American region was equivalent to aggression against all of the Americas.

Despite his accomplishments, Rockefeller's appointment as assistant secretary came to an end eight months after the death of Roosevelt. President Truman felt no strong loyalty to Rockefeller, and when Truman's newly appointed secretary of state wanted to chose his own assistant, the president gladly accepted Rockefeller's resignation in 1945.

Returning to New York, Rockefeller again took control of Rockefeller Center. Unsatisfied and eager once again to command global attention, he launched the American International Association (AIA) in 1946, a nonprofit and philanthropic organization designed to aid in the modernization of Brazil's and Venezuela's health, education, and agricultural infrastructure. Over time, the AIA helped to build roads and reduce infant mortality. In conjunction with the AIA, Rockefeller also started the International Basic Economy Corporation (IBEC) in 1947, a private, commercial organization whose mission was to introduce Latin America to such U.S. enterprises as supermarkets and mass distribution. As a result of the IBEC, hundreds of U.S. businesses invested in Latin America.

Rockefeller's private ventures regarding cultural and technological progress in Latin America again gained him entry into the White House. In 1949, President Truman announced his Point Four program to introduce scientific advances into underdeveloped areas. With some prodding by Rockefeller, Truman invited him in 1950 to chair the International Advisory Board (IAB) to enact that program. The board's recommendation to consolidate all overseas economic functions currently distributed among twenty-three agencies into a single office, the Office of Overseas Economic Administration, antagonized Special Assistant to the President Averell Harriman. Harriman wanted an organization that stressed military rather than economic assistance in Latin America. When Truman approved the Harriman agency, Rockefeller resigned from the IAB in 1951.

When the Republican Party regained the White House a year later with the election of Dwight Eisenhower, Rockefeller again seized the opportunity to return to Washington. He enjoyed much success in the Eisenhower administration. As chair of an advisory committee to study the reorganization of the federal government, Rockefeller helped establish the Department of Health, Education, and Welfare and in 1953 became its first undersecretary. His position, which involved improving health and educational facilities, soon gave way to yet another coveted position in 1953: special assistant to the president concerning foreign affairs. In this role, Rockefeller developed programs that would increase understanding and cooperation among countries; the media popularly termed his work psychological warfare. Rockefeller persuaded Eisenhower to adopt a plan proposed to him by his consultant, Harvard professor of government Henry Kissinger. Called Open Skies, the Rockefeller-Kissinger plan not only proposed that the United States and the Soviet Union allow inspectors from each country to examine military establishments as a necessary step to nuclear disarmament, but it also proposed that both countries allow aerial inspections of their territories to reduce the risk of surprise attacks. Rockefeller again waited for recognition of his service by being appointed to a cabinet post and was again disappointed.

Frustrated, Rockefeller resigned and left Washington in 1955. From his experiences in the Eisenhower White House, he recognized the limitations of being in someone else's power and now sought the power that derives from being popularly elected. With the announcement of his candidacy for governor in 1958, Rockefeller staged an aggressive and expensive media campaign that highlighted his dedication to work diligently for the public welfare. This, coupled with his inherent charm, won him the governorship of New York for the first of four times.

During his fifteen years as New York governor, Rockefeller achieved an impressive record of accomplishments. To tackle the urban problems of the state, he created the Urban Development Corporation to clear slum areas and aid in the construction of low-income housing. His antidrug program, initially opposed from almost all quarters due to the harsh penalties Rockefeller called for, was eventually instituted with only minor changes. Regarding education, he expanded the New York State university system to the point that it was the largest system of higher education anywhere in the world at that time. He successfully pushed for legislation that outlawed racial discrimination in housing and the lending practices of financial institutions. His youth centers served to provide training and jobs for troubled young adults. He also promoted construction on a grand scale. To make Albany worthy of being the capital of New York, Rockefeller initiated the South Mall project; by its completion, the Empire State Plaza had been constructed and constituted an eighteen-acre complex of government buildings, a cultural center, and a shopping mall. To attract industry and business, Rockefeller oversaw the building of the twin 110-story towers of the World Trade Center. Other benefits New Yorkers received because of Governor Rockefeller included a State Council on the Arts that promoted cultural development in the performing arts, establishment of the first mandatory police training course, and the development of open land as recreational areas.

Rockefeller's terms as governor were not without their moments of controversy. Perhaps the most dramatic involved the Attica prison riot in September 1971 and Rockefeller's response to it. For five days, inmates seized control of the prison, taking thirty-nine guards hostage. Despite repeated pleading by the prison commissioner and others on the scene, Rockefeller refused to come to Attica personally. He did, however, order the state police to retake the prison. In the assault, thirty-nine inmates and hostages were killed, constituting the highest loss of life in U.S. penal history. The McKay Commission, authorized to study the riot and its aftermath, criticized both the amount of force used in retaking the prison and Rockefeller's failure to appear on the scene and take charge personally.

His triumphs and trials as governor, however, did not slow his drive for achieving his most sought after goal: the presidency.

Buoyed by his landslide victory for the governorship in 1958, Rockefeller turned his attention to winning the White House in 1960. He recruited a large personal staff, which he divided between speech writing, research, image management, and logistics. After two months of cultivating support and generating headlines, Rockefeller decided that he could not stop Richard Nixon from winning the primaries, given the latter's position as vice president to the immensely popular President Eisenhower. Rockefeller withdrew from the race but he was not silent. In 1959, he issued a statement that essentially condemned the Republican Party for its failure in leadership. This plus the revelation of Rockefeller's plan to coerce Nixon into accepting several Rockefeller-platform elements caused Rockefeller to be viewed as a party spoiler.

Despite this 1960 election image, Rockefeller found himself a leading contender for his party's nomination in the 1964 election. After Nixon's defeat in 1960 and his subsequent defeat in a California race for governor, Rockefeller became the favorite, given the new and untested faces in the GOP, but his front-runner status failed to last because of several questionable decisions. Support began to erode when he reneged on a campaign promise not to raise taxes as governor of New York. His support continued downward when he attacked the Republican Party's conservative right in an attempt to associate himself with the civil rights issue. Finally, he angered the morally concerned citizenry when in 1962 he divorced his wife after three decades and fourteen months later married a woman nineteen years his junior. Margaretta Fitler Murphy, nicknamed Happy, was a thirty-six-year-old divorcée who appeared to have given up her own four children to indulge her romance with Rockefeller. When the votes were counted, Rockefeller had lost the chance for the presidency again.

Rockefeller's third try at the presidency in 1968 also proved abortive. As that presidential election neared, Rockefeller assured his supporters in February 1967 that he would run again;

however, he stunned them weeks later when he formally declared that he would not seek the nomination. The events of late March and early April worked to lead Rockefeller back into the race: President Johnson refused to seek another term and Dr. Martin Luther King, Jr., was assassinated, with the ghettos in many major cities erupting in turmoil as a result. In yet another reversal, Rockefeller believed it was his duty to resume running, but his on-again-off-again campaign, coupled with his increasing alienation of Republican delegates by attempting to capture the poor and black constituencies after Robert Kennedy's assassination in June 1968, placed him behind Nixon in the primaries again.

Rockefeller's governorship and bids for the presidency did not prevent him from continuing his service to the presidency. Having a strong friendship and mutual respect with Lyndon Johnson, Rockefeller frequently brought the president's attention to civil rights, water pollution, and education. From 1965 to 1970, Rockefeller served as a Johnson appointee to the Advisory Commission on Intergovernmental Relations, allowing him to bring together mayors and other country officials in order to pressure Washington into overhauling the federal grant system and to focus national attention on such issues as welfare reform. Even his enmity toward Nixon did not prevent Rockefeller from aiding his chief rival, nor did it stop Nixon from utilizing Rockefeller's talent. Nixon and Rockefeller met frequently to discuss domestic legislation. When Nixon asked Rockefeller to undertake a special mission to develop a successful U.S. policy toward Latin America, Rockefeller accepted. After a seven-month trip through Latin America, considered by some to be ill conceived, Rockefeller presented Nixon with a critically acclaimed "Report on the Americas" that proposed the refinancing of Latin America's foreign debt and that called for a more-tolerant attitude toward the military regimes in that region of the world.

It was perhaps fitting that Rockefeller served in the Nixon White House when his rival faced his greatest crisis. In 1972, the police arrested five men during a break-in at Democratic National Committee offices in Washington's Watergate Hotel and office complex. Later that year, and despite repeated denials from the president, suspicions rose that Nixon himself had personal knowledge of that event before the fact. With the release of the White House tapes contradicting Nixon's assertion that he knew nothing about Watergate, and facing impeachment, Nixon became the first person to resign the presidency on August 9, 1974.

With Vice President Gerald Ford's ascension to the presidency, Rockefeller immediately became the subject of speculation regarding Ford's choice for his vacated office. However, the New York governor was not the president's first choice; these were Wisconsin Representative Melvin Laird with whom Ford had had a long congressional relationship and Republican National Committee Chairman George Bush. With Bush the target of reports that linked him to a secret "slush fund" in the Nixon White House and Laird's refusal of the appointment, Ford turned to Rockefeller. In spite of Rockefeller's reluctance to be the vice president and his current work with the Commission on Critical Choices for Americans (an organization that he created in 1973 to brought together the best minds of the time to address the problems facing the country), he believed it his duty to work with the untried president to alleviate the economic and social problems facing the nation.

The first test of that duty came in fall 1974 with the vice-presidential confirmation process. The country eagerly awaited the hearings that would reveal the specifics regarding Rockefeller wealth and power. No one at the time knew that the process would go on for four grueling months, taking their toll on Rockefeller's wife Happy as she underwent a radical mastectomy and on Rockefeller himself as he defended his finances, explained his personal transgressions, and awaited to begin work in the White House.

The length of the confirmation process stemmed from the need for Congress to satisfy its concern that there would be no conflict of interest given Rockefeller's vast holdings in major corporations—corporations that worked almost daily with the executive branch. If he succeeded the president, Congress reasoned, the Rockefeller fortune merged with the power of the presidency could be economically unsettling.

On the first day of hearings before the Senate Rules and Administration Committee in September, Rockefeller attempted to lay to rest what he considered the erroneous belief concerning his family's fortune and their economic power. According to him, he personally owned less than 1 percent and his family combined owned less than 3 percent in any oil company. To help lessen the supposed conflict of interest issue, Rockefeller offered to place all his securities in one blind trust while vice president, keeping only his real estate and art in his name. Although less than what many people anticipated, Rockefeller estimated his total worth at $178 million.

For three days, Rockefeller's confirmation went smoothly; then the trouble began. During October, two potentially damaging revelations came to light. The FBI disclosed that Rockefeller had funded a disparaging book about his opponent, former Supreme Court Justice Arthur Goldberg, during his 1970 reelection bid for governor. This seemingly "dirty trick" raised the specter of Watergate in the public's mind. Rockefeller explained that he did not know what the book was going to say; he just referred the backers of the project to his brother Laurence for financing. Rockefeller admitted that he had made a hasty error and he apologized to his former opponent. The Senate concluded that Rockefeller was only guilty of poor judgment. The second revelation involved large financial gifts and loans Rockefeller had given to New York State officials while he was governor. On this point, Rockefeller made no apologies. To him, his gifts reflected no more than the respect and admiration he felt for many of those officials. In addition, Rockefeller maintained that these gifts could not be bribes because the recipients were already working for him. The Senate committee disliked Rockefeller's practice but found no evidence of any wrongdoing. With the Senate's vote of 90 to 7 to confirm, and the House's vote of 287 to 128 in favor, Rockefeller officially became vice president on December 19, 1974.

The vice president has traditionally undertaken certain tasks, and Rockefeller's vice presidency was no different. As a vice president, Rockefeller presided over the Senate. He learned there that, unlike in the New York State legislature, the Senate would not meekly bow before him. In a representative episode, Rockefeller, attempting to facilitate a decision in the Senate, refused to recognize two senators who wanted to speak before the roll call for votes was continued. A senator informed Rockefeller that he had the authority to ignore members of the Senate but that it was discourteous of him to exercise that authority. Two months passed before Rockefeller apologized for his breach of Senate etiquette. Rockefeller also toured foreign countries on goodwill missions and traveled throughout the United States promoting the administration. For example, regarding his tour of U.S. cities, Rockefeller made a series of speeches during the bicentennial year that acquainted Americans with the administration's concerns about the energy crisis, national health, and religion.

Other traditional vice-presidential duties included membership on several national commissions. As chairperson of the Commission on CIA Activities within the United States, Rockefeller investigated whether any of the CIA's activities were illegal and beyond the scope of its charter. The National Commission on Productivity and Work Quality sought to increase the productivity and morale of the American worker. The Commission on the Organization of Government for the Conduct of Foreign Policy worked to clarify the relationship between the legislative and executive branches regarding foreign policy making. Finally, as chairperson of the President's Panel on Federal Compensation, Rockefeller developed recommendations that would make compensation practices fair to both the employees and the public.

For Rockefeller, however, commission work took too much time away from cultivating a central role in the Ford White House and in developing program policies. Contrary to vice-presidential tradition, Rockefeller wanted a substantive policy role, so he preferred his assignments as vice chairman of the Domestic Council, as the panel chairman responsible for achieving the nation's energy independence, and as the chairman of an advisory group whose task was to establish a White House Science Advisory Unit.

The Domestic Council had been created to evaluate domestic programs, to integrate them for maximum efficiency, and to determine how they could be funded. Under John Erlichman's direction during the Nixon administration, the Domestic Council became such a powerful entity that it dominated the domestic cabinet secretaries and involved itself in departmental program activities. With the Watergate scandal and Erlichman's resignation, the council found its power severely limited. In addition, the newly created Economic Policy Board (EPB) and the Energy Resources Council (ERC) overlapped responsibilities with the Domestic Council, creating the potential for further weakening of the council's power.

From this weakened position, Rockefeller hoped to establish the Domestic Council to a prominent position regarding domestic matters. He first proposed to become the council's executive director, but this met with strong opposition. Not only did President Ford's legal advisers publicly conclude that it was legally impossible for Rockefeller to hold the vice-chair and executive director's position simultaneously, but White House Coordinator Donald Rumsfeld privately informed Rockefeller that he and he alone would be responsible for the paper flow to and from the president. Unable to maneuver himself into the coveted position, Rockefeller proposed that two of his associates, James Cannon and Richard Dunham, assume the roles of executive directive and deputy directory, respectively. His new proposal similarly agitated the White House staff. Rumsfeld countered by proposing his own nominee for the executive directorship and lobbied his choice to President Ford. Angered by Rumsfeld's actions, Rockefeller sent a memo to the president stating that he would withdraw from the Domestic Council if his proposal was not met. To prevent a major division in his administration, Ford backed Rockefeller.

With his associates in place, Rockefeller worked next to regain the Domestic Council's position over the EPB and the ERC. To that end, the vice president called for and got those offices to agree to become part of the council's task force to establish long-range goals for the administration regarding social programs and subordinate their power to Rockefeller's unit.

Rockefeller, however, failed to achieve control over the Domestic Council, as it had been created to serve the president's needs, not the vice president's. As a result, Cannon, Rockefeller's associate, made it clear that as executive director he worked for and gave his loyalty to Ford. Furthermore, when Ford offered Deputy Director Dunham the opportunity to chair the Federal Power Commission, he accepted. Rockefeller had lost the means to control the council and so largely withdrew from it.

Rockefeller's involvement with the Domestic Council did not mark the end of his attempt to influence domestic policy programs. He believed that he could still direct those policies with the authority he derived from the vice-president's office. Rockefeller began by establishing a group to review the nation's social programs and by getting that group recognized by the Domestic Council; this latter action ensured the legitimacy of the review group as more than a Rockefeller operation. With this authorization, Rockefeller's group developed detailed proposals concerning economic growth, resource development, and human welfare and for improving the national infrastructure. These proposals, Rockefeller hoped, would become the basis for Ford's 1976 State of the Union message. A few months before that message, however, Ford announced a budget cut that would all but destroy any chance of the review group's proposals from being accepted. Daunted but not defeated, Rockefeller instructed the group to revise its proposals to meet the new budget limitations. The vice president then sent a memo to the president that outlined the group's revised recommendations. Sensing the futility of having his proposals accepted, Rockefeller officially withdrew from the Domestic Council in December 1975. Just as Rockefeller had guessed, less than one month later, Ford's State of the Union address contained not one of his recommendations.

Another controversial episode in Rockefeller's quest to direct domestic policy involved his proposal to create a federal energy development corporation to aid in making the nation energy independent. In early 1975, Ford warned the nation that it was too dependent on importing foreign oil to meet its rising energy demands. The process by which the nation could achieve energy independence intrigued Rockefeller, and he set his staff to the task of determining how that could be done. After months of investigation, Rockefeller presented to Ford his proposal for the creation of the Energy Resources Finances Corporation (ERFCO). According to the vice president, ERFCO would act as a federally sponsored corporation to stimulate the private sector to generate investment needed to help the administration achieve its goals regarding energy independence. Those goals included oil-imports reduction and energy-technology and resources development to make the United States a leading supplier of the world's energy needs. Opponents of Rockefeller and ERFCO informed the president that the corporation would not solve the energy problem and that its broad power would be disruptive to the investment community; their doubts caused Ford to hesitate in authorizing ERFCO but not to deny it outright. Thus, Rockefeller began to work with the Federal Energy Administration to revise ERFCO and to generate support for it on Capitol Hill.

In August 1975, Rockefeller submitted a revised proposal for ERFCO, now called the Energy Independence Authority (EIA), for a smaller version of the initial federally sponsored corporation. Ford accepted this proposal and publicly declared the EIA as the means to make the nation energy independent. To promote the EIA, Rockefeller became one of only three vice presidents to appear in the Senate to give congressional testimony in its behalf. However, his EIA would not be realized: just as the Democratic majority in Congress had stalled other of Ford's energy programs, the EIA suffered the same fate.

Another assignment Ford gave to Rockefeller late in 1974 concerned whether the White House needed to revive its science advisers' board and, if so, in what form. Rockefeller began by tapping his Commission on Critical Choices for Americans for the members of his advisory group. In February 1975, the vice president submitted to Ford recommendations that included the chief executive's need to have an independent source of scientific judgment available to him and the establishment by congressional action of an Office of Technology and Science (OTS). Ford supported the creation of an OTS but balked at the scale suggested by Rockefeller, for example, a support staff of seventeen professionals; Ford wanted five. After several discussions with his advisers, Ford submitted a proposal to Congress that was virtually identical to Rockefeller's: instead of seventeen professionals, Ford agreed to fifteen, and the name was changed to the Office of Science and Technology Policy (OSTP).

With the proposal moving through Congress, albeit slowly, Rockefeller next tackled the areas on which the OSTP would focus. Rockefeller recommended to Ford that he be allowed to bring together a contingent from the scientific community that would advise the OSTP on anticipated advances in technology and on technology policy and their affect on economic growth; Ford approved the recommendation. In early May 1976, Ford signed the National Science and Technology Policy, Organization, and Priorities Act into law, which created the OSTP within the executive office, establishing its director as a presidential adviser on matters of science and technology who also sat on the Domestic Council. Essentially, Rockefeller took an assignment that called only for recommendations regarding the reestablishment of the White House's science advisory unit and expanded that unit's scope and influence.

Rockefeller's dual positions as a White House staff assistant and as the vice president gave him the ability to push beyond the limits usually associated with each individual role. In the former position, he prepared and developed various proposals that were adopted as administration initiatives; with his latter position, he generated support for those initiatives in Congress and in the private sector. This benefit from the duality of roles also came with several costs. First, the number of assignments given to and personally undertaken by Rockefeller strained his ability to give adequate attention to any of them, and despite the vice president's ability to surround himself with the most capable people, he found himself extended as never before. Second, Rockefeller's domestic policy development and the zeal he showed in attempting to push past any opposition threatened senior White House staff so much that Rockefeller's ideas were resisted in varying degrees regardless of their merit. Third, Rockefeller's understanding with Ford that the president wanted an active vice president proved illusory. Rockefeller learned that Ford was unwilling to redefine the vice-presidential role in domestic policy development until Rockefeller threatened to withdraw from an active role on the Domestic Council.

What successes Rockefeller won during his twenty-five months as vice president came at perhaps the greatest cost. His constant clashes and frequent frustrations with key personnel in the Ford White House won him virtually no friends and no allies, so when the Ford camp looked to the 1976 election, it decided that the president would be better off without Rockefeller. Ford approached Rockefeller and explained that he was not asking Rockefeller to withdraw from the Republican ticket but that if he did some problems might be eliminated. On November 3, 1975, ever vigilant to do his duty for the nation, Rockefeller agreed. Despite his dismissal from the ticket, the vice president continued to do his job dutifully. When asked to nominate Senator Robert Dole for the vice presidency, Rockefeller complied and introduced Dole to New York State voters. But Rockefeller's acquiescence was short lived: at State University Rockefeller, being taunted by some students, responded by "giving them the finger"—a moment captured by a newspaper photographer that could have symbolized his long-suppressed frustration with his vice presidency.

Once again a private citizen in January 1977, Rockefeller withdrew from active involvement with politics and busied himself with various private enterprises over the next two years. He created The Nelson Rockefeller Collection, Inc., to market reproductions of his artwork, started a second company to publish books regarding his artwork, and remade his property at King Ranch in Texas into a jungle by stocking it with exotic African animals. Furthermore, Rockefeller assisted the soon-to-be deposed Shah of Iran in finding a home in the United States.

In his own mind, Rockefeller believed that he was a failure because he never reached his most-sought-after goal—the presidency—but his advocates as well as his critics would have to disagree. He almost single-handedly rehabilitated his family's reputation by promoting numerous philanthropic causes in the Rockefeller name, aided several chief executives in developing U.S. foreign and domestic agendas that still influence the country today, governed the most politically and socially complex state in the country and did so successfully, and left a legacy that few people could ever hope to repeat.

Nelson Rockefeller died of a heart attack on January 26, 1979, while in the much-publicized private company of a young female "research assistant."

REFERENCES

Stewart Alsop, *Nixon & Rockefeller: A Double Portrait* (Garden City, N.Y.: Doubleday & Company, Inc., 1960); Elizabeth A. Cobbs, *The Rich Neighbor Policy: Rockefeller and Kaiser in Brazil* (New Haven, Conn.: Yale University Press, 1992); Robert H. Connery and Gerald Benjamin, *Rockefeller of New York: Executive Power in the Statehouse* (Ithaca, N.Y.: Cornell University Press, 1979); Frank Gervasi, *The Real Rockefeller: The Story of the Rise, Decline and Resurgence of the Presidential Aspirations of Nelson Rockefeller* (New York: Atheneum, 1964); Michael Kramer and Sam Roberts, *"I Never Wanted To Be Vice-President of Anything!": An Investigative Biography of Nelson Rockefeller* (New York: Basic Books, Inc., 1976); Joseph E. Persico, *The Imperial Rockefeller: A Biography of Nelson A. Rockefeller* (New York: Simon and Schuster, 1982); Nelson A. Rockefeller, *The Future of Federalism* (Cambridge, Mass.: Harvard University Press, 1962); Nelson A. Rockefeller, *The Future of Freedom: Vice President Nelson A. Rockefeller Speaks out on Issues Confronting Americans in Bicentennial 1976* (Washington, D.C.: U.S. Government Printing Office, 1976); Nelson A. Rockefeller, "Overview," *Critical Choices for Americans: Reports on Energy, Food & Raw Materials—Vital Resources*, Volume 1 (Lexington, Ky.: D.C. Heath and Company, 1977); Nelson A. Rockefeller, *The Rockefeller Report on the Americas: The Unofficial Report of a United States Presidential Mission for the Western Hemisphere* (Chicago, Ill.: Quadrangle Books, 1969); Michael Turner, *The Vice President as Policy Maker: Rockefeller in the Ford White House* (Westport, Conn.: Greenwood Press, 1982); James E. Underwood and William J. Daniels, *Governor Rockefeller in New York: The Apex of Prag-*

matic Liberalism in the United States (Westport, Conn.: Greenwood Press, 1982).

LEROY G. DORSEY holds a Ph.D. from Indiana University and is an assistant professor of speech communication at Texas A&M University in College Station. His research has been published in the *Western Journal of Speech Communication*. Dr. Dorsey specializes in and teaches courses in presidential rhetoric, argumentation and debate, and American oratory.

WALTER F. MONDALE (b. 1928)

Vice President, 1977–1981

(President Jimmy Carter)

WALTER F. MONDALE
(Library of Congress)

By Frank Kessler

Those who study the institution of the vice presidency and its rising stature will no doubt point to Walter F. Mondale as a man who, more than any of his predecessors, remade the much-maligned graveyard of the executive branch into an office to be sought after. Unlike some of his predecessors in this one-time dead letter office, Mondale did not fit the stereotype of a ticket balancer. Perhaps his varied career in politics gave him the vision to see more in the office that has provided many a one-liner for starving stand-up comics. He decided to try to make something of a position that had been characterized as a "fifth wheel of the vehicle of government" and an afterthought of the Constitutional convention.

Mondale became a close, trusted adviser to President Jimmy Carter, and it is evident that Carter valued Mondale's intellect and breadth of experience with the Democratic Party constituent groups and Washington political scene. He knew his place in the administration and that was not merely cowering in the wings. Mondale saw himself as "in the loop" as he noted in a *National Journal* interview:

> I'm automatically included in things, invited to things. That was not the case in the beginning . . . but now we've got institutional experience. The next Vice President is going to say, "Well, I should be in the White House (too.)" I may have more influence now than I ever had in the Senate. I'm able to be heard on any matter I want to be heard on.

Mondale was able to make statements like this because of his lifelong ties with labor, minority groups, and traditional Democratic Party leaders. These ties offered potential reservoirs of support and savvy under the party umbrella for Jimmy Carter, whose limited experience as Georgia governor left him lacking the necessary network to govern effectively. During the campaign and throughout the four years of the Carter administration, Mondale served as a special liaison with unions and party honchos, especially in the urban Northeast where Carter's poll numbers were so deficient.

Given the disrepute surrounding the vice president's office, one might wonder why Mondale sought it. First of all, he had nothing to lose by running because he could return to his seat in the Senate, but, more than that, it fit his pursuit of politics as a career. In the forward to his book on the power of the presidency, *Accountability of Power* (1975), Mondale writes about the early Nixon years: "The sense of helpfulness and humanity that underlay the Great Society was already gone, having been destroyed by the [Vietnam] war." He also complained that this new attitude was due to "a new national strategy to create suspicion, division, and a sense of selfishness in the American people." This point speaks volumes on Mondale's acceptance of the positive role of government and led him to the view that public servants should aspire to bring out the noble in their constituents rather than pandering to their basest, most selfish instincts.

Mondale's family heritage and political lineage provide much of the explanation for his political career.

He was born in 1928 to Theodore Mondale, son of a Norwegian immigrant, and his second wife, Claribel. His father became a Lutheran minister but left the church because of its insistence on predestination and denial of free will and lack of social concern. The elder Mondale later joined the Methodists. Young Walter Frederick (known as Fritz) was raised with the Social Gospel at home and in church. The painful slow death from encephalitis of Reverend Mondale's first wife, Jessie, along with his inability to pay for care after going bankrupt in the Depression no doubt reinforced the message of social justice that he imparted to his family. Possibly because of his father's move from Lutheranism to Methodism and his older brother's decision to become a Unitarian minister, Mondale developed an openness to other religious views and traditions. As one of his biographers, Finlay Lewis, wrote: "While religion pervaded almost every aspect of family life, it was a happy and optimistic faith. . . ."

Mondale demonstrated leadership in high school and seems to have decided on a political career during those formative years. When the time came just after World War II for him to attend college, he chose Macalester College in St. Paul, Minnesota. The school, even though undergoing a change of direction from its Presbyterian roots, was still hardly a political hotbed. While Mondale was a freshman, though, he became involved with Students for Democratic Action (SDA), affiliated with the Americans for Democratic Action (ADA), and campaigned for the reelection of Minneapolis reform mayor Hubert H. Humphrey, a one-time Macalester professor whose enthusiasm, boundless energy, optimistic spirit, and deep compassion for the poor and minorities were most attractive to Fritz. Humphrey eventually became his mentor and provided an introduction for young Mondale to eventual Minnesota governor Orville Freeman, among other state party leaders, and national Democratic leaders whose company Humphrey frequented. Humphrey's election as mayor of Minneapolis in fact had been a testament to the success of his and the ADA's efforts to unite the old Farmer–Labor Party with its labor union ties to the state Democratic Party, a coalition that came to be known as the Democratic Farmer–Labor Party (DFL).

As one might expect from a person with career aspirations, Mondale was involved in political and international organizations and debate clubs at college. His years at Macalester were volatile ones for the Minnesota Democratic Party and college liberals in general because communist influences threatened the party, the campus ADA, and the Farmer-Labor coalition. Mondale was honing his world view in the fight against McCarthy-era paranoia about communism. Communism and activism against it divided liberals from the late 1940s forward.

While in college, at the age of twenty, Mondale offered his services to help manage what would be the successful Humphrey race for the U.S. Senate. The candidate's positions were a perfect fit for Mondale because both were New Dealers and both had a deep sense of commitment to ameliorating social injustice (no doubt deepened by Mondale's days working the farm harvest fields shoulder to shoulder with migrant workers). In addition, both felt at home with the major constituent interest groups of the party, especially labor, and both were committed to an active role for the federal government in dealing with social problems. He took on a Republican stronghold, organized it with no funds from the state organization, and helped ring up solid majorities for both Humphrey and President Truman there.

After Humphrey's election, Mondale dropped out of college (a sabbatical of sorts) to take a job in Washington, D.C., to help pay his mounting debts from attending Macalester, which was an expensive private school. He worked as secretary for the SDA but became disenchanted with its paucity of resources both in staff and finances. His biographers would note that this was a period of frustration and self-doubt for Mondale. A certain need to please his father seemed to pressure him toward success in politics; in addition, his small-town upbringing encouraged insecurities about the big city life that was required in national politics. All this led to self-doubt and personal reflection and compensation

via bouts of extraordinary and unremittingly hard work.

Within two years, Mondale returned from Washington, D.C., to finish college at the less-expensive University of Minnesota. There he became involved in trying to take the stodgy, more conservative state Democratic Party to the Left, where it could meet the more liberal Farmer–Labor party. He worked to recruit new young progressive candidates to run for office. In the process, he was building his contacts for a race of his own at some later date.

Upon completion of a political science degree from the university, Mondale considered his options and concluded that the armed services would provide the means for him to finish his education through the GI Bill. He enlisted in the army but proved too "radical" for some of his senior officers, and after being rejected for training in the Counter Intelligence Corps because of "loyalty" reasons, Mondale served his commitment uneventfully. On his discharge, he returned to attend the University of Minnesota law school before embarking on a legal career. To him, law was the perfect way to both make a living and permit him to dabble in politics. He commented once to a biographer that he felt that a person needed something other than politics to fall back on—if something offended one's conscience too deeply in politics, one could just walk away.

At his core, Mondale was a populist who distrusted people born into wealth and privilege. He viewed himself as the quintessential champion of the common man against the greed of corporate barons bent on profit regardless of the impact on the human condition. He was also raised in a state that valued a civil service of policy development and reform instead of the patronage systems commonly associated with party organizations in the majority of the states.

After graduation from law school, Mondale and his wife, Joan Adams, settled in Minneapolis. His first job was with a firm known for the political careers of its members. For the next few years, he spent his time helping others be elected. Then, in 1960, Mondale was appointed by Governor Orville Freeman, whose state campaign Mondale had managed, to fill out the unexpired term of the flamboyant Minnesota Attorney General Miles Lord, who had resigned.

Ever the party stalwart and unwilling to divide the Democratic Farmer-Labor Party, Mondale decided not to run in 1962 for the governorship against then Lieutenant Governor Karl Rolvaag, though others had urged him to do so after his impressive win in his race to retain the job of attorney general in 1960. Some would suggest this decision demonstrated that Mondale was unwilling to take a gamble, but he had given his word to support Rolvaag two years earlier and, he told others, he felt unprepared to make the leap to the governor's mansion.

As luck would have it, had he taken the governor's job, he might not have been called upon by Hubert Humphrey to mediate successfully a critical impasse that developed at the Atlantic City Democratic national convention in 1964. Mondale's skills as a conciliator were showcased as the party grappled with the mostly black Mississippi Freedom Democratic Party's challenge, which sought to have the freedom slate of delegates rather than the regular Democrats seated as the rightful convention delegates from the state.

Mondale's next step up the political ladder could be more accurately characterized as a prodigious leap. With the selection of Hubert Humphrey in 1964 to share the national ticket with Lyndon Johnson, Humphrey's U.S. Senate seat fell vacant. The line of suitors was long indeed and contained some state party heavyweights, including Governor Rolvaag himself; former governor and U.S. Secretary of Agriculture Orville Freeman; Walter Heller, John Kennedy's chair of the Council of Economic Advisers; Carl Rowan; and even Miles Lord, whom Mondale had replaced as Minnesota attorney general.

In a 1962 speech, Mondale had placed himself clearly on the liberal side of most public policy issues because he believed that the United States had enough determination to remove the remaining vestiges of poverty and racism in society by using current institutions. He put it this way: "We in America have now all the wealth, the sociological and political know-how to root out poverty and its causes." He viewed it to be primarily government's responsibility to see that every citizen had an equal chance to succeed. His liberal credo had a conservative side as well because he tended to view job training and education as possible solutions to the problems of race and poverty. With Humphrey's backing and Rolvaag's gratitude that Mondale had not challenged him for the governorship, Mondale garnered the coveted appointment as senator. Once again he was in the right place at the right time; still, he had put himself in the right place via loyalty and determination and successful efforts on other people's behalf.

The new young senator arrived in the nation's capital during one of the most intense periods in American history. Goldwater conservatives seemed to be in retreat, and the heady days of the Great Society saw the liberal Democrats living up to promises the party had made since 1948 in education, health care, and civil rights for black Americans.

Mondale, the Senate neophyte, quickly learned that the flowcharts of the legislative process and Senate rules were not as crucial as understanding the political culture of the place. He learned from his predecessor that having a hide like an armadillo was a definite political asset in the clubby atmosphere of the U.S. Senate. Because he had only two years left in Humphrey's term before he would have to stand for election in his own right, Mondale was forced to moderate his potential impact on the Senate. More than most of his colleagues who had six years to work with when they came in, Mondale had to pick his battles carefully, set his priorities, and calibrate his legislative votes with an eye toward the way they would sell back home. His biographers note that working in his Senate office in those days was akin to having Attila the Hun for a boss. In fairness to him, though, he pushed himself every bit as hard.

During his Senate years, Mondale tended to view Vietnam War as something that the president and the executive branch were more capable of dealing with than the Congress. Mondale believed that expert advisers to the president were honest and correct in their assessment of the winability of the conflict. His real areas of interest and expertise were more domestic than foreign. When the day for his reelection came, Mondale retained the loyalties of Minnesota's New Deal Democrats and won with almost 54 percent of the vote. He would later admit that he had not been as critical of the war as he should have been. With Humphrey in the vice presidency, Mondale evidently felt constrained from criticizing the administration on foreign policy, an area that had not been his own personal strong suit. Mondale would later concede that he had miscalculated on supporting the war and that it was the greatest mistake of his career.

On his return to Washington for a full Senate term of his own, Mondale was unwilling to back down from the Great Society and civil rights programs despite the fact that public opinion seemed to hold that too much effort and treasure was going into those areas and not enough into crime prevention and success in Vietnam. He pressed for a fair housing bill, education, job training programs, and housing supplements and rent subsidies. His position was the opposite of the views that Nixon would galvanize as those of the "silent majority" in 1968.

Other pro–civil-rights leaders feared white backlash from Mondale's proposed "open housing" initiatives. Still Mondale, instead of seeking compromise as one might have predicted from him, pressed forward on principle. The concern at that time centered around whether the old FDR coalition could be melded with the new antiwar types. The November elections could demonstrate whether the coalition, which had held sway since the 1930s, was so badly frayed that the very fabric of the party itself seemed to be beyond repair. The coalition of minorities, labor, and big city machines could still nominate candidates but could no longer automatically elect them. The movement of antiwar Democrats, with its outreach to youth, suburbanites, and the academic community, helped create the historic riot-tainted Chicago Democratic national convention that helped to seal Humphrey's fate despite the incredible comeback that Mondale as one of Humphrey's campaign managers had helped to engineer. In almost a prophetic comment about his own situation later, Mondale

tried to defend Humphrey from student hecklers by noting that no one is ever at his best in the vice presidency: "No man has ever done well there. You must judge Humphrey on his entire record, not just his years in the vice presidency." No doubt Humphrey's defeat chastened his protégé about the efficacy of governmental efforts when executive bureaucracies can lead the nation astray, as happened over Vietnam.

In the aftermath of Humphrey's defeat and his own return to the Senate, Mondale began to reexamine previous standard liberal solutions to social problems publicly, much in the way he had moved away from support for the Vietnam conflict. He felt the frustration of the United States being the richest nation on earth and yet having so many children in poverty. He lectured his fellow liberals, complaining that it was time for them to face the fact that their approaches had been too Washington centered, insensitive to public concern, overlooking of recipients' needs. His solution was to propose for the children of the poor alternative federally funded programs in the nutrition, health, and educational services. Nevertheless, as he traveled the nation giving speeches for House and Senate candidates in the off-year elections, Mondale intoned more traditional party mantras. In his partial term as senator, he focused most of his time on domestic concerns, and little of his energy was spent on foreign policy, with the exception of trade matters that affected the agricultural constituencies in his state. Within a year or so of the beginning of his second term and with his opposition to the Vietnam War becoming more recognized, he began to examine foreign policy, as several of his biographers assert, to position himself to run for president someday soon.

Any success in his aspirations to a chair in the Oval Office depended on his ability to mount a credible coalition behind him. Mondale was unprepared for the reality of the New Deal coalition's fragmentation. It was as if he expected the demographics of Minnesota's Democrats would be the same across the nation. As he traveled the nation in support of Democratic House candidates, he preached an orthodox New Deal gospel to a flock that had lost a number of its sheep. Some erstwhile middle-class Democrats made up what Nixon deftly categorized as the silent majority and began to do what Mondale had never imagined—join the party of the "rich and the powerful." As they departed their urban neighborhoods, fleeing taxes, political corruption, blight, and crime, they became the new Republicans of the inner suburbs. Issues like those and new ones like integration, busing, school choice, school prayer, and (after *Roe v. Wade*) abortion became the new hot-button issues. Southern Democrats and suburban Catholics were especially vulnerable to breaking away. Richard Nixon's call to the "forgotten American," with its emphasis on patriotism, law enforcement, and a call for a return to "traditional values" resonated well with many of the one-time Democrats. Unlike other senators, who such as Gary Hart of Colorado had incorporated these shifts into their campaign rhetoric, Mondale was a latecomer to this reality, though he had become increasingly skeptical whether the liberal creed would work in practice by the 1970s.

Earlier in his Senate career, Mondale had recognized a need to find a middle ground in policy areas while not abandoning his lifelong principles. He called for the creation, for example, of a Senate Select Committee on equal educational opportunity to see if the problems in education for minorities could be catalogued and thoroughly examined and if a middle ground between liberals and disenchanted conservative Democrats could be found. His move to the political center might well have been partly in response to the decision of Hubert Humphrey to do so to win Eugene McCarthy's old Senate seat in 1970 and his warnings to the DFL that such changes were necessary. This recognition that a more centrist message was more salable did not daunt Mondale's concern for poor children. His child-care initiatives had broad party support in 1971, but his $2 billion program for dealing with children whose parents had to work was stymied by Nixon's veto pen. Interestingly enough, the vote for override in the Senate was only seven votes short of the needed two-thirds. It did not do much for Mondale's attempt to be seen as more moderate to lead a coalition made up of labor, civil rights groups, the women's liberation forces, big city mayors, and advocates of zero population growth.

Unfortunately for his children's initiative, Mondale's own polls in his races for the Senate in 1972 were showing a white backlash, and as a result, his campaign for the Senate tried to downplay his past role in advancing liberal agendas. He kept his political distance as far as possible from his neighboring senator from South Dakota, George McGovern, whose capture of the Democratic Party nomination in 1972 left the party's national wing in a shambles. Mondale's campaign-manager experience left him with the discernment to realize that the coalition that McGovern cobbled together by ingenious crafting of the party rules could not get him into the White House.

As noted earlier, Mondale the principled champion of the people could also be Mondale the cautious, as the situation dictated. He was not eager to play the ant trying to move the rubber-tree plant; high hopes gave way to foundational pragmatism. One of his biographers, Steven Gillon, notes that on a number of occasions Mondale was known to say that he didn't like "to waste his time slaying windmills," a phrase he must not have cleared with his speechwriters. From this point on, he was not noted for tilting at dragons either. He seemed to sense intuitively that some melding of these new and the old traditional Democrats would be required for a successful pursuit of the Oval Office. For these reasons, he told McGovern that he would not want to be considered as vice-presidential candidate on the ticket. Why should he sacrifice a Senate seat so he could win in 1972 to rearrange deckchairs on the *Titanic*? He expected that other opportunities for national office would come along when he would not have to gamble to consider them. Of course, we know that his instincts were quite correct. Unfortunately for Mondale, his pragmatism made him the target of sarcasm, especially from the political Left. One DFL wag reportedly commented, when Mondale had an emergency appendectomy in 1974: "I hope the surgeon inserted some guts before sewing him up."

Mondale's success in getting early childhood education programs through the Senate made him the darling of national media and added him to the list of names put forward by the "great mentioners" in the national press corps who could anoint presidential candidates as possibles or curse them to political oblivion by merely providing no ink or airtime. Mondale's longtime Senate office chief of staff Dick Moe and compatriots Mike Berman and Jim Johnson were his political brain trust, drafting the plan for Mondale's self-positioning to be the Democratic nominee in 1976. Like a fair damsel holding suitors at arm's length, Mondale would tell the press he was thinking of running, he was 99 percent sure he would, that probably he would run but not give a definitive yes.

As Moe, Berman, Johnson, and the Mondale family prepared to clear the decks so they could give their undivided attention to the campaign, Mondale became increasingly unsure whether he had the desire, stamina, and masochism to make the race. Six months of cat and mouse with the press corps and giving speeches across the nation did not appreciably improve his standing in the Gallup and Harris polls in November. Reminiscent of his decision not to seek the governor's race earlier, Mondale seemed to be wimping out. Hindsight is always 20/20, but it would have been interesting to see if, after Ted Kennedy dropped out and Senator Henry "Scoop" Jackson and Governor George Wallace's support began to falter, Mondale could have knocked an unknown governor from Georgia named Jimmy Carter out of the race.

In a *Minnesota Tribune* interview, Mondale indicated that his heart was not in the effort. He explained his stunning decision not to run by saying:

> In order to be a serious presidential candidate, I was going to have to ask others to commit themselves—to pledge parts of their lives to the campaign. Being uncertain myself as to whether I really wanted to seek the office, I just didn't feel I could ask others to make the commitment. I did not have the overwhelming desire to be president which is essential for the kind of campaign that it required. I don't think anyone should be president who is not willing to go through fire.

In looking back on his decision, Mondale told a friend that it was the indignity of it all in campaigning that soured him on the process. Every place he went, he was someone new to the voters there. He was constantly having to sell himself. He was never the fascinating speaker that the age of instant communications required.

As the election of 1976 approached, Jimmy Carter surprised virtually everyone except himself as he represented the Democratic Party in the quadrennial contest with the Republicans for the Oval Office. Unlike his predecessors, he spent quite a bit of time thinking about who ought to be his vice president and who would bring the most to the ticket and the job itself. During a November 1991 meeting of the Miller Center for Public Policy's Commission on the Selection for Vice President, Center Director Kenneth Thompson recorded Carter's recollections on the matter. According to Thompson's synopsis, Carter first assessed the people running against him. As Georgia governor, he had the 1972 candidates down to the capital to visit with him. He had aspirations to run for president or vice president himself. It had been reported that Carter's close aide Hamilton Jordan and his friend Dr. Peter Bourne had approached the McGovern camp, offering the governor as a vice-presidential candidate.

In summer 1976, after the Carter nomination was all but assured and weeks before he won on the first ballot at the New York Democratic national convention, he began to talk to Jordan and old friends like Charles Kirbo about how to select a running mate. He reported fifteen years later to those gathered at the Miller Center Forum that he put together a list of thirty candidates in a leather-bound book, along with a list of names of his choices for high cabinet positions. He had Kirbo interview some of the vice-presidential possibilities and later winnowed the list down to ten or so. He invited Senators Jackson of Washington, Church of Idaho, Muskie of Maine, and Mondale and two others to visit with him at Plains.

Carter realized that he needed someone with major Washington experience, a quality clearly lacking in his personal entourage. He finally chose between Muskie and Mondale. To Carter, the issue beyond experience was compatibility or chemistry between him and his choice, rather than the standard philosophical or geographic balance factors commonly used by his predecessor candidates for president. Mondale had impressed him by doing his homework on the issues, and ultimately, the phone call and invitation to join the ticket went out to him. When Carter was asked about the vice presidency during the 1976 campaign, he expressed an unprecedented view of the vice president's role, evidently with a Mondale-type in mind. He indicated that he was:

> certainly determined to make the Vice Presidency a substantive position. . . . I hope to have the kind of Vice President, if I am elected, who would share with me all the purposes of the administration in an easy and unrestrained way. . . . I think the country loses when a competent Vice President is deprived of any opportunity to serve in a forceful way.

During the campaign, Mondale participated in a first: He and Republican counterpart Bob Dole traded jabs in the first televised vice-presidential debate, organized by the League of Women Voters. When the joust was finished, Dole had scored debating points, but Mondale had shown himself to be not only a worthy candidate for vice president, but also a person of intelligence and finesse capable of being president on his own should the worst occur.

Mondale served as an important bridge to the liberal constituencies among which he had labored for his entire political career. Those same labor, minority, and other activist liberal groups were concerned about Carter's lack of specificity on issues and tendency to sound like a Republican in Democrat's clothing, with his calls for budgetary austerity, cutting bureaucracy, and civic virtue. It was Mondale's ties to the groups that Carter had seemingly run against in primaries that helped the ticket get out the vote necessary to win

by one of the smallest margins in American history on election day. The big-city political organizations and labor unions delivered the needed turnout for the narrow victory. Mondale put on the final push in Illinois, New Jersey, Ohio, Pennsylvania, New York, and Wisconsin that combined to total 147 of the necessary 270 electoral votes to win. Pundits would note later that the Democrats in 1976 had resurrected the old New Deal coalition, with Carter bringing back the South and Mondale cementing the other traditional groups. By 1980, it would be clear that 1976 might have been an apparition of the ghost of victories past, but the body of the old coalition did not rise.

Given the rough road Mondale knew both Nelson Rockefeller and Hubert Humphrey had to travel as vice presidents and the psychological abuse to which they had been subjected by the presidents or their staff, he made sure that he and Carter were on the same wave length about the office very early in the game. In fact, Moe (in an interview on the Mondale staff as a part of the Carter Presidency Project oral histories, January 15 and 16, 1982 under auspices of the University of Virginia's Miller Center), reported that both Carter and Mondale felt that the vice presidency had been wasted in the past. They determined that if Mondale would be on the ticket, the two of them would talk over his role right after the election. Moe noted that Hamilton Jordan met with Moe and Mike Berman with the suggestion that the two staffs be fused. This experience of working together in the campaign would make the transition to governing in an integrated staffing mode much easier. Carter asked Mondale after the election to draft a memo of what he thought his role ought to be.

Mondale, after talking with Rockefeller and Humphrey and their staffs, concluded that it was a mistake for vice presidents to have institutional responsibilities because these impinged on other people's turf and created other problems. Also, responsibilities for specific programs and issues would keep the vice president from being useful as an adviser on more crucial issues. For Mondale's perception of the office to work, he told Carter he would need three things: unimpeded access to the president, access to all the information to which the president had access, and no make-work duties. In an interview after he had assumed the office, Mondale noted that "in the past Vice Presidents often took on minor functions in order to make it appear their role was significant, when if they were President they wouldn't touch them at all."

Few would argue that Mondale was anything but a respected adviser who had both the experience and stature to handle almost anything for the president. Both the vice president and his staffers were permitted to see virtually every paper that went through the Oval Office. He and his staff interacted regularly with the president, his staff, and key cabinet-level personnel. These interactions included a weekly lunch with the president; attending with the president weekly congressional leadership sessions; twice-weekly intelligence briefings with the White House chief of staff, the National Security assistant, and the CIA director; and participating in Friday foreign-policy breakfasts with Carter, National Security Assistant Brzezinski, Jordan, and the secretary of state (first Muskie, then Vance).

The integration of the two staffs was virtually unprecedented and permitted Mondale access to decision making even when he was not in the country. Carter had suggested that they share a common staff, but Mondale had sense enough to know he would want the independence of having his own people. At one point Carter had said publicly that he wanted Mondale to be his staff chief; as if to make the point that the staffs would be integrated, Mondale suggested and Carter agreed that Moe be both chief of staff to the vice president and senior adviser to the president. There was no precedent for such a move. Carter also told the White House staff: "If you get a request from Fritz, treat it as from me." On another occasion Carter, according to Moe, told the staff: "If I hear anybody critical of Fritz, you're out of here." Carter did not always follow Mondale's advice or that of the staff, but he always sought it out and listened.

It was Mondale who supervised a combined staff effort to set the early agenda of the incoming administration. The report suggested, on December 28, 1976, to the assembled cabinet-staff level personnel and the president fourteen key agenda points for the administration in the first hundred days, and it proposed the image the president would want to project. Carter acknowledged to the assembled administration personnel: "Fritz has done a good job." That good job would be rewarded with the ultimate indication of clout, an office in the West Wing near the Oval Office. Mondale was the first vice president to even have an office in the White House, a precedent that has been followed ever since.

Mondale is credited with being able to influence the president to select several key cabinet and major staff personnel including Health, Education, and Welfare Secretary Joseph Califano. Mondale also lobbied successfully to get people loyal to him in key administration positions: David Aaron, Mondale's chief foreign policy adviser in the Senate, became deputy national security adviser in the new administration. Close Mondale staffer Bert Camp became presidential deputy for domestic policy. So closely were the staffs intermingled that Hamilton Jordan, early in the administration, said: "I consider that I work for Mondale. He is my second boss, the way Carter is my first boss." Unlike his predecessors Humphrey and Rockefeller, Mondale was given no special project types of things to administer. Carter was especially concerned that Mondale be able to assume the presidency prepared in foreign affairs.

As vice president, Mondale took it upon himself to try to improve administration relations with the civil rights community, organized labor, and traditional liberal party leaders, whose support he would need to govern effectively. He encouraged Carter to accept a little pork barrel (eighteen water-control projects) to retain congressional support for his other initiatives. His recommendations and those of Domestic Policy Adviser Stu Eisenstadt convinced Carter to stand for affirmative action as a principle when confronted with the *Baake* case, which claimed reverse discrimination against white students seeking admission to medical school. Attorney General Griffin Bell had planned to argue the case entirely differently until the president intervened.

While Mondale had a good batting average early in the administration in being able to convince Carter to follow his suggestions, he was not an insider. The vice president found that, though he always had access, he was not assured that the president would either turn to him for advice or agree with his assessments of situations. Carter was more of an economic conservative than his more liberal vice president. Mondale fought for a higher minimum wage and lost; he advocated a $50 tax rebate and lost again to Carter's commitment to balance the budget before the end of the term; and he had no better luck advocating increased farm price supports.

During fall 1977, Carter commented on Mondale's role in the administration, saying: "Fritz doesn't waste his influence. He does excellent background study. And his staff is superb. He also uses my staff, some of whom are his former staff members, very effectively." Further, Carter noted, "And it's really kind of a rare thing for me not to go along with his position because Fritz tries to put himself in the role of a president and not just present a fairly radical argument one way or the other in an irresponsible way."

Unfortunately for Mondale's traditional liberal views on the economy and public policy, continuing inflation encouraged Carter to follow his more conservative instincts and constrict the growth of new programs. Moe would later comment that he "spent a lot of time trying to keep domestic initiatives adequately funded and to prevent the marginal cuts that would do nothing for the economy but would create a firestorm of resentment and opposition."

The Carter regulars from Georgia and his media guru, Gerald Rafshoon, all urged belt tightening. Rafshoon once commented: "We were giving them ninety percent of their agenda and all they talked about was the ten percent they were not getting." Cutting back on spending and slowing the economy presented the danger of some unintended consequences such as unemployment. The Carter austerity package without massive cuts in defense opened the door for a Ted Kennedy challenge at the 1980 convention. Mondale's political instincts had proven correct. Once again, he found himself placed in the me-

diator's role that had characterized his career going back to college days. His liberal colleagues in the Senate, representing interest groups from the left of the party spectrum, were expecting that Mondale would successfully do their bidding when pressure for cuts came; instead they concluded that he caved in to pressure to please the president.

Liberals were also frustrated with Carter foreign policy in the Middle East because it tilted too much toward solutions that addressed Arab concerns without sufficiently bringing U.S. Jewish leaders into policy formulation. Language in a joint U.S.-Soviet declaration on solutions in the Middle East called for efforts to "ensure the legitimate rights of the Palestinian people." The language was highly incendiary to the U.S. Jewish community, which had tended to vote strongly Democratic in key electoral college states. Mondale was expected to put out the fire without being able to change the policy.

Mondale also expressed serious misgivings about the president's request that all staff and cabinet people tender their resignations in late July to prepare for a second-half of the term review. Even though the vice president thought the firings were a bad idea and expressed that to key presidential staffers, he was unable to halt the process and was out of town on a vice-presidential road show when the ax fell on so many "non-loyal" appointees. Unfortunately for Mondale, as the president and his staff became more knowledgeable about Washington, they felt the need to bypass the very constituencies Mondale was supposed to be a bridge to for the administration. Though he had advanced the role of the vice presidency far beyond anything his predecessors had been able to do, he realized, as he told a *National Journal* interviewer: "Jimmy Carter is the President; I know that." Though Mondale was required to pick up the campaigning slack left by Carter's decision not to campaign while Americans were being held hostage in Iran, it would not be his last presidential campaign.

From his selection to be Carter's running mate, Mondale wrote a new chapter in the history of the vice presidency. Carter's selection process, his suggestion that he felt that the office had been wasted, the merger of campaign staff, and the close ties between presidential and vice-presidential staff after the inauguration represented a new direction for the number-two office. In addition, Mondale's ability to write his own job description, see everything the president saw, have an office in the West Wing, and avoid make-work commission roles positioned the vice president to be an adviser to the president instead of a "Secretary of Catchall Affairs," as Nixon had characterized his duties in the Eisenhower years. Mondale would advise subsequent vice presidents how to get the most out of the office and in enhancing the role of the office to better serve the person who selected him as running mate. Mondale's proximity to power illustrates an important point about power and influence: Just being there doesn't always mean you will have influence.

Even as the campaign of 1980 was winding down, Mondale seemed to be looking ahead in a speech at the Woodrow Wilson Center at Princeton. In speaking to true-believing liberals, Mondale with sobering candor said, "Progressives need to adjust the liberal values of social justice and compassion to a new age of limited resources."

After the dust settled from the drubbing that Carter and Mondale took at the hands of Reagan and Bush, one might have expected Mondale's comment that he needed time to study and rethink the party message instead of making a bid for the Senate, as Hubert Humphrey had done. In fact, his attendance at numerous issue seminars across the country and trips overseas lent credence to his comments. At the same time, though, he was considering a run for the presidency in his own right. He made sure that he had representatives on the Democratic Party commission that wrote the party rules on convention delegation selection and seating criteria, and he reinvigorated his contacts with the old party constituencies. Though he tried to project the image of a new progressive, he was still perceived in poll after poll as being an old-line liberal Democrat. It was that perception that encouraged Senator Gary Hart of Colorado to toss his hat into the ring and give Mondale the fight of his life in the party primaries.

Mondale's campaign seemed to be an uphill climb. His choice of Geraldine Ferraro as his running mate was indeed precedent shattering. Though he criticized PACs and their influence, he was embarrassed to have to respond to press and Hart complaints that Mondale had, in fact, created several PACs to funnel money into the campaign. Hart embarrassed him across the nation with the taunt: "Give the money back, Walter." Both Jimmy Carter and Ronald Reagan had won on their first general election by projecting the "outsider" image. Obviously Mondale, with all his Senate experience, was destined to be seen as just another tainted insider. He did not help his new-Democrat image when he announced in his convention acceptance speech: "If you elect me, I'll raise your taxes; so will Mr. Reagan; he won't tell you, I just did."

Some would attribute his eventual loss in 1984 to his positions on issues, while others saw Reagan as an incumbent president whose messages resonated well with larger segments of the increasingly conservative national constituency. As Mondale and his campaign staff realized, if the Democrats were to reclaim the White House in 1984, they would have to bring the middle class voters into the coalition of labor, citizen lobby groups, feminists, civil rights supporters, and old traditional urban Democrat machines. That promised to be no easy proposition. Some would fault Mondale's campaign style as the root of his problems: His message was not focused enough to some; he never learned how to use the media the way Reagan had, others would complain. His strength was within the traditional Democratic coalition put together around FDR, but that strength proved also to be a weakness because it labeled him as a traditional liberal at a time when a conservative middle class was turning elections.

Mondale's loss in 1984 then, in the main, was more due to an inability to articulate a new message for the Democratic Party, which had worn out its welcome to many of its past constituents who left the city ethnic neighborhoods for the suburbs. Six months after his defeat, he held a press conference in St. Paul to indicate that he did not intend to run for another term in the Senate. He withdrew from elective and appointed public life, but President Bill Clinton plucked him from the private sector in 1992 to serve as U.S. ambassador to Japan.

While it could be argued that his race for president will ensure his place in the history books, Mondale deserves recognition for the way his incumbency affected the ability of the vice presidents of the United States to advise the president and prepare the junior partner of the presidential ticket should the unthinkable happen. History may also record him, as well, as the last of a New Deal breed capable of getting the Democratic nomination for president. His message of compassion and civil rights in an age of middle-class consumerism and personal self-fulfillment became the ultimate hard sell.

REFERENCES

Steve M. Gillon, *The Democrats' Dilemma: Walter F. Mondale and the Liberal Legacy* (New York: Columbia University Press, 1992); Finley Lewis, *Mondale: Portrait of An American Politician* (New York: Harper and Row, 1980); Kenneth Thompson, ed., *The Selection of Vice Presidents* (Charlottesville, Va.: Commission to Study Vice Presidential Selection, The Miller Center, University of Virginia, 1990–92); Interview with Richard Moe (including Michael Berman), Miller Center Interviews, Carter Presidency Project, v. XII, January 15–16, 1982, Jimmy Carter Library, Atlanta, Georgia. The author wishes to thank both the Miller Center at the University of Virginia and its director Kenneth Thompson and Martin J. Elzy, assistant director of the Jimmy Carter Library, for their help in making the oral history interviews available.

FRANK KESSLER is a political scientist with a Ph.D. from the University of Notre Dame. He has been recipient of NEH and NSF research grants, is author of *Dilemmas of Presidential Leadership: Of Caretakers and Kings* (Prentice Hall, 1983), and has been on the National Steering Committee of the Presidency Research Group and Board of Editors for *Presidential Studies Quarterly*. He teaches political science at Missouri Western College in St. Joseph, Missouri.

GEORGE HERBERT WALKER BUSH (b. 1924)

Vice President, 1981–1989

(President Ronald Reagan)

GEORGE H.W. BUSH
(Courtesy of Bush Presidential Materials Project)

By L. Edward Purcell

After George Bush returned to his Detroit hotel room on the evening of August 16, 1980, and changed into casual clothes, he settled in to wait for delegates to the Republican Party convention, to which he had just delivered a speech, to nominate Ronald Reagan as the party's candidate and for Reagan to then name Gerald Ford as his running mate. Before that could happen, however, the Secret Service phoned to say several agents had taken over a room two floors below in Bush's hotel. Bush understood

what the call meant: he was likely to become vice president of the United States.

For Bush, the vice presidency was the penultimate stop on his way to the White House. It would fill out a sterling résumé that had only two more slots left open at the top, and it would position Bush to run for the White House. As he wrote: "everybody belittles the office of the Vice President, not many people turn it down."

Born in Milton, Massachusetts, in June 1924, Bush was the second son of a wealthy New

385

England family. His father, Prescott Bush, was a tall, handsome, well-to-do member of the northeastern social and economic elite, a gifted amateur golfer and singer and eventually a U.S. Senator from Connecticut (the family moved to Greenwich not long after George's birth). The elder Bush worked in his father-in-law's investment banking firm of Brown Brothers, Harriman. Bush's mother, Dorothy Walker, was less public than her husband but just as much a part of the genteel establishment. The family summered at Kennebunkport, Maine, where George's namesake grandfather owned the beachfront "Walker's Point," and where George acquired his love of boating, fishing, swimming, and tennis.

Bush was precocious and began his education at Greenwich Country Day School a year earlier than the norm. At age twelve, he was sent to Phillips Academy at Andover, Massachusetts, where by all accounts he developed into an extremely likeable young man, gifted in athletics and more than respectable in the classroom. His graduation from Andover was delayed by a serious illness, but during his senior year he was class president, captain of the baseball team, a member of the soccer and basketball varsity squads, and editor of the school newspaper.

Although he was speaking of a slightly later period of Bush's life, Rhode Island Senator John F. Chafee once described George as

> . . . one of those fellows who was sort of a golden boy: Everything he did he did well. . . . My first impression was that he was—and I don't mean this in a derogatory way—in the inner set, the movers and shakers, the establishment.

Bush finished prep school six months after the Japanese bombed Pearl Harbor, and against the wishes of his parents and the advice of his mentors, he spurned college and enlisted in the Navy, applying immediately for a commission and aviator's training. The Navy waived its usual requirement that demanded two years of college from pilots and allowed Bush to become—at eighteen years of age—the country's youngest flight trainee. Within a year, Bush earned his wings as a torpedo bomber pilot and headed toward the war in the Pacific.

He was assigned to a squadron aboard the carrier *San Jacinto* (known to its crew as the "San Jack"), flying a three-man TBM torpedo bomber. In June 1944, during an attack on Japanese bases on the Mariana Islands, Bush and his crew were forced to take off from the deck of their carrier into heavy fire. They were hit and the aircraft went down, but all survived the ditching and were rescued. In September, they were not so lucky. Bush and his crew were flying a combat mission against a Japanese radio station on the island of Chichi Jima (part of the same group as Iwo Jima) when the plane took a severe antiaircraft hit during a strafing run. After completing his attack, Bush turned his crippled plane toward the open sea. As the aircraft went down, Bush and his crew bailed out. The two crewmen were never seen again. Bush escaped alive but discovered that his life raft was slowly drifting toward the Japanese base and certain capture, perhaps death. Rather miraculously, the American submarine USS *Finback* appeared from the depths and rescued the downed pilot. After a month aboard the sub, Bush was put ashore at Pearl Harbor and, after a brief return to the *San Jacinto*, he was shipped home to the United States. For his heroism, he received the Distinguished Flying Cross. Bush was thus one of the five twentieth-century American presidents who were combat veterans when they became commander in chief.

Shortly after arriving home, Bush married Barbara Pierce, the daughter of a New York publisher. He had met her before the war when she was a student at Ashley Hall girls' school, and she dropped out of Vassar to marry Bush. The newlyweds moved to Norfolk, Virginia, where Bush was assigned as a flight instructor until the war's end. Eventually, the union produced four sons and two daughters, one of whom died tragically from childhood leukemia.

After his discharge from the Navy in 1945, Bush returned to Connecticut and enrolled at Yale, his father's alma mater. He was one of the thousands of veterans who descended on American campuses in the years immediately after the war. Many of whom, like Bush, were married and mature and eager to pick up lives interrupted by duty during the conflict.

Bush was again in a hurry, and he was admitted to an accelerated degree program at Yale. Despite the pressures of extra courses and the distractions of marriage and a family (his eldest son, who in 1994 was elected governor of Texas, was born in 1947), Bush managed to participate in extracurricular life at the Ivy-League school. He was captain of the excellent school baseball team, playing in the finals of the national collegiate world series twice, and he played varsity soccer. He also was a member of a social fraternity and elected to Yale's famed secret society, the Skull and Bones. He graduated as a Phi Beta Kappa economics major in the spring of 1948.

At this stage, Bush took a surprising decision about a career. With his many family connections in the eastern business world, he could have chosen among many gilt-edged job offers. Instead, he arranged for an entry-level position with a Texas oil company and moved his fledgling family to Odessa, in the heart of the oil patch, a major disjuncture from his previous country-club life in Connecticut. The Bushes at first lived modestly in a shotgun-style house while George learned the oil business from the ground up. After a short tour as a salesman in California, Bush settled in Midland, Texas. In 1951, he and a friend, John Overbey, formed an oil development company with financial backing from George's uncle. Two years later, the duo merged their interests with the Liedtke brothers, William and Hugh, to form Zapata Petroleum.

Bush was a hard-working businessman in an industry having one of its periodic boom spells, and the company prospered. In 1959, Bush's interest in offshore drilling rigs prompted him to move to Houston and become head of a split-off business, Zapata Offshore, which rented equipment to producers. The new firm was a profitable enterprise that eventually employed more than 200 workers.

The success of his oil-rig business coincided with Bush's growing interest in politics. As a Republican in heavily Democratic Texas, Bush was not well placed for a quick rise, and he at first devoted himself to hard work at the grass-roots level. Most of his interests revolved around the Harris County Republican Party (which encompassed conservative districts in Houston), and he was selected as county chairman in 1963. The following year, Bush decided to try for elective office and mounted a campaign for the U.S. Senate. He won the GOP primary, but when pitted against popular Democrat Ralph Yarborough, Bush was no match, despite heavyweight campaign help from Senator Barry Goldwater and Vice President Richard Nixon.

Realizing the futility of running statewide in Texas as a Republican, Bush refocused his ambitions and in 1966 entered the race for the newly reapportioned seat in the U.S. House of Representatives from the prosperous Seventh District of Houston. At the same time, Bush decided to get out of the oil business, and he sold his interest in Zapata Offshore for around $1.1 million—a modest fortune by Texas standards but nonetheless a tribute to his business energy and acumen. Henceforth, Bush would devote himself to politics and officeholding as he began to build a spectacular record of public service. The first step was taking the House seat by winning more than 57 percent of the district's vote.

When he moved his family to Washington, D.C., early in 1967, Bush began a twenty-five year period of nearly uninterrupted officeholding. Except for a few years in the late 1970s, his next quarter-century revolved around national government and politics. The Bush ties to Texas were strong, but because the family moved so frequently, the most stable residence was probably the compound at Kennebunkport, Maine, where the Bushes vacationed often during the years of public life. (Eventually the Bushes were able to buy Walker's Point from George's family and take over the main house.)

During Bush's first term in the House, he was favored by the party leadership and got a superior appointment for a freshman representative to the House Ways and Means Committee. He was a strong supporter of American participation in the war in Vietnam, and although he voted for the Fair Housing Act in 1968, he was no more than lukewarm in supporting other causes backed by black Americans.

In all of this, as well as the rest of his political career, Bush confirmed his own nature and reflected what would become his public image: he was a good party man of deep loyalty. He could count on moving to the top through good connections and he could handle any job assigned to him, but he was unmotivated by any deep conviction or fire in the belly.

Bush won a second House term in 1968, and emboldened by the national Nixon–Agnew Republican victory—he had been briefly considered as Nixon's running mate before the election—he decided to once again try for the Texas Senate seat held by Ralph Yarborough. Bush's conclusion that Yarborough was vulnerable proved correct when the latter was beaten in the Democratic primary by Lloyd Bentsen. The contest between Bentsen and Bush proved a lively affair, with President Nixon throwing all his support behind the congressman from Houston. Nixon also privately promised Bush an appointment to a high post if he lost. In the end, Bentsen won the Senate seat by nearly six percentage points, a result attributed to Bush's failure to attract even token support among black Texas voters.

True to his word, President Nixon rewarded Bush by appointing him to the post of U.S. ambassador to the United Nations. Bush enjoyed his duties in New York but discovered that he was being used by the administration—headed on foreign policy matters by Secretary of State Henry Kissinger—as a diplomatic decoy. Bush vigorously pursued the longtime American policy of defending Taiwan as the official representative of China to the UN, while behind the scenes, Kissinger and Nixon prepared to recognize the mainland Communist Chinese, which they eventually did, leading to the expulsion of Taiwan from the world body.

Despite the seeming embarrassment of his term at the UN, Bush was still in political favor, and in 1972, Nixon appointed him to head the GOP as chairman of the Republican National Committee. The most important event during Bush's watch as head of the party was the infamous break-in at the Watergate by operatives of Nixon's reelection committee. Bush was not involved, but he was placed in the uncomfortable position of having to defend Nixon throughout the subsequent investigation and scandal. Bush's loyalty was tested, but he remained steadfastly a supporter of the president to the bitter end, crisscrossing the country to make speech after speech in defense of Nixon. Not until the day before Nixon's resignation did Bush formally withdraw his support and acknowledge the president's guilt.

When Gerald Ford became president on Nixon's departure, Bush hoped to be named vice president. With Nelson Rockefeller's selection instead, Bush was placated by the offer of his choice of ambassadorships to either Great Britain or France—the two posts generally considered to be the plums of the foreign service. Instead of accepting either, Bush surprised Ford and asked to be named to the relatively less important post of head of the U.S. mission to Communist China. He and Barbara moved to Beijing in 1974, and although they were tireless travelers and consumers of tourist culture, George himself had little to do. Kissinger handled almost all important communications with the Chinese government and usually consulted Bush only as an afterthought.

In December 1975, Bush was offered an escape to a job with real responsibility when Ford asked him to take over as head of the besieged Central Intelligence Agency. The CIA had come under heavy attack for lying to Congress and for concealing bungled attempts to assassinate several world leaders, including Fidel Castro. Bush had few if any qualifications for the job except for his well-known charm, loyalty, and capacity for hard work. After he became director in January 1976, however, Bush was successful in improving agency operations and did a good deal to improve internal morale and to resuscitate the CIA's reputation, especially on Capitol Hill. With Jimmy Carter's election victory in November, however, Bush's days at the CIA were numbered. When the Democrats swept into office, he was replaced and moved back to Houston, out of a government job for the first time in a decade.

Bush joined the executive committee of Houston's First International Bank and gained several lucrative seats on corporate boards, but his main occupation from 1977 to 1979 was campaigning on behalf of Republican candidates and laying plans for his own political future. Bush's goal, of course, was the White House.

In May 1979, he announced his intention to run for the G.O.P. presidential nomination in 1980. Although he was well known nationally in some party circles from his days as Republican Party chairman, Bush's name was not much of a public commodity. He had held only one elective office—his seat in the U.S. House—and despite his tours in diplomatic posts and at the CIA, the general population knew very little about him. Even in his home territory, he was something of a cipher. His introduction to a 1978 Dallas Republican Men's Club luncheon meeting as a "prospective Republican nominee for president" was met with disbelieving silence.

Nonetheless, Bush mounted a spirited campaign for the nomination. He assembled a group of consultants and a staff and set up a campaign headquarters in Alexandria, Virginia, just across the Potomac from Washington, D.C. His chief advisers were his old friends James A. Baker III, a former undersecretary of commerce under Gerald Ford, and Robert Mosbacher. Bush also used the family compound at Kennebunkport as a meeting center to plan strategy.

The Republican front-runner for the nomination was former movie star and California governor, Ronald Reagan. Behind Reagan came a cluster of hopefuls including Bush, Robert Dole, John Connally, Howard Baker, Phil Crane, and John Anderson, but none of them had the public recognition or momentum of Reagan. Bush's main task was to separate himself from the pack and become Reagan's chief competitor. He took a step toward this by coming in first in a Maine straw poll of Republicans (Reagan was not on the ballot), but the high point of Bush's campaign for the nomination came in late January 1980 when he actually beat out Reagan and the others in the Iowa party caucuses. He basked in the fame of his Iowa "victory," appearing on the cover of *Newsweek*, but a strong showing by Reagan in the New Hampshire primary all but finished the campaign. By May, even though Bush had won primaries in Massachusetts, Connecticut, Pennsylvania, and Michigan, it was clear that Reagan, with a thirty-point lead in the polls, would be the choice of the party, and the best Bush could hope for was to get the call as vice president.

Bush went to the Republican convention in Detroit prepared to accept the vice presidency, but as he later commented, he "knew you don't campaign for the vice presidency, because it's a calling. And the caller is whoever happens to be the presidential nominee." Reagan's first choice for his vice president was former president Gerald Ford, whom Reagan's pollsters told him would be the strongest addition to the GOP ticket. Plans to nominate Ford were well advanced when Ford shot himself in the foot during a TV interview with Walter Cronkite. Ford outlined his idea of what in his mind was to be nearly a copresidency, with Reagan handling domestic matters and Ford in charge of foreign affairs. The Reagan camp was outraged and turned immediately to Bush, despite lingering resentment of some of Bush's anti-Reagan primary campaign tactics (especially a crack Bush made about Reagan's "voo-doo economics").

When the call from Reagan finally came to his hotel room that night in Detroit, George Bush was happy to accept the second spot on the ticket. He did not know Reagan well personally—historically, few vice presidents seem to have had much acquaintance with their running mates—but Bush believed they were close enough in political philosophy to make the combination work. "The bottom line," he wrote, "both politically and economically, was that Reagan and I agreed that solving the country's economic problems would require not only tax cuts but massive cuts in government spending, along with a wholesale reduction in federal red tape and overregulation."

The election itself was not much of a contest. Jimmy Carter appeared to a majority of American voters to have lost his grasp on government and policy, and the Reagan-Bush ticket swept into office with a plurality of almost 9.5 million popular votes and a margin of 489 to 49 in the electoral college. In January, Bush moved back to Washington, D.C., and into the vice presidential residence on the grounds of the Naval Observatory, although his vice-presidential schedule allowed for frequent visits to Kennebunkport.

Bush's two terms as vice president saw him take on the sort of tasks that have come to characterize the office in the late twentieth century: heading task forces to cut government paperwork and to combat drugs and attending state funerals around the globe (he once quipped "You die; I fly"), but his tenure was also marked by very dramatic episodes.

During his first year in office, Bush was circumspect and intentionally low key. He knew that several of the president's longtime California supporters mistrusted him and that the ultraconservatives in the party thought him unsound even though he consistently refused to take a stand or comment on ideology. He quietly set out to establish a personal relationship with Reagan in the hope that it would solidify his political position. As Bush later commented that " . . . even when Presidents and Vice Presidents see eye to eye on the issues, their long-term political relationship can only be as strong as their personal relationships." The tactic worked, and within a few weeks Reagan had warmed to Bush. The two shared a private lunch weekly, where the president relaxed, talked about issues, and auditioned new jokes. As have other recent vice presidents, Bush had an office in the West Wing of the White House and had access to all documents and classified communications of the president, allowing him to maintain a high state of preparedness to step forward if need be.

The need arrived suddenly on March 3, 1981, when Reagan, White House press secretary Jim Brady, a Secret Service agent, and a policeman were shot down on the street outside the Capital Hilton by a would-be assassin. Reagan was seriously wounded and rushed to George Washington Hospital with a bullet lodged in his chest. Brady had taken an even more grievous wound to the head and barely survived.

At the time of the attack, George Bush was in Fort Worth, Texas, dedicating a historic site. He was airborne in Air Force Two when a rather cryptic message came through the communications net from Secretary of State Alexander Haig that the president had been shot. A certain amount of chaos reigned at the White House in the hours immediately after the attack on Reagan—Haig made an unfortunate appearance before the press, for example, in which he claimed to be in charge, an assertion that displayed an incredible ignorance of the constitutional line of succession—and not much clear information made its way from Washington to Bush's plane. Most of what he learned about the situation came from commercial television broadcasts monitored on Air Force Two on a tiny black-and-white set.

When the plane landed at Andrews Air Force Base, south of Washington, Bush was pressured to take a Marine helicopter directly to the White House in order to avoid the delay of rush-hour traffic, but he firmly declined and insisted on being flown to the Naval Observatory and then traveling by limousine. For Bush this was an important symbolic action. He wanted to be certain that Americans and foreign friends and foes knew that the government in Washington would continue to function in steady hands, but he wanted to avoid all appearance of impudence or impropriety. He told his advisers: " . . . only the president lands on the South Lawn."

At 7:00 P.M., Bush called a meeting of the cabinet and then spoke to a press conference where he reassured the nation and the world that the United States government was still functioning.

As his friendly biographer Fitzhugh Green has noted, Bush showed a nice touch in his willingness to assume authority as needed, without giving an unseemly appearance of a thirst for power. On the other hand, some former Reagan aides have criticized Bush for being too passive during his term as vice president. The truth is that Bush was very cautious in almost every situation to avoid an aggressive or self-seeking stance, but he was more than willing to speak out or take on responsibility if asked, and President Reagan came to rely on him in important situations. When Secretary of State Haig and National Security Adviser Richard Allen got into an exceedingly acrimonious power fight, for example, Reagan resolved the problem by appointing Bush as head of the White House crisis management team, which gave the vice president a limited but crucial position of power within the administration.

Bush was always very clear about his understanding of the vice president's role. He was firm in stating his view that a vice president must be circumspect at all times, and intense loyalty is the highest of vice-presidential virtues. In his autobiography, Bush listed his five rules of the vice presidency:

1. There is only *one* president.
2. No political opportunism.
3. No news leaks.
4. All interviews must be on the record.
5. The vice president owes the president his best judgment.

In the 1984 election, the Reagan-Bush team ran against former Vice President Walter Mondale and his running mate, Geraldine Ferraro. The result was a monumental landslide for the incumbent Republican team. The weather in Washington turned nasty for the Reagan-Bush second inauguration and the ceremony was moved inside to the Capitol Rotunda, but otherwise the slide into a second term was almost uneventful.

By mid-1985, however, events again turned dramatic. During a routine physical, doctors discovered that Reagan had suspicious-looking polyps attached to his intestines. A biopsy showed the growths to be cancerous, and the president was scheduled for surgery. The question then arose whether to evoke the provisions of the Twentieth Amendment to the Constitution, which called for the president to turn over powers temporarily to the vice president in case of physical incapacity. Reagan would be under anesthetic for the surgery and for a while, at least, unable to function. Reagan's advisers decided to hedge the situation slightly, and at 11:30 A.M. on July 13, Reagan signed a letter (just before going under anesthetic) temporarily transferring the power of the presidency to Bush. When the president regained consciousness six hours later, he signed a second letter to reclaim his office. Although the episode may have been little more than a footnote to history, it demonstrated a vastly different ap-

proach to the question of a president's fitness for office than had been the case many times before, most notably the two-and-a-half years of Woodrow Wilson's complete debility.

Perhaps the only controversial aspect of Bush's vice presidency revolved around what came to be known as the Iran-Contra Affair. Members of the Reagan team, notably Marine Colonel Oliver North, put into play a scheme to sell missiles to Iran and send the proceeds to finance right-wing guerrillas in Nicaragua, who were trying to overthrow the elected government of the left-wing Sandinistas. When the illegal maneuvers became a public scandal and led to congressional hearings and criminal convictions, some Democrats and members of the news media wanted to explore Bush's knowledge of the affair and possible involvement. He had been, after all, head of the CIA and of task forces dealing with terrorism and drugs and therefore might be expected to have had a hand in the administration's clandestine activities. Although his role has never been explained to his critics' complete satisfaction, Bush denied involvement in the Iran-Contra exchange, although he did admit to learning of North's activities. Subsequent official inquiries little focused on Bush.

As the end of Reagan's second term approached, Bush stepped forward and claimed the GOP nomination for president, despite a challenge from Robert Dole, who shook Bush with an early victory in the Iowa caucuses. The Democrats nominated Massachusetts Governor Michael Dukakis, who chose Bush's old Texas political nemesis Lloyd Bentsen as his vice-presidential running mate. Coming out of the Democratic convention in late July, the Democratic candidates had a seventeen-point lead in the polls.

Bush selected Dan Quayle, a relatively obscure senator from Indiana, to fill out the Republican ticket and set forth on a masterfully crafted campaign to defeat the Democrats. By focusing on what his pollsters and strategists said were Dukakis's perceived weaknesses, especially a supposed softness on crime, and emphasizing brisk, positive media sound bites, Bush closed the gap. He was especially effective in calling attention to "a kinder, gentler America," and telling Americans to "Read my lips. No new taxes." When combined with a brutal attack on Dukakis's record on crime—most famously involving an ad about furloughed black Massachusetts rapist and killer Willie Horton—the positive strategy worked. Bush and Quayle won the election by claiming nearly 54 percent of the popular vote and taking forty of the fifty states. Bush thus became the first sitting vice president to be elected directly to the presidency since Martin Van Buren took over from Andy Jackson in 1836.

Bush's term as president proved to be eventful, to say the least. Within the first year, Communist control of Eastern Europe collapsed with shocking suddenness. The Berlin Wall came down, Communist regimes fell everywhere, and the Russian empire itself disintegrated. Bush's administration managed to negotiate this new situation and reached arms-reduction agreements that heralded the end of the Cold War, a situation that would have seemed unthinkable only a few years earlier.

Bush also led the nation into a full-scale war—the first since Vietnam—after the army of Iraqi dictator Saddam Hussein invaded Kuwait in 1990 and threatened Saudi Arabia. With the West's oil supplies on the line, Bush skillfully built a United Nations coalition, including several Mideastern Arab nations, that demanded Hussein's withdrawal. In early 1991, the coalition, comprised mostly of American forces, carried out a massive air war followed by a devastating ground attack that crushed the Iraqi army in Kuwait, although the coalition stopped short of occupying Baghdad and ousting Hussein. Bush's popularity soared as he justly claimed credit for what most Americans saw as a chest-puffing victory that laid to rest the ghostly legacy of failure in Vietnam.

It was somewhat shocking, therefore, that by 1992 Bush's standing with the voters had been pummeled and that the relatively obscure Democratic governor of Arkansas, Bill Clinton, was able to chase Bush out of office after only one term.

The cause was almost certainly a sharp downturn in the economy and Bush's need to renege on his loud campaign promise not to raise taxes. Even though the economy was well along toward recovery, Bush ran a lackluster campaign until close to the end, and he was unable to catch Clinton.

Following his defeat, Bush moved back to Houston, where he and his wife built a new house in a posh section of town and settled in to a comfortable retirement. Bush has been active on the speechmaking circuit and reportedly commands up to $100,000 a speech. He worked on a book with former foreign policy advisor Brent Scowcroft, and in 1993, he visited Kuwait at the invitation of the nation's ruler and narrowly avoided an assassination attempt by the Iraqis. In general, George Bush has kept a low public profile since 1992, spending much time with his family (including thirteen grandchildren), both in Houston and Kennebunkport.

REFERENCES

George Bush (with Victor Gold), *Looking Forward: An Autobiography* (New York: Doubleday, 1987); Michael Duffy and Dan Goodgame, *Marching in Place: The Status Quo Presidency of George Bush* (New York: Simon and Schuster, 1992); Fitzhugh Green, *George Bush: An Intimate Portrait* (New York: Hippocrene Books, 1989); Haynes Johnson, *Sleepwalking Through History: America in the Reagan Years* (New York: W.W. Norton, 1991); Pamela Kilian, *Barbara Bush: A Biography* (New York: St. Martin's Press, 1992); Nicolas King, *George Bush: A Biography* (New York: Dodd, Mead, 1980); Jane Mayer and Doyle McManus, *Landslide: The Unmaking of the President, 1984–1988* (Boston: Houghton Mifflin, 1988); Edwin Meese, *With Reagan: The Inside Story* (Lanham, Md.: Regnery Gateway, 1992); Peggy Noonan, *What I Saw at the Revolution: A Political Life in the Reagan Era* (New York: Random House, 1990); Ronald Reagan, *An American Life* (New York: Simon and Schuster, 1990); Larry Speakes, *Speaking Out: The Reagan Presidency from Inside the White House* (New York: Scribner's, 1988); David Stockton, *The Triumph of Politics: How the Reagan Revolution Failed* (New York: Harper & Row, 1986).

See the entry for George Clinton for a biographical note on L. Edward Purcell

J. DANFORTH QUAYLE (b. 1947)

Vice President, 1989–1993

(President George Bush)

J. DANFORTH QUAYLE
(Courtesy of the Dan Quayle Center and Museum)

By Shirley Anne Warshaw

The Republicans dominated the White House throughout the 1980s, first with the Reagan–Bush administration and then the Bush–Quayle administration. Elected in 1988, George Herbert Walker Bush and J. Danforth Quayle continued the Reagan legacy of fiscal conservatism, slimming the federal bureaucracy, and deficit reduction, in addition to a continued defense buildup. By the 1992 election cycle, however, the tide of public opinion had turned against the Republican agenda and moved toward the domestic and economic stimulus themes of the Democrats. The Democratic ticket of Bill Clinton and Al Gore defeated the one-term Republican Bush/Quayle team and turned the reins of government over to the Democrats for the first time in twelve years.

When George Bush chose the relatively obscure junior senator from Indiana as his vice-presidential running mate in 1988, he had taken a calculated risk that Dan Quayle could galvanize the conservative right wing of the Republican Party for an electoral victory. Quayle and Bush hardly knew each other, but Quayle had forged a reputation as a strong supporter of family values, the prolife movement, and conservative principles. Quayle solidified for the Bush–Quayle ticket the conservative vote that had supported Ronald Reagan for the past two elections. Bush, himself a moderate, needed to balance the ticket in order to maintain conservative support.

The November 8, 1988, election proved Bush's risk of Dan Quayle to be well taken, for the voters handily turned away Democrat Massachusetts Governor Michael S. Dukakis and his running mate, senior Texas Senator Lloyd Bentsen. Bush controlled the election, carrying 40 states with 48.9 million votes, 53 percent of the total, and an impressive 426 electoral votes. Dukakis carried only 10 states, with 41.8 million votes or 46 percent of the total, and 111 electoral votes.

The emergence of Dan Quayle as a national political figure was part of a concerted effort on his part to move into the national scene. As Bush became the clear front-runner for the Republican nomination in 1988, Quayle embarked on a campaign to capture the vice-presidential nomination. As early as 1986, just after being reelected to the Senate, he had begun to explore ways to become a contender for the nomination. He gave high-profile speeches on the Senate floor throughout spring 1988, became an active participant in the weekly lunches of Senate Republicans that George Bush regularly attended, and frequently stopped in Bush's office in the Senate.

Quayle's most deliberate move toward gaining the vice-presidential nomination was lobbying to give the keynote address at the 1988 Republican convention. Quayle commented that "I lobbied a little bit, very discreetly. . . . I thought I'd be . . . good." In late spring, Quayle began actively to garner the support of the Republican Party's conservative wing through his opposition to the INF (Intermediate Nuclear Forces) Treaty being debated on the Senate floor. He later became a major opponent of the 1988 defense budget, arguing that the Democrats had cut the budget beyond acceptable limits. When the de-

fense bill was passed by the Democratic-controlled Senate, Quayle became the leading advocate of a presidential veto and frequently met with Vice President Bush. Bush eventually supported the Quayle position and convinced President Reagan to veto the bill.

The decision to consider Dan Quayle for the 1988 Republican ticket came on July 25, 1988, as the Democratic convention was ending. Bush phoned Quayle at his McLean, Virginia, home and told him he was one of several people under consideration as the vice-presidential nominee. By August 16, when the New Orleans Republican convention was in full operation, Quayle emerged as the successful candidate. Quayle's addition to the ticket provided Bush with not only political and geographic balance but also the increasingly important generational balance. Dan Quayle represented the politically active postwar generation. At the relatively young age of forty-one, Quayle had become one of the nation's youngest vice-presidential nominees, representing burgeoning baby boomers. Only Richard Nixon, who was elected in 1952 at age thirty-nine with Dwight D. Eisenhower, had been younger when elected to the nation's second highest office.

J. Danforth Quayle entered the world as part of a prominent Indianapolis publishing family. Born to James and Corinne Quayle on February 4, 1947, in Huntington, Indiana, Dan Quayle grew up in a small midwestern town where his father was a second-tier manager of a newspaper owned by his father-in-law, Eugene Pulliam. When he was eight years old, the Quayle family moved to Arizona, where Jim Quayle joined another newspaper. Finally, in 1963, when Quayle was sixteen years old, the family returned to Huntington when his father bought the *Huntington Herald-Press* from Pulliam.

Quayle's childhood was one of strong family ties and conservative values. His father, a John Birch Society member, had been a powerful influence on the development of Quayle's conservative value system. Life was comfortable for the Quayles and included such luxuries as a country-club membership and, as one family friend recalled, "plenty of time to play golf." It was also a childhood full of politics, with both his parents serving on precinct committees and heavily involved in Republican politics. In 1968, Quayle signed on as a volunteer at the Republican national convention and became a driver for the Nixon staff, all of which was encouraged by his parents.

Quayle's strong family ties were a key reason for his decision to attend DePauw University in Greencastle, Indiana, where both his parents and his grandfather had gone. After graduating there in 1969, he entered the Indiana National Guard to meet his military obligation before he could be drafted. A year later, Quayle entered the Indiana University–Indianapolis Law School with the class of 1973. His interest in politics was fueled during his tenure at law school; he held jobs in both the attorney general's and the governor's offices.

While in law school Quayle met another law student, Marilyn Tucker, whom he married in 1972. After graduation, they returned to Huntington, Indiana, where Quayle took over the family newspaper as associate publisher of the *Huntington Herald-Press*, which was owned by his grandfather and run by his father. In addition, he opened a law firm, known as Quayle and Quayle, with his wife.

The political career of Dan Quayle began as soon as he left law school, with his decision to buy a house in Huntington because of its location. Quayle wanted to run for the state legislature and sought a house in a district from which he thought he could be elected. However, he subsequently chose to bypass the state legislature and make a run for the U.S. House of Representatives in 1976. Marilyn Quayle served as his campaign strategist and became the liaison with Republican state leaders, meeting with county party leaders and organizing local political events. She was widely credited with managing the campaign and ensuring its political and financial success.

Quayle's 1976 campaign for the House focused on the issues of welfare reform, increased defense spending, and criticism of the New York City bailout. Rather than run on the president's coattails, Quayle chose to distance himself from Gerald Ford, whose popularity had fallen after his pardon of Richard Nixon. Quayle ousted Democrat J. Edward Roush, who had represented the Fourth Congressional District for 16 years, winning the election by a margin of 19,000 votes, 55 percent to 45 percent, despite trailing Roush by 16 points during the summer before the election.

Quayle's congressional victory was a combination of clever attacks on a tax-and-spend liberal Congress, of which Roush was a prominent member, and actively seeking support from the Christian right. A Fort Wayne newspaper noted that "Congressman-elect Quayle called for a limited government, an end to deficit spending, and a stop to the federal bureaucracy's cancerous growth." In January 1977, at the tender age of twenty-nine, Quayle was sworn into the U.S. Congress and focused his energies on what he called "excessive government spending."

Quayle's voting House record reflected the conservative values that he had espoused during the campaign and was scored by the conservative Americans for Constitutional Action as one of the highest in the Congress, averaging in the mid-ninetieth percentile. The liberal Americans for Democratic Action scored his voting record as unacceptable, averaging in the fifteenth percentile. After two House terms, Quayle took a major political risk by challenging the Democratic incumbent, Birch Bayh, for the U.S. Senate. When the leading Republican contender to challenge Bayh, Governor Otis Bowen, announced that he would not run for the Senate seat, Quayle announced that he would. On May 14, 1979, Quayle entered the race.

Quayle's decision to challenge Bayh, an eighteen-year Senate veteran, was based on his belief that the public was ready for a new generation of leadership committed to reducing federal expenditure. During seven televised debates during the 1980 campaign, Quayle repeatedly hammered away at the liberal voting record that Bayh had maintained.

Quayle's attacks were in step with the conservative trend of the 1980 election: Republican presidential candidate Ronald Reagan was similarly attacking President Jimmy Carter's administration. Quayle tried to draw parallels between Democrats Bayh and Carter, including their support for a gasoline tax. Quayle adeptly used the media in his drive for the Senate; for example, he held a press conference using a local McDonald's as the backdrop for presenting a chart that listed the onerous federal regulations that governed making a hamburger. Indiana supported Quayle, as it did Ronald Reagan, with 54 percent of the vote to Bayh's 46 percent. Four years after being elected to the House, Quayle had been elected to the Senate. In January 1981 when the Ninety-seventh Congress convened, Indiana had two Republican Senators, Richard Lugar and J. Danforth Quayle.

The Reagan Revolution ushered Quayle into the Senate along with the first Republican majority since Dwight Eisenhower, and the new majority was committed to cutting taxes, reducing federal regulation, and increasing national defense. The Republicans' goal was to restructure the federal government's role in policy making by both ending numerous programs and devolving other programs to the state level. The Reagan Republicans were also committed to a major buildup in national defense, including military hardware and manpower.

Quayle's 1980 campaign had been a natural fit with the conservative Republican trend of the Reagan Revolution. Quayle campaigned as an advocate of prayer in public schools and tuition tax credits for private schools. He opposed abortion and supported voluntarism to replace government services.

His committee assignments were generally a solid mix with his electoral base and his ambition toward higher office. His appointment to the Labor and Human Resources Committee provided input into social legislation, his appointment to the Budget Committee allowed constant overview of budget cutting, and his appointment to the Armed Services Committee ensured national attention.

During his first year in office, it was the Armed Services Committee that dominated Quayle's attention as it held hearings on the proposed sale of AWACS surveillance airplanes by the Reagan administration to Saudi Arabia. The debate became heated, as Israel brought pressure on the Senate to abandon the sale. Relatively early

in the debate, Quayle tried to broker a satisfactory deal between the opponents of the AWACS sale and those in favor of it. A deal was forged and the Senate voted to support Reagan's plan of sale, giving Quayle instant credibility as a knowledgeable, active player who was willing to deal in high-stakes issues.

Although the Armed Services Committee had served Quayle well in his bid to move past freshman status and gain credibility among his colleagues, he decided to focus his attention on the Labor and Human Resources Committee, where he would immediately gain control of a subcommittee. Committee Chair Orrin Hatch, a Republican from Utah, assigned Quayle the Subcommittee on Employment chairmanship, which controlled the $8 billion Comprehensive Employment and Training Act (CETA), which would expire on September 30, 1982. The focus of the subcommittee would be to determine whether to extend CETA and, if extended, at what level.

Quayle was extremely sensitive to the issues of unemployment and job training. Indiana, which had a large auto manufacturing base, suffered from nearly an 18 percent unemployment rate among autoworkers. During his 1980 campaign against Birch Bayh, Quayle had said that "300,000 people were without jobs and that Birch Bayh was to blame." Now Quayle moved aggressively to seek ways to spur the economy and to protect the unemployed. He immediately pored over the CETA program, trying to understand its assets and liabilities. The Reagan administration had recommended significant program cuts and restructuring of the remaining programs primarily into block grants.

After a detailed review, Quayle recommended continuing the program, essentially in its previous form but with a trimmed down budget, and not moving toward block grants. The White House was not eager to support his proposal but viewed it as acceptable and moved on with its own legislative agenda. As he had in the Armed Services Committee AWACS issue, Quayle had mastered the details of the CETA issue and gained bipartisan respect for his ability to move swiftly to resolution. One of Quayle's strengths during his early tenure on the Labor and Human Resources Committee was his ability to build such bipartisan support both on the subcommittee and within the full committee. With a nominal 9–7 Republican majority, which included the liberal-leaning Connecticut Republican Lowell Weicker, success depended upon such bipartisan support.

As Quayle moved to become a leading player in labor and employment issues, he needed the aid of longtime labor supporter Democrat Edward Kennedy of Massachusetts. By early 1983, Quayle had forged an alliance with Kennedy, Labor and Human Resources Committee's senior member, to replace the CETA bill and to introduce a replacement Senate bill, S2036, focusing on job training for the unemployed. Headlines read that the unlikely alliance of conservative Dan Quayle and liberal Ted Kennedy would work together for the "Quayle–Kennedy Training for Jobs Bill."

The Reagan administration opposed the bill primarily because of its costs but additionally because of general opposition to any bill supported by Kennedy. Reagan's economic cabinet council, chaired by Treasury Secretary Donald Regan, opposed the jobs training bill, so Quayle found himself being opposed by the White House and supported by Kennedy, a position he was uncomfortable maintaining. Surprisingly, Quayle chose to remain loyal to S2036 and to continue his alliance with Kennedy in the Senate.

Quayle successfully convinced Orrin Hatch, chair of the full committee, to lend his support to the bill on the grounds that the Republicans had to provide leadership in economic issues. Hatch, who was running for reelection, finally moved into the Quayle camp and began to lobby the White House. The intense lobbying by Hatch and Quayle proved successful, and on September 21, 1983, Reagan endorsed the Job Training Partnership Act to replace the CETA program. The Senate quickly approved the bill, 97–0, followed by a House vote of 339–12 in favor of the bill. It became Public Law 97–300, largely due to Quayle.

Quayle's leadership had resulted in one of the few pieces of significant legislation passed by the divided Ninety-seventh Congress. He noted of the Ninety-seventh Congress that "we've passed the two budgets, the two tax bills, and the voting rights bill. Add the job training bill and that's just about it for this Congress."

The jobs training bill proved to be central not only to the Ninety-seventh Congress's legislative record but also to Quayle's legislative accomplishments. When he campaigned for reelection in 1986, he focused his campaign on his success in providing a key piece of economic legislation. He often cited "the 163,000 people in Indiana who have been trained" as a result of the act.

Quayle's opponent in the 1986 senatorial race was Valparaiso University Professor Jill Long. Being essentially unknown, she was able to raise only $100,000, compared to the $2 million raised by Quayle. The election result was predictable, with Quayle garnering 61 percent of the vote, the largest percentage margin any Indiana Senator had ever received in a general election. As Quayle's campaign manager noted, the jobs bill "was the whole campaign."

By 1988, Dan Quayle was beginning to look toward what he called "career advancement." He aggressively pursued the second seat on the Republican presidential ticket. Six months before the Republican convention, Quayle began to leak his interest in the job, noting his solid conservative credentials, his success at building bipartisan coalitions, and his support within his own generation. When the call came from George Bush on the night of August 16, 1988, it was the result of a highly orchestrated effort by Dan Quayle, his wife Marilyn, and the Quayle Senate staff.

Although Bush had called Quayle in July to test his interest in the job, no one on the Bush campaign had contacted Quayle since then, and no one had alerted Quayle that he would be the final choice. Bush had not had a single substantive conversation with Quayle about the campaign's goals and objectives. When Quayle was finally contacted during the convention, he was as surprised as the nation.

Quayle's first public appearance as the vice-presidential nominee at the Republican convention, however, was less than ideal. He entered the convention hall out of breath, having walked several blocks from his hotel. He was hot, tired, and overly eager to please. Once next to

Bush, he continually grabbed Bush's arms and said, "Let's go get them." The media disparagingly described Quayle not as a major asset to the ticket but as a cheerleader for the presidential nominee.

Quayle's performance during the first days after the convention continued to support the image of the ticket's minor player. Quayle floundered through questions about his personal wealth (appraised in 1988 at $859,700 by Price Waterhouse), average academic achievements, country-club background, and service in the National Guard. The question of military service was repeatedly raised as the press sought to learn why Quayle had chosen the National Guard rather than an active-duty assignment that might have led to a tour in Vietnam.

In spite of his initial high profile, Quayle stayed out of the limelight throughout most of the 1988 campaign. Bush dominated the national media and generally moved Quayle into state political and fund-raising activities. Quayle's most visible campaign moments came in October during the nationally televised vice-presidential debate with Democratic nominee Lloyd Bentsen. Both Bush and Quayle had agreed to debate their individual opponents through the nonpartisan Commission on Presidential Debates. When Quayle and Bentsen were on the stage together, Quayle tried to draw attention to their age and generational difference. Just when this tactic might have been successful, Quayle went the extra step and tried to draw a parallel between himself and the youthful John F. Kennedy during the 1960 presidential debates. Bentsen retorted that he had known John F. Kennedy and that Quayle "was no John Kennedy." This was the lasting impression of the debate, one in which Bentsen had gained the upper hand.

Although Bentsen won the vice-presidential debate, presidential candidate Michael Dukakis did not gain the same advantage in his debates with Bush. The electorate saw Bush as the more experienced statesman and leader and by the November election had turned its support to the Bush–Quayle team in spite of a 17 percent lead by Dukakis–Bentsen during the summer. In large measure, the election had turned on a negative campaign, particularly the charge made by Bush that Dukakis's liberal approach to crime as governor of Massachusetts had allowed a convicted murderer, Willie Horton, to be furloughed. Horton was later convicted of committing rape and torture while on furlough. Bush and Quayle capitalized on public intolerance of crime and eventually garnered 53 percent of the popular vote and 426 electoral votes.

Once in office, Bush did not seek to bring Quayle into the inner circle. In an effort to gain status among administration members, Quayle sought avenues for gaining attention. One of the more obvious tactics was to try to meet with international leaders, which would bring national media attention and ensure frequent briefings with Bush. This idea, however, was quickly derailed by Secretary of State James Baker, who saw diplomatic initiatives as the State Department's sole province. Quayle, who had only a limited personal relationship with the new president, would always be outmaneuvered in policy issues by Baker, who enjoyed a thirty-five year friendship with Bush.

With both domestic and foreign policy involvement moved out of the scope of routine responsibilities, Quayle returned to his roots in Congress and within the Republican Party. He regularly met with members of the Senate Republican leadership in his Senate office, provided for his Constitutional role as the president of the Senate, to discuss bills in progress. He served both to relay presidential positions on major bills and to lobby on their behalf. During the 1990 battle over the budget, Quayle became a key member of Bush's congressional liaison staff as he worked to build conservative support for the budget bill. In spite of a campaign promise not to raise taxes in the famous "Read my lips" statement, the Bush administration supported tax increases as a means to curb the mounting deficit crisis. The White House assigned Quayle to meet with members of Congress to build support and sooth the tensions that were mounting over a sense of betrayal. Although Quayle did not support the budget bill (which he called "the most serious test of loyalty I'd experience during the administration"), he lobbied on behalf of the tax increase.

In addition to his role as congressional liaison, Quayle took up the mantle of political liaison for the White House, meeting with key Republican leaders and raising millions of dollars for the National Republican Committee and for state and local Republican candidates.

Throughout his term of office, Quayle contributed to two major policy areas: federal regulation and space research. As chair of the National Space Council, Quayle worked to protect NASA's programs and to continue support for the Freedom space station.

In the more high-profile Council on Competitiveness, Quayle and his staff reviewed every new federal law and oversaw the departmental production of the regulations to implement the law. Their task was to minimize the number of regulations imposed on either private business or state and local government as means of reducing the cost of doing business. The business community had repeatedly complained in recent years that the federal government had imposed too many regulatory mandates to allow a competitive environment.

Among the many regulatory issues that the Council on Competitiveness addressed were those raised by the Environmental Protection Agency (EPA). Under William Reilly's leadership, the EPA moved to support aggressively the reauthorization of the Clean Air Act in 1991 and often battled with both White House Chief of Staff John Sununu and Quayle's Competitiveness Council on clean-air standards to be incorporated into the new bill. Quayle fought with Reilly over the biodiversity treaty signed in Rio de Janeiro, Brazil, and over wetlands legislation. The public saw both the EPA and Quayle as overly zealous, seeking to address environmental problems in less-than-satisfactory ways.

The Persian Gulf War in 1991 was the single area that provided cohesiveness among the senior White House staff and the vice president. As a National Security Council member, Quayle was regularly briefed on Iraq's movements and about U.S. troop buildup. In less-structured discussions among senior White House staff, Quayle was consistently included. He was, however, generally a passive member of the group as Sununu dominated the questioning of national security advisor Brent Scowcroft and Joint Chiefs of Staff Chairman Colin Powell.

By 1992, Dan Quayle had not worked his way into the Bush inner circle, a circle generally dominated by Sununu and, after Sununu's ouster, Samuel Skinner. Quayle had to be content traveling the nation on behalf of Republican candidates (a task he hoped would pay off when he moved into a presidential campaign as the ticket's lead member) and managing the Competitiveness Council.

Although sitting presidents rarely have vigorous opposition during the second-term reelection campaign, in 1992 the Democrats attacked what they perceived to be a relatively weak Republican administration. Democratic presidential nominee Bill Clinton and his running mate, Senator Al Gore, charged the Bush–Quayle administration for its failure to manage the domestic economy. The Bush–Quayle campaign focused on its Persian Gulf War success but never gained broad-based public support. Clinton won the election with 43 percent of the popular vote. Ross Perot, millionaire industrialist from Texas, similarly challenged Bush and gained 19 percent of the popular vote.

George Bush and Dan Quayle gracefully acknowledged their defeat in the 1992 election and offered their support to the fledgling Clinton–Gore administration. Both Bush and Quayle opened their offices during the transition to provide advice and information to the new tenants of 1600 Pennsylvania Avenue.

After the Clinton administration's January 20, 1993, inauguration, Quayle returned to his native Indiana and joined the conservative Hudson Institute, a think tank near Indianapolis. There, he focused on issues of competitiveness in the marketplace, continuing his efforts from the Competitiveness Council.

Although Quayle was widely viewed as a major contender for the 1996 Republican presidential nomination, he pulled his name out of contention during the fall of 1995. He had suffered several health problems during 1995, including a hospitalization for a blood clot in the leg, and appeared to have difficulty raising the necessary funds for a national election. His formal withdrawal from the race, however, was based on his decision to remain close to his wife and three teenage children, Tucker, Benjamin, and Corinne. Citing his deep commitment to his family, Quayle explained that his children came first in his life. He left the door open to a continuing political career, noting that he was still a young man with many years remaining to pursue politics.

The legacy of Dan Quayle is one of consistency: throughout his political career Quayle remained loyal to his personal values of family and church and to his conservative political values of a reduced role for government. His political future, however, remains in question; the U.S. public will not easily forget the vice president who erroneously "corrected" the spelling of an elementary school child. The child had spelled "potato" on the blackboard at his school, but Dan Quayle made him change it to "potatoe"

Although accuracy in spelling is not a criteria for attaining national office, most Americans prefer their candidates to be able to spell "potato" correctly.

REFERENCES

David S. Broder and Bob Woodward, *The Man Who Would Be President* (New York: Simon and Shuster, 1992); Richard F. Fenno, Jr., *The Making of a Senator: Dan Quayle* (Washington, D.C.: Congressional Quarterly Press, 1989); Dan Quayle, *Standing Firm* (New York: HarperCollins, 1994).

SHIRLEY ANNE WARSHAW is associate professor of political science at Gettysburg College, specializing in presidential decision making. Her latest books are *Powersharing: White House-Cabinet Relations in the Modern Presidency* (1996) and *The Domestic Presidency: Decision Making in the White House* (1997).

ALBERT ARNOLD GORE, JR. (b. 1948)

Vice President, 1993–2001

(President Bill Clinton)

ALBERT A. GORE, JR.
(Office of the Vice President)

By Scott W. Rager

During his tenure in the vice presidency, Al Gore, Jr., played a more substantial role in decision and policy making than many of his recent predecessors. Highly regarded for his energy and competence, Gore, with President Bill Clinton's encouragement, redefined the office, expanding both its power and influence. He served as one of Clinton's main advisers on foreign policy and became strongly identified with several key administration domestic issues, including the reorganization of government, the environment, and communications technology.

Born on March 31, 1948, in Carthage, Tennessee, Al Gore was the second child of Albert and Pauline LaFon Gore. His parents and older sister, Nancy, were dynamic individuals who set high standards of personal achievement for Gore to emulate.

Albert Gore, Sr., a former educator and lawyer, was a protégé of Franklin Roosevelt's secretary of state, Cordell Hull. First elected to Tennessee's Fourth Congressional District in 1938, he served seven terms in the U.S. House of Representatives (1939–1953) and three terms in the Senate (1953–1971). Pauline LaFon Gore was the second woman ever to graduate from Vanderbilt University Law School and practiced law for a year prior to her marriage on April 17, 1937. Nancy Gore, ten years older than her brother, was also a graduate of Vanderbilt University and became one of the founding members of President John F. Kennedy's Peace Corps.

Al Gore, Jr., was raised in two entirely different environments. One was the family cattle farm in rural Carthage, Tennessee; the other was Washington, D.C. Until the age of nine, he lived and attended school in Carthage. After moving to the capital, Gore's formal education continued at St. Albans School for Boys, a prestigious Washington prep school where he excelled in both academic and athletic pursuits. Equally valuable, however, was the informal tutelage he received in American politics and government while living in Washington.

Upon graduation from St. Albans in 1965, Gore, who had won a National Merit Scholarship, was admitted to Harvard, where he majored in political science and became active in student government. His senior thesis, written under the direction of Dr. Richard Neustadt, was titled: "The Impact of Television on the Conduct of the Presidency, 1947–1969" and dealt with the effect of presidential debates on elections. Gore appeared headed for a career in politics. His parents, particularly his father, had encouraged him in that direction, but upon graduating in 1969, Gore made a decision that sidelined all his career plans for several years; he enlisted in the army.

This decision, one of the most difficult of his life, had nothing to do with approval or support for the Vietnam War—like many of his Harvard classmates, Gore had been a war protester. Obtaining exemption from the draft would have presented no particular problem for him, but he sensed the severe ramifications avoidance of military service might have for Al Gore, Sr., who had

already been severely criticized for his own antiwar stance. Despite the fact that he later campaigned in uniform for his father, Gore was unable to prevent the senator's defeat in 1970. Still, military service, which included a tour of duty as an army journalist in Vietnam, would later prove invaluable for his own political career.

Upon completing Army enlistment in May 1971, Gore returned to Tennessee to find a career. Deeply disillusioned by the war, he abandoned the idea of entering politics and was left without a clear idea of what he intended to do. Shortly after enlisting, Gore had married the former Mary Elizabeth "Tipper" Aitcheson in May 1970. Reunited with his wife, Gore settled in Nashville, where he became a reporter for the *Tennessean*. That fall he also entered Vanderbilt School of Divinity, hoping to resolve some spiritual questions raised by his war experiences.

While covering the local and state political beat for the *Tennessean*, Gore found his interest in political activity rekindled and realized that his own abilities qualified him to be involved in government. In preparation for a political career, Gore transferred to Vanderbilt Law School in 1974 but never completed the degree because an opportunity came for him to run for the House of Representatives. The Fourth District congressional seat held by Joseph L. Ervin for thirty-two years was being vacated, and Gore could not pass up the chance to represent his home district. Despite his youth and lack of experience, he easily defeated an independent with 96 percent of the vote, winning the seat his father had once held.

At twenty-eight, Gore was the youngest man ever elected to Congress from the Fourth District. During his four terms in the House, he earned a reputation for responsibility, competency, and hard work. So genuine was his desire to keep in touch with the electorate, he held more than 1,600 town meetings. His agenda in Congress included nuclear arms control, health, communications, and environmental issues. With respect to the latter, as member of the Energy and Commerce Oversight Subcommittee, Gore led the investigation on illegal hazardous-waste dumping and helped bring about the creation of the Superfund in 1980, which provided $1.6

billion for toxic waste cleanup. Recognition for his dedication and diligence as a legislator came from several quarters, most notably from the *Washington Monthly*, which named him among the six most effective members of Congress, and from the Jaycees, who chose him as one of the "Ten Most Outstanding Young Men in America."

In 1983, Senator Howard Baker, the Republican majority leader from Tennessee, announced that he would not seek reelection for another term. Again, following in his father's footsteps, Gore ran for the Senate. In the fall 1984 election, despite a Republican landslide in other races, he handily defeated his Republican opponent, Victor H. Ashe, winning 61 percent of the vote. Although the victory was a triumph, with it had come sadness; during the campaign Gore's sister, Nancy, to whom he was very close, died of cancer.

In the Senate, Gore maintained the agenda he had set for himself in the House. Still dedicated to nuclear arms control, as a member of the Armed Services Committee he was able to play an instrumental role in working out a Democratic agreement with the Reagan administration to limit the deployment of MX missiles. Gore also proposed a $1.2 million trimming of Reagan's $3.7 million budget for development of the Strategic Defense Initiative but failed to generate enough support for his compromise measure with either the liberal or conservative camps.

As a member of the Commerce, Science, and Transportation Committee, Gore sponsored the National High Performance Computer Technology Act, which set into motion the creation of a national super computer network.

Continuing his advocacy for improved health care, Gore worked for the creation of a computerized network to match organ donors with patients needing transplants. Another of his causes involved placing stronger warnings on cigarettes and warnings on alcoholic beverages.

Gore further enhanced his reputation as one of Congress's leading experts on the environment. Fact-finding trips to gather information on the state of the environment took him to both the North and South poles and to Brazil. In June 1992, he led the Senate delegation to the Earth Day Summit. His best-selling book, *Earth in the Balance: Ecology and the Human Spirit*, published in 1992, expressed his thoughts on the environment and laid out a comprehensive plan for global action.

The high-profile and excellent legislative record achieved by Gore while in Congress provided him with an impressive base from which to launch a bid for the Democratic presidential nomination in 1988. The competition was stiff: Senator Gary Hart of Colorado, Senator Joe Biden of Delaware, Governor Michael Dukakis of Massachusetts, Representative Dick Gephardt of Missouri, and Reverend Jesse Jackson of Illinois. Gore initially focused on the environment as the chief issue of his campaign, but that tactic failed to attract as much public attention as he had hoped. His performance in the New Hampshire primary was lackluster. Determined campaigning and a refocus of his agenda helped Gore to rebound to win five of fourteen Super Tuesday states in March, but disappointing results in the crucial New York primary finally convinced him to suspend his efforts. The Democratic nomination ultimately went to Michael Dukakis, who lost the election to George Bush, Ronald Reagan's vice president.

By no means did his failure to win the Democratic Presidential nomination in 1988 diminish Gore's desire to seek the office again. He very likely would have pursued it in 1992 if a life-changing event had not intervened. In April 1989, Gore's six-year-old son Albert was struck and nearly killed by a car. The boy sustained massive internal and external injuries that required extensive surgery at Johns Hopkins Hospital in Baltimore and took months to heal. His son's recuperation eventually was complete, but the experience caused Gore to do serious soul searching, and the entire family went through therapy to overcome the trauma. This experience was the most important factor in Gore's decision not to run for president during the 1992 cycle.

That Gore might instead consider being a candidate for the vice presidency in 1992 seemed at best a remote possibility; based upon his past remarks, he considered the second position a political dead end. But this assessment obviously changed. When Warren Christopher, head of Arkansas Governor Bill Clinton's vice-presidential search team, contacted Gore about his availability as a potential candidate, he consented to have his name added to a list which, in its final form, included forty individuals. At the end of June, Gore met privately with Clinton. Subsequent to that meeting the Tennessee senator secured a place on the vice-presidential shortlist that had five others: Congressman Lee Hamilton and Senators Harris Wofford, Bob Kerry, Jay Rockefeller, and Bob Graham.

The decision to choose Gore was not difficult for Clinton, who recognized a man of exceptional drive, ability, and intellect. Also important was the fact that on a personal and political level Gore suited Clinton almost perfectly. The two shared many similarities. In addition to being from the same region, they were both Southern Baptists, both baby boomers in their forties (Gore is nineteen months younger than Clinton), and both graduates of prestigious universities. More significant, both Clinton and Gore were so-called New Democrats, a group whose core philosophy was based in making government more efficient and responsible. It did not seem to worry Clinton that Gore might be perceived as being too much like him, which could give rise to an argument that the ticket lacked diversity, particularly in respect to region. He was more concerned that the South and border states went solidly for him, and Gore's participation made that outcome more probable.

The ticket was also strengthened by Gore in a critical area where Clinton was thought to be weak: personal character. The Gores' marriage, unlike the Clintons', was one of the most solid in Washington. Furthermore, Al and Tipper, the parents of one son and three daughters, were strong proponents of "family values." Their reputation was further bolstered by Tipper Gore's crusade for labeling rock music to inform parents about obscene lyrics.

Finally, Gore's acknowledged expertise on environmental matters and foreign affairs made a Clinton presidency more attractive to several key groups within the electorate. His outstanding record as an environmental advocate meant Gore could potentially win the support of affluent suburbanites and West Coast voters. Equally important, he was also an expert and a moderate on foreign policy issues. During the Gulf crisis, Gore was among only ten Democrats who voted to authorize President Bush to use U.S. forces to drive Iraqi strongman Saddam Hussein's forces from Kuwait. This and the fact that he had served in the army during the Vietnam War (unlike Bill Clinton who had avoided military service) would provide reassurance to both veterans' groups and Reagan Democrats who might otherwise be wary of a Clinton-led administration.

Before he was officially offered the vice-presidential slot, Gore had consulted with his family, and together they had agreed that he should accept if asked to join Clinton on the ticket. Gore realized that if all went well, he would stand a very good chance of becoming the Democrats' next nominee for the presidency. When Clinton called with the offer on July 20, Gore was ready with his answer.

Clinton's choice was widely applauded at the Democratic convention and served to win the support of some of his former critics. Only Jesse Jackson expressed concern with the selection, remarking: "It takes two wings to fly but here you have two of the same wing." The selection seemed to strike a responsive chord with the public as well. A *Newsweek* poll showed that 44 percent of those surveyed expressed a greater willingness to vote for Clinton after Gore was added to the ticket, compared with 21 percent who indicated they were less willing and 27 percent who indicated no change in their position.

The main issue of the Clinton–Gore program was the need for change and fresh ideas, particularly regarding a solution to revive the country's then sagging economy, but from the beginning of the campaign it was clear that the Democratic strategy would also involve making an issue of the vice presidency and the two individuals seeking that position. At their first news conference, Clinton focused on this issue, saying that in choosing Gore he had "tried to take political considerations out" of the selection process "and ask (instead) who would be the best person." He stressed that Gore would be a vice president immediately prepared to assume the presidency if anything happened to him. A poll subsequently taken by *Time* magazine indicated that the public did perceive Gore as more qualified than Dan Quayle to become president by a margin of 61 percent to 21 percent.

A televised debate between Gore and Quayle at Georgia Tech in Atlanta on the evening of October 13, 1992, served to further enhance Gore's position. Also participating in the debate was Admiral James Stockdale, the running mate of Ross Perot, whose on-again-off-again campaign was once more on. While Quayle did a much better job than many had expected, polls taken afterward showed that Gore fared best when people were asked who had won. Fifty percent of the respondents chose him over Quayle, who received 27 percent, and Stockdale, who received 7 percent.

Energetic and enthusiastic during the often grueling three-and-a-half-month race, veteran campaigner Gore was a true asset to the team and regularly demonstrated the improvements he had made in relating to an audience; less in evidence was the Al Gore who had once been described as somewhat "wooden," "obsequious," and "boring." Together, he and Bill Clinton displayed a dynamism often missing from the campaign of their Republican opponents.

Bush, particularly, seemed to lack his old fire and fighting zeal. Perhaps due to overconfidence, the incumbent president had begun his campaign too late. In October, he and Quayle were still running ten points behind Clinton and Gore in the polls, and a desperate Bush resorted to calling his opponents names. Hoping to cast aspersions on the Democratic team's grasp of geopolitics, the president said that his dog Millie knew more about foreign affairs than those "two bozos." Bush also attempted to make a jest out of Gore's dedication to environmental matters by calling him "Ozone Man." Such tactics, however, only succeeded in calling attention to the failing Bush–Quayle campaign and swayed little support toward the Republicans.

The November 4 election went much as had been expected; Clinton–Gore won 43 percent of the vote. Bush–Quayle took 38 percent and Perot-Stockdale trailed far behind with 19 percent.

President-elect Clinton fully appreciated the important part Al Gore had played in winning the election and publicly expressed his desire to have him take a more substantial role in governing than had many of his predecessors in the vice presidency. Before the January 20 inaugural, Gore assisted in picking the subcabinet and the White House staff and from the first days of the new administration was integral to the decision-making process. He became a general adviser to the president and counseled Clinton on nearly all major issues.

Gore's input on foreign policy was particularly sought after by the president. The former Senate Armed Services Committee member's advice tended to be that of a moderate hawk. After the June 1993 assassination attempt made on the life of George Bush during a visit to the Middle East, Gore was in the vanguard of those advisers urging Clinton to order a retaliatory military strike against Saddam Hussein. Gore also initially argued that aggressive force should be used to solve the crisis in Bosnia-Hercegovina but relented when President Clinton was unable to rally support among the allies. By midterm, the president had increased his reliance on Gore, who was devoting 25 percent of his working hours to foreign policy. Diplomatic trips to Russia helped Gore to develop a relationship with his counterpart, Prime Minister Victor Chernomyrdin, and led to the creation of the Gore–Chernomyrdin Commission, formed by Presidents Clinton and Boris Yeltsin to encourage greater economic cooperation between the United States and Russia. Gore's carefully cultivated relationship with Chernomyrdin became a back channel for communications between Washington and Moscow. The vice president further eased tension in Eastern Europe through his secret negotiations with Ukranian President Leonid Kravchuk, which resulted in the surrender of the Ukraine's nuclear weapons stockpile.

During fall 1993, the vice president also played a vital role in winning support for the North American Free Trade Agreement (NAFTA), which allowed free trade with Mexico. Opponents of the controversial policy maintained that U.S. companies would be likely to move their factories to Mexico to take advantage of the cheap labor. The anti-NAFTA rhetoric of Ross Perot was particularly poisonous. Heading the administration's damage control operation was Al Gore, who challenged Perot to a televised debate. The forum was CNN's *Larry King Live*. On November 9, 1993, Gore and Perot debated the pros and cons of NAFTA and took phone-in questions from the audience. The outcome of the debate was a clear win for Gore. The NAFTA agreement subsequently passed, and Gore was sent to Mexico to discuss implementation of the plan with President Carlos Salinas de Gortari.

Gore played a no-less-significant role in the planning and implementing of the Clinton administration's domestic policy. His highest-profile activity involved heading the National Performance Review, which was initially charged with conducting an examination of every department in the federal government and then formulating recommendations for "reinventing government." This process, according to Gore, would involve "not just cutting wasteful spending, but also improving our services and making our government work better." "We want," he concluded, "major reforms and major innovations." Typically thorough, Gore hired expert consultants; sought advice from federal, state, and local government officials; and held town meetings with employees from each cabinet department. Within six months, by early September 1993, the report was ready. Contained in it were 800 recommendations expected to save $108 billion in five years and to eliminate a quarter-of-a-million federal jobs within fifteen years. The plan was announced without much fanfare but resonated with the public in a way that the White House never anticipated it would. When national health care reform, the administration's greatest effort, stalled in Congress, Gore's efficiency project was given a higher priority and was destined to become a major issue in the second half of Clinton's term.

Acting as the administration's chief spokesman for the environment and for technological advancement rounded out Vice President Gore's duties. In pursuit of the latter, he played a major role in planning and promoting a new telecommunications strategy for development of the national information superhighway. The proposal, dubbed the National Information Infrastructure, called for connecting libraries, schools, and other public institutions to computer networks and increasing the federal support for research into online technologies.

Without question, Gore established himself as a Clinton administration key player, becoming "a vice-president who counts," according to a *U.S. News and World Report* article of July 1993. Unfortunately, the mediocre overall record of the administration's first two years tended to obscure Gore's successes. Little progress had been made with health care and welfare reform, and by midterm President Clinton was plagued with personal problems. Polls indicated low public approval for the president, an outcome in part linked to ongoing investigations into financial arrangements made while he was governor of Arkansas. Dissatisfaction with the administration was registered in the 1994 elections, when the Republican party took over control of Congress for the first time in forty years. Vice President Gore's reputation and personal integrity remained unblemished through all of the Clinton administration's first-term trials, however.

His long-term political future seemed to be in serious doubt in 1994 when the president's chances for reelection appeared to be slight, but in a remarkable political comeback, Bill Clinton fought off the defeats of midterm and along with Gore took a commanding lead in the election polls by mid-1996. The Republicans, who had appeared to be completely in command when they took control of Congress, fumbled the presidential race badly. Senate Majority Leader Robert Dole, a candidate for the vice presidency twenty years before, won the GOP nomination but failed to ignite any sparks among the electorate. He was one of the oldest presidential candidates ever and showed what seemed to be campaign weariness from the beginning. His selection of the energetic Jack Kemp did little to combat the effective public team of Clinton and Gore.

Having maintained a double-digit lead in the polls right up until election day, Clinton and Gore won easily with 49 percent of the vote to 41 percent for the Republicans and 8 percent for H. Ross Perot.

Editor's Addendum to Updated Edition:

The come-from-behind victory put Al Gore into position to become the Democratic Party candidate for president in the 2000 election, if he could avoid political pitfalls during his second term. However, this proved to be difficult, as a series of remarkable events overtook Gore and the Clinton presidency in the four years following the 1996 victory, only to be capped by one of the most closely contested and hotly disputed elections in the nation's electoral history.

Gore was scarcely into his second term when his theretofore squeaky-clean image began to tarnish. He had been unusually active in raising campaign funds for the election (Republicans in Washington referred to Gore as the "Solicitor in Chief"), and it appeared that he had overstepped or trod close to the bounds of legality in two cases. In 1995, both he and President Clinton had made political fund-raising calls from their official offices in the West Wing of the White House, which was in violation of federal laws governing fund-raising by elected officials. The following year, Gore had attended a questionable fund-raising event at a Buddhist temple in California, where thinly disguised campaign contributions slipped through the legal cracks.

In March 1997, the Justice Department began an investigation of Gore's fund-raising activities. He was forced to respond publicly, and he fumbled badly in explaining his presence at the Buddhist temple, where it was determined illegal activity had taken place although there was no direct link to the vice president. Worse, when Gore appeared in a televised press conference to defend the fund-raising calls made from his White House office, he insisted that he had been under "no controlling legal authority," a phrase that the Republicans immediately pounced on with withering ridicule.

Compounding his political difficulties, when Gore traveled to China later the same month, he appeared in public with Chinese premier Li Peng, widely believed in the West to have ordered the crackdown and massacre in Tiananmen Square in 1989. Gore was shown on American television clinking champagne glasses in what appeared to be a jolly toast.

These highly public missteps might have been, to an impartial observer, counterbalanced by Gore's solid record of accomplishments as vice president, but his activities on behalf of the environment, deficit reduction, the regulation of tobacco as a dangerous drug, and support for "v" chip technology to shield children from harmful television shows lacked glamour in the political arena and seldom reached the same level of public consciousness as his gaffes. Unfortunately for Gore, his boldness and forcefulness as a behind-the-scenes adviser in the second Clinton administration were seldom matched in his public appearances, where he appeared to remain stiff and wooden.

Gore continued to work with Viktor Chernomyrdin, even though the latter was ousted as Russian prime minister. In 1999, the vice president was crucial in working out an agreement with Chernomyrdin, who was Russia's envoy to Yugoslavian dictator Slobodan Milosevic, a tactic to persuade the Yugoslavs to withdraw from Kosovo. Chernomyrdin and Gore met in Washington at Gore's official residence to hammer out the proposal that Milosevic finally accepted.

Most of Gore's efforts were overshadowed, however, by the national political crisis precipitated by the revelation that President Clinton had probably lied under oath about his relationship with a young White House intern named Monica Lewinsky. The allegations stemmed from a deposition Clinton gave in January 1998 in regard to a suit for sexual harassment brought against him by state employee Paula Jones when he had been governor of Arkansas. Special Prosecutor Kenneth Starr, who for years had been investigating an allegedly crooked land deal in Arkansas involving President and Mrs. Clinton without success in pinning anything on the First Couple, discovered that the president and Lewinsky had probably carried out a series of sexual liaisons in the White House, and the prosecutor maneuvered Clinton into what appeared to be perjury. Clinton, who had taken the bait during his testimony—he denied ever being alone with Lewinsky—exacerbated his problems by apparently trying to cover up the mess and buy off Lewinsky with a cushy job.

Gore felt shock and betrayal over the Lewinsky scandal. He had been brought onto the Clinton ticket originally to balance the president's reputation as a womanizer, and now the vice president was faced with the need to back a president whose personal behavior was completely at odds with Gore's beliefs and lifelong example of marital fidelity. Moreover, as the year wore on, Gore came under more and more pressure. By fall, when Starr released a report with graphic details of the president's sexual exploits, Gore was forced to take a public stand of support for Clinton, despite his personal feelings. When Clinton was finally impeached by the U.S. House of Representatives in December, Gore appeared on the White House lawn with Clinton and loyally declared him to be "one of our greatest presidents."

Clinton was acquitted of the articles of impeachment after a trial in the U.S. Senate in 1999, but the cloud of the affair hung over the remaining months of the Clinton-Gore administration and created a big problem for Gore as he began to outline his plans for a run at the presidency. Clinton was a powerful campaigner and fund-raiser who, in the normal course of things, could have been relied on to boost Gore's candidacy, but after the impeachment scandal, Clinton was perceived as a political liability with much of the electorate. Although Gore had shown unwavering public loyalty as Clinton's vice president, he decided to keep Clinton at arm's length during the 2000 presidential campaign.

Gore's chief rival for the Democratic nomination was Bill Bradley, the former U.S. senator from New Jersey and a star college and professional basketball player. Bradley had high visibility, especially among those who remembered his days on the court, but he was uninspiring as a speaker and campaigner, and if anything even stiffer in public than Gore. Nonetheless, polls in fall of 1999 showed Bradley tied with Gore in New Hampshire, the site of the first presidential primary. Gore eventually moved ahead of Bradley, however, and not only won the highly publicized Iowa party caucuses in January 2000 but also took the prize in New Hampshire and by March chased Bradley out of the running. *Newsweek* commented that Gore had been "lucky to face a Democrat even less personable than himself."

Gore originally set up his campaign headquarters in Washington, D.C., but when it became apparent that his organization was top heavy with expensive consultants and was apparently bogged down in the political culture of the capital, Gore moved his headquarters to Nashville, Tennessee. He had named former U.S. official Tony Coelho as chief campaign manager but changed other staffers frequently during the early months of the campaign. At one point, in order to change his image, Gore dumped his trademark blue suits and began to appear in earth-toned knit shirts, and he tried to incorporate personal anecdotes into his speeches.

In May, President Clinton, who was mostly relegated to giving advice to his wife, Hillary Rodham Clinton, who was running for the U.S. Senate from New York, burst forth into the presidential campaign when he was quoted in the *New York Times* as criticizing Gore's strategy and organization. When this blow was coupled with polls that showed him badly trailing George W. Bush, son of the former president and presumptive G.O.P. nominee for president, Gore was motivated to shake up his campaign again. He fired Coelho and hired William Dailey, a former cabinet member and son of the famous Chicago mayor, as his new campaign manager, and almost the entire campaign was re-staffed and refocused during the slow summer weeks before the national conventions. The new strategy was to concentrate on Gore's experience and accomplishments before he became vice president and to sharpen the message about the nation's prosperity during Gore's time in the administration.

In early August, Gore took a bold step by naming Joseph Lieberman, a moderate Democratic senator from Connecticut, as his running mate. Lieberman was an Orthodox Jew—the first of his religion to be nominated to such a high post—and had been one of the most vocal Democrats in condemning President Clinton during the Lewinsky affair. Not only was Lieberman an animated speaker who gave renewed life to the campaign, but his selection helped Gore distance himself even further from the president. Gore neglected to inform Clinton of his choice before leaking the news to the press.

At the Democratic National Convention in Los Angeles, later in August, Gore made perhaps his biggest impact of the campaign. As he arrived on the speakers' platform to give his acceptance speech, he spontaneously embraced Tipper and gave her a prolonged, lusty kiss, which received cheers from the crowd and favorable media comment for weeks after. Overall, Gore came out of the convention with a much bigger bounce in the polls than expected—they showed him ahead of Bush by as much as ten points, which proved to be his high point.

During the weeks following the conventions, the rival candidates seemed to take turns fumbling. Bush in particular had trouble when speaking informally, and he often mangled the English language in ways that the television commentators and late-night comedians found irresistible. Gore was at the opposite end of the scale, still appearing stiff and unbending (a physical pose he adopted in part to deal with chronic back trouble) and criticizing and shaking up his campaign staff with frequent changes in advisers.

Gore also did surprisingly poorly during the three presidential debates in early October, by which time the polls showed the race to be a dead heat. He had long been a skilled debater—he had demolished Ross Perot on live television—and his staff hoped Gore could show up Bush as an inarticulate intellectual lightweight. During the first debate in Boston, however, Bush did well in his presentation, and Gore hurt his own performance by too audibly sighing and shaking his head while Bush was speaking. Gore also made two slim exaggerations about his record, which the Bush camp jumped on immediately. Since Gore had previously been caught making exaggerated claims, most famously that he "invented" the Internet, the new problems hurt.

Gore fared better during the second debate a few days later, although he may have overcompensated for his previous podium manner by retreating into his accustomed stiffness. The debate was overshadowed by affairs in the Mideast, where renewed violence between Palestinians and Israelis claimed the headlines and the evening news. The third debate, conducted in town meeting style, was inconclusive according to media pundits, but the poll numbers narrowed between Gore and Bush even further.

It became clear during the final weeks of the campaign that the race was too close to call ahead of time. The undecided voters would be the key: whichever way they leaned on Election Day would probably decide the winner. Although the polls showed Bush with a slight lead, it was within the pollsters' margin of error. At this stage, the fringe candidacy of Ralph Nader, a long-time consumer advocate and government gadfly who carried the banner of the Green Party, took on new significance, since most analysts—including those on Gore's staff—felt he would take votes from Gore. Both of the major candidates began to carefully calculate their chances in the large states with big numbers of electoral votes, since it appeared the final numbers would be close.

A few of his staff and consultants urged Gore to bring Clinton from under wraps and unleash his proven ability to mobilize black voters, a group that appeared to be crucial to victory, but in the end the vice president decided to keep Clinton away from the spotlight. Gore pushed himself mercilessly during the final days of the campaign, hopscotching from place to place and putting in incredibly long hours in an effort to swing the key states.

When Election Day finally arrived, everyone expected a close contest, but no one anticipated the prolonged drama that ensued.

As the returns began to come in on November 7 and were tabulated by the television networks, the closeness of the election became clear to all. What was unclear was who the winner was. The nation had grown accustomed to relying on television commentators to project winners in specific states, based on exit interviews at polling places and early returns, but this election completely confounded this process. All the networks fumbled and they began to waffle, awarding key states to either Gore or Bush and then taking them away. As the night wore on, the confusion become greater and greater.

By the last hours of Election Day, it appeared that the contest would be settled for whoever got the twenty-five electoral votes of Florida, where margins of victory seemed to be razor thin. Gore followed the returns from his headquarters in Nashville, and when the networks and his own staff decided at around 2:00 A.M. that Florida would go to Bush, Gore called his opponent and offered his concession. He then started in a motorcade toward Nashville's War Memorial Park to make his concession speech to a crowd of supporters who had been waiting through the rainy, cold night.

As the cars drove through the streets toward the memorial, however, Bill Dailey began to receive new reports from Florida that Bush's margin in the swing state—where the Republican candidate's brother, Jeb, was governor—was narrowing to the vanishing point. Dailey frantically called Gore on his cell phone and told him to stay away from the platform. When Gore and the campaign staff finally arrived at the park and conferred, Gore decided he should wait out the decision in Florida, and he then called Bush and rescinded his concession in a tense phone conversation.

As dawn broke the following day, one of the most dramatic stories in United States election history began to unfold, and the election process was "clouded by uncertainty" over who had won the electoral votes of Florida and would therefore become the next president.

It appeared that Bush had won by fewer than 300 votes out of a total of nearly 6 million cast in the state. However, there were reports of irregularities or at least confusion over thousands of votes in key counties, and thousands of overseas absentee ballots were still to arrive and be counted. Moreover, Florida state law called for recounts if an election was close, so the process of recounting the hand-punched ballots would be crucial.

In a rare occurrence, the margin of victory in a presidential election appeared to be smaller than the margin of error in the electoral process. Literally a handful of votes would make the difference, and the actual physical process of voting was too crude to accurately handle this margin.

Both Gore and Bush sent small armies of lawyers and advisers to Florida. Gore selected former secretary of state Warren Christopher to head his team. Christopher faced off against James Baker, himself a former cabinet officer and long-time political operative.

At first, machine recounts of disputed ballots narrowed Bush's lead even further but did not reverse the outcome. However, it was discovered that 19,000 ballots in Palm Beach County alone had been disqualified. The Gore campaign began immediately to demand hand recounts there and in other key counties, which were traditionally Democratic. To complicate matters further, although the elected state officers in Florida were Republicans, including Katherine Harris, the secretary of state, and the state legislature was controlled by the G.O.P., the local canvassing boards, which were charged under state law to conduct the manual recounts, were controlled by Democrats.

As the hand recounts began, in full view of the television cameras, the public came to know every permutation of the term *chad*, referring to the tiny rectangle of paper that was punched out by voters as a way to indicate their preferences. Since Florida recount law allowed recount canvassers to determine the intent of the voter, many chads that were partially punched (said to be "pregnant," "dimpled," or "hanging") were counted as votes after agonizing scrutiny by the canvassers.

It was soon evident that although Bush's lead was likely to increase when all the absentee ballots were in, the hand recounts in Democratic counties could well reverse the victory and give the state to Gore. As a result, Bush's campaign brought suit in federal court to stop the hand recounts. Gore's team countered with its own suits (joined by many individual Florida voters who brought suits of their own). Within days of the election, it appeared that the courts would play a significant role in deciding the election.

Two deadlines further complicated matters. Under a federal law, which had been passed in response to the contested 1876 election, if Florida's electoral votes were certified and submitted to Congress before December 12, then they could not be contested. The final deadline was December 18, when the electors around the country were due to cast their votes and actually elect a president.

Florida secretary of state Katherine Harris, who had close ties to the Bush camp, stepped forward a week after Election Day and announced that she was preparing to certify the state's election for Bush, based on his initial 300-vote lead. However, she was immediately placed under a court order restraining her from making arbitrary decisions about the official vote count. Two days later, the Florida Supreme Court, most of whose members were Democratic appointees, ruled that the hand counts should continue at all possible speed toward the deadline of December 12, but the court provided no guidelines for how to count partially punched ballots.

More potential constitutional and legal complexities were raised when the leaders of the Republican state legislature announced plans to convene and select its own slate of electors, without regard to the balloting, which appeared on the face of it to be constitutionally possible.

After more give and take, and the entry of an appeal to the United State Supreme Court by the Bush campaign to vacate the Florida Supreme Court's rulings, Katherine Harris certified the Bush victory on November 26, giving a total margin of 537 votes. Four days later, the Florida legislature called a special session. At this stage there were more than forty-five lawsuits in the Florida courts concerning the election. On December 8, the state supreme court ordered a massive hand recount of 45,000 votes, which when begun started to whittle down Bush's tally, rapidly approaching a reversal of the election totals. The recount was halted, however, by the U.S. Supreme Court, which agreed to hear arguments and make a final ruling.

On December 12, the justices of the United States Supreme Court voted five to four to overturn the rulings of the Florida Supreme Court, and, since there was no time for the recount procedure to be redefined and begun again, the Court's ruling effectively awarded the election in Florida, and therefore the presidency, to Bush, marking the only time the Supreme Court decided a national presidential election.

Gore, forced to accept defeat by the Court, finally conceded the election to George W. Bush and adopted a gracious and dignified demeanor. He was the overall winner of the national popular vote by more than half a million votes, but he fell four electoral votes short of the required majority. Gore thus became the fourth presidential candidate in U. S. history to win more votes than his opponent but still lose the election. He had roughly 49 percent of the vote to Bush's 48.

Gore had the unenviable duty of presiding over a joint session of Congress that tallied the electoral votes. He received 266 to Bush's 271. An elector from the District of Columbia withheld her vote as a protest against the district's lack of congressional representation.

On inauguration day, a month later, Gore left office and became a private citizen for the first time in nearly twenty-five years. His future remained undefined for the time being, although he announced in a January 24, 2001, interview that he planned to teach at three universities—Middle Tennessee State, Fisk, and Columbia—and work with Tipper to write a book.

REFERENCES

David Maraniss and Ellen Nakashima, *The Prince of Tennessee: The Rise of Al Gore* (New York: Simon & Schuster, 2000); Bill Turque, *Inventing Al Gore: A Biography* (Boston: Houghton Mifflin, 2000); Bob Zelnick, *Gore: A Political Life* (Washington, D.C.: Regnery Publishing Company, 1999); Hank Hillen, *Al Gore, Jr.: His Life and Career* (New York: Carol Publishing Group, 1992); Betty Burford, *Al Gore: United States Vice President* (Hillside, N.J.: Enslow Publishers, Inc., 1994); *Biography of Vice President Al Gore*, Press Office, Vice President of the United States; Peter J. Boyer, "The Political Scene: Gore's Dilemma," *The New Yorker*, November 28. 1994, 101–10; Kenneth T. Walsh, "A Vice President Who Counts," *U.S. News and World Report*, July 19, 1993, 29–33; Bill Turque, "The Three Faces of Al Gore," *Newsweek*, July 20, 1992, 30–31; Walter Shapiro, "Gore: A Hard Won Sense of Ease," *Time*, July 20, 1992, 28-29.

SCOTT W. RAGER is a historian of U.S. politics and of congressional development who received his Ph.D. from the University of Illinois in 1991. His main research focus has been on Joseph Gurney Cannon, Speaker of the U.S. House from 1903 to 1911. He is a contributor to a forthcoming book on leadership in the House of Representatives sponsored by the Everett McKinley Dirksen Center. Rager has also taught history at several midwestern colleges and universities.

RICHARD B. CHENEY
(©AFP/CORBIS)

By L. Edward Purcell

$\mathcal{R}$ichard Cheney came to the vice presidency as dency as part of a ticket that won office with half a million fewer votes than its opposition and only by virtue of a split decision of the United States Supreme Court that awarded Cheney and his running mate, George W. Bush, one of the most disputed elections in American history. Nonetheless, Cheney was widely perceived, even by his enemies, as a man with a sterling résumé and qualifications whose term as vice president might well be one of the most significant in the history of the office.

Cheney had a long career in government and high office in Washington, D.C., before his selection as Bush's running mate, and he moved to his new position directly from a Fortune 500 oil services company that he had taken to new heights of prosperity, yet he came from quite ordinary, if not to say humble, origins and was almost the antithesis of Bush, who had been born into a political family that was financially well off.

The forty-sixth vice president was born in Lincoln, Nebraska, the eldest of three children.

His parents were native Nebraskans. His father was a soil conservation agent for the U.S. Department of Agriculture. The family lived on a pleasant dead-end street that provided Cheney with a childhood playground.

When Cheney was twelve or thirteen (accounts vary), the family moved to the oil-boom town of Casper, Wyoming. There he entered high school, where he excelled in football, becoming captain of the team despite his short stature and light build, and met his future wife, Lynn Vincent, who was a baton twirler and homecoming queen. Cheney traced his life-long love of the outdoors to his adolescence spent hunting and fishing in Wyoming.

Even as a boy, Cheney impressed people with his seriousness and purposefulness. He was capable of boyish pranks but was regarded by his classmates as someone destined for high achievement. One companion later said: "He was decent and everything, not serious but earnest, just straight as a die, just true."

In fall 1959, after graduating from high school in Casper, Cheney traveled to the East Coast to take up a scholarship he had won to Yale University. Unfortunately, he was unhappy at the Ivy League school and soon flunked out. He commented later in life that "I had a lack of direction, but I had a good time."

Cheney returned to Casper and worked for a while as a lineman for the local utility company, but his romantic relationship with Lynn spurred him to return to school. She was herself an exceptional student, and Cheney concluded that she would never be happy married to him if he neglected his education. He attended Casper Community College for one semester and then enrolled at the University of Wyoming, where he settled down to serious work. He and Lynn were married in August 1964, and he received his bachelor's degree at the end of the following school year. He stayed at the university for another year, earning a master's degree.

In 1966, the couple moved to Madison, Wisconsin, and entered graduate school, Dick in a Ph.D. program in political science and Lynn in British literature.

Cheney—a future secretary of defense—avoided service in the Vietnam War through a series of student deferments, although he was reclassified in mid-1964 into the top category and was probably close to being drafted when Lynn gave birth to the couple's first child, Elizabeth, in 1966. As a father, Cheney received an additional deferment that lasted until he reached the age of twenty-six and passed out of the draft pool. When quizzed in later life about his deferments, Cheney maintained that he would have served if called up.

In 1968, Cheney interrupted his Ph.D. program—his dissertation on various models of roll-call voting remained unfinished (Lynn got her degree, however)—and moved to Washington, D.C., for a one-year internship sponsored by the American Political Science Association. He never resumed academic pursuits but instead began a government career that had a steep upward spiral.

While an intern, Cheney wrote a memo that caught the attention of Donald Rumsfeld, a U.S. representative from Illinois. Cheney was soon on Rumsfeld's staff and moved along with his mentor when Rumsfeld became director of the Office of Economic Opportunity under President Richard Nixon. Within a year, Cheney was a staff assistant in the White House and eventually was appointed as assistant director of the Cost of Living Council.

Despite its rapid rise, Cheney's career was short-circuited for a time by the Watergate scandal and the collapse of the Nixon administration. In 1973, Cheney took a job with a Washington, D.C., investment firm, where he forged the beginnings of his personal fortune and waited out the end of the Watergate drama. After Nixon's resignation, Cheney returned to government service as staff assistant and head of the transition team for Gerald Ford, the new president. In late 1975, Cheney became Ford's chief of staff (replacing Rumsfeld, who moved on to become secretary of defense), one of the youngest people ever to hold that position.

When Ford lost to Democrat Jimmie Carter in the election of 1976, Cheney, who had been at the center of Ford's campaign and received some of the blame for the Republican candidate's narrow defeat, returned to Wyoming. The thinly populated state had only a single U.S. representative, so the political opportunities of the position for someone of Cheney's precocious record were limited; however, the Democrat who held the office decided to retire, and Cheney entered the race.

During the primary campaign, Cheney suffered the first of three heart attacks, a serious event for someone only thirty-seven years old. The attack proved to be relatively mild, but Cheney was forced to the sidelines to recuperate for nearly six weeks, although with the help of a California ad agency, he cleverly turned the episode into a campaign positive by stressing the philosophical maturity he had gained during his brush with mortality. Despite charges that he was a carpetbagger, having been absent from the state for so long, Cheney easily defeated his Republican primary opponent and won the general election in a landslide, claiming the first of what proved to be five terms in the U.S. House.

Cheney's record in Congress was a model of consistency. He predictably voted on the conservative side of almost every issue, opposing abortion rights for women and voting against welfare, for example. He won a very high rating from the American Conservative Union and one of the lowest possible scores from the liberal Americans for Democratic Action, although he eventually joined the moderates on environmental policy when parts of Wyoming were threatened by development under Reagan's secretary of interior James Watt.

Shortly after arriving in the House, Cheney resumed his rise to higher office when he became Republican minority whip. By all accounts he handed his duties with an effective combination of firmness and low-key charm that contrasted sharply with some of the G.O.P.'s subsequent whips, such as Newt Gingrich. Cheney kept the party's troops in line, but he made few enemies and many admirers, although he was reported to be extremely tough in private when facing down the opposition.

While in Congress, Cheney suffered two more heart attacks, in 1984 and again in 1988.

After the third attack, he underwent quadruple bypass surgery and appeared to enjoy a full recovery, although as the years went on, the repairs grafted to the arteries of his heart could be assumed to start to wear out.

Meanwhile, Lynn Cheney forged an enviable Washington career of her own, being appointed by President Reagan in 1986 to become chairperson of the National Endowment for the Humanities, a post she served in until the end of the Bush administration in 1993. She and Dick also collaborated on a study of congressional leaders, published as *Kings of the Hill: How Nine Powerful Men Changed the Course of American History* (a book that was reissued in paperback in 2000 shortly before Dick was nominated for the vice presidency).

In 1989, Cheney returned to the administrative side of government when President George Bush nominated him as secretary of defense. Cheney was Bush's second choice, after the Senate turned down Senator John Tower, a notoriously heavy drinker, but the selection proved to be sound. Cheney, although not a veteran of military service himself, immediately took hold of the job, studying assiduously and bringing to office his capacity for hard work and skillful management. With his background in Congress, Cheney proved to be an effective spokesperson for the administration's proposals to expand military spending for expensive programs such as the B-2 Stealth bomber. He also oversaw the planning and execution of the American incursion into Panama to oust dictator Manuel Noriega.

Cheney's grandest moments, however, came in 1990 and 1991, when the United States and its allies carried on the biggest military operation since the Vietnam War. When Iraqi dictator Saddam Hussein invaded oil-rich neighbor Kuwait in August 1990, he threatened the oil supply of the West and appeared poised to roll on down the Arabian Peninsula into Saudi Arabia—the United States's closest ally in the region. President Bush immediately declared that the United States would resist the incursions, and while the president set about forging an alliance against Iraq and galvanizing support in the United Nations, Secretary Cheney began to mobilize American ground, air, and naval forces to descend on the region. Four days after Hussein's move across the border of Kuwait, Cheney flew to Saudi Arabia and met with King Fahd, persuading the Saudis to accept the presence of tens of thousands of American troops on Saudi soil and to fight alongside the Western allies against a fellow Arab state.

Over the following months, Cheney and his handpicked head of the Joint Chiefs of Staff, General Colin Powell, organized and helped plan a campaign to reclaim Kuwait and defeat Saddam Hussein, even though the Iraqis had what appeared on paper to be a large and powerful army and a significant air force. The American plan was to build up a large force in the Gulf region as rapidly as possible and then launch a massive air attack on Iraq, followed by a ground assault across the desert.

The air assault began in January 1991, news of which was dramatically brought to the American public by live reports from Baghdad by CNN correspondents who described the first-night bombing runs by American warplanes. Over the following days, the war plans engineered in part by Cheney appeared to be moving toward a huge success, despite Iraqi missile attacks on Israel (Cheney helped quell Israel's desire for direct retaliation). A sanitized version of the war played out each night on U.S. television. When the ground assault was launched in February, the allied forces rapidly overran Iraqi positions and swept around the main Iraqi force in a giant flanking maneuver. Tens of thousands of Iraqi soldiers were killed on the "Highway of Death" while trying to escape from Kuwait.

Cheney's role in what was called Operation Desert Storm brought him into the limelight and raised his public stock extremely high, along with Colin Powell and General Norman Schwartzkopf, the crusty theater commander. Despite some nagging criticism that the ground attack was called off too soon before ousting Hussein from power, the Gulf War marked a high point of popularity for the Bush administration in general.

The fall from power was, therefore, all the more difficult when President George Bush was defeated in the national election of 1992 by the Democratic team of Bill Clinton and Al Gore.

Cheney was suddenly out of office. He remained in Washington for a time, working as a senior fellow at the American Enterprise Institute, a conservative think-tank, along with Lynn. In 1995, the couple moved to Dallas, Texas, and Dick became chief executive of Halliburton Company, which provides engineering and construction services to oil-industry clients worldwide. Halliburton prospered under Cheney's leadership, expanding its share of the market (it acquired one of its main rivals along the way) and increasing annual revenues. Cheney's salary and stock options made him a very wealthy man over the course of the five years he was head of Halliburton. He also served on the corporate boards of such large companies as Union Pacific, Electronic Data Services, and Proctor and Gamble.

Despite his sojourn in private life, Cheney kept open his many channels of influence among his old colleagues and associates in Washington and from the first Bush administration. As Bush's son George W. Bush, who was governor of Texas and also a former oil industry executive, began to assemble advisers for a run at the Republican nomination for president in 2000, Cheney was drawn into the campaign. After George W. Bush defeated his main Republican opponent, Senator John McCain of Arizona, in the spring primaries, he asked Dick Cheney to head the search for a vice presidential candidate.

After two months of looking for potential running mates for Bush, Cheney finally decided to consider the post for himself, despite his pledge to the Halliburton board that he would not be a candidate.

In mid-July, Cheney signaled that he would be Bush's choice by changing his voter registration back to Wyoming, where he had not lived for decades but where he still owned a vacation home. The Twelfth Amendment to the U.S. Constitution bars a state's electors from voting for both presidential and vice presidential candidates from their state, so in order to not risk losing the thirty-two electoral votes from Texas, Cheney and Bush had to appear to be from different states.

A few days later, Bush announced Cheney's selection for the G.O.P. ticket.

The choice was greeted by the nearly universal opinion that Cheney would bring a wealth of high-level experience and seriousness to the ticket—elements that Bush seemed to lack—but that he was too stolid and boring to enliven the campaign. It was clear that Bush had decided to forgo a running mate who would be a vigorous campaigner in favor of someone whom he could rely on for advice and who could be trusted to carry out even the heftiest assignments. It was widely commented that Cheney would supply "gravitas" to the G.O.P. ticket. Cheney's connection to George W. Bush's father's administration was another plus, since in a real sense the younger Bush was hoping to redeem the loss his father suffered at the hands of the Democrats in 1992.

Questions were raised almost immediately about Cheney's history of heart problems, but the Bush-Cheney campaign got famed Texas heart surgeon Denton Cooley to testify to Cheney's good health, based on a call by Cooley to Cheney's doctor.

Cheney proved to be—as predicted—a very low-key campaigner for the most part. He appeared less than completely comfortable at times when giving speeches, but he was direct and effective in meeting people and discussing issues. His opposite number, Connecticut Senator Joe Lieberman, chosen as Al Gore's running mate, was an ebullient figure to whom the news media gave much favorable attention, contrasting the rather somber Cheney to the lively Lieberman.

However, when the two vice presidential candidates met for a televised debate in October, Cheney's strong points and depth of background and character were prominently displayed. The debate was a friendly, unstructured, sit-down encounter between Lieberman and Cheney, and they covered a great deal of substance and displayed considerable knowledge. Both candidates demonstrated intelligence and wit. Several pundits expressed the opinion after the debate that the two vice presidential candidates were more impressive than the figures at the head of their respective tickets.

Cheney suffered a few distressing moments during the campaign, when the news media brought up unpleasantries such as his arrest in the 1960s for drunken driving (a particularly sensitive issue since George W. Bush openly admitted to a serious drinking problem during his younger days), the fact that he had failed to vote during most of the previous two decades, and his earlier admission that he passed a series of bad checks through the notorious Capitol bank when he was a congressman. He was also attacked for the $13 million dollar retirement package he stood to receive from Halliburton and his contrastingly puny charitable contributions during his years in private life. On the whole, however, the media gave Cheney almost a free pass on personal issues.

During the confused and contentious period following the election (see the entry on Al Gore for a detailed narrative of the election dispute), Cheney initially stayed out of public view. Bush assigned him the major task of overseeing a potential transition of power, and Cheney spent most of his time organizing for what he hoped would eventually become the Bush-Cheney administration. His efforts to deal with the monumental tasks of transition were made difficult, of course, by the decreasing amount of time available between a conclusion to the election and the inauguration.

On the morning before Thanksgiving, Cheney awoke early with chest pains. Lynn rushed him to a Washington, D.C., hospital, where the first tests were negative, but follow-ups showed he had experienced a slight heart attack. His doctors performed an angioplasty and inserted a stent (a small device designed to reinforce arteries) to ease the flow of blood to Cheney's heart.

At first, Bush, who may simply have been ill-informed at that early stage, denied that Cheney had a heart attack, but within hours, the campaign issued a full statement.

Luckily, Cheney recovered rapidly from the episode, and within a few days of leaving the hospital appeared to be back to business, although vowing to follow his doctor's advice.

As the election dispute over Florida's crucial electoral votes wound to a conclusion before the U.S. Supreme Court, Cheney's value to the Bush administration—already thought by some to be virtually on the level of a prime minister, owing to Bush's inexperience—grew even greater when an extremely close election recount in Oregon's senatorial race resulted in an even split among Republicans and Democrats in the U.S. Senate. The only constitutional duty of any vice president, that of presiding over the Senate, which during most of U.S. history has been purely ceremonial, suddenly became crucial to the Republican Party's control. In the event of a fifty-fifty tie on any issue, Cheney would have cast the deciding vote.

As he assumed office on January 20, 2001, alongside President George W. Bush, having already been instrumental in the transition and in bringing Colin Powell and Donald Rumsfeld into the new cabinet, Cheney appeared poised to become one of the nation's most important vice presidents ever.

REFERENCES

As this book went to press in early 2001, Richard Cheney has yet to find a biographer. His life and career must be pieced together from newspaper accounts and profiles, many of which were published during the 2000 campaign and the extended election. The best general coverage may be found in the pages and on the web sites of the *New York Times* (http://www.nytimes.com) and the *Washington Post* (http://www.washingtonpost.com) and the web site of the Associated Press (http://dailynews.yahoo.com). Also useful were articles based on broadcast news reporting and found on the web sites of CNN (http://www.cnn.com) and CBS News (http://www.cbsnews.com). Other specific news articles of interest are Carla Marinucci, "Cheney Seen as Possible VP for Bush," *The San Francisco Chronicle*, July 22, 2000, p. A1; Glen Johnson, "Campaign 2000/ Profile," *The Boston Globe*, July 26, 2000, p. A12; Michael Kranish, "Cheney's Low-Key Style," *The Boston Globe*, September 10, 2000, p. A1; Michael Cooper, "Cheney, After a Slow Start, Warms to Campaign Role," *The New York Times*, November 5, 2000, p. 33; and Jodi Enda, "Cheney May Be Most Powerful VP Yet," Knight Ridder Washington Bureau, December 27, 2000 (published in various Knight Ridder papers).

L. EDWARD PURCELL, a historian, is the author, coauthor, or editor of 15 books, including Facts On File's *Who Was Who in the American Revolution* and *Encyclopedia of Battles in North America*. Purcell holds history degrees from Simpson College and the University of Iowa. He was previously editor in chief of publications at the Iowa State Historical Society. He has taught history at several colleges and universities, most recently at Drake University in Des Moines, Iowa, and his journalism has been nationally syndicated.

APPENDICES

1774

September–October
The First Continental Congress, with representatives from all the American colonies except Georgia, meets in Philadelphia to discuss grievances with Great Britain.

1775

April
American militiamen at Lexington and Concord in Massachusetts clash with British regulars, setting off six years of warfare.

May
The Second Continental Congress convenes in Philadelphia and takes responsibility for fighting the war and serving loosely as a central government for what become the thirteen states. The body becomes the Confederation Congress in 1781 with the adoption of the Articles of Confederation and remains in existence until superseded by the first U.S. Congress in 1789.

1776

July
Congress adopts the Declaration of Independence.

1781

March
The Articles of Confederation, first proposed in 1775, finally go into effect, thereby establishing a new form of government for the United States.

October
Commander in chief George Washington forces the surrender of the British army commanded by Lord Cornwallis at Yorktown, Virginia, bringing

to an end most of the actual fighting, although the treaty-making process drags on for two more years.

1783

April
Congress ratifies the treaty of peace with Great Britain; the treaty is not signed officially until September, ending the Revolutionary War.

1785

May
Congress passes the Land Ordinance that specifies how public land is to be sold to the public. The law calls for a survey of land into rectilinear townships and sections, which are then to be sold in 640-acre lots at $1 an acre. Specific size and price of lots are changed frequently in future decades, but the principles and procedures of selling public land follow this precedent.

1786

September
Armed malcontents, led by former Revolutionary War officer Daniel Shays, confront state militia near Springfield, Massachusetts, setting off widespread fears of civil insurrection and a crisis of confidence in the government of the Confederation. Shays's Rebellion, as it is known, is eventually put down by federal troops in February of the following year.

1787

May–September
Delegates from the states (Rhode Island is missing) assemble in Philadelphia to consider revising the form of national government. The result is

the Constitution of the United States. The new plan calls for a national executive consisting of a president and a vice president to be chosen by electors from the states. The candidate receiving the highest number of electoral votes will be president and the second highest will be vice president. The duties of the vice president are to succeed to the presidency on the death, resignation, or removal of the president and to preside as president of the Senate, one of the two bodies of the new U.S. Congress.

July

The Confederation Congress gives final approval to the Northwest Ordinance, one of its greatest accomplishments. The law sets forth the steps and requirements for admitting new states to the Union from the Old Northwest Territory (the modern states of Ohio, Indiana, and Illinois) and provides a blueprint for further political expansion.

October

The proposed Constitution is submitted to the state legislatures for ratification. Nine of the thirteen states must approve if the plan is to go into effect, and a political struggle ensues in several key states during the following months.

1788

June–July

The Constitution is officially ratified with the approval of New Hampshire in June, but success of the new government is not assured until the Virginia and New York legislatures concur a month later.

1789

February

Electors chosen by the states (in a variety of ways) cast their votes for president and vice president.

April

The new U.S. Senate meets in New York City (the temporary capital) and counts the electoral votes: George Washington is elected as the first president with 69 votes; John Adams is vice president with 34. Adams arrives in New York before Washington and takes his oath of office on April 21. Washington is inaugurated on April 30. He chooses Thomas Jefferson of Virginia as his first secretary of state; Alexander Hamilton of New York is secretary of the Treasury.

1790

June

A site for the new national capital is chosen in northern Virginia on the Potomac River; meanwhile, the government will convene in Philadelphia, to which it moves in December.

1791

December

The first ten amendments to the Constitution, known as the Bill of Rights, are ratified and go into effect. Several states insisted that such a list of rights be added before they agreed to ratify the new form of government.

1792

February

Congress passes the first of several Succession Acts, which specify who will ascend to the presidency if both the president and vice president die, resign, or are removed from office. Neither this law, which puts the president pro tem of the Senate and the Speaker of the House in line, nor subsequent laws alter the vice president's first right of succession.

October

The cornerstone of the White House is laid in Washington, D.C.

November

The second national election for president and vice president is held. When the votes are counted a month later, Washington again wins with 132 votes, with Adams repeating as vice president with 77.

1793

April

"Citizen" Edmond Genêt arrives as the minister from the revolutionary government of France. His presence galvanizes the developing political parties in the United States, with the Jefferson-Madison Democratic Republicans enthused about the French Revolution and the Hamilton-Adams Federalists distrustful and anxious. Genet's silly behavior and offenses toward Washington over the summer months discredit him and his cause. He is recalled in August but seeks political asylum in the United States, eventually marrying future vice president George Clinton's daughter.

1794

August–November

Farmers in western Pennsylvania stage violent protests against the federal tax on whiskey. Washington counters the so-called Whiskey Rebellion with a show of force, and the protesters back down.

November

John Jay, chief justice of the Supreme Court, concludes a treaty with Great Britain that attempts to settle American and British claims arising from the Revolution, as well as several other issues such as the closing of British posts in the Old Northwest. The treaty becomes a controversial political issue when its provisions are made public several months later. It is narrowly ratified by Congress in June of the following year but continues to divide the country.

1796

February

France is outraged at the provisions of the Jay Treaty between the United States and Great Britain and brings relations with the United States almost to the point of war. During the following months, there will be armed conflict at sea between ships of the two countries.

May

A new Land Act establishes a system by which public land can be bought on credit at auction. The minimum price set is high enough to eliminate many potential small buyers.

September

Washington issues his Farewell Address, signaling his withdrawal from public life.

December

John Adams, a Federalist and the sitting vice president, wins the national election for president with seventy-one electoral votes. His rival, Thomas Jefferson, comes in second with sixty-eight votes and thereby becomes vice president, although of the opposing party from the new president. Several others receive electoral votes, including Federalist Thomas Pinckney, who is only nine votes behind Jefferson.

1797

March

Adams and Jefferson are inaugurated. The Constitution calls for this long interval between election and taking office, which has potential for causing problems if and when the office of president changes hands from one party to the next. The original framers of the Constitution did not foresee the formation of parties and have made no allowance for them or the conflict they imply.

October

Three U.S. diplomats, Charles C. Pinckney, Elbridge Gerry, and John Marshall, arrive in Paris on a mission to patch up differences with the French and conclude a peace treaty. Instead, French foreign minister Talleyrand attempts to extort nearly a quarter-million-dollar bribe before opening negotiations. The incident becomes known as the XYZ Affair, after the pseudonyms of the three French agents sent by Talleyrand with the demand for money. Pinckney and Marshall return to the United States, but Gerry is forced to stay. Americans are outraged when the affair is reported.

1798

May

The United States and France enter a period of active but undeclared war known as the Quasi War. President Adams has overseen a build up of American naval forces and is authorized by Congress to raise a new army and to have U.S. warships capture French naval vessels if they attempt to stop U.S. shipping.

June–July

The Federalists use the Quasi War as an excuse to pass a series of Alien and Sedition Acts, aimed at stifling government critics from the opposing Democratic-Republican Party. Several politicians and journalists are arrested and jailed under the repressive laws, but in the end, the measures backfire and turn voters against the Federalists.

1799

December

George Washington dies at Mt. Vernon and is mourned by the entire nation.

1800

April–May

Candidates for president and vice president are chosen by congressional party caucuses. Incumbent John Adams will run again as the Federalist candidate with Charles C. Pinckney as his running mate. The Democratic Republicans nominate Thomas Jefferson for president and Aaron Burr for vice president.

May

President Adams recognizes that some of his cabinet members are secretly working against him in conjunction with Alexander Hamilton. He dismisses several disloyal officers but loses the broad support of his Federalist Party, in part because he works toward peace with France.

November

The government leaves Philadelphia for the new capital of Washington City on the Potomac, where John and Abagail move into the president's residence, later known as the White House.

1801

February

The presidential electoral ballots, cast the previous December, are finally counted, resulting in a potential political catastrophe. Thomas Jefferson and Aaron Burr have tied with 73 votes each. It was intended that some Democratic–Republican electors refrain from voting for Burr, thereby making him vice president, but there has been a slip-up. To Jefferson's consternation, Burr sees a chance to achieve his ambition to become president, and he refuses to concede to Jefferson. The contested election is thrown into the House of Representatives, which is controlled by Jefferson's Federalist enemies. After a prolonged deadlock, some Federalists decide that Jefferson is the lesser evil and swing enough votes to make him president. The affair reveals a major defect in the electoral system.

1801

March

Jefferson and Burr are inaugurated in Washington City, the new national capital.

1802

February

Congress appropriates funds to arm U.S. vessels in the Mediterranean Sea against the pirate nation of Tripoli. The United States has paid tribute to pirate kingdoms along the Barbary coast of North Africa for several years, but the Pasha of Tripoli has declared war. The conflicts with the pirate states will continue off and on for many years—the current war with Tripoli drags on until 1805—and the problems are not settled until 1815 when U.S. naval hero Stephen Decatur defeats Algiers, Tunis, and Tripoli and secures American rights.

1803

May

American envoys in Paris agree to a treaty with France that will transfer a huge area west of the Mississippi River to the United States. The French offer to sell the land has come as a surprise, but President Jefferson seizes the opportunity. In exchange for about $15 million, the United States acquires a region between the river and the Rocky Mountains that eventually will be carved into thirteen states. The Louisiana Purchase is the largest and most significant single act of expansion in American history. The Senate approves the purchase in October.

August

An expedition put afoot by Jefferson and led by Meriweather Lewis and William Clark sets off to explore a route across the newly acquired Louisiana Purchase to the Pacific Ocean.

December

Congress passes the Twelfth Amendment, which alters the flawed presidential electoral process. The new amendment calls for presidential and vice-presidential candidates to run as a paired ticket, with separate electoral votes for each office. No longer will the vice president be elected by the second-highest number of votes for president, thereby eliminating the possibility of a repeat of the Aaron Burr–Thomas Jefferson conflict that arose after the election of 1800. Final ratification of the change will come from the states in the fall of 1804.

1804

February

Democratic–Republican members of Congress meet in a caucus to nominate candidates. They pick Jefferson to run for a second term and replace Burr with veteran New York governor George Clinton.

July

Vice President Aaron Burr has lost a bid for the governorship of New York State, and he blames the opposition of former Secretary of the Treasury Alexander Hamilton, who is the leader of the Federalist Party. Burr challenges Hamilton to a duel. When the two meet at Weehawken, New Jersey, the Vice President shoots his opponent dead and is forced to flee arrest warrants in New York and New Jersey. Later in the year, he resumes his place in Washington as president of the Senate, despite the warrants.

December

The Democratic–Republican ticket of Jefferson and Clinton smashes the Federalist candidates, Charles Cotesworth Pinckney and Rufus King, taking the presidency and vice presidency by a margin of 162 electoral votes to 14.

1805

March

Jefferson is inaugurated for a second term; Clinton for his first.

1806

January

When Secretary of State James Madison reports to Congress on the British practice of impressment—stopping U.S. merchant ships and forcibly recruiting sailors—he draws attention to what has been and will continue to be a long-term source of conflict between the two nations. The struggle over impressment and the right of free passage at sea will continue for several years and eventually become a major reason for the War of 1812.

1807

February

Former Vice President Aaron Burr is arrested in Alabama and charged with a conspiracy to attack Spanish territory in the West in order to form an independent nation. His murky motives seem nefarious, and he is eventually indicted in Virginia on a federal charge of treason. He is acquitted in September at a trial presided over by U.S. Chief Justice John Marshall, and he escapes prosecution on the old charges of murdering Hamilton by sailing to Europe.

December

At the request of President Jefferson, Congress passes the Embargo Act, which makes it illegal for Americans to trade with foreign nations or to sail ships to foreign ports. Jefferson hopes thereby to avoid further conflict over freedom of the seas and impressment and at the same time to stimulate regional U.S. manufacturing. The result, however, is an economic disaster for the United States. Mercantile states of the Northeast are particularly hard hit.

1808

January

The African slave trade is finally banned by law. The Constitution had contained a provision that stalled ending the trade until this year. Slavery itself, of course, remains legal in all the southern states; most northern states eliminated it during or soon after the Revolution.

December

A complex political situation develops over the question of who will succeed Jefferson as president. The Democratic–Republican congressional caucus has nominated James Madison (with Jefferson's blessing) for president and renominated Vice President George Clinton. However, a separate faction opposes the southern leadership of the party, and it nominates Clinton for president, making him simultaneously the running mate of Madison and one of his chief opponents. The Federalists again put up Charles Cotesworth Pinckney and Rufus King. Madison easily wins the presidency, although Clinton gets a few electoral votes for the top office. By a margin of 113 to 47, Clinton is elected as vice president for a second term, once again beating King.

1810–1811

In a series of confusing events, the British and French pass conflicting and devious regulations about trade and seizures of American ships. The United States responds with aggressive stances against first one and then the other. Deceived by the French, the U.S. government finally focuses on a policy of nonintercourse with the British, which brings on increased conflict and confrontation.

1811

November

A new generation of politicians, known as War Hawks, takes over control of Congress and begins to press for war against Great Britain. John C. Calhoun of South Carolina and Henry Clay of Kentucky are leaders of the war faction.

1812

April

Vice President George Clinton dies in Washington, D.C.

May

Democratic–Republican congressmen from the southern states caucus and renominate Madison for president and choose John Langdon for vice president, but Langdon refuses and the vice-presidential nomination then goes to Elbridge Gerry. Dissident, antiwar Democratic-Republicans in the North nominate DeWitt Clinton for president with the backing of the waning Federalists. The Federalists put up Jared Ingersoll for vice president.

June

The United States declares war on Great Britain. Ironically, the British government rescinds its aggressive policy on the high seas, which is the pretext for the American declaration of war, before Congress acts, but the news fails to reach the United States in time. Western and southern states enthusiastically support the war, but almost all of New England is bitterly opposed. The country has a difficult time recruiting an army (many state militia units refuse to fight outside their state boundaries) and leadership is for the most part dismal. Even though the British are distracted by their prolonged war against Napoleon, they nonetheless succeed in almost all the land campaigns against the Americans. Only at sea do U.S. forces enjoy repeated victories, including the destruction of a British frigate in August by the USS *Constitution* ("Old Ironsides").

December

Madison wins a second term as president by defeating DeWitt Clinton. Gerry wins the vice presidency, actually garnering more electoral votes than Madison due to the split in the Democratic–Republican Party over the war.

1813

April

After a series of defeats, the U.S. land forces finally have some success and momentarily capture the city of York in Canada (now Toronto). They burn the government buildings and then retreat.

September

British victories during the summer are to a degree negated by Commodore Oliver Hazard Perry's naval victory on Lake Erie. He sends the message: "We have met the enemy and they are ours." Three weeks later, General William Henry Harrison defeats the British and their Indian allies at the Battle of the Thames.

1814

August

With resources freed by the temporary defeat of Napoleon, the British launch a reenvigorated campaign to win the war in America. They invade Maryland and defeat the American army at Bladesburg. President Madison and the U.S. government flee Washington as the British advance. Temporarily taking control of the city, the British burn the Capitol and White House, although neither are destroyed. The British withdraw after a few days, and Madison returns to Washington.

September

The British attack Baltimore from the sea, but are beaten back after bombarding Fort McHenry

with rockets and artillery, inspiring "The Star Spangled Banner."

November

Vice President Elbridge Gerry dies in Washington, D.C., becoming the second consecutive vice president to die in office.

December

American and British peace commissioners in Europe sign a treaty ending the war, but news of the peace travels slowly.

1815

January

Unaware that the war is officially over, a British army attacks American forces outside New Orleans. The Americans inflict a terrible defeat on the British, killing or wounding more than 2,000, while suffering only eight dead themselves. U.S. general Andrew Jackson emerges as the nation's greatest military hero, even though the battle was pointless.

1816

March

After considerable debate, Congress charters the second Bank of the United States as a quasi-public, quasi-private financial institution to help regulate the national currency and to some degree allow control of aspects of the economy. It is a controversial creation, seen by some in American society as a satanic device used by the rich class to keep the common man down. Others see the bank as necessary for financial order, although it usually favors the property-holding portions of society. The bank will frequently be at the center of political controversy over the next twenty years.

March

The Democratic-Republicans nominate Secretary of State James Monroe for president through the congressional caucus system. Daniel Tompkins of New York, a strong wartime governor, is selected as his running mate. The Federalists, their days in American politics nearly at an end, nominate old reliable Rufus King for president and John Howard for vice president.

December

Monroe and Tompkins win with 183 electoral votes.

1819

January

The nation is hit with a severe economic crash (known in the nineteenth century as a panic) when Congress passes a law restricting credit. Many in the West and South have gone into debt to buy land, and the panic hits them hard. By year's end, many Americans have lost everything. This is only the first in what proves to be a recurring series of financial panics.

1820

February–March

As the United States expands westward, the central divisive question of slavery pushes itself forward onto the national agenda. The slave South wants to take slavery into the new territories; the North wants the new regions to be free. At stake is the essence of what the United States will become and adherents on each side will find it increasingly difficult to compromise. In 1820, however, when the admission of Maine into the Union as a free state is at issue, opponents manage to work out a trade-off by admitting Missouri as a slave state, thus maintaining the national political balance for the time being. The law also bans slavery north of latitude 36 degrees 30 minutes (the Missouri border).

December

Monroe and Tompkins run for reelection virtually unopposed because the Federalists opposition has collapsed and no new party has formed to take its place. Monroe wins with 231 electoral votes to just 1 for Massachusetts's John Quincy Adams (son of former president John Adams).

1822

May

Denmark Vesey, a free black man, plots an uprising of black slaves in South Carolina, but the plan is foiled before it gets off the ground. Vesey and thirty-four others are executed. Revelation of the plan frightens white slaveholders who begin to build an even more repressive legal system to lock blacks into slavery. More uprisings, many involving considerable bloodshed, continue over the next four decades, and southern white response is increasingly harsh and preemptory.

July

War hero Andrew Jackson is nominated for the presidency in 1824 by his home state legislature in Tennessee. The old system of nomination by caucus has collapsed with the demise of the party system. Several months later, the Kentucky legislature nominates Henry Clay.

1824

February

The absence of well-organized political parties results in a chaotic presidential nomination process. Andrew Jackson and Henry Clay have been nominated two years previous. In February, a small minority of the Democratic-Republicans in Congress hold a rump caucus and nominate Secretary of the Treasury William Crawford. The next day, John Quincy Adams is nominated by a political meeting in Boston. John C. Calhoun also has presidential ambitions, but he stands aside and agrees to accept the vice presidency no matter who is elected president.

December

As might have been predicted with the nation so split among candidates, the election turns sour. Jackson has a clear plurality in the popular vote, but he has only ninety-nine electoral votes, not enough to reach the constitutionally required majority. Adams has eighty-four; Crawford forty-one; and Clay thirty-seven. Calhoun, however, receives 182 electoral votes for vice president and is elected, albeit without a president. The contest must go to the House of Representatives for resolution.

1825

February
The House votes for president, and John Quincy Adams wins even though he was significantly outpolled by Jackson in the popular vote. When Henry Clay is named as Adams's secretary of state, the Jackson faction howls that there was a "corrupt bargain" to deprive Jackson of the prize. New parties are formed in the wake of the dispute: Jackson's followers become the precursors of modern-day Democrats, and Clay's adherents join with other political factions to form first the National Republicans and then the Whig Party.

March
John Quincy Adams and John C. Calhoun are inaugurated. Adams and his father are the only father-son combination to win the presidency.

1826

July 4
John Adams and Thomas Jefferson die within hours of each other on the fiftieth anniversary of the Declaration of Independence.

1828

May
An unusually high tariff (import tax) is passed by Congress. The tariff, along with the national bank and the federal land sales office, is one of the principal factors in the national economy (there is no central financial system and no income tax at this time), so a high tariff is a matter for great political controversy. This 1828 "Tariff of Abominations" and its successors will spark trouble for years to come.

December
John C. Calhoun, although he is the incumbent vice president under President John Quincy

Adams, is elected for a second term as the running mate of Andrew Jackson. Adams and his running mate, Richard Rush, are soundly defeated. Adams will later return to Washington as a long-serving representative from Massachusetts.

1829

March
Andrew Jackson's inauguration is capped by a boisterous reception at the White House, symbolizing the transition of the American political system from the more sedate era of the Early Republic to a period dominated by the political power of the "common man."

1830

September
Henry Clay receives an early nomination for the presidency from a convention of a faction of the National Republicans.

1831

April
What is known as the Peggy Eaton Affair comes to a head in Washington with the resignation of all but one of Jackson's cabinet members. Secretary of War John Eaton's wife, Peggy, had been deemed to be low in social standing and deficient in morals (she was a former barmaid) by the wives of most of the other cabinet members, and they refused to receive her socially. Jackson was outraged, in part because of the experience of his own late wife, Rachel, who had suffered public scorn because of revelations of a defective divorce from her first husband. Only Martin Van Buren among Jackson's cabinet supports the president and Mrs. Eaton. What may seem a trifling matter becomes a serious political split between Jackson and his cabinet. Jackson is an extremely pugnacious man who thrives on confrontation and conflict, and he pushes the feud to the end. Vice President Calhoun's sharp differences with the president come to the surface during this episode.

1831

August
Vice President John C. Calhoun is nominated for president in next year's election by a public meeting in New York City.

September
The Anti-Mason Party, a third-party splinter group founded on the basis of a widespread belief in a conspiracy by the Masons, holds a convention and drafts the first party platform. The Anti-Masons eventually merge with other factions to help form the Whig Party.

1832

May
The Democratic Party, which has evolved from the original Democratic–Republicans of Thomas Jefferson and James Madison, holds its first convention. The delegates nominate Andrew Jackson as their presidential candidate and Martin Van Buren of New York for vice president. The convention method of nomination will dominate until the late twentieth century.

July
President Jackson vetoes a bill to recharter the National Bank, which he sees as a corrupt enemy of the people. This sets off a fierce political debate, but the Senate fails to override the veto. The bank is dead and with it all mechanisms to control the currency and the national economy. Jackson further demolishes the national economy the following year when he withdraws federal deposits from the national bank and distributes them to "pet" (favorite) private banks around the country.

November
South Carolina precipitates a national crisis by passing a law that nullifies the high import tariffs of 1828 and 1832, which have hurt the agricultural South. The state prepares troops and declares it will leave the Union if opposed by the federal government. Vice President Calhoun is the intellectual force behind the nullification movement.

December
Jackson and Van Buren win easily over Clay and John Sergeant. A few days later, Vice President Calhoun resigns to take up a seat as senator from South Carolina. The nullification controversy heats up with warnings from Jackson that no state can secede.

1833

January–February
After both sides bluster and rattle sabers, the controversy over nullification and the national tariff is settled with a compromise that lowers the tariff and saves face all around.

December
The growing antislavery and abolitionist movements gain momentum with the organization of the American Anti-Slavery Society in Philadelphia. During the next thirty years, the abolitionist forces, centered in the northern states, come to exert increasing social, cultural, and political pressure on the slaveholding South. The activities of the abolitionists will do much to bring about the Civil War.

1834

April
A growing coalition of political interests is christened the Whig Party (named after a faction of the British Parliament) by Henry Clay, one of its leaders. The party is made up of anti-Jackson factions of the old National Republican and the Democratic parties. They are joined by pro-states' rights supporters of nullification and slavery and by the Anti-Masons. Until its demise in the political convulsions of the 1850s, the Whig Party is a major factor in U.S. political life, managing to elect two presidents (both of whom die in office) and many members of Congress.

1835

January
The Whig Party has adopted a strategy of disruption that encourages states and regions to

nominate several people for the presidency, hoping to throw the election into the House of Representatives. Daniel Webster is nominated in January by a meeting in Massachusetts and later by other northeastern states. The month before, Hugh L. White of Tennessee has been nominated by a small congressional caucus and then by several southern state legislatures. John L. McLean is nominated by the legislature in Ohio, but declines. William Henry Harrison, a war hero from Ohio, is nominated by several state legislatures. The vice-presidential situation is also clouded and complex. There are two major Whig nominations: Frances Granger and John Tyler. Philip Barbour is nominated in Georgia but declines. The electoral possibilities seem endless.

May

The national Democratic convention nominates Vice President Martin Van Buren for president and Kentuckian Richard Johnson for vice president.

October

A group of dissident Democrats, known as Loco Focos, meets in New York City and adopts an anti-Jackson platform, further confusing the national political scene.

1836

March–April

Open warfare breaks out in the Mexican province of Texas, which is largely populated by slaveholding former U.S. citizens. A Mexican army under President Santa Anna captures and kills garrisons at the Alamo and Goliad and seems poised to defeat the ragtag Texas army. However, on April 21, Texas commander Sam Houston surprises the Mexicans at San Jacinto and achieves complete victory, capturing Santa Anna and killing hundreds of Mexican soldiers. Texans and many in the United States assume that the United States will recognize and eventually absorb the new independent Republic of Texas, but the matter proves over the coming decade to be controversial and divisive, in large part because of the issue of slavery.

December

The Whig strategy is foiled when Martin Van Buren wins 170 electoral votes, 97 more than his closest Whig rival and enough to make president. He is the last sitting vice president to succeed to the White House until George Bush does it 152 years later. Van Buren's running mate, Richard Johnson, is not so lucky. Enough electoral votes are siphoned off by the Whig vice-presidential candidates so that Johnson just fails to get the required majority. For the first and only time, selection of the vice president goes to the House of Representatives.

1837

February

The House of Representatives votes 33–16 to make Richard Johnson vice president.

May

Another financial panic hits the country, probably as the result of Jackson's policies, especially his move late in his last term to tighten credit by requiring payment for land sales in hard currency. Van Buren is blamed, however.

1839

November

Abolitionists form the Liberty Party and nominate James B. Birney for president and Thomas Earle for vice president.

December

The Whig Party nominates William Henry Harrison, a military hero of the War of 1812, for president and John Tyler, a Virginia slaveholder, for vice president.

1840

May

Meeting in convention, the Democrats renominate Martin Van Buren for president, but there is enough opposition to Richard Johnson to stifle a formal renomination by the convention, which votes to leave the vice-presidential candidacy up to the states. No serious rivals to Johnson emerge, however, after James K. Polk drops out.

December
The Whig ticket of Harrison and Tyler sweeps to victory, and the Whigs capture a majority in Congress. The new party should be able to control national policies for several years to come.

1841

April
Only a month after taking office, President Harrison dies of pneumonia, making John Tyler the first vice president to succeed to the presidency. For a while, Tyler's status is unclear—some in Washington want to declare him merely acting president—but he demands and receives full status as the chief executive. To the dismay of the Whigs, Tyler proves to have little in common with the rest of the party, and he usually backs measures supported by the Democrats. Within a short while, Tyler lacks all support of his own party.

1844

May
The Whigs hold a national convention and nominate Henry Clay for president and Theodore Frelinghuysen for vice president. Clay has waffled on the major issue of annexing Texas, so the party ignores the question when drafting a platform.

The Democrats have a fierce convention struggle. Van Buren cannot gain enough votes for the nomination, despite an early lead, and a relative long shot, James K. Polk, eventually wins. His running mate is George M. Dallas of Pennsylvania. The Democratic platform stresses annexing Texas at all costs and takes an aggressive stance toward Great Britain on the question of the Oregon border.

Dissident Democrats simultaneously nominate incumbent President John Tyler, who was originally elected to the vice presidency as a Whig, but he withdraws from the campaign three months later.

December
Polk and Dallas win the election. Clay's strength has been drained to some degree in the North by the strong showing of James G. Birney the antislavery Liberty Party candidate.

1845

February–December
Through a series of complicated legal and political maneuvers, Texas becomes a state. President James K. Polk has pushed hard for annexation, which becomes a reality after some constitutional legerdemain by Congress and a vote for annexation by a convention in Texas. Annexation is certain to mean war with Mexico.

1846

May
Provocations on each side lead to a violent clash along the Mexican border. At President Polk's urging, Congress declares war on Mexico and authorizes the raising of an army. The war is bitterly opposed by many in the northern and western free states but strongly supported by southerners. U.S. troops invade Mexico almost immediately, opening what will be a bloody contest.

June
Wishing to concentrate on matters with Mexico, Polk agrees to a treaty with Great Britain over the Oregon border question. Americans in California declare a revolt against Mexico and proclaim the Republic of California, although they agree to transfer power to a U.S. military officer a few weeks later.

August
When passing an appropriation to pay for land anticipated to come to the United States from Mexico after the war, Congress considers but eventually rejects the Wilmot Proviso that would assure that all territories acquired must exclude slavery. U.S. forces take Los Angeles in California and Santa Fe in New Mexico, consolidating control over the former Mexican provinces, although

they must put down a revolt later in summer by Mexican residents in Southern California.

September
The U.S. army of invasion under General Zachary Taylor takes Monterrey. By the end of the year, he holds a large area in northern Mexico.

1847

February
General Taylor wins a major victory at Buena Vista against large odds.

March
General Winfield Scott takes Veracruz after an amphibious assault.

April
General Scott wins at Cerro Gordo and two other smaller battles.

August
Initial peace negotiations between the United States and Mexico fail.

September
The antiimmigrant American Party (called the Know Nothings) organizes and nominates General Zachary Taylor for president and Henry Dearborn of Massachusetts for vice president.

September
After a fierce battle at Chapultepec, General Scott captures Mexico City, effectively bringing the war to a close.

1848

March
By the Treaty of Guadalupe Hidalgo, the United States acquires a vast region in the West and Southwest from Mexico, including most of the modern-day states of New Mexico, Arizona, California, Utah, and Nevada.

May
The Democratic convention nominates Lewis Cass of Michigan for president (Polk declines to run for a second term) and William O. Butler of Kentucky for vice president.

June
The Whigs nominate war hero Zachary Taylor, with New York's Millard Fillmore as his running mate. The fragmentation of national politics that comes to characterize the next dozen years is prefigured this year by nominations from several splinter groups, none of which are yet serious contenders, however.

July
The first national convention supporting women's rights meets at Seneca Falls, New York. Although not successful at the national level for several generations to come, the women's suffrage movement exerts a powerful influence on American life and politics from this time on.

August
Antislavery supporters form the Free Soil Party and nominate former President Martin Van Buren for president and Charles Francis Adams of Massachusetts for vice president.

December
Whig candidates Zachary Taylor and Millard Fillmore win the election when the Free Soilers drain support for the Democratic ticket.

1849

February
News of the discovery of gold in the northern California hills ignites a huge rush of fortune seekers. Tens of thousands of "Forty-Niners" set out by sea and overland for the goldfields. While some miners strike it rich, most fail and eventually leave broke.

1850

January–September
Henry Clay leads a fight for a political compromise that will defuse the issue of extending slavery into the new territories taken from Mexico. After prolonged negotiations, debate, and maneuvering, Congress finally passes a series of measures that are known as the Compromise of 1850 and include admitting California as a free state, organ-

izing the territories of New Mexico and Utah, allowing Texas to remain a slave state, abolishing slavery in the District of Columbia, and putting in place a strong new Fugitive Slave Act.

July
President Zachary Taylor dies in office and Millard Fillmore becomes president.

1851

February
Reflecting resistance to the Fugitive Slave law in northern states, citizens of Boston rescue an escaped slave from jail. In several other places, antislave mobs frustrate U.S. marshals and southern slave hunters.

1852

March
Harriet Beecher Stowe publishes *Uncle Tom's Cabin*, which becomes immensely popular and helps to galvanize northern public opinion against slavery.

June
The Democratic national convention nominates Franklin Pierce of New Hampshire for president and William Rufus King of Alabama for vice president. The party backs the Compromise of 1850.

August
The Free Soil Party nominates John P. Hale of New Hampshire for president and George Julian of Indiana for vice president. The party platform condemns the Compromise of 1850.

November
The Democratic slate wins in a landslide, 254 electoral votes for Pierce to Winfield Scott's 42. The Free Soil candidates fare poorly in the popular vote.

1853

March
Franklin Pierce is inaugurated in Washington, D.C. Vice President William King is inaugurated

(by special dispensation of Congress) in Cuba, where he has gone to seek better health.

April
Vice President King dies at his home in Alabama, never having taken up his duties.

December
The United States signs a treaty with Mexico for the purchase of a small parcel of land along the southern Arizona and New Mexican borders, which becomes known as the Gadsden Purchase.

1854

January
Hope for a peaceful solution to the question of slavery in the West evaporates when Illinois Senator Stephen Douglas introduces the Kansas-Nebraska Act, which would organize these two territories as a preliminary to statehood and would allow territorial residents to vote on whether to be slave or free (a concept known as "popular sovereignty"). Because both territories would be above the 36 degrees 30 minute limit on slavery established by the Missouri Compromise in 1820, the act is destined to reopen the political conflict between free and slave states, North and South.

February
Antislave opponents of the Kansas-Nebraska bill form the Republican Party at a meeting in Wisconsin. The new party grows rapidly and brings under its banner a variety of antislavery factions, including the Free Soilers, northern Democrats, and antislavery Whigs.

1855–1858

Factions in Kansas Territory fight over adopting a constitution and applying for statehood as a free or a slave state. The conflicts are complex and increasingly violent. The region will come to be known as Bleeding Kansas and is seen as the cockpit of the great struggle for the soul of the nation. By the end of 1856, there is open warfare in Kansas with armed attacks by pro-slavery forces on the antislavery capital at Lawrence and murderous retaliation by antislavery advocates such as John Brown.

Both sides draft their own constitutions and ask for statehood. The situation is so volatile that neither side wins. Kansas remains a territory until after the outbreak of the Civil War.

1856

February
The Know-Nothing Party nominates former president Millard Fillmore.

June
The Democrats meet in a stormy convention and nominate James Buchanan of Pennsylvania for president. Buchanan has been out of the country, and his views on slavery have not been widely reported. John C. Breckinridge is selected as the vice presidential candidate. The party hopes to avoid a split over slavery and the Kansas-Nebraska question.

Later in the month, the new Republican Party meets in its first national convention and nominates John C. Frémont of California and William L. Dayton of New Jersey.

December
Buchanan and Breckinridge win the national election in a race that is divided clearly along slave versus free lines. The Democrats have managed to eke out enough votes for an electoral college win, but the regional split seems likely to grow worse and spell trouble for the older party, especially in face of growing Republican strength. The Whig Party, strong enough to elect two presidents during the 1840s, is virtually dead.

1857

March
The Missouri Compromise is rendered unconstitutional by the decision of the U.S. Supreme Court in the *Dred Scott* case, in which a black slave had sued for his freedom after his owner had taken him into free territory in Illinois. The effect is to say that the federal government has no power to bar slavery from northern or western states and

territories. The ruling also declares slaves ineligible to be citizens.

August
Businesses start to fail with the onset of another of the nation's periodic financial panics.

1859

October
Fanatical Kansas abolitionist John Brown and a small group of followers attempt to seize the federal arsenal at Harper's Ferry, Virginia, hoping to set off a massive slave insurrection. Brown is captured by federal troops (led by Virginia colonel Robert E. Lee) and hanged for treason in early December. The incident becomes a focal point for conflict over slavery.

1860

April
The final split of the nation is presaged by presidential politics. The Democratic Party holds a convention but is unable to select a candidate after southern delegates walk out.

May
Fragmentation continues with the formation of the Constitution Party and the nomination of John Bell of Tennessee and Edward Everett of Massachusetts.

The most significant political development comes in Chicago, where the Republican Party nominates Illinois lawyer and former Congressman Abraham Lincoln, with Hannibal Hamlin of Maine as his running mate. The southern slave states, especially the so-called fire-eaters such as South Carolina, have made it clear they will not remain in the Union if Lincoln is elected.

June
A second Democratic convention nominates Stephen Douglas for president, but only because all but his supporters have left the party. Southern Democrats meet separately and nominate their own candidate, Vice President John C. Breckinridge with Joseph Lane of Oregon as his running

mate. The election will turn solely on the issue of slavery and which section shall dominate the federal government. The Democrats are badly divided along sectional lines and the way is clear for a Republican victory, although in general probably only a minority of voters support the party.

November

Lincoln and Hamlin win with a majority of electoral college votes but a minority in the popular vote.

December

A convention in South Carolina votes to secede from the Union. Despite some attempts to find a new compromise, it is clear that with Lincoln in the White House, the nation will break apart.

1861

January

More Southern slave states vote for secession. Eventually eleven states—all in the slave South—will withdraw from the Union to form the Confederacy.

March

At his inauguration, Lincoln calls for unity, but the Confederacy has already come into being with Jefferson Davis of Mississippi as its president.

April

Warfare begins as Confederate artillery batteries in Charleston, South Carolina, fire on federal troops at Fort Sumter in the harbor. President Lincoln calls for volunteers to put down the rebellion of the Confederate states.

July

The first great battle of the Civil War is fought near Manassas, Virginia, not far from Washington. The larger Union army is routed by the better-led and tougher Confederate troops, although the Southerners fail to follow up their victory with a march on the national capital. The first years of the war reflect the basic confrontation established early in the conflict: the Union will have huge numbers of well-equipped and well-trained soldiers but few good generals, including the blustering but timid commander George McClellan; the Confederacy will have limited resources in manpower (slaves are not allowed to fight) and matériel but discover a corps of superb generals, headed by Robert E. Lee, which allows them to win battle after battle and stave off overall defeat for years.

1862

Although eventually winning major victories in the West, the Union forces in the East have little success and retreat ignominiously from a failed attempt to invade Virginia from the coastline. Lee assumes command of the Army of Northern Virginia and decides on an invasion of Maryland, after defeating a Union Army in a second battle at Manassas. In September, Lee's troops meet McClellan's at the Battle of Antietam. The result is a stalemate after the bloodiest single day of combat in American history. Lee is forced to retreat, but McClellan fails to follow up.

1863

With the important but mostly symbolic declaration of the Emancipation Proclamation in January, Lincoln isolates the Confederacy from potential British support and explicitly makes slavery one of the major issues of the war. More costly battles continue, both in the West and the East. The war approaches a kind of climax in midyear. Union forces under General Ulysses S. Grant take Vicksburg, Mississippi, and gain control of the great river. Lee attempts another invasion of the north and meets a huge Union army near Gettysburg, Pennsylvania, where a horrendous three-day battle ends with the Confederate Army broken on federal defensive positions. Lee is forced to retreat south, but again the Union generals fail to pursue and allow him to regroup. There is no longer any possibility that the South can win the war in the field, but Lee can prolong the bloody conflict for many months.

1864

The Union forces begin a costly but inevitable advance across the South from Tennessee, moving toward Atlanta, which falls in September. Grant is given overall command by Lincoln and begins to move toward the Confederate capital at Richmond, Virginia. The eastern theater turns into a horrible meatgrinder, with battle after battle resulting in huge casualty lists. After reaching the outskirts of Richmond, the Union army sets up a trench-warfare siege. At the end of the year, Union general William T. Sherman leads his army from Atlanta on a destructive march to the seacoast cities of Savannah and Charleston.

June

The Republican Party (calling itself the National Union Party) renominates Abraham Lincoln for president but discards Vice President Hamlin in favor of Tennessee's Andrew Johnson, a former Democrat.

August

The Democrats nominate General George McClellan for president and George Pendleton of Ohio for vice president.

November

Lincoln and Johnson win a narrow popular victory over the Democrats, with the soldier vote the likely crucial factor.

1865

March

Lincoln delivers a conciliatory speech at his second inauguration in Washington. He expresses the desire to bind the nation's wounds "with malice toward none and charity for all."

April

Union troops occupy Richmond. Lee surrenders his army to Grant at Appomattox Court House, Virginia. The war is essentially over.

President Lincoln is shot in the head by prosouthern sympathizer John Wilkes Booth while attending a play in Washington. He dies the next day, and Andrew Johnson becomes president.

December

The thirteenth Amendment, abolishing slavery and involuntary servitude, is ratified.

1865–1876

The death of President Lincoln marks the beginning of a long struggle to reconstruct the nation, a struggle that centers on the issues of how to extend political, social, and economic rights to black former slaves and how to reincorporate the states of the Confederacy into the Union. The struggle is sharp, played out against a background of corrupt and incompetent leadership and in the end reaches no satisfactory conclusions. President Andrew Johnson begins immediately to implement his vision of accepting the southern states back into national life, but he is thwarted by powerful antisouthern figures in Congress. He is impeached and nearly convicted. The strident reconstructionists pass several constitutional amendments and laws that extend citizenship and voting and economic rights to former slaves, and they punish the former Confederate states with military occupation and withheld sovereignty. Eventually, however, the power of the reconstructionists wanes, and more cynical men take charge. By 1876, Reconstruction is dead and the South has managed to resubjugate the region's black population and to regain its political potency.

1866

April

Congress passes a civil rights bill over President Johnson's veto. The law grants citizenship and full civil rights to former slaves.

1867

March

Congress passes, over the president's veto, a reconstruction act that sets up military governments in the southern states and requires ratification of the proposed fourteenth Amendment, which protects blacks' rights and punishes former Confederates, before a state can be readmitted to the Union. Congress also passes the Tenure in Office Act that weakens the president and will be used against Johnson.

In the same month, Secretary of State William Seward concludes a treaty with Russia for the purchase of Alaska for $7.2 million.

1868

February
Congress impeaches President Andrew Johnson on the formal grounds that he has violated the Tenure in Office Act by his attempts to fire his secretary of war. In fact, the struggle is over reconstruction policies and political control of the nation.

March
Johnson is tried on impeachment charges in the Senate and is effectively acquitted by one vote in a highly dramatic scene.

May
The Republicans nominate war hero Ulysses S. Grant for president with Schuyler Colfax of Indiana as his running mate.

July
The Democrats nominate New York's Horatio Seymour and Francis P. Blair of Missouri.

Later in the month, the Fourteenth Amendment is formally ratified.

November
Republicans Grant and Colfax win by a large margin in the electoral college, although the popular vote is relatively close and turns on the votes of former slaves.

1869

May
Crews working from different directions meet in Utah and complete the first transcontinental rail line.

1870

March
The Fifteenth Amendment to the Constitution is ratified. It says a citizen's right to vote may not be abridged by the states on account of race, color, or previous servitude. However, the exclusion of women voters continues.

1872

May
A group of splinter Liberal Republicans nominate Horace Greeley of New York and Gratz Brown of Missouri as a rival ticket to President Grant. Two months later, the Democrats also nominate the Greeley–Brown ticket.

June
The regular Republican convention renominates Grant for president but discards Vice President Schuyler Colfax, who has been touched by the many scandals of the Grant administration, in favor of Henry Wilson of Massachusetts.

September
The worst of the Grant-era scandals becomes public when it is revealed that several influential members of congress have set up a phony construction company, called the Crédit Mobilier, in order to grab millions of dollars of public money from railroad-building contracts.

November
Despite the scandals, Grant and Wilson are elected by 286 electoral votes to 66.

1873

September
A new financial panic hits the country with massive numbers of business failures. The New York Stock Exchange closes its doors temporarily.

1876

June
The Republicans nominate Rutherford B. Hayes of Ohio for president and William Wheeler of New York as his running mate.

Flamboyant General George Armstrong Custer and 260 men and officers of his 7th Cavalry are killed in a battle with a large number of Sioux and Cheyenne warriors at the Little Big Horn River. Public reaction prompts a massive campaign against the remaining free Indians of the West.

The Democrats nominate Samuel Tilden of New York for president and Thomas Hendricks of Indiana for vice president.

November

Disputed and possibly fraudulent voting in some of the former Confederate states clouds the election. Tilden has won majority of the popular vote, but contested returns throw the election into the House of Representatives.

1877

January

The House selects a special commission to settle the disputed presidential election. Originally, the commission was to have been divided evenly between Democrats and Republicans with the deciding vote held by an independent, but the balance is upset when the independent is appointed to a Senate seat and the Republicans gain control. A deal is finally struck between Republicans and white southern Democrats: Hayes and Wheeler are put in office in return for final withdrawal of federal troops from the South and a free hand for whites to subjugate blacks.

1877

July

A series of nationwide strikes opens what becomes a prolonged struggle between labor and business owners.

1878

February

The Greenback Party, which favors paper money and free silver, joins with members of the Labor Party. The coalition will elect more than a dozen members to Congress.

Congress passes the Bland-Allison Act that calls for limited silver coinage.

1880

June

The Republicans nominate James A. Garfield of Ohio for president, defeating a movement to nominate Grant for a third term. New Yorker Chester A. Arthur is Garfield's running mate. The party has split into factions called Stalwarts (supporters of Grant) and Half-Breeds (led by James G. Blaine). Garfield is the Half-Breed candidate and Arthur is a Stalwart.

The Greenback-Labor Party nominates James B. Weaver and B.J. Chambers.

The Democrats nominate Pennsylvania Civil War general Winfield Scott Hancock and Indiana's William H. English.

November

Republicans Garfield and Arthur win 214 electoral votes to 155.

1881

July

President James A. Garfield is shot at a train station in Washington, D.C. The assailant is a deranged office seeker inflamed by the political rhetoric of the Stalwart and the Half-Breed conflicts.

September

Garfield dies after painful suffering, and Chester A. Arthur becomes president.

1883

January

Congress passes the landmark Pendleton civil service reform act. Somewhat surprisingly, President Arthur, who has been thought of as the exemplar of the political spoils system, supports the reform movement.

1884

June

The mainline Republicans again nominate James G. Blaine for president, pairing him this time with

John Logan of Illinois.

The dissident Liberal Republicans vote to support the Democratic candidate, who has not yet been selected. These splinter Republicans, known as Mugwumps (supposedly an Indian term for "big chief"), despise Blaine.

July

The Democratic Party nominates New York Governor Grover Cleveland and Indiana's Thomas Hendricks. The Republican Mugwumps give their support.

November

Cleveland and Hendricks narrowly defeat the Democrats after a nasty campaign marked by scurrilous personal attacks.

1885

November

Vice President Thomas Hendricks, who has been in poor health for months, dies in Indianapolis.

1886

January

Congress passes a Presidential Succession Act that defines the succession of cabinet members to the presidency if both executives and heads of Congress die or are disabled.

May

A labor meeting in Chicago's Haymarket Square is disrupted by a bomb that kills several police. Spurred by widespread fear of political terrorism, authorities arrest, convict, and hang several accused anarchists.

1887

February

A new law governs contested elections: states will now determine the validity of their own vote totals. Congress will become involved only in extreme cases.

In the same month, the Interstate Commerce Act becomes law. It has far-reaching effects in allowing the federal government to regulate business in the public interest.

1888

June

The Democratic national convention renominates President Grover Cleveland and names Allen Thurmand of Ohio as his running mate.

The Republicans nominate Benjamin Harrison of Indiana and Levi P. Morton of New York.

November

In another of the weird presidential elections that plague the second half of the nineteenth century, Harrison and Morton are elected, although Cleveland and Thurmand receive 5,000 more popular votes nationwide. The Republicans have won in key electoral states and win easily in the electoral college, 233 to 168.

1890

July

The Sherman Antitrust Act is passed and signed. It is intended to limit the size and power of big corporations but is frequently used against labor unions in coming years. Later in the month, Congress passes the Sherman Silver Purchase Act, increasing the coinage of silver.

1891

May

The Populist Party is founded, basing its strength on western and southern farmers and laborers. The party uses inflammatory rhetoric to urge a variety of "radical" measures such as government ownership of the railroads and the eight-hour day.

1892

June

Amid increased national agitation between labor and business, the Republicans again nominate

President Benjamin Harrison. Vice President Levi P. Morton is replaced on the ticket by New York's Whitlaw Reid.

The Democrats nominate former President Grover Cleveland with Illinois's Adlai Stevenson as his running mate.

July

The Populists nominate old war horse James B. Weaver for president and James Field of Virginia for vice president.

November

Cleveland and Stevenson win the election. Cleveland becomes the only president to serve two nonconsecutive terms.

1893

February–June

A financial crisis grows rapidly after the failure of a major railroad. The nation's gold reserves have been drained due to the silver purchase policy, and the economy collapses in the worst panic of the century. The dislocations are long lasting, even after revocation of the Sherman Silver Purchase Act.

July

President Grover Cleveland has secret surgery for cancer of the mouth aboard a yacht off Long Island, New York. Vice President Stevenson is not informed of Cleveland's illness or operation, although the hugely corpulent president goes under a dangerous general anesthetic. The president recovers and resumes his duties.

1894

April

Hundreds of protestors, known as Coxey's Army after leader Jacob Coxey, march on Washington, D.C., to agitate against unemployment caused by the financial depression.

May

Workers for the Pullman rail-car company in Illinois go out on strike. The confrontation with ownership develops into a violent struggle involv-ing the federal and state governments and the U.S. Army. Several people are killed and much property is damaged before the strike is called off.

1896

May

The U.S. Supreme Court upholds the "separate but equal" doctrine that allows public facilities and schools to be segregated on racial lines.

June

The Republican national convention nominates William McKinley of Ohio for president and Garret Hobart of New Jersey for vice president.

July

There is no clear choice for the presidential nomination at the Democratic convention until Williams Jennings Bryan captures the delegates with his "cross of gold" speech in which he extols the free coinage of silver. His running mate is Arthur Sewell of Maine.

September

Breakaway Democrats who favor the gold standard instead of free silver meet in a separate convention and nominate John Palmer of Illinois and Simon Buckner of Kentucky.

November

McKinley and Hobart win easily.

1897

June

The United States signs a treaty that annexes the territory of the Hawaiian Islands (although the official act is delayed for nearly a year). The islands have been in the grip of powerful U.S. planters for some time.

1898

February

After the U.S. battleship *Maine* blows up in Havana harbor, agitation increases for a war with Spain over Cuba.

April

After months of posturing, Spain and the United States declare war on each other. The struggle during the coming weeks will be one sided, although the U.S. Army is ill prepared and suffers badly from poor organization and disease during its invasion of Cuba. The Navy, on the other hand, performs well against a weak Spanish fleet in the Philippines. The United States wins before the summer is out, creating an instant overseas empire.

May

The U.S. Asiatic Fleet under Admiral George Dewey destroys the Spanish fleet at the battle of Manila Bay.

June

U.S. Marines land at Guantanamo Bay, Cuba, followed by a large army invasion force near Santiago.

July

U.S. troops suffer heavy casualties in taking strategic hills surrounding Santiago. Theodore Roosevelt achieves lasting heroic fame for leading a prominent assault near San Juan Hill. Later in the month, the Spanish capitulate, and the United States formally accepts surrender in August. The peace allows Cuban independence and passes control of Puerto Rico, the Philippines, and Guam to the United States.

1899

November

Vice President Hobart dies in Paterson, New Jersey.

1900

June

The Republicans renominate McKinley for president with war hero and former New York Governor Theodore Roosevelt for vice president.

July

The Democratic convention again selects William Jennings Bryan as the party's standard bearer. Former vice president Adlai Stevenson joins him on the ticket.

November

McKinley wins a second term with Roosevelt as his vice president.

1901

September

President McKinley is shot by an anarchist while visiting an exhibition in Buffalo, New York. He dies thirteen days later, and Theodore Roosevelt is sworn in as president.

1904

June

The Republican Party nominates President Theodore Roosevelt to head the election ticket, although his vocal opposition to monopolies and large business combinations has created some dissention among party's leaders. Charles Fairbanks of Indiana, a conservative, is chosen as vice-presidential candidate.

July

The Democrats nominate Alton B. Parker of Illinois and Henry G. West of West Virginia.

November

Republicans Roosevelt and Fairbanks win with a plurality of a quarter-million popular votes. Roosevelt sees the victory as confirmation of his policies and, during his second term, pushes for more restrictions on big business, including a flurry of new laws and court decisions.

1906

November

President Theodore Roosevelt travels to the Isthmus of Panama to view progress on the great canal project he has strongly supported. The canal is completed seven years later.

1907

October

A major financial panic hits the country. Complete collapse of the economy is avoided, but a year-long depression follows.

1908

June

Roosevelt is seen as having already served two terms, so the Republicans nominate William Howard Taft of Ohio as his successor. John Sherman of New York is his vice-presidential running mate.

July

The Democrats again nominate reliable William Jennings Bryan with John W. Kern of Indiana for vice president.

November

Taft and Chairman win with a large margin of more than 1.2 million votes. Taft will expand on Roosevelt's anti–big-business and trust-breaking policies but without Roosevelt's flair for publicity.

1911

January

Reformers organize the Progressive Party to rally opponents of big business from both of the traditional parties. Former president Theodore Roosevelt, anxious for power once again, becomes a prominent member.

June

The mainline Republicans reject Roosevelt and reinominate President Taft and Vice President Sherman. Roosevelt thereupon bolts and later in the summer forms his own third party, the Bull Moose Party, based on the Progressive Party. Hiram Johnson of California is chosen as TR's running mate.

July

The Republicans stage an exhausting convention fight in which warhorse William Jennings Bryan finally gives way to New Jersey's reform governor, Woodrow Wilson. Thomas Marshall of Indiana is nominated for vice president.

October

Vice President Sherman dies and is replaced on the Republican ticket by New York's Nicolas Butler. During the same month, ex-president Roosevelt is shot and wounded by a would-be assassin in Milwaukee. He miraculously survives the attack.

November

Wilson and Marshall win by a large margin, surpassing the combined total of Roosevelt and Taft. The electoral vote is 435 for Wilson, 88 for Roosevelt, and 8 for Taft.

1913

February

The Sixteenth Amendment, which imposes an income tax, is ratified.

May

The Seventeenth Amendment passes, providing for the popular election of senators (who have been chosen by state legislatures until now).

1914

August

A general war breaks out in Europe with all the great powers in opposing alliances—the Central Powers against the Allies. Vicious fighting during the first weeks of the war establish a stalemated line of battle that stretches north to south across Western Europe. The United States led by President Wilson, declares neutrality.

October

Congress passes the Clayton Antitrust Act which proves to be a milestone in economic and business legislation. One effect of the law is to free labor unions from persecution under antitrust restrictions.

1915

May

Germany attempts to counter Great Britain's naval blockade of the Continent by using a deadly new sea weapon, the modern submarine. The British passenger ship *Lusitania* is sunk without warning, taking more than a 100 Americans to their deaths. The United States is outraged and moves closer to favoring war against the Central Powers.

1916

March

Mexican bandit Pancho Villa raids into New Mexico. President Wilson sends an expeditionary force under General John Pershing to chase Villa. The force crosses into Mexico but has no success. The invasion nearly sets off a war between the two countries.

June

The Progressives hold a convention and offer the nomination to Roosevelt, who declines. They then nominate a ticket of Charles Evans Hughes and John Parker.

The Republican convention also nominates Hughes, but selects Charles Fairbanks as the vice-presidential candidate. Many Progressives come back into the Republican fold after the joint nomination for president.

President Woodrow Wilson and Vice President Thomas Marshall are renominated by the Democrats. The party slogan claims that Wilson "kept us out of war."

November

Wilson and Marshall win again.

1917

January

Germany resumes unrestricted submarine warfare, which has been on hold, and announces it will sink neutral civilian ships without warning. Four days later, Wilson breaks diplomatic relations with Germany.

April

President Woodrow Wilson asks Congress to declare war on Germany. This marks the first time the United States has entered into a conflict in Europe and will alter temporarily the historic isolationist stance of the nation. Although the United States is completely unprepared to fight on a large scale, within months the country will

mobilize and train an army and begin to gear up industrial production to help the Allies. By any absolute measure, the U.S. contribution to the Allied effort in Europe is modest, but it comes at a crucial time when all the long-term combatants are depleted and exhausted; it will help to decide the contest.

June

The first contingent of U.S. troops under Commander John J. Pershing lands in France. By year's end, there will be close to 200,000 American soldiers in France; by war's end two million.

1918

January

President Wilson announces his program of Fourteen Points that he insists be the basis for any peace after the war. To his European allies, the declaration seems irrelevant and naive.

June

U.S. Marines and soldiers win a battle at Belleau Wood, but at a horrendous cost in casualties.

September

The Americans win a significant victory at St. Mihiel.

November

The Central Powers give up the struggle and conclude an armistice with the victorious Allies, bring the "war to end all wars" to a conclusion. Making a lasting peace will prove impossible.

1919

January

The peace conference to set terms for postwar Europe meets in Paris. Wilson will attend with high hopes of implementing his Fourteen Points, but diplomats from France and Great Britain will brush him aside and impose harsh terms on the defeated Central Powers, especially Germany. Wilson will be rebuffed as a hopeless idealist.

In the same month, the ill-considered Eighteenth Amendment to the Constitution reaches ratification, outlawing the manufacture and sale of liquor in the United States.

June

The Treaty of Versailles concludes the war. The treaty includes a League of Nations, one of President Wilson's pet ideas, but the U.S. Senate will refuse to ratify the agreement in a fit of isolationist reaction to the war and to the loss of more than 130,000 American lives in Europe.

September

President Wilson suffers a stroke after touring the country in an unsuccessful attempt to drum up support for the League of Nations. He is incapacitated, but his wife and advisers refuse to let the nation know of his true condition, even keeping Vice President Thomas Marshall in the dark. Wilson never really recovers, and the nation is left without a true chief executive until the next inauguration. Mrs. Wilson and a few advisers run the country in Wilson's name.

1920

January

As a part of the continuing reaction against the war, the nation enters a paranoid phase of public fear and oppression, known as the Big Red Scare. Using the Bolshevik revolution in Russia as an excuse, the U.S. Attorney General arrests and persecutes hundreds of innocent people on suspicion of subversive activities.

June

The Republican Party nominates Warren G. Harding of Ohio for president and Calvin Coolidge of Massachusetts for vice president.

July

The Democrats nominate James M. Cox of Ohio and Franklin Delano Roosevelt (a cousin of TR) for vice president.

August

The Nineteenth Amendment gives women the vote, a victory achieved only after decades of struggle.

November

Harding and Coolidge win with an margin of more than 7 million votes.

1923

August

President Warren Harding dies of pneumonia in a San Francisco hotel room on his way back from a visit to Alaska. Vice President Calvin Coolidge is sworn in as president by his father, a rural Vermont justice of the peace.

October

The Teapot Dome oil scandal breaks into the news. Government officials, including the secretary of interior and cronies of former President Harding, are guilty of selling strategic oil reserves for profit.

1924

May

Congress passes the first comprehensive legal restrictions on immigration. Although the full force of the law will not go into effect until 1929, the act marks a major change in U.S. policy and shuts down the massive movement of people from Europe to the United States.

June

The Republicans nominate President Coolidge to run for a term on his own with Charles Dawes of Illinois as his running mate.

July

The Democrats nominate John Davis of West Virginia and Charles Bryan of Nebraska as the party's national ticket. The fading Progressives have previously nominated Robert La Follette and Burton K. Wheeler.

November

Coolidge and Dawes win by a large margin: 382 electoral votes to 136 for Davis and Bryan and 13 for the Progressives.

1928

June

Interpreting Coolidge's statement that he does not choose to run as declining nomination, the Democrats select Herbert Hoover of California to head their ticket. Charles Curtis of Kansas is nominated for the vice presidency.

The Democrats nominate New York Governor Al Smith as the first serious Roman Catholic candidate for president. His running mate is Joseph T. Robinson of Arkansas.

November

The Republicans win the election easily with 21.3 million votes to the Democrats' 15 million.

1929

October

The New York stock market collapses in a single day, and the price of shares goes into a free-fall decline that will eventually wipe out billions of dollars of paper wealth. The crash heralds the beginning of the Great Depression, which will last a decade and not be reversed until the outbreak of war in Europe stimulates the U.S. economy.

1932

January

The Reconstruction Finance Corporation is created to use federal funds to prop up banks, financial institutions, and other key parts of the economy. Most see this as too little and too late on the part of the Hoover administration.

May–July

A so-called Bonus Army of World War I veterans descends on Washington, D.C., to demand full payment of their war bonuses. After camping out in the capital, they are ruthless dispersed by the Army.

June

The Republicans renominate Hoover and Curtis.

The Democrats nominate Franklin Delano Roosevelt of New York and John Nance Garner of Texas.

November

The Democrats sweep into office with a Roosevelt–Garner landslide. They take 472 electoral votes to the Republicans' 59.

1933

February

The Twentieth Amendment, known as the lame-duck amendment, is ratified, changing the inauguration date for the president and vice president from March to January. This will eliminate the traditional long waiting period between election and taking office.

Later in the month, Franklin Delano Roosevelt, who is waiting out the time until his inauguration under the old arrangement, is shot at while riding in an open car in Miami, Florida, by a would-be assassin. The president-elect escapes harm, but Chicago mayor Anton Cermak, who is with FDR, is fatally wounded.

March–June

President Franklin Delano Roosevelt launches his New Deal, a comprehensive program of executive action and legislation, aimed at economic recovery and relief. He closes the nation's banks temporarily in order to stop a panic, reorganizes the federal government, creates a Civilian Conservation Corps to employ young workers, takes the country off the gold standard, promotes the Federal Emergency Relief Act and the Agricultural Adjustment Act as instruments of direct relief, sets up federal regulation of the stock market, creates a federal employment service, and gains passage of the National Industrial Recovery Act that in turn spawns the National Recovery Administration and the Public Works Administration. These and other agencies, such as the Resettlement Administration and the Works Progress Administration, form the basis for the New Deal and, although often modified and added to, the fundamental policies and programs influence American life for decades to come.

December

The states ratify the twenty-first Amendment, which repeals the Nineteenth Amendment and ends Prohibition.

1935

May

The U.S. Supreme Court strikes down the National Industrial Recovery Act, bringing FDR's New Deal into question and beginning a struggle between the Court and the president.

July

Congress passes the National Labor Relations Act, which allows unions to organize freely.

August

President Roosevelt signs the Social Security Act, probably the most far reaching of all New Deal programs, which provides unemployment insurance, disability benefits, and pensions to almost all workers. During the same month, he also signs an act that establishes federal taxes on inheritances and gifts.

1936

January

The Supreme Court rules that the Agricultural Adjustment Act, a key part of the New Deal for farmers, is unconstitutional.

June

The Republican Party nominates Alf Landon of Kansas for president and Frank Knox of Illinois for vice president.

The Democrats renominate FDR and Vice President John Nance Garner.

November

FDR and Garner score a huge landslide over the Republicans. The Democratic incumbents win 523 electoral votes to 8 for Landon and Knox. The margin of the popular vote is more than 11 million.

1937

January

President Franklin Delano Roosevelt and Vice President John Nance Garner become the first to be inaugurated in January following a previous November election.

February

FDR announces a plan to "pack" the Supreme Court by creating places for up to six new judges. He ultimately fails to get the legislation passed.

1938

February

The Agricultural Adjustment Act is revived in a new form.

1939

September

Germany invades Poland, setting off war in Europe. The United States has remained neutral under law as the belligerents have jostled toward the outbreak of war, but FDR openly favors the British.

1940

March–June

German military forces roll over all opposition and occupy much of France and northern Europe. Only Great Britain, which has evacuated its small army across the English Channel, remains as a viable opponent to Hitler, and FDR moves to strengthen ties with the British, but stops well short of armed support.

June

The Republican national convention selects relative unknown Wendell Wilkie of Indiana as presidential nominee with Charles McNary of Oregon as his running mate.

July

FDR breaks the tradition set by George Washington and is nominated for a third term. He discards

John Nance Garner in favor of Henry Wallace of Iowa as his vice presidential choice.

September
The United States begins the Lend Lease program to supply the British with what is essentially the gift of fifty destroyers. The country edges further and further from neutrality. At the end of the month, FDR announces an embargo of steel to all belligerents except Britain. The real target of the embargo is Japan, which is also hit with a U.S. embargo on oil.

November
FDR and Wallace win a relatively narrow victory in the popular vote, with a margin of less than 2 million votes, although the electoral college vote is 449–82. FDR becomes America's only three-term president.

1941

January
Speaking at his third inaugural, President Roosevelt announces his "Four Freedoms": freedom of speech, freedom of worship, freedom from want, and freedom from fear.

December
The Americans are stunned on December 7 by a devastating sneak air attack by the Japanese Imperial Fleet on U.S. military bases at Pearl Harbor, Hawaii. The next day, President Roosevelt asks Congress for a declaration of war against Japan. A few days later, the United States also declares war on Germany and Italy. America's neutrality is ended, and a titanic international struggle begins. The war will be fought on two major fronts, Europe and the Pacific, with significant conflicts in the China–Burma–India theater. It will consume unimaginable amounts of energy and matériel and result in millions of casualties worldwide. At the beginning, the nation is ill prepared for war and things go badly, especially in the Pacific. Eventually, America's natural resources, industrial capacity, and manpower are mobilized and expanded on a huge scale, and these factors ultimately tip the military balance in favor of the United States and its allies. The Italians and Germans are defeated after bloody invasions of Europe by the Allies, and Japan is forced to surrender by the explosion of atoms bombs over two Japanese cities. By the end of the war in 1945, the United States will have become the dominant world power, armed with nuclear weapons, and ready to assume a role in international affairs that would have been impossible to imagine only a few years previous.

1942

February
The U.S. Navy in the Pacific attempts to regroup after the Philippines, Wake Island, Guam, and a host of lesser-known islands fall to the Japanese, but a major defeat in the Java Sea further weakens U.S. forces. On the home front, President Roosevelt organizes wartime government control and administration of key parts of the economy and authorizes a program to intern Japanese Americans.

April
The United States forces a stalemate in the naval battle of the Coral Sea and stalls further Japanese advances on Australia.

May
In a huge battle near Midway Island, the U.S. carrier fleet defeats a large Japanese naval force and turns back an invasion plan.

August
U.S. ground forces land on Guadalcanal Island and begin a prolonged, costly campaign against the Japanese who hold the island. Both sides pour resources into the series of land, air, and sea battles, which the Americans eventually win.

During the same month, U.S. bombers flying from England make their first air strikes on German bases in France. A large buildup of air forces in England is underway as well as planning for the assembly of a cross-Channel invasion.

November
American and Allied forces under General Dwight Eisenhower land in North Africa and

seize former French territories in Morocco and Algiers.

In Eastern Europe, German forces are turned back at Stalingrad, but the campaign into Russia has resulted in extreme casualty rates among both armed forces and civilians.

1943

January

After more than a year of war, the home front looks vastly different than during peacetime. The federal government controls prices, wages, and production in almost all industrial and manufacturing segments of the economy. Scarce or strategically important goods are rationed. The Selective Service System (the draft) and patriotic enthusiasm have pulled hundreds of thousands of young men and women into the armed forces, and they are replaced in the domestic workforce mostly by women who have never worked outside the home before. Almost every family in the America is affected by wartime separation and disruption.

President Roosevelt travels to North Africa for a conference with the leaders of the Allies at Casablanca. They set policy for the continuation of the war, including an agreement to demand unconditional surrender from the Germans.

May

After a long teeter-totter struggle, the Germans withdraw from North Africa and leave the Allies victorious there.

July

The Allies invade the island of Sicily as a preamble to invasion of Italy. Later in the same month, Benito Mussolini, the Italian fascist dictator, gives up power.

September

The Allies invade Italy, and the new Italian government effectively ceases to resist. The Germans, however, move into the breach and will eventually stop the Allied advance up the Italian peninsula.

November–December

President Roosevelt meets other Allied leaders in a series of conferences in Cairo, Egypt, and Teheran, Iran. They agree to demand unconditional surrender from Japan and on the timing of the war in Europe. The president later announces that U.S. General Dwight Eisenhower will become the Supreme Allied Commander for the anticipated invasion of Europe.

1944

January–February

U.S. forces capture Japanese bases in the Marshall Islands in the Pacific, beginning a long and exceedingly costly campaign of "island-hopping" aimed at taking all of Japan's strategic bases and eventually attacking the Japanese home islands.

January–March

Allied attempts to advance through central Italy are stopped by the Germans, and a stalemate develops. Massive daylight air raids are launched against German cities from bases in England, but very little strategic damage results despite horrendous casualty rates among air crews. U.S., British, and Canadian forces continue an unparalleled build-up of power in England in preparation of the planned invasion of Europe.

June

On D-Day, June 6, the Allies invade France at beaches in Normandy. Air superiority allows the landings to succeed, despite high casualty rates. When the invasion forces join and begin to move inland, the end of the war in Europe can be glimpsed even though many months of death and destruction remain. Hitler and the German nation are also pressed from the East by the advancing Russian Red Army.

In the Pacific later in the month, the Japanese are decisively defeated at the naval battle of the Philippines, and U.S. forces continue a costly advance toward the Japanese islands.

The Republicans nominate New York Governor Thomas Dewey as their candidate for the presidency with governor John Bricker of Ohio for vice president.

July

The Democratic Party convenes and renominates President Roosevelt for a fourth term. Few can imagine pursuing the war without him in the White House, although in reality he is very ill. Vice President Wallace is removed from the ticket in favor of Missouri Senator Harry S. Truman.

August

Guam falls to a U.S. invasion in the Pacific, and the Allied advance in Europe continues to push the Germans back. Late in the month, the Allies enter Paris, which the Germans have abandoned intact.

October

U.S. forces land in the Philippine Islands, led by General Douglas McArthur, who had vowed to return when forced to flee the Japanese in 1942. A decisive naval victory in Leyte Gulf destroys a major portion of the remaining Japanese fleet, and the Japanese turn to suicide kamikaze air attacks on U.S. ships.

November

Roosevelt and Truman win with a 3.5 million popular-vote edge. The president will enter a fourth term with his third vice president.

December

A desperate German attack in Belgium momentarily halts Allied advances with the Battle of the Bulge.

1945

February

At a conference at Yalta in the Crimea, President Roosevelt and other Allied leaders plan for the postwar international organization that eventually becomes the United Nations.

March

In the Pacific, Americans capture Iwo Jima and move on to attack Okinawa as the last step before invasion of Japan itself. In Europe, Allied troops cross the Rhine into Germany as the Russians close in from the East.

April

President Franklin Delano Roosevelt dies of a massive stroke while at his resort home in Warm Springs, Georgia. Vice President Harry S. Truman, relatively unknown to the public and a sharp contrast to FDR in style and personality, assumes the office of the president at a crucial time in U.S. and world history. He pledges to continue FDR's wartime policies.

May

Germany surrenders, bringing the war in Europe to an end. The Allies divide Berlin and occupied Germany into four sectors.

July

After a massive secret research and development program, U.S. scientists explode the world's first atom bomb at a base in New Mexico. President Truman is informed of the successful test while at a conference with Allied leaders at Potsdam, Germany.

August

On August 6, an American B-29 bomber drops an atom bomb on the Japanese city of Hiroshima, resulting in extraordinary casualties and destruction. The United States immediately calls on Japan to surrender, but the demand is rejected. President Truman has ordered the bomb dropped in hope of forestalling a bloody invasion of the Japanese home islands. He orders another bombing, and the city of Nagasaki is hit with an atom bomb on August 9. Five days later, the Japanese government agrees to end the war.

September

Japan formally surrenders. The war is over.

1946

January

America begins a series of social and economic postwar adjustments. Several industries are hit by major strikes, for example, as unions try to upgrade wages and working conditions held in check during the war. As hundreds of thousands of veterans are demobilized and return to the civilian world, national leaders fear economic dislocation, but the fears prove wrong. Using the benefits granted under the so-called G.I. Bill of Rights, veterans enroll in college in record numbers and many buy houses, propelling an economic expansion.

March

British Prime Minister Winston Churchill, during a speech in the United States, draws attention to the "Iron Curtain" that has descended across Eastern Europe where the Soviet Union has established political and military control. Churchill's analysis points to a growing international conflict between the communist East and the democratic West. As the world's first atomic power and in the aftermath of the devastating war that impoverished Britain and France, the United States is forced to assume leadership of what its politicians call the "free world."

1947

March

President Truman announces the Truman Doctrine that will provide American aid to anticommunist regimes. At the same time, he institutes a loyalty program to guard against Communists in the federal government.

June

Secretary of State George Marshall, formerly the commanding general of U.S. forces, announces a massive program of aid to rebuild the nations of Western Europe. The policy becomes known as the Marshall Plan and is the nation's first large-scale involvement in peacetime European affairs. During the same month, Congress passes the Taft-Hartley Act over President Truman's veto. The act outlaws closed union shops.

July

Amendments to the Presidential Succession Act of 1886 places the Speaker of the House as next in line for the presidency after the vice president.

1948

March–April

Strikes in the coal and rail industries hamper the economy, but the forecast postwar depression fails to materialize.

June

The Republicans again nominate Thomas Dewey for president with Governor of California Earl Warren as his running mate. The party hopes to regain the presidency for the first time since 1932.

A few days after the convention makes its choice, the Soviets create a European crisis by blocking access to the occupied German capital of Berlin. The United States responds with a massive airlift of supplies, food, and fuel. This marks the first major confrontation between the United States and the Soviet Union and begins the so-called cold war, a forty-year period of mutual antagonism and aggression. Because the Soviets now have the secrets of the atom bomb (gained through spies in the United States), mutual global destruction is a growing possibility, but the cold war always stops just short of warfare.

July

The Democrats meet in a convention full of conflict and put a civil rights plank into their platform. They nominate President Truman for a full term with Alben Barkley of Kentucky as his running mate. Democratic delegates from the southern states walk out in protest of the civil rights plank, and later in the month, they convene their own convention as the States' Rights Party—known as the Dixiecrats—and nominate Senator Strom Thurmond of South Carolina for the presidency and Fielding Wright as his running mate. Dissatisfied left-wing Democrats form a fourth party, resurrecting the name Progressive, and nominate former vice president Henry Wallace. The Democrats seem to be fragmented and at the mercy of the strong Republican ticket.

At the end of the month, President Truman signs an executive order that ends segregation in the armed forces and the federal government.

August

A growing anticommunist trend gains momentum when journalist Whittaker Chambers accuses state department official Alger Hiss of being a Soviet spy.

November

Against all odds and in the face of polling reports to the contrary, Truman and Barkley win the election. Truman's attacks on Congress during a train-tour campaign have had their effect. He and Barkley poll more than 24 million popular votes to slightly less than 22 million for the Republican ticket. The Dixiecrats and the Progressives between them get 1.3 million.

1949

January

President Truman calls his package of domestic proposals the Fair Deal. They include expansion of social security, a hike in the minimum wage, a national health insurance system, more federal aid to education, civil rights legislation, and government-sponsored housing. Little is actually passed during his administration, but the proposals extend the domestic ideas of FDR's New Deal.

April

The United States signs the first treaties that eventually form the North Atlantic Treaty Organization (NATO), a key factor in the cold war military stalemate.

1950

February

Senator Joseph McCarthy begins a loud campaign against communists in government with unsubstantiated charges of communists in the State Department. Before the movement known as McCarthyism is finished and McCarthy himself discredited four years later, a wave of communal hysteria will turn the nation on its head. McCarthyism will destroy the lives of hundreds of innocent victims while leaving real spies and subversives little affected.

June

The communist government of North Korea launches an invasion of the Republic of South Korea. The United States immediately sends troops and planes to help defend the South and secures a UN resolution authorizing armed intervention by a United Nations force. The resulting conflict is a vicious, costly war (although labeled only as a "police action") that will eventually involve massive combat between the United States and Communist China and end in a standoff at the original borders.

November

Puerto Rican nationalists try to kill President Truman in an attack on Blair House, where the president and his family are living during renovations to the White House. A guard and one of the would-be assassins are killed, but the president is safe.

1951

February

The Twenty-second Amendment is ratified, limiting presidents to two elected terms.

April

Soviet spies Ethel and Julius Rosenberg are sentenced to death in a controversial case that polarizes much of the nation. During the same month, President Truman removes General Douglas McArthur from command in Korea. McArthur has defeated the North Koreans but baited the Chinese into entering the war and now refuses to heed Truman as commander in chief. The removal further disrupts national unity, as many conservatives support McArthur as a symbol of anti-Communism. The dismissed general is asked by Congress to address a joint session, an extraordinary occurrence.

1952

March

President Truman publicly declines to run for renomination, although he is still eligible under Twenty-second Amendment.

June

The Supreme Court overrules President Truman's recent takeover of the steel industry, setting off a massive strike in a crucial industry. Later in the month, Congress passes an immigration restriction law over the president's veto. The new act sets national origin quotas.

At their convention, the Republicans nominate World War II commander Dwight "Ike" Eisenhower for president with Californian Richard Nixon as running mate.

July

The Democrats nominate Adlai Stevenson of Illinois and Alabama's John Sparkman.

November

The Republican ticket wins easily with 442 electoral votes to 89 for the Democrats. Eisenhower becomes the first Republican president in twenty years. Less than two weeks after the balloting, the United States successfully tests the first hydrogen bomb in the Pacific.

December

Fulfilling a campaign pledge, President-elect Eisenhower travels to Korea to visit the troops and assess the United States position there. The fighting has diminished, but the truce talks are at stalemate.

1953

July

The belligerants sign an armistice in Korea but cannot agree on an official end to the war. Both sides will continue indefinitely to face each other across an uneasy border. The United States will permanently station 40,000 troops in South Korea.

1954

April

The Senate begins hearings on the U.S. Army, which has been accused by Senator Joseph McCarthy. During the course of the televised hearings, McCarthy will be completely discredited and his hold on the nation will be finally broken.

May

The U.S. Supreme Court in the *Brown v. Board of Education* decision declares separate-but-equal segregation unconstitutional and sets the stage for a long struggle to end legal racial discrimination in the United States.

1955

September

President Eisenhower suffers a heart attack while in Denver. The seriousness of his condition is shielded from the general public, but he eventually recovers after a three-week hospital stay.

December

Rosa Parks refuses to give up her seat on a bus to a white man and sets in motion a long campaign by black citizens in the South to challenge and vanquish public segregation laws. The decade-long series of activities comes to be known as the Civil Rights movement and brings leaders such as Martin Luther King, Jr., to national prominence. In general, the movement uses nonviolent means, such as boycotts, demonstrations, and "freedom" marches, to protest discrimination in housing, transportation, education, and voting rights.

1956

June

President Eisenhower again falls ill, this time with a bout of ileitis. He undergoes surgery and recovers normally.

August

Despite his two episodes of ill health, President Eisenhower is renominated by the Republican Party, as is Vice President Nixon. The Democrats again nominate Adlai Stevenson, but put Estes Kefauver of Tennessee up as his running mate.

November

Eisenhower and Nixon win again, outpolling their opponents by a landslide margin of almost 10 million votes.

1957

September

The state National Guard is called out by the governor in Little Rock, Arkansas, to prevent black students from integrating the high school. Violence escalates until President Eisenhower sends in U.S. Army troops to enforce the law and escort black students to class.

October

Americans are shocked when the Soviet Union successfully launches the space satellite *Sputnik*. Efforts to respond with a U.S. launch fail when the U.S. rockets explode on their pads. The humiliation stimulates massive spending on a space-and-rocket defense program and on heightened educational efforts in science and mathematics.

1960

March–July

John F. Kennedy, a wealthy young senator from Massachusetts, uses the state primary system to gain enough delegate votes to win the Democratic nomination. His bold tactics spell the end of the party convention system as the mechanism to nominate presidential candidates.

May

Soviet missiles shoot down a U.S. U–2 spy plane over Russia and capture the CIA pilot. The incident precipitates a crisis in cold war relations but leads to nothing more than threats.

July

The Democratic convention names Lyndon Johnson of Texas as Kennedy's running mate. The Republicans nominate Vice President Nixon and Henry Cabot Lodge of Massachusetts.

September

Nixon and Kennedy stage the first televised presidential campaign debate. Kennedy, the more telegenic candidate, is thought to have "won."

November

Kennedy and Johnson win by a very thin margin of not much more than 100,000 votes. Widespread rumors of voting fraud in Illinois and Texas do not change the outcome.

1961

March

The Twenty-third Amendment to the Constitution is ratified, giving voters in the District of Columbia the vote.

April

An armed force of Cuban refugees from Florida attempts to invade Cuba, hoping to oust Communist dictator Fidel Castro. The Central Intelligence Agency has trained and armed the invaders, but the Cuban military crushes the landings at the Bay of Pigs.

May

Alan Shepard, Jr., becomes the first American in space when he rides a rocket-propelled capsule in a looping, suborbital flight to the edge of the Earth's atmosphere.

1962

October

The Soviets precipitate the worst cold war crisis by attempting to install missiles in Cuba. U.S. intelligence detects the building of sites and the shipment of missiles, and President Kennedy orders a naval blockade of Cuba and aggressively warns the Soviets to withdraw the weapons. After a tense confrontation, the Soviets back down.

1963

April–May

Black civil rights activists stage large-scale demonstrations and marches in Birmingham, Alabama. Leader Dr. Martin Luther King, Jr., is jailed. Violence continues while U.S. Attorney General Robert Kennedy (the president's brother) tries to intervene.

June

Alabama Governor George Wallace attempts to keep black students out of the state university but finally is forced to allow two to enroll.

August

Dr. Martin Luther King, Jr., addresses a large civil rights rally on the Mall in Washington, D.C. He tells the crowd that "I have a dream. . . ." This becomes one of the central events of the civil rights campaign.

November

President John F. Kennedy is assassinated by a sniper while traveling in a motorcade in Dallas, Texas. The nation is stunned by his death and the subsequent events, which are widely seen on television. Vice President Lyndon Johnson is sworn in aboard a plane bound for Washington, D.C. The alleged assassin, Lee Harvey Oswald, is killed publicly by a bystander while in police custody, giving rise to decades of speculation about conspiracy.

1964

March

President Johnson begins an ambitious domestic program with his war on poverty. His overall program of welfare spending, civil rights legislation, and education improvements will try to implement his vision of what he calls the Great Society.

July

The president signs a civil rights act that ends legal discrimination.

The Republicans nominate Arizona Senator Barry Goldwater for the presidency. William Miller of New York is his running mate.

August

U.S. destroyers off the coast of Communist North Vietnam in the Gulf of Tonkin are reportedly attacked by North Vietnamese boats. They retaliate and U.S. planes bomb the mainland.

Congress subsequently passes resolutions authorizing further armed attacks by U.S. forces.

This sequence ushers in the beginning of serious American involvement in what proves to be the most disastrous foreign war in U.S. history. President Lyndon Johnson is persuaded by his advisers that the United States has vital interests in stopping a takeover of South Vietnam by the nationalist communist regime of Ho Chi Minh in the north, which is allied with southern Vietcong rebel guerilla fighters and supplied by the Soviet Union. The United States props up a series of weak governments in the south and begins a massive infusion of troops, planes, and ships by which it is hoped the technologically unsophisticated Communists can be defeated. The hope proves false, however, and no amount of manpower, technology, or bombing can ultimately dissuade or defeat the Vietcong and the North Vietnamese. During Johnson's administration, the United States pours more and more into Vietnam, reaching a high point of more than a half-million troops by 1968. The home front, however, proves a complete disaster as conflict over the war erupts everywhere in American society, particularly on college and university campuses. While many Americans support the war effort, millions do not, and protests, draft evasion, and desertion take on major political and social power. Johnson is chased from office by the dissention and replaced by Richard Nixon, who tries to wind down America's direct involvement on the ground and negotiate a peace. The war stretches on and on, however, and no peace is reached until 1973. The regime in the south collapses and the United States has to face the trauma of a defeat in war and in spirit.

August

The Democrats nominate incumbent President Johnson and name Minnesota's Hubert Humphrey as the vice-presidential candidate.

November

Johnson and Humphrey win by a huge margin of nearly 16 million popular votes, taking 44 states to 6 for the Republicans.

1965

February
The conflict in Vietnam begins to escalate as Vietcong guerrillas attack a U.S. base and the president orders bombing in retaliation.

Radical black leader Malcom X is assassinated in New York City by members of the Black Muslim organization, of which he was previously a principal leader.

March
State troopers in Selma, Alabama, attack civil rights marchers. President Johnson eventually nationalizes the state National Guard and sends federal troops to protect the demonstrators.

July
President Johnson signs an act creating Medicare, a national health insurance program for the elderly and disabled.

August
Large-scale race riots erupt in the Watts section of Los Angeles. These are the first in a series of destructive riots in urban black ghettos over the following three years.

October
An immigration reform bill becomes law. It abolishes the quota system and opens the way for renewal of larger-scale immigration and for the first time allows significant immigration from Asia.

1966

January
President Johnson orders bombing of North Vietnam, which had been suspended since December, to resume.

March
Protestors in several cities stage large demonstrations against the war in Vietnam.

June
The U.S. Supreme Court rules in the *Miranda* decision that accused criminals must be informed of their rights.

U.S. planes begin to bomb the North Vietnamese capital of Hanoi.

July
One of decade's the most violent and destructive race riots takes place in Detroit. Damage is in the hundreds of millions of dollars, and thousands of inner-city residents are left homeless by fire. President Johnson sends in Army troops to help restore order.

1967

October–December
Massive antiwar demonstrations in Washington, D.C., and many other cities, including New York, result in large-scale arrests of demonstrators.

1968

January
The Vietcong and North Vietnamese unleash a series of attacks on the eve of the Tet New Year. The attacks destroy the American perception that the war is going well. Antiwar student riots renew in the United States.

March
Anti-war Democratic presidential candidate Eugene McCarthy wins a primary in New Hampshire and shakes the Democratic Party. Attorney General Robert Kennedy announces his candidacy in the wake of evidence of President Johnson's unpopularity. Former Vice President Richard Nixon has previously announced his run for the Republican nomination. President Lyndon Johnson surprises the nation with a declaration that he will not seek the nomination for another term.

April
Civil rights leader Martin Luther King, Jr., is assassinated in Memphis, Tennessee. Rioting and protests result.

Students seize administration buildings at Columbia University to protest the war.

June

Robert Kennedy is assassinated in Los Angeles, where he is campaigning for the presidential nomination.

August

The Republican convention nominates Richard Nixon and he names Maryland Governor Spiro Agnew as his running mate.

The Democratic party convention in Chicago nominates Vice President Hubert Humphrey and Maine Senator Edmund Muskie, but the convention and the city are totally disrupted by brutal street battles between police and antiwar demonstrators.

November

Nixon and Agnew win a tight race with a margin of slightly more than 800,000 million votes out of nearly 80 million cast. Third-party segregationist candidate George Wallace pulls almost 9.5 million votes.

1969

June

President Nixon announces a new policy of Vietnamization that is planned to place the burden of ground fighting on the South Vietnamese regime and will mean gradual withdrawal of U.S. troops.

July

U.S. astronauts Neil Armstrong and Buzz Aldrin set foot on the moon, marking one of humankind's greatest technological achievements. A second lunar landing follows in November.

1970

May

Ohio national guardsmen fire on student demonstrators at Kent State University, killing four and wounding nine. A few days later, two students are killed at Jackson State College in Mississippi in a similar incident.

1971

April

The twenty-sixth Amendment is adopted, granting the right to vote to eighteen-year olds.

1972

January

President Nixon announces a peace proposal for Vietnam.

February

Nixon visits Communist China and announces resumption of partial diplomatic and economic relations.

March

The North Vietnamese reject the U.S. peace proposals and stage a massive attack into South Vietnam. President Nixon orders the mining of major North Vietnamese ports and the resumption of bombing.

May

The president visits the Soviet Union and signs an agreement to freeze nuclear weapons.

June

Operatives of the Committee to Reelect the President break in to Democratic National Party headquarters at the Watergate building in Washington, D.C. They are caught in the act, and the subsequent investigation snowballs until eventually the president and almost all of his key aides and associates are implicated in a series of illegal actions. The break-in becomes part of the greatest political scandal in American history. Nixon will resign the presidency in the face of imminent impeachment, and many of his coconspirators will serve prison time.

July

The Democratic convention nominates South Dakota's George McGovern, who wins on the strength of primary victories and manipulation of delegate rules. He chooses Missouri Senator Thomas Eagleton as his running mate.

August

Eagleton is forced to withdraw from the Democratic ticket when it is revealed that he has suffered psychiatric disorders and has been treated with electroshock therapy. He is replace by Sargeant Shriver.

The Republican Party renominates President Richard Nixon and Vice President Spiro Agnew.

November

Nixon and Agnew are reelected for a second term with one of the most emphatic victories in American political history. They win more than 60 percent of the popular vote. McGovern and Shriver win electoral votes only from Massachusetts.

December

After peace talks break down, President Nixon orders new bombing of North Vietnam. Most of the ground fighting is now in the hands of the South Vietnamese.

1973

January

In *Roe v. Wade*, the U.S. Supreme Court rules that state laws against voluntary abortion are unconstitutional. The decision legalizes abortion and touches off a long, rancorous, sometimes violent debate over the next two decades.

A peace agreement is signed in Paris that will end the war in Vietnam. The United States is to withdraw all of its troops. The agreement tacitly acknowledges the victory of the Vietcong and the North Vietnamese.

June–July

Testimony before the Senate committee investigating the Watergate break-in implicates high White House and reelection committee officials, including the president himself. The break-in was authorized at the highest levels as were attempts to cover up. A White House aide reveals that all conversations are routinely recorded by order of the president.

October

Vice President Spiro Agnew is forced to resign his office after pleading "no contest" (a legal admission of guilt) to charges of corruption and bribe taking while governor of Maryland. Some of the illegal payments were made to Agnew after he took office as vice president. President Richard Nixon, himself under intense investigation for political wrongdoing, appoints Michigan Representative Gerald Ford as vice president, using the Twenty-fifth Amendment for the first time. Previous vacancies in the vice presidency have remained unfilled.

A few days later, Nixon precipitates another crisis in what is known as the Saturday Night Massacre. He orders his attorney general to fire a special prosecutor who has been seeking the secret White House tapes. When the attorney general refuses and resigns along with his assistant attorney general, the solicitor general finally agrees to fire the special prosecutor. This sequence is greeted with a storm of outrage.

During the same month, an economic crisis threatens as the result of an oil embargo by Arab oil-producing nations. The nation reacts with a burst of interest in energy saving during the year-long embargo. Long lines at the gas pumps and other signs of distress mask the fact that actual shortages are negligible.

December

After intense hearings prompted by the possibility of a presidential impeachment, Gerald Ford is sworn in as vice president.

1974

March

High-ranking members of the president's staff are indicted on criminal charges connected with Watergate. President Nixon is named as an "unindicted co-conspirator."

July

After a favorable Supreme Court ruling, the House Judiciary Committee finally gets tapes of White House conversations about Watergate from the president. The committee then approves articles of impeachment that charge the president with criminal misconduct in obstructing justice and violating his oath of office in connection with the Watergate cover-up.

August

Richard Nixon resigns as president in order to avoid impeachment and trial. Vice President Gerald Ford is immediately sworn in as the new president. Before the end of the month, Ford nominates New York's Nelson Rockefeller as vice president.

September

President Ford gives former President Nixon a full pardon. Later in the month, he grants amnesty to Vietnam War draft evaders and deserters.

December

Nelson Rockefeller takes the oath of office as vice president. His confirmation has been delayed by long and critical investigative hearings.

1975

January

The North Vietnamese move to take Saigon, and the final U.S. evacuees flee the country.

September

President Gerald Ford narrowly escapes an assassination attempt in San Francisco when a woman shoots at him with a handgun from a crowd. Her arm is jostled by a bystander as she fires.

1976

May

President Gerald Ford wins Republican presidential nomination primaries in several key states. Georgia governor Jimmy Carter takes similar victories in crucial state Democratic Party primaries. The party conventions no longer have a meaningful role in selecting party candidates as the focus has shifted almost entirely to state

caucuses and primaries, which can be influenced by media campaigns.

July

Jimmy Carter officially receives the Democratic nomination and selects Minnesota's Walter Mondale as his running mate.

August

President Gerald Ford is nominated by the Republican convention and chooses Kansas Senator Robert Dole for the vice presidential nomination.

November

Carter and Mondale beat Ford and Dole in a relatively close race. The Democrats take 297 electoral votes to the Republicans' 241.

1978

June

The Supreme Court rules in the *Bakke* case that affirmative action racial quotas are illegal, although affirmative action guidelines that favor racial or ethnic minorities are not in themselves against the Constitution.

1979

January

The United States ends diplomatic relations with the government of Taiwan and resumes full normal relations with Communist China.

November

Following a takeover in Iran by radical Muslims and the ouster of the U.S.-backed Shah, students in Tehran seize the U.S. embassy and take sixty-six hostage when the Shah is allowed into the United States for medical treatment. The resulting prolonged crisis cannot be solved by U.S. diplomacy, and an attempt at a military rescue mission fails miserably. President Carter's popularity suffers as a result.

1980

July

California's former Governor Ronald Reagan takes the Republican nomination for the presidency and selects George Bush as his running mate.

August

The Democrats renominate incumbents Carter and Mondale.

November

Reagan and Bush score a smashing victory. They win 489 electoral votes to the Democrats' 49.

1981

March

President Reagan is shot down by a would-be assassin on the street in front of a Washington, D.C., hotel. Vice President Bush flies back from a visit to Texas and temporarily takes control of the U.S. government. Reagan recovers from his wounds after surgery and resumes the powers of his office.

1982

August

Hundreds of U.S. Marines are sent to Beirut, Lebanon, to as part of a multinational peacekeeping force.

1983

April

The U.S. embassy in Beirut is destroyed by a terrorist car bomb. Seventeen U.S. embassy personnel and sixty-three people in total are killed.

October

Islamic terrorists strike again in Beirut, blowing up the Marine headquarters with a suicide truck bomb. Two hundred forty-one Marines are killed in the attack.

Two days later, the United States invades the tiny Caribbean island nation of Grenada, responding to a Cuban communist take over of the the island's government.

1984

April–May

President Ronald Reagan makes a five-day visit to mainland China.

July

The Democrats nominate former vice president Walter Mondale as their presidential candidate. He selects New York's Geraldine Ferraro as his running mate, the first woman to be so nominated by a major party. The Democratic ticket's chances seem slight in view of President Reagan's overwhelming popularity.

August

The Republicans again name Reagan and Bush as their candidates.

November

Reagan and Bush win in a huge landslide with nearly a 16.9-million-vote plurality. They take 49 of the 50 states (Mondale and Ferraro win only in Minnesota) and claim 525 electoral votes to the Democrats' 13.

1985

June

President Reagan has surgery for cancer of the colon. While he is under anaesthetic and during the first hours of recovery, Vice President George Bush takes over the powers of chief executive.

1986

January

The space shuttle *Challenger* explodes and crashes shortly after takeoff, killing the entire crew. It is the worst disaster of the entire U.S. space program.

April

The United States hits Libya with an air attack in retaliation for Libya's sponsorship of terrorism.

August

Congress approves a request from the president for financial aid to the anticommunist Contra rebels in Nicaragua. The White House policy is to unseat the communist government in the Central American nation.

October

A major tax code revision becomes law, lowering taxes for many U.S. taxpayers. At the same time, a record national deficit of $220.7 billion is announced. This comes despite the passage five years earlier of a law mandating deficit reduction.

November

The first details of the so-called Iran–Contra Affair become public. The president's national security adviser and his assistant have engineered a complicated deal that involved secretly selling arms to Iran and diverting the proceeds to the anticommunist rebel army in Nicaragua. The president claims ignorance of the entire affair. Congress investigates, as does a special prosecutor. The scandal eventually causes a major shake-up in the administration and criminal indictments of former White House officials, but the president himself evades widespread blame.

1987

October

The stock market crashes spectacularly in the greatest single-day loss in history. The Dow-Jones market average falls more than 500 points. Although the fall is vastly worse than the 1929 crash, the long-term effects are slight and no major economic dislocation results. By December, the market rebounds and finishes up overall for the year.

1988

May

The U.S. Senate approves a major arms-reduction treaty with the Soviet Union, calling for elimination of many land-based missiles.

July

The Democrats nominate the winner of the primaries, Massachusetts governor Michael Dukakis for the presidency with Texan Lloyd Bentsen as his running mate.

August

The Republicans nominate Vice President George Bush, who has easily defeated his rivals in the primaries. He selects a representative from Indiana, Dan Quayle, as the vice-presidential candidate.

November

The Republican ticket wins easily, taking 426 electoral votes to 112 for the Democrats. The popular vote margin is close to 7 million votes.

1989

August

As the result of a free election, Tadeusz Mazowiecki, an official of the Polish labor union, Solidarity, is named as the nation's first non-communist prime minister since World War II. This is the beginning of a series of astonishing events that culminate in the transformation of eastern Europe. One by one during 1989 and 1990, communist bloc nations throw out their communist governments and install freely elected officials. The decades-old restrictions on travel, commerce, and political life disappear as the Iron Curtain lifts. The most important symbolic event is the destruction of the Berlin Wall in November 1989, followed within a year by the reunification of East and West Germany. By 1991, even the Soviet Union is dissolved and replaced by rampantly nationalistic new countries. In Russia, Boris Yeltsin takes office as an elected democratic president. All of this has a huge impact on U.S. foreign and domestic policy: the cold war is over and the United States is the only remaining world superpower.

August

Congress approves a $166-billion bailout for the failed savings-and-loan industry. More and more tax money is required before the end of the hugely expensive affair.

December

U.S. forces invade Panama and seek to arrest Panamanian dictator Manuel Noriega, who has bellicosely threatened U.S. interests and is accused of drug trafficking. Twenty-three U.S. soldiers are killed in the invasion, but Noriega is eventually taken into custody in January.

1990

August

Iraqi strongman Saddam Hussein invades Kuwait and threatens the Western world's oil supply. President George Bush pushes resolutions through the United Nations and organizes a coalition against Iraqi. The coalition builds a huge military force—mostly from the United States—in the Persian Gulf region, basing the ground troops in Saudi Arabia. It is clear by the end of the year that a massive attack is imminent. The United States alone has more than 500,000 military personnel in the region by December.

1991

January

A series of air attacks on Iraq employ long-range cruise missiles, stealth bombers, and high-tech "smart" bombs to devastate Iraqi defenses and offensive capability. The Iraqis retaliate with "Scud" missile attacks on Israel but do not dissuade the coalition. After flying more than 40,000 air sorties, the U.S.-led coalition launches a ground attack than crushes the Iraqis in a battle of 100-hours duration. The defeated Iraqis set fire to the Kuwaiti oil fields, and the coalition in an ill-advised move stops short of taking Baghdad and deposing Hussein. The Persian Gulf War has preserved U.S. access to relatively cheap oil but has failed to dislodge a persistently irritating Mideast foe and achieves little lasting benefit.

October

Despite President Bush's extremely high standing in the popularity polls after the Gulf War, the economy begins to erode, and Arkansas Governor Bill Clinton announces he will make a run for the Democratic nomination in the 1992 primaries. Clinton's main opponents for the nomination will be Jerry Brown and Paul Tsongas.

President's Bush's appointment of judge Clarence Thomas to the Supreme Court proves to be controversial when the jurist is accused of sexual harassment. Televised hearings eventually result in his confirmation.

December

Conservative Republican Pat Buchanan announces a primary challenge to President George Bush for the presidential nomination.

The Soviet Union officially disbands after more than 70 years of existence.

1992

March–April

President Bush and Bill Clinton win respective party primaries and take the leads in the races for their party nominations. Texas millionaire H. Ross Perot announces he will run for president as an independent. Polls show Bush has a lead over Clinton, with Perot surprisingly strong.

In Los Angeles, destructive riots break out after several L.A. policemen are acquitted by an all-white jury of beating black motorist Rodney King at the scene of a traffic arrest the previous March. The beating was videotaped by an onlooker, and the police have been seen repeatedly on television viciously assaulting King. The riots continue over several days and result in the deaths of fifty-two victims and cause at least $1 billion damage. Federal troops and state National Guard are called into quell the violence.

May

The Twenty-seventh Amendment to the Constitution is finally ratified when Michigan becomes the thirty-eighth state to approve. The amendment, which says that sitting Congress may not raise its own salaries, was proposed and first put to the ratification process in 1789 by James Madison. The measure has been pending for more than 200 years.

June

More primary victories clinch the Democratic nomination for Bill Clinton.

July

Clinton is officially nominated at the Democratic national convention, and he chooses Tennessee Senator Al Gore as his running mate. Perot surprises the nation and his supporters by dropping out of the race. Clinton begins an attack on President Bush that centers on the poor state of the economy—economic indicators continue to decline and unemployment remains high.

August

President Bush and Vice President Quayle are renominated by the Republican convention.

September

Perot declares he will reenter the race. The three candidates stage a televised debate, as do the vice-presidential candidates.

November

Clinton and Gore are elected with 43 percent of the popular vote, taking thirty-two states and 370 electoral votes. Bush and Quayle win only eighteen states and 168 electoral votes. Perot finishes strongly with almost 19 percent of the popular vote but no electoral votes.

December

The United States sends troops to Somalia as part of a UN peacekeeping force, hoping to stifle civil war and ameliorate a war-induced famine among the civilian population. President Bush visits the troops late in the month.

1993

February

Islamic terrorists bomb the World Trade Center in New York City. Six people die, and more casualties are avoided by sheer luck when the terrorists misposition their explosive-laden truck. This is the first major attack by foreign terrorists on U.S. soil. The FBI arrests the plotters and later in the year averts further attacks in the New York area by more arrests.

April

An FBI assault on the stonghold of the Branch Davidian religious cult outside Waco, Texas, results in the death of seventy-two of the cult members, including several children. The incident becomes a rallying point for violent antigovernment militias.

November

Congress narrowly ratifies the North American Free Trade Agreement, which will open trade borders with Canada and Mexico.

December

Fifteen U.S. troops are killed in a clash with warlords in Somalia. The United States decides to withdraw.

1994

September

The United States sends peacekeeping troops to Haiti to help a restore a U.S.-backed president after engineering the ruling junta's withdrawal.

1995

April

A massive truck bomb destroys a federal office building in Oklahoma City, killing 168 men, women, and children. Two radical antigovernment domestic militia terrorists are arrested and accused of the attack shortly after the blast.

December

The United States sends troops into Bosnia as part of a United Nations force that will try to enforce a truce between the Bosian Serbs, the Muslims, and the Croatians, who have been at war since the breakup of Yugoslavia.

1996

January

Senate leader Robert Dole begins a primary campaign for the Republican nomination. He will beat back a minor challenge from ultraconservative Pat Buchanan in the coming months and take the nomination easily. President Clinton has seemed vulnerable, but a rapidly improving economy strengthens the president's position.

August

Robert Dole is nominated by the Republicans, and he chooses New York's Jack Kemp as his vice presidential running mate. They are well behind the Democratic incumbents Bill Clinton and Al Gore in the polls. Ross Perot is also again in the race, but trailing his popularity of four years previous.

November

President Clinton and Vice President Gore easily defeat Dole and Kemp, taking 49 percent of the popular vote and claiming 373 electoral votes. The Republicans have 41 percent of the popular vote and 113 in the electoral college. Perot has dropped to 8 percent of the popular vote.

1997

January

Bill Clinton and Al Gore are sworn in as president and vice president for second terms. Having beaten the odds to win the national election, they now embark on campaigns to advance their domestic agenda while facing a U.S. House and Senate still controlled by Republicans. Gore, who appears to be the heir apparent to Clinton as a presidential candidate, hopes to spearhead domestic issues that will keep him favorably in the public eye.

June

The jobless rate hits 4.8 percent, the lowest figure in more than twenty years, signaling the robust health of the American economy. Over the next three years, the stock market indexes and all other measures of economic activity reach extraordinary heights, pushed most publicly by the rapid formation and growth of new Internet-based businesses (known as "dot coms" because their names include the Internet designation

".com" at the end). Almost all sectors of American society seem to share in the record-breaking prosperity, which gives a strong boost to the approval ratings of President Clinton.

December

U.S. Attorney General Janet Reno, who has been held over in office despite widespread criticism of her actions during the first Clinton-Gore term, absolves both Clinton and Gore of legal responsibility for making what appear to have been illegal campaign fund-raising calls from their official White House offices. She rules out charges and further investigation.

1998

January

President Clinton is called to testify privately in a sexual harassment case brought against him by former Arkansas state employee Paula Jones, who during the 1992 campaign had accused the president of making improper sexual advances toward her when he was Arkansas governor. Clinton later turns down an offer by Jones's attorneys to settle the case because he is reluctant to make an embarrassing public apology. During his deposition, Clinton denies a sexual relationship with a young White House intern named Monica Lewinsky.

June

President Clinton makes an official visit to China, a nation he has attempted to woo into closer ties with the United States. Clinton's domestic opponents accuse him of ignoring the well-documented human rights abuses of the Chinese government in order to advance economic trade and easier diplomatic relations.

July

Special Counsel Kenneth Starr, who has taken over the long-running investigation into fraudulent land deals in Arkansas in which both President Clinton and First Lady Hillary Rodham Clinton appear to have been involved, although no evidence of impropriety by either has surfaced, subpoenas President Clinton to testify to the Whitewater grand jury.

August

Monica Lewinsky testifies to the grand jury, alleging she took part in a series of sexual encounters with President Clinton in the White House while she was an intern there. Public revelations of her testimony set off a national uproar, and Starr—supported by the president's political enemies—pushes forward his case against the president for perjury under oath during his grand jury testimony and obstruction of justice, based on the president's alleged attempts to cover up his relationship with Lewinsky and to suppress her testimony.

Terrorists blow up U.S. embassies in Kenya and Tanzania, killing and injuring dozens of people. The attack is suspected to be the result of a plot by Muslim terrorist mastermind Osama ben Laden, an immensely rich Saudi who hates the United States and is said to train terrorists from a base in Afghanistan.

After first publicly denying during a national telecast that he had sexual relations with Monica Lewinsky, President Clinton is forced to admit his involvement.

September

Special Counsel Kenneth Starr's report to the U.S. Congress on President Clinton's false grand jury testimony and his relationship with Lewinsky is released to the public. It describes in explicit detail a series of sexual acts between Clinton and the intern, which the Republican members of Congress conclude make Clinton guilty of perjury since he denied the relationship under oath.

December

The U.S. House of Representatives brings articles of impeachment against President Bill Clinton, marking only the second time in U.S. history that a president has been impeached. The vote, which is mostly along political party lines, claims Clinton committed perjury before the Whitewater grand jury and attempted to obstruct justice during the investigation.

1999

January

The trial of President Clinton on articles of impeachment opens in the U.S. Senate, which the Republicans control. Chief Justice of the U.S. Supreme Court William Rehnquist presides. If convicted, Clinton will become the first U.S. president to be officially ousted from office.

February

After considerable debate, oratory, and legal wrangling, the Senate votes fifty-five to forty-five to acquit the president. Ten Republicans have joined the Senate Democrats.

April

Three teenage high school students arm themselves with a small arsenal and attack their classmates and teachers at Columbine High School in Colorado. They kill thirteen and then commit suicide. The carnage and the televised aftermath shock the nation, but it is only one of a series of school shootings by teenagers during the 1990s.

March

NATO launches a series of air attacks, carried out mostly by the U.S. Air Force, against Yugoslavia after the Serb-dominated nation begins what observers fear is a war of extermination against Muslims in the province of Kosovo. The air strikes continue for seventy-eight days and visit serious destruction on Belgrade and other cities before the Yugoslavian president, Slobodan Milosevic, relents and agrees to pull out of Kosovo.

June

A NATO peacekeeping force enters Kosovo on the heels of a Yugoslavian pullout.

September

Widespread and highly publicized fears about the so-called Y2K problem, which holds that computers will shut down or malfunction on January 1, 2001, reach a loud pitch that will continue until the end of the year, when all the anxieties prove to be groundless.

November

The Coast Guard rescues a six-year-old Cuban boy, Elián Gonzáles, from the waters off Florida where he is found floating in an inner tube, the survivor of an ill-fated attempt by refugees to flee Communist Cuba. His mother has drowned in the escape attempt, so he is turned over to anti-Castro relatives in Miami, even though his father is still in Cuba and claims custody of the boy.

2000

January

The presidential campaign hits high gear with the Iowa party caucuses, which supply the news media with the first slight but concrete signs of the electorate's preferences. Vice President Al Gore defeats his only serious Democratic opponent, former U.S. senator and basketball star Bill Bradley. On the Republican side, Texas governor George W. Bush (the son of former president George Bush, who was defeated by the Clinton/Gore ticket eight years previous) defeats Arizona senator and Vietnam P.O.W. hero John McCain.

February

In the New Hampshire primary election, the first actual voting for the candidates, Gore again defeats Bradley, but Senator McCain soundly whips Governor Bush, confounding most pundits and predictions.

In the subsequent primary in South Carolina, where Bush ducks comment on the hot topic of whether to remove the Confederate flag from the state capitol, the Texas governor beats McCain, but McCain returns the favor and beats Bush in the Michigan primary.

March

Despite his strong early showing, McCain concedes defeat after Bush takes more primaries. He was unable to match Bush's massive campaign chest. Bill Bradley also concedes his party's nomination to Al Gore, who will attempt to become only the second vice president since Martin Van Buren to succeed to the presidency by election (Bush's father was the other).

April

Federal agents raid the home of Elián González's relatives in Miami and forcibly remove the boy from his uncle's custody. The relatives have refused to return the boy to his father despite a court order. The move enrages the Cuban exile community in Florida.

June

A federal judge orders the breakup of computer software giant Microsoft. Although the decision is suspended pending a drawn-out appeal process, the uncertainly caused by the judgment underscores a decline in the stock market, particularly the high-flying technology stocks and "dot coms" that have driven the U.S. economy to extreme highs. By year's end, many of the most publicized dot coms go out of business, and the nation appears to slip into a recession or near recession after years of expansion and prosperity.

July

The Middle East peace talks between Israel and the Palestinians break down. President Clinton has been the chief sponsor of the talks, which were held at his presidential retreat at Camp David, Maryland.

Texas Governor George W. Bush announces former Secretary of Defense Richard B. Cheney as his choice as a vice presidential running mate. Cheney is seen as an undynamic but highly experienced and respected choice, a good counterbalance to the slightly lightweight reputation of the presidential candidate.

August

The Republican National Convention nominates Bush and Cheney as the G.O.P. ticket.

Vice President Al Gore selects Senator Joseph Lieberman as his running mate, making Lieberman the first Jewish candidate for the office of vice president. The Democratic Convention nominates the pair, who lead their Republican opponents in the national polls.

September

The six-year-long investigation of the Whitewater Arkansas real estate affair—which touched off the impeachment of President Clinton—comes to an end with an announcement that no charges will be brought against the president or First Lady Hillary Rodham Clinton, who is running for a U.S. Senate seat from the state of New York.

October

Fighting breaks out on the West Bank and in the Gaza Strip, bringing the Mideast peace process to an end and dashing hopes for an American brokered peace.

The U.S.S. *Cole* is attacked by suicide terrorist bombers while in port for refueling in Yemen. Seventeen U.S. sailors are killed and thirty seven wounded.

The presidential candidates meet in their first campaign debate in Boston. They cover foreign policy, tax cuts, and Medicare. Green Party candidate Ralph Nader is not only barred from participating but also turned away at the door when he tries to attend the debate.

Two days later, the vice presidential candidates meet for their only debate. The affair is low-key and extremely cordial, showing off the two men to considerable advantage.

Bush and Gore debate for the second time and forego the contentiousness that characterized their first meeting. Bush later calls the debate a "love fest."

The final debate between the presidential candidates takes place in St. Louis and is organized in the style of a town hall meeting, as Bush and Gore respond to questions from the audience. Overall, Bush does much better than expected against Gore, who entered the campaign with a strong reputation as a formal debater.

November

National polls show the campaign to be extremely close and getting closer as November 7 approaches. The actual election proves to be the most confused and disputed in more than a century, with neither candidate able to claim a victory at day's end. The national news media's exit polling techniques break down entirely, and the television commentators swing back and forth during their reporting, first awarding the victory to one candidate and then the other. At one point, Vice President Gore believes he has lost the race, and he calls Governor Bush to concede. However, on his way to make his concession speech, Gore learns that the key state of Florida, whose twenty-five electoral votes will provide the margin of victory in the Electoral College, is still very much in doubt, so the vice president calls Bush and rescinds the concession.

The Republicans hold their control of the U.S. House of Representatives, but the Senate appears to be split fifty-fifty, pending a contested race in Oregon, making the final selection of a vice president crucial to control of the national legislature, since the new vice president will most likely have the deciding vote in the Senate if the even split holds up (as it does). Hillary Rodham Clinton takes the U.S. Senate seat for New York, making her the first wife of a U.S. president ever to hold elected office.

Following election night, a long, drawn-out series of events surrounding the counting of the popular votes in Florida, where Bush has a very slim margin—only a few hundred votes out of nearly 6 million cast—grips the nation for weeks. No one can say for certain who has won the key Florida electoral votes, not even George W. Bush's brother, Jeb, who is governor of the state, but lawyers, political-party operatives, state officeholders, and judges wrangle over the validity of punchcard ballots, hand recounts in key counties, and disqualified absentee ballots. Recounts are on and off again as the two campaigns turn to the courts. The state's Republican secretary of state, Katherine Harris, certifies Bush as the winner, but her action is challenged. The Republican-controlled state legislature appears ready to select its own slate of electors. During the weeks of confusion, vice presidential candidate Dick Cheney suffers a mild heart attack but appears to recover quickly.

December

Although Vice President Al Gore and Senator Joe Lieberman appear to be closing the gap on Bush and Cheney in the recount of Florida votes, their hopes for victory in the Electoral College are dashed when a Bush appeal is upheld by the U.S. Supreme Court in a five-to-four decision that rules the recounts must stop and Bush will therefore win the state's electoral votes. Gore finally concedes defeat. Bush wins the Electoral College vote, 271 to 266 (one Gore elector from the District of Columbia withholds her ballot), even though Gore and Lieberman have won the overall popular vote by more than half a million votes. Only three other times has the winner of the popular vote lost the presidency in the Electoral College, and never with such a huge popular plurality.

2001

January

George W. Bush and Richard B. Cheney are inaugurated. Cheney has overseen the Bush administration transition and played a major role in selecting the Bush cabinet, and his will be the deciding vote in the evenly divided U.S. Senate.

VICE PRESIDENTS OF THE UNITED STATES

(In Alphabetical Order with Years of Service)

Adams, John (1789–1797)

Agnew, Spiro T. (1969–1973)

Arthur, Chester Alan (1881)

Barkley, Alben W. (1949–1953)

Breckenridge, John Cabell (1857–1861)

Burr, Aaron (1801–1805)

Bush, George H. W. (1981–1989)

Calhoun, John Caldwell (1825–1832)

Cheney, Richard B. (2001–)

Clinton, George (1805–1812)

Colfax, Schuyler (1869–1873)

Coolidge, Calvin (1921–1923)

Curtis, Charles (1929–1933)

Dallas, George Mifflin (1845–1849)

Dawes, Charles Gates (1925–1929)

Fairbanks, Charles Warren (1905–1909)

Fillmore, Millard (1849–1850)

Ford, Gerald R. (1973–1974)

Garner, John N. (1933–1941)

Gerry, Elbridge (1813–1814)

Gore, Albert (1993–2001)

Hamlin, Hannibal (1861–1865)

Hendricks, Thomas A. (1885)

Hobart, Garret Augustus (1897–1899)

Humphrey, Jr., Hubert H. (1965–1969)

Jefferson, Thomas (1797–1801)

Johnson, Andrew (1865)

Johnson, Lyndon Baines (1961–1963)

Johnson, Richard Mentor (1837–1841)

King, William Rufus de Vane (1853)

Marshall, Thomas Riley (1913–1921)

Mondale, Walter F. (1977–1981)

Morton, Levi Parsons (1889–1893)

Nixon, Richard M. (1953–1961)

Quayle, J. Danforth (1989–1993)

Rockefeller, Nelson A. (1974–1977)

Roosevelt, Theodore (1901)

Sherman, James Schoolcraft (1909–1912)

Stevenson, Adlai Ewing (1893–1897)

Tompkins, Daniel D. (1817–1825)

Truman, Harry S. (1945)

Tyler, John (1841)

Van Buren, Martin (1833–1837)

Wallace, Henry Agard (1941–1945)

Wheeler, William A. (1877–1881)

Wilson, Henry (1873–1875)

VICE PRESIDENTS OF THE UNITED STATES

(Listed by State)

("b" indicated state of birth; "c" location of career)

ALABAMA

King, William Rufus (c)

CALIFORNIA

Nixon, Richard M.

INDIANA

Colfax, Schuyler
Hendricks, Thomas A. (c)
Fairbanks, Charles W.
Marshall, Thomas R.
Quayle, J. Danforth

ILLINOIS

Stevenson, Adlai E. (c)
Dawes, Charles G. (c)

IOWA

Wallace, Henry A.

KANSAS

Curtis, Charles

KENTUCKY

Johnson, Richard Mentor
Breckenridge, John C.
Stevenson, Adlai E. (b)
Barkley, Alben W.

MAINE

Hamlin, Hannibal
Rockefeller, Nelson A. (b)

MASSACHUSETTS

Adams, John
Gerry, Elbridge
Wilson, Henry
Bush, George (b)

MICHIGAN

Ford, Gerald R.

MISSOURI

Truman, Harry S.

NEBRASKA

Cheney, Richard B. (b)
Dawes, Charles G. (c)
Ford, Gerald R. (b)

NEW YORK

Burr, Aaron (c)
Clinton, George
Tompkins, Daniel D.
Van Buren, Martin
Fillmore, Millard
Wheeler, William A.
Arthur, Chester (c)
Morton, Levi P. (c)
Roosevelt, Theodore
Sherman, James S.
Rockefeller, Nelson (c)

NEW JERSEY

Hobart, Garret A.
Burr, Aaron (b)

NORTH CAROLINA

King, William Rufus

OHIO

Hendricks, Thomas A. (b)
Fairbanks, Charles W.
Dawes, Charles G. (b)

PENNSYLVANIA

Dallas, George M.

SOUTH CAROLINA

Calhoun, John C.

SOUTH DAKOTA

Humphrey, Hubert H. (b)

TENNESSEE

Johnson, Andrew
Gore, Albert A., Jr.

TEXAS

Garner, John Nance
Johnson, Lyndon B.
Bush, George (c)

VERMONT

Arthur, Chester (b)
Morton, Levi P. (b)
Coolidge, Calvin

VIRGINIA

Jefferson, Thomas
Tyler, John

WYOMING

Cheney, Richard B. (c)

Unsuccessful Vice-Presidential Candidates

By Year of Contest

1792 George Clinton (Antifederalist)
1796 Thomas Pinckney (Federalist)
Aaron Burr (Democratic-Republican)
1800 Charles C. Pinckney (Federalist)
1804 Rufus King (Federalist)
1808 Rufus King
1812 Jared Ingersoll (Federalist)
1816 John Howard (Federalist)
1820 no opponent
1824 Nathan Sanford (no party)
Nathaniel Macon (no party)
1828 Richard Rush (National Republican)
1832 John Sergeant (National Republican)
1836 Francis Granger (Whig)
John Tyler (Whig)
1840 Richard M. Johnson (Democrat)
1844 Theodore Frelinghuysen (Whig)
1848 William O. Butler (Democrat)
Charles Francis Adams (Free Soil)
1852 William A. Graham (Whig)
1856 William L. Dayton (Republican)
1860 Edward Everett (Constitutional Union)
Hershell V. Johnson (Democrat)
Joseph Lane (National Democrat)
1864 George Pendleton (Democrat)
1868 Francis P. Blair (Democrat)
1872 B. Gratz Brown (Liberal Republican and Democrat)
1876 Thomas Hendricks (Democrat)
1880 William English (Democrat)
1884 John A. Logan (Republican)
1888 Allen G. Thurman (Democrat)

1892 Whitlaw Reid (Republican)
1896 Arthur Sewell (Democrat)
1900 Adlai Stevenson (Democrat)
1904 Henry G. Davis (Democrat)
1908 John W. Kern (Democrat)
1912 Nicolas Butler (Republican)
Hiram W. Johnson (Progressive)
1916 Charles W. Fairbanks (Republican)
1920 Franklin D. Roosevelt (Democrat)
1924 Charles W. Bryan (Democrat)
Burton K Wheeler (Progressive)
1928 Joseph T. Robinson (Democrat)
1932 Charles Curtis (Republican)
1936 Frank Knox (Republican)
1940 Charles McNary (Republican)
1944 John Bricker (Republican)
1948 Earl Warren (Republican)
Felding Wright (States' Rights)
1952 John Sparkman (Democrat)
1956 Estes Kefauver (Democrat)
1960 Henry Cabot Lodge (Republican)
1964 William Miller (Republican)
1968 Edmund Muskie (Democrat)
1972 Sergeant Shriver (Democrat)
1976 Robert Dole (Republican)
1980 Walter F. Mondale (Democrat)
1984 Geraldine Ferraro (Democrat)
1988 Lloyd Bentsen (Democrat)
1992 J. Danforth Quayle (Republican)
James Stockdale (Independent)
1996 Jack Kemp (Republican)
2000 Joseph Lieberman (Democrat)

Alotta, Robert I. #2: *A Look at the Vice Presidency.* New York: Julian Messner, 1981.

Barzman, Sol. *Madmen and Geniuses: The Vice Presidents of the United States.* Chicago: Follett Publishing Co., 1974.

Biographical Directory of the American Congress, 1774–1971. Washington, D.C.: U.S. Government Printing Office, 1971.

Byrne, Gary C., and Paul Marx. *The Great American Convention: A Political History of Presidential Election*s. Palo Alto, Calif.: Pacific Books, 1976.

Cleere, Gail S. *The House on Observatory Hill: Home of the Vice Presidents of the United States.* Washington, D.C.: Department of the Navy, 1989; reprinted, Diane Publishing Co., 1993.

Curtis, Richard, and Maggie Wells. *Not Exactly a Crime: Our Vice Presidents from Adams to Agnew.* New York: Dial Press, 1972.

Diller, Daniel C., and Stephen L. Robertson. *The Presidents, First Ladies, and Vice Presidents.* Washington: Congressional Quarterly, 1989.

Di Salle, Michael V., and Lawrence G. Blockman. *Second Choice.* New York: Hawthorne Books, 1966.

Dorman, Michael. *The Second Man.* New York: Delacorte Press, 1968.

Dunlap, Leslie W. *Our Vice Presidents and Second Ladies.* Metuchen, N.J.: Scarecrow, 1988.

Durbin, Thomas M., and Michael V. Seitzinger. *Nomination and Election of the President and Vice President of the United States.* Washington, D.C.: Government Printing Office, 1980.

Greenstein, Fred S., et al. *Evolution of the Modern Presidency: A Bibliographic Survey.* Washington, D.C.: American Enterprise Institute for Public Policy Research, 1977. (Chap. 19)

Goldstein, Joel K. *The Modern Vice Presidency: The Transformation of a Political Institution.* Princeton, N.J.: Princeton University Press, 1982.

Harwood, Michael. *In the Shadow of the Presidents.* New York: J.B. Lippincott, 1966.

Hatch, Louis C., and Earl L. Shoup. *A History of the Vice Presidency of the United States.* Westport, Conn.: Greenwood Press, 1970.

Healy, Diana Dixon. *America's Vice-Presidents.* New York: Atheneum, 1989.

Hoopes, Roy. *The Changing Vice-Presidency.* New York: Crowell, 1981.

Kane, Joseph N. *Facts About the Presidents.* New York: H.W. Wilson, 1989.

Lanman, Charles. *Biographical Annals of the Civil Government of the U.S. during Its First Century.* Washington, D.C.: 1876; reprinted, Gale Publishing, 1976.

Levin, Peter. *Seven By Chance: The Accidental Presidents.* New York: Farrar, Straus, & Co., 1948.

Levy, Leonard W., and Lewis Fisher, eds. *The Encyclopedia of the American Presidency.* New York: Simon and Schuster, 1994.

Light, Paul C. *Vice Presidential Power: Advice and Influence in the White House.* Baltimore: Johns Hopkins University Press, 1984.

Natoli, Marie D. *American Prince, American Pauper: The Contemporary Vice Presidency in Perspective.* Westport, Conn.: Greenwood Press, 1985.

Nelson, Michael. *A Heartbeat Away.* New York: Priority Press Publications, 1988.

Schindler, Allan P. *Unchosen Presidents: The Vice-Presidency and Other Frustrations of Presidential Succession.* Berkeley, Calif: University of California Press, 1976.

Schlesinger, Arthur M., Jr., and Fred L. Israel, eds. *History of American Presidential Elections, 1789–1968.* 4 vols. New York: Chelsea House, 1971.

Sobel, Robert, ed. *Biographical Dictionary of the U.S. Executive Branch, 1774–1989.* Westport, Conn.: Greenwood Press, 1990.

Southwick, Leslie. *Presidential Also Rans and Running Mates, 1788–1996.* Jefferson, N.C.: MacFarland & Co., 1998.

Tally, Steve. *Bland Ambition: From Adams to Quayle—The Cranks, Criminals, Tax Cheats, and Golfers Who Made It to the Vice Presidency.* San Diego, Calif.: Harcourt Brace Jovanovich, 1992.

Vexler, Robert I. *The Vice-Presidents and Cabinet Members: Biographies Arranged Chronologically by Administrations.* Dobbs Ferry, N.Y.: Oceana Publications, 1975.

Waldrup, Carole Chandler. *The Vice Presidents: Biographies of the 45 Men Who Have Held the Second Highest Office in the Land.* Jefferson, N.C.: MacFarland & Co., 1996.

Waugh, Edgar W. *Second Consuls: The Vice Presidency; Our Greatest Political Problem.* Indianapolis, Ind.: Bobbs-Merrill, 1956.

Williams, Irving G. *The Rise of the Vice Presidency.* Washington, D.C.: Public Affairs Press, 1956.

Witcover, Jules. *Crapshoot: Rolling the Dice on the Vice-Presidency.* New York: Crown, 1992.

Young, Donald. *American Roulette: The History and Dilemma of the Vice Presidency.* New York: Holt, Rinehart and Winston, 1965.

Young, Klyde, and Lamar Middleton. *Heirs Apparent: The Vice Presidents of the United States.* Freeport, N.Y.: Books for Libraries Press, 1969.

INDEX

Page numbers in **boldface** indicate extensive treatment of the subject.
Page numbers in *italics* represent illustrations.